macromedia®
DREAMWEAVER® MX
2004
with asp, coldfusion, and php

jeffrey bardzell

training from the source

macromedia®
PRESS

Macromedia Dreamweaver MX 2004 with ASP, ColdFusion, and PHP: Training from the Source

 Published by Macromedia Press, in association with Peachpit Press, a division of Pearson Education.

Macromedia Press
1249 Eighth Street
Berkeley, CA 94710
510/524-2178
510/524-2221 (fax)
Find us on the World Wide Web at:
http://www.peachpit.com
http://www.macromedia.com

Printed and bound in the United States of America

ISBN 0-321-24157-6

9 8 7 6 5 4 3 2 1

CREDITS

Author
Jeffrey Bardzell

Editor
Wendy Sharp

Copyeditor
Peggy Gannon

Production Coordinator
Becky Winter

Compositors
Rick Gordon, Emerald Valley Graphics
Debbie Roberti, Espresso Graphics
Myrna Vladic, Bad Dog Graphics

Indexer
Julie Bess

Technical Review
Robert Crooks, Director of Training and Curriculum, Macromedia

Cover Production
George Mattingly, GMD

table of contents

introduction

Macromedia Dreamweaver has been the market leader in visual HTML editors for years, combining ease of use, power, and unusually high quality code writing. But since version 1 was first released, the Web has changed. Over the years, numerous technologies, many developed quite independently of the Web, have emerged as critical Web authoring tools, including JavaScript, databases, SQL, Java, WML, WSDL, cascading style sheets, XML, XSLT, CGI scripting, and above all, a group of new server languages that enable developers to turn Web pages into powerful, data-driven, interactive Web applications: these include Macromedia ColdFusion, Microsoft ASP and ASP.NET, as well as JSP and PHP. Without compromising its ease of use or the quality of code it has always generated, Macromedia Dreamweaver has absorbed these technologies, not only making it possible to work with each of them in isolation, but also making it possible to build sophisticated applications combining these technologies.

PREREQUISITES

While Dreamweaver has managed to keep up with the rapid evolution of Web technologies, many developers have not fared so well. HTML, image editing, and cascading style sheets are one thing: document object models, for loops, relational data, concatenation, recordsets, cookies, and methods are something else. Yet for many of us, our careers depend on our ability to make the jump from static HTML to full-fledged dynamic Web applications—and that means gaining competence with several of the technologies listed in the previous paragraph.

That's where *Macromedia Dreamweaver MX 2004 with ASP, ColdFusion, and PHP: Training From the Source* comes in. In a series of hands-on tutorials, you'll build competence in working with three of today's hottest dynamic application development languages: Microsoft ASP (VBScript) and Macromedia ColdFusion Markup

Language (CFML), and the open source PHP. Along the way, you'll also learn about database design, writing SQL queries, cascading style sheets, the new XHTML standard, and more.

The book takes a novel strategy of mixing enough hand-coding for you to become competent with programming in these languages, while also providing extensive coverage of the dialog- and wizard-based server behaviors and pre-built application objects that Dreamweaver provides to speed up application development. The goal is not simply to build dynamic applications, but for you to gain a deep understanding about how they work, even when you are relying on GUI-based server behaviors.

The lessons assume the following:

- You have basic familiarity with your operating system, including using the menu system and file management.

- Dreamweaver MX is installed, and your system meets the requirements needed to run it.

- You are familiar with working in Dreamweaver, including the use of the Property inspector, various panels, and the main menu. You should also understand the site definition process and Site panel.

- You understand how HTML code works, and you are familiar with its most common tags and attributes, such as the `<p>`, `<table>`, `<tr>`, `<td>`, `<ol>`, `<ul>`, `<h1>`, `<h2>`, and `<img>` tags. You should also understand common HTML concepts, such as absolute versus relative links, validly nested tags, and the difference between the document head and body.

OUTLINE

This Macromedia training course steps you through the projects in each lesson, showing you how to create database-driven, interactive Web applications in Dreamweaver MX 2004 using ASP, ColdFusion, and PHP. The curriculum of this course should take you 20 to 24 hours to complete and includes the following lessons:

Lesson 1: Introducing Newland Tours
Lesson 2: Upgrading to XHTML
Lesson 3: Creating the Presentation Layer
Lesson 4: Dynamic Web Sites
Lesson 5: Passing Data Between Pages
Lesson 6: Sending Email From a Web Form
Lesson 7: Building a Tour Price Calculator
Lesson 8: Databases on the Web
Lesson 9: Completing the Price Calculator
Lesson 10: Filtering and Displaying Data

THE PROJECT SITE

In the course of completing the book, you will build a site for a fictional travel tours company, called Newland Tours. Newland Tours offers travel tours to numerous countries throughout the world. Currently, tours are listed on a static HTML Web page. Unfortunately, new tours are added, old tours are removed, and tour details (especially their prices) change frequently. Newland Tours, having no dedicated Web developer on staff, is having trouble keeping the site up to date, and they are looking for a better way to keep content up to date on the Web. In addition, site users are complaining that tours are hard to find, as there is no way to search for tours short of scrolling through long pages of tour listings.

The solution, of course, is to store data about the tours in a database, and enable users to search database records over the Web. Likewise, as you will learn, Web forms can be used to update the database from any computer with access to the Internet. Of course, exposing the Newland Tours database to the general public (via Web forms) would not be a good security practice, so you'll also implement an authorization framework for the site, which blocks users from seeing pages unless they have logged in.

Along the way, you'll build a number of common Web applications, including a tour price calculator, a Contact Us form that automatically generates an email message, search interfaces, and a forms-based content management system that enables Newland Tours employees to insert, update, and remove country profiles.

ELEMENTS AND FORMAT

Each lesson in this book begins by outlining the major focus of the lesson at hand and introducing new features. Learning objectives and the approximate time needed to complete all the exercises are also listed at the beginning of each lesson. The projects are divided into short exercises that explain the importance of each skill you learn. Every lesson will build on the concepts and techniques used in the previous lessons.

Tips: Alternative ways to perform tasks and suggestions to consider when applying the skills you are learning.

Notes: Additional background information to expand your knowledge, as well as advanced techniques you can explore in order to further develop your skills.

Boldface terms: New vocabulary that is introduced and emphasized in each lesson.

Italic text: Text that is italic indicates that you will need to type it.

Menu commands and keyboard shortcuts: There are often multiple ways to perform the same task in Dreamweaver. The different options will be pointed out in each lesson. Menu commands are shown with angle brackets between the menu names and commands: Menu > Command > Subcommand. Keyboard shortcuts are shown with a plus sign between the names of keys to indicate that you should press the keys simultaneously; for example, Shift+Tab means that you should press the Shift and Tab keys at the same time.

CD-ROM: The files you will need to complete the projects for each lesson are located in a folder named for the lesson: Lesson01, Lesson02, etc. The CD can be found in the back of the book. Inside the lesson folders are Start and Complete folders, which represent the state of the Newland Tours project at the beginning and ending of that lesson, respectively. After the first few lessons, which use the same files regardless of the server model you plan to use (ASP, ColdFusion, or PHP), the Start and Complete folders have subfolders for each server model—newland-asp, newland-cfm, and newland-php.

The files you will use for each of the projects are listed at the beginning of each lesson.

IF YOU GET STUCK

One frustrating aspect of learning dynamic Web site development is the errors that you will encounter. A dynamic Web site is typically the fusion of many technologies, and some of them, especially ASP, ColdFusion, and PHP themselves, depend on the configuration of the server. If the server (or database) is not configured correctly, you will see error messages even if you entered all the code correctly in Dreamweaver. Worse, the error messages that you see are often hard to interpret (especially those in ASP), and in some cases, misleading.

The following are some strategies you can use to resolve these problems:

Use the files in the lesson's Complete folder. One reason these are provided is so that you can use them if something goes wrong with your files. You can also print out the code for your file and the one in the Complete folder for a comparison.

Consult Macromedia's TechNote on common server errors. Though created initially for Dreamweaver UltraDev, the predecessor to Dreamweaver MX, this page contains a listing of some of the most common server errors and their solutions: http://www.macromedia.com/support/ultradev/ts/documents/common_server_errors.htm

Verify that the page you are testing has all of the data that it needs. Some pages depend on the presence of form or querystring/URL variables to work. For example, a SQL query on a detail page might filter database records based on a querystring or URL variable that it is expecting from a related page. If you test that detail page directly, without going through the related page first, the data ASP, ColdFusion, or PHP is expecting won't be present, resulting in an error. Always test starting from an application's starting page, rather than a page in the middle of the process.

Know when to move on. While you should try to resolve any errors that you encounter, don't beat your head against the wall. The goal of the book is really for you to learn dynamic Web site development, and not literally to build every aspect of the Newland Tours site. If you get stuck, at a certain point, it's better to swap in the file from the Complete folder and move on.

Try to determine whether the problem is due to code or configuration. With static HTML development, if a page doesn't look right, it's almost always because of something in your code. When they see a server error, many beginners assume that they made a mistake in their code, and while that is possible, it's just as likely that there is a configuration problem, such as the wrong permissions, a service that's not available, or a missing DSN. The easiest way to test is to swap in the file from the Complete folder—if it doesn't work either, then your code is probably fine. Take up the matter with your server administrator.

Check the book's Web site. Because ASP, ColdFusion, and PHP errors are so common and hard to troubleshoot, the author and the editorial team took extra pains to ensure that the code in the book and on the CD-ROM are bug free. However, no book is completely without errors, and if we learn of any, we will post them on the book's page at http://www.allectomedia.com.

Ask your questions in the appropriate Macromedia Dreamweaver forums. Macromedia has a number of free forums where anyone can go to ask questions or search previous posts. The forums are frequented by Macromedia tech support staff and Dreamweaver/ASP/ColdFusion/PHP veterans and gurus, and you can often get an answer to your questions within a matter of minutes. To access the forums, visit http://www.macromedia.com/support/dreamweaver/ts/documents/dream_newsgrp.htm. I visit the Dreamweaver Application Development newsgroup periodically and pay special attention to posts that reference this book in the title. I cannot guarantee to provide support for every problem every reader might encounter, but the community in that forum is sufficient to help most people get what they need.

MACROMEDIA TRAINING FROM THE SOURCE

The Macromedia Training from the Source series is developed in association with Macromedia, and reviewed by the product support teams. Ideal for active learners, the books in the Training from the Source series offer hands-on instruction designed to provide you with a solid grounding in the program's fundamentals. If you learn best by doing, this is the series for you. Each Training from the Source title is designed to teach the techniques that you need to create sophisticated professional-level projects. Each book includes a CD-ROM that contains all the files used in the lessons, completed projects for comparison and more.

MACROMEDIA AUTHORIZED TRAINING AND CERTIFICATION

This book is geared to enable you to study at your own pace with content from the source. Other training options exist through the Macromedia Authorized Training Partner program. Get up to speed in a matter of days with task-oriented courses taught by Macromedia Certified Instructors. Or learn on your own with interactive, online training from Macromedia University. All of these sources of training will prepare you to become a Macromedia Certified Developer.

For more information about authorized training and certification, check out *www.macromedia.com/go/training1*

WHAT YOU WILL LEARN

You will develop the skills you need to create and maintain your own Web sites as you work through these lessons.

By the end of the course, you will be able to:

- Update an existing site so that it uses maintainable, standards-compliant XHTML and CSS code

- Understand the limitations of the HTTP protocol, and how ASP, ColdFusion, and PHP work with it to enable Web applications

- Pass data between pages and make data persist over time, using form, querystring/URL, cookie, session, and application variables

- Collect and process information entered by users via Web forms

- Validate data entered into forms using both client-side (JavaScript) and server-side (ASP, ColdFusion, or PHP) code

- Write code to evaluate expressions and perform simple mathematical calculations

- Connect your Web site to a database, so that it displays database contents

- Filter data retrieved from a database

- Build search interfaces that enable users to access only the information they need

- Authenticate users and restrict access to pages

- Build content management systems that enable site owners to maintain Web content using Web forms, rather than HTML editors and FTP

- Hand-code common ASP, ColdFusion, and PHP scripts that you can reuse in future projects

- Learn core SQL statements, enabling you to build pages that interact with data in sophisticated ways

- Control the flow of scripts, using conditional statements and loops

- Work with Dreamweaver's server behaviors, Recordset dialog, and pre-built application objects to rapidly develop dynamic Web applications

MINIMUM SYSTEM REQUIREMENTS: WINDOWS

- Macromedia Dreamweaver MX 2004 (A 30-day trial version is on the CD-ROM.)

- Intel Pentium III processor or equivalent 600+ MHz

- Windows 98 SE, Windows 2000, or Windows XP

- 128 MB RAM (256 MB recommended)

- Internet Explorer or Netscape Navigator 4.0 or higher

- Internet access (for Lesson 6 only)

- Access to a server capable of processing the desired application language, as follows:

  - ASP/VBScript users must have access to Microsoft Internet Information Services (IIS). IIS comes bundled with Windows 2000 and Windows XP Professional, so you can run it on your local system. Alternatively, you can connect to an IIS server over a network or over the Web via FTP.

  - ColdFusion users must have access to the ColdFusion application server in addition to a Web server, such as IIS, Apache, or ColdFusion's own standalone server. A single IP developer's edition of ColdFusion can be downloaded for free from http://www.macromedia.com.

  - PHP users must have access to a Web server, such as the open source Apache Web server, with the PHP module loaded. It is possible to run PHP in an IIS environment, though Apache is recommended for PHP.

8

MINIMUM SYSTEM REQUIREMENTS: MACINTOSH

- Macromedia Dreamweaver MX 2004 (A 30-day trial version is on the CD-ROM.)
- 500 MHz Power Mac G3 Processor
- Mac OS 10.2.6
- 128 MB computer RAM (256 MB recommended)
- Internet Explorer 4.0 or Safari 1.0 or higher
- Internet access (for Lesson 6 only)
- Access to a server capable of processing the desired application language, as follows:

    ♦ ASP/VBScript users must have network or Internet access to a Microsoft Internet Information Services (IIS) Web server. IIS and ASP cannot be run locally from a Macintosh.

    ♦ ColdFusion users must have network or Internet access to a ColdFusion server. ColdFusion cannot be run locally from a Macintosh (unless it is running on top of a J2EE server, such as Macromedia JRun).

    ♦ PHP users must have access to a PHP-enabled Web server, such as the open source Apache. You can connect to a PHP-enabled Apache server over a network or over the Internet. In addition, Mac users can now run Apache with PHP locally, without having to connect to a separate server over a network or the Internet.

introducing Newland Tours

LESSON 1

The Web is changing. HTML is no longer a new technology, and most established organizations are no longer seeking attractive Web presence sites, that is, sites that establish a static presence on the Internet but do little else. They already have sites, and in many cases, these sites have been around for several years. Web designers and developers today increasingly face a different set of problems than they did a few years ago.

- Rather than creating brand-new sites, today's designers and developers need to maintain existing sites in the face of changing standards, new technologies, and evolving content.

The homepage of the Newland Tours site looks good enough, but certain parts of it, such as the weekly Traveler's Journal column (at right) require a lot of work to maintain.

- The variations among different browsers, now including assistive technologies for the millions of users with impairments, have become so pronounced that it is no longer acceptable to simply check the page in both Netscape and Internet Explorer.

- Modern Web sites should respond to users' needs, which often means that Web sites must react on-the-fly to user interaction.

- Today's designers and developers often need to build content management systems, which facilitate the movement of site content maintenance from IT departments to non-technical business users by creating Web forms that post content.

Needs such as these raise a series of practical questions. What is the fastest way to update the look or structure of a site? How can one design a site so that a non-technical content expert can contribute to it? How does one develop a site that customizes itself to the needs and interests of the user? And finally, how does one accomplish all these goals at the same time?

In response to these issues, a whole new series of technology solutions have appeared as solutions to Web development problems: cascading style sheets (CSS), ColdFusion, ASP, SQL, database servers, XHTML, DHTML, XML, Web services, ADO, CDO, JavaScript, Flash, PHP, Java, .NET, XSLT, and more. Web development software, such as Macromedia Dreamweaver MX 2004, has kept up so that developers can create sites using any of the technologies just mentioned. But for the HTML jockey of yesteryear, this onslaught of technical solutions may seem as problematic as the problems they purport to solve.

Increasingly, mastering many of these technologies is part of the core skill set of today's Web developers. The goal of this book is to set you well on your way to that goal. The central project of this book transforms a static Web site into an interactive, easy to maintain, and standards-compliant site. The site is for a fictional travel tour operator, called Newland Tours. By the time you are done, site visitors will be able to home in on the content they are looking for quickly and easily. In addition, the non-technical users who own the site will be able to update it without having to know any HTML code. These are ambitious but attainable goals; and thanks to Dreamweaver's tools and environment, they are easier to achieve than you might think.

In this lesson, you will get familiar with the book's starting and ending points. You'll open the site as it exists today within Dreamweaver. The first task will be to create a new page; imagine that before you start overhauling the site, the client needs you to create a missing page immediately. Once the immediate crisis is passed, you'll go over the site's shortcomings. These shortcomings can be divided into two categories: technical shortcomings, such as the outdated and non-compliant code used throughout the site, and business shortcomings, where the site no longer meets the needs of its business. Finally, you'll hop onto the Web and see the completed version of the site that you'll build over the course of the book.

WHAT YOU WILL LEARN

In this lesson, you will:

- Define a static site in Dreamweaver
- Work in the Dreamweaver environment to create and lay out a new page of content
- Explore the existing HTML code
- Learn about the client's needs
- Explore the completed project as it appears at the end of the book
- Outline a strategy for upgrading the site

APPROXIMATE TIME

This lesson takes approximately 60 minutes to complete.

LESSON FILES

Starting Files:

Lesson01/Start/newland/about.htm
Lesson01/Start/newland/contact_text.txt
Lesson01/Start/newland/index.htm
Lesson01/Start/newland/profiles.htm
Lesson01/Start/newland/tours.htm

Completed Files:

Lesson01/Start/newland/contact.htm

DEFINING A STATIC SITE

The Newland Tours site as you are inheriting it is a static HTML site. For this reason, you can easily pull it into Dreamweaver and start working on it.

Working with Web sites often involves hundreds or even thousands of individual files, including Web pages, images, cascading style sheets, multimedia assets, and more. These files are linked together via HTML. Unfortunately, even a small typo can create ugly (or indecipherable to users) error messages and even block access to portions of your site. Dreamweaver provides many sophisticated site management tools to help ensure the overall integrity of your site, both during development and once it is launched. To take advantage of these features, you must first define a site, a process in which at a minimum you tell Dreamweaver where the site's root folder is located on your hard drive.

Defining a site has several benefits, many of which you will see quickly. It helps prevent broken links, automatically updating files site-wide if you move or rename a file. The Site Manager also enables you to perform site-wide operations, such as Find and Replace, which greatly boosts productivity. Another key advantage of the Site Manager is that it has built-in file uploading capabilities (including FTP), which means you can publish your files to the Web whenever you want, with the click of a single button. You can even synchronize local files (on your hard drive) and remote files (on the Web or a staging server), to ensure that the most up-to-date versions of the files are in the right place.

In this task, you'll define a regular, static site in the Site Definition dialog box, a process involving little more than giving the site a name and telling Dreamweaver where it is stored on the local disk. In a few lessons, once you've made appropriate preparations, you'll return to this dialog box and define a dynamic site. Dynamic site definition is a little more involved, and the additional overhead won't do us any good at this early stage. Fortunately, you can always change a site definition, so we've nothing to lose by defining a static site for now and getting right to work.

1) Create a new directory on your hard disk called dw_dynapps.

You'll store the local version of the site in this folder.

2) Copy the newland folder (and its contents), found in the Lesson01/Start folder on the CD-ROM, into this new directory.

Often enough in real life, you'll inherit an existing site and be asked to upgrade it. With any significant upgrade, it's best to make a copy of the existing site and work on that. You should never directly edit a site in production (that is, the site that the public sees).

3) Open Dreamweaver MX 2004.

Once the files are visible in Dreamweaver, you should edit them exclusively in Dreamweaver. Any text editor can open any HTML file, and every operating system has a file management utility (such as Macintosh Finder or Windows Explorer) that lets you move and delete files. But you should avoid using these tools, because any change is likely to foil Dreamweaver's Site Manager, which is likely to cause broken links. So once the files are there, go straight to Dreamweaver and avoid the temptation to do anything to them by any other means.

4) On the Start page, click the Create New Dreamweaver Site link.

NOTE *You can also choose Site > Manage Sites and click the New button.*

Though the files are on your hard disk, Dreamweaver doesn't yet see them. By defining a site, you enable Dreamweaver to see—and manage—the files. You define a site in the Site Definition dialog box. If the dialog you see doesn't look like the one in the screenshot, it's probably because you are in advanced view. Click the Basic tab near the top of the dialog to bring up the basic view shown in the screenshot.

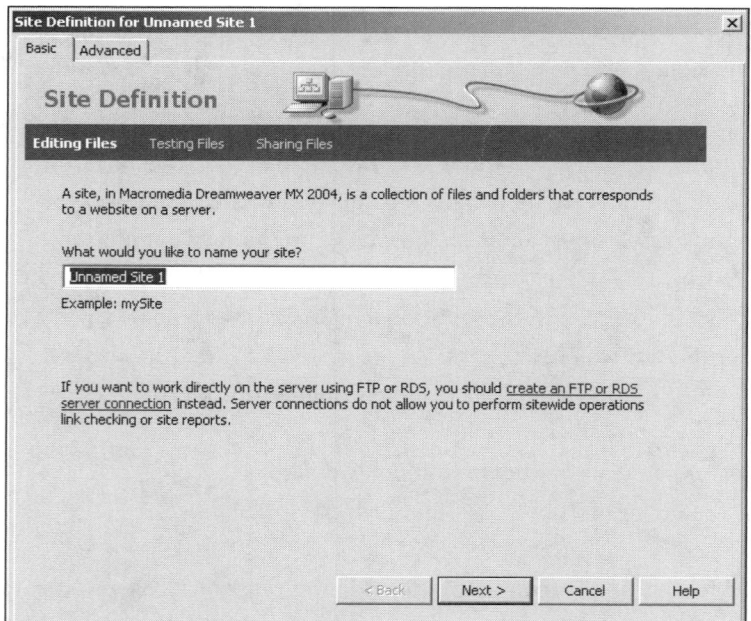

5) Enter *Newland Tours* in the only field on the screen, and click Next.

The Site Definition dialog's basic view uses a wizard-like approach, unlike the more complex dialog box in previous versions of Dreamweaver.

TIP *If you prefer the old-style Site Definition dialog better, you can access it by clicking the Advanced tab.*

6) On the Editing Files, Part 2 screen, select "No, I do not want to use a server technology." Click Next.

Later in the book you will use a server technology. But by choosing No now, you get to skip several complex steps.

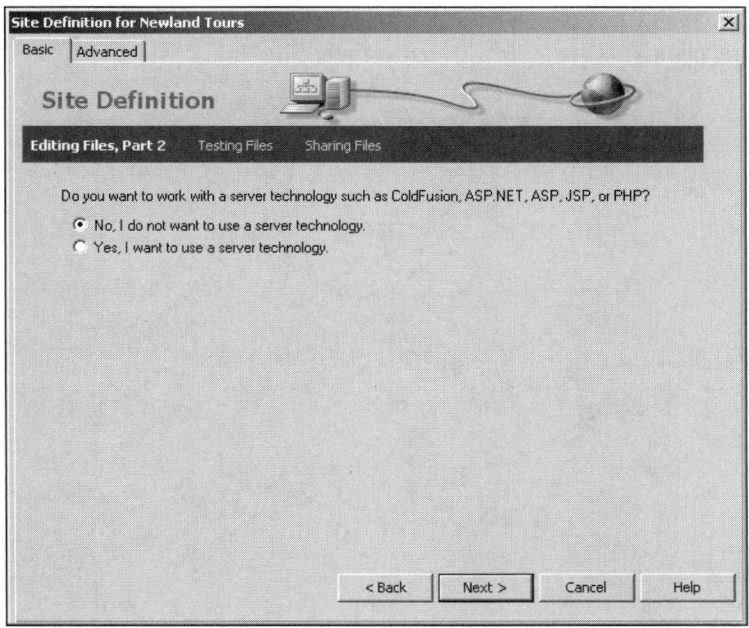

7) On the next screen, select the first option: Edit local copies on my machine, then upload to server when ready (recommended).

As a result of this decision, there will always be two sets of files for the site—one local (usually on your hard drive, though you can put it in a network folder if you want) and one remote (usually on a server). This is safer, because you always have at least one backup copy of your file. More importantly, it means that the files you work on will be stored on your hard drive, where customers will never see them.

Most professional sites work using a 3-tier setup. The local site contains all the files in development on the Dreamweaver user's hard drive. A *staging server* contains a mirror of the site used for testing and development purposes only. The public never sees content on the staging server, but it is a real Web server environment, which is typically identical or nearly identical to that of the *production server*. The production server is the public version of the site. Only tested, edited, polished, and approved files should be published on the production server.

8) Click the folder icon beside the "Where on your computer do you want to store your files" field, and browse to the newland folder within the dw_dynapps folder, and click Select to select the folder and return to the Site Definition dialog box.

In this step you are defining the local site—this is where all the action takes place. Whenever you edit a file, you will be editing the file as it appears in the local site. The local site is generally not seen by the public, which means if you temporarily break the functionality of the site as you work, no harm is done.

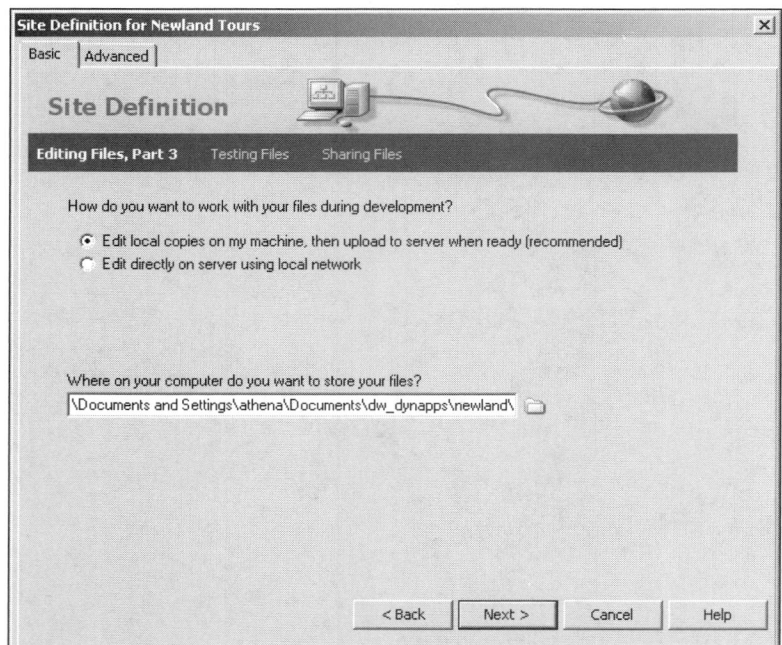

9) On the next screen, choose None in the drop-down menu.

Normally, you specify either a staging server or production server as the Remote site. When working with dynamic, database-driven content, a staging server is an absolute necessity.

Later in the book, you will define a remote site, which you will use as a staging server. That staging server will be able to handle fully dynamic sites, which the local site you are defining can't do—as you'll see later. But for now, a remote site is an unnecessary complication.

NOTE *There is no production server for the site you are building in this book because Newland Tours is fictional.*

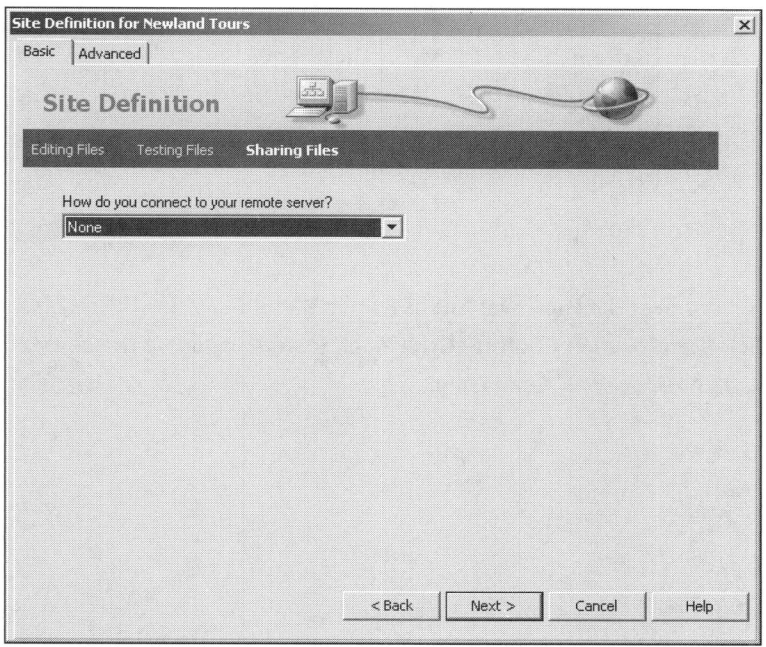

10) Click Next. Review the summary, and click Done.

When you are finished, a dialog box appears, indicating that Dreamweaver is building the site cache. What this means is that Dreamweaver is analyzing all of the files in the site, checking all of the links, and storing them in memory. This way, if you do decide to rename a page or move an asset to a different folder, Dreamweaver will automatically update all of the files that link to the modified file. Once Dreamweaver has built the site cache, the dialog disappears on its own.

When you are finished, the Site panel (by default, in the lower-right corner of your screen) should be filled with files. You'll probably also notice that a lock icon appears beside each of the files. This lock indicates that the files are read-only, which means you can't modify them.

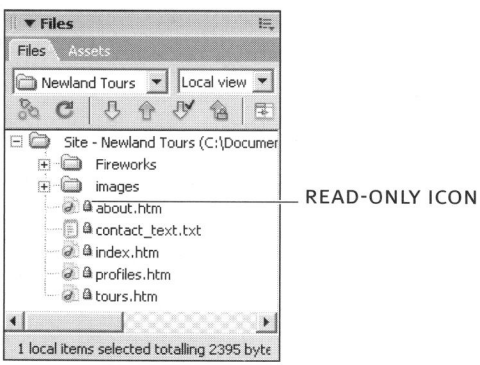

READ-ONLY ICON

This is obviously not the behavior you want—the whole point of working with files in Dreamweaver is to change them. The reason why they appear as read-only is that you copied them from a CD-ROM, and CD-ROMs are read-only (in fact, that's what the *RO* of CD-ROM stands for). If you click to expand the Fireworks or images folders, you'll see that all of those files have lock icons as well.

Before you start working on the files, you'll need to turn off the read-only status.

11) Position your cursor over the top-level folder (which should say Site – Newland Tours) and right-click (Windows) or Control-click (Macintosh) to open up the context menu. In that menu, choose Turn off Read Only.

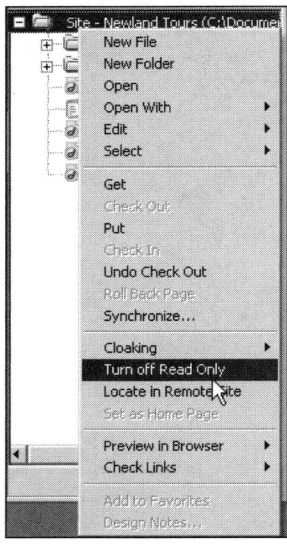

If you glance through the site at this point, you'll notice that all of the lock icons have been removed. The site is defined and you're ready for action!

CREATING THE CONTACT US PAGE

As is often the case with Web projects, before you can dig in and overhaul the Newland Tours site, you must address a more pressing need: the site's Contact Us page is missing and needs to be recreated.

This exercise is mainly intended as a crash course/quick review in the basics of creating and editing Web pages in Dreamweaver. If you are already very comfortable with developing static pages in Dreamweaver, you can skip this exercise—the final result is on the CD in this chapter's Complete folder, as well as all subsequent chapters' Start folders. If you do skip this exercise, begin reading again two sections ahead, "Assessing the Site: The Code."

This quick exercise is only intended to give you a basis for working in the Dreamweaver environment. It is not intended as a comprehensive guide for developing static Web sites using Dreamweaver. For that, see *Macromedia Dreamweaver MX 2004: Training From the Source* (Macromedia Press) or *Macromedia Dreamweaver MX 2004: Visual Quickstart Guide* (Macromedia Press/Peachpit).

1) In the Files panel, double-click the file contact_text.txt to open it in Dreamweaver. If the Files panel is not visible, choose Window > Files to show it.

As you can guess from the contents, this file contains all the text that needs to go on the Contact Us page.

This is a plain text file, and not an HTML document. It doesn't contain any HTML tags, and though it appears formatted in Dreamweaver, if you were to view it in a browser, all the formatting would be lost and it would be collapsed into a single, large paragraph. The reason for the collapse is that browsers disregard white space—paragraph returns, spaces (beyond the first space used to separate words), and tabs. To create white space in a page displayed in a browser, you use HTML tags, such as the paragraph (<p>) tag. In the next few steps, you'll make a copy of an existing page in the site (about.htm) and replace its contents with the contents of this file, format these contents using HTML, and save the page as contact.htm.

SHOW CODE VIEW

SHOW CODE AND DESIGN VIEWS

SHOW DESIGN VIEW

FILES PANEL

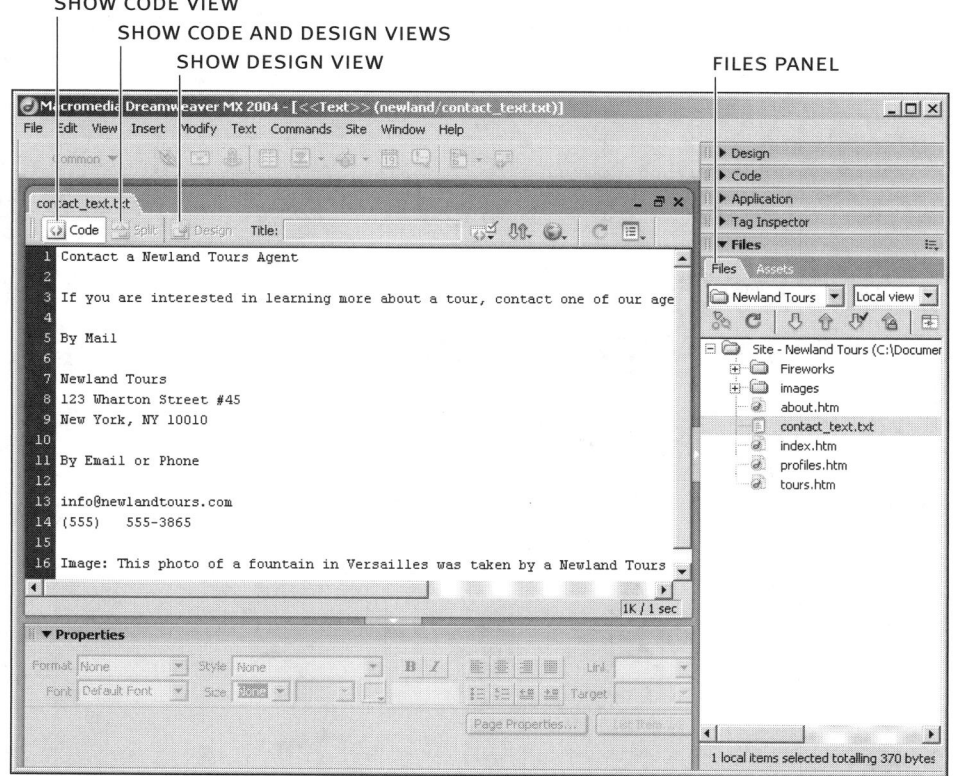

Notice that on the View toolbar, the Code button is selected, and the two buttons beside it, Split and Design are grayed out. Because the document lacks any HTML, Dreamweaver can't open it in design view. You'll switch back and forth between code and design views often in this book.

2) Click anywhere in the text, and choose Edit > Select All. Choose Edit > Copy to place all the text on the Clipboard.

The text is now ready to dump in the destination document—only you don't have a destination document just yet.

3) In the Files panel, double-click about.htm to open it. If necessary, click the Design button to see the page rendered, as opposed to its code.

You'll use this page as a guide for creating the new page.

4) Choose File > Save As, and name the file contact.htm.

You are about to modify this version of about.htm. To ensure that you don't overwrite the original version, you make a copy by using Save As and giving it a new name.

Each of the pages has a button in its navigation bar called Contact An Agent. Clicking that button loads contact.htm, which up until this moment didn't exist.

5) Drag to select everything from About Newland Tours down to and including the image caption. Press the Delete key.

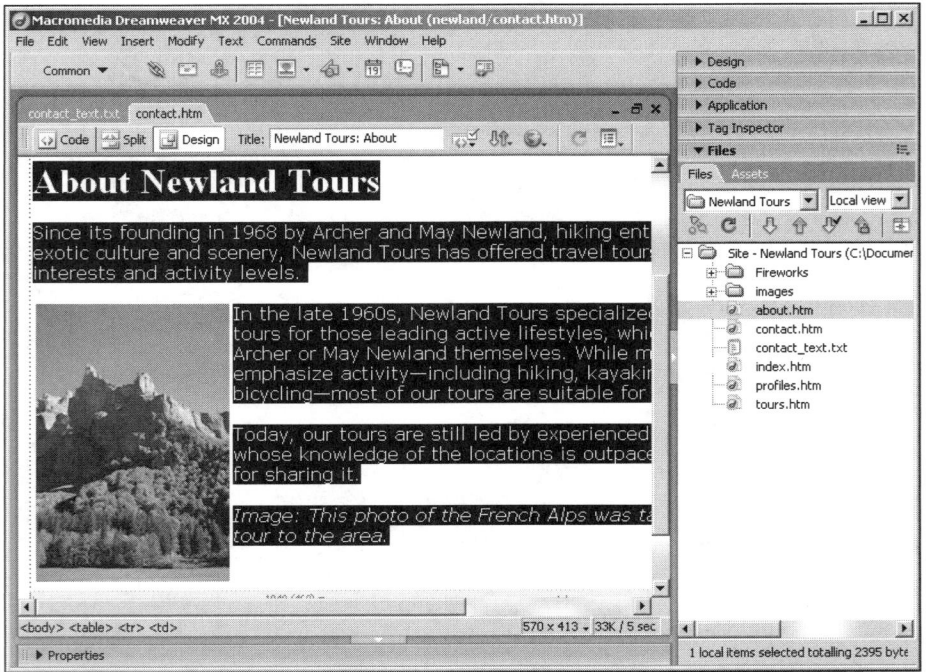

This content is unique to about.htm. You'll replace it with the content on the Clipboard.

After you press the Delete key, you'll notice that the image, which was placed inline with the rest of the text, is also deleted.

6) With the cursor blinking in the main (and now blank) content area of the page, switch into code and design views (henceforth referred to as split view), by clicking the Split button.

By working in both modes simultaneously, you can design visually and also ensure that Dreamweaver will write code the way you expect it to.

Notice that in code view, the cursor is located inside an <h1> tag. The <h1> tag tells the browser to render the enclosed contents using a level 1 heading. Below the document window, in the Property inspector, notice that the Format drop-down menu displays Heading 1. In other words, the Property inspector is showing what you've just seen in code view: the insertion point is formatted as a level 1 heading. If you paste in the contents on the Clipboard now, all the content will be formatted as level 1 headings.

A more sensible choice as a default paragraph format would be the regular paragraph format, indicated by the <p> tag.

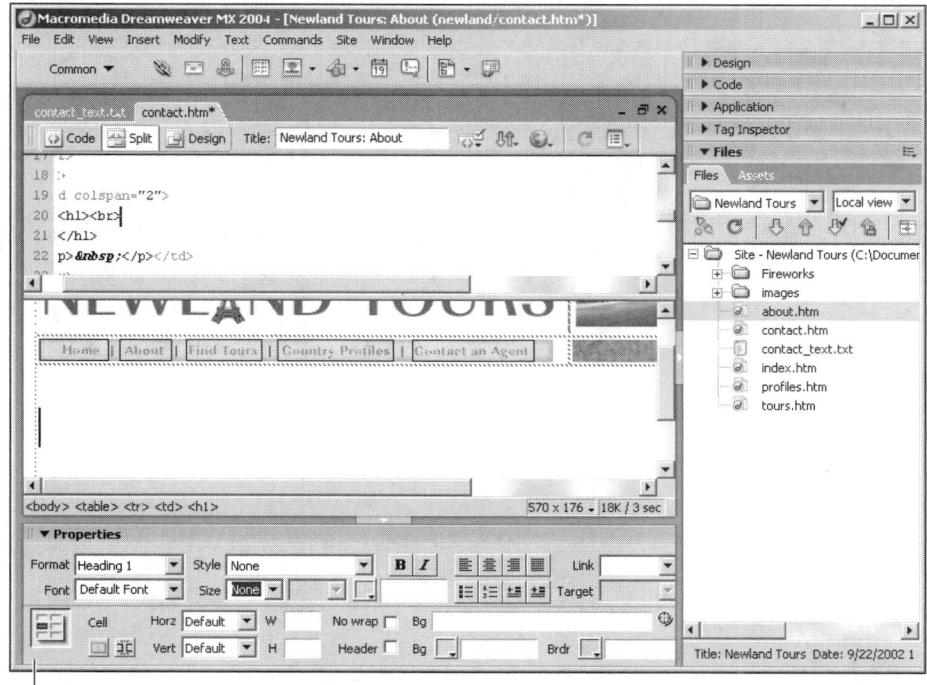

PROPERTY INSPECTOR

7) In the Format drop-down menu of the Property inspector, choose Paragraph.

In code view, notice that the <h1></h1> tags have been replaced with <p></p> tags. Now if you paste the contents on the Clipboard, they'll be formatted as regular paragraphs.

8) If a <br> tag appears between the <p></p> tags in code view, select and delete it.

This tag is a relic of about.htm that may or may not get left behind, depending on how you selected and deleted the original page contents.

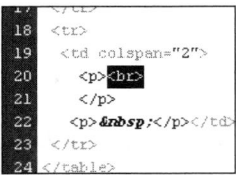

9) With the cursor in between the <p> and the </p> tags in the code half of the window, choose Edit > Paste.

The text from contact_text.txt is pasted in, and is formatted the way it was in the original file. If you compare the text and code in design and code views, you'll see that Dreamweaver has automatically inserted line break characters (<br>) to create the appearance of paragraph breaks.

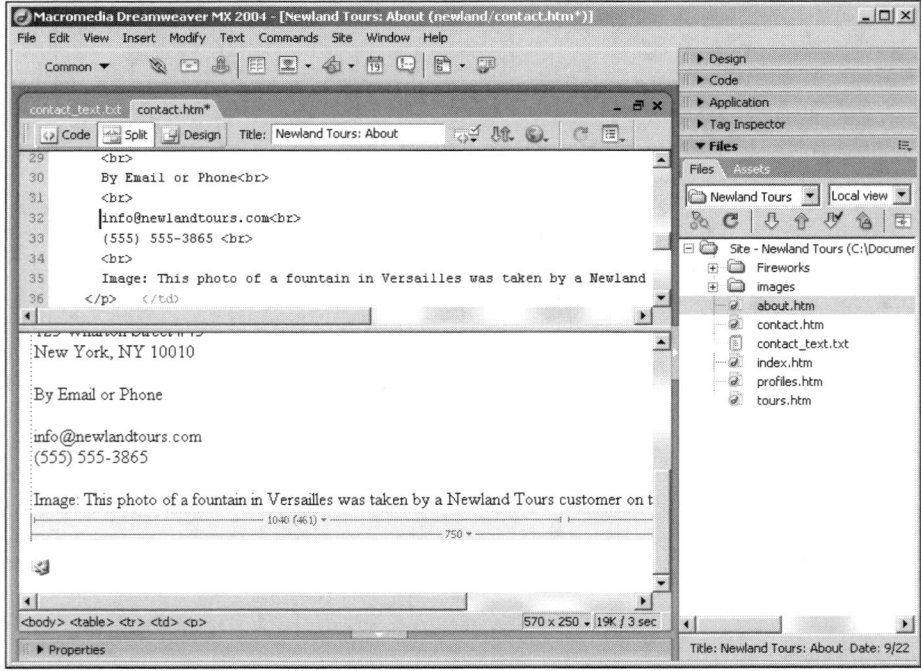

The content is in the new page, and you're now ready to start formatting the content.

FORMATTING THE CONTACT US PAGE

In this task, you'll format the text, converting Dreamweaver's line breaks into proper paragraphs as well as using some of Dreamweaver's layout features. You'll begin by separating the paragraphs from one another.

1) In the Design half of split view, position the insert point between Contact a Newland Tours Agent and If you are interested, press Delete three times to remove the line breaks, and press Enter (Windows) or Return (Macintosh) on your keyboard.

Dreamweaver separates the text into two paragraphs, wrapping each in its own set of <p></p> tags.

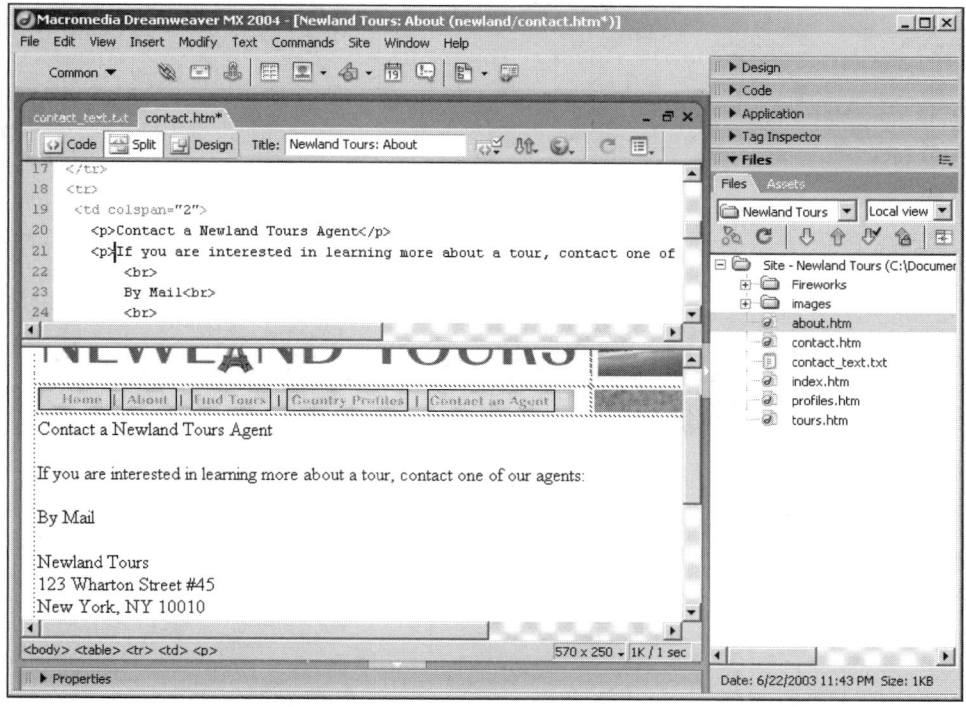

2) Repeat step 1 to create a paragraph break before each of the following words: By Mail, Newland Tours, 123 Wharton, New York, By Email, info@newlandtours.com, (555), and Image.

23

When you are done with this step, you should have ten separate paragraphs in the main content area of the window. They may not be pretty yet, but at least they are separate.

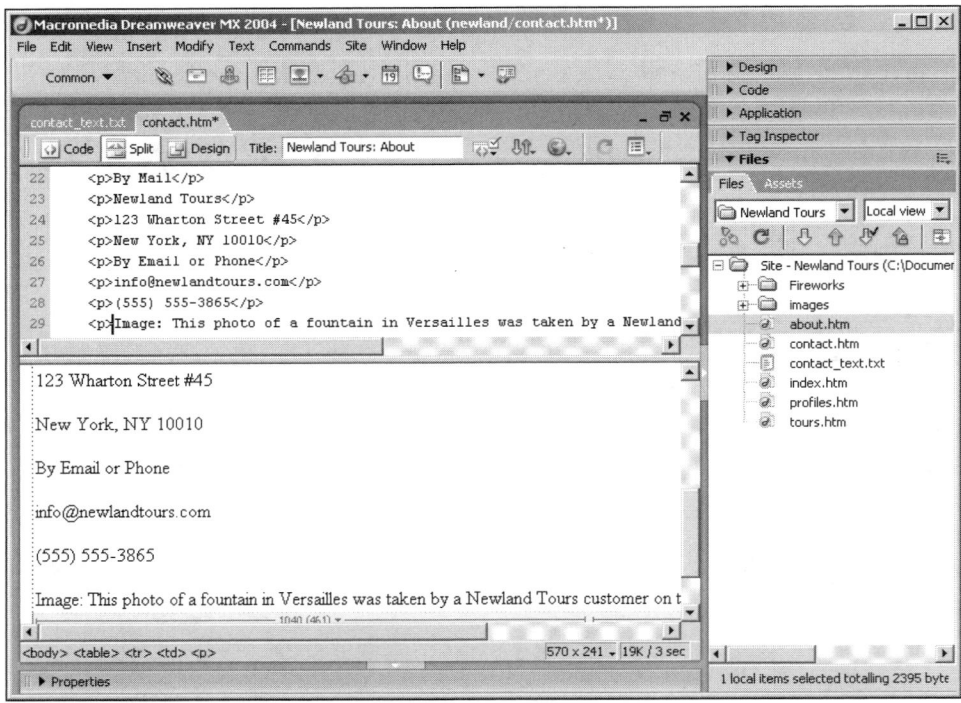

3) In design view, position the insertion point anywhere within the first paragraph, Contact a Newland Tours Agent. In the Property inspector's Format menu, choose Heading 1.

Notice that the page heading now looks like a page heading. In code view, you'll see that the <p> tag has been replaced with an <h1> tag for that paragraph.

Also notice that the page heading appears very close to the banner. You can space it a little further from the banner by entering in a line break tag, <br>.

4) In code view, between the opening <h1> tag and the word Contact, type <br> to create a line break.

To see the results updated in design view, click in the design view half of the document window.

5) In design view, position the cursor just before If you are interested, and click the Insert Image button from the Common category of the Insert bar.

Images are inserted inline with the HTML and text that surrounds them, so it is important to choose the insertion point carefully.

Notice that beside the Insert Images button is a small arrow, indicating a drop-down menu. Clicking the arrow reveals many other image-related assets that you can insert from this menu, including image placeholders, interactive Fireworks HTML/images, rollovers, hotspots, and more. You won't use these features in this book, but be aware that they are there. Several other buttons in the Insert bar hide similar commands.

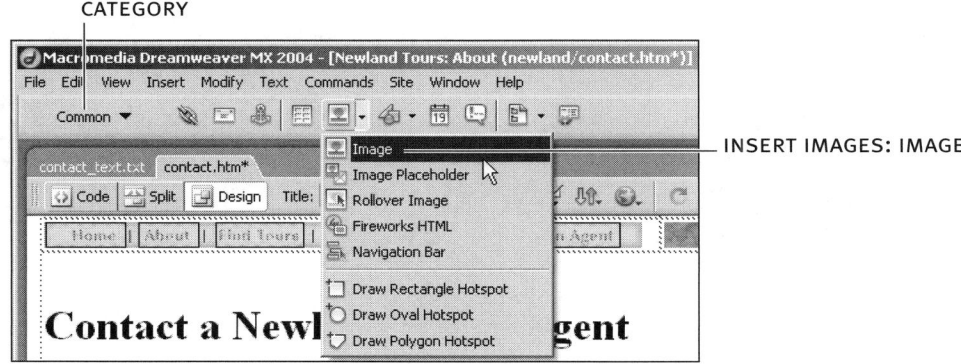

25

6) In the Select Image Source dialog, browse to fountain_versailles.jpg, in the site's images folder. Click OK.

In addition to enabling you to browse to the image, so Dreamweaver can write the correct path to it from contact.htm, this dialog contains several other features and options. These include an image preview, information about the size and dimensions of the image, and options regarding the type of link, document or site root relative (it defaults to document relative, which is what you want).

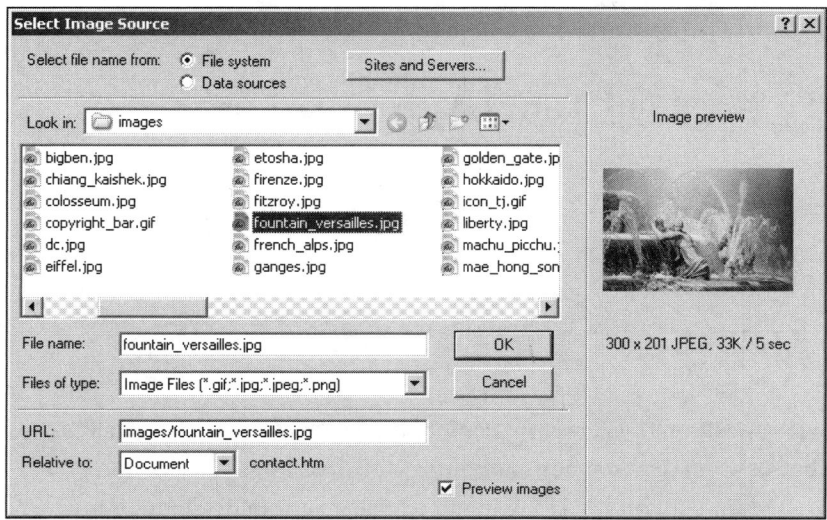

At the top of the dialog, there is an option, Select File Name From. Your choices are File system (that is, you browse to the file on your computer) or Data sources (that is, you dynamically pull the URL from a database); you'll work extensively with both approaches throughout the book. In this step, verify that File system is selected.

7) With the image selected on the page, use the Property inspector to change the image's Align setting to Left.

The default setting usually causes the image to render to the left of one line of text, with all other text wrapping beneath the image. The result is a considerable amount of wasted page space. By choosing Left (or its opposite, Right), the image is rendered so that text wraps around it.

8) Position the insertion point before the words By Mail, and click the Insert Table button from the Insert bar.

In this step, you are preparing to insert a table, which will hold information on how users can contact Newland Tours. Tables can be used to present tabular data, as one would expect. Tables can also be used as a page layout tool. In the next steps, you will create a simple table that presents street address, email address, and phone in a two-column format.

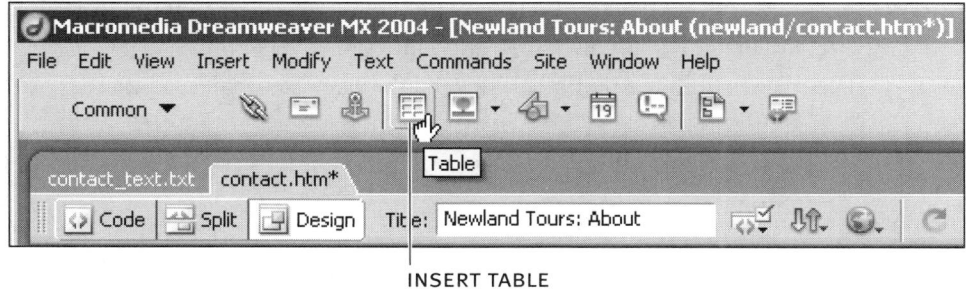

INSERT TABLE

9) In the Insert Table dialog, specify 2 Rows, 2 Columns, a Table width of 400 pixels, a Border thickness of 1, Cell padding of 3, and Cell spacing of 0. In the Accessibility section, enter *Newland Tours contact information* as the Summary. Click OK.

27

These settings will result in a 4-cell table that is 400 pixels wide. Cell padding measures the space between cell borders and cell contents. Cell spacing measures the distance between cells. When you fill out the Summary information, Dreamweaver adds a summary attribute to the <table> tag that screen readers use to give vision-impaired users a quick glance at what the table contains.

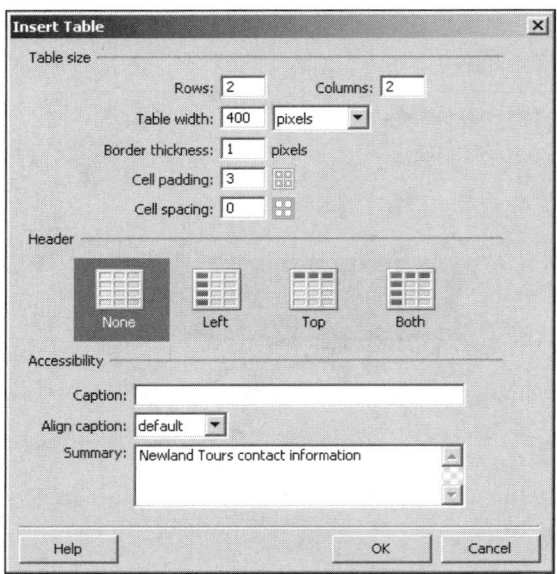

10) Triple-click the words By Mail to select their entire paragraph (just those two words). Drag the selected paragraph into the top-left cell of the table. Likewise, triple-click to select and then drag the words By Email or Phone into the top-right cell. Drag to select the three paragraphs with the mailing address into the lower-left cell, and drag the email and phone information into the lower-right cell.

Dreamweaver moves both the text blocks and all the enclosing <p> tags into the appropriate cells.

Notice that the address, phone, and email information have a lot of extra white space in between their lines.

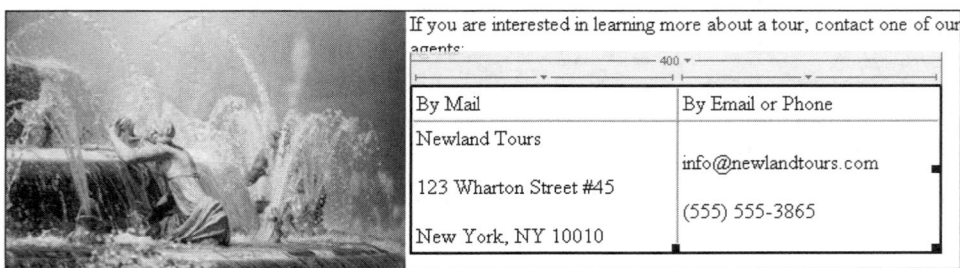

11) Position the insert point just before 123 Wharton Street, and press Backspace (Windows) or Delete (Macintosh) to remove the paragraph break separating 123 Wharton Street from Newland Tours; that is, they should be on one line. With the insertion point between the two former lines of text, hold down the Shift key and press Enter (Windows) or Return (Macintosh).

Whereas pressing Enter or Return causes Dreamweaver to create a new paragraph (<p>), Shift+Enter/Return causes Dreamweaver to insert a line break character (<br>).

12) Repeat step 11 to remove the extra white space between the street address line and the city/state/zip line in the left cell, and likewise remove the white space between the phone and email address lines in the right cell.

The table is now complete. All that remains is to remove the superfluous white space below the table (if applicable), and to format the caption using italics.

13) Position the insertion point before Image: This photo..., and press Backspace (Windows) or Delete (Macintosh) as many times as necessary until the image caption appears in the paragraph just below the table.

The additional spaces are a relic of removing the original address paragraphs and placing them in the table. If you look in the code, you'll see a series of <p> </p>

blocks. This is how Dreamweaver creates empty paragraphs. It is illegal in HTML to have opening and closing <p></p> tags with nothing in them. Dreamweaver therefore enters a space character as an empty placeholder. Because HTML ignores whitespace in code, Dreamweaver enters the character entity for the space character: , which stands for non-breaking space.

14) Triple-click anywhere in the caption line, and once it's selected, use the Property inspector to apply italics.

Notice in the code that Dreamweaver applies italics using the <em> tag, rather than the <i> tag. The significance of this is discussed later in the book.

15) Save contact.htm.

You are done designing the new page. In the real world at this point, you would publish the page to a Web server, but for now, don't worry about it. With the missing contact page crisis resolved, you can now turn your attention toward the more ambitious task of reworking the site.

30

ASSESSING THE SITE: THE CODE

In this task, you won't make any changes to the files; rather, you'll customize the Dreamweaver environment to make it more friendly to the kind of work we'll be doing, and then you'll explore the code in the index page of the start files so you can learn about its shortcomings.

These shortcomings will not show up at all if you view the page in a browser. That is, the page should look just fine in most major browsers. If the page looks fine in a browser, you might wonder how could the code have any shortcomings? The answer is that the starting code in this project is outdated and noncompliant with recent standards. We'll explore the significance of code and standards at the end of this task.

Often a Web redesign project will begin with outdated, non-compliant code, so you might as well learn how to spot it. Later, you'll learn how to fix it.

1) Double-click index.htm to open it.

Depending on whether you did the Contact Us exercise, you may be viewing the document in design view (if you did not do the exercise) or split view (if you did do the exercise).

Back in the late 1990s, when the HTML editor market was crowded with editors that either did code well and design badly, or vice versa, the introduction of Dreamweaver, which excelled at both, caused a revolution. Several years later, Dreamweaver remains the only editor in its league when it comes to doing both design and code. Many designers, knowing that Dreamweaver was writing clean HTML in the background, were content to design sites in design view and never worry too much about the code.

But working exclusively in design view is a luxury of the past.

If you are serious about Web development, and need to develop database-driven Web content, you have to get involved with the code. Moreover, if you want to upgrade older HTML code to standards-compliant XHTML code, you need to roll up your sleeves and do some hand-coding.

2) If necessary, click the Split button.

Split view is a best-of-both-worlds feature. It gives you access to the code, so you can hand-edit code when necessary, even while it leaves the traditional design view open, which makes some kinds of edits, such as edits to body text, much easier than working in code view.

SHOW CODE AND DESIGN VIEWS

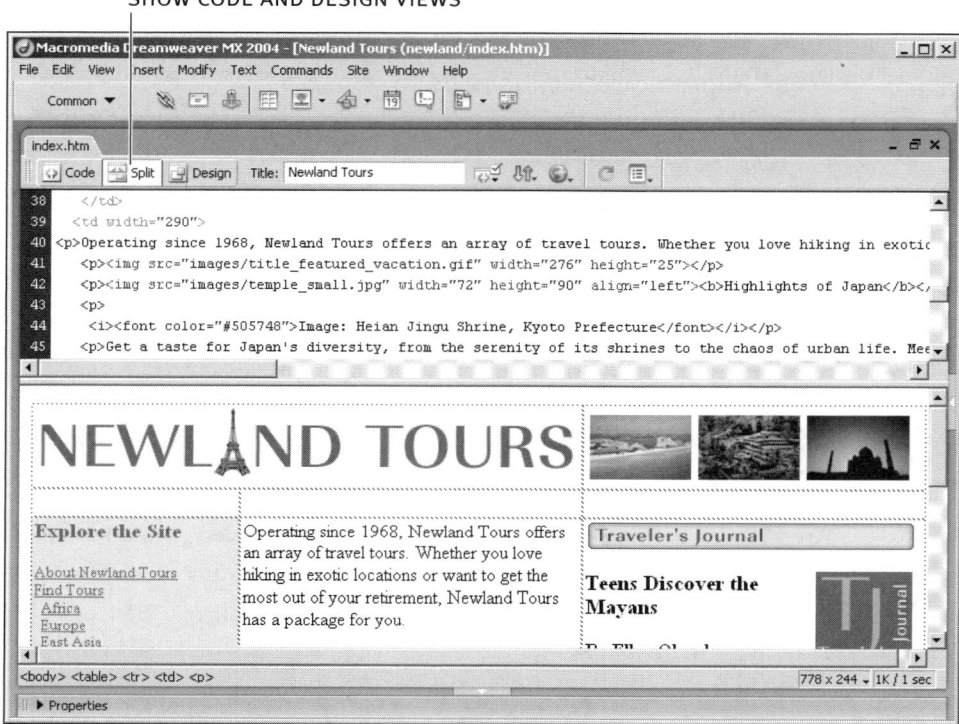

Split view is indispensable for working with dynamic sites. While Dreamweaver enables you to accomplish many tasks using wizard-based server behaviors and its built-in visual SQL builder, you still need to edit code directly. You'll also find that some edits are much faster in code view than they are in design view. Yet another benefit is that it will teach you code. While I assume if you are reading this book, you are familiar with HTML, you may have forgotten some of the details; for example, you might not remember all of the attributes of a given tag. Split view will help you master HTML. From now on (and for all your future projects), make split view your default view. You should avoid using either the code view or the design view alone unless you have a specific reason to do so. And when you are done, switch back to split view.

All of the problems specified in the subsequent steps in this task are revealed only in code view—they are all invisible in design view. Split view is already paying dividends.

TIP *Another benefit of working in split view is that you can easily find a piece of code in code view by clicking its corresponding object in design view. For example, to see the code for a given image, click the image. All of the relevant HTML will be centered in the window and highlighted in code view. This is especially helpful in pages with hundreds of lines of code.*

CODE AUTOMATICALLY HIGHLIGHTED AND CENTERED

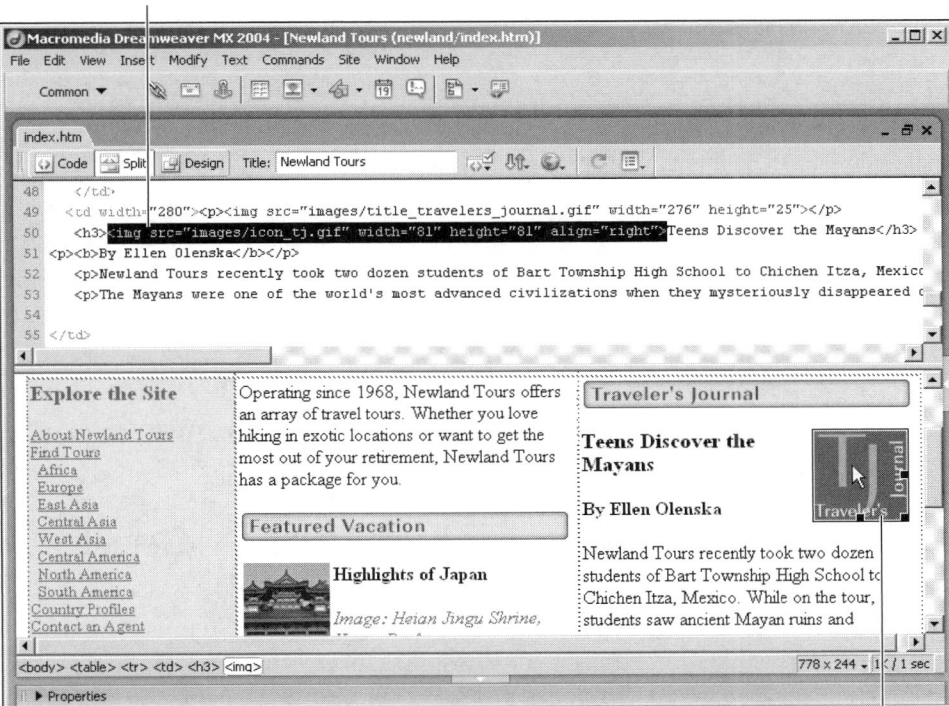

SELECTED IMAGE

3) If necessary, turn on line numbering in code view by choosing View > Code View Options > Line Numbers.

This setting displays line numbering beside the code in the code section of your screen. Line numbering makes it easier to communicate about portions of code to others. (I'll make use of line numbering quite often in this book.) It also makes troubleshooting much easier, because when they encounter problems, ASP and ColdFusion, send back error messages that specify the line number of the code that caused the problem.

4) Determine which version of HTML the document currently uses (scroll to line 1).

This task is difficult in design view, but split view shows right away that the document's code is HTML 4.01 transitional. How do we know that? It says so in the DOCTYPE declaration, in line 1. This declaration tells the browser which version of HTML the document uses, so the browser can render it properly. All well-formed HTML documents should have a DOCTYPE declaration.

HTML 4.01 transitional is now an outdated version of HTML. It still renders as well as ever in every major browser. But it has since been replaced with XHTML, and future browsers may not support it. In Lesson 2, you'll upgrade the site to XHTML.

Upgrading to XHTML means more than changing the DOCTYPE declaration, of course. XHTML is a major revision of HTML, and several coding practices have been changed. One such change, for example, is that all elements must be closed. In HTML 4 and earlier, empty elements were acceptable. Empty elements have no closing tags; or they have nothing between opening and closing tags. Example of empty tags include <br>, <hr>, <input>, and <img>. In XHTML, all tags must be closed. To accomplish this with empty tags, just add a space and a forward slash (/) before the closing angled bracket, so <br> becomes <br />, and <img src="picture.jpg"> becomes <img src="picture.jpg" />. If you take a look at the end of line 32, you'll see a <br> tag. It is one of hundreds of empty elements in the site. We'll deal with them later.

5) Check for compliance with accepted accessibility practices (scroll to lines 11 and 12).

For years, many Web developers neglected the needs of those with impairments that interfere with their ability to use sites. For example, users with visual impairments that prevent them from seeing the site had no way to access the site's content. Given that much of a site's content is text, a special kind of browser, called a screen reader, was developed that reads Web page content aloud. One problem with these readers, though, is that they have no way to articulate visual content, such as graphics. If these graphics communicate any important information about the site—and most graphics do—then users accessing sites with these browsers were not accessing that content.

A simple way to enable screen readers to articulate all of the information that your page communicates is to add a text caption to describe the contents of the image. If you put in a description of each image, including both graphics of substance (such as a diagram) and those used for mere decoration or even spacing, then users will never have to wonder what they're missing.

You can accomplish this in code by adding an attribute to each image element that associates a text string with that image. The attribute in question is alt. To use it,

34

you'd add alt="A description of the image" to each <img> tag in the document. The screen reader reads the alt description aloud and the user has access to the content.

```
 6  </head>
 7
 8  <body link="#3D7030" vlink="#505748" alink="#009900">
 9  <table width="750" border="0" cellpadding="3" cellspacing="0">
10   <tr>
11    <td colspan="2" width="470"><img src="images/banner_left.gif" width="451" height="68"></td>
12    <td width="280"><img src="images/banner_right.jpg" width="276" height="68"></td>
13   </tr>
14   <tr valign="top">
15    <td width="180"> </td>
```

When you scroll to lines 11 and 12 of the current document, you'll see two images in the first row of the table. These images are the Newland Tours banner and a single graphic holding the three photos (the beach, forest, and mosque). As you can see, they lack alt attributes, which means these images are inaccessible to users accessing the page with screen readers.

NOTE *Adding the Image* alt *attribute is not the only accessibility concern. For example, to make pages accessible, you might add shortcuts at the top of the page that enable users to skip over navigation bars to the page content. Another code feature that undermines accessibility is the abuse of HTML tables. While there is nothing intrinsically inaccessible about HTML tables, their overuse breaks up content and may make it hard for a screen reader to present your page's content in a logical sequence.*

The overriding goal of accessibility is to ensure that all users have equivalent access to all of your content. An extended discussion of accessibility is beyond the scope of this book, but you can learn more about it at Macromedia's Web site: www.macromedia.com/macromedia/accessibility/.

6) Check for obsolete and deprecated HTML code (scroll to line 21).

In line 21 of the code, you see:

```
<p><b><font color="#505748" size="4">Explore the Site</font></b></p>
```

While this line of code is rendered just fine in Dreamweaver and in a browser, the code is dated and problematic.

As we'll discuss in more detail later, one of the goals of recent versions of HTML has been to separate HTML markup from the details of presentation. In other words, HTML markup should describe the structure and content of the document, but it should not attempt to describe how the content should be presented. Two tags in the line of code above are deprecated for this reason. The term "deprecated" refers to a technique or code structure that has been removed from the standard but which is still (albeit temporarily) supported.

The <b> tag, which stands for bold, is a presentation tag. For users with screen readers, bold may not mean anything. Sometimes when we put something in bold we are trying to communicate that the content is somehow stronger or more emphatic than regular text. In this case, though, "Explore the Site" is not emphatic at all; it's simply a section title. Use of the <b> tag makes it unclear whether something is emphatic or just needs to stand out.

The other bad tag in the snippet is the <font> tag. This tag was used in HTML 3 and earlier to enable HTML developers to specify how their documents should appear. It has since been replaced with the much more powerful and efficient cascading style sheet. The <font> tag creates significant problems for developers, because they are attached to single blocks of text. Imagine, for example, that you use the <font> tag to specify how to present all of your level 2 headings throughout the site. To do so, you'd have to add this tag to every instance of a level 2 heading. If you make a mistake, your site is no longer consistent. Worse, if you do a site redesign, you have to manually change every single instance of that tag. Every <font> tag in the site needs to be removed, and, now that you know it's a problem, you can do so.

To summarize what we've found here, the code is old and no longer compliant with current standards. It is not XHTML (we saw that in the DOCTYPE declaration). Its empty tags are not closed. The images don't have alt attributes. The code is loaded with presentation tags, such as <b> and <font>, that need to be replaced. These are not all of the problems in the code, but it is a good enough sampling to give you an idea of what you are up against.

Now, you might be asking, "It all looks fine in a browser, so why bother? It seems like such a headache to fix—can't we just ignore it and move onto the dynamic stuff?" There are several answers to this question.

Just because it renders fine in Netscape and Internet Explorer today, doesn't mean it will appear well in the future. If your code breaks when the next version of Internet Explorer comes out, your client won't be impressed with your work.

In fact, the code *doesn't* render in all current browsers now. You have to think of screen readers, in which, as you have already seen, all of the images are inaccessible.

In addition, emerging technologies, such as XSLT (eXtensible Stylesheet Language Transformations), require XHTML compliance to function. XSLT is not a part of this book, nor is it likely to be implemented in a small business site such as this at the time of this writing, but it may be in the future. Since the first edition of this book was published, I have seen several major sites begin using XHTML with XSLT.

Taking the easy route now could create massive headaches later. Newland Tours is a small site at the moment—five HTML pages. By the end of this book, the Newland Tours site will contain about 30 pages, and if it were a real world project, it would quickly grow beyond that number as well. Before beginning its overhaul, it's best to whip it into shape while it's still easy to do so.

ASSESSING THE SITE: BUSINESS PROCESSES

Many clients are unaware of how well their code stacks up against current standards, and it is unlikely that you'll get many projects where the client is willing to pay you simply to upgrade the code from HTML 4.0 to XHTML. In fact, most Web redesign jobs occur because the current site no longer fits the business needs of the site owner. Common examples of a mismatch between the business needs and the site are as follows:

- The navigation is confusing. Site users can't find what they are looking for.
- Updating the site is too difficult. Many small businesses don't have large IT departments that can update their sites. A small-business owner may need to update site content, but lack the knowledge and tools to do so. The site begins to fall behind the business, or the business has to spend disproportionate money to pay for IT human resources.
- The look is outdated. Graphic design, like fashion, goes through cycles, and what was cutting-edge a few years ago may look stale today. An outmoded look communicates the wrong message to the business' target constituencies.
- The business wants to migrate certain services to the Web that are currently handled through other resources. Many clients want their sites to provide sufficient information to the public to decrease the number of phone calls coming in. For example, many companies deploy Web Knowledge Bases to decrease technical-support calls, while others provide online pricing and sales to decrease sales calls and/or to provide 24-hour service without hiring a whole night crew.
- The business is expanding or changing its offerings. If a business offers a whole new class of products or services, the Web site needs to reflect that. In such situations, adding a paragraph or two to an existing page isn't going to cut it. The site needs many new pages, requiring a new site map, navigation system, and so on.

This list, obviously, is not exhaustive, but it illustrates some of the relationships that exist between business processes and Web sites. In most cases, the client wants a site upgrade for many of these kinds of reasons. Ultimately, it is this information that should drive the entire site-revision process. It should enable you and your client to identify the scope of the upgrade as well as each of the particulars about what you should do.

TIP *Take the time to get this information from the client. Some clients are a little lazy about defining what they want. If you don't prompt them for more information, the site you deliver may not meet their needs. Do not expect them at that point to be self-critical enough to recognize that they were not sufficiently forthcoming: The burden is on you to work out all of this up front.*

In this task, you'll take a guided tour of the site as it exists. Along the way, I'll role-play the client and point out some of the shortcomings of the site. In this way, this task represents meeting with the client and identifying how the site is out of sync with business needs and processes. As these problems are identified, solutions—the specific changes and enhancements that you need to make to the site—begin to materialize. This way, the primary force driving the site upgrade process is the needs of the client, and not something else, such as your own opinion about what the site could be or, as is too often the case, the hottest technology on the market.

1) Still viewing index.htm, press F12 to open the site in a browser.

The F12 shortcut automatically opens the active file in a browser. Given that what the browser displays often varies from what you see in Dreamweaver, especially when you are working on dynamic content, you need to test often. The F12 shortcut is one of the most used keyboard shortcuts in all of Dreamweaver.

2) Look over the main homepage.

FONTS TOO PLAIN   TRAVELER'S JOURNAL COLUMN

Graphically, the site design is not bad. The client is not intending to overhaul the look. This particular design is also used in several print advertisements, so the client wants the site to reinforce that branding.

One design aspect that could be improved, though, is the type. The site sticks to HTML tags at their defaults, and as a result, they look a little plain. The client would like the headings to be a little more prominent and possibly in color.

Aside from the design, the page has a significant practical problem. The column entitled "Traveler's Journal" needs to be updated about once a week. Sometimes the business owners update this column, other times travel agents update the column. Not everyone knows how to work with the code or upload the files to the site. In addition, the owner does not want to give out the password to enable people to upload new pages. Currently, the journal is written in a word processor and handed off to one of the travel agents who knows how to revise and upload the pages. But this bottleneck prevents the site from being updated promptly, especially when that one agent is busy or not in the office. The client would like to find a way to make the weekly posting of the Traveler's Journal easy enough for everyone to contribute to it, without compromising security.

3) In the navigation bar on the left side of the screen, click the About Newland Tours link.

Beyond the font issues, discussed previously, this page doesn't need to change. Its content is almost never changed, and the client is happy with it as-is. Beyond upgrading the code to XHTML, a change that won't be visible in most browsers, this is the one page you won't change at all.

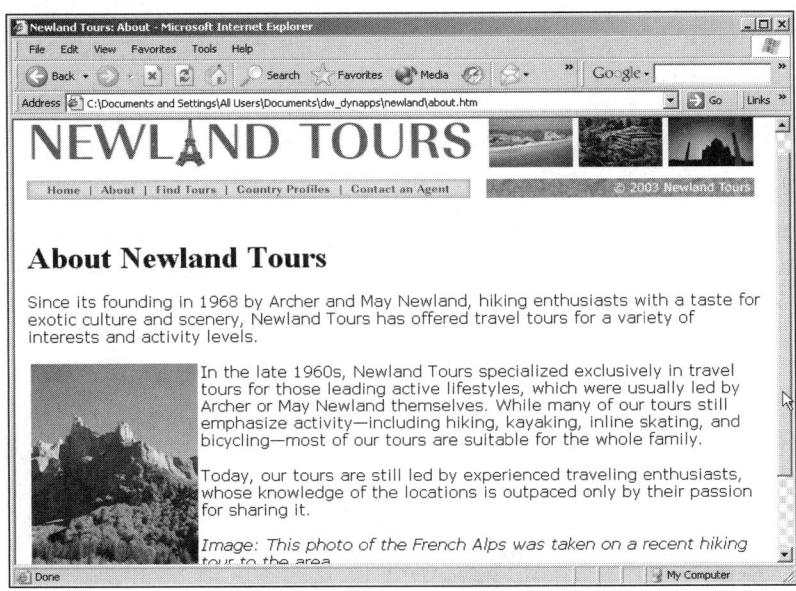

4) In the navigation bar at the top of the screen, click Find Tours. Scroll up and down the page, or use the internal navigation links near the top, to look over the tours.

This page is problematic in many different ways.

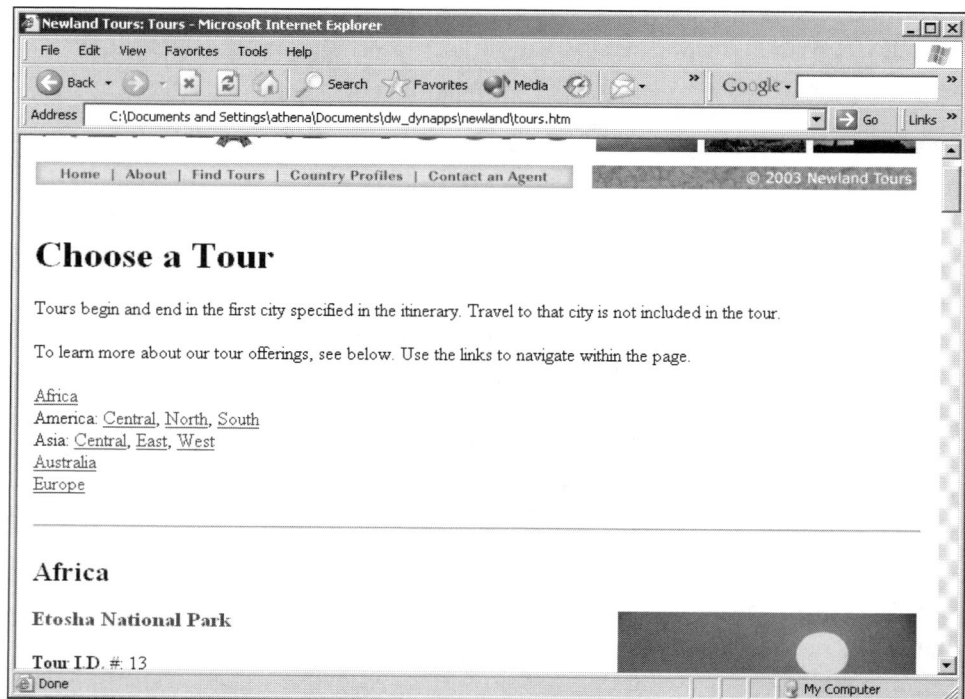

Let's start with the problems that the client faces with a page like this. Once again, the page is hard to maintain, because Newland Tours doesn't have an IT department. This issue is a serious problem from the client's point of view, because the information on this page is the primary source of information users have about the tours. The business problem that the client faces is that the tours change—some get added, some get removed. Worse, prices fluctuate so often that the client decided not to post them at the site, given the difficulty of keeping them up to date and the consequences if they did not. In addition, Newland Tours offers several more tours than listed here, but no one has had the opportunity to add them. This means that the client is losing business, thanks to the Web site's difficulty to maintain.

From the user's standpoint, the page is not very usable. It is extremely long, and it is hard to find tours of interest. There is no way to filter tours, other than checking out the tours listed in a particular region. For example, Newland Tours offers some tours that are exercise-intensive and others that are not; users have no way to filter out only those that are exercise-intensive. And, of course, the fact that the prices aren't

40

listed doesn't give the users any way of knowing how much the tours cost, unless they make a phone call.

As developers, we should observe that much of the information on this page is structurally redundant. That is, every tour has a title, an image, a description, and so on. Such a predictable structure should make us think that this information would be better stored in a database and pulled in on the fly. This would simplify maintenance and create the possibility of filtering, which would enhance the page's usability.

5) In the navigation bar at the top of the page, click the Country Profiles button.

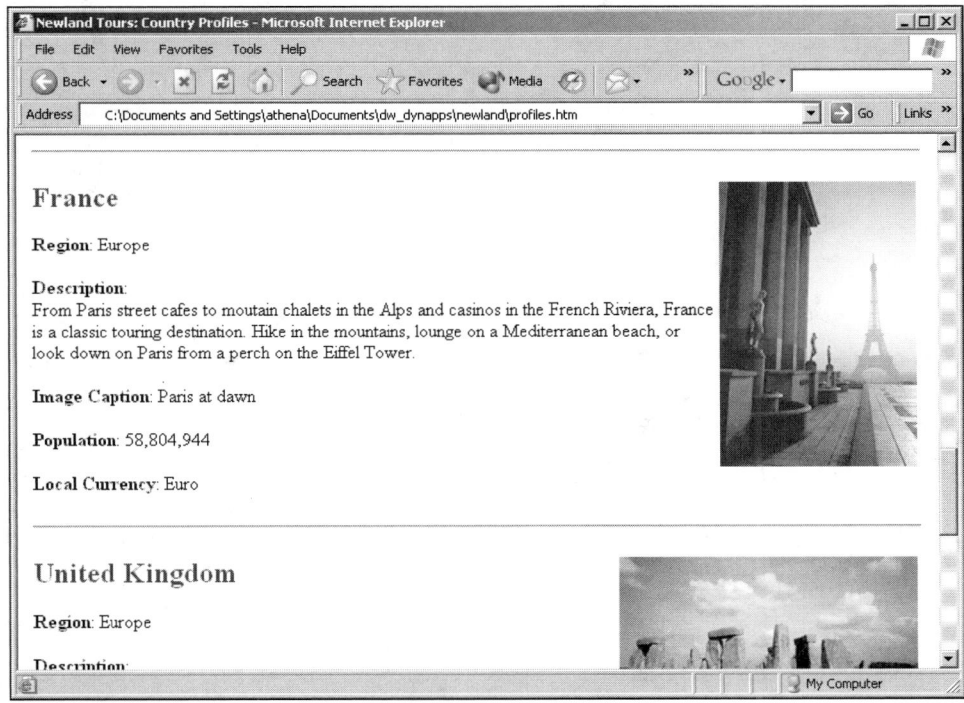

Almost every problem identified on the previous page also exists here. The page is hard to maintain, making it hard for Newland Tours staff to add countries to which they now offer tours. Users may incorrectly assume that Newland Tours doesn't offer any tours to, say, Italy, because it's not on this list. But Newland Tours does offer a tour to Italy, so the Web site is sending a counter-productive message to its users.

The problem also persists for users. Few users will want to learn about *all* of the countries that Newland Tours serves; they'll just want to see the ones they are interested in. Again, a simple filtering mechanism would make all the difference.

Another usability issue is that to go from a tour about Namibia's Etosha National Park to the Namibia country profile, the user has to scroll back up to the navigation bar, click Country Profiles, and scroll down to Namibia. It would be nice to automatically link from the Etosha National Park information to the Namibia country profile. But that would require extra coding using static HTML.

6) Return to the navigation bar, and click the Contact an Agent link.
This is the file that you developed earlier in the lesson to replace the version that was lost.

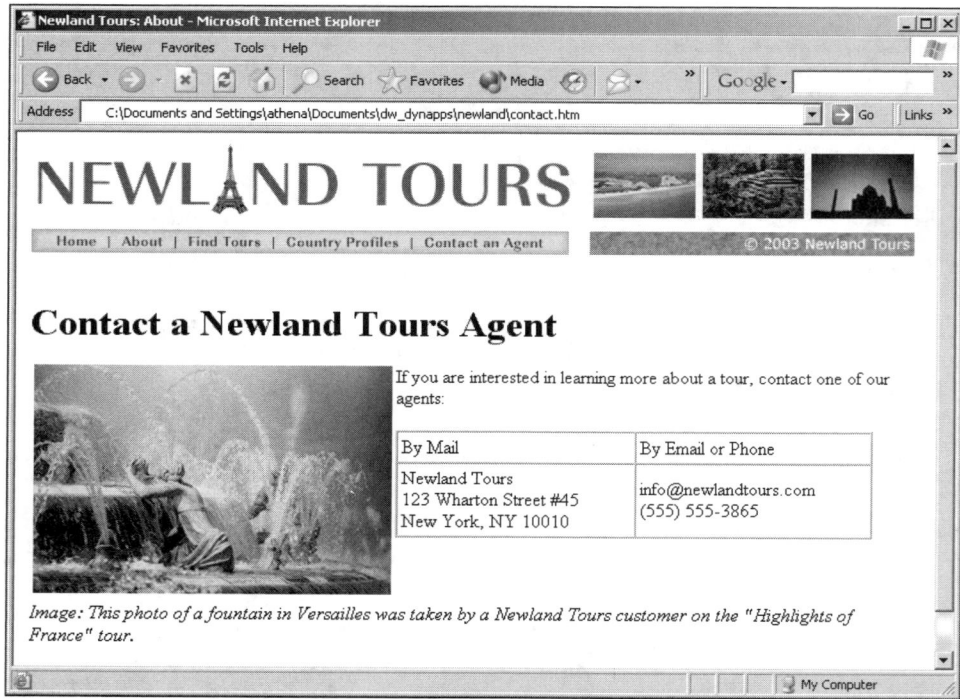

This simple table doesn't change very often, and it's easy enough to use. One thing about this page that the client doesn't like is the fact that the email address appears directly on the page: About a week after the page was posted with this email address, spammers started flooding the account with weight loss, debt reduction, and other less savory messages.

Another problem is that some of Newland Tours' customers don't have email clients automatically configured or were confused when the email client opened.

The client would like some way for customers to be able to contact Newland Tours without having to rely on an email client configuration. Also, the client would like to find a way to discourage spammers from flooding the accounts with junk.

The solution, of course, is to use a Web form. A form is perfect because it demands very little of the user, and it is possible to hide the email address, which will prevent spam bots (automated programs that crawl the Web "harvesting" email addresses for spammers) from finding Newland Tours agents' email addresses. Forms also make it possible to send the email address to a different address depending on its contents. For example, if a form asks the user to select a region, you can create a script that emails the form data only to the agent specializing in that region. You won't create that functionality in the course of this book, but by the time you are done, you should certainly have the wherewithal to do it.

A GLIMPSE OF THE FUTURE

Though this lesson has yielded only a static Web page to show for itself, you have actually done more than you may realize, and you have worked through a step that is too often shortchanged—with disastrous consequences. You've conducted a thorough assessment of the site, including code, business processes, and (indirectly) usability. You have a clear idea about what you need to do. For convenience, here is a summary of the site upgrade project goals:

- Upgrade HTML code to XHTML
- Improve site accessibility and usability
- Store structured and/or frequently updated content in a database
- Provide search and/or filtering mechanisms to enable users to find tours and country profiles more easily
- Develop a Web form that enables users to contact Newland Tours staff, without having to use email
- Develop a series of Web forms that enable Newland Tours staff to add, update, and delete content stored in the database (remember that the content stored in the database is also the source material that appears on the Web site)

If some of this sounds a bit abstract, look at the final version of the site as it will appear at the end of the book.

1) Point your browser to `http://www.allectomedia.com/newland_dynamic/`.
The index page should look almost the same as the version you just opened in Dreamweaver. However, it is quite different behind the scenes. For example, the Traveler's Journal column is actually retrieved and formatted on the fly from a database. In addition, the text is formatted more nicely on this version of the page.

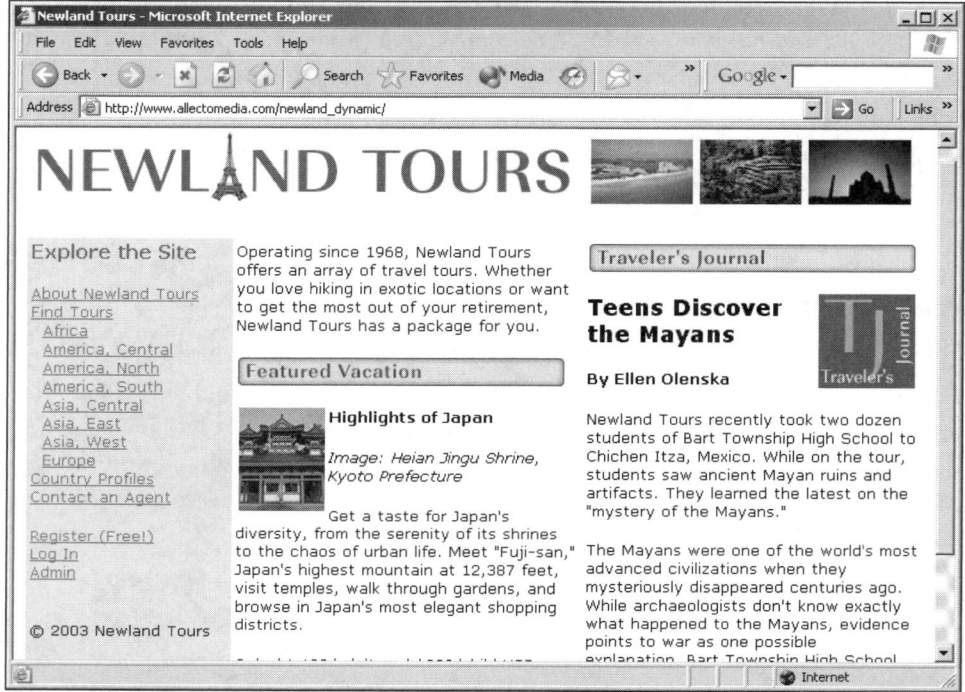

2) Click the Find Tours link in the navigation bar on the left side.
Instead of seeing the Find Tours page, as you expected, you are interrupted with a log-in screen. The previous site obviously had no such functionality. This was added because the client wanted users to register before accessing the site so the client has a way of learning about customers, as well as contacting them with offers and promotions. You can log in using the following credentials:

Email address: *osiris@allectomedia.com*

Password: *osiris*

NOTE *This is a fictional account created for the purpose of giving readers access to the site without having to register. There is no such account, so please don't send email to it.*

Once you authenticate, you are sent to the page you requested earlier.

3) Explore the site as much as you like.

At this point, I'll turn you loose and let you explore on your own. You will see that the site offers several methods of filtering content, linking to related content (from tours to country profile, for example), and even a price calculator utility.

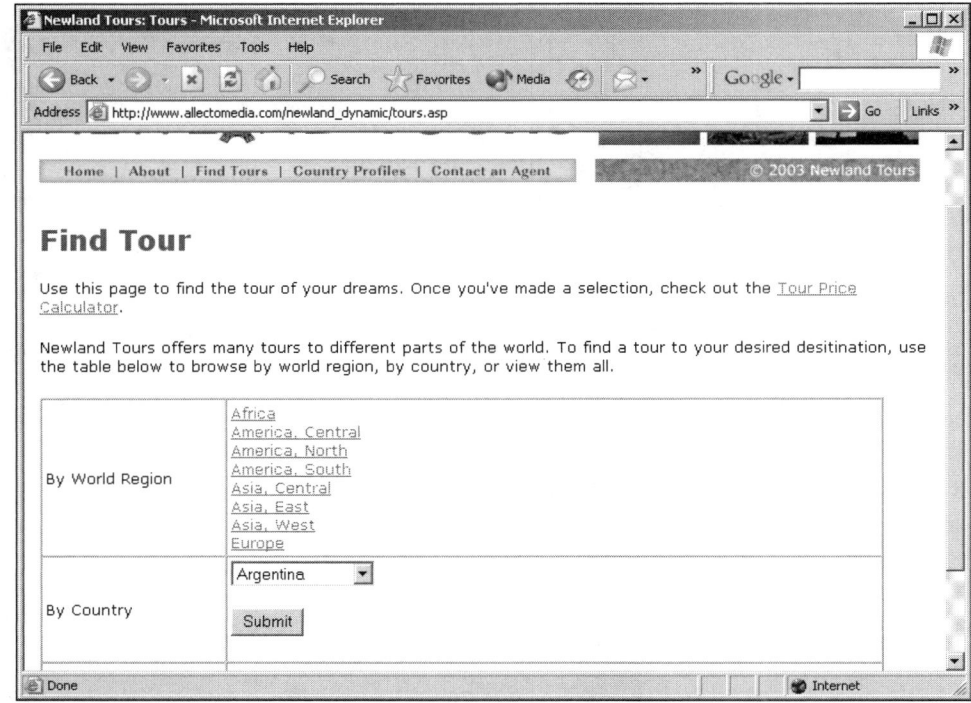

You'll notice that the Admin section is off-limits to the osiris@allectomedia.com account. That section enables users to change the content of the database, and hence much of the site. Obviously, I can't publish that in a book! As you'll see later, what's inside is the content management system—that is, the Web forms that enable Newland Tours staff to update site content.

The accompanying screenshot shows one of these forms. Using this form, the staff can create a new Traveler's Journal entry just by filling out the form, following the directions that appear onscreen. As soon as the staff member clicks Submit, the database entry is added, and the staff member is redirected to the site's homepage, where she or he will discover that the Traveler's Journal has already been updated on the public Web site in the split second between the time the Submit button was clicked and the index page was loaded.

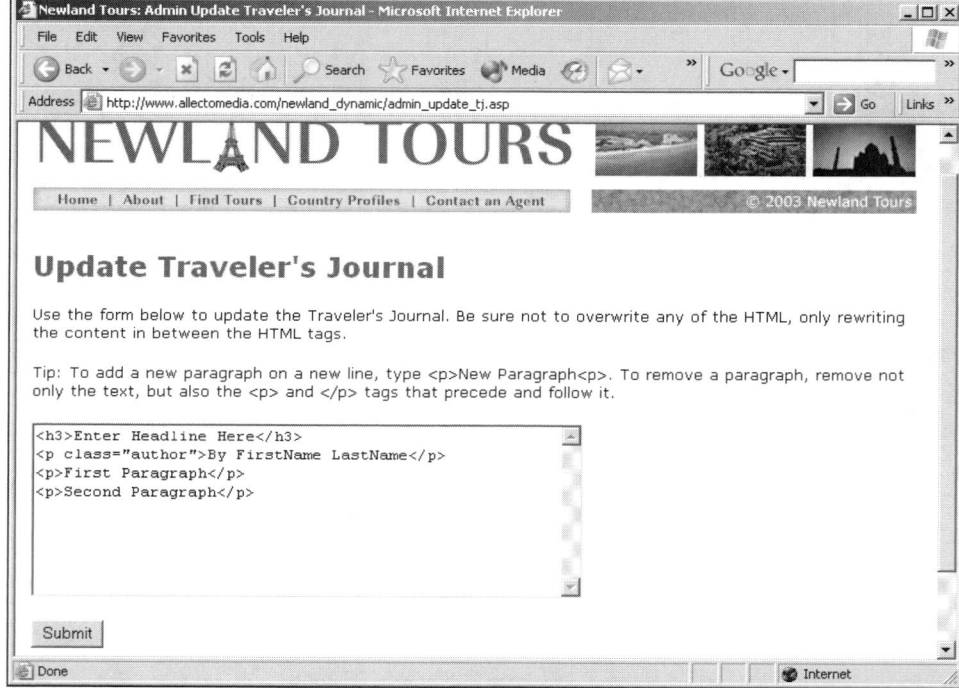

WHAT YOU HAVE LEARNED

In this lesson, you have:

- Defined a static site in Dreamweaver (pages 13–18)

- Created a basic static page (pages 18–22)

- Formatted a page (pages 23–30)

- Assessed the existing code and identified several problems with it (pages 31–37)

- Compared the client's business needs with the current site and identified several shortcomings (pages 37–43)

- Plotted out several site enhancements that will make it a better fit for the client's needs (page 43)

- Previewed some of these enhancements, to get a better sense of what you'll be doing for the rest of the book (pages 44–46)

upgrading to XHTML

LESSON 2

In the previous chapter's assessment tasks, you identified two categories of problems that need addressing in this site revision: outdated code and mismatches between the existing site and the business processes it should support. In this lesson, you'll take care of the first of these problems: You'll convert the site to XHTML. It will take the rest of the book (and more) to take care of the business process issues. Before jumping into building dynamic Web applications, though, you should first take care of the code issues. This way, rather than proliferating the existing code problems, you can eliminate them up front.

I'll delve into the specifics of XHTML—what it is and what code needs to be changed to get there—inside the lesson itself. For now, let's take a look at the big-picture task of upgrading code. Because of the similarities between HTML and XHTML, the primary task of this chapter is to find outdated code and replace it with current code. Strictly speaking, the simplest way to do this is to use Dreamweaver's conversion feature (File > Convert > XHTML). However, we're going to use Find and Replace instead. Why

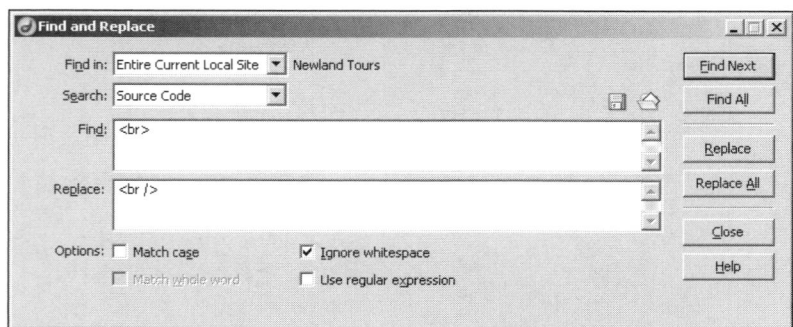

Dreamweaver's Find and Replace dialog is a powerful utility that automates large-scale changes, such as upgrading to XHTML.

bother with this when there's an easier alternative? The lesson covers several critical Dreamweaver skills. You should read this lesson to learn about the following:

- **HTML in general.** Those rusty with HTML or who want some practice refreshing their memory with it will benefit from the HTML code orientation of this chapter.

- **XHTML in particular.** Those new to XHTML, not sure how it differs from HTML, or not understanding why XHTML is so important will know all of this by the end of the lesson.

- **The power of Find and Replace.** Most Dreamweaver users have dabbled with it, but few take the time to master what is one of Dreamweaver's most powerful automation and productivity tools.

- **The site we'll be using throughout the book.** Working through the site in this lesson will make you intimately familiar with the current pages at the code level. Dynamic Web site development is intrinsically code-oriented, especially as taught in this book, and it will make more sense to you if you have worked through this lesson.

If you have already mastered hand-coded XHTML and understand the directions the W3C is taking XHTML, and you have considerable experience working with the more advanced and out-of-the-way features of the Find and Replace dialog, then you can skip this lesson and move onto Lesson 3. Before you go, however, open each page in Dreamweaver, and one at a time, choose File › Convert › XHTML to upgrade it to XHTML.

Word processor users are probably familiar with the Find and Replace function. Using a simple dialog, you specify the string that needs replacing and the string to replace it with. At its core, Dreamweaver's Find and Replace function works the same way. But Web sites are different from word processor documents—site content is spread out across files, strings can be either document text or document code, and so on. Dreamweaver's Find and Replace dialog offers a host of options that enable you to customize the tasks in ways that result in unbelievable productivity gains.

Dreamweaver's Find and Replace dialog also has another feature, called **regular expressions**, which enables you to search for text patterns, rather than specific strings of text. Regular expressions use placeholder characters that represent other characters. They are useful when you want to search for a certain kind of text, without being able to specify the exact text itself. For example, imagine you wanted to search for email addresses, or verify that an email address has been entered. You obviously can't spell out for Dreamweaver every email address that has ever been (or ever could be) entered. But you do know that but all valid email addresses have the following syntax: username@domain.com (or other extension, such as .org or .edu). And thanks to regular expressions, you can tell Dreamweaver to look for a pattern that meets the following criteria: "find any text string without spaces, followed by an @ character, followed by another text string without spaces and including zero or more period characters (.), followed by a period character (.), followed by another text string of up to three characters without spaces." Such directions would find any valid email address. Unfortunately, regular expressions can be hard to use. For example, the regular expression to catch any email address looks as follows:

```
^([a-zA-Z0-9_\-\.]+)@((\[[0-9]{1,3}\.[0-9]{1,3}\.[0-9]{1,3}\.)|
(([a-zA-Z0-9\-]+\.)+))([a-zA-Z]{2,4}|[0-9]{1,3})(\]?)$
```

Source: Todd Moon at `http://www.regxlib.com`

Many regular expressions aren't quite so crazy, but they can still be hard to use. Fortunately, Dreamweaver has built in the equivalent functionality of dozens of regular expressions in the Find and Replace dialog. You'll work with quite a few of these built-in search expressions in this lesson, and you'll see how their power can add to your productivity. If you are already competent with regular expressions, know also that you can type them in directly to the Find and Replace dialog.

Find and Replace is obviously a powerful productivity tool, and its applicability extends beyond upgrading HTML sites to XHTML. For example, Find and Replace would be an ideal solution for changing a navigation bar sitewide, dealing with a company name change (e.g., a law firm that adds a new partner), or updating the address in every page's footer.

The power of Find and Replace notwithstanding, you might be wondering how you can be sure that you didn't overlook anything, that the site really is, in fact, XHTML-compliant. At the end of the lesson, you will validate your pages using Dreamweaver's Validator, proving that your pages are fully XHTML-compliant. If the Validator catches any deviations, it will show you exactly where the problem occurred—and any problems you find will be, of course, only a Find and Replace away from correct.

WHAT YOU WILL LEARN

In this lesson, you will:

- Learn about the relationships among HTML, XHTML, XML, and CSS
- Replace obsolete HTML tags with their XHTML counterparts using Find and Replace
- Use Dreamweaver's Specify Tag/Action utility to find and replace sophisticated text patterns
- Force Dreamweaver to write XHTML code, rather than HTML code, henceforth
- Validate the XHTML code using Dreamweaver's built-in code validation utility

APPROXIMATE TIME

This lesson takes approximately 90 minutes to complete.

LESSON FILES

Starting Files:

Lesson02/Start/newland/about.htm
Lesson02/Start/newland/contact.htm
Lesson02/Start/newland/index.htm
Lesson02/Start/newland/profiles.htm
Lesson02/Start/newland/tours.htm

Completed Files:

Lesson02/Complete/newland/about.htm
Lesson02/Complete/newland/contact.htm
Lesson02/Complete/newland/index.htm
Lesson02/Complete/newland/profiles.htm
Lesson02/Complete/newland/tours.htm

UPGRADING TO THE XHTML DOCUMENT TYPE

The goal of this lesson is to upgrade the site's HTML code to XHTML, and ensure that all subsequent code you add while working in Dreamweaver is XHTML-compliant. You might be wondering what exactly XHTML is and how it differs from HTML. XHTML is the current standard for HTML, which means that the relationship between the two is historical: XHTML replaces HTML.

Perhaps the most significant change to come with XHTML has little to do with code at all; it's the new conceptual thrust of XHTML, bringing HTML in line with XML, or eXtensible Markup Language. XML is a meta-language—a set of rules that developers can use to develop their own custom language in line with a common standard. XML is markup-based, like HTML, so its syntax should be familiar, as in the following: `<authorname type="first">Jeffrey</authorname>`. Several variants of XML have already appeared, such as MathML, a markup language that mathematicians use to encode mathematical expressions. XHTML is a variant that developers use for (drum roll) marking up Web pages.

One of the central tenets of XML is that the tags describe the content of a document, *but not its presentation*. Presentation of XML content is handled with a separate type of code (such as CSS, XSLT, or XSL-FO). Previous versions of HTML mixed content and presentation markup. Elements such as `<font color="green" size="+1">` lack semantic value. For this reason, they are **deprecated**, which means that their use is discouraged and they will eventually be dropped from the standard, but they'll still work for now. They tell the user (or browser) nothing about what was enclosed inside them. Rather, these tags merely tell the browser how to present whatever is enclosed, unlike the `<authorname>` element in the preceding paragraph, which leaves little to the imagination about what it contains.

In short, you should use XHTML to describe the structure of your document: headings (`<h1>`, `<h2>`, etc.), lists (`<ol>`, `<ul>`, `<li>`), body text (`<p>`), emphatic text (`<strong>`, `<em>`), anchors (`<a>`) and so on. To specify how graphical browsers (such as Internet Explorer and Netscape) should present this information, you should use cascading style sheets, rather than presentation tags, such as `<font>` or `<b>`.

This separation of code from content and presentation has more than just theoretical benefit. First, it enables a broader variety of browsers, including screen readers for the visually impaired, to render the content without having to weed out (or worse, attempt to interpret) presentation tags. Second, the proper use of XHTML and cascading style sheets greatly speeds up the development and maintenance of Web sites.

As you probably know, XHTML looks mostly like HTML. Many of the tags are the same, including `<body>`, `<head>`, `<h1>`, `<p>`, `<ol>`, `<a>`, `<table>`, `<tr>`, `<td>`, `<form>`, and so on. In fact, most HTML code is unchanged in the transition. That limits how much you actually have to change when upgrading to XHTML.

NOTE *XHTML is backward-compatible. That is, browsers created before the XHTML specification can still display XHTML code nearly perfectly.*

But XHTML code is not exactly the same as HTML code. Your task in this lesson is to find these differences and change the code accordingly. The most significant differences, beyond the enforced separation of logic and presentation already discussed, are as follows:

- All XHTML tags and their attributes must be lowercase. In HTML, both `<p>` and `<P>` are equally acceptable, and many developers capitalized HTML tags to help them stand out. But in XHTML, following XML rules, all tags must be lowercase, so only `<p>` is acceptable. Likewise, tag attributes, such as the `cellpadding="3"` attribute of the `<table>` tag, must also be in lowercase. The Newland Tours site already uses lowercase tags, so you won't have to worry too much about this issue.

- All XHTML tags must be closed. For example, if you have an `<h1>` tag, somewhere else there should be a closing `</h1>` tag. However, some elements lack closing tags. Examples of these empty tags include `<br>`, `<img src="xyz.gif">`, `<hr>`, and `<input>`. In addition, some tags could be closed or empty in HTML, including the `<p>` and `<li>` tags. In XHTML, however, the `<p>` and `<li>` tags need corresponding `</p>` and `</li>` tags. As for the empty tags, they are closed in a special way. The syntax is `<my_empty_tag />`. Thus, you should convert the empty tags above to `<br />`, `<img src="xyz.gif" />`, `<hr />`, and `<input />`. The added space and backslash replace the closing tag.

- Because so many different flavors of HTML exist side-by-side on the Web, developers have for years preceded HTML documents with a document type declaration. For example, Dreamweaver adds the following to the top of most new documents: `<!DOCTYPE HTML PUBLIC "-//W3C//DTD HTML 4.01 Transitional//EN">`. This tells browsers which version of code (HTML 4.01 Transitional) the document uses as well as its language (English). XHTML not only has a different document type statement, but as a valid form of XML, it also has an XML declaration.

- As discussed previously, presentation tags are no longer allowed. Instead, use cascading style sheets to handle presentation.

With that background, let's get started!

1) Open index.htm in Dreamweaver.

The Find and Replace operations you'll be doing are sitewide, so theoretically it makes no difference which file you open. In fact, you can have a blank, unsaved document open. Dreamweaver doesn't care. As long as you have a file open, you can access the Find and Replace dialog.

In a moment, you'll use Find and Replace to formally convert the site to XHTML. To do so, you will replace the document type definition from HTML 4.01 Transitional to XHTML 1.0 Transitional. Your document won't be fully XHTML-compliant, since all of the noncompliant code will still be there. But by changing the document type information, you'll not only tell browsers that the document is XHTML, you'll also tell Dreamweaver. Once you do so, Dreamweaver will automatically write XHTML-compliant code from that point forward, as you'll see for yourself.

2) Still in split view, place your cursor at the end of the Featured Vacation segment in the design pane (after $899/child USD) and press Shift+Return (Macintosh) or Shift+Enter (Windows).

This keyboard shortcut inserts a line break element (the <br> tag in HTML). This is an empty element, and as you can see, it is not inserted in the correct XHTML format. This is proof that Dreamweaver is writing, by default, non-XHTML compliant code. The reason Dreamweaver does this is that the document type is HTML 4.01 Transitional, and in that version of HTML, <br> is the correct way to code a line break element.

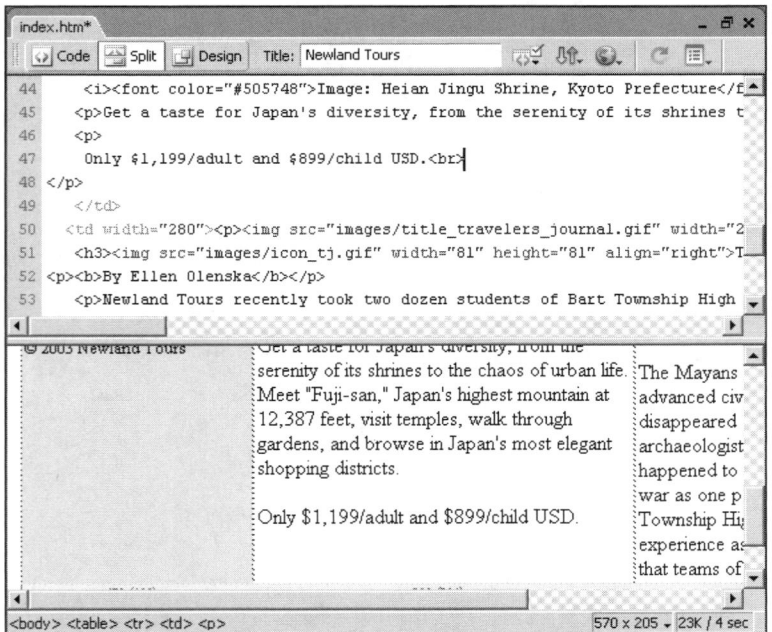

Let's change the document type information.

3) Choose File > New to create a new document. Make sure Basic Page is the selected category and that HTML is the file selected in the second pane. Near the bottom-right corner, check Make Document XHTML Compliant. Press Create.

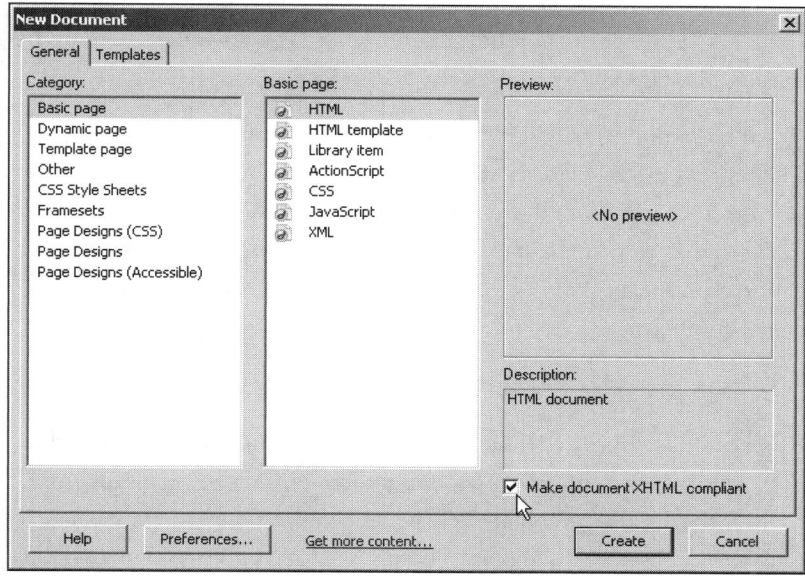

When you create a new document that is XHTML-compliant, Dreamweaver writes the proper document type information at the top of the new document. We'll copy that code and use it to replace the existing code in the HTML 4.01 Transitional site.

4) Select lines 1–2 of the new document, and choose Edit > Copy to copy the code to the clipboard. You can close the new file without saving.

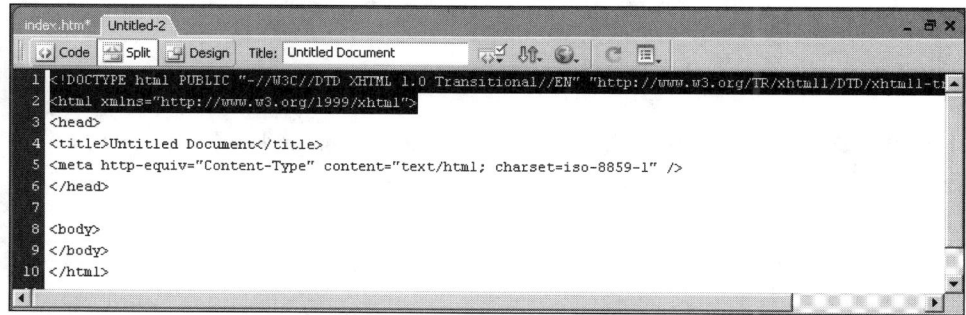

Let's take a look at the code you just copied.

```
<!DOCTYPE html PUBLIC "-//W3C//DTD XHTML 1.0 Transitional//EN"
"http://www.w3.org/TR/xhtml1/DTD/xhtml1-transitional.dtd">
<html xmlns="http://www.w3.org/1999/xhtml">
```

The first line is the DOCTYPE declaration, which looks much like the one for HTML 4.01. Only the HTML version has changed. One new difference is a URL that points to a DTD file. A DTD, or document type definition, is a document containing all the rules specifying the tags and attributes allowed in a particular version of XML.

The second line is the opening <html> tag that all HTML documents must have. This one is special, in that it has an xmlns attribute. This attribute, short for XML Name Space, specifies the source of all the tags. It is required in XML because it is conceivable that two different XML-based languages will use the same tag. By specifying a default name space, the rendering program (in this case, the browser) can resolve any such conflicts.

5) Choose Edit > Find and Replace.

The Find and Replace dialog appears. The factory default settings are shown in the accompanying screenshot, but yours may vary, depending on the settings from any previous use. If either the Replace With area or the area above it already has any text in them, delete it. Both fields should be empty before you proceed to the next step.

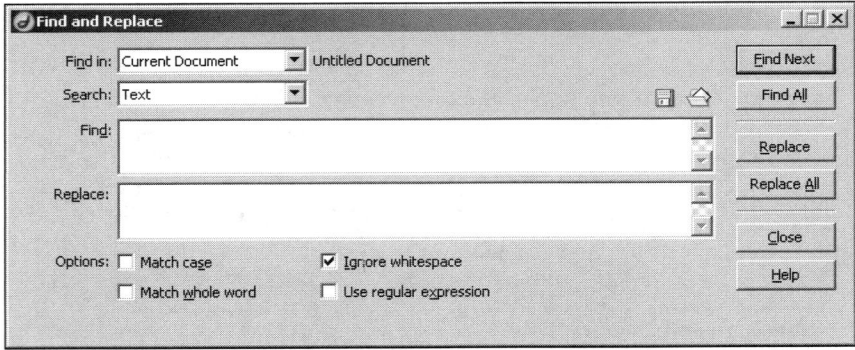

6) Click inside the Replace With text area and press Command+V (Macintosh) or Ctrl+V (Windows) to paste in the two lines of code.

The code may wrap inside the dialog so it appears to be more than two lines, but don't worry about that.

What you're doing in this step is telling Dreamweaver what to replace the searched text with. Of course, you haven't yet told Dreamweaver what to search for in the first place. You also haven't told Dreamweaver which files you want it to search.

56

7) Index.html should still be open. Scroll to the top of code view, select lines 1–2, choose Edit > Copy, click in the text area above the Replace With text area, and paste in these two lines of code.

Again, the lines of code may wrap, but that is no concern.

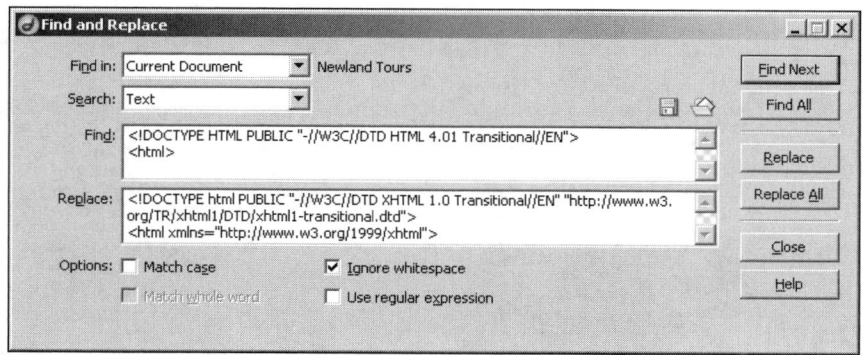

At this point, you've told Dreamweaver what to find and what to replace it with. So far, so good. But you still haven't told Dreamweaver in which files it should search for the strings.

8) In the Find in drop-down menu (at the top), select Entire Current Local Site.

Here you are telling Dreamweaver to look for the string in every HTML file in the site. This means that rather than upgrading one page at a time to XHTML, you can update every file at once.

NOTE *Making multiple-file replacements is a potentially dangerous action, because changes made to site files currently closed (which is all files besides index.htm) are permanent and not Undo-able. Be careful when running Find and Replace operations on multiple files.*

9) In the Search drop-down menu, choose Source Code. Uncheck Match case, Match whole word, and Use regular expressions. Check Ignore whitespace.

The Search For drop-down menu is important. By default, Find and Replace looks in the text, which is the text that will be displayed in a browser for the user to see. The Text option does not include the code. Since you are upgrading the code of the pages, and not the text, it is vital that you choose Source Code.

Match case takes case (a versus A) into account in the search. Case differences are ignored if the box is unchecked.

Match whole word forces Dreamweaver to find only a whole word. With this option unchecked, searching for design would match for design, designer, and designed. With it checked, this option will only match design.

Ignore whitespace ignores any white space, such as hard returns, tabs, and indentation between text or elements. Because HTML ignores white space, many programmers use white space to make code more legible.

Use regular expressions causes Dreamweaver to interpret reserved characters used in regular expressions (such as /d) as regular expression characters. If unchecked, and Dreamweaver encounters /d, it will search for /d, rather than any single numeral, which is what /d means in regular expressions.

The final version of the Find and Replace dialog should appear as in the accompanying screenshot.

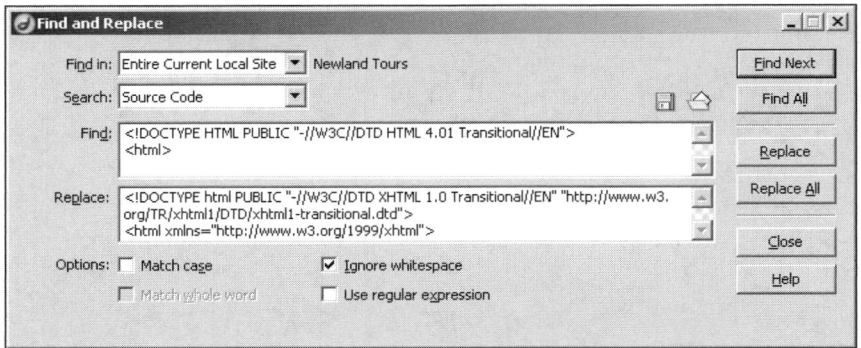

10) Click Replace All. When the warning dialog appears, click Yes.

The operation is run. By default, the Dreamweaver Results panel opens to show you which files were changed. As you can see, five files were changed. Since there are five files in the site, you know you were successful.

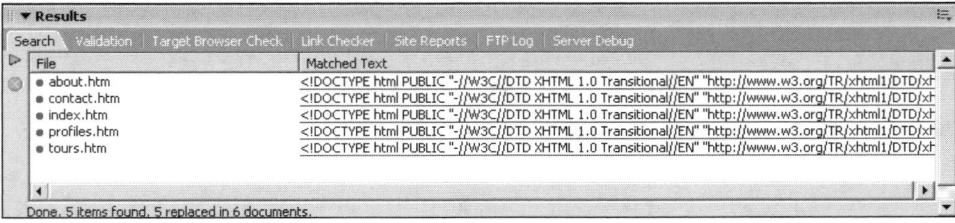

11) To wrap up the line break experiment, return to the bottom of the Featured Vacation section where you inserted a line break earlier, and press Shift+Return (Macintosh) Shift+Enter (Windows) again.

When you look in code view, you will see that Dreamweaver this time added a <br /> tag beside the <br> tag it added earlier. Remember, the <br /> syntax is used for empty elements; it is equivalent to
</br>, and is not simply a closing </br> tag. This proves that Dreamweaver knows that the document is an XHTML document, and you can be assured that henceforth Dreamweaver will not add any non-XHTML-compliant tags to your code.

NOTE *Dreamweaver may still add <font> tags, depending on how you format text. It's best to discipline yourself not to format text using the Property inspector for such attributes as color and size. Instead, rely on CSS as much as possible.*

NEW LINE BREAK TAG   ORIGINAL LINE BREAK TAG

```
44        <i><font color="#505748">Image: Heian Jingu Shrine, Kyoto Prefecture</font></i></p>
45      <p>Get a taste for Japan's diversity, from the serenity of its shrines to the chaos of urban life. Me
46      <p>
47        Only $1,199/adult and $899/child USD.<br>
48      └─<br />
49   </p>
50      </td>
51      <td width="280"><p><img src="images/title_travelers_journal.gif" width="276" height="25"></p>
52      <h3><img src="images/icon_tj.gif" width="81" height="81" align="right">Teens Discover the Mayans</h3>
53   <p><b>By Ellen Olenska</b></p>
```

Changing the document type information at the top ensures that new tags are XHTML-compliant. Of course, it does nothing about the existing tags. You'll have to fix those yourself.

12) Remove the two line breaks, if you like, and save the file.
Any time you make a significant change, you should save index.htm. You don't need to save any of the closed files—as soon as Dreamweaver replaced the document type information, it saved those files.

REPLACING STRINGS IN SOURCE CODE
In this task, you will replace a handful of simple tags. For example, you will replace all instances of <br> with <br />. These changes are straightforward, because there are no attributes or variations to throw off the search. (In contrast, tags such as <img src="images/imagename.gif"> are going to be a little more work, thanks to their attributes; we'll wrestle with these harder ones shortly.)

1) Choose Edit > Find and Replace to open the dialog once again.
This time, rather than pasting information in, you can just type directly in the text areas.

59

2) Type `<br>` **in the upper text area, and type** `<br />` **in the lower one (don't forget the space between the** r **and the** / **character). Be sure that you have completely removed the text that was in these windows from before.**

The Find In drop-down should still say Entire Current Local Site, which is what you want, as is Source Code in the Search drop-down.

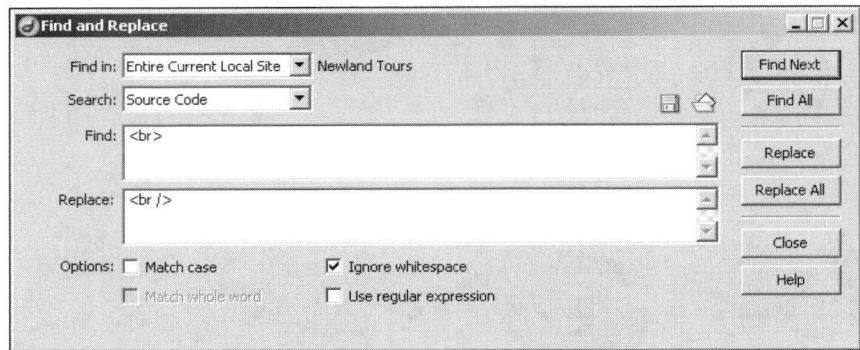

3) Click Replace All.

Once again, you see the warning, and the Results panel displays the changes. In this case, there were quite a few changes made throughout the site.

4) Repeat steps 2 and 3 to replace `<hr>` **with** `<hr />`**.**

Find and Replace makes quick work of what otherwise would be a very tedious task.

5) Repeat steps 2 and 3 to replace `<meta http-equiv="Content-Type" content=` `"text/html; charset=iso-8859-1">` **with** `<meta http-equiv="Content-Type"` `content="text/html; charset=iso-8859-1" />`**.**

TIP *To avoid typing this string, you can copy it from line 6 on any of the pages.*

The original Newland site was created in Dreamweaver, and it automatically added the `<meta>` tag you are replacing here. Generally, developers use the `<meta>` tag to convey information about a document. You'll often see `<meta>` tags with descriptions and keyword lists. Since these obviously vary, they can be a challenge to update through Find and Replace. But in this particular case, that's not a problem. On each page, Dreamweaver added only one `<meta>` tag, each time with the same contents. You can therefore be confident that you fixed them all.

6) Repeat steps 2 and 3 to replace `<map name="navbarMap">` **with** `<map name=` `"navbarMap" id="navbarMap">`**.**

TIP *index.htm doesn't have this tag. You can manually type it in, or you can open any of the other four site files and copy it from there. This tag is found near the bottom of each of those pages.*

Certain Web page objects have identifying attributes, which, among other things, enable the object to be accessed and even manipulated by scripts. In previous versions of HTML, you'd use the name attribute to give an object a unique identifier. In XHTML, the proper identifier has changed from name to id. Unfortunately, a lot of older browsers don't yet recognize id. And you can assume that newer browsers eventually won't recognize name. The way to work around this problem is to include both name and id attributes set to the same values, so that all browsers can recognize them.

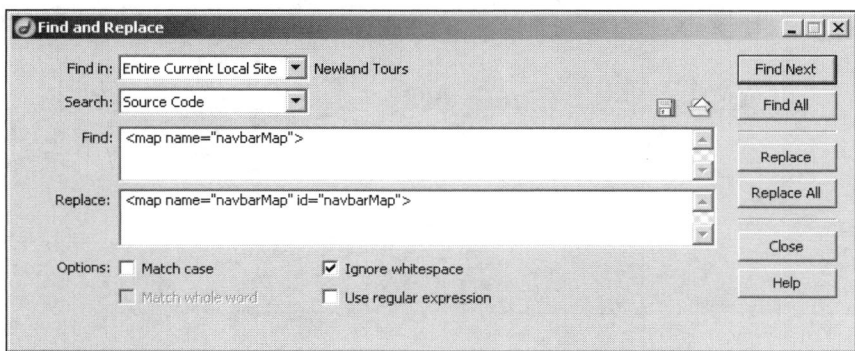

7) Save index.html.

REPLACING TAGS

As a part of the migration from presentation-oriented HTML tags to content-descriptive HTML tags, the <b> (bold) and <i> (italic) tags have fallen out of favor. Both have been replaced with the content-descriptive tags <strong> and <em>. Most major browsers render the <strong> tag in bold and the <em> tag in italics. In other words, by upgrading from <b> to <strong> and <i> to <em>, you can achieve standards compliancy and enhance accessibility without changing the appearance of your documents in major browsers.

Because this change is a simple one-to-one change, and because none of the four tags involved have any attributes, you could easily find <b> and replace it with <strong>, find </b> and replace it with </strong>, and so forth. But Dreamweaver has an even easier way to replace tags: the Change Tag action in the Find and Replace dialog.

1) With index.htm still open, choose Edit > Find and Replace. Make sure the Find in drop-down specifies Entire Current Local Site.

So far, the setup is just like the searches you have already done, but that's about to change.

2) Choose Specific Tag from the Search drop-down.

The rest of the Find and Replace dialog changes drastically.

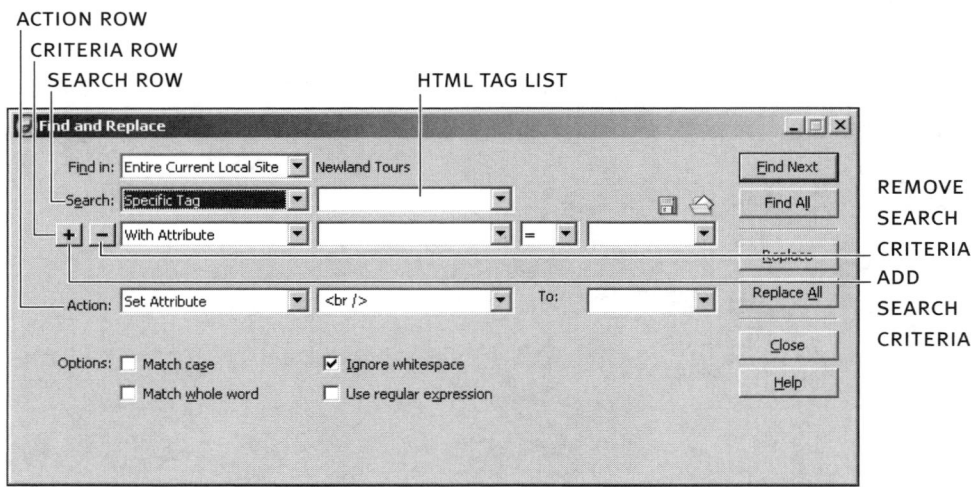

The Specific Tag setting opens up a number of options that enable you to manipulate tags. Since our goal is to update the tags from HTML to XHTML, the options displayed here are incredibly useful.

3) Choose b from the HTML tag list drop-down, which is just to the right of the Search drop-down.

Your first goal is to upgrade the <b> tag to the <strong> tag. You'll take care of the <i> tag in a moment. By specifying the b element, you are in effect telling Dreamweaver to find not just the opening <b> tag, but also the closing </b> tag.

4) Click the Remove Search Criterion button to remove the With Attribute line that was added by default.

You can add multiple additional criteria to further refine your search. You will use this feature later in the lesson, but for now, it is not necessary, so remove it.

5) Select Change Tag in the Action drop-down menu. In the To drop-down menu that appears, select strong.

The action list contains all of the actions that you can have Dreamweaver do to the tag you specified in the HTML Tag List drop-down. You'll get to see a few of these in action. Right now, you are telling Dreamweaver to search for all <b> and </b> tags and change them to <strong> and </strong> tags, without changing whatever's between them at all. Your screen at this point should match the one shown in the screenshot.

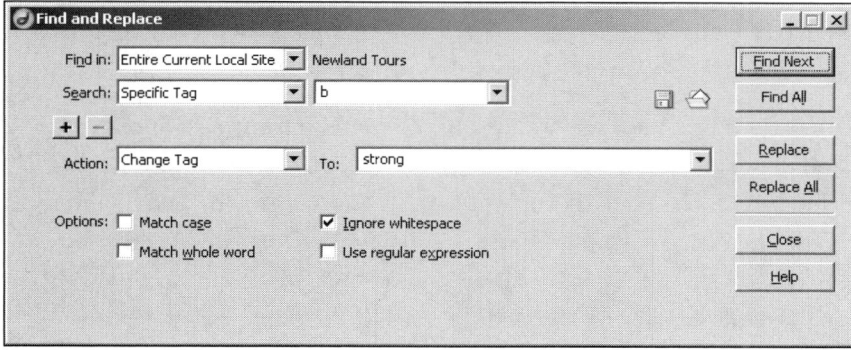

6) Click the Replace All button, and click Yes in the warning dialog that appears.
The Results window opens, and you can see that Dreamweaver replaces quite a few of these tags throughout the site.

7) Repeat the preceding steps to change the <i> **tags to** <em> **tags.**
Thankfully, when you reopen the Find and Replace dialog, Dreamweaver remembers the preceding operation, so there is little you have to do to customize the operation for these new tags.

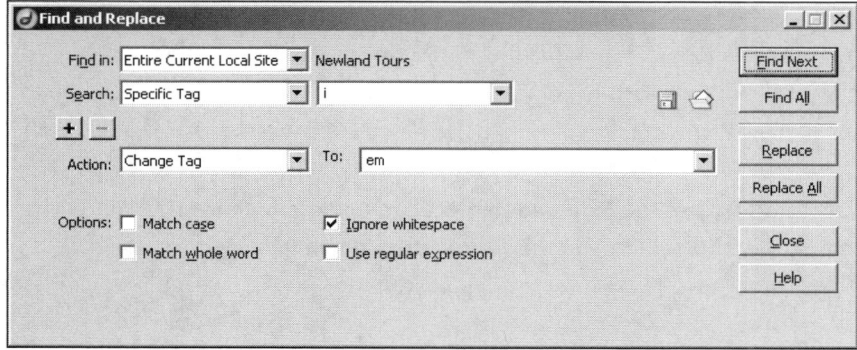

8) Save index.htm.

STRIPPING UNWANTED TAGS

As you know by now, the <font> tag has become obsolete, but unlike the <b> and <i> tags, it has no easy counterpart with which you can replace it. The presentation details that the <font> tag was once used to specify are now handled with an entirely new technology: CSS. Thus, rather than a one-to-one fix as you did in the previous task, solving this problem requires two steps. First, you need to strip out all of the old tags. Second, you need to develop and apply CSS. You'll do the first of these two steps in this task. The second step forms the basis of Lesson 3.

Stripping out <font> tags might seem to be difficult. After all, given their many attributes, and the many possible values you can enter in the attributes, you can't just do a search for the <font> tag as you can with the <b> tag. You'd need to find a way to catch differences like the ones between <font color="#00FF00"> and <font size="+1">. Two workarounds to this issue spring to mind. You could search for the string "<font" without the closing ">," and then manually delete each instance. Alternatively, you could use regular expressions to construct a search for the font tag that includes any possible variation of attributes and their values.

NOTE *Regular expressions enable you to have the Find function look for patterns in text strings, rather than hard-coded strings. Regular expressions work by substituting wildcard characters for real characters and by providing other ways of describing patterns in strings. You can find a substantive introduction to regular expressions at the following URL: http://www.webreference.com/js/column5/. For the curious, the regular expression needed to find every instance of the <font> tag, in all of its variations, is as follows:* `<(font)[^>]*>`

Dreamweaver makes what would otherwise be a difficult task an easy one. Its Strip Tag action does all the work of generating the right regular expression for you, invisibly, behind the scenes. When it is finished, it removes every instance of the <font> tag, regardless of its attributes and their values. At the same time, of course, it also removes the closing </font> tags.

1) Still in index.htm, open the Find and Replace dialog again, and verify that Entire Current Local Site is still selected in the Find in drop-down menu.

Once again, this step prepares you for the main work of this task.

2) With Specific Tag still selected in the Search drop-down menu, select font in the HTML Tag List drop-down menu. If necessary, click the Remove Search Criterion (minus sign) button beneath the Search drop-down menu.

As before, you are here telling Dreamweaver what to look for, in this case all instances of the <font> and </font> tags.

3) In the Action drop-down menu, choose Strip Tag.

No other attributes appear, so you are ready to run the operation. First double-check to make sure your screen matches the screenshot. Mistakes made during Find and Replace operations can have painful consequences.

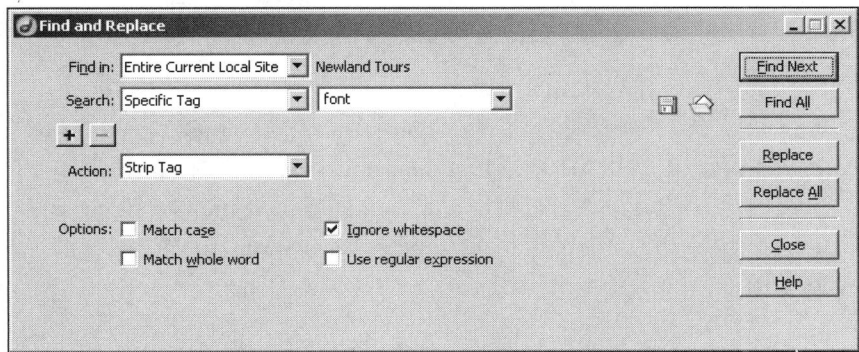

4) Click Replace All and then click Yes when the warning dialog appears.

As expected, the Results panel shows a fair amount of activity sitewide.

But the Results panel is not the only indication that the Find and Replace operation worked. Some of the text on index.htm changed. The Explore the Site heading at the top of the navigation bar is now smaller and has changed fonts. The point to notice here is that this operation actually affects more than just the code; it changes the outward appearance of your page as seen in a browser (or Dreamweaver's design view).

5) Save index.htm.

CLOSING EMPTY TAGS THAT HAVE ATTRIBUTES

Earlier in the lesson, you easily closed the empty tags that lack attributes; for example, you had Dreamweaver find `<br>` and replace it with `<br />`. But closing empty tags that have attributes is a different story. That is, closing off `<img src="images/image.gif" width="200" height="150">` poses the same challenge that the `<font>` tag did: the differing attributes and their values make them harder to search for.

As with the `<font>` tag, Dreamweaver can write the regular expressions needed to successfully find all of the `<img>` tags. You accomplish that by choosing Specific Tag and by picking img from the HTML Tag List drop-down menu. Unfortunately, there is no "Close Empty Tag in XHTML Style" action in the Find and Replace dialog, which means that the finding is going to be easier than the replacing. Still, there is a workaround, which, if somewhat ugly, gets the job done.

Once you've closed the `<img>` tags, you'll also need to close the other empty tags that have attributes. In this task, you'll also close the `<area>` tags used on each page in the image map. If the site had forms (it doesn't, yet), you'd also use this method to close `<input>` tags, which are also empty and loaded with attributes.

1) With index.htm open, open the Find and Replace dialog, and verify that Entire Current Local Site is selected. Verify that Specific Tag is selected in the Search drop-down menu, and choose img from the HTML Tag List drop-down menu. If necessary, click the Remove Search Criterion button, so that no additional search criteria are specified.

This part of the routine is probably getting familiar.

2) In the Action drop-down menu, choose Add After.

The strategy here is to find every `<img>` tag, regardless of its attributes and their values, and add a special string of text after it. As soon as you choose Add After, a text area appears, which enables you to type in that extra string.

3) Type *QWERTY* in the text area.

When you run this Find and Replace operation, Dreamweaver will append QWERTY directly after the `<img>` tag's closing angle bracket (>). This closing > is the problem that you are trying to fix, since it should be " />" rather than just ">". But you can't go through and find all ">" and replace it with " />", because that search would change all angled brackets, including those in tags such as the `<p>` tag that are used correctly. You need to be able to identify all of the angled brackets that close `<img>` tags only.

By appending the unique QWERTY text string after the angled bracket, you have in effect marked every closing > of every `<img>` tag in the site. Then you can run a second Find and Replace operation that replaces `>QWERTY` with `/>`, which is the correct closing syntax. Take the time to be a little creative with Find and Replace, and you can solve all sorts of large problems.

NOTE *QWERTY is not a keyword or special term. It was just a unique string that I know doesn't appear anywhere else in the site. You could, for example, use your name (as long as it isn't Newland) and achieve the same effect.*

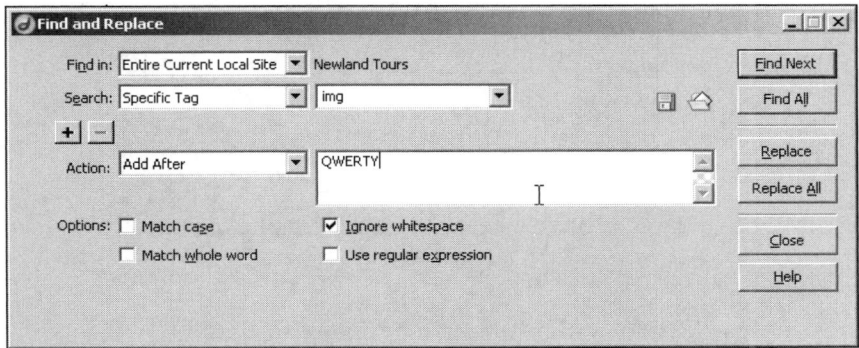

4) Click Replace All, and, as usual, Yes in the warning dialog that appears.
If you take a moment to look at the document in design view, you'll see QWERTY appear after all of the images in the document. It's not pretty, but you know it worked.

5) Reopen Find and Replace, and in the Search For drop-down menu, choose Source Code. Type *>QWERTY* in the top text area (don't forget the angle bracket), and then type */>* in the lower text area (don't forget the space).

Now that you've told Dreamweaver to look for the angled brackets that close <img> tags only, you can tell Dreamweaver to replace that bracket with the proper XHTML closing syntax.

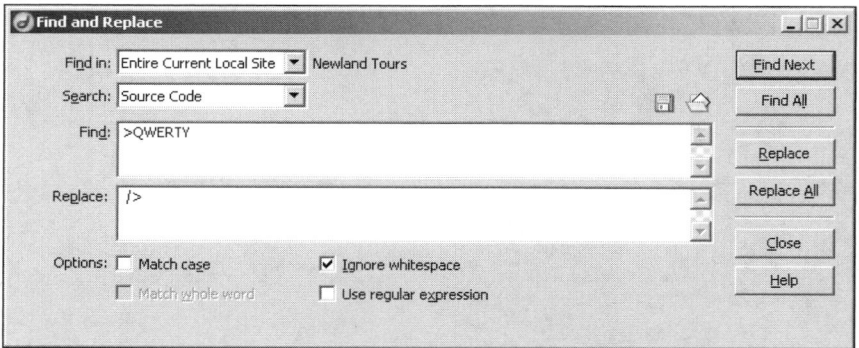

6) Click Replace All, and click Yes when the warning dialog appears.

Click a handful of images in design view, and look at the corresponding code in code view. You should see perfectly normal <img> elements in XHTML style. No one has to know about the whole QWERTY thing.

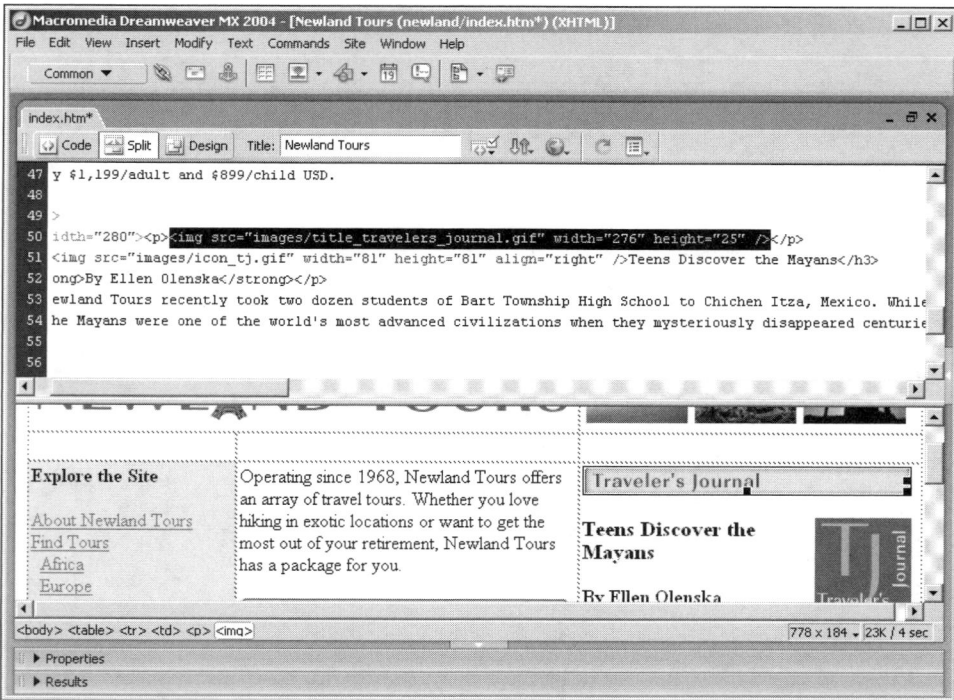

7) Repeat the QWERTY process to properly close all of the <area> **tags in the site.**

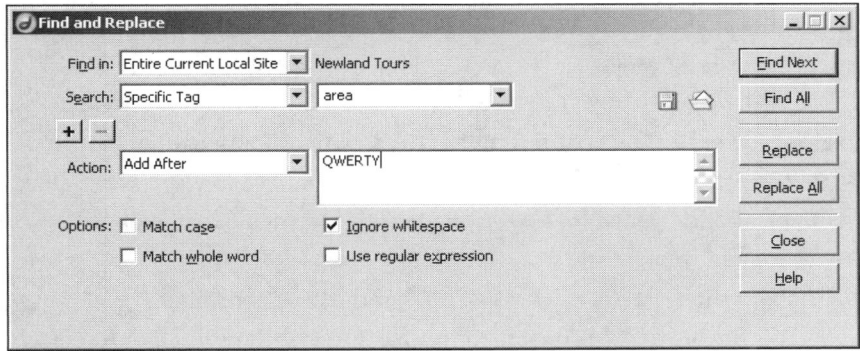

If you want to verify that this change worked, you'll need to open any page other than index.htm. The <area> tags are used as a part of the image map on the navigation bar. The code for the image map is at the very bottom of the document, just above the closing </body> tag.

```
113 <map name="navbarMap" id="navbarMap">
114    <area shape="rect" coords="1,0,62,20" href="index.htm" alt="Home" />
115    <area shape="rect" coords="71,0,117,20" href="about.htm" alt="About" />
116    <area shape="rect" coords="129,0,196,20" href="tours.htm" alt="Find Tours" />
117    <area shape="rect" coords="209,0,311,20" href="profiles.htm" alt="Country Profiles" />
118    <area shape="rect" coords="327,0,434,20" href="contact.htm" alt="Contact An Agent" />
119 </map>
120 </body>
121 </html>
```

8) Save index.htm.

FINDING IMAGES WITHOUT THE alt ATTRIBUTE

At this point, the Newland site meets the XHTML standard, so you've succeeded in the main goal of the lesson, which was to upgrade the site to XHTML. One problem remains, and while it's not strictly speaking related to XHTML, it is a code issue: Many of the images lack the alt attribute. As you recall, the alt attribute of the <img> tag provides a description of an image, which is used by those who have no access to the image, for instance, because they are using a screen reader or because they are using a text-only browser.

This change is also hard to automate, since every image should have a different alt attribute. You'll use Find and Replace a couple of different ways in this task. First, you'll use it to add alt text to the four images that make up the banner on all of the pages. Second, you'll use it to find the remaining images that are lacking the alt attribute.

69

1) Open about.htm.

The homepage, index.htm, doesn't have the full navigation bar that the other pages have, so by switching to about.htm, you ensure that you can take care of all the images used in the navigation bars.

2) Click the Eiffel Tower to select the left half of the Newland Tours banner in design view. Its corresponding HTML should be highlighted in code view. Right-click (Windows) or Control-click (Macintosh) over the highlighted code, and choose Copy from the context menu.

This method is about the fastest way that you can get the code for a given object onto the clipboard, which makes it convenient for pasting into the Find and Replace dialog or reusing on other pages. It works not just for images, but also for other objects, from image maps to Macromedia Flash movies.

AUTOMATICALLY HIGHLIGHTED CODE

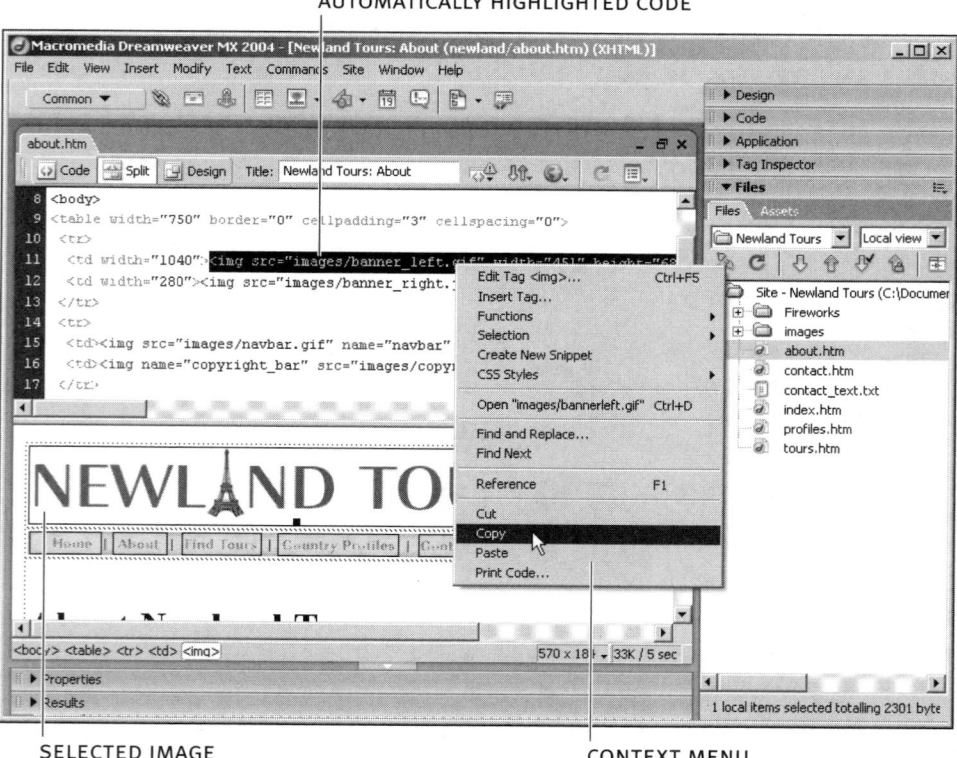

SELECTED IMAGE   CONTEXT MENU

3) Press Ctrl+F (Windows) Command+F (Macintosh) to open the Find and Replace dialog, remove any existing text (from previous searches) in the upper text area, and paste in the HTML code for the image.

Don't forget to double-check that Entire Current Local Site is selected in the Find in drop-down menu and that Source Code is selected in the Search drop-down menu.

TIP *You can resize the Find and Replace dialog to accommodate long text strings.*

4) Paste the same HTML code in the Replace With (lower) text area. Somewhere inside the tag, add the following text: `alt="Newland Tours Banner, Left"`
The order of the attributes doesn't matter. Just make sure that the attribute is typed in lowercase and that the attribute's value is in quotation marks.

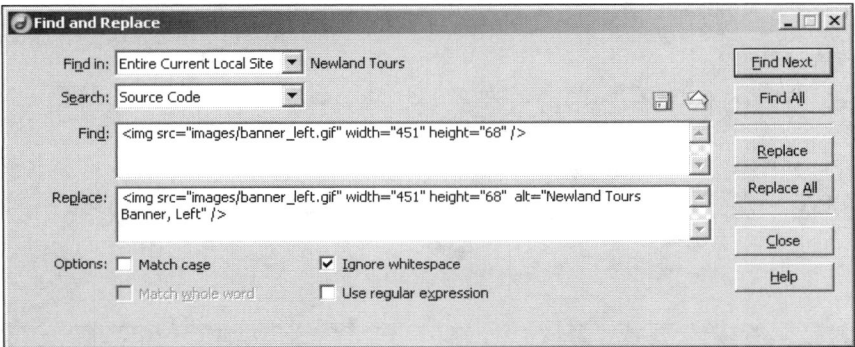

5) Click Replace All, and click Yes when the warning dialog appears.
The `alt` tag has now been updated for the left side of the banner throughout the site.

6) Repeat the preceding steps for the right-hand graphic on the banner (the three photos). The `alt` **tag should read as follows:** `alt="Newland Tours Banner, Right"`**. Click Replace All.**

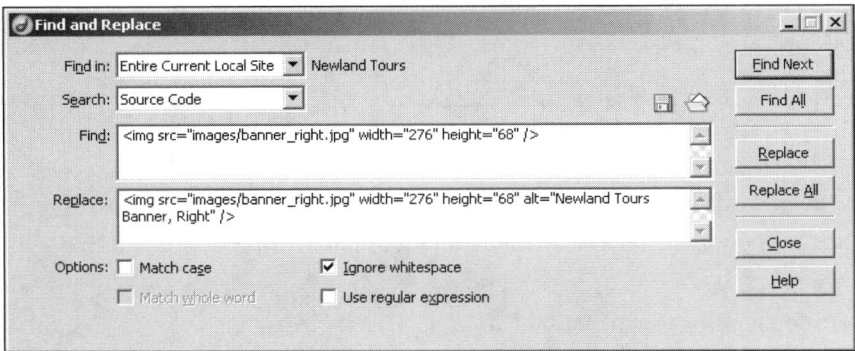

Both halves of the banner now have `alt` attributes.

7) Repeat the preceding steps to add an alt **attribute to the button bar beneath the Newland Tours banner. The** alt **attribute should read** alt="Navigation Bar".

The file index.htm lacks the banner navigation, so you have to open one of the other pages to modify it.

The navigation bar is an interesting problem, because it is not the navigation bar as a whole, but rather the individual button graphics on the bar that matter. Adding an alt attribute to this image doesn't convey what each of the buttons does. Remember, though, that what makes the buttons do something (namely, load another page when clicked) is the image map, and not the image itself. For this reason, it is necessary to add the alt attribute to each of the <area> tags within the image map. I have already done this for you.

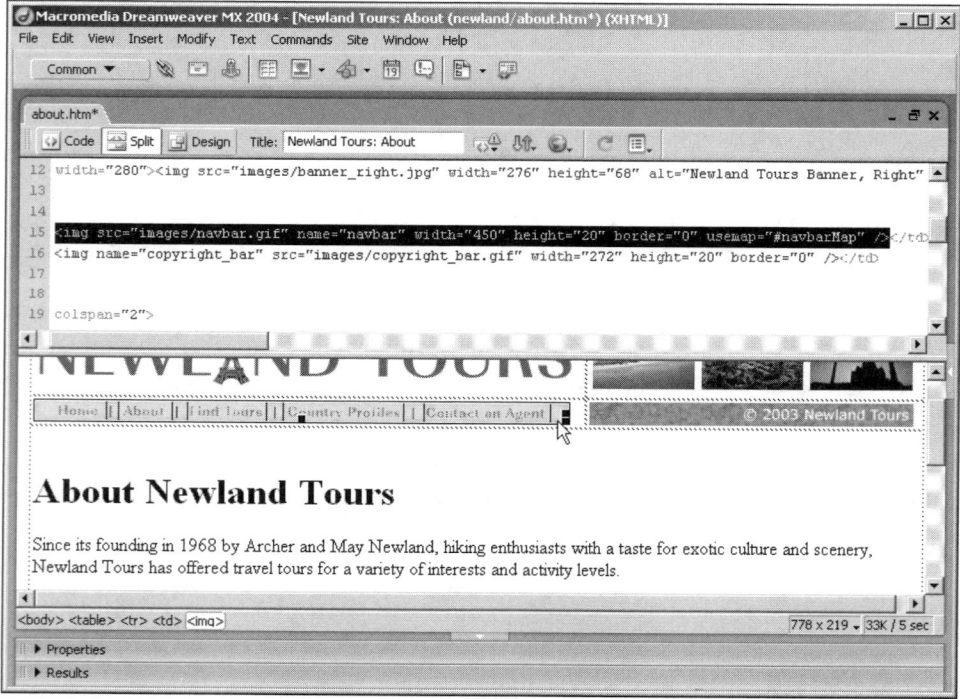

8) Repeat the preceding steps to add an alt **attribute to the marbleized bar beneath the three photos. The** alt **attribute should read** alt="Copyright 2004 Newland Tours".

That's it for the banner and navigation bar.

The next step is to identify the remaining graphics that don't have an alt attribute. None of the remaining images appears on multiple pages, so you can't automate the replacement process with Find and Replace. Fortunately, you can automate the finding process, which will make it easy for you to identify the pictures still needing alt attributes.

9) Open Find and Replace again, and choose Specific Tag from the Search drop-down menu. Choose img **from the HTML Tag List drop-down menu. A new row for additional search criteria appears automatically, and it defaults to With Attribute. Change that to Without Attribute, and choose** alt **from the next drop-down menu. Don't worry about the Action row.**

These settings tell Dreamweaver to find all instances of images that do not have an alt attribute. This should make it easy to ensure that you find all of the images without alt attributes. You don't need to specify anything in the action row, because you are taking no action. You are not replacing anything. You are simply using Dreamweaver tools to find tags that meet a certain criterion.

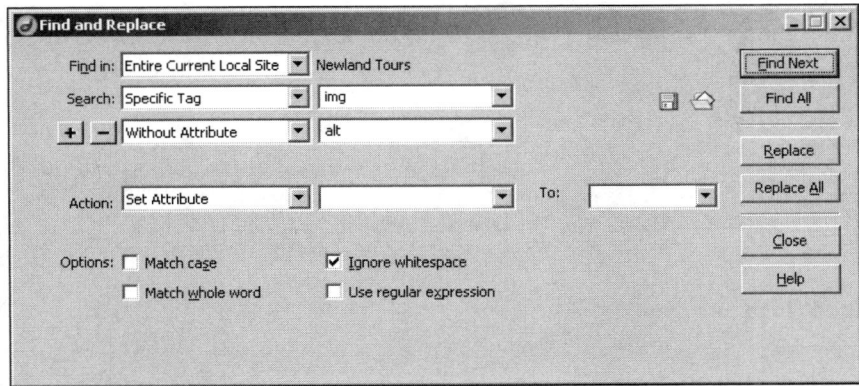

10) Press Find Next.

You will be taken automatically to an image without an alt tag. Which one you are taken to depends on the location of your cursor when you initiated the search.

11) Add alt **attributes to each of the images you find on all of the pages except tours.htm and profiles.htm. Several of the images have captions or descriptive text embedded in them, so use those as a guide.**

It doesn't matter all that much what you enter, so long as it is descriptive and conveys textually what the image conveys visually.

73

The reason you don't need to enter alt attributes on tours.htm and profiles.htm is that these pages will be upgraded to dynamic pages, and you'll implement a more radical solution to the alt attribute later in the book.

CAPTION   CORRESPONDING ALT ATTRIBUTE

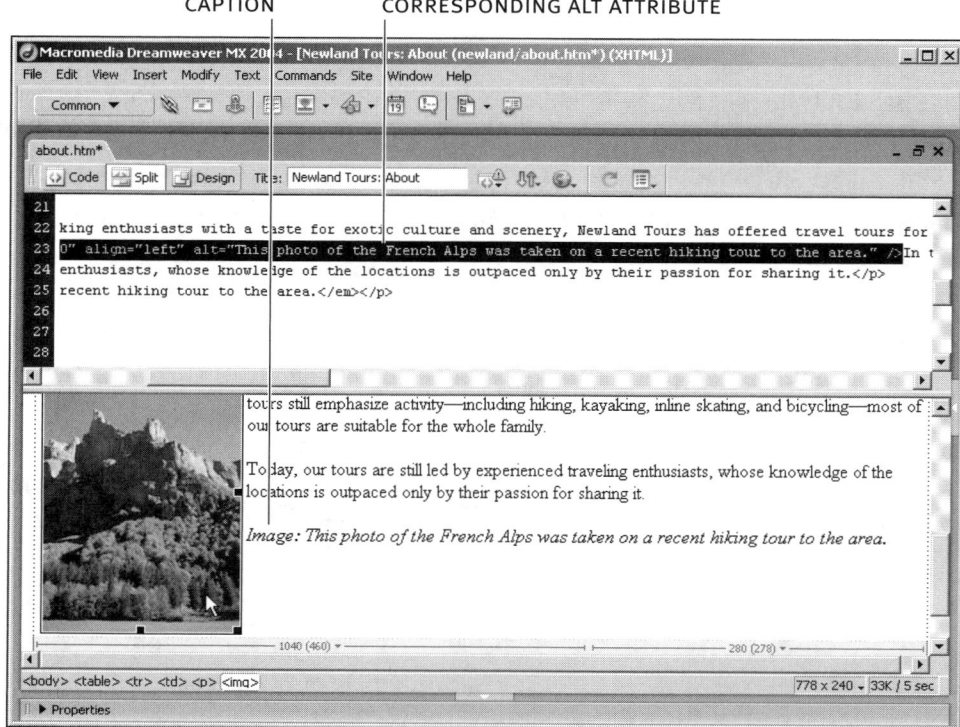

12) Save and close any open files.

VALIDATING YOUR XHTML

You have done a lot of work in this lesson to whip the code into shape. Now it's time to find out how well you did. Dreamweaver has several built-in code validation tools that you can use to check your code. In this task, you'll verify that you successfully upgraded the code throughout the site to XHTML.

1) Choose Window > Results > Validation.

This opens the Results panel, if it isn't already open, and switches it to the Validation tab.

VALIDATE

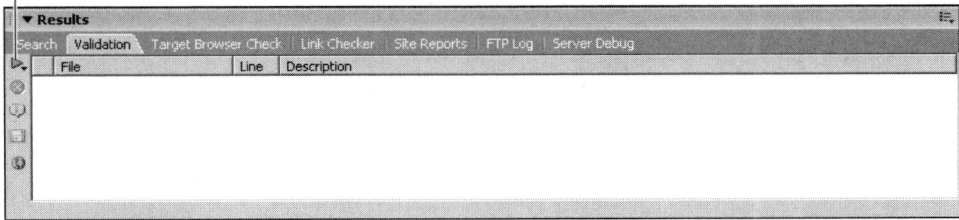

2) Click the Validate button, and from the pop-up list, choose Settings.

This option is a shortcut to the Preferences dialog's Validator category, where you see a list of several different versions of HTML and proprietary language code. Before you can validate your code, you need to tell Dreamweaver which version of code you want to validate against.

3) In the validate against list, choose XHTML 1.0 Transitional. Uncheck all other options. Click OK to proceed.

By choosing XHTML 1.0 Transitional, you are aligning the Validator with the settings you specified at the beginning of this lesson, when you pasted the DOCTYPE declaration at the beginning of the document.

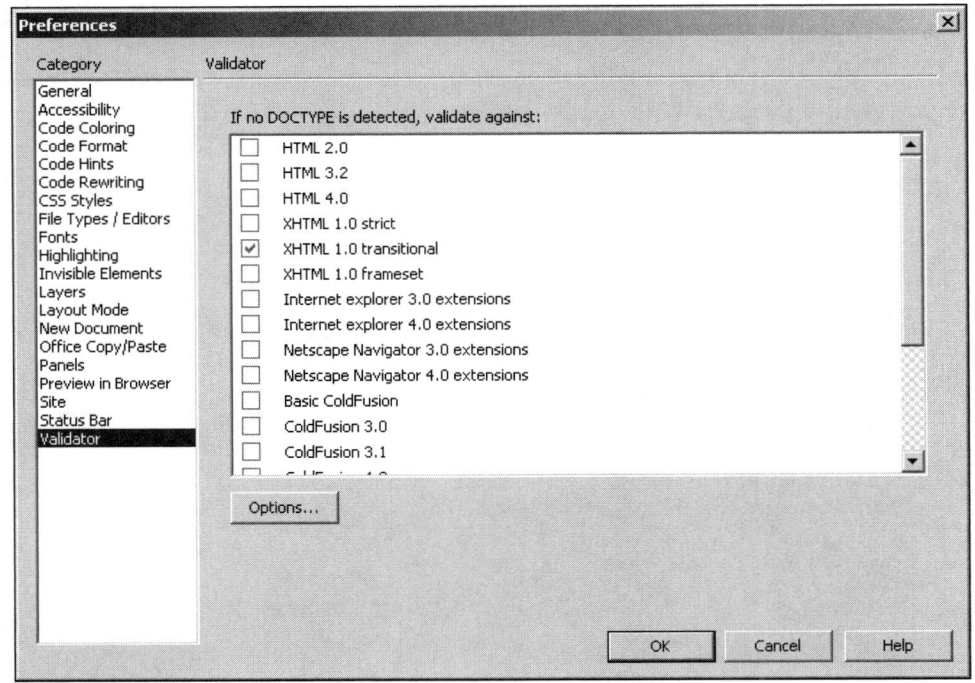

4) Click the Validate button again, and this time, choose Validate Entire Site from the list.

The Validator may take a few moments to run, and when it does, it will list any problems in the Validation tab, including the file, the line, and the nature of the problem. If you followed all of the steps in this lesson, you should see the message "No errors or warnings found" for each of the site's five files.

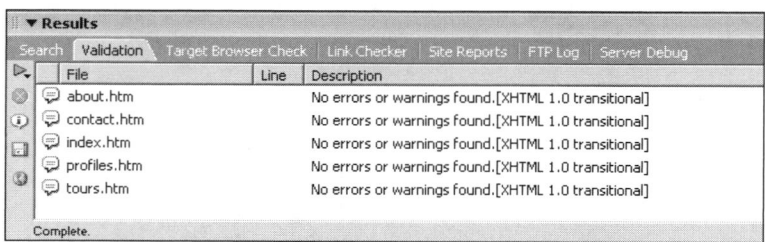

If you did encounter problems, then double-click the error, and Dreamweaver will open the file at the line in question, and you can inspect the code for yourself.

5) If problems remain, study the code until you figure out what went wrong, and then use what you learned in this chapter to fix it using Dreamweaver's Find and Replace tools.

In the worst-case scenario (not to encourage sloth), don't forget that the completed files for this lesson on the CD-ROM are clean, so feel free to replace your files with the files on the CD if you just want to move on.

WHAT YOU HAVE LEARNED

In this lesson, you have:

- Upgraded the document type to XHTML (pages 52–59)
- Used Find and Replace to automate changes to source code (pages 56–61)
- Replaced obsolete tags with current tags (pages 61–63)
- Stripped tags from code (pages 64–65)
- Closed empty elements in proper XHTML syntax (pages 66–69)
- Found and fixed images lacking alt attributes (pages 69–74)
- Validated your page for XHTML 1.0 Transitional compliance (pages 74–76)

creating the presentation layer

L E S S O N 3

In the past, when designers were developing static HTML pages, they would often copy and paste several pages of plain text into Dreamweaver, and then go about the task of marking it up to make it presentable. In other words, roughing out the content preceded much of the design work, which came only at the end of the process.

In a way, that workflow is turned on its head when working with dynamic Web sites. The content that users see when they visit your site is often added to the HTML pages in the split second between the request for the page and its appearance in the browser. That means that you have to create your designs with placeholder content. In the dynamic Web site development workflow, then, you deal with design and presentation issues up front, and let the server model (ASP, ColdFusion, PHP, etc.) pour the right content into it.

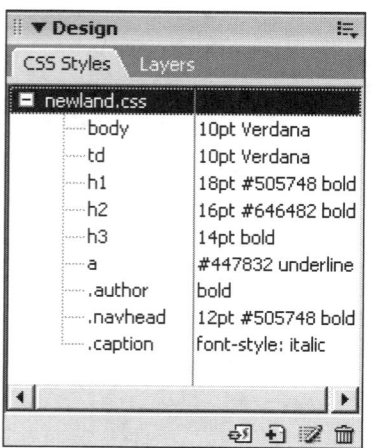

Use the improved CSS Styles panel to manage all your CSS styles, whether they're redefined HTML tags or custom CSS classes.

After completing this lesson's tasks, you'll have specified nearly all of the stylistic and design information used in the Newland site. A few issues will come up during the application development stages—they always do—but by and large you'll nail down the main graphic design decisions by the end of this lesson. The most important task is to create and apply a cascading style sheet, which controls most of the presentation issues in the site. In a related exercise, you'll also create an all-purpose page template that you can use as the basis for any new pages that you'll need to add to the site.

WHAT YOU WILL LEARN

In this lesson, you will:

- Create and apply a cascading style sheet to the site
- Build a reusable template for all new pages added to the site
- Enhance each page's accessibility with a hidden navigation layer

APPROXIMATE TIME

This lesson takes approximately 75 minutes to complete.

LESSON FILES

Starting Files:

Lesson03/Start/newland/about.htm
Lesson03/Start/newland/contact.htm
Lesson03/Start/newland/index.htm
Lesson03/Start/newland/profiles.htm
Lesson03/Start/newland/tours.htm

Completed Files:

Lesson03/Complete/newland/about.htm
Lesson03/Complete/newland/contact.htm
Lesson03/Complete/newland/index.htm
Lesson03/Complete/newland/generic_template.htm
Lesson03/Complete/newland/profiles.htm
Lesson03/Complete/newland/tours.htm
Lesson03/Complete/newland/css/newland.css

REDEFINING HTML ELEMENTS WITH CSS

One of the advantages to HTML is that it includes a wide range of logical tags, flexible enough to describe the logic of most basic documents. With its six built-in levels of heading (<h1>, <h2>, <h3>, and so on); tags for regular text (<p>); lists (<ol> and <ul>) and list items (<li>); tables (<table>, <tr>, <td>); block quotes (<blockquote>); address (<address>) tags and more, you can mark up documents quickly and in such a way that the tags actually describe the content and structure of the document. In addition, browsers recognize these styles and know how to render them. For example, content in the <h1> tag is large and bold with extra space above and below it, while content inside <p> tags is rendered in a normal body font, such as a 12-point system font.

Because every page relies on the browser for rendering, it might seem that all HTML pages would look the same. For example, every level one heading on the Internet might be in 18 point Times New Roman bold. Such a uniform appearance prevents organizations from differentiating themselves and bores users. For this reason, early on in the development of HTML, coders demanded some way to control the presentation of content. To meet this need, special presentation tags, such as the <font> tag, were added to the standard. As you know from the preceding lesson, the <font> tag has since fallen out of favor, largely because it is inefficient. It requires developers to add special formatting attributes to each and every paragraph that needs to diverge from the standard browser template.

With the emergence of CSS, developers have a much more powerful and flexible way of handling presentation. Perhaps the simplest, and ultimately most powerful, feature of CSS is that you can use it to tell browsers how to render standard HTML tags. For example, you can specify that the browser renders all content enclosed in <p> tags in Verdana 12 point black, and all level 2 headings as Verdana 16 point purple bold. What makes this so useful is that you specify these directions in one place, and every single <p> tag and <h2> tag in your site is automatically formatted correctly, without the need for any additional code. Further, if you make a change later to this small bit of code, the change will cascade throughout your entire site instantly. Anyone who came from the 20th century world of desktop publishing or even professional word processing would be familiar with the benefit of automatic styles.

In addition to the ability to define the appearance of existing HTML tags, CSS also enables developers to create custom styles, called **classes**, which can be applied to any portion of text, whether it's a block level tag such as <p>, or a span of characters within a regular paragraph. The only catch to using classes is that not only must you define custom styles, you also have to add a small bit of code to apply them (in contrast to redefining HTML tags, which update as soon as you save the style).

Conveniently, Dreamweaver enables you to apply custom CSS classes without having to type out the code manually, unless you want to.

In the first task, you will create a series of CSS styles that redefine the most common HTML tags used in the site. You will also attach these styles to each of the existing pages. When you are finished, you will have formatted the vast majority of the text for the site—as it stands now and as it will stand at the end of the book. In the next task, you will create and apply custom styles, which will take care of some of the remaining exceptions. Others will be added at appropriate times in the book. But for now, let's redefine the HTML elements to give the site the Newland Tours look.

1) Open index.htm and choose Window > CSS Styles to open the CSS Styles panel (if necessary).

You create and (in some cases) apply styles using the CSS panel. You can also access the same commands and any custom CSS classes from the Property inspector.

The CSS Style buttons at the bottom of the panel are sometimes grayed out, unless you select the style name (or, as in this case, the placeholder text, "no styles defined").

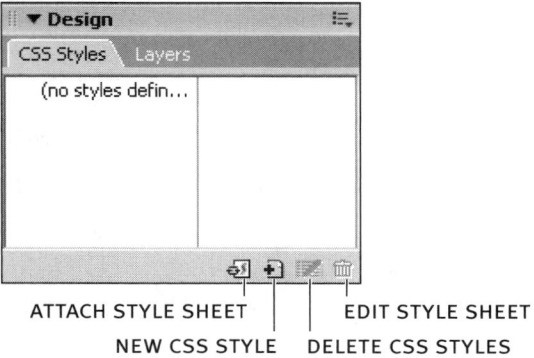

ATTACH STYLE SHEET | EDIT STYLE SHEET
NEW CSS STYLE | DELETE CSS STYLES

2) Click the New CSS Style button. In the New CSS Style dialog, select Tag in the Selector Type radio group, and select (New Style Sheet File) in the Define in radio group. From the Tag drop-down menu, choose the body element. Click OK.

In this step, you are preparing to redefine the <body> tag. To do so, you have to tell Dreamweaver that the style you want to create redefines an HTML tag, and that you are not creating a custom style. The Define in radio group enables you to specify whether you want the styles stored in index.htm only (This document only) or in an external style sheet ([New Style Sheet File]).

The benefit of storing styles in an external style sheet is that multiple pages in the site can reference that same file, which means that a change made to that external file instantly affects every page that refers to it (which in the Newland Tours site will be every page in the site).

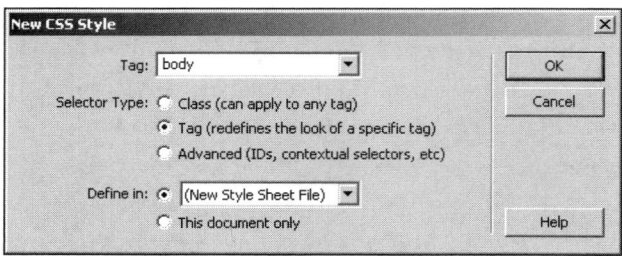

3) In the Save Style Sheet File As dialog, verify that you are looking in the newland folder and create a new folder called css. Double-click to open this new css folder. Name the file newland.css, and click Save.

Though Newland Tours does not, some sites require multiple style sheets. It's a good idea to keep them all in one place. For this reason, I always create a css folder that sits parallel with the images folder.

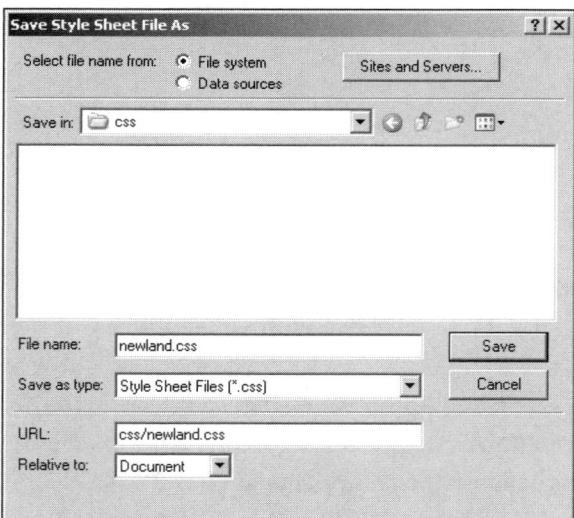

Notice near the bottom of the dialog that Dreamweaver writes the path of the style sheet relative to the currently active document in the URL field. In this case, it's css/newland.css.

4) In the CSS Style Definition for body in newland.css dialog, in the Type category, select Verdana, Arial, Helvetica, sans-serif from the Font drop-down menu, and 10 points (not pixels!) from the Size drop-down menus. Click OK.

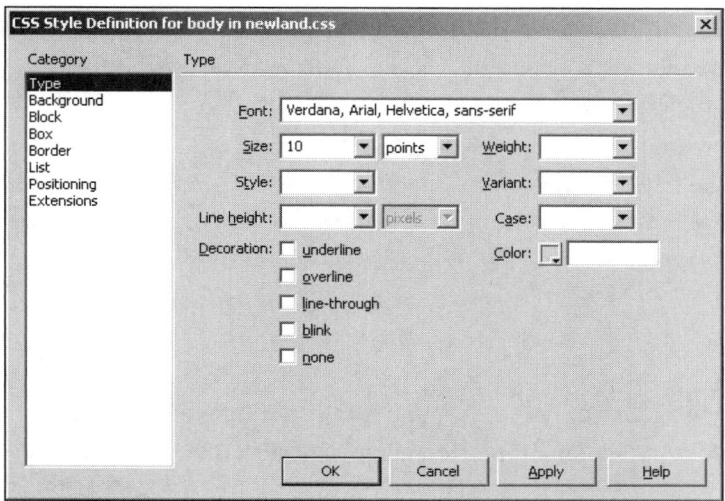

In this step, you are creating a default text setting for all of the text on the page. How does this work, since generally all text inside the <body> tag is also inside another set of tags, such as <p> or <h1>? The answer revolves around the concept of **inheritance**. Tags nested inside other tags inherit (theoretically) the styles of their parent tags. Since all page content appears within the <body> tags, all page content should inherit the CSS style information from those tags.

Does this mean that text inside an <h1> tag will now be formatted using 10 point Verdana? No, because browsers have a default set of formatting instructions for the <h1> tag. Where this formatting information conflicts with the formatting information in the <body> tag, it overrides it. Whether (and which) formatting is overridden is determined based on the order of precedence. In general, the closer a tag is to the text, the more heavily weighted are its formatting attributes. Since the content in an <h1> element is closer to the <h1> tags than it is to the <body> tags, the <h1> formatting takes precedence.

That's the theory, anyway. But browsers don't uniformly respect this CSS hierarchy, and sometimes formatting attributes get ignored when they aren't supposed to be. So in practice, you often have to define more information than you should have to in theory.

Due to varying implementations of CSS across browsers, you may discover with enough testing that regardless of the size you specify for the <body> tag, a browser may disregard it. The reason this happens is that some browsers ignore body formatting information if it conflicts with formatting information intrinsic to the <td> (table cell) tag. In other words, the formatting of the <td> tags in some browsers may override the size you specified in the <body> tag. But this is not a major problem: To fix it, you just need to redefine the <td> tag.

NOTE *Whenever you create a new style, DW actually opens the CSS file in the background. This enables you to edit your CSS file directly. In addition, consider it a learning opportunity: look at the CSS code that Dreamweaver writes. Try changing some values or adding new properties (in the expression font-size: 10pt;, font-size is the property, and 10pt; is the value). Use Dreamweaver's code hints to ensure that you get the syntax right.*

5) Click New CSS Style again, verify that the type is Tag, and Define in is set to newland.css. Select td from the Tag drop-down menu, and click OK.

NOTE *If newland.css is not available in the Define in menu, try closing the dialog, closing the file newland.css, and then starting over by clicking New CSS Style.*

This dialog will become very familiar to you over time.

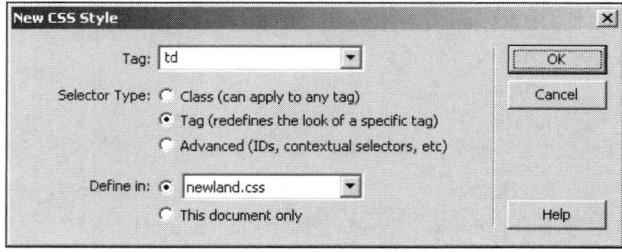

6) In the CSS Style Definition for td in newland.css dialog, select Verdana, Arial, Helvetica, sans serif as the font and 10 points (not pixels) as the size. Click OK to create the new style.

These are the same settings you associated with the <body> tag, and no change is visible in Dreamweaver, but you've added some insurance for older browsers. In Netscape 4.x, for example, text inside a <td> tag for some odd reason doesn't inherit the formatting from the <body> tag. This is a bug, of course, but a bug that millions of users likely still experience. You circumvent it with this step.

We need to redefine several more HTML styles using CSS, but index.htm doesn't actually have that many styles, so in the next step, you'll open a different file.

7) Save and close index.htm. Open tours.htm.

This more structured document makes use of <h1>, <h2>, and <h3> tags as well as some plain-looking <a> elements.

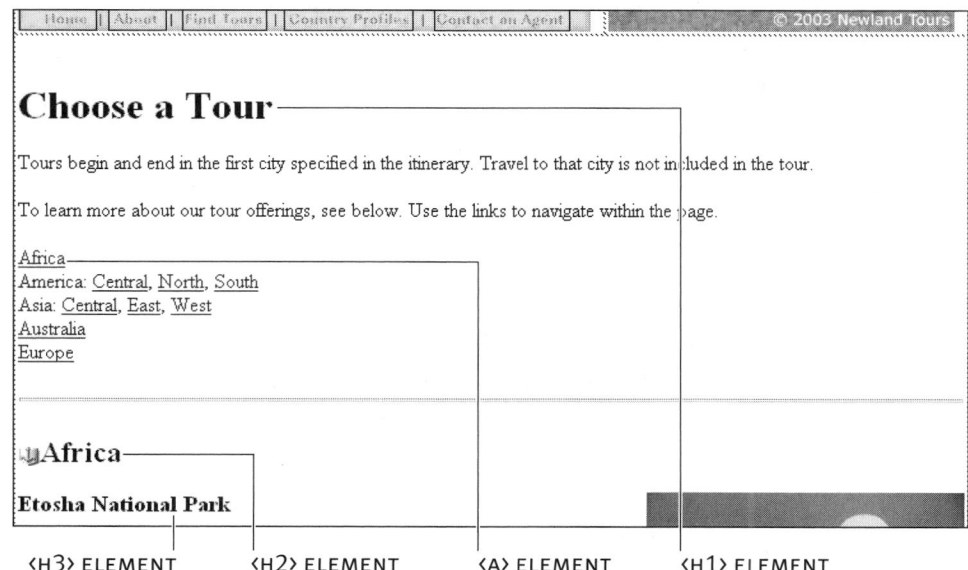

8) In the CSS Styles panel, click Attach Style Sheet, and in the Attach External Style Sheet dialog, browse to newland.css in the css folder and click Open. Verify that Add as Link is selected, and click OK.

Before you start defining new styles, you need to attach to the style sheet you already created. Otherwise, you'd end up creating a second style sheet. Again, the goal is to create a single style sheet to which all files in the site refer.

Why choose Link, rather than Import, to apply the external file? Had you chosen Import, Dreamweaver would have copied the styles in newland.css into the header of this file. In other words, importing replicates the style sheet on each page, negating one of the primary benefits of using style sheets. Importing style sheets is useful when you want a page to have its own unique styles, which should override those of the default style sheet. But that's not the behavior you want, so choose Link.

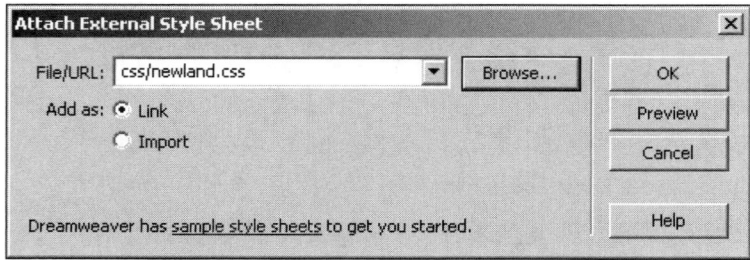

You should now see that all of the text on the page is converted to Verdana, and that the body text is 10 points. When you see that, you know the style sheet has been attached and applied.

Still, the three levels of heading are somewhat bland. Let's spruce them up with some color.

9) Click the New CSS Style button, and make the appropriate settings to redefine the h1 element, saving it in newland.css. Once in the CSS Site Definition dialog, set the size to 18 points; the weight to bold; and the color to #505748. Click OK.

You should be getting comfortable creating style definitions at this point. The only new thing here is that you are specifying a color. You can click the color box to choose a color from a pop-up, or you can enter the color value directly.

TIP *Another way to select a color is to pick it up from somewhere else onscreen. To do so, click the color box pop-up, and then click with the eyedropper tool anywhere onscreen, and Dreamweaver will select that color. In this step, if you click any of the letters in the Newland Tours banner, the correct color value should appear automatically.*

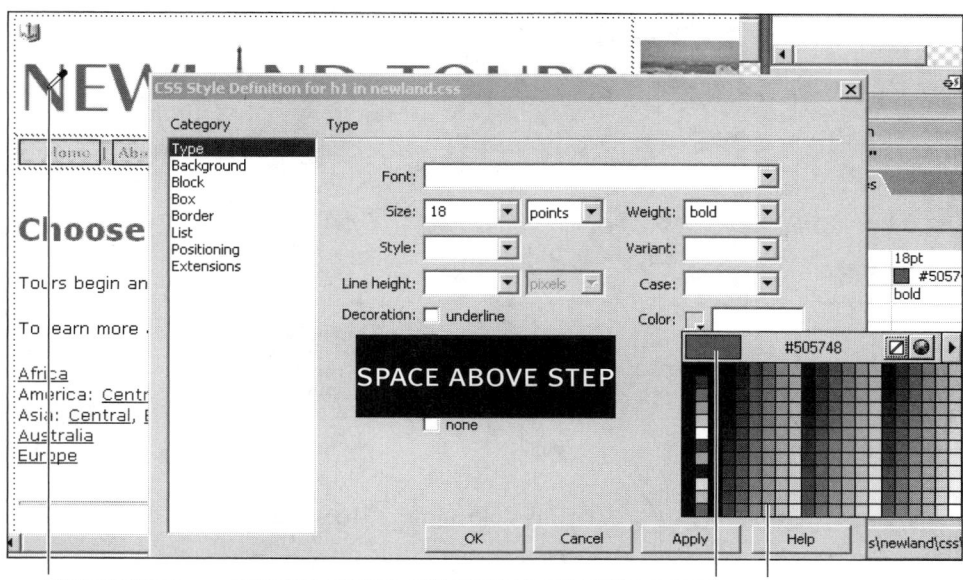

EYEDROPPER   CORRECT COLOR SELECTED FROM EYEDROPPER   COLOR BOX POP-UP

10) Redefine the \<h2> tag using the following settings: Size = 16 points; Weight = bold; Color = #646482.

Look at the continent names on the page to see the results. They should appear dark purple.

11) Redefine the \<h3> tag using the following settings: Size = 14 points; Weight = bold.

On the tours.htm page, this setting affects the tour names. You'll probably notice little difference. We only redefine this HTML style to ensure it fits in consistently with the two headings you just defined.

12) Redefine the `<a>` tag using the following settings: Decoration = underline; Color = #447832.

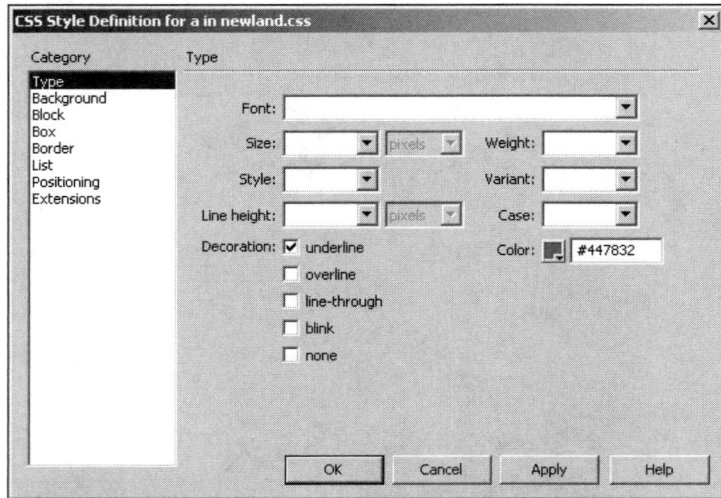

You probably know you can specify link colors in the `<body>` tag in HTML (or in the Dreamweaver Modify > Page Properties dialog). But, again, why specify the same information on every page, when you can specify it once in a CSS and have it apply to all pages?

When you are finished, the links at the top of the page should become green, which suits the color of the site better than the default blue color.

13) Save and close tours.htm.

We are done redefining all of the HTML tags used in the site. We have yet to create our custom styles—that's covered in the next section—but first, take a moment to attach newland.css to each of the remaining files.

14) One at a time, open about.htm, contact.htm, and profiles.htm, and use the Attach Style Sheet button in the CSS Styles panel to attach newland.css to each of these pages.

Take a quick look at the contents of the pages to verify that the styles have indeed been applied. If you are successful, not only will you see that the text is in Verdana and in the appropriate color, but you'll also see a series of styles listed in the CSS Styles panel.

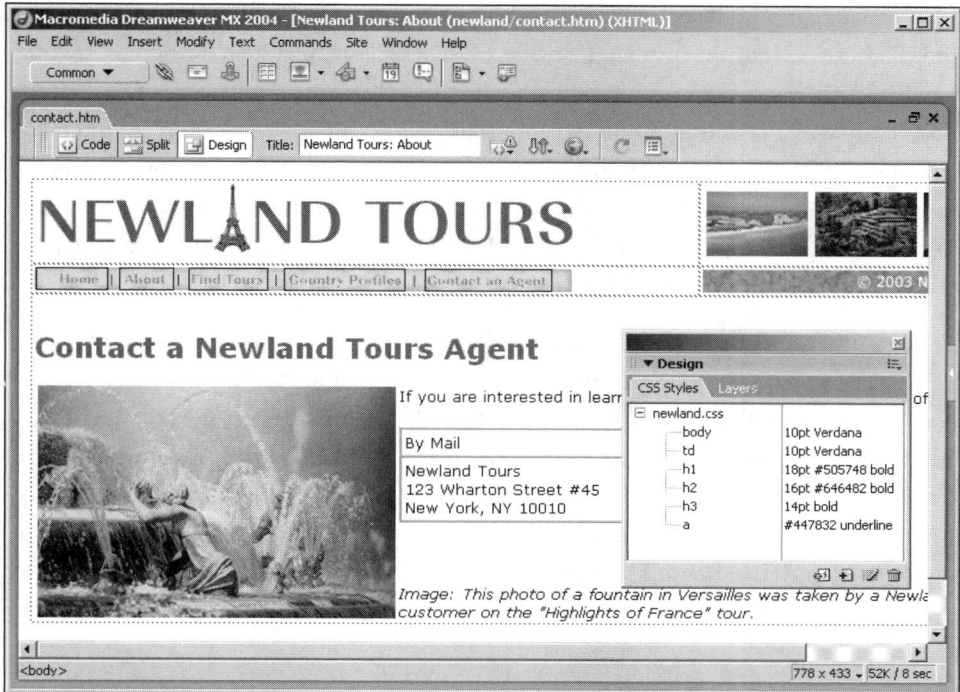

CREATING AND APPLYING CUSTOM CSS STYLES

By providing presentation specifications for HTML styles, you have quickly formatted the vast majority of your site, both as it stands now and as you will develop it during this book. Better yet, you've also optimized the site for maintenance, since to update the look of the site, you need only change the CSS file. You can do this using Dreamweaver's CSS Styles panel from any page in the site, and the settings update instantly throughout the site. If the site is already loaded on a server, all you need to upload is the updated CSS file; you do not need to re-upload each of the pages.

The only drawback to what you have done so far is that you've been limited to redefining the look of pre-existing HTML styles. You haven't been able to create custom styles for text elements that aren't part of the HTML specification. For example, there is an author by-line in the Traveler's Journal of the index page, but HTML has no <authorbyline> tag. In this task, you will learn how to create and apply custom styles, or classes.

1) Open index.htm. Make sure you can see the Traveler's Journal section at the right side of the page.

89

The Traveler's Journal section is composed of three parts: a title, an author byline, and the body text of the article. The title is enclosed in a heading, and the body text is marked up in <p> tags, so in both cases the HTML markup represents the content reasonably well. The author byline is not so easy to categorize. It's represented in bold, using the <strong> tag. However, the author byline is bolded not because it is stronger, or more emphatic, than the surrounding text, but because it performs another function; it gives credit to the author. Again, since HTML doesn't have an <author_byline> tag, this is a good opportunity to create a custom CSS style.

The result of this new style, which we will call .author, will merely add bold to the element to which it is attached (in this case, a <p> tag), and it won't look any different in a browser than it does now. But making this change will make the code describe the text a little more meaningfully, and you'll also see the concept of inheritance in action again.

2) Click New CSS Style. In the New CSS Style dialog, select Class in the Selector Type group, and verify that newland.css is still specified in the Define in group. In the Name field, type .author. Click OK.

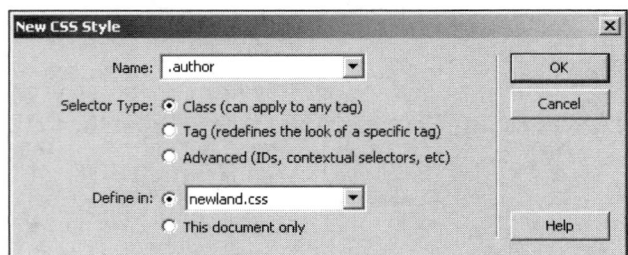

These settings should, at this point, all make sense to you, with one exception: Why does the class name begin with a period (.)? The period indicates that the style does not redefine an HTML tag in its own right, as in "all <p> tags should look like XYZ," but rather that it defines an element subordinate to an HTML tag. One practical application of this is that you can use a custom class to specify the appearance of *some* <p> tags, but not all of them. That makes sense in this particular case—only some paragraphs should be designated as author paragraphs.

Another benefit to custom classes is that they can be applied to different HTML elements. For example, not only could you apply the .author class to any <p> tag, but you could also apply it to a <span> or <div> tag.

3) In the CSS Style Definition dialog, set the weight to bold and click OK.
You don't need to specify any other information here, such as the font face or size, because that information is already specified in a parent tag (in this case, the <td> and <body> tags). So all we need the style to do is inherit all of that presentation information and add bolding.

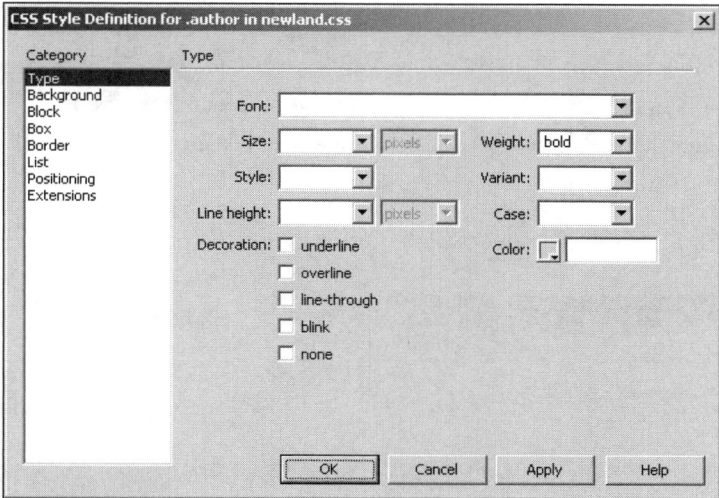

4) Create a new class called .navhead **with the following settings: Size = 12 points; Weight = bold; Color = #505748.**
This style will be used as the navigation header at the top of the navigation bar in the left-hand column of index.htm.

5) Create a new class called .caption **with the lone attribute of Style = italic.**
This style will be used for all of the image captions used in the site. Currently, they are formatted using <em>, which most browsers render as italics. Again, .caption

better describes that content than <em>, and creating this style gives us precise control over the presentation of all the captions in the site (or will, once we apply the style).

At this point, your CSS Styles panel should display nine styles. These are sufficient for now, though you'll add to this list as needed during development.

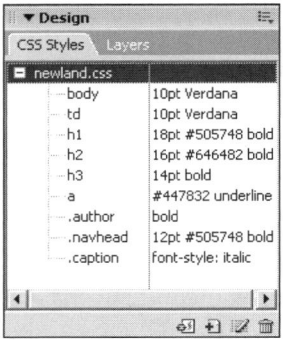

The next step, of course, is to apply these custom styles.

6) Back on the index.html page, click once anywhere in the Explore the Site text at the top of the navigation bar. Right-click (Windows) or Control-click (Macintosh) the `<strong>` tag in the tag selector and choose Remove Tag from the context menu.
In this step, you are stripping the `<strong>` tag out of the code. It's no longer needed, since the `.navhead` class you created has bold already built in.

Make sure you are clicking in the tag selector, not in the text on the page.

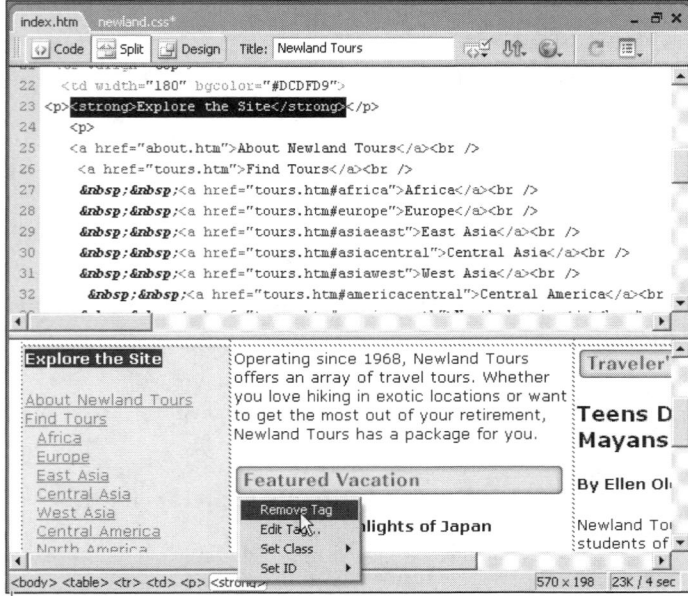

TIP *The tag selector is a very useful tool for specifying which tag you want to affect in a Dreamweaver operation. One of the challenges when working with a graphical program to edit HTML code is that it is often hard to tell the editor which element in a group of nested elements you want to affect. For example, if you want to add background color to a string of text, how does the editor know that you are not actually trying to change the background color of a <td> cell that the string of text happens to be nested in?*

TIP *A related problem is getting Dreamweaver to display the version of the Property inspector that you want. Imagine you want to change the* cellpadding *attribute of a table used for page layout. How can you get the Property inspector to show the settings for the <table> element, rather than the settings for one of the dozens of elements nested inside it? The answer is the tag selector. Click anywhere on the page that's inside the attribute you are trying to affect, and then select the desired tag from the tag selector. The Property inspector shows settings for that tag, and the context menu provides several additional options for modifying it.*

7) Click the <p> tag in the tag selector, and then click navhead in the Style drop-down menu in the Property inspector.

Not only does the heading update in design view, but the new style is reflected both in the source and in the tag selector itself.

CLASS ATTRIBUTE APPEARS IN HTML CODE

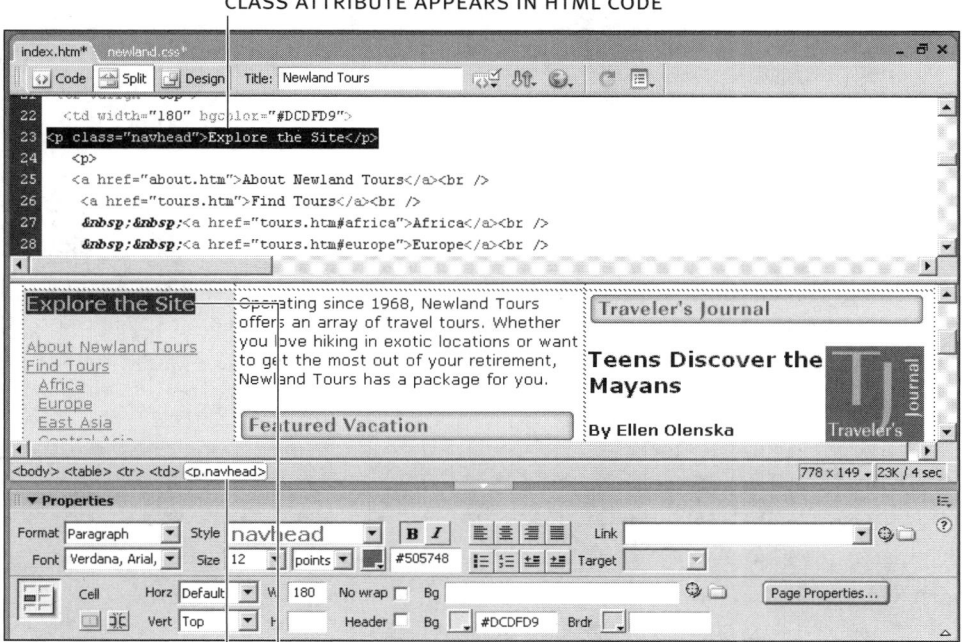

APPEARANCE OF THE NAV BAR HEADER UPDATES IN DESIGN VIEW
TAG SELECTOR DISPLAYS THE ATTACHED STYLE

93

Let's take a moment to look at the code:

```
<p class="navhead">Explore the Site</p>
```

In the previous task, when you redefined HTML tags, the pages updated instantly, and you did not need to update the code. To apply a CSS class, however, you need to change the HTML code. Specifically, you add the `class` attribute to the desired HTML tag, and list the style name (without the period) as the value of the attribute. The class is attached to the whole tag, and everything inside it, including text, images, and other tags, is affected by the style.

You cannot, therefore, attach a class to a portion of a tag. For example, if you wanted to attach the navhead style just to the word *Explore*, you could not do so by attaching the style to the `<p>` tag, because the style would be applied to everything else in the tag as well. However, you can get the same effect by creating a new tag around Explore and attaching the class to that tag. To do so, you'd use the inline tag `<span>` since it is used to create arbitrary inline containers that you can use to specify a part of a larger element. So, to complete the example, if for some reason you wanted to put just Explore in the `.navhead` style, the code would look as follows: `<p><span class="navhead">Explore</span> the Site</p>`.

NOTE *Another convenient way to apply CSS styles is through the Property inspector. Position the insertion point inside any paragraph of text, and in the Property inspector, click the A icon between the Format and Font fields, which toggles the Property inspector into CSS Mode. Once in CSS Mode, the most common HTML tags and custom CSS classes become available inside the Property inspector.*

8) Repeat steps 7 and 8 to remove the `<em>` tag around the image caption beside the picture of the Japanese shrine, and then apply the `.caption` class to that paragraph.
The display in design view shouldn't change, since the `<em>` tag you are removing is represented with italics, and since the `.caption` style you are attaching specifies only italics. But you should see the changes reflected in the tag inspector and in the source code itself.

9) Remove the `<strong>` tags around the author byline (By Ellen Olenska), and attach the `.author` class to that paragraph.
Again, the page appearance won't change, but the class should be reflected in the tag inspector and in the source code.

10) Save and close index.htm.
You've completed the design and presentation of index.htm. All changes made to it from this point forward will affect its content and functionality, but not its design.

And of course, the site contains more than index.htm.

11) One at a time, open about.htm and contact.htm, and replace the <em> tags with the `.caption` **class in the captions on those two pages. Save and close both pages.**

Neither about.htm nor contact.htm has a navigation bar heading or an author byline, so you won't need to use the `.navhead` or `.author` classes.

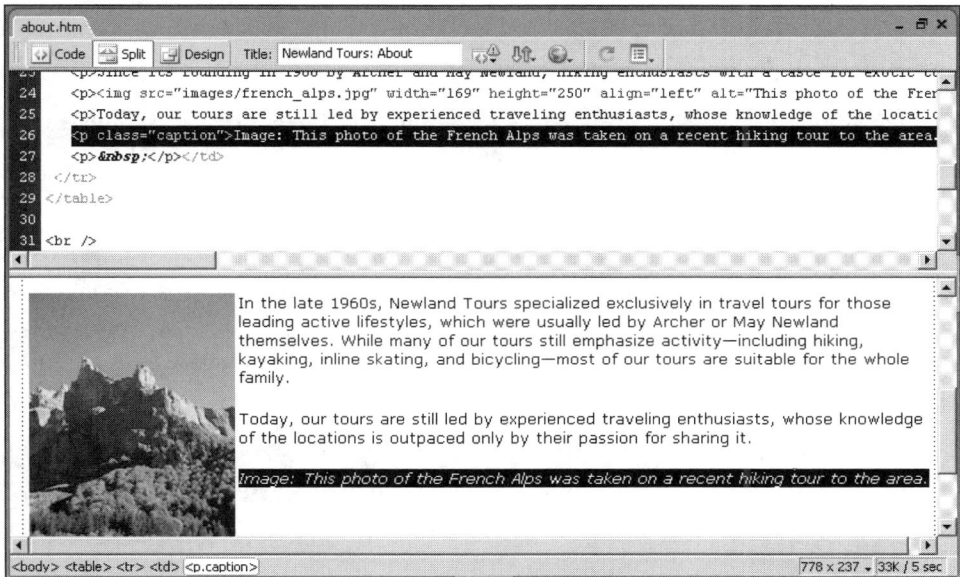

You won't need to update the classes on profile.htm or tours.htm, because both pages will undergo fairly radical overhauls later in the book, and any effort expended now would be wasted.

CREATING A REUSABLE TEMPLATE

For the most part, the presentation aspect of the Newland Tours site is complete. As I mentioned, minor tweaks and additions will be necessary along the way, but by and large the site design is stable.

Once you reach this point in development, you should usually pause to create a generic site design template for all new files. For example, all of the pages within this site will share the same banner, basic layout, style sheet, and so on. Rather than re-creating all of that every time, if you create a generic page template, you can get straight to work.

In this task, you'll create such a template, which you will use throughout the rest of the book as the basis for all new pages in the site.

Before continuing, it's important to clarify that the template you are about to build is *not* a Dreamweaver Template file. Dreamweaver Templates is a special feature that enables designers to build page templates and then lock specified regions to prevent users from modifying their content. Other regions remain editable, so users can go in and change the content as needed without undermining the site look or navigation across pages. Dreamweaver Templates is a powerful feature, especially when combined with Macromedia Contribute, enabling non-technical content experts to take control over page content and maintenance, while minimizing both their need for Web development skills and the chance that they will mess up the code.

Though an interesting and useful feature, working with Dreamweaver Templates is beyond the scope of this book. Be sure to keep Dreamweaver Templates in mind whenever you are creating a large site, especially if you are working in a collaborative environment.

To conclude, the word *template* used in this lesson and throughout the book is used in the common sense, not in the specialized sense of the Dreamweaver Template feature.

1) Open about.htm.

To create the template, you'll strip out all of the unique content from one of the pages of your site. Obviously, the fastest way to do that is to begin with the page that has the least unique content. The file about.htm is the simplest page in the site, so it's a good place to start.

2) Choose File > Save As and save the file as *generic_template.htm*.

Before you start destroying the content of your file, you should save it under a new name. Sooner or later, if you wait until the end, you'll save over the source file and have to rebuild it from scratch.

3) Click to select the large photo of the French Alps and press Delete. Select the final two paragraphs of body text and the image caption, and press Delete.

All of this content is unique, so it needs to go. We'll deal with the title and the first paragraph of body text in a moment.

You may find that after Dreamweaver removed the content, it did not resize the table (although Macromedia Dreamweaver MX 2004 is much better at dealing with this problem than prior versions), resulting in an absurd amount of white space. However, this is not a code problem, but rather a screen refresh problem; it will display as you would expect it to in a browser.

If you experience this problem, simply click the `<table>` tag in the tag selector to force Dreamweaver to redraw the table.

NOTE *A lot of users attempt to fix the white space problem by dragging the bottom border of the table up. However, this often causes Dreamweaver to specify the table's (or possibly a table cell's)* `height` *attribute. In other words, you are in effect attempting to solve a display problem by changing the code. In reality, this method causes new problems and still doesn't solve the original problem. Leave the bottom border of the table alone!*

4) Select the text About Newland Tours and replace it with *Page Title Goes Here*.

Placeholder text in your templates will make it faster to enter standard content and to ensure consistency across pages: For example, every page should have a title, and this title should be in the redefined `<h1>` style. By capitalizing each initial word, you remind yourself, or others working on the template, that page titles use initial capitalization.

5) Replace the first paragraph of body text with *Body text goes here*. Press Delete several times, until all of the empty lines beneath the body text are removed.

Click `<table>` in the tag selector, if necessary, to force Dreamweaver to redraw the table.

The page template should appear as in the screenshot.

6) Save generic_template.htm.

ENHANCING ACCESSIBILITY WITH INVISIBLE NAVIGATION

In creating a page template, you spared yourself the redundant task of reconstructing the basic page content every time you want to create a new page. In this task, you'll extend a similar courtesy to visitors accessing your site via screen readers.

As you know by now, screen readers are browsers that read page contents out loud, so that users with visual impairments can still access the site. The problem is that screen readers start at the beginning of the page and work their way down. This means that visitors using screen readers will have to sit through a description of your navigation bar, along with all of its hotspots, over and over again as they browse through the site.

In this task, you will implement an easy solution to this problem, using a tiny, invisible graphic and a link. This will enable these visitors to jump straight to the page's main content. And users accessing your site through traditional browsers need never know that this feature exists.

Here's how it works: You will insert a 1× 1 pixel graphic and add a link to it that skips to the page title on each page. You will place this at the very top of the <body> element, so that it is the first element that a screen reader will encounter.

1) With generic_template.htm still open, click anywhere inside the main table, and click the `<table>` **tag in the tag selector. Then, using the keyboard arrow key, press left once.**

This should position a rather large insertion point just to the left of the page table, which indicates that the insertion point is now the first item after the opening <body> tag.

INSERTION POINT

2) Click the Insert Image button in the Insert bar, with the Common category active. Browse to spacer.gif in the images folder, and click OK.

The file spacer.gif is only 1-pixel in width and height, making it a fast download. In addition, that pixel is set to 100% transparency, so that it is invisible. Though it is invisible, it still has the two features you need most: the ability to add a hyperlink to it, and the ability to add an alt description.

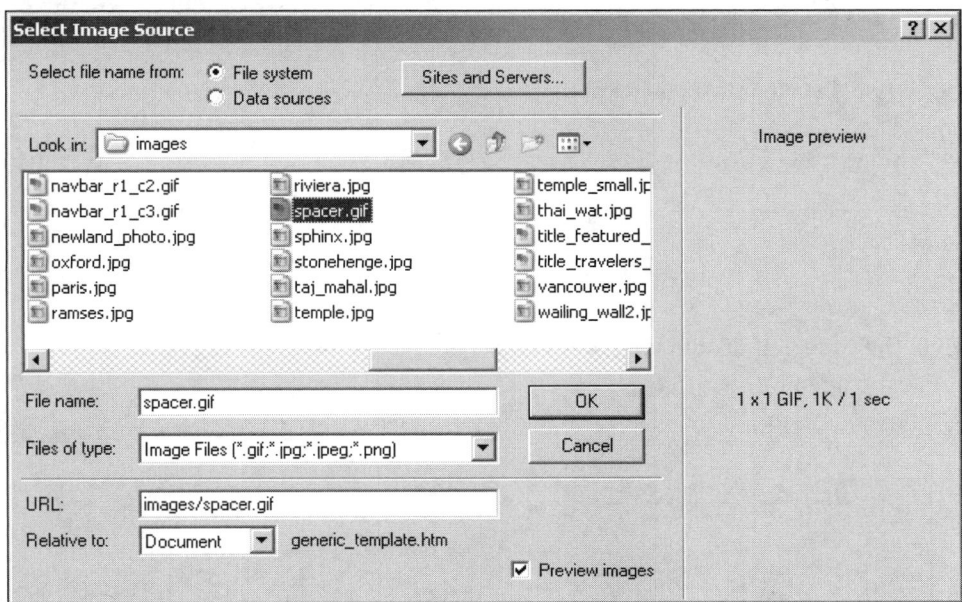

3) Position the insertion point just to the left of the word Page in the page title. Choose Insert > Named Anchor. In the Named Anchor dialog, name it *top*, and click OK.

Dreamweaver inserts the anchor in the code. Depending on your view settings, you may also see a yellow anchor icon beside the page title. This icon is a Dreamweaver visual aid only; it will not appear in a browser. One other visual aid is already on the page, for the image map in the navigation bar.

99

TIP *You can toggle these icons on or off by checking or unchecking View > Visual Aids > Invisible Elements.*

ANCHOR ICON

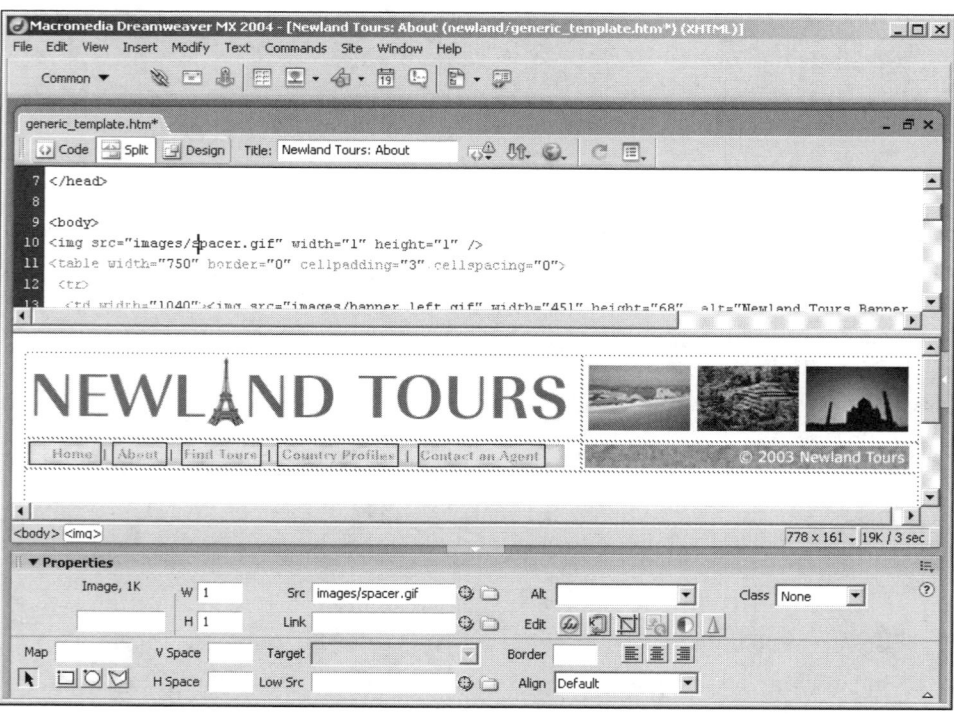

IMAGE MAP ICON

4) In the code half of split view, click anywhere inside the <img> **tag immediately below the opening** <body> **tag.**

Notice that the Property inspector updates to show the options for this image.

5) In the Alt field of the Property inspector, type *Skip to main page content*.

You are using the alt attribute to provide directions to the user.

6) In the Link field, type #top.

This option creates a link to the named anchor you entered a few minutes ago.

7) In the Align drop-down menu, choose Left as the alignment.

This setting causes the table to appear beside the 1-pixel graphic. The default setting causes the table to start a line lower, and introduces unwanted white space at the top of the page.

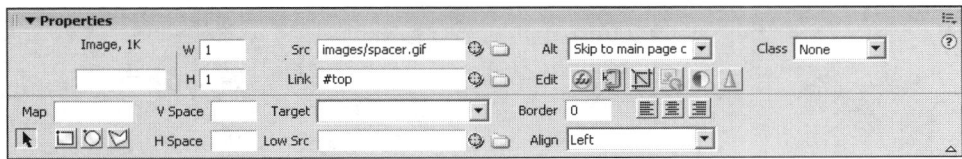

8) Save generic_template.htm.

The template is ready to use.

9) In the code half of split view, copy the entire line below the <body> tag, which should include both the <a> and <img> tags that create the accessibility feature.

Though the template is ready for reproduction, the existing pages lack the accessibility feature that you just created. You can replicate it easily enough by pasting this line of code into each of the existing pages and inserting a named anchor at the top of each page.

TIP *The following steps walk you through copying and pasting this line in each of the five existing files. But you should know a better way: If you are up to it, skip the remaining steps and use Find and Replace to update all five of the pages in one try. Also remember to use Find and Replace to insert the anchor tag as well.*

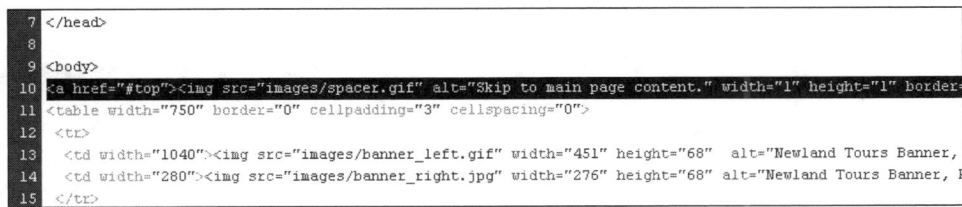

101

10) Open about.htm, click anywhere inside the main table on the page, select `<table>` **from the tag selector, and press the left arrow key once. Choose Edit › Paste.**

This pastes the accessibility spacer graphic into the correct place on the page. Because it is invisible, you won't see it in design view.

11) In Design view (or the design half of split view) position the insertion point just to the left of the page title, and press Ctrl+Alt+A (Windows) or Command+Option+A (Macintosh) to insert a named anchor. Once again, name it *top*, and click OK.

Obviously, for the link to work, the named anchor needs to be inserted!

12) Repeat steps 10 and 11 for each of the remaining pages, except index.htm.

Index.htm has a different structure, so it won't work the same way. If you want to insert the accessibility spacer anyway, go ahead, but it's optional on this page.

WHAT YOU HAVE LEARNED

In this lesson, you have:

• Used Cascading Style Sheets to redefine several HTML tags used in the site (pages 80–89)

• Created custom CSS styles, or classes, and applied them to specific places on the page (pages 89–95)

• Created a generic template that you can use to generate future pages in the site (pages 95–97)

• Added an accessibility spacer image to enable users with screen readers to skip the navigation bar (pages 98–102)

dynamic web sites

LESSON 4

You have reached a significant milestone in the revision of the Newland Tours site. You have upgraded to XHTML, stripped out inefficient presentation code, created a cascading style sheet for the entire site, built a template, and enhanced the site's accessibility. Glancing at the site in a browser, it may not seem like you've accomplished three lessons' worth of work. But you know what important things are going on behind the screen: You've laid the foundations for a standards-compliant, future-proof, maintainable site.

Beginning with this lesson, you'll cast aside (for the most part) traditional, static Web development, and move into database-driven, interactive, dynamic site development. Before you can start developing, though, you need to work through some prerequisites, of both a conceptual nature and a technical nature. By the end of this lesson, you'll have an idea of how dynamic sites work, and what they are created to do; you'll have Dreamweaver configured to work with dynamic data; and you'll have created your first page that uses dynamic content.

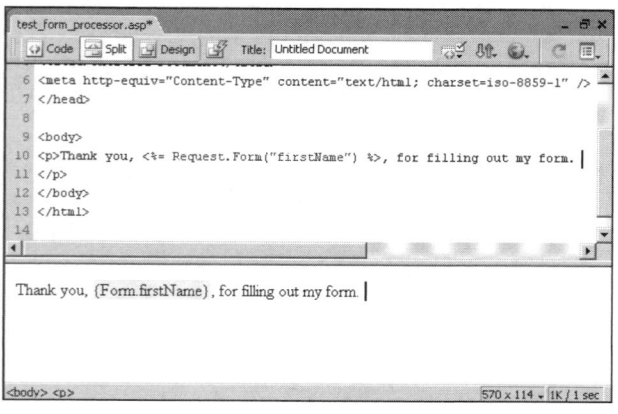

Developing dynamic Web pages often means mixing and matching regular text with placeholder variables.

WHAT YOU WILL LEARN

In this lesson, you will:

- Learn foundational dynamic site concepts

- Choose a server model (ASP, ColdFusion, or PHP)

- Configure your computer to run a Web server with a server model (optional)

- Reconfigure the Newland Tours site definition for dynamic Web site production

- Develop a simple dynamic application

APPROXIMATE TIME

This lesson takes approximately one hour to complete.

LESSON FILES

Starting Files:

Lesson04/Start/newland/about.htm

Lesson04/Start/newland/contact.htm

Lesson04/Start/newland/css/newland.css

Lesson04/Start/newland/generic_template.htm

Lesson04/Start/newland/index.htm

Lesson04/Start/newland/profiles.htm

Lesson04/Start/newland/tours.htm

Completed Files:

Lesson04/Complete/newland-asp/about.asp

Lesson04/Complete/newland-asp/contact.asp

*Lesson04/Complete/newland-asp/css/
newland.css*

*Lesson04/Complete/newland-asp/
generic_template.asp*

Lesson04/Complete/newland-asp/index.asp

Lesson04/Complete/newland-asp/profiles.asp

Lesson04/Complete/newland-asp/test_form.asp

*Lesson04/Complete/newland-asp/
test_form_processor.asp*

Lesson04/Complete/newland-asp/tours.htm

NOTE *If you are using ColdFusion or PHP, and you want to access the completed files, then use the mirror folder (newland_cf or newland_php) included on the CD. All of the file names are the same, except the extension is .cfm or .php rather than .asp.*

DYNAMIC WEB SITE BASICS

Setting aside, for a moment, the specifics of the Newland Tours site, in the preceding lessons you explored several concepts that are critical to dynamic site development. One of these is the separation of logic and presentation. The site logic at this point is handled exclusively by XHTML, while the presentation is handled by the cascading style sheet. You have also explored the concept of merging two different documents (an HTML page and a CSS) on the fly to create something different than either of the two source documents alone. These concepts are fundamental to creating dynamic Web sites.

To understand these interactions, and to prepare you for the tasks ahead, let's take a moment to analyze the relationship among the three different major sources of information that make up every Web page: the content (text, images, etc.), the logic (the document hierarchy, such as headings and body text), and the presentation (the colors, font sizes, positioning, and other cosmetic effects).

In earlier versions of HTML, text, markup, and presentation code all exist in the same place: the HTML document itself. In a meaningful way, the document that a developer creates on her or his hard drive is the same as the document viewed in a browser by the site visitor. This simple relationship is shown in the following figure.

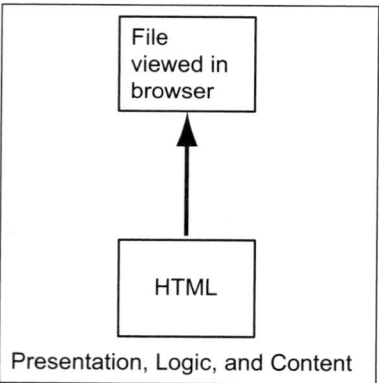

As a result of the upgrades you made in Lessons 2 and 3, the relationships have changed: You have separated a document's presentation from its logic and content. Presentation information is now stored in the CSS. Document content is stored as text within the XHTML markup, which also provides the document logic. Only when the XHTML document and the CSS are merged is the "real" page created. This new relationship is represented in the following figure.

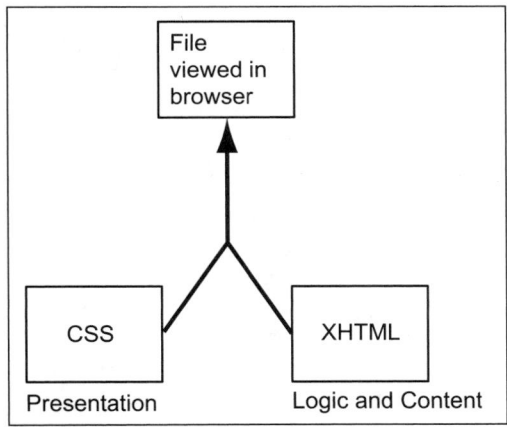

Beginning with this lesson, you are going to add yet another layer of sophistication to this relationship—one that's more profound and more powerful even than migrating from HTML to XHTML and CSS. Specifically, when you add database content to the site, you will separate the content from the logic. What this means is that all three levels—presentation, logic, and content—are quasi-independent of each other, which means you can make radical changes to one without needing to make changes to another. The relationship—and the basic blueprint for the rest of the book—is shown in the following figure.

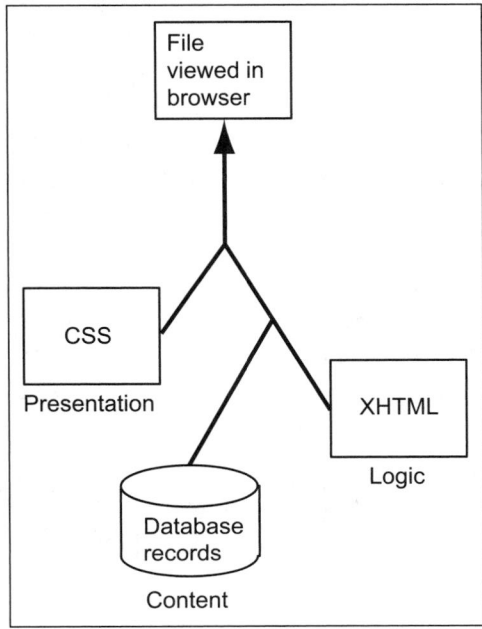

HTML cannot separate content from document logic. Even in its fifth major revision as XHTML 1, HTML is ultimately intended to mark up a plain text document. It cannot process scripts, evaluate expressions, do math, interact with a database, or send and receive information to or from a user. Yet separating logic from content requires, at times, each of these abilities and more. To accomplish these tasks, you need to give HTML some help, and this is where server-side technologies such as Microsoft ASP, Macromedia ColdFusion MX, and PHP fit in.

NOTE *A stylesheet language (think CSS on steroids), XSLT (eXtensible Stylesheet Language for Transformation) is capable of looping, data conversion, and much more. One of its most useful features is its ability to convert one type of XML document (for example, a proprietary XML language developed for internal use) to another type of XML document (such as a standard type of XML document that can be shared with others), and vice-versa. In spite of its utility, XSLT is not as powerful or flexible as server-side applications built using ASP, ColdFusion, or PHP.*

Server technologies like ASP, ColdFusion, and PHP (and there are others, including JSP and ASP.NET) are able to handle programming tasks such as evaluating expressions, doing math, and processing scripts. In addition, they are capable of interacting with data sources, including databases, structured text files, and in some cases XML data. They also have special abilities that pertain only to the Web, such as the ability to collect data sent by the user and control the information that gets sent back to the user.

But there's a catch. Browsers are limited to handling HTML, CSS, and JavaScript—they don't understand server scripts (by server scripts, I am referring to code written in ASP, ColdFusion, PHP and so on). Whatever the server sends to the browser has to be in standard HTML. All server scripts must be processed on the server and output as standard HTML before they get sent to the browser.

To put it more plainly, to view a page with dynamic content, you need to run the page through a server capable of processing the code. This is in contrast to standard HTML pages, which you can view directly in a browser, regardless of whether they go through a server. You can open Internet Explorer or Netscape and browse to any of the HTML pages in the Lesson04/Start folder, and they will display as expected. If you attempt to browse to the pages in the Lesson04/Complete folder, you'll discover that the pages don't open (or they open in Dreamweaver MX, rather than in the browser). The browser sees code it doesn't understand, and refuses to open the file. This is why, in Lesson 1, you viewed the final version of the site at allectomedia.com, rather than from the CD.

Normally, when we think about servers on the Web, we use the term server to refer to the computer that holds the HTML file. This server is properly named the Web server. The most common Web servers include Apache, used on Unix/Linux systems, including Mac OS X; and Microsoft Internet Information Services (IIS), which is used on Windows Web servers.

In addition to the Web server, you will probably use other servers to deliver dynamic data. You may use a database server, such as MySQL or Microsoft SQL Server. You may also use an application server. An application server processes server scripts. ColdFusion is an application server. The application server that processes ASP scripts is actually built into IIS, so you might say that IIS is a hybrid Web and application server. PHP is an application server that runs as a module inside of Apache.

CHOOSING A SERVER MODEL

You know already that there are several common server-side languages. This begs the question (often asked by those new to dynamic site development), "which server model should I use?" The following list summarizes the main functions, pros, and cons of each:

Active Server Pages (ASP): ASP is a Microsoft technology that ties together its IIS (Internet Information Services for Windows 2000 and XP) or PWS (Personal Web Server for Windows 98) servers with VBScript (Visual Basic Script) for dynamic Web site development (you can also use Microsoft's implementation of JavaScript, JScript). ASP is free and built into all IIS and PWS servers, which means that virtually all Windows users can develop ASP sites for free with little configuration. Its code, VBScript, can be somewhat daunting for those with little to no programming experience. ASP is currently being replaced with Microsoft's much-ballyhooed ASP.NET (see below).

ColdFusion: ColdFusion is Macromedia's server technology. Its tag-based syntax is much easier to use than VBScript, and it certainly requires fewer lines of code. Most designers find it the most accessible of all the server models. Newbies aside, ColdFusion is a powerful language that makes dynamic site development rapid. With the release of Macromedia ColdFusion MX 6.1, ColdFusion's performance— oft complained about in earlier versions—is greatly improved. The disadvantage to ColdFusion is that it is not free, though the boost to productivity it affords usually means it pays for itself. It is also extremely easy to set up and configure.

PHP Hypertext Processor (PHP): A recursive acronym, PHP is a fast-growing server model for a variety of reasons. As an open-source solution, it is free and ties in well with other excellent open-source products, including the Apache Web server and MySQL database management system. In PHP 4, used in this book, its code is comparable in difficulty to that of ASP—possibly a little easier. In the newly released PHP 5, the language has been upgraded to a more object-oriented approach, and as a consequence, it is much harder for newbies (though considerably better for seasoned object-oriented programmers). One disadvantage—and this is true of many open-source products—is that setting up and configuring PHP-Apache-MySQL can be difficult.

ASP.NET: The Web authoring portion of the .NET phenomenon, ASP.NET is a powerful new technology that holds a lot of promise for rapid, powerful Web development. Like its predecessor ASP, it runs on any Microsoft IIS server that has the free .NET extensions installed. But ASP.NET is conceptually and architecturally different from classic ASP, ColdFusion, and PHP. Whether you know only HTML, or you have experience with JavaScript or even ASP, you will need to do some adjusting to work with ASP.NET effectively. ASP.NET supports numerous development languages, but by far the two most prevalent are VisualBasic.NET and C#.

Java Servlet Pages (JSP): JSP is the Java-based solution to dynamic Web site development, requiring a Java server (such as a J2EE server) to interpret the code. JSP is fast, providing impressive response times. It is also extremely powerful—certainly the most powerful solution until the appearance of .NET, and certainly powerful enough to compete head-on with .NET. But its code, once again, is daunting for those new to dynamic Web site development.

This book provides coverage of ASP classic (hereafter just ASP), ColdFusion, and PHP. However, this is not specifically an ASP, ColdFusion, or PHP book. The book is designed to initiate readers into the concepts and practices of building database-driven, dynamic Web sites using Macromedia Dreamweaver MX 2004. You will learn lots of code and coding concepts along the way, and you will also make use of Dreamweaver's server behaviors to speed up and simplify development. When you are done, you will have a solid sense of what's possible, how several different technologies merge to create dynamic pages, and how to plan and build sites that use these technologies effectively. Most likely, you will not in the end be an ASP, ColdFusion, or PHP expert per se, but you should be able to get a code-oriented, non-beginner's ASP, ColdFusion, or PHP book at that point and understand it well enough to push forward and develop ambitious Web projects.

Having summarized the advantages and disadvantages of the various server models, I'll let you in on a secret. Web developers seldom choose based on rational criteria, such as which model fits their needs better than another. I certainly have rarely had that opportunity. In reality, the choice is usually driven by the available technology, your budget, the technologies used in an existing site, and the skills and experience of the available human resources. Going a step further, unless you develop for one organization and one organization only, and you intend to stay there for a very long time, you probably don't have the luxury of learning just one. I initially learned ColdFusion and ASP simultaneously, because both were required for different projects I was working on.

SIDE BY SIDE WITH ASP, COLDFUSION, AND PHP: A STRATEGY FOR LEARNING

Don't be alarmed at the prospect of learning all three at the same time. The truth is, in the vast majority of situations, if you need to add a block of ASP to handle some functionality, then you would also need to add an equivalent block of ColdFusion or PHP to handle the same functionality. And the hardest part is not the syntax of one or the other type of code, but rather understanding what data is available, where it is available, and deciding how to get it to do what you want. If you know that much, the syntax isn't that hard.

For this reason, this book uses ASP, ColdFusion, and PHP side by side. While you don't need to develop the same site three times so you can use all three server models, you should make an effort to understand all three sets of code. That is, if you decide to develop in ColdFusion, don't just skip the ASP and PHP code. Take a moment to see how the ASP and PHP code accomplishes the same thing as the ColdFusion code. If you can understand how all three code blocks accomplish the same task, you will accelerate your mastery of Web programming.

For example, the following three code snippets perform the same function: They output (or display) a value that the user entered in an XHTML form field, called "firstName."

In ASP:

```
<p>Thank you, <% Response.Write(Request.Form("firstName")) %>, for your
⇒submission.</p>
```

In ColdFusion:

```
<p>Thank you, <cfoutput>#form.firstName#</cfoutput>, for your submission.</p>
```

In PHP:

```
<p>Thank you, <? php echo $_POST['firstName']; ?>, for your submission.</p>
```

Let's review the similarities between these three code snippets.

- All use a special set of tags to indicate server markup. ASP uses <% and %>, ColdFusion uses <cf[tagname]> and </cf[tagname]>, and PHP uses <? php and ?>.

- All indicate that they are outputting data: ASP uses Response.Write, ColdFusion uses <cfoutput>, and PHP uses echo.

- All make explicit reference to the variable name (firstName).

- All specify that this is a form/POST variable (form variables, as discussed later, are sent using POST): ASP uses Request.Form("firstName"), ColdFusion uses #form.firstName#, while PHP uses $_POST['firstName'].

- Neither contains any additional code beyond these four points.

You don't need to memorize this code; there won't be a quiz on it, and you'll get plenty of practice with it later. The point for now is to see the deep similarity between what the three snippets are doing: All are requesting a form variable named firstName, and outputting it in the middle of a string of otherwise regular XHTML code. The differences between the three code snippets are therefore completely cosmetic: a matter of syntax and a matter of looking up something in a reference. The hardest part is understanding in the first place that you *can* capture a value entered in a form and send it back mixed in with plain-old XHTML code.

Throughout the book, then, I will present all three sets of code side by side. In all cases, I will deconstruct what the code blocks are doing, so you should understand exactly what is going on. All you have to do is read the three sets of code, and see how each accomplishes in its own way the functions that I outline in the main text.

But before you start getting neck-deep in code, you need to configure your system for dynamic site development.

REDEFINING THE NEWLAND TOURS SITE FOR DYNAMIC DEVELOPMENT

Configuring Dreamweaver to work with dynamic Web sites is somewhat more complicated than configuring it to work with static Web sites. Either way, you use the Site Definition dialog to configure the site. What makes defining dynamic sites so difficult, then, is external to Dreamweaver: To develop dynamic sites, you need access to (and permissions on) a bona fide Web server, with (if applicable) an application and/or database server.

This may be a new workflow for many readers. In the past, you may have developed a site locally on your hard drive, and then uploaded it to the production (or public) server when you were ready to publish. When developing dynamic Web sites, you can still develop locally on your hard drive, but you also need access to a development server. Only when you have completed the site using the development server do you upload it to the public Web server.

NOTE *The only difference between a development Web server and a regular Web server is that the development server is not publicly accessible. But from a technical standpoint, a development server is identical to a regular Web server: it processes and outputs code in the same way.*

You can connect to servers in two different ways: you can set up servers on your local machine and develop everything on your machine, or you can develop using a remote machine, such as a network server or using FTP to a machine out on the Web, such as at your ISP.

If you want to work locally, then you first need to spend some time configuring your computer; instructions follow. If you want to work remotely, then you don't have to do any configuration to your machine, but you will need several pieces of information from your server administrator to configure Dreamweaver to work with that machine.

Depending on your setup, you'll need to work through the lesson as follows:

- If you are developing locally, read the section immediately following, "Developing with a Local Server."

- If you are developing remotely, skip to the section, "Developing With a Remote Server," later in the lesson.

- Once you have finished the appropriate section, regardless of the server model or configuration you set up, you need to configure Dreamweaver to work with the server and server model you have chosen; this topic is discussed in the section, "Defining a Dynamic Site in Dreamweaver (All Users)."

DEVELOPING WITH A LOCAL SERVER

Developing with a local server has advantages and disadvantages. Benefits of developing locally include the following:

- The control and autonomy you have over your own computer: you never have to go through a server administrator.

- No need for an Internet or network connection throughout development.

- No lag time for logging in, authenticating, and transmitting data over a network.

The primary disadvantages to developing locally are the following:

- Running a server opens your computer to security risks, and the less you know what you are doing, the more vulnerable you are to attacks, viruses, hacks, and worms.

- If you have a problem with configuration, or something is not working as expected, you are usually on your own.

TIP *The best way to protect your server from hacks, viruses, and worms is to run Windows Update (Windows) or Software Update (Macintosh) regularly—at least twice a week—and to install all the security patches. This is especially important for Windows users, because Windows is more commonly targeted by malicious code. Windows Update can be found in the Start Menu, while Macintosh Software Update can be found in the System Preferences.*

If you decide to develop the Newland Tours site locally, then you must choose the server model you want to use and configure your system accordingly. Use the bolded headings below to select the directions that meet your needs. When you are finished, skip directly to the section later in the lesson entitled, "Defining a Dynamic Site in Dreamweaver (All Users)."

NOTE *Macintosh OS X users developing locally have only one choice: PHP, using the Apache Web server. Macintosh OS 9 users as well as OS X users who want to develop ASP or ColdFusion sites can do so, but not locally. They will have to connect to a remote server that is already running these technologies.*

NOTE *Strictly speaking, it is possible to develop ColdFusion sites locally on a Macintosh. If you have the Macromedia JRun 4 server for Macintosh installed, you can install ColdFusion on top of it and develop locally. This setup is highly atypical for beginners and requires a substantial investment, especially if all you are doing is getting your feet wet with Newland Tours. However, Mac-centric organizations that want to run Macintosh servers should seriously consider this option. Developing ColdFusion over JRun on the Macintosh is not explicitly covered in this book, though most of the steps and code would be the same.*

SETTING UP A LOCAL ENVIRONMENT FOR IIS/ASP

ASP users need to ensure that Internet Information Services (IIS) is installed and running on their system. IIS comes free with Windows 2000 and XP Pro.

NOTE *Windows 98 and ME can use Personal Web Server (PWS) in place of IIS. However, this Web server, now retired, has substantially fewer features and less reliable security. If you are developing dynamic, database-driven Web sites, you need a professional environment, which PWS is not. Upgrade to Windows 2000 or Windows XP Professional and use IIS. Windows XP Home users are likewise out of luck: Microsoft officially states that if you need a Web server, you must use Windows XP Professional. See the following article for a workaround (I have not tested this approach; do so at your own risk): http://www.15seconds.com/issue/020118.htm.*

Depending on how Windows was first installed, you may already have IIS up and running. To determine whether you have IIS installed, look in Control Panel >

Administrative Tools (Windows XP users need to switch to Classic View to see this option). If you see an icon in the list called Internet Information Services, then it is already installed. To verify that it is running, double-click the icon, and in the left side of the dialog, navigate down to Web Sites. In the right pane, you should see Default Web Site listed, and beside it, you should see the word Running. If it says Stopped, click the Start button to restart it.

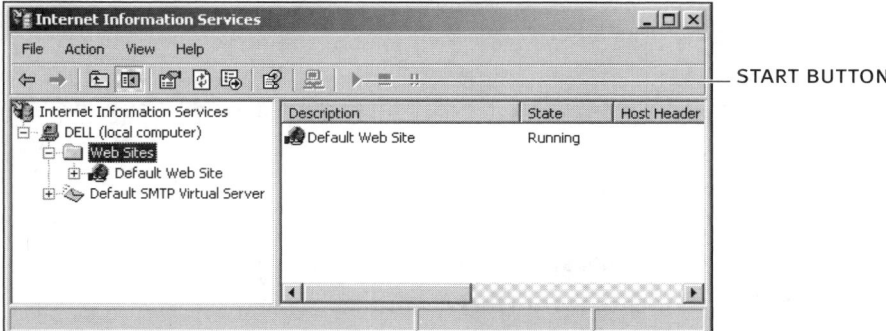

To install and run IIS, follow these steps:

1) Use the Add/Remove Programs utility in the Control Panel, and from there, select Add/Remove Windows Components.

It takes Windows a couple minutes to analyze your machine and determine what is already installed. Once it has built a profile, you will see the Windows Components Wizard.

2) From the list, check Internet Information Services, and click Next.

The default setup should work fine for our purposes, so no further customization is needed. Once you click Next, Windows installs and starts IIS.

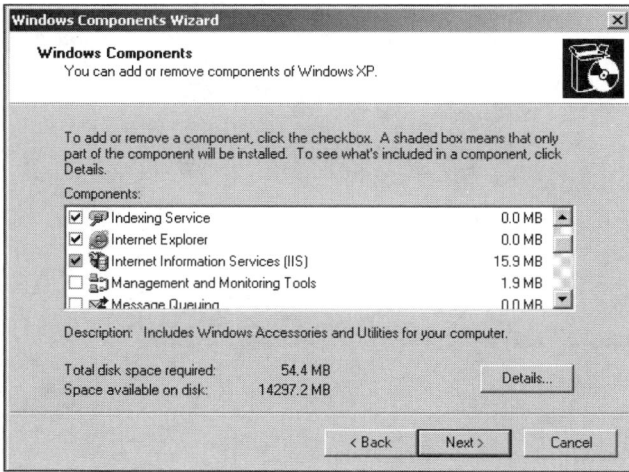

115

SETTING UP A LOCAL ENVIRONMENT FOR COLDFUSION

Setting up ColdFusion locally for development purposes is quite easy, thanks to its installer.

NOTE *This option is only for Windows users.*

1) Initiate the ColdFusion installer from the CD.

After a few moments, the installation begins.

2) Read through and click Next twice to proceed through the Introduction and License agreement sections.

These both contain important information, so don't just skip them.

3) In the Install Type screen, you are prompted to enter your serial number. Check the Developer Edition checkbox and click Next.

You can use the Developer Edition indefinitely for free. The key limitation is that it can only be tested from the local machine. That is, if a different computer on your network attempts to access a ColdFusion Web page that is powered by the Developer Edition, the user will see an error indicating that the maximum number of IP addresses has been exceeded.

If you were installing the Enterprise edition of the ColdFusion server, you would have a serial number, and the limit of one machine would be lifted.

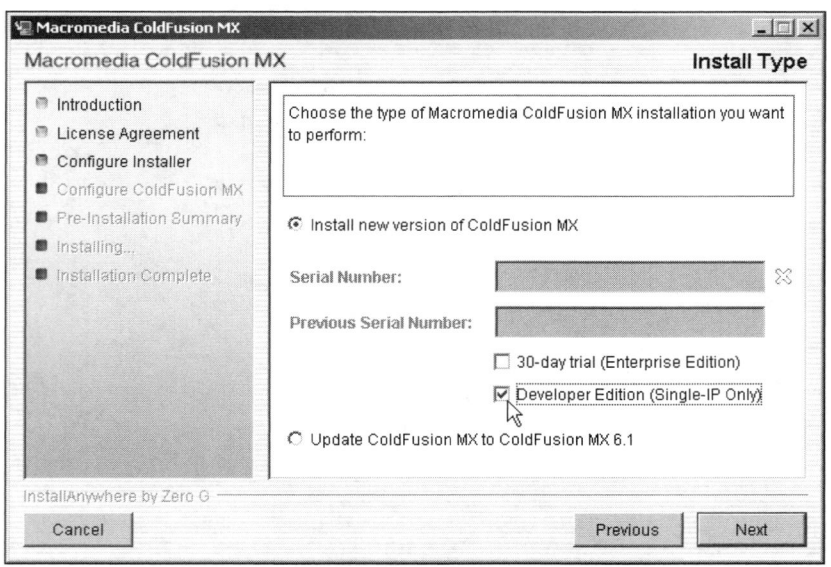

4) In the Install Configuration screen, leave the default at Server configuration. Click Next.

The other two options are for configuring a ColdFusion server to run on top of a J2EE server.

5) Accept the default and click Next in the Choose Install Directory screen.

This screen enables you to specify where the ColdFusion application files are installed.

6) In the Web Server Selection screen, choose Built-In Web Server (if you are not running a Web server, such as IIS), or (if you are running a Web server) choose Configure web server connector for ColdFusion MX and verify that your server is listed in the Web Servers/Sites box.

As an application server, ColdFusion is not intended to fulfill the role of a Web server. On a real production site, another server, such as IIS or Apache typically fulfills this role.

In the development environment, one may not have a bona fide Web server available. Macromedia enables you to let ColdFusion also fulfill the role of Web server for development purposes if you need; to activate it, choose built-in web server.

If you already have a Web server installed, such as IIS or Apache, you can let that continue as your main server, and enable ColdFusion to connect to it, so that when that Web server sees ColdFusion code that it does not understand, it knows to send it to the ColdFusion application server for processing.

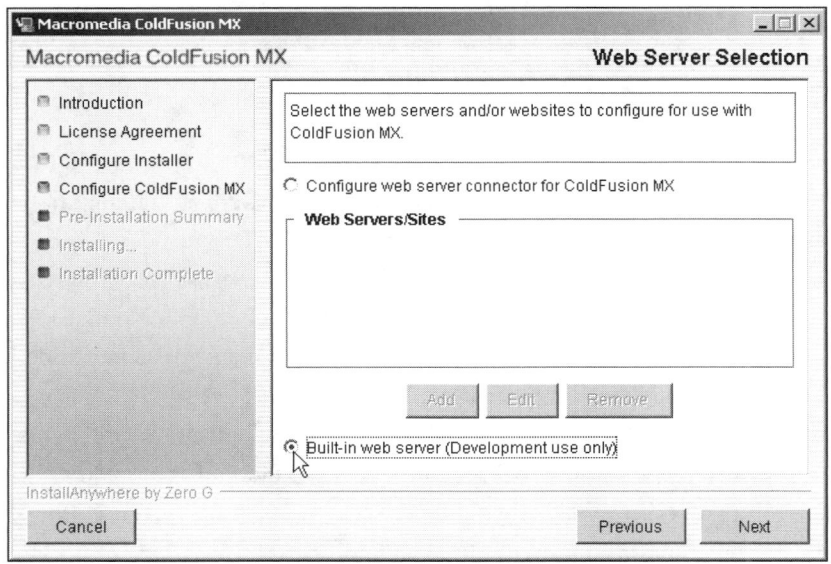

117

Your choice here ultimately affects the URL you use to view ColdFusion pages, which is important when configuring Dreamweaver later in the lesson.

7) Continue to finish the wizard, which is self-explanatory from this point forward.

NOTE *During the installation, you will be asked to enter a password. Do not forget this password! You will need it to configure the ColdFusion server, and you will also need it to access ColdFusion from within Dreamweaver during development time.*

The installation process may take several minutes to run, as it installs the ColdFusion server and starts it up.

When you are finished, a browser opens, which lets you into the ColdFusion administrator application. This application is itself running in ColdFusion. After logging in, you'll be prompted to enter a password for RDS login. You will need this password to use many application development features in Dreamweaver, so do not disable this feature here, and enter a password that you can remember.

You'll need to click Next a couple more times and wait a few more minutes as ColdFusion finalizes the setup process. When you are dumped into the ColdFusion administrator application, you have finished the setup and can begin developing.

SETTING UP A LOCAL ENVIRONMENT FOR APACHE/PHP

Setting up a local environment using the open source Apache and PHP setup can be difficult and frustrating for Windows and Macintosh users who are largely unfamiliar with Unix systems. Two reasons for the frustration are that there are often multiple versions of the same software available, and there are usually multiple ways of installing and configuring it.

But the biggest reason why Windows and Macintosh users are often intimidated by Apache/PHP setup is that the way users interface with the software is fundamentally different from what they're used to. Windows and Macintosh users are accustomed to interfacing with the computers through dialogs, windows, and wizards. To set up IIS, for example, you access a dialog through the Windows Control Panel. To configure ColdFusion, you access a special Web page, where you fill out nicely designed and well documented Web forms. To configure PHP, Apache, and (later) MySQL, you will need to open and manually edit text files buried in nested application directories. A single typo can cause the system to malfunction or cease functioning altogether (until you fix it), and you'll be given little guidance what to do while you are in the text document. Such is the price of open source technologies.

This section walks both Windows and Macintosh users through the process, albeit at a slightly generalized level. The reason for this is that the exact steps are likely to change (in minor ways) between the time I write this and the time you read it.

You begin by downloading the latest versions of the Apache Web server and the PHP module software, both available for free on the Web. You should install Apache before attempting to install PHP, because PHP is dependent on a Web server.

NOTE *Windows users with IIS running on their machines may be tempted to just install the PHP module directly into IIS, and skip installing Apache altogether. This approach is certainly workable, but it has a drawback: Very few ISPs that offer PHP have it running on an IIS server. That is, PHP is almost invariably paired with Apache. Since it is generally desirable for your development environment to resemble, as closely as possible, your eventual production environment, it is worth installing Apache. Also, it is good practice, just to familiarize yourself with the Apache environment—the permissions structures, the commands, the interface, and so on.*

When you download Apache, PHP, or MySQL, in addition to different versions for different operating systems, you'll also usually see options to download the **Source** or the **Binary** files. The source code is the non-compiled code that actually runs these products. Before it can be installed and used, it must be compiled, that is, converted to 0s and 1s, also known as binary code. The binary code has already been compiled for you, and it is ready to install on your system. With commercial products, such as Microsoft or Macromedia products, you never have the option of seeing the source code—what comes on the CD is the binary file. One benefit of being able to access the source code is that you can change it. However, I assume that if you are reading this book, you are probably not at a point where you want to rewrite portions of the programming code behind Apache or PHP! Also, if you get the source code, you have to go through the additional trouble of converting it to a binary file. Thus, for the purposes of this book, I strongly recommend that you take the easy way out and download the binary file.

INSTALLING APACHE FOR WINDOWS

To download and install the Apache Web server for Windows, follow these instructions.

NOTE *The following instructions assume that IIS is not already running as the local Web server. Setup and configuration varies if Apache is not the only Web server.*

1) Go to the following URL, read the instructions, and click the Download link.

```
http://httpd.apache.org/
```

In addition to downloading the Web server itself, this site contains numerous useful resources for Web developers.

2) Find the Windows Binary file for the most current production release, and click its link.

At the time of this writing, the most current production release was 2.0.47.

3) Save the file to disk, and wait for it to download.

At the time of this writing, the Windows binary for Apache was under 6 MB.

The application downloads in a single installer file.

4) Double-click the installer file, which is called something like apache_2.0.47-win32-x86-no_src.msi to launch the installation wizard.

The installer file is on your hard drive, in the directory you saved it in the preceding step.

5) Complete the installation wizard. In the Server Information screen, enter localhost in both the Network Domain and Server Name fields. Leave the default For All Users option selected.

The Apache installer is entirely self-explanatory, with one exception: the Server Information screen. This screen tells Apache how developers and users alike should access the server. If you were installing Apache on a network server, you'd have to specify the computer name and domain, but since you are only installing it for use on a single machine, you can just enter localhost.

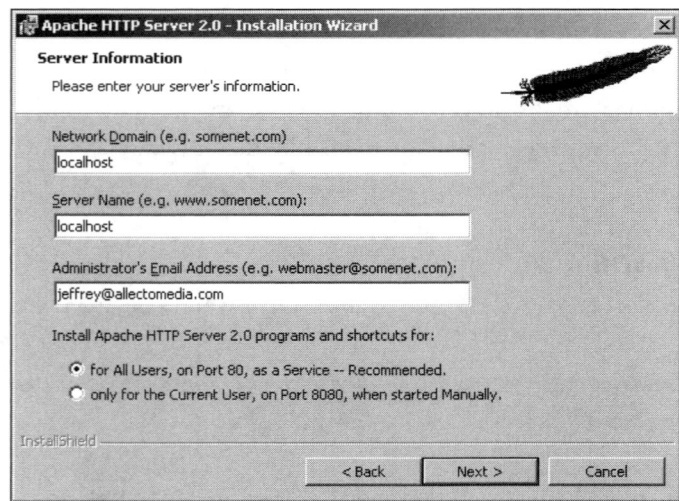

6) To verify the successful installation of your server, open a browser and go to the following location:

```
http://localhost/
```

You should see a placeholder page, as follows.

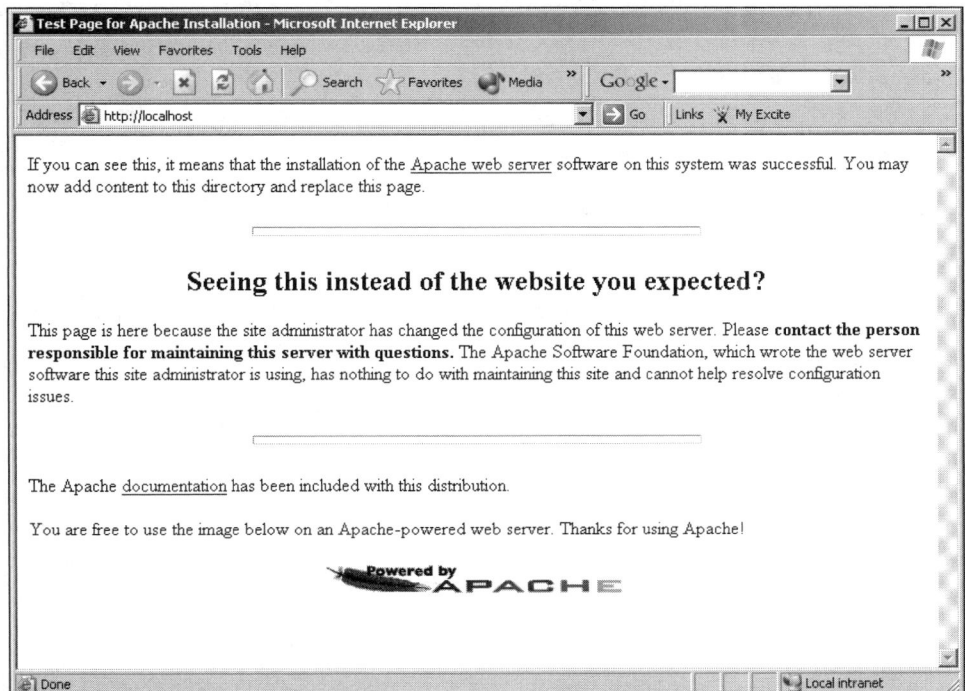

Installing PHP in Windows

Installing PHP in Windows is slightly more complex than Apache, because the files don't come with an installer. Instead, the files needed for the program come zipped. After you unzip them, you must manually move a few files to different locations.

1) Go to `http://www.php.net/downloads.php` **and download the latest stable (not beta) version of PHP, choosing the Windows binary version.**

At the time of this writing, the latest stable version is PHP 4.3.2. A beta is available for PHP 5, and it may be a stable release by the time you read this. Its release may also change some of the steps below. If you install PHP 5, check the book's Web site (at http://www.allectomedia.com) for errata and addenda.

As long as you have PHP 4.2 or higher, the code in this book should work as described.

2) Open the directory into which you downloaded the file, and unzip the file. Specify that the extracted files go to the C: drive.

In my setup, PHP resides in C:\php-4.3.2-Win32. You will need to refer to this location later, so make sure you remember where you put it!

3) Open your PHP directory on the C: drive, find the file php.ini-dist, and move it into the c:\windows (Windows XP) or c:\winnt (Windows 2000) folder. Once it's there, rename it php.ini.

The php.ini file enables you to specify how PHP runs on your computer; that is, it is the primary configuration file for PHP.

4) Returning to the PHP directory, find the file php4ts.dll and move it into the folder, c:\windows\system32.

All the files are now in place. The next step is to tell Apache that PHP is there.

5) Find the file httpd.conf on your computer, and open it in a text editor.

In my configuration, it is in the following directory: C:\Program Files\Apache Group\Apache2\conf\httpd.conf.

Much as php.ini does for PHP, this file enables you to configure Apache. Most Windows programs use dialog boxes for this type of information, but open source programs, following the Unix way of doing things, typically have users interface with the applications via a text file.

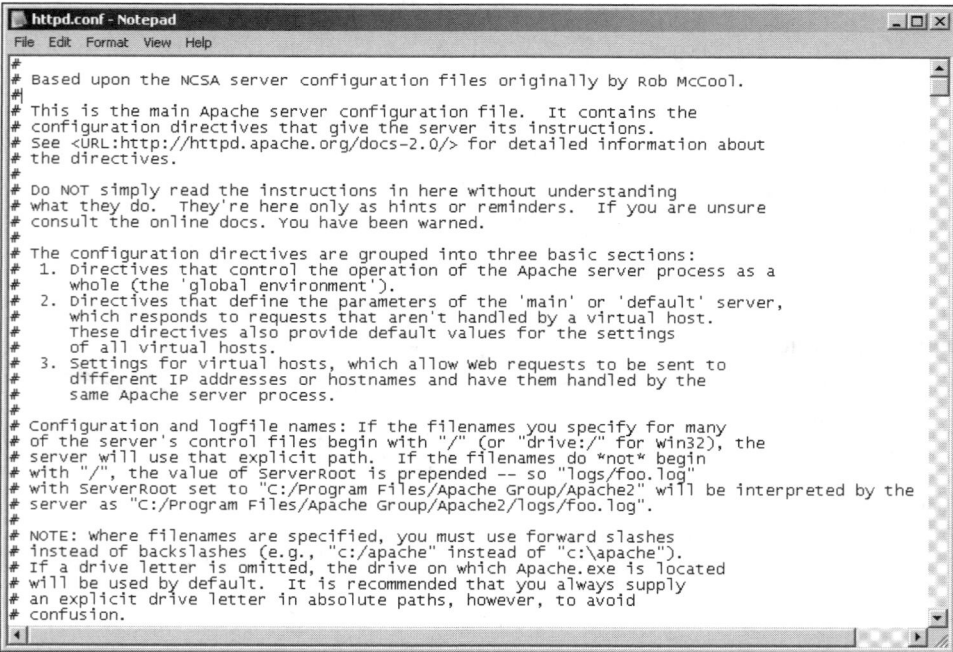

6) Use the Find feature, or simply scroll until you see a number of lines that begin with LoadModule **or** #LoadModule**.**

As the name suggests, LoadModule causes extensions, including PHP, to be activated on the Apache server.

The hash mark (#) that precedes some lines signals a comment. That is, the interpreter ignores any lines preceded by a hash mark.

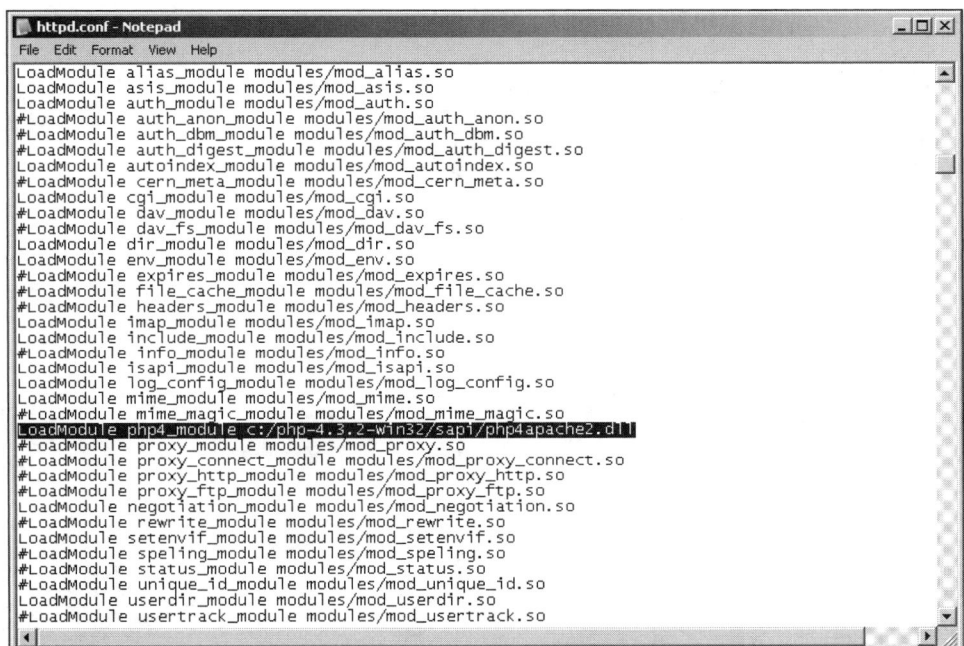

7) Look through the LoadModule **section for the following line of code. If it exists and is preceded with a** # **sign, remove that sign and verify that the version number is the same as the one you just installed. If the version is different, simply edit the file to correct the version number. If no such line exists, type it in at the end of the** LoadModule **block, exactly as you see below, substituting your version number, if it differs.**

```
LoadModule php4_module c:/php-4.3.2-Win32/sapi/php4apache2.dll
```

At the end of this step, regardless of whether the LoadModule line for PHP was there initially, you should have the line printed above in your LoadModule section, and it should appear exactly as it is printed above, except for the version number, which may change.

8) Save and close the file httpd.conf.

You'll need to restart Apache for these changes to take effect.

9) Open the Apache monitor by double-clicking its icon in the task bar. Click the Restart button.

When you restart the server, you'll see a confirmation message in the dialog. Also note in the lower-left corner of the monitor, it says something like Apache/2.0.46 (Win32) PHP/4.3.2. This information confirms that PHP has been successfully loaded.

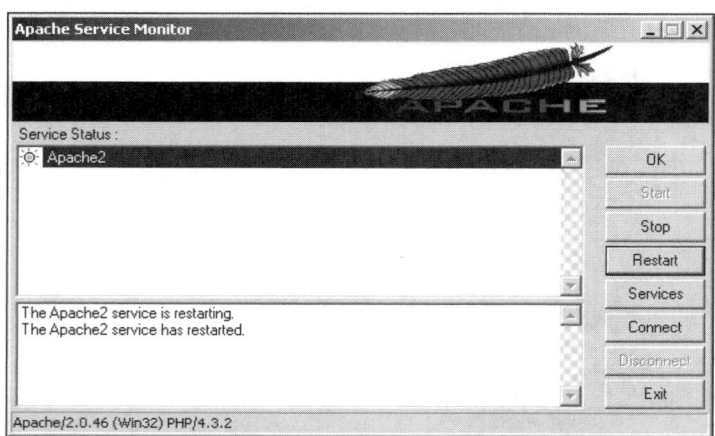

10) Close the Apache monitor and skip ahead to the section, "Defining a Dynamic Site in Dreamweaver."

You have configured your local system to run PHP on Apache.

SETTING UP APACHE IN MAC OS X

Apache comes preinstalled as the default on Mac OS X and higher, so there is literally nothing to install. You do, however, have to turn it on, because by default, the Apache Web service is stopped.

1) Open System Preferences and click the Sharing folder.

The sharing folder is used to control file sharing, Web services, FTP access, printer sharing, and firewalls, among other features.

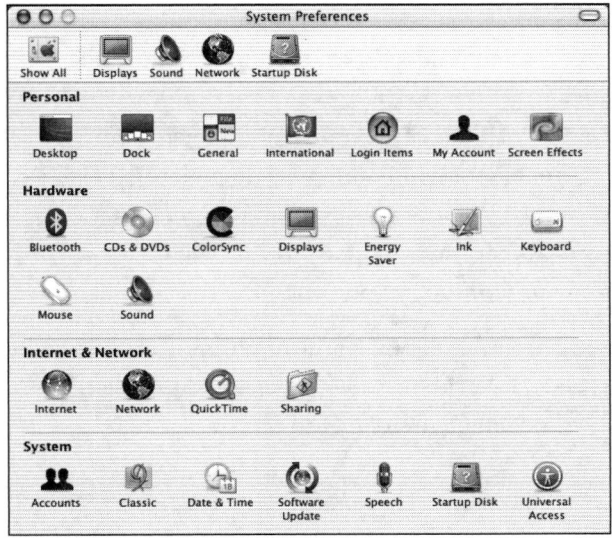

2) In the Services tab of the Sharing folder, check the Personal Web Sharing option.
Checking this box starts Apache. That's it!

NOTE *The version of Apache that ships with Mac OS X is 1.3.x. At the time of this writing, the current version is 2.0.x. Version 1.3 works fine for the purposes of this book. If you want the latest version of Apache, go to http://www.apache.org/ and follow the instructions there for the latest install.*

NOTE *Macintosh has a useful site for configuring the Mac for Web development: http://developer.apple.com/internet/macosx/intro.html.*

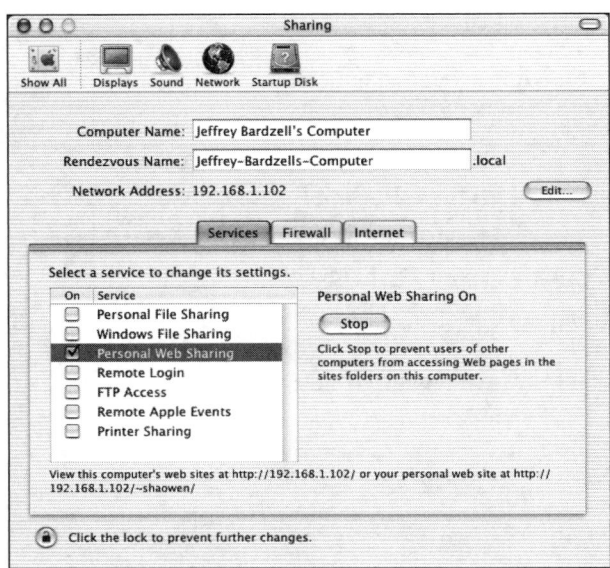

SETTING UP PHP IN MAC OS X

Like Apache itself, PHP comes preinstalled in Mac OS X, so you don't need to install it. Also like Apache, the version of PHP that ships with Mac OS X (PHP 4.12) is not current. You can download and install the latest and greatest version of PHP (to do so, see the Apple developer site, mentioned in the preceding Note). That requires some extra work, and it is sufficient for the purposes of this book to use the shipping version. In the remaining chapters, only one line of code won't work in this version, and it has an easy workaround that I'll point out when the time comes.

To use PHP on Mac OS X, you need to turn it on. In contrast to turning on the Apache Web server, you can't just click a checkbox, though; you need to type some code in the Apache Web server's configuration file, httpd.conf.

NOTE *To develop for the Web on the Mac platform requires more than a passing familiarity with the Macintosh implementation of Unix, called Darwin, including using the Terminal window, navigating directories, using the permission system and the root user, as well as editing text in common Unix text editors, such as pico. The directions in this section assume you are competent working in the command line Unix interface. If this is new to you, I highly recommend* Unix For Mac OS X: Visual QuickPro Guide *(Peachpit), which is my personal favorite book on OS X.*

1) In the Terminal window, open the file httpd.conf in a text editor.
Typically, this file can be found in the following location /etc/httpd/httpd.conf.

2) Search or simply scroll until you see a number of lines that begin with LoadModule **or** #LoadModule.
As the name suggests, LoadModule causes extensions, including PHP, to be activated on the Apache server.

The hash mark (#) that precedes some lines signals a comment. That is, the interpreter ignores any lines preceded by a hash mark.

3) Look through the LoadModule **section for the following line of code. If it exists and is preceded with a # sign, remove that sign. If no such line exists, type it in at the end of the** LoadModule **block, exactly as you see below.**

```
LoadModule php4_module libexec/httpd/libphp4.so
```

This is one of two lines in httpd.conf that activates PHP in Apache.

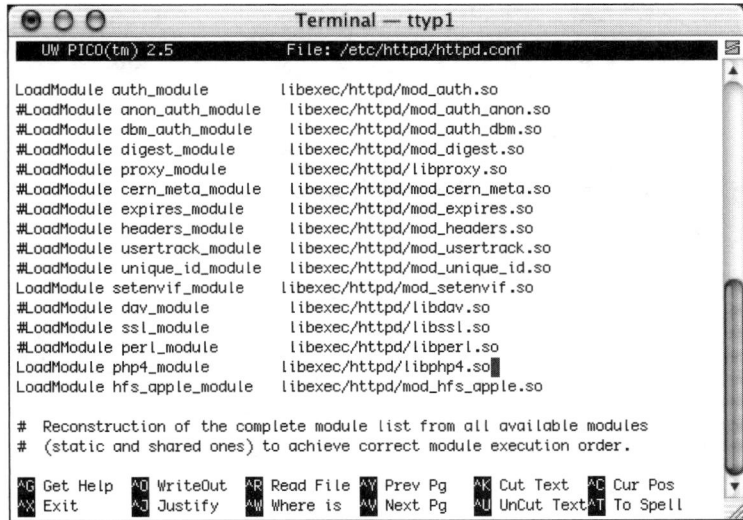

4) Shortly after the block of `LoadModule` lines, you'll see a block of lines that all begin `AddModule` or `#AddModule`. **The following line of code needs to appear in that block. It may already be there, commented; if so, remove the comment (#) preceding it. If the line of code is not there at all, then type it at the end of the** `AddModule` **block.**

```
AddModule mod_php4.c
```

Between this and the `LoadModule` line entered in the previous step, we have given Apache enough information to activate PHP.

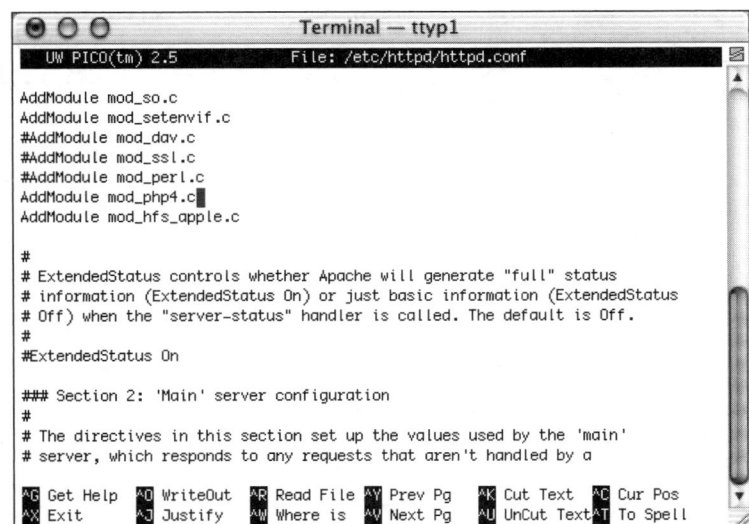

5) Search or scroll much later in the file, until you see a group of AddType **statements.**

The AddType group is a little harder to spot, but you can find it by searching for the comment that precedes it, shown in the following screenshot.

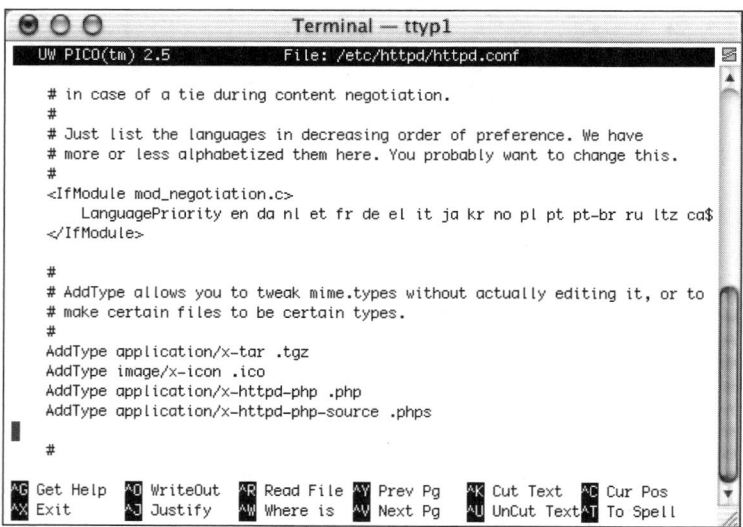

6) Verify that the following two lines of code appear in this AddType **group, and that they are not commented. If they are not there initially, type them in yourself.**

```
AddType application/x-httpd-php .php
AddType application/x-httpd-php-source .phps
```

These two lines tell Apache to treat all files ending with the .php extension as PHP files, and likewise to treat all .phps files as PHP source files. PHP source files actually display the PHP code in the HTML document, complete with code coloring, rather than interpreting and outputting them. This option is useful for debugging.

7) Save and close httpd.conf.

You have now configured Apache to work with PHP. Before you can use it, though, you must restart Apache.

8) To restart Apache, return to the Services tab of the System Preferences, select Personal Web Sharing from the list at left, click the Stop button, and then click it again once it becomes the Start button.

Your system is now configured to process and serve PHP files.

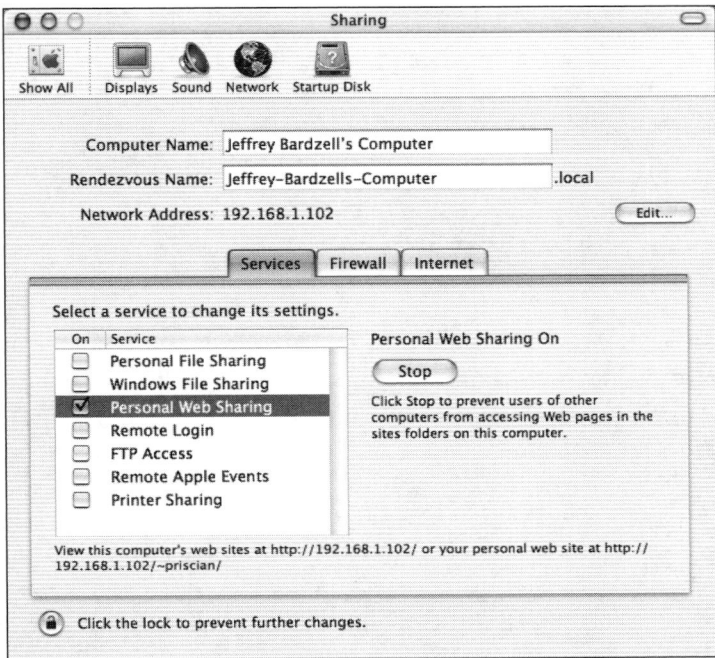

DEVELOPING WITH A REMOTE SERVER

The local server configuration is not for everyone. Macintosh users obviously have no access to IIS or ColdFusion. Further, many Windows and Macintosh users are not permitted to install and run Web servers. Even behind a university firewall, I am not allowed to run IIS on my XP machine. The reason for this is security. Web servers need regular maintenance to deal with the viruses and security holes that make corporate or university networks vulnerable. To prevent, or at least minimize, the chance of infiltrators circumventing an overall security system, administrators often forbid users from installing Web servers on their own machines.

Obviously, if you don't have access to a local server, you'll need to find access to some other development server. This may be a dedicated development server (which is what I use at the university), or it may be a nonpublic folder inside your public Web server. You can access the server over a network, if you have a network connection to the server, or by using FTP. Either way, you will need to get the network path or FTP specifics from the server administrator before you can continue and define your site in Dreamweaver. The server needs to be IIS (for ASP development), have ColdFusion MX installed (for ColdFusion development), or have Apache or IIS installed with the PHP module loaded (for PHP development).

In addition to an account, and permission to add and remove files and folders within that account, you'll also need *one* of the following pieces of information from the site administrator:

- The path to the folder on the network, which could look like one of the following:

```
\\webdev.bigcompany.com\your_site\
\\serverName\your_site\
```

NOTE *If you have network access to a server, you should map a network drive to your account on that server.*

- The FTP information to access the site, including the Host Name/Address, which is usually an IP address (and looks something like 123.12.123.12) and a username/password combination to access your account on that server.

The preceding information is enough to give you access to upload your content to those folders. But you will also need some way to browse the content. Specifically, you need a URL to access your content on the server. Typically, the URL will look something like http://webdev.bigcompany.com/your_site/ or http://serverName/your_site/. When you migrate your site into production, the production URL (in this example) would be http://www.bigcompany.com/your_site/. The important thing to look for is a complete URL that includes http://. Only your server administrator can give you this information.

DEFINING A DYNAMIC SITE IN DREAMWEAVER (ALL USERS)

Regardless of which section above applied to you, use the following steps to define your site in Dreamweaver. Before you begin, you must have access to a fully configured Web server, with the desired application server/module loaded and running.

1) With the Newland site open in Dreamweaver, choose Site > Manage Sites. In the Manage Sites dialog, make sure Newland Tours is selected, and click Edit.
Remember, the Newland Tours site is already defined. You don't need to start from scratch. You just need to add the remote and testing server information to the existing site.

2) In the Site Definition for Newland Tours dialog, click the Advanced tab. Then, select the Remote Info category from the Category list on the left side. From the Access drop-down menu, make a selection and enter the appropriate information in the fields that appear, using the guidelines below.

If you are developing on a computer with a local version of IIS installed (ASP or ColdFusion via IIS), choose Local/Network from the Access drop-down menu. Next to the Remote Folder field, click the browse button, and browse to the C:\Inetpub\wwwroot\ folder. Click the Add New Folder button to create a new folder, called newland. Double-click this folder to select it as the Remote folder.

NOTE *The Inetpub/wwwroot folder is IIS' root Web folder on your system. When you browse to your site (http://localhost/), you will be served pages from this folder.*

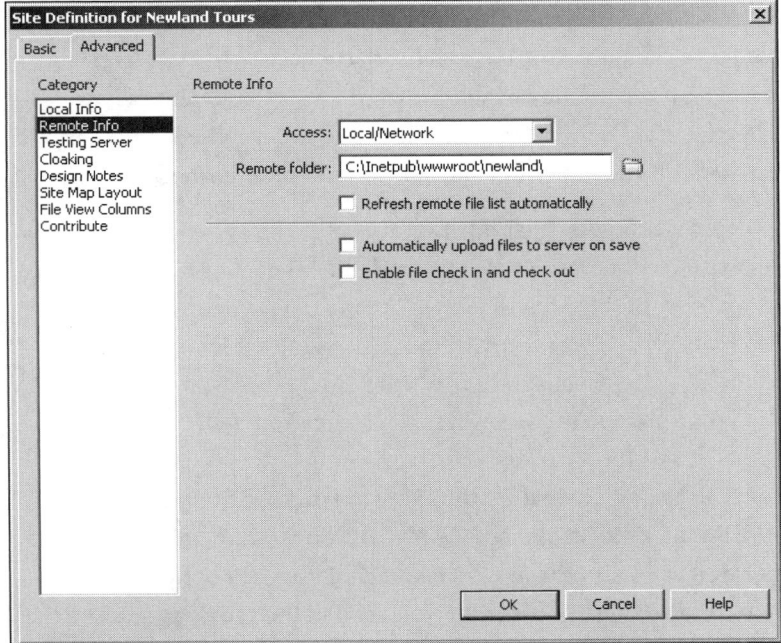

If you are developing on a computer with a local version of the standalone ColdFusion Web server, choose Local/Network in the Access drop-down menu. Next to the Remote Folder field, click the browse button, and browse to the C:\CFusionMX\wwwroot\ folder. Click the Add New Folder button to create a new folder, called newland. Double-click this folder to select it as the Remote folder.

NOTE *The CFusionMX/wwwroot folder is the standalone ColdFusion server's root folder on your system. When you browse to your site (http://localhost:8500/), you will be served pages from this folder.*

If you are developing on a computer with a local version of Apache running, choose Local/Network in the Access drop-down menu. Next to the Remote Folder field, click the browse button, and browse to the C:\Program Files\Apache Group\ Apache2\htdocs folder (Windows) or to HD:Library:WebServer:Documents folder (Macintosh). Click the Add New Folder button (Windows) or New Folder button (Macintosh) to create a new folder, called newland. Double-click this folder to select it as the Remote folder.

NOTE *The Program Files\Apache Group\Apache2\htdocs folder is Apache's root folder on Windows. The HD:Library:WebServer:Documents folder is Apache's root folder on Macintosh. When you browse to your site (http://localhost/), you will be served pages from this folder.*

If you are developing on a computer that has a network connection to the server, choose Local/Network in the Access drop-down, and browse to your folder on the server. Most likely, this appears in a mapped network drive. Use the Choose Remote Folder dialog to add a new folder called newland, and select that as the Remote folder.

If you are developing on a computer that has FTP access to the server, first make sure that there is a folder in your account called newland. Then, in Dreamweaver's Site Definition dialog, select FTP from the Access menu, and type the IP or Web address in the FTP Host field. Enter the path to the newland folder in the Host Directory field. Then fill in the Login and Password fields. When you have done all this, click the Test button to make sure you have configured it all correctly.

3) From the Category list at left, select Testing Server. From the Server Model menu, select ASP VBScript, ColdFusion, or PHP MySQL, depending on which server model you have decided to use. In the Access menu, and also any options that appear beneath it, enter the same information you used in the previous step.

NOTE *Do not choose ASP JavaScript. Though the server model works fine in general, it is incompatible with most of the code you will use in this particular book.*

For the Newland Tours site, the Remote site and the Testing Server site are essentially the same. The difference is that the Remote site exists to enable Dreamweaver to save files to the correct folder, while the Testing Server enables Dreamweaver to test files after they have been processed on the server, so you can verify that they actually work.

4) In the URL Prefix field near the bottom of the Testing Server category tab, enter the site's URL.

If you are using IIS locally on your computer (all ASP and some ColdFusion users), enter http://localhost/newland/.

132

If you are running ColdFusion locally as a standalone server without IIS, enter `http://localhost:8500/newland/`.

If you are running Apache locally in Windows or on a Macintosh, enter `http://localhost/newland/`.

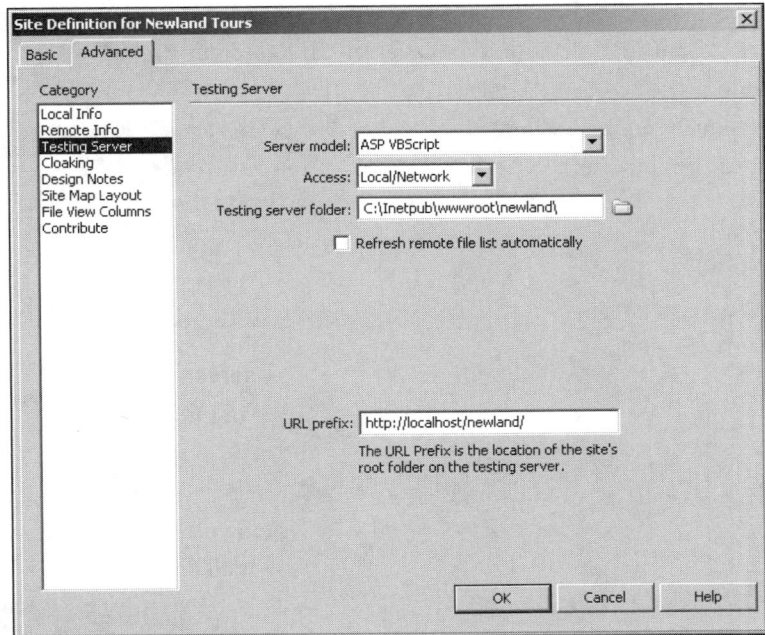

As indicated earlier, the word localhost *is a shortcut that activates the Web server on your computer, and tells it to look in the server's root folder (the wwwroot folder for IIS and the standalone ColdFusion Web server, or htdocs on Apache), in which you created a newland folder in a previous step.*

If you are using a remote server, whether through a network or through FTP, enter the server's URL, which the site administrator should have given you. It probably looks something like `http://www.bigcompany.com/newland/`.

Either way, the URL prefix must begin with http:// and should not have any drive letters (such as h:\) anywhere in it. Also note that the slashes in the URL are forward slashes, not backslashes.

TIP *If the site doesn't display properly later in the lesson, the URL prefix is the first place you should look when troubleshooting. If this information is wrong, you will not be able to browse your site and see it in action, even if all your code is correct and your server and server models are correctly configured and running.*

5) Click OK to save and close the dialog, and then click Done to close the Edit Sites dialog.

The site is now redefined and should be ready for dynamic development.

6) One at a time, right-click (Windows) or Control-click (Macintosh) each of the HTML files in the Site panel, choose Edit > Rename, and change the extension from .htm to .asp, .cfm, or .php as appropriate. Whenever the Update Files dialog appears, click Update.

Changing the extension is required when you upgrade to dynamic sites, because the server uses the extension to determine whether to process any special code on the page.

When you change the extension, all of the links that point to that page are broken. Dreamweaver's site manager catches this and fixes the problem when you choose Update.

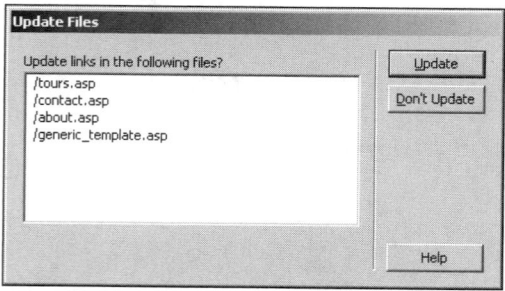

7) Click once on the top-level folder, and click the Put File(s) button.

This uploads the entire site to the remote folder and testing server.

NOTE *If a dialog appears asking whether you want to Put the entire site, click OK.*

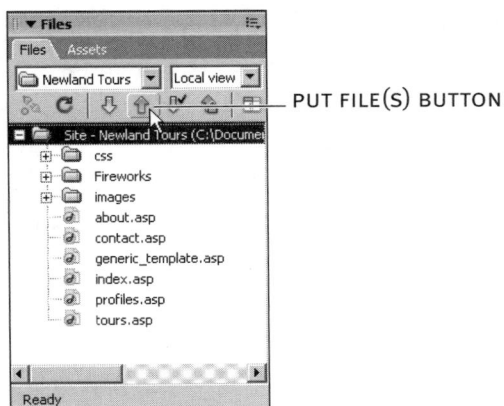

PUT FILE(S) BUTTON

8) Click once to select index.asp, index.cfm, or index.php in the Site panel, and press F12.

Pressing F12 tests the site as it runs through the server. This test results in either good news or bad news. If you can see the Newland Tours index page, then you have correctly configured the site, and you are ready to start developing. If you get an error message or the site doesn't display properly, then something has gone amiss. To troubleshoot, take a second look at the URL prefix. Also, use Windows Explorer or Macintosh Finder to make sure that the files really were uploaded to the remote site. If you are still hung up, talk to your site administrator, who should be able to help you resolve this problem.

SITE URL DISPLAYS IN ADDRESS BAR

BUILDING A SIMPLE, DYNAMIC APPLICATION

You have now tested the site going through the remote server, and—assuming you saw index.asp, index.cfm, or index.php in your browser—you have everything correctly configured. But nothing in the Newland site is actually dynamic yet. At this point, you've done all the work and haven't seen any of the benefits. In this task, you will create a very simple dynamic application, which will reward you with a taste of what's to come, both conceptually (how dynamic sites work) and behaviorally (the sequence of steps needed to create the functionality).

CREATING THE INPUT PAGE

You're going to build a page containing a form that asks users their names. Then they will click Submit, at which point they will be redirected to a second page, which will display the name they entered. No, this application doesn't exactly push the limits of ASP, ColdFusion, or PHP. It does, however, introduce you to building forms, dealing with dynamic data, and distinguishing between server-side and client-side code.

1) With the Newland site open, choose File > New. In the New Document dialog, choose Dynamic Page in the Category list on the left side, and then choose ASP VBScript, ColdFusion, or PHP on the right. Make sure Make Document XHTML Compliant is checked. Click Create.

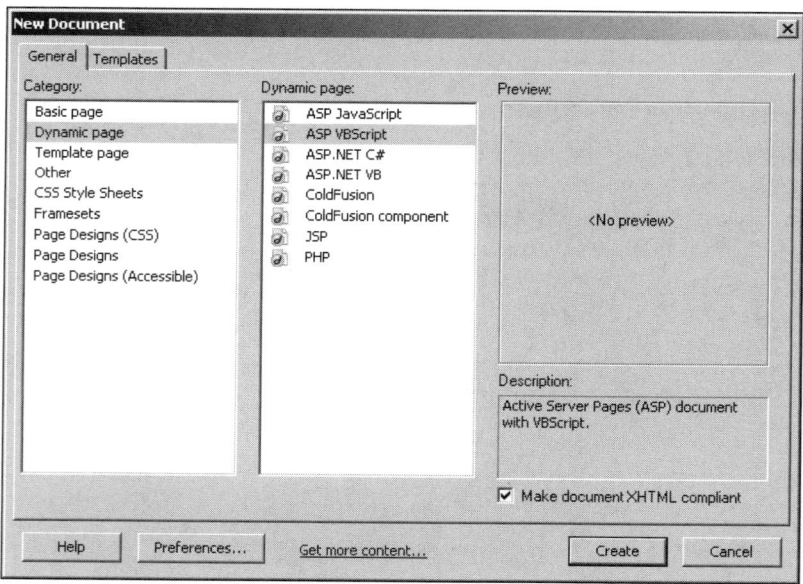

In this step, you are creating a new dynamic page. By specifying the type of dynamic page, you tell Dreamweaver what code to use when you use Dreamweaver's ready-made server behaviors, which extension to use when you save the file, and in some cases, which additional code to add to the document header.

ASP users will see `<%@LANGUAGE="VBSCRIPT" CODEPAGE="1252"%>`; this line specifies whether you are using VBScript and JScript, either of which you can use with ASP. For the exercises in this book, though, you must work with VBScript. ColdFusion and PHP don't have multiple scripting languages, so a new ColdFusion or PHP page has no equivalent for this line.

2) Click anywhere in the design window, select the Forms category in the Insert panel, and click the Form button to insert a form. Click the Text Field button, and then click the Button button.

You have just added a basic form to your page.

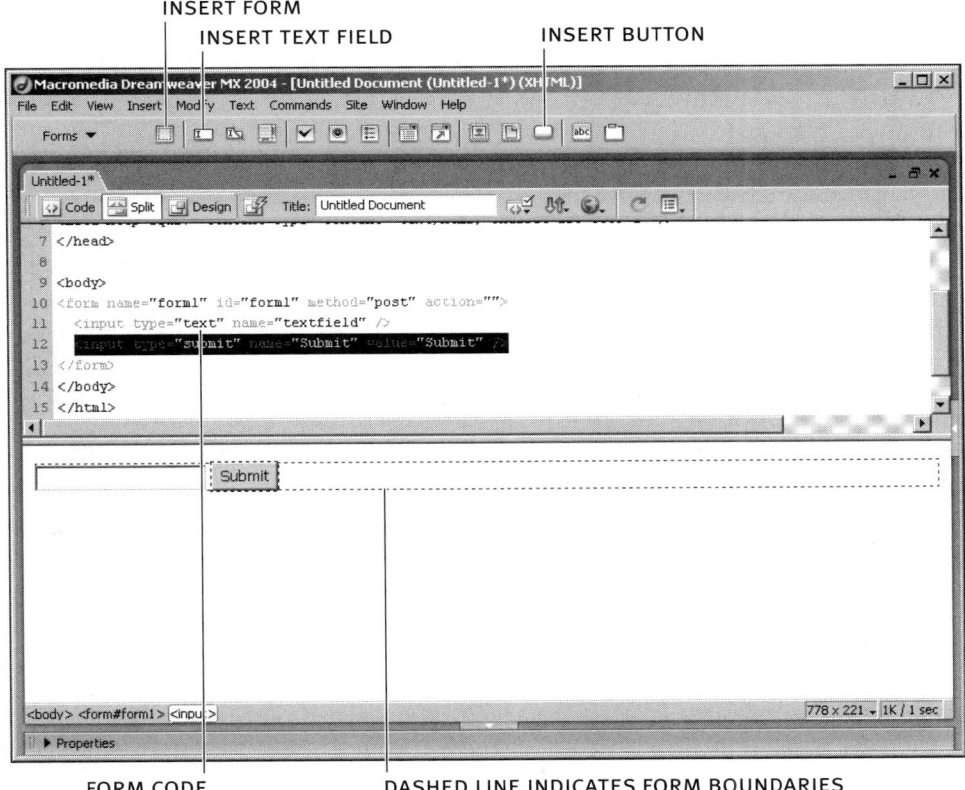

INSERT FORM
INSERT TEXT FIELD   INSERT BUTTON

FORM CODE   DASHED LINE INDICATES FORM BOUNDARIES

The red dashed line indicates the form's boundaries. This will not appear in the browser; it is there just to help you know where the form begins and ends on the page.

The form at this stage is not yet customized and does not do anything. Lacking even a text label beside the text field, it doesn't tell you anything about itself.

3) Click the text field, and then press the left keyboard arrow once to position the insertion point before the text field. Type *First Name*.

If you don't label your text fields, no one will know what to type in them.

4) Click the text field, and in the Property inspector, name it *firstName* and press Tab or Enter/Return.

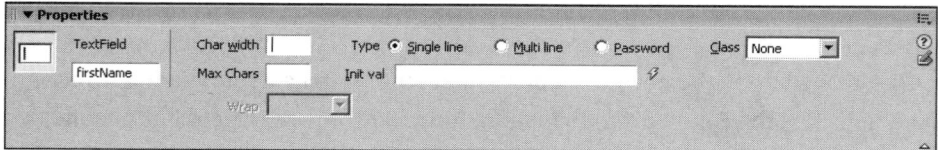

You will use this name to retrieve the value in ASP, ColdFusion, or PHP in a few minutes. Always give your form fields meaningful names. Code is hard enough to write as it is—don't make it worse by sticking with Textfield1, Textfield2, and Textfield3, which Dreamweaver inserts by default.

You press Tab or Enter/Return to apply a setting entered in the Property inspector.

5) Click `<form#form1>` in the tag selector, to activate the Property inspector for the form. Name the form *frm_name*, and type *test_form_processor.asp* (or .cfm or .php) in the Action field.

The Action field points to the page (or other resource) that contains the script that can process the form data. It is always a URL. In this case, it points to a URL that doesn't exist, because you haven't created test_form_processor.asp (or .cfm or .php) yet. The method should be set to POST. I'll explain what POST means in a later lesson.

NOTE *Henceforth, I will assume you can figure out your own extensions. It wastes space and insults your intelligence for me to specify "(or .cfm or .php)" every time I refer to a file. I will always use .asp, so if you are using ColdFusion, just use the .cfm extension instead, and if you are using PHP, use the .php extension instead.*

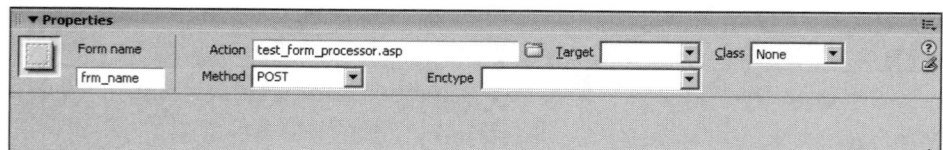

6) Choose File > Save As and name the file test_form.asp.

This is a throwaway file that you are creating just to test a simple dynamic site feature. I often prefix such files used for testing purposes with "test_"; that way, when I am finished, I can easily find and remove them.

CREATING THE OUTPUT PAGE

You have completed the input page. Now it's time to show how ASP or ColdFusion can collect that information, insert it into regular XHTML code, and return it to the client browser.

1) Create a new dynamic page.

See step 1 from the previous task if you forgot how.

2) Save the new file as test_form_processor.asp.

I often use the suffix "_processor" for pages that exist to process some sort of data. This page will process the data entered by the user in the form.

3) In design view, type *Thank you, , for filling out my form*. With the cursor anywhere inside this paragraph, choose Paragraph from the Format menu in the Property inspector.

Eventually, this text will say, *Thank you, [whatever the user's first name is], for filling in my form*. Most of the sentence is just static text. The dynamic part will be the actual value of the first name, which will be pulled in from the form.

By selecting Paragraph as the Format, you wrap the text string in <p></p> tags.

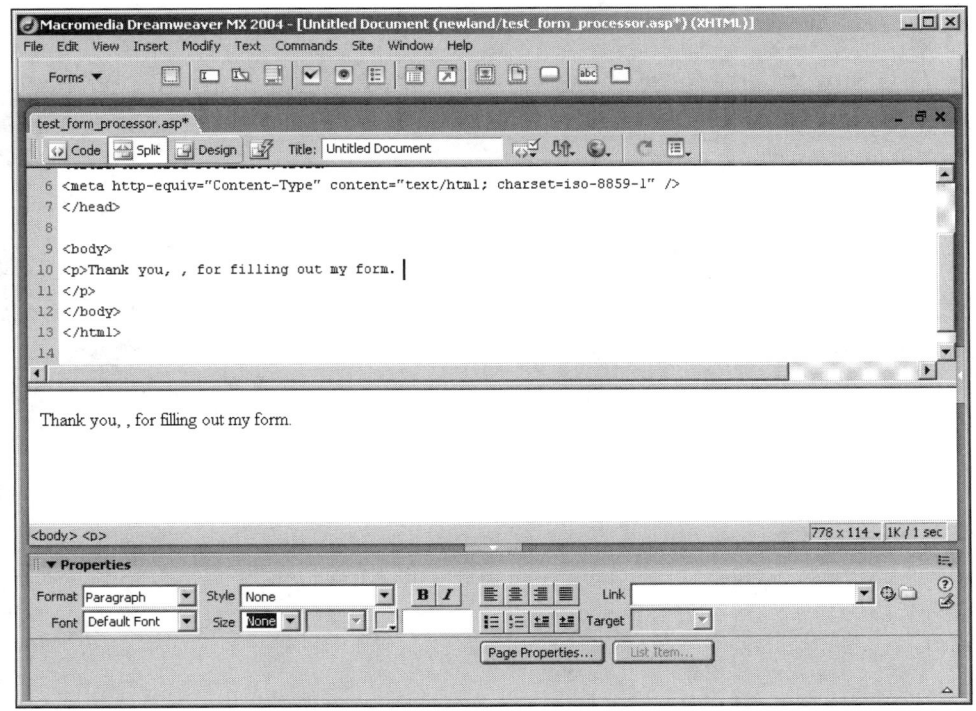

4) Position the cursor in between the commas, where you would enter someone's name. Open the Bindings panel (Window > Bindings).

The Bindings panel is used to specify all of the data that is available to the page. Data is typically stored in a name-value format. In this particular case, the name is firstName. The value doesn't yet exist—it won't exist until someone fills out the form. Remember also that this value comes to the page from a form on the test_form.asp page. Other possible sources besides forms (and you'll get quite familiar with these later) include the URL, a recordset (data retrieved from a database), a cookie, and more. But this time, it's from a form.

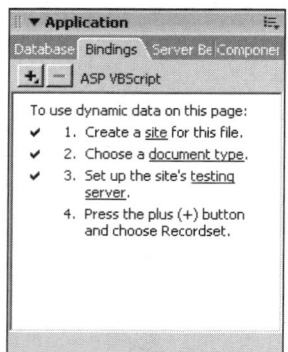

5) Click the + button to add a new binding. From the menu, choose Request Variable (ASP) or Form Variable (ColdFusion and PHP). In the resulting dialog, for ASP, select Request.Form in the Type Menu and type *firstName* in the Name field, or for ColdFusion or PHP type *firstName* in the Name field. Click OK.

The first screenshot shows the Request Variable dialog, which ASP users see, while the second one shows the Form Variable dialog, which ColdFusion and PHP users see.

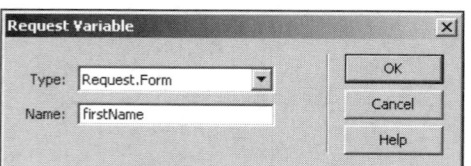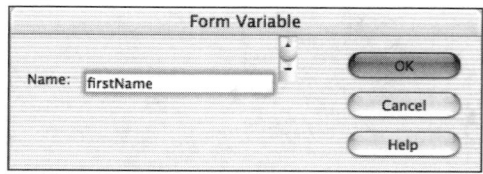

The Bindings panel is updated to show the firstName variable. The screenshot shows what the Bindings panel looks like in ASP. It looks slightly different in ColdFusion and PHP (the word Request is replaced with Form, and the word Form.firstName is replaced with firstName).

140

You might be wondering what exactly you've just accomplished. If you take a look at your code, you'll see that you haven't changed the document at all: The code is the same as it was before you opened the Bindings panel. What you've done is use Dreamweaver's graphic interface to tell Dreamweaver how to write a block of dynamic code.

Back at the beginning of the chapter, I listed three code snippets side by side: one in ASP, ColdFusion, and PHP. The code in those snippets specified a variable (firstName); its origin (a form); and what to do with it (output it to XHTML). What you've just done in the Bindings panel is specify that logic in a way that Dreamweaver can understand and translate into code.

For ASP, you specified a Request variable. In ASP, the Request object is used to retrieve information from a given location. In the dialog, you then specified Request.Form, which tells ASP to look in the Request object for the variable in a form. Finally, you specified the name of the variable itself. In a word, you have provided a road map for Dreamweaver/ASP to find the value of the firstName variable.

For ColdFusion and PHP, you specified a form variable, which is sufficient for ColdFusion to look in the right place (no need to worry about Request objects and such). Then you provided the name of the variable. Again, to summarize, you have provided a road map for Dreamweaver/ColdFusion or PHP to find the value of the firstName variable.

At this point, though, you have told Dreamweaver only *how* to find the variable. You haven't actually *asked* it to find that variable; nor have you asked Dreamweaver to do anything with that value once it has it.

6) Make sure that the variable Form.firstName (ASP) or firstName (ColdFusion/PHP) is selected in the Bindings panel, and click the Insert button at the bottom.

A blue highlighted {Form.firstName} appears on the page, in between the commas. Blue highlighted text signifies the presence of dynamic content in Dreamweaver. The text won't appear blue when viewed in a browser. For that matter, it also won't display {form.firstName}, either: It will display instead the user's first name.

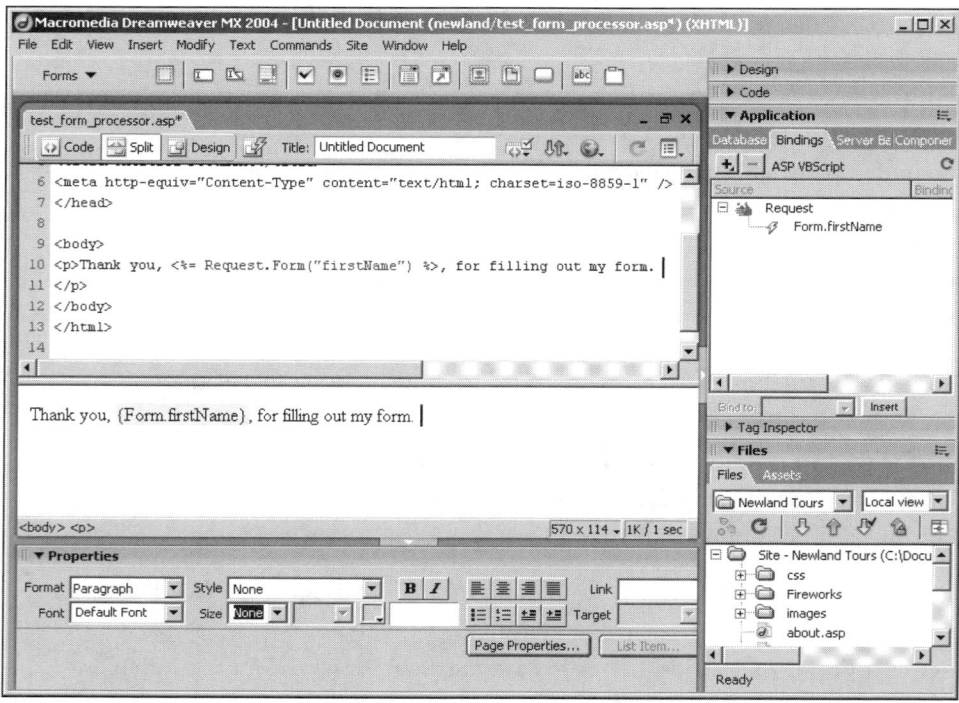

NOTE *Though {Form.firstName} looks like code, it's actually pseudocode. This appears the same regardless of server model. One assumes Macromedia used pseudocode to create a generic and descriptive language to communicate what was actually specified in the dynamic content. That's fine as long as you don't attempt to use that syntax to write code.*

If you look in the actual code, you should see that `<%= Request.Form("firstName") %>` (ASP), `<cfoutput>#form.firstName#</cfoutput>` (ColdFusion), or `<?php echo $_POST['firstName']; ?>` (PHP) has been added. These are the same snippets I showed you earlier in the chapter, with one small exception in the ASP code.

The way to tell IIS to output an expression is to use the Response object. The most common use of the Response object is Response.Write(). This is a command that tells IIS to insert whatever's inside the parentheses into the document. With a few nuances, Response.Write() is more or less the equivalent of <cfoutput> or echo. Response.Write() is so popular that it has a shortcut. When you see an ASP code block that begins <%= rather than simply <%, it means <% Response.Write(). In other words, the following two lines of code mean the exact same thing:

```
<% Response.Write(Request.Form("firstName")) %>
<%= Request.Form("firstName") %>
```

To summarize what you have done in the last two steps, you told Dreamweaver/ASP, Dreamweaver/ColdFusion, or Dreamweaver/PHP how to find the firstName variable, using the Bindings panel's + button. Then, you inserted that binding onto the page, which told ASP, ColdFusion, or PHP how to find the variable and also to display the current value of the variable.

7) Save and close all open documents. In the Site panel, hold down the Shift key and select both test_form.asp and test_form_processor.asp. Click the Put File(s) button in the toolbar at the top of the panel.

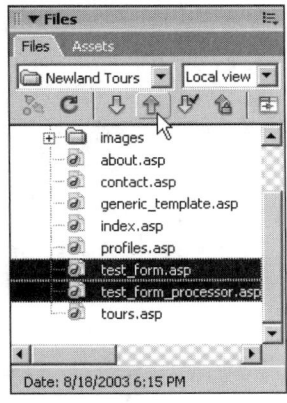

You can't test the site unless you run it through a server, and your server is not your local site. So, to test your site, you have to upload, or Put, your file to the server.

TIP *This is a step I forget about time and time again. If you get an unexpected error during development, your first point of troubleshooting should be to verify that you uploaded all of the requisite files.*

8) Select test_form.asp in the Site panel, and press F12 to test it in a browser. When the page loads, type your first name in the field and click Submit.

You are redirected to the test_form_processor.asp page. As I hope you anticipated, the first name you entered in the form now appears on the screen.

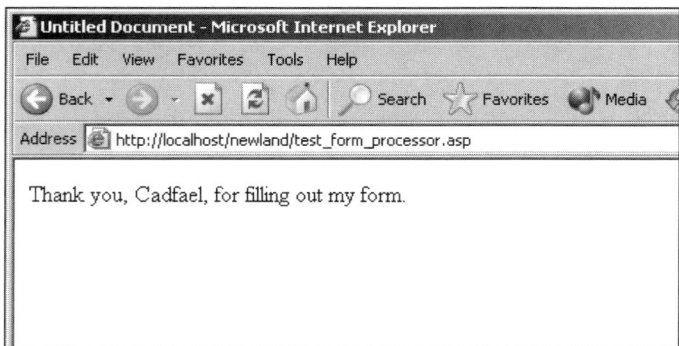

9) Still in your browser, choose View > Source (or your browser's equivalent). Look at the line enclosed in <p> tags.

This is the interesting part. The dynamic code has been completely removed! The code for this page is that of a static XHTML Web page. Even the dynamic part, the first name, looks as though it were hard-coded in there. But of course, you know it wasn't.

```
test_form_processor[1] - Notepad
File  Edit  Format  View  Help

<!DOCTYPE html PUBLIC "-//W3C//DTD XHTML 1.0 Transitional//EN" "http://www.w3.org/TR/xhtml1/
<html xmlns="http://www.w3.org/1999/xhtml">
<head>
<title>Untitled Document</title>
<meta http-equiv="Content-Type" content="text/html; charset=iso-8859-1" />
</head>

<body>
<p>Thank you, Cadfael, for filling out my form.
</p>
</body>
</html>
```

Our review of the output code brings up a critical concept. The page you code in Dreamweaver is different from the page the user sees in a browser, even though they both have the same name (and still, of course, a great deal in common).

The difference between the two versions of the page is that all of the original page's ASP/ColdFusion/PHP code is processed and removed, with its output values written into the XHTML as regular XHTML.

The two versions of the page also share some similarities: All of the standard XHTML code written into the original, including the <body> and <p> tags, and most of the text, are passed unchanged to the output version of the page.

WHAT YOU HAVE LEARNED

In this lesson, you have:

- Learned about the relationships between presentation, document logic, and content (pages 106–109)
- Explored the pros and cons of five major server models (pages 109–112)
- Set up a local Web server and server model (pages 112–130)
- Defined a dynamic site in Dreamweaver (pages 130–135)
- Developed a Web form (pages 136–138)
- Created a page that collected and displayed data from the Web form (pages 139–144)

passing data between pages

LESSON 5

The hallmark feature of dynamic Web pages is that the contents displayed in the browser are not coded in the page, as in static HTML, but rather inserted into the page on the fly as it is served. The implication of this is that the core skill in developing dynamic Web applications is knowing how to capture and embed data, so that it can be inserted into Web pages when they are served.

At the end of the preceding lesson, you got a taste of this process, when you displayed the first name that users entered on a form on a different page. To accomplish this task, you used ASP, ColdFusion, or PHP code to capture the firstName variable and inserted it inline into regular XHTML code. Though it was a simple little application, the form-to-Web transfer you achieved at the end of Lesson 4 is representative of a good portion of dynamic site development.

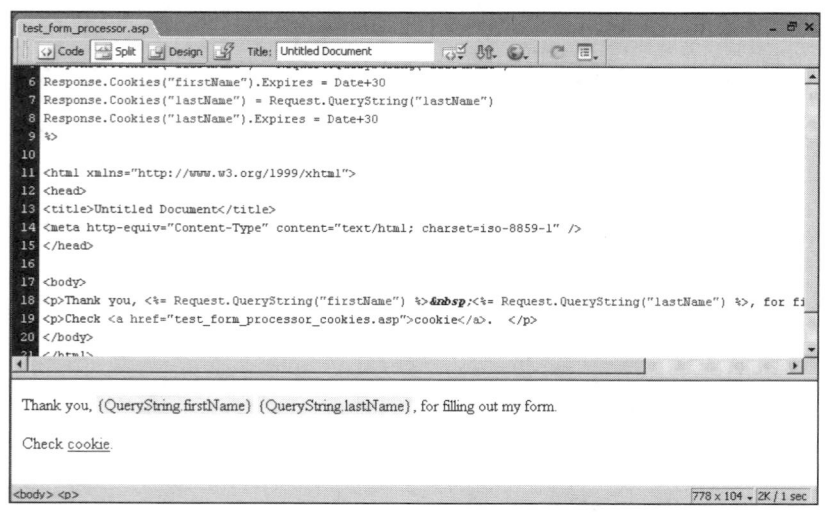

*In this lesson, you will pass data from a URL into a cookie on the user's hard drive to create **persistent dynamic data**.*

You probably already know that there's a lot more to dynamic Web site development than forms and form variables. You know that you can embed database content in a Web page, and you have probably also heard of cookies, which store little bits of information on client computers for later use. Building dynamic Web pages, then, usually means working with several different types of data, coming from different sources, and outputting them into a standard XHTML page.

In this lesson, you will explore two other ways of capturing and embedding data in Web pages (also called **binding**). In doing so, you will discover how similar each of these approaches to binding data is to the other, from the perspective of coding. And yet you will also see that each approach offers unique benefits that the other approaches don't have. You will not do anything for Newland Tours in this lesson; nor will the files be particularly attractive or useful in themselves. But they will teach you quite a bit about the core skill of binding data to Web pages.

As you learn each of these approaches to binding data, you'll also learn more about the HTTP protocol that the Web uses. The nature of this protocol shapes the ways we bind data to Web pages, and understanding HTTP protocol basics takes a lot of the mystery out of the inner workings of dynamic Web pages. As the book progresses, in addition to form, database, and cookie data, you'll learn several more ways to bind data to Web pages, and when and why to use each technique.

WHAT YOU WILL LEARN

In this lesson, you will:

- Learn about the HTTP protocol, and how it enables developers to create dynamic sites
- Discover the difference between GET and POST
- Encode and retrieve querystrings or URL variables
- Encode and retrieve cookies
- Create a cookie using dynamic data

APPROXIMATE TIME

This lesson takes approximately 75 minutes to complete.

LESSON FILES

Starting Files:

Lesson05/Start/newland/about.asp

Lesson05/Start/newland/contact.asp

Lesson05/Start/newland/generic_template.asp

Lesson05/Start/newland/index.asp

Lesson05/Start/newland/profiles.asp

Lesson05/Start/newland/test_form.asp

*Lesson05/Start/newland/test_form_
processor.asp*

Lesson05/Start/newland/tours.asp

Completed Files:

Lesson05/Complete/newland/about.asp

*Lesson05/Complete/newland/animal_home_
page.asp*

*Lesson05/Complete/newland/animal_
questions.asp*

Lesson05/Complete/newland/contact.asp

*Lesson05/Complete/newland/generic_
template.asp*

Lesson05/Complete/newland/index.asp

Lesson05/Complete/newland/profiles.asp

Lesson05/Complete/newland/test_form.asp

*Lesson05/Complete/newland/test_form_
processor.asp*

*Lesson05/Complete/newland/test_form_
processor_cookies.asp*

Lesson05/Complete/newland/tours.asp

UNDERSTANDING THE HTTP PROTOCOL

Pages on the Web are transferred using the HTTP protocol. This protocol specifies how users (or, in some cases, systems) make requests of servers over the World Wide Web, and how these servers respond to these requests. Understanding the basics of this protocol will help you understand how dynamic pages work.

At its core, the HTTP protocol is a transactional system. A client sends a request to a server, and the server sends a response back to the client. One part of the request is the URL, or Uniform Resource Locator. When you click a link in a browser, a request is sent to the server that contains the desired file.

What most people don't realize is that the client's computer sends a lot more to the server than simply the URL request. It also sends quite a bit of information about itself, including the browser (referred to as the **user agent**), username, IP address, file types it can accept (such as GIF and JPEG), and several sources of data. The request contains a header and a body; most of the information just specified is sent in the header. The reason people don't realize this is happening, of course, is that the header is not visible to the human user.

Once the server receives the request, it responds if it can. It looks at the requested document, and if that document has any server-side code on it (such as ASP VBScript, ColdFusion Markup Language, or PHP code), the server processes those instructions. When it is finished, it removes the server-side code and combines the output from the server-side code along with the XHTML in the document, and sends it all back to the client in the body of the response. The response, like the request, has a header, which contains information for the client system (such as the document size and type and the date and time of the response). About all a user can see of this transaction are the URL and the output XHTML page.

The following figure represents an HTTP transaction. Solid rectangles show documents visible to the user, while dashed rectangles represent documents hidden from the user.

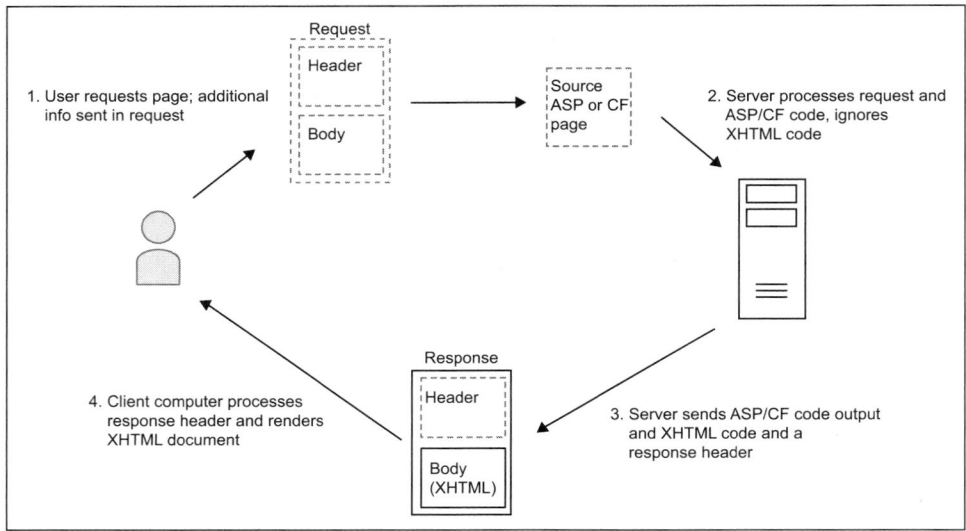

If you wondered at the end of Lesson 4 exactly how test_form_processor.asp gained access to the data that the user entered in the form on that page, the request is your answer. The firstName variable and its value were sent in the body of the request message when you clicked the Submit button. In other words, the hidden portions of the HTTP request and response messages make it possible to send data values back and forth between the client and server, which makes them available to ASP, ColdFusion, or PHP scripts on the server. It also means, as you'll see in this lesson, that the server can send data back to the client with directions to store the data in a cookie.

Before we start looking at how to take advantage of the HTTP protocol to facilitate dynamic Web development, there is one more vital behavior you need to know about the protocol: *Once the server sends its response to the client, it forgets about the entire transaction.* That is, if the client makes a second request of the server, the server has no idea that this is the same client who made a request a moment ago. For this reason, HTTP is known as a **stateless protocol**.

The statelessness of the HTTP protocol is a significant problem for those developing Web applications. If the Web forgets who you are in between every page, how can you get through the successive screens of an online shopping cart? If you have a multipart survey, how can you ensure that the data entered on page 1 is inserted into the database along with the data entered on page 4? You have seen online shopping carts and probably taken multipage surveys, so you know there are solutions to these problems.

It is hard to develop dynamic Web sites without an awareness of the request-and-response transaction and the statelessness of HTTP. Binding data to pages takes place within this context, and the differences between querystring (or URL) variables and form variables, POST and GET, and setting and retrieving cookies—all of which you are about to become familiar with—are considerably less obscure when you understand how they relate to the HTTP protocol.

RETRIEVING DATA FROM THE URL

At the end of the previous lesson, users filled out a short form and submitted it to a page that displayed the value they entered in the form. As you know from the preceding section, the variable sent from the form to the test_form_processor.asp page was enclosed in the body of the request. There are other ways to send data between pages. You can send variables through URLs, cookies, and (depending on your server technology) session and application variables. You'll learn all about each of these during the course of the book, but for now it is sufficient to understand that there are many ways to share data among pages.

The logical question that follows from this is, why are there so many different ways, and how do you know which one to use? The answer is that each has unique capabilities and limitations.

For example, the form variable you sent in Lesson 4 in the body of the request sent the data from the form page to the page that processed and displayed the information. One limitation of this approach is that once the server completes this transaction, it forgets the firstName name-value pair. So though it outputs the user's first name to that page, if the user goes to a different page, the server no longer knows the value of the firstName variable, which means that this name-value pair is no longer available to your code. If you were developing a multiple-page shopping cart or survey, you'd soon encounter the limitations of form variables.

In this task, you'll pass data from the form to the test_form_processor.asp page in a different way: You'll use a querystring. A querystring is a list of variables appended to the end of a URL. You have probably noticed as you surfed the Web that sometimes URLs are quite long and seem to contain much more information than the page address; that information is a querystring. Let's modify the Web form you created in Lesson 4 so that it sends information using a querystring, rather than a form variable.

1) Open test_form.asp.

At the moment the form is somewhat minimalist.

2) Position the insertion point after the text field, and press Enter/Return. Type *Last Name* and add a second text field. Use the Property inspector to name the new field *lastName*. Position the insertion point after the lastName text field and press Enter/Return again to move the Submit button below the new field.

In this step, you are adding and formatting a second form field. Just because you are placing content in a form doesn't mean you can't format it as needed. You can insert just about any valid HTML element inside of a form.

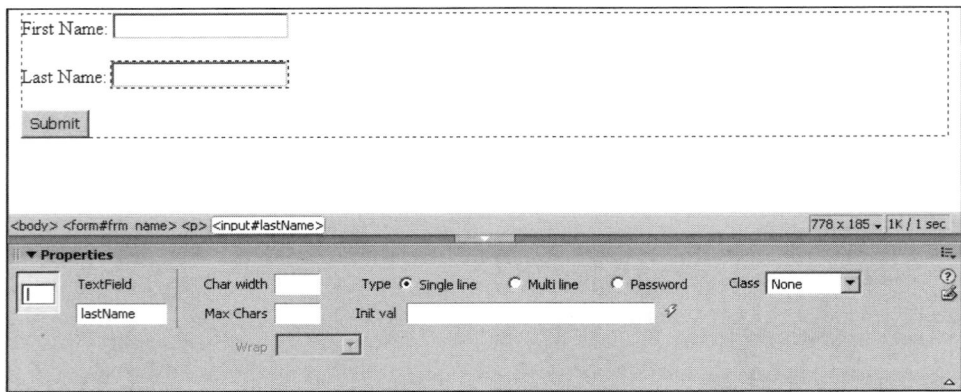

3) Click `<form#frm_name>` in the tag selector to select the whole form and also to bring up the form options in the Property inspector.

The easiest way to modify an element's attributes—especially an element with several child elements, such as the `<form>` element—is to select it in the tag selector.

4) In the Property inspector's Method drop-down menu, select GET.

Initially, the value is set to POST, which you specified in the previous lesson. By changing the method from POST to GET, you are changing the way that the data is sent to test_form_processor.asp. With POST, the data is sent in the request body, as discussed before. But with GET, the data will be sent as a querystring, which means that you see the firstName and lastName name-value pairs appended to the URL, as you will see in a moment.

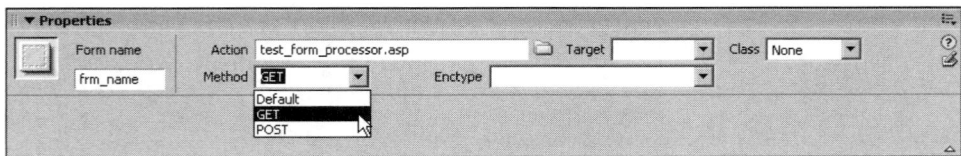

152

5) Save and close test_form.asp. Open test_form_processor.asp.

You need to modify the test_form_processor.asp page because the dynamic text on that page is looking for the firstName value to come to the page as a form variable. Now that you have changed POST to GET, the firstName value won't be available as a form variable; it will be available only as a querystring. That means that you have to return to the Bindings panel and define a new binding.

6) In the Bindings panel, for ASP click the New Binding (+) button, choose Request Variable, and in the Request Variable dialog specify Request.Querystring as the type. Type *firstName* as the name. For ColdFusion and PHP, click the New Binding (+) button, choose URL variable, and enter *firstName* as the name. Click OK.

"Querystring" and "URL variable" are two variations of the same thing: a variable appended to the URL. There are some subtle differences between the way ASP and ColdFusion handle these types of variables, but for the purposes of this book, we'll treat them as if they are no more than two different names for the same thing.

When you are finished, the change should be reflected in the Bindings panel. The screenshot is for ASP. ColdFusion and PHP users will see two categories of variable: Form (with firstName nested inside) and URL (with firstName nested inside).

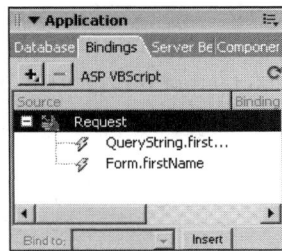

7) Repeat step 6 to add a Request.Querystring/URL Variable for the lastName variable.

Again, the Bindings panel should update, and you should now see three variables defined: two versions of firstName and one of lastName.

153

It might seem odd to have the same variable—firstName—listed twice. But as far as ASP, ColdFusion, and PHP are concerned, these are two completely different variables. One is a form variable, and is only retrievable from the body of the HTTP request. The other is a querystring variable, which is only retrievable from the URL itself. This concept—where variables are available only in a designated place—is known as **variable scope**. A variable's scope includes the place(s) where the variable exists, and excludes the places it does not. The lastName variable exists only as a URL querystring. If ASP, ColdFusion, or PHP looks for it in the request body, it won't find it: The request body is outside of the querystring scope.

Scoping variables is a fundamental task in any programming language. Without it, you would have no way of ensuring both that data is available when you need it and that two different pieces of data don't inadvertently share the same name.

By changing the form's method from POST to GET, you change the firstName variable's scope. By making these changes in the Bindings panel, you gave your server-side code access to the appropriate scope. There are many more scopes than form and querystring variables (as you doubtless noticed when working in the Bindings panel), but conceptually, they all work the same way.

8) Click to select the blue-shaded {Form.firstName} dynamic text on the page, and press Delete to remove it. Position the insertion point just before the second comma, click QueryString.firstName (ASP) or URL > firstName (ColdFusion and PHP) in the Bindings panel, and press Insert.

When you are finished, you should see a new blue-shaded dynamic text block that contains {QueryString.firstName} (ASP) or {URL.firstName} (ColdFusion and PHP).

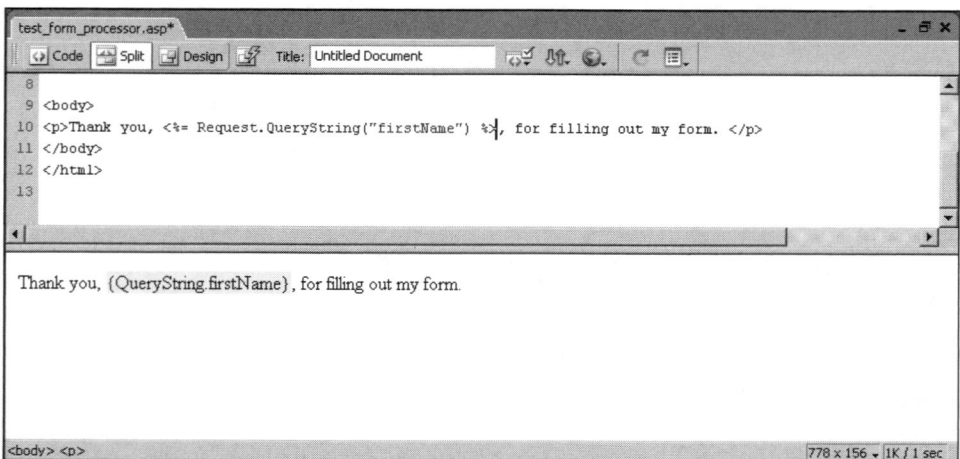

Now that you understand scope, you probably also can read Dreamweaver's dynamic text pseudocode. The curly braces {} represent a dynamic code block, and inside is listed the scope, followed by a period, followed by a variable name. Dreamweaver pseudocode gives you quick access to the scope and name of all dynamic text.

Looking beyond the pseudocode at the real code, you should see `<%= Request.QueryString("firstName") %>` embedded in the HTML on the ASP page, `<cfoutput>#URL.firstName#</cfoutput>` on the ColdFusion page, and `<?php echo $_GET['firstName']; ?>` on the PHP page.

> **N O T E** *In ColdFusion, values enclosed in #pound signs# are variables that ColdFusion must resolve before outputting. In the preceding example, if you omitted the pound signs, ColdFusion would write: "Thank you, URL.firstName, for filling out my page." Once in pound signs, ColdFusion knows it needs to evaluate the variable in the pound signs—in this case, by outputting whatever value is stored in the firstName variable in the URL.*

9) Position the insertion point after the firstName block, and bind the QueryString.lastName or URL.lastName variable to the page.

The two variables should appear side by side, so that the output displays the user's entire name.

> **N O T E** *If the first and last names run together, which seems to happen in ASP but not ColdFusion or PHP, insert a non-breaking space character ( ) between the two.*

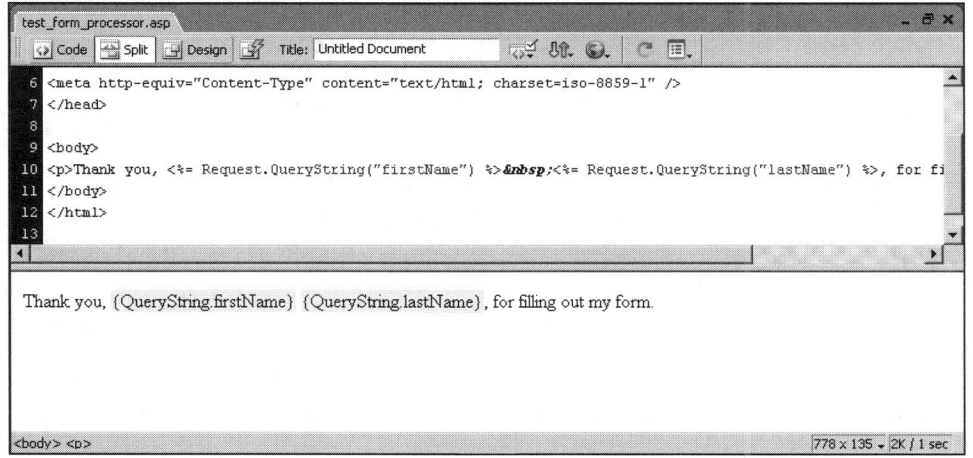

10) Save test_form_processor.asp, and in the Site panel, Shift-select test_form.asp and test_form_processor.asp and click the Put File(s) button.

Remember, you can't test your files unless you upload them to the server.

11) Click test_form.asp in the Site panel, and press F12 to test in a browser. Enter your first name and your last name, and click Submit.

As you've anticipated, the page now thanks you, using your first and last name.

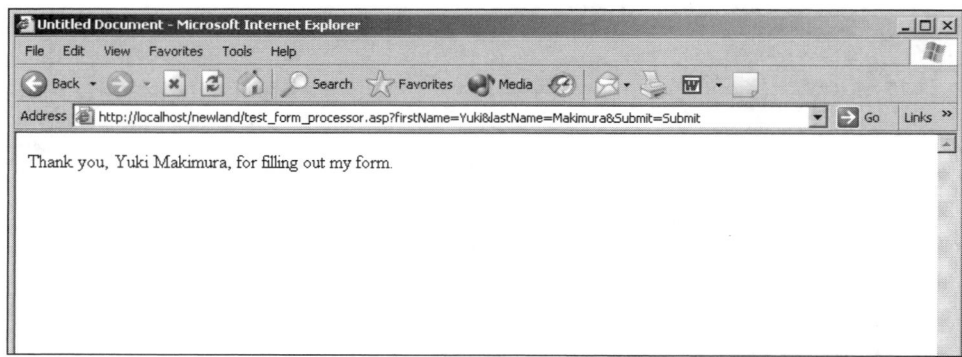

What's more of interest, though, is the URL. Appended to the page address is a question mark followed by three name-value pairs:

```
http://localhost/newland/test_form_processor.asp?firstName=Yuki&lastName=Maki
mura&Submit=Submit
```

The appended three variables are the querystring. The output first and last names are pulled directly out of the URL. This URL appears the same, regardless of server model, because querystrings are a part of the HTTP protocol itself, rather than a dynamic Web page technology.

Generally, you should use POST, rather than GET, to send form data to be stored in a database, because with POST the data is not visible to the user. Imagine if your form requests that the user enter a username and password combo, and then that password is displayed for all to see in the URL! Also, you can embed quite a bit more data in the request body (using POST) than you could in a URL (using GET). For the sake of this exercise, though, GET is sufficient. As you will see momentarily, though, querystrings have some advantages that form variables don't.

12) Close your browser. In Dreamweaver's Site panel, click test_form_processor.asp, and press F12.

156

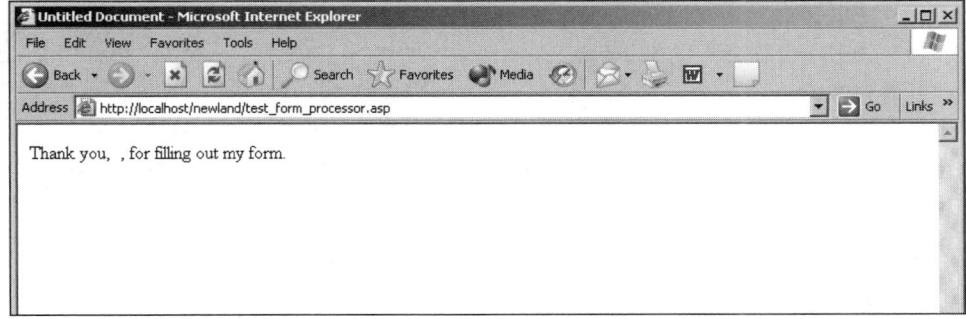

This time, when you test the page, it lacks the querystring data that ASP, ColdFusion and PHP are expecting, because you closed the browser and flushed that data from memory. Interestingly, ASP and PHP handle this problem differently than ColdFusion. ASP and PHP display, "Thank you, , for filling out my form." ColdFusion refuses to display the page at all, showing an error: "The page cannot be displayed."

One of the challenges of dynamic site development is to make sure that no user enters a page without all of the data that the page needs to process. If this happens, the result is often an error that confuses and frustrates users. The solution to this problem is twofold: Prevent users from accessing pages without sufficient data in the first place, and if that fails, catch the error and redirect users to an all-purpose error page that enables them to notify the Webmaster, which is better than them seeing a cryptic ASP, ColdFusion, or PHP error message. We'll use several different types of validation during the course of this book to prevent users from accessing pages without the required data.

SENDING DATA WITH HYPERLINKS

The querystring's open display of data, though a problem for confidential information, has certain benefits. One of them is that you can embed data in hyperlinks. That is, you can collect information from users without requiring them to fill out a form. In this task, you will build a simple page, which, though a bit silly superficially, exhibits a couple of key dynamic Web site concepts in action.

You will build a two-page mini-application that lets each user specify whether she or he is a cat person or a dog person. The first page contains two links—one for cats and one for dogs. The interesting thing about these links is that they both point to the same page. The links are differentiated in that each has a querystring appended to it with the chosen animal preference. On the second page, dynamic text is output, based on the selected link. If you first choose one animal, and then go back and choose the other, it will appear as if you went to two different pages, while in fact you went to only one, with different dynamic text values displaying.

This is an important concept. Think about a large e-commerce site, such as Amazon. Rather than having a different page for every single book they sell, they have only one product detail page, and the page is populated dynamically when the user selects a book. In other words, dynamic pages enable developers to drastically reduce the number of pages they must create and maintain, while simultaneously expanding the amount of content that their pages can show.

So set aside the impracticality of this application for the time being. It forms the basis of the site maintenance functionality that you'll build later in the Newland site.

1) Choose File > New, and create a new dynamic page using ASP/VBScript, ColdFusion, or PHP. Make sure it's XHTML-compliant.

By choosing the correct document type in this dialog, you ensure that Dreamweaver will write the correct type of code for your site.

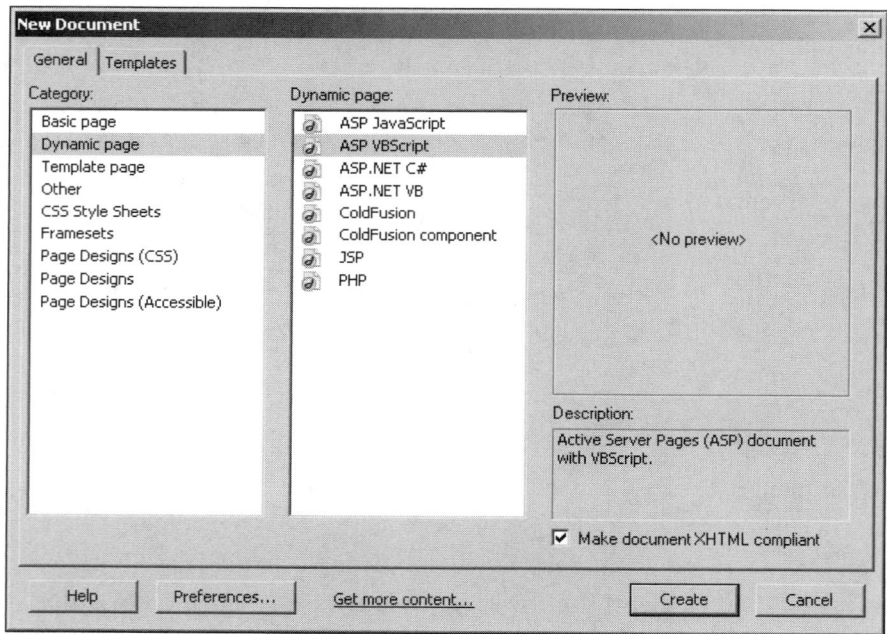

2) In design view, type the text shown in the accompanying figure. Format the first one as an <h1> heading and the second two as body paragraph elements <p>.

In this step, you are marking up just the static portion of the application.

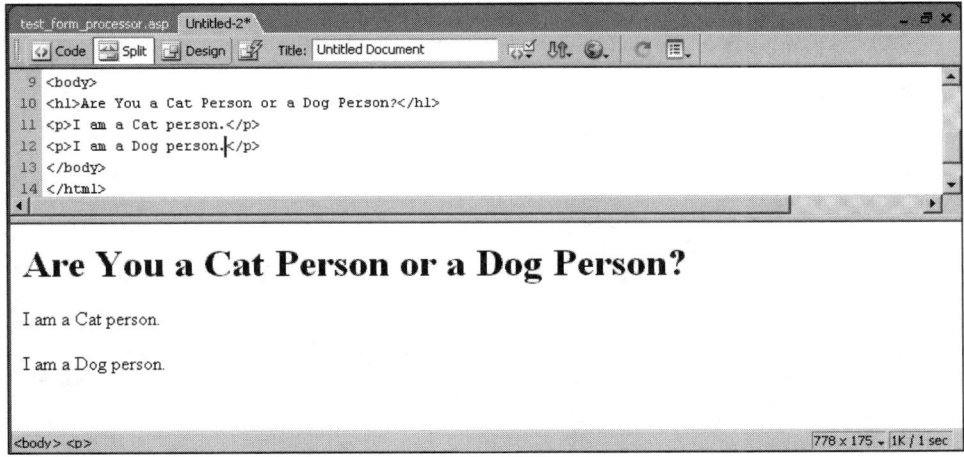

3) Save the file as *animal_questions.asp*. Then choose File › Save As and save the page again, this time as *animal_home_page.asp*.

Here you are both saving the file and creating a second page based on the first.

4) Still in animal_home_page.asp, replace the existing heading with *The Person Home Page*, and replace the first statement with *You are a person*. Remove the second statement.

Again, you are setting up the static portion of this page. As it now stands, it's nonsensical. In a moment, it will make more sense when you add functionality that will place Cat or Dog before the word person in each paragraph.

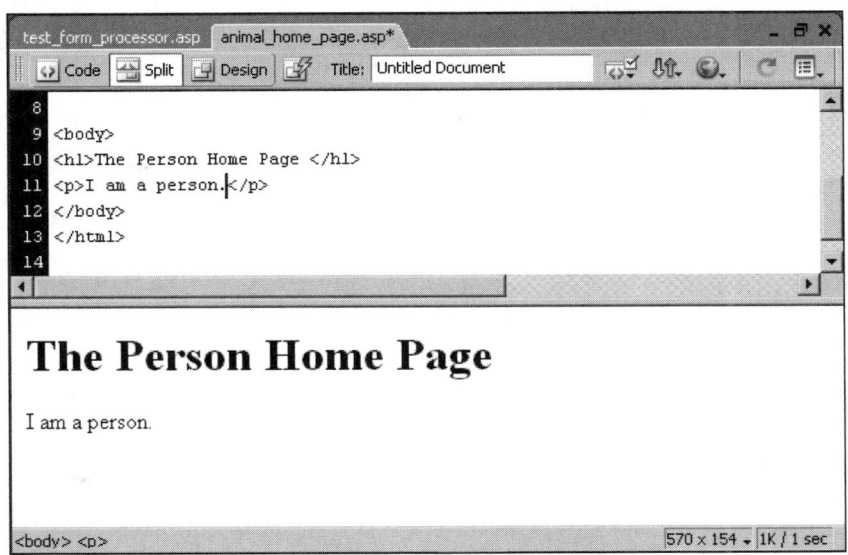

5) Open animal_questions.asp. Double-click to select the word Cat in the second paragraph. In the Link field of the Property inspector, type the following: *animal_home_page.asp?mypet=Cat.*

Here you are manually adding a querystring to the URL. When the user clicks this link, both the URL and the querystring will be sent, and the querystring's contents will be available on animal_home_page.asp.

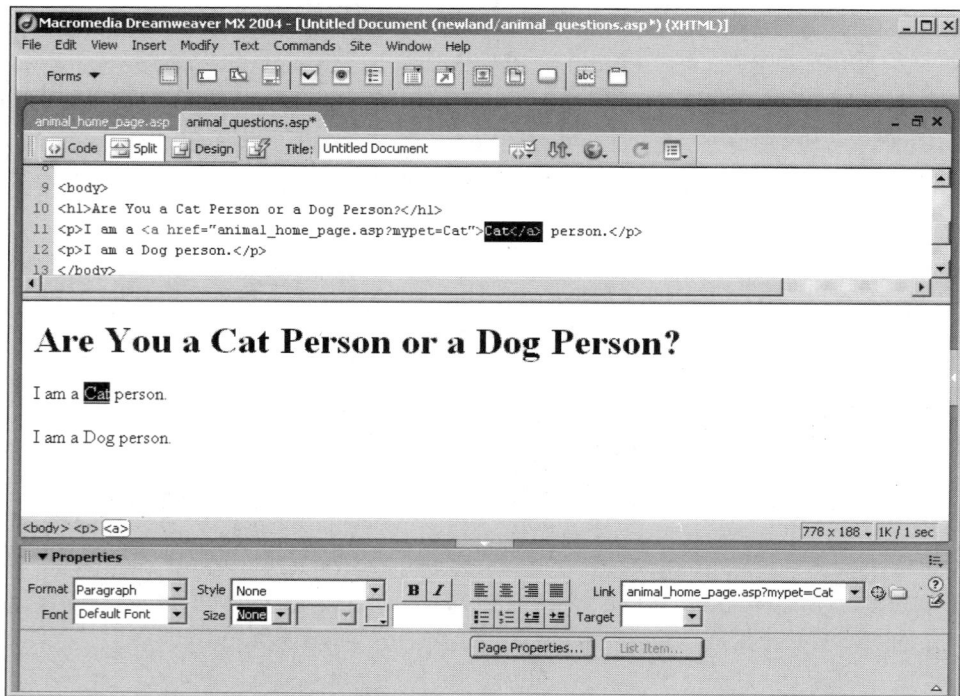

6) Repeat step 5 to add a link to the word Dog, with the appropriate querystring added to the link. Save and upload (Put) the file.

You are finished with this page.

7) Return to animal_home_page.asp. In the Bindings panel, add a QueryString/URL variable named *mypet*.

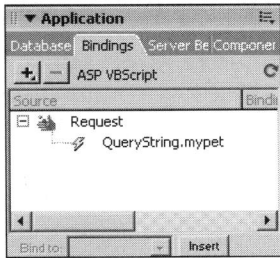

This is the variable that you coded into the each link's URL on the previous page. But you set each one to a different value—Cat or Dog. In this step, you are using the Bindings panel to retrieve this name-value pair.

8) Position the cursor just ahead of Person in the heading. Click the mypet variable in the Bindings panel, and click Insert. Add another instance of this variable before person in the body paragraph. Save and upload the page.

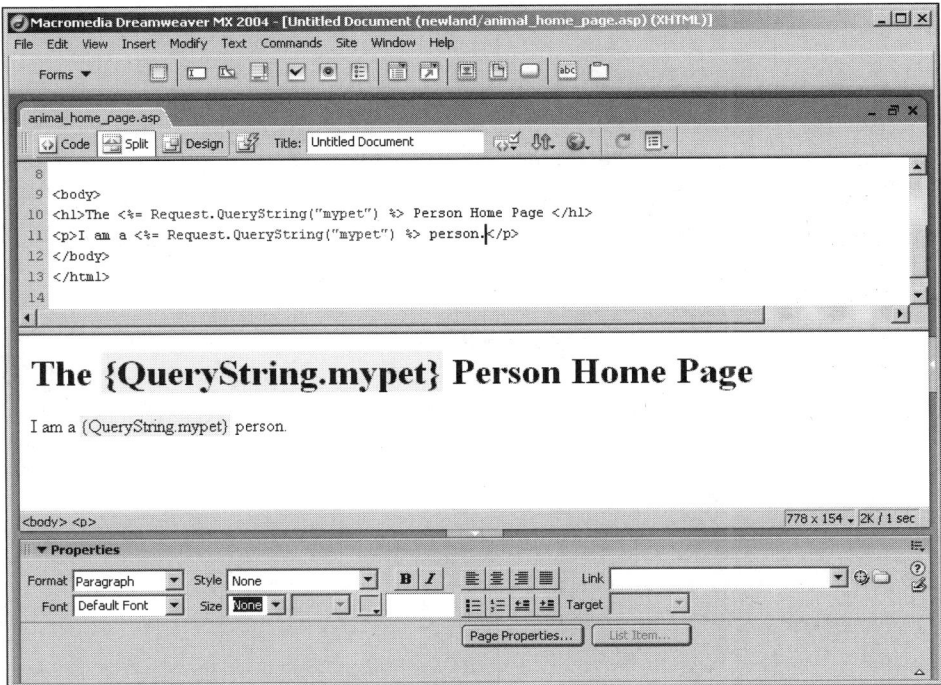

The application is complete.

9) Select animal_questions.asp in the Site panel, and press F12 to test the application.

In turn, click both Cat and Dog, so you can see that the page does indeed change.

As you can see, animal_home_page.asp is a template that can hold any content. You could easily add links on animal_questions.asp for iguanas, tropical fish, and pythons, and animal_home_page.asp would function without any changes to the code. And this is the ultimate power of dynamic Web pages: You can present infinite content—as well as add to or change that content—without having to redo the XHTML pages. Change the content in the source, and the update takes place seamlessly in the output XHTML page.

SETTING AND RETRIEVING COOKIES

Up to this point, you've seen different ways to use forms and simple links to collect user data, to make that data available to another page, and to make use of it on that page. In spite of their differences, though, form and querystring variables have something important in common: Each is good for sending data from one page to another, but after that they vaporize into the forgetfulness of the HTTP protocol.

When you build Web applications, you will often want certain pieces of data to persist beyond a single request/response transaction, and forms and querystrings won't do for that. However, other variable types do persist beyond a single transaction. How is that possible, given the limitations of the HTTP protocol? The answer is that their data is stored on a hard drive—the user's or the server's—and retrieved or set as a part of every request/response transaction that requires that data.

One such variable type is the **cookie**. Cookies are tiny text files that are written onto user's hard drives. You can save cookies on user's hard drives and retrieve them across multiple pages. In this manner, you can maintain state in spite of the stateless HTTP protocol.

NOTE *Many users are concerned about cookies and security. In many instances, this concern is unfounded, since cookies can't be used to infect a computer with a virus, and the only site that can read a cookie is the site that set the cookie. However, cookies persist on a computer's hard drive, regardless of which actual user is logged in. Thus, storing credit card information in a cookie becomes dangerous when the user is working from a public terminal or a workstation that is shared with other colleagues. Developers should either not store anything sensitive in a cookie, such as a credit card number or a password, or the site should at least provide users with the option of whether to save the information.*

In this task, you will learn how to set and retrieve cookies. You'll use the form application again, but this time, when the form is submitted and the user is redirected to test_form_processor.asp, their first and last name will be stored in a cookie on their hard drive. Then, you'll create a third page that requests these values—without using form or querystring variables—to demonstrate how the firstName and lastName variables can persist beyond a single HTTP request/response transaction.

1) Open test_form_processor.asp.

As you'll recall, this page is expecting the firstName and lastName variables to appear as a querystring; in fact, it outputs these values in the page's lone line of text: "Thank you, {QueryString.firstName} {QueryString.lastName}, for filling out my form."

In a moment, you'll capture those same values, not for the purpose of outputting them in body text, but rather to save them as cookies to the user's hard drive.

2) In code view, ASP and ColdFusion users should place the insertion point at the end of the line of code that precedes the opening <html> tag (line 2 in ASP and line 1 in ColdFusion). PHP users should place the insertion point at the very beginning of the document. Press Enter/Return three times to add some blank space.

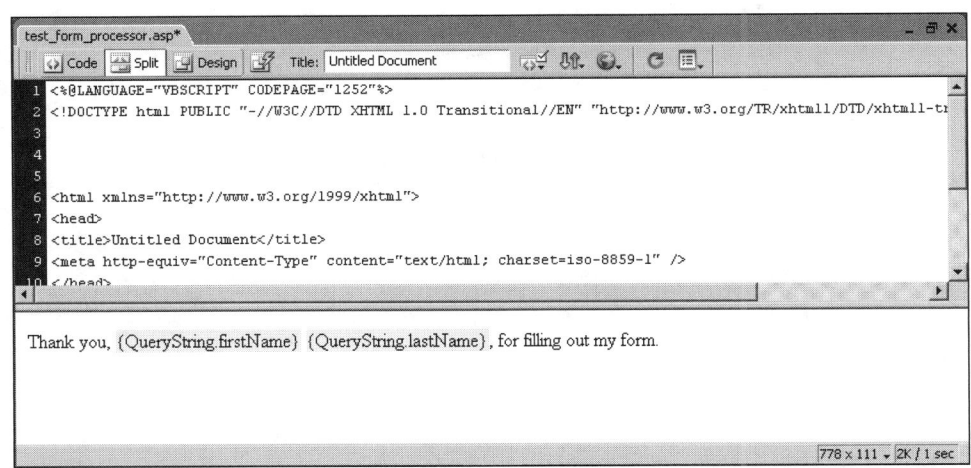

In a moment you will manually add some code, so you need to make space for it. Notice that you're adding the code before the HTML document proper, which begins with the <html> element. Server code is often placed outside the HTML document, which makes it easier to find and edit. And don't forget: When the page is output from the server to the client, the server code is stripped out, so users will never see this code.

NOTE *In PHP, any time you attempt to send content back to the browser via a header—and setting cookies is one example of this—you must add this script before the first line of XHTML code, or you will see an error along the lines of "cannot add header information." The simple solution to this problem is to put such content at the very beginning of the file.*

3) Type the code block below, as appropriate.

In ASP:

```
<%
Response.Cookies("firstName") = Request.QueryString("firstName")
Response.Cookies("firstName").Expires = Date+30
Response.Cookies("lastName") = Request.QueryString("lastName")
Response.Cookies("lastName").Expires = Date+30
%>
```

In ColdFusion:

```
<cfcookie name="firstName" expires="never" value="#url.firstName#">
<cfcookie name="lastName" expires="never" value="#url.lastName#">
```

In PHP:

```
<?php
setcookie('firstName', $_GET['firstName'], time() + (60*60*24));
setcookie('lastName', $_GET['lastName'], time() + (60*60*24));
?>
```

```
1  <%@LANGUAGE="VBSCRIPT" CODEPAGE="1252"%>
2  <!DOCTYPE html PUBLIC "-//W3C//DTD XHTML 1.0 Transitional//EN" "http://www.w3.org/TR/xhtml1/DTD/xhtml1-t
3
4  <%
5  Response.Cookies("firstName") = Request.QueryString("firstName")
6  Response.Cookies("firstName").Expires = Date+30
7  Response.Cookies("lastName") = Request.QueryString("lastName")
8  Response.Cookies("lastName").Expires = Date+30
9  %>
10
11 <html xmlns="http://www.w3.org/1999/xhtml">
12 <head>
13 <title>Untitled Document</title>
14 <meta http-equiv="Content-Type" content="text/html; charset=iso-8859-1" />
15 </head>
16
```

Before discussing the particulars of this code, I'd like to point out that there is no visual way to write a cookie using Dreamweaver, so you have to write the code yourself. While Dreamweaver can help you develop dynamic Web sites, you have to be willing to do some hand-coding if you really want to build dynamic sites. If you've been studying the code, you can probably already understand how the code works.

Though the syntax varies markedly when you compare ASP, ColdFusion, and PHP, all three sets of code work the same way. They create two new cookie variables, one named firstName and the other named lastName. As before, we are naming two completely different variables with the same names (QueryString.firstName and Cookies.firstName, with a comparable pair for the last name), but their different scopes prevent any possible confusion. Both specify expiration dates (30 days from today in ASP, never in ColdFusion, and one day for PHP). Finally, all three specify the new cookie variable's value as the current value of QueryString.firstName and QueryString.lastName.

In other words, the values of the new cookie variables are dynamically set. Not only can you set variables to static, hard values, such as Cat or Dog, but you can also create variables to hold contents drawn from other variables. Here, the cookie variables are dynamically set with the contents of the querystring/URL variables.

4) Back in design view, create a new paragraph below the existing one, and type *Check cookie*. Link the word cookie to a page named *test_form_processor_cookies.asp*. Save and upload this page.

```
1  <%@LANGUAGE="VBSCRIPT" CODEPAGE="1252"%>
2  <!DOCTYPE html PUBLIC "-//W3C//DTD XHTML 1.0 Transitional//EN" "http://www.w3.org/TR/xhtml1/DTD/xhtml1-t
3
4  <%
5  Response.Cookies("firstName") = Request.QueryString("firstName")
6  Response.Cookies("firstName").Expires = Date+30
7  Response.Cookies("lastName") = Request.QueryString("lastName")
8  Response.Cookies("lastName").Expires = Date+30
9  %>
10
11 <html xmlns="http://www.w3.org/1999/xhtml">
12 <head>
13 <title>Untitled Document</title>
14 <meta http-equiv="Content-Type" content="text/html; charset=iso-8859-1" />
15 </head>
16
```

This new page, test_form_processor_cookies.asp, doesn't exist yet, but you'll create it in a moment.

Before you create this new page, based on what you have learned so far in this lesson, can you guess what you'll need to do to display the two cookie variables on that page?

5) Create a new dynamic, XHTML-compliant page, and save it as
test_form_processor_cookies.asp.
Creating new dynamic pages should be familiar to you now.

6) In design view, type *Hi, !*
Typing text to be used with dynamic pages often looks bizarre, because a portion of the text is hard-coded, and a portion of it is going to be loaded dynamically.

NOTE *Because your text is coming from two different sources (static XHTML and a dynamic data source), be sure to double-check your grammar and punctuation, to ensure that the text works as a unit once it is all assembled.*

7) In the Bindings panel, click the New Binding (+) button. ASP users should choose Request Variable, and then specify Request.Cookies and firstName. ColdFusion and PHP users simply choose Cookie Variable and type *firstName* in the dialog.
Adding cookie bindings is just like adding querystring and form bindings.

8) Repeat step 7 to add the lastName cookie to the Bindings panel.
As ever, the Bindings panel updates to show you the variables that you've added.

One difference in the Bindings panel between ASP and ColdFusion/PHP is that ASP displays variables on a page-by-page basis, whereas the bindings ColdFusion users created on other pages are available throughout the site. The practical consequence is that while an ASP user's Bindings panel at this point shows only the two cookie variables, a ColdFusion user's Bindings panel at this point shows all of the bindings you have created for the site.

9) Position the insertion point before the exclamation point, select Cookies.firstName (ASP) or Cookie › firstName (ColdFusion) in the Bindings panel, and click Insert. Repeat to add the last name as well.

At this point in the lesson, you should be familiar with this routine.

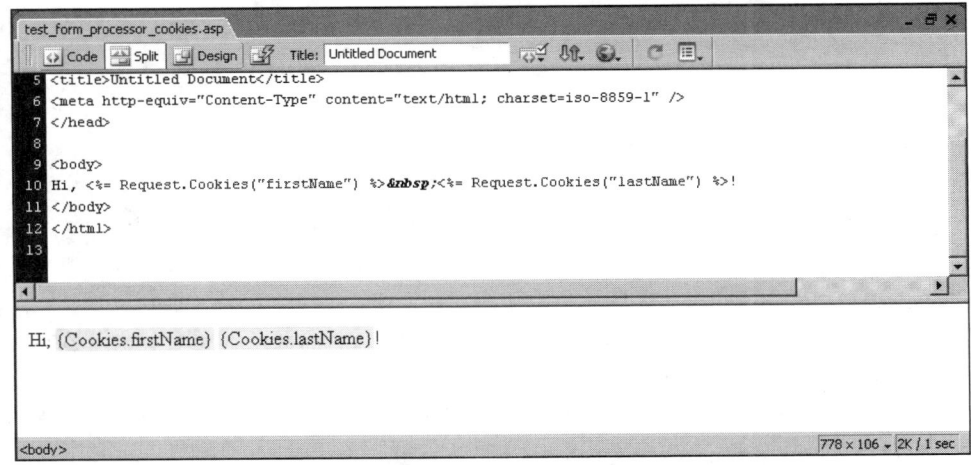

10) Save and upload the page. Click test_form.asp in the Site panel, and press F12 to test. Fill out the form, click Submit, then follow the Check cookie link.

As you would expect, it works. Even though the data started on the first page, you got it to display on the third. The information was pulled not from the URL or the request body as form variables, but rather from your hard drive.

167

NOTE *As before, ASP users may need to add a non-breaking space character ( ) between the first and last names, to prevent them from running together.*

NOTE *Because HTTP is limited to request/response transactions, the server does not have direct access to the hard drive, so the cookie variables are passed from the hard drive to the server through the request. However, the source value itself is on the hard drive.*

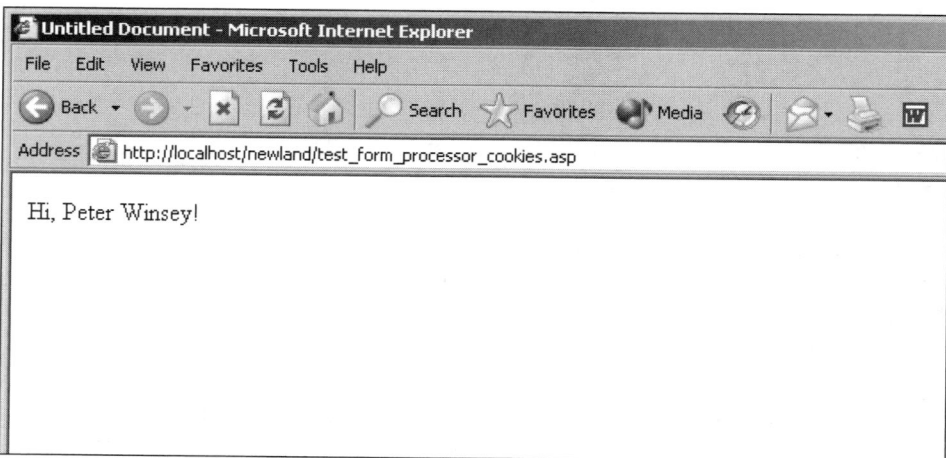

11) Close your browser. Return to Dreamweaver, select test_form_processor_cookies.asp in the Site panel, and press F12.

Earlier, when you did this experiment with test_form_processor.asp, it didn't work, because there was no data in the querystring—that data was lost as soon as you closed your browser. ASP and PHP left the text blank, while ColdFusion threw an error. But when you try the same experiment using cookies, even though you closed the browser, the data persisted, because it was saved on your hard drive as a cookie. As you can see, cookies are a powerful way to create a set of persistent data that you can access across multiple pages throughout the site.

WHAT YOU HAVE LEARNED

In this lesson, you have:

- Learned some specifics about the HTTP protocol's request/response transaction model (pages 149–151)
- Captured and displayed data embedded in a querystring (pages 151–157)
- Collected user data and output dynamic results using links and querystrings (pages 157–162)
- Written the code to cause ASP, ColdFusion, and PHP to set cookie variables (pages 162–165)
- Retrieved and output data stored in cookies (pages 165–168)

sending email from a web form

LESSON 6

You are now experienced at sending data between pages in several different ways. Sending data between pages is helpful to users, because it creates a cohesive experience. Sending data is even more useful for Web site owners, since it allows them to offer customized services via the Web, based on choices users make. In a word, sending data between pages enables a group of pages to function together as a single unit—no mean accomplishment given the forgetfulness of the HTTP protocol.

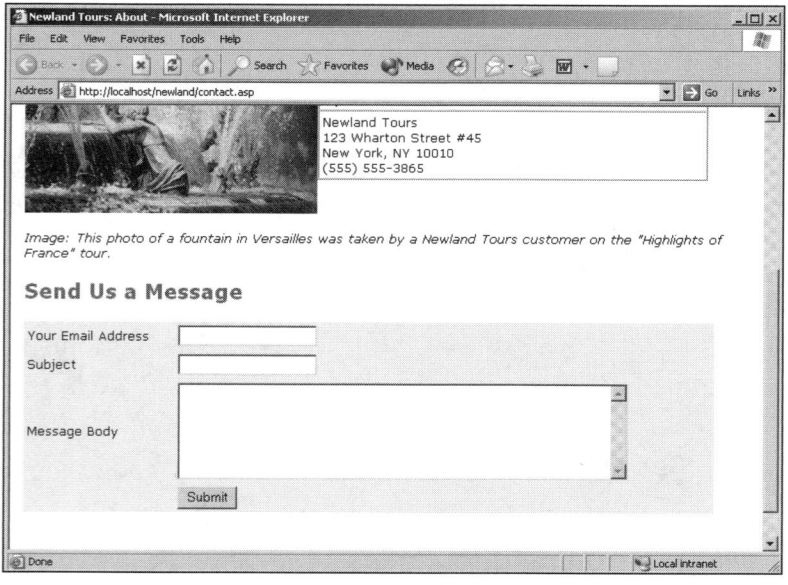

You'll use the data collected from this form to generate an email message to yourself.

Though passing data between pages is useful, pages are not the only places you'll need to send your data. Sometimes, you'll want to send it to an information storage warehouse, such as a database. Other times, you'll want to send the information directly to a reader. In this lesson, you'll see how to collect information from the user at the Newland Tours Web site and send it to a Newland Tours travel agent. (Of course, since Newland Tours doesn't really exist, you'll have to settle for sending the messages to yourself to test the functionality.)

In this lesson, you'll learn how to configure your system to send email messages, if you are running IIS or ColdFusion locally.

If you are running Apache and PHP locally, on Windows or Macintosh, you unfortunately won't be able to send messages. PHP is fully capable of sending messages, and instructions are provided in this chapter. However, Apache doesn't have a built-in mail server, unlike IIS and ColdFusion. Most ISPs hosting Apache/PHP sites have dedicated mail servers, so in a real world PHP implementation, you should be able to use the code discussed in this lesson. You just won't be able to actually test it, unless you are using ASP/IIS, ColdFusion, or you are already saving your files at an ISP (any server model) that offers mail service.

In addition to configuring a mail server, if applicable, you'll make use of special mail objects. You may have heard the term "objects," as in "object-oriented programming," and not known exactly what that means. When working with ASP, you encounter many objects and have to deal with the initially unfamiliar syntax.

To those new to programming, objects can be intimidating. But the truth is, the objects in object-oriented programming (OOP) are conceptually modeled on tangible objects in the real world. That is, the whole point of OOP is to make programming easier, more approachable, and easier to maintain. But at first, you may feel that objects are unnecessarily complex. This, despite the fact that most of their complexity is deliberately hidden, even as their power is made available to you. ColdFusion and PHP users don't work explicitly with objects the way ASP users do, but objects are never far, sometimes hidden in the underlying code.

This lesson requires some hand-coding. Again, as user-friendly as Dreamweaver's interface is, sometimes you have to go behind the page design, behind the wizards and dialogs, and type your own code. Don't worry: I assume you have no programming experience and will walk you through it, step-by-step with detailed explanations.

WHAT YOU WILL LEARN

In this lesson, you will:

- Configure IIS or ColdFusion to send email messages, if you are developing locally using IIS or ColdFusion

- Use mail objects to generate an email from a Web page

- Create a form to collect data from the user

- Populate the email message with form data

- Deploy client-side form validation

APPROXIMATE TIME

This lesson takes approximately one hour to complete.

LESSON FILES

Starting Files:

Lesson06/Start/newland/contact.asp
Lesson06/Start/newland/generic_template.asp
Lesson06/Start/newland/index.asp

Completed Files:

Lesson06/Complete/newland/contact.asp
Lesson06/Complete/newland/messageSent.asp
Lesson06/Complete/newland/generic_template.asp
Lesson06/Complete/newland/index.asp

172

INTRODUCING SMTP EMAIL SERVICE

The mail service that you will use in this chapter is SMTP. SMTP, or Simple Mail Transfer Protocol, is an Internet standard for sending email messages that can be received and correctly interpreted by a number of different clients, including POP3 and IMAP.

Perhaps the most important thing to understand about SMTP is that it is used for sending mail, not for receiving it. Thus, in this chapter, when you configure your server to use SMTP mail, you are enabling your Web applications to send messages. But you are not creating a full-fledged email service. There are extensions and other solutions that enable you to make your local workstation able to send and receive messages, but doing so is beyond the scope of this book.

The goal in this lesson is to make it possible to generate messages from within your Web applications and send them over the Internet—a useful capability, as you will soon see.

CONFIGURING YOUR SYSTEM TO SEND SMTP EMAIL MESSAGES

Before you can send email from within a Web application, you need to ensure that the server hosting the application can send email. Some of you are using IIS locally to develop ASP pages, some are using ColdFusion locally, some are using Apache locally, and some are connecting to remote servers that have any combination of ASP, ColdFusion, and/or PHP on them. Depending on how you are connecting to your server, you need to follow a different set of steps in this task, as outlined in the following list:

- ASP users developing locally with IIS (Windows 2000 or Windows XP) should read the section, "Configuring IIS to Send Email (ASP Users)."

- ColdFusion users developing locally should skip ahead to the section, "Configuring ColdFusion to Send Email."

- PHP users developing locally with Apache, unfortunately, are out of luck. Apache does not support SMTP mail. You can (and should) still work through this chapter, but you won't be able to actually send messages. However, if at some later point you can upload to a production Web server at an ISP, then the pages will work as intended. Go ahead and skip to the section, "Writing the Code to Send a Message."

- ASP, ColdFusion, or PHP users developing on remote servers (using a mapped network drive or FTP) need to verify with their server administrator that the server is SMTP email-enabled, and likewise verify that their folder on that server has permission to send SMTP email messages. Once verified, skip ahead to the section, "Writing the Code to Send a Message."

CONFIGURING IIS TO SEND EMAIL (ASP USERS)

You should read this section if you are using ASP on a local copy of the IIS server (Windows 2000 or XP). Chances are your system is already configured to use SMTP email, but you need to verify that. And if for some reason SMTP service is not installed, you'll need to install it, following the steps provided below.

1) Open the Windows Control Panel, and access the Add/Remove Programs dialog. Click the Add/Remove Windows Components button.

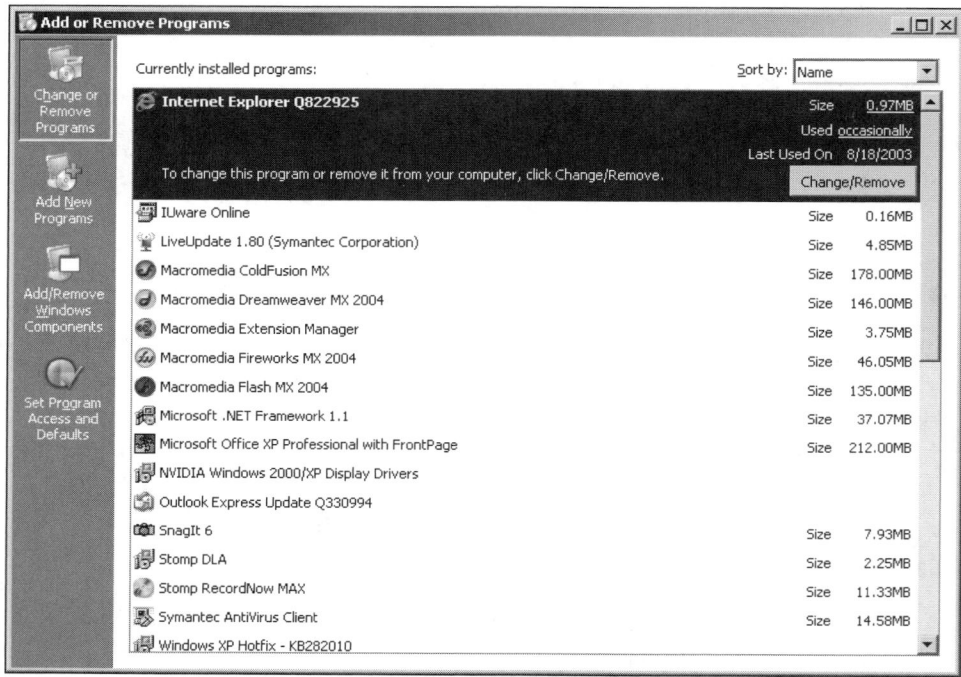

When you click the Add/Remove Windows Components button, a second dialog, the Windows Components Wizard, appears.

As you probably know, you not only maintain installed programs through the Add/Remove Programs portion of the Control Panel, but you also maintain the installation and configuration of Windows. Since IIS is a part of Windows 2000 and Windows XP, you can add and remove its installed components through this dialog.

2) In the Windows Component Wizard, click to select Internet Information Services (IIS), and click the Details button.

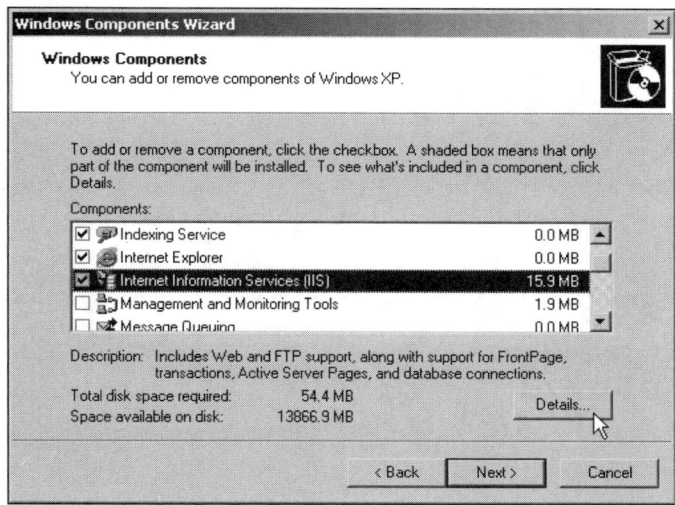

The Internet Information Services (IIS) dialog opens. Use this dialog to install and uninstall IIS components, including SMTP service.

3) Scroll down (if necessary) and verify that SMTP Service is checked.

If it is already checked, then SMTP outgoing email service is already installed.

If it is not checked, then SMTP is not installed. When you check it, Windows will install it and start it for you.

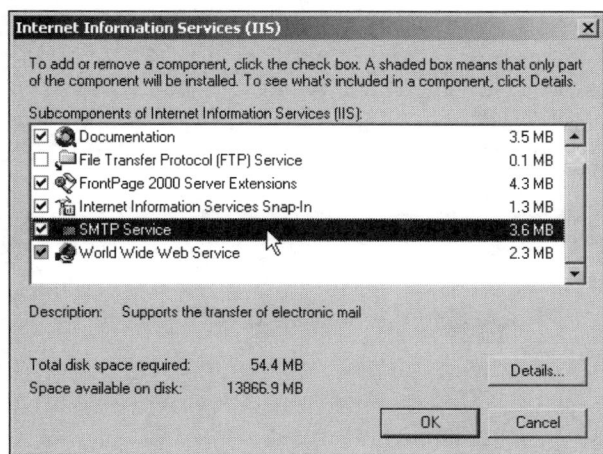

4) Click OK to accept the changes in the Internet Information Services (IIS) dialog, and then click Next to have Windows finish the installation.

At this point, outgoing SMTP mail service is installed. You can skip ahead to the section, "Writing the Code to Send a Message."

175

CONFIGURING COLDFUSION TO SEND EMAIL

You should read this section if you are using ColdFusion locally on your workstation. Configuring outgoing SMTP service for ColdFusion is easily handled using ColdFusion's Administrator application.

1) From the Start menu, open Macromedia > Macromedia ColdFusion MX > Administrator.

The path within your Start menu may vary, if you have customized it.

When the page opens, you'll need to log in. Once you do, you will see the ColdFusion administrator. You use this page for a number of ColdFusion administration settings, and you'll use it later in the book to create a datasource, which will enable you to use database content on the Newland Tours page.

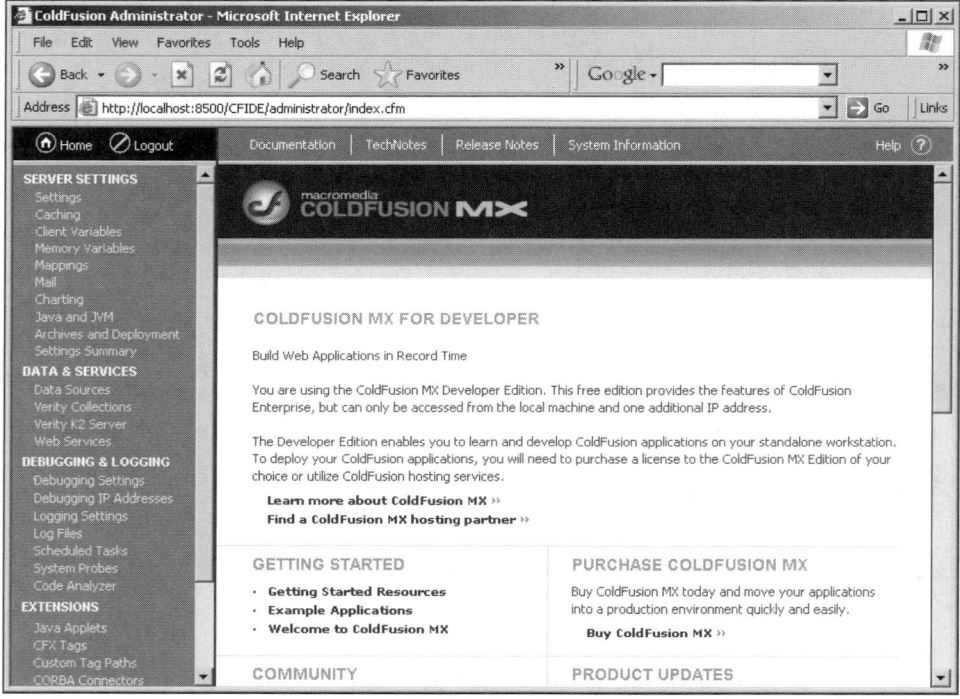

2) Click the Mail link from the left navigation bar, in the Server Settings category.

You see a page containing several settings for the mail server. You can leave all of them, with the exception of the Internet or IP address of your outgoing mail server, at their defaults.

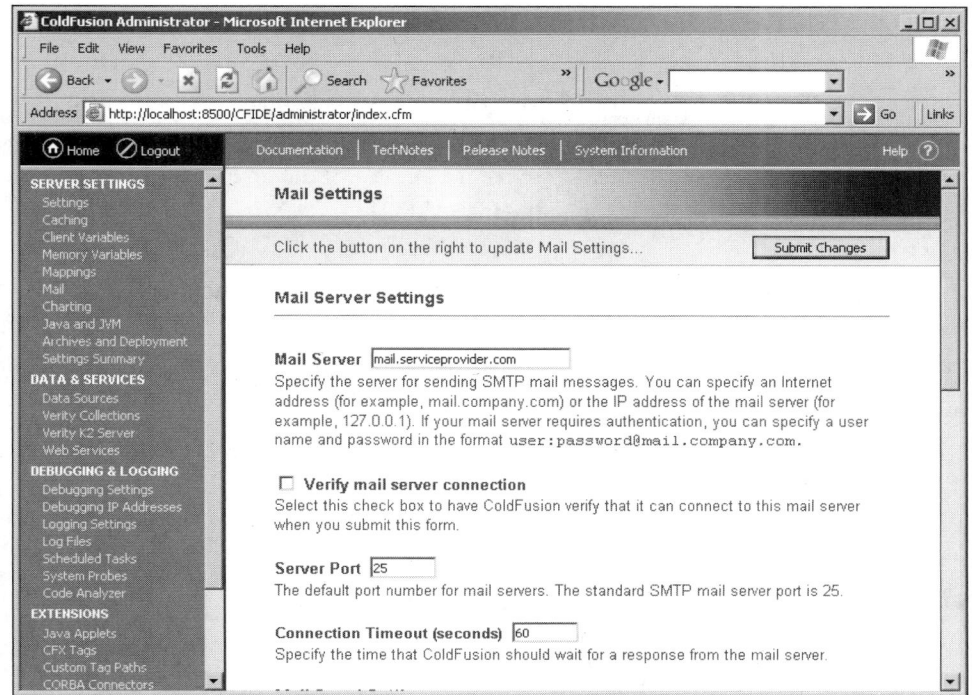

3) In the Mail Server field, enter the Internet or IP address of your outgoing mail server.

If you are not sure of your outgoing mail server's address, look inside the account settings of your email software. They should be the same.

For example, in Outlook Express, look in Tools > Accounts. Select your email account, and click Properties. Click the Servers tab, and copy the address in the Outgoing mail (SMTP) field. The menus and commands in other email clients may vary, but the outgoing Internet or IP address information should be available somewhere in the interface.

4) Click the Submit button at the top or bottom of the page.

ColdFusion updates the settings, and as long as the SMTP address you entered is valid, it will work as expected.

WRITING THE CODE TO SEND A MESSAGE

In this task, you'll create a page that sends an email message to your email address. The content of the message will be hard-coded initially. That is, if you send yourself 20 messages, they'll all have the same subject and body content. Once you have verified that it works, you can build a front-end form for the mail message and change the hard-coded values to dynamic form values.

1) Open generic_template.asp, choose File › Save As, and name the new file
messageSent.asp.

This new file will do the work of generating and sending the email message and will inform the user that the message has been sent.

2) Replace the placeholder title with *Message Sent*. Replace the placeholder body text with *Your message has been sent. You should hear from us within two days.* Insert a new paragraph with the text, *Return to Newland Home*, and link the word *Home* to index.asp.

You can see the payoff for having created the template already. The new page literally takes seconds to create and customize.

What's lacking at this point is the functionality that will generate and send the email. Before dealing with this issue, let's pause for a moment to discuss objects. Many modern computer languages—including most languages used for Web programming—contain them, so it's a good concept to master.

UNDERSTANDING OBJECTS, METHODS, AND PROPERTIES

Programming languages are developed to solve certain problems or enable certain functionalities—they don't just pop up from nowhere. For example, Flash ActionScript was created to enable developers to get the most out of native Flash capabilities and features. For this reason, several features of ActionScript are unique to Flash, and these features distinguish ActionScript from languages similar to it, such as JavaScript.

ASP, ColdFusion, and PHP are no different. Each was designed to enable dynamic Web site functionality within the context of the HTTP protocol. Their respective developers knew that you would want to do certain tasks, such as send data between pages, connect to databases, and generate email messages. To simplify these tasks, each language includes built-in objects. Objects are generic entities created for the purpose of simplifying a given task. For example, ASP's Message object makes it easy to create and send new mail messages from within ASP.

TIP *Strictly speaking, the Message object doesn't belong to ASP, but rather to a larger class of objects built into Windows 2000 and XP, and available to IIS. This nuance has little consequence for our purposes, and I only mention it here for accuracy.*

To use an object, you must first create an **instance** of it. If you've ever used a Library in Macromedia Flash, Fireworks, or Dreamweaver, you are already familiar with the relationship. The object, or more properly, **class**, exists in potential only; you can't directly use the class itself. When you make an instance of it, you make a unique copy of that class, but you also customize it for its surroundings. You might think of it as the difference between the scientific definition of homo sapiens on the one hand, and an individual person on the other. All members of homo sapiens have height, hair color, and weight attributes. But these values differ for each person.

Most object classes have built-in features. Generally, these fit into two categories: **properties** and **methods**. Some objects even have child objects with their own properties and methods. Properties are descriptive attributes. To use the homo sapiens example, height, hair color, birthday, present location, and weight are all properties. Methods are what the object can do. Humans can walk, dance, sing, and sleep; each of these would be a method of the homo sapiens. When you create an instance of an object, you often define its properties. When you want something to happen, you **call** one or more of its methods.

Finally, when you create an object instance, you usually need to give it a unique ID, or name. This name enables the script to keep track of it, since you can usually use multiple instances of the same object in the same script or document. Once again, humans have names for the same reason—names help us identify and refer to each other.

To summarize, you can achieve specific kinds of functionality in scripts by using built-in objects. To use an object, you must create an instance of it. To enable the script to properly identify your instance, you give it a unique name. Finally, to make use of the instance (and accomplish your task), you set its properties and call its methods.

In the steps that follow, ASP users will write a script in which they can see each of these steps in action. ColdFusion and PHP users will discover that their respective languages hide much of this complexity, though traces of it are still visible.

The following steps are separated to reflect the different stages of using an object.

NOTE *These steps continue from the last task, "Writing the Code to Send a Message."*

3) Using the code view, position the cursor at the beginning of line 2 (that is, just before the opening `<html>` tag) and press Enter/Return several times.

In this step, you are merely making room for a new script.

4) ASP and ColdFusion Users Only: To instantiate and give identity to a new mail object, enter the following code:

For ASP:

```
<%
theSchema="http://schemas.microsoft.com/cdo/configuration/"
Set cdoConfig=server.CreateObject("CDO.Configuration")
cdoConfig.Fields.Item(theSchema & "sendusing")= 2
cdoConfig.Fields.Item(theSchema & "smtpserver")="your.SMTP.server.com"
cdoConfig.Fields.Update

set cdoMessage=Server.CreateObject("CDO.Message")
cdoMessage.Configuration=cdoConfig
%>
```

For ColdFusion:

```
<cfmail>
</cfmail>
```

ASP users: be sure to replace the highlighted code "your.SMTP.server.com" with the name or IP address of your actual SMTP server. This is most likely the same server as the one listed for outgoing email in your email client, such as Microsoft Outlook Express.

The ColdFusion code is fairly self-explanatory: These two tags tell ColdFusion to create a new mail object. It still needs help before it's useful, but at least you've created it. Behind the scenes, ColdFusion also gives this mail object a unique ID, so in this simple step you have accomplished several tasks.

The ASP code is (not surprisingly) somewhat more cryptic. In the first code block, you provide the information ASP needs to actually connect to the mail server. It's cryptic, to be sure, but you should be able to use it as-is on any modern Windows server.

The second code block in ASP, which you'll add to momentarily, instantiates the Message object.

```
1  <!DOCTYPE html PUBLIC "-//W3C//DTD XHTML 1.0 Transitional//EN" "http://www.w3.org/TR/xhtml1/DTD/xhtml1-t
2
3  <%
4  theSchema="http://schemas.microsoft.com/cdo/configuration/"
5  Set cdoConfig=server.CreateObject("CDO.Configuration")
6  cdoConfig.Fields.Item(theSchema & "sendusing")=2
7  cdoConfig.Fields.Item(theSchema & "smtpserver")="mail.insightbb.com"
8  cdoConfig.Fields.Update
9
10 set cdoMessage=Server.CreateObject("CDO.Message")
11 cdoMessage.Configuration=cdoConfig
12
13 %>
14
15 <html xmlns="http://www.w3.org/1999/xhtml">
16 <head>
```

5) Customize the instance so that it can send desired information to the proper email address. To do so, add the following code just above the closing `%>` (ASP) or `</cfmail>` (ColdFusion). PHP users: enter the line of PHP below, in the empty space you created in step 3 above.

For ASP, enter the following code, substituting yourname@yourserver.com with your actual email address:

```
cdoMessage.From="yourname@yourserver.com"
cdoMessage.To="yourname@yourserver.com"
cdoMessage.Subject="This is the message subject"
cdoMessage.TextBody="This is the message body"
cdoMessage.Send
```

Then, ASP users should add two new lines, as follows:

```
Set cdoMessage=Nothing
Set cdoConfig=Nothing
```

For ColdFusion, amend the <cfmail> tag so that it reads as follows, substituting [enter your email address] with your actual email address:

```
<cfmail from="yourname@yourserver.com" to="yourname@yourserver.com"
⇒subject="This is the Message Subject">
```

ColdFusion users should then add a new line between the opening and closing <cfmail> tags and type:

```
This is the message body.
```

For PHP, type the following code:

```
<?
mail('yourname@yourserver.com','This is the message subject','This is the
⇒message body.');
?>
```

Both ASP and ColdFusion require you to specify who the message is from, to whom it is being sent, the subject, and the body text itself.

- ColdFusion uses easy-to-read attribute="value" syntax. The body of the message appears between the <cfmail> tags (as opposed to inside the opening <cfmail> tag, like the other attributes). The action of the message—the fact that you want to send it—is implied in ColdFusion.

NOTE *For ASP, you call the Send method, which means that you are explicitly telling ASP to send the message. Before doing that, you populate a number of the* Message *object's properties, including the sender and recipient's email addresses, as well as the subject line and message body. After invoking the Send method, you destroy both the* cdoMessage *and* cdoConfig *objects. In doing so, you make it possible for the page to send a different message using the same objects in the future.*

The completed script for ASP looks as follows:

```
<%
theSchema="http://schemas.microsoft.com/cdo/configuration/"
Set cdoConfig=server.CreateObject("CDO.Configuration")
cdoConfig.Fields.Item(theSchema & "sendusing")= 2
cdoConfig.Fields.Item(theSchema & "smtpserver")="your.SMTP.server.com"
cdoConfig.Fields.Update

set cdoMessage=Server.CreateObject("CDO.Message")
cdoMessage.Configuration=cdoConfig
cdoMessage.From="yourname@yourserver.com"
cdoMessage.To="yourname@yourserver.com"
cdoMessage.Subject="This is the message subject"
cdoMessage.TextBody="This is the message body"
cdoMessage.Send

Set cdoMessage=Nothing
Set cdoConfig=Nothing
%>
```

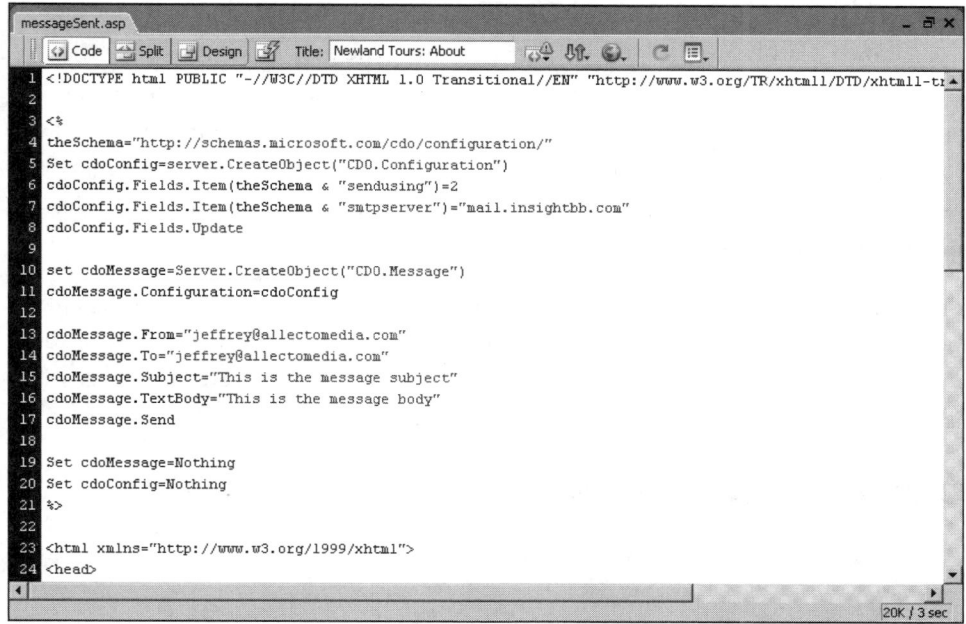

```
messageSent.asp                                                    _ ☐ x
  ◇ Code  ⊟ Split  ⌨ Design  ⎙  Title: Newland Tours: About  ⌯◆ ⑬. ◎.  C ⊟.
 1  <!DOCTYPE html PUBLIC "-//W3C//DTD XHTML 1.0 Transitional//EN" "http://www.w3.org/TR/xhtml1/DTD/xhtml1-tr▲
 2
 3  <%
 4  theSchema="http://schemas.microsoft.com/cdo/configuration/"
 5  Set cdoConfig=server.CreateObject("CDO.Configuration")
 6  cdoConfig.Fields.Item(theSchema & "sendusing")=2
 7  cdoConfig.Fields.Item(theSchema & "smtpserver")="mail.insightbb.com"
 8  cdoConfig.Fields.Update
 9
10  set cdoMessage=Server.CreateObject("CDO.Message")
11  cdoMessage.Configuration=cdoConfig
12
13  cdoMessage.From="jeffrey@allectomedia.com"
14  cdoMessage.To="jeffrey@allectomedia.com"
15  cdoMessage.Subject="This is the message subject"
16  cdoMessage.TextBody="This is the message body"
17  cdoMessage.Send
18
19  Set cdoMessage=Nothing
20  Set cdoConfig=Nothing
21  %>
22
23  <html xmlns="http://www.w3.org/1999/xhtml">
24  <head>
◀                                                                       ▶
                                                              20K / 3 sec
```

The completed script for ColdFusion looks as follows:

```
<cfmail from="yourname@yourserver.com" to="yourname@yourserver.com"
subject="This is the Message Subject">
This is the message body.
</cfmail>
```

Like those of ASP and ColdFusion, the PHP block also requires you to specify the recipient, subject, and message. However, it does not require you to specify the sender. In addition, the ability to specify a sender depends on external factors, most importantly, the operating system and mail server that you are pointing PHP to use. For the sake of this book, you won't need to specify a sender. You can learn more about specifying a sender in PHP's mail() function at the following URL: http://www.php.net/manual/en/function.mail.php.

6) Save and Put the file on your remote server. Click anywhere in the document and press F12 to test it.

When your browser opens, you should see the message indicating that the message has been sent. If you see an error message, and you've double-checked the spelling in your code, there is something wrong with your server's mail configuration. If you are using a staging or production server with your work or ISP, you can contact the server administrator for troubleshooting.

If you are working on a standalone machine running IIS, you can try to troubleshoot on your own. In this instance, troubleshooting this issue may be more trouble than it's worth. The point is that you should understand the code and know that it will work on a production server, provided that it is configured to allow email to be sent. But dropping everything to spend potentially several frustrating hours debugging your server is not the most effective way to learn dynamic Web development; you might just want to move on.

Now for the acid test: Check your email. You should have a received a message, like the one shown in the screenshot, except with your own email address. Needless to say, this is not the most exciting email message you've ever received, and since it's hard-coded to contain that text, it's not likely to improve.

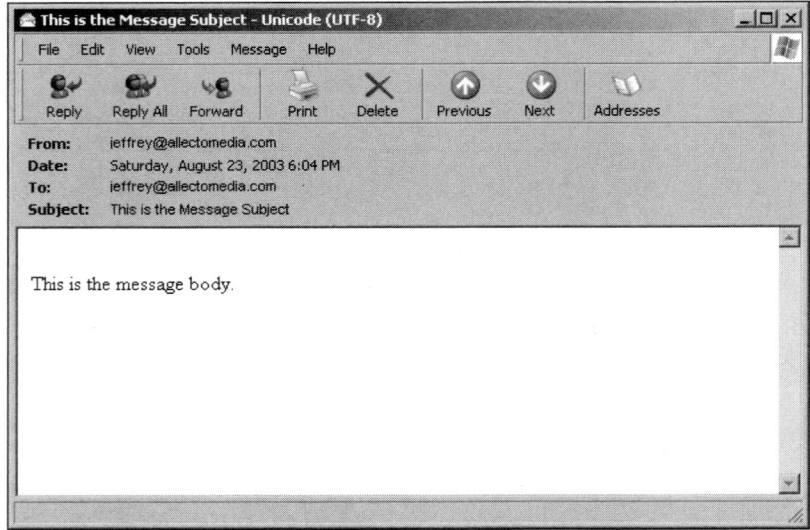

If you did not receive the message, then one of several things could have gone wrong. By far the most likely is that your server is not properly configured to send SMTP email messages. Users with IIS might check Control Panel > Administrative Tools > Services and make sure that Simple Mail Transport Protocol is listed as Started. You can also look in Control Panel > Administrative Tools > Internet Information Services (XP) or Internet Services Manager (Windows 2000), select the computer with the server, and explore the Default SMTP Virtual Server's properties.

If you are using ColdFusion, most likely you did not enter the correct Internet or IP address of your outgoing SMTP mail server.

7) Close messageSent.asp.

Now that you have the messaging itself working, you need to make it useful, by putting meaningful content into the message. To do that, you'll use a form to collect the message data from the user, and then you'll send that data to the mail object, which in turn will send it (ostensibly) to Newland Tours staff.

CREATING THE WEB FORM

In this task, you will create a form to collect data from the user, and you will send that data to messageSent.asp. Before you continue and start reading through the steps, test your knowledge. How do you send data to messageSent.asp? Should you use GET or POST? What fields should the form contain?

1) Open contact.asp. Change the table on the page containing the mailing, phone, and email information so it appears as in the screenshot. Also, change the first body paragraph so it reflects the new page structure.

One benefit of placing your email address in server-side code is that spammers have no access to it. If you put your email address on the page, as in the current version of the site, spammers' automated email address harvesting tools have easy access to it and can (and will) add it to their lists. By switching to a mail-based form, you keep your email address more private.

Contact a Newland Tours Agent

If you are interested in learning more about a tour, contact one of our agents by mail or phone, or use the form below to send us an email.

By Mail or Phone
Newland Tours 123 Wharton Street #45 New York, NY 10010 (555) 555-3865

Image: This photo of a fountain in Versailles was taken by a Newland Tours customer on the "Highlights of France" tour.

2) Position the insertion point below the image caption, and choose Insert › Form › Form to create a new form. Without moving the insertion point, choose Insert › Table, providing the following settings. Click OK.

Rows: 4

Columns: 2

Width: 95 Percent

Border: 0

Cell Padding: 3

Cell Spacing: 0

People often forget that they can put all sorts of HTML inside tables. By using a table, you can present your form in a more structured way.

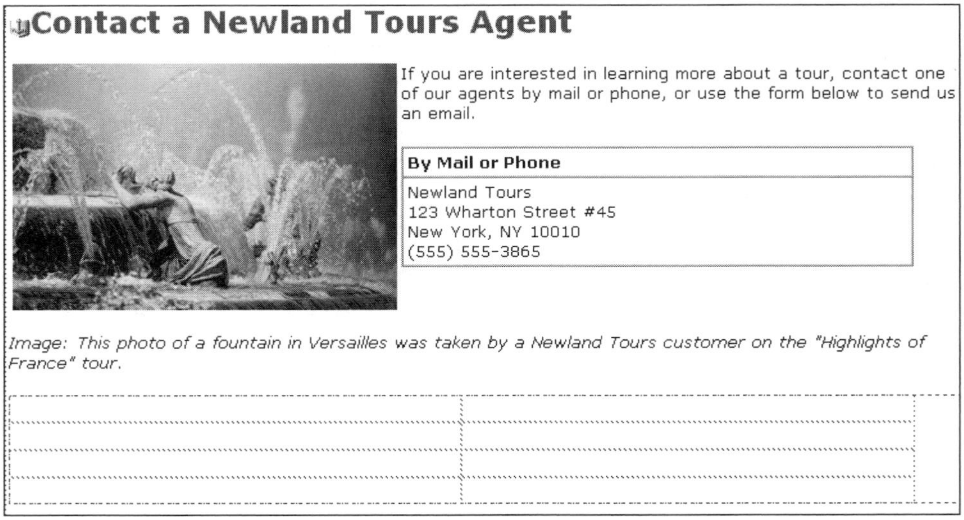

Image: This photo of a fountain in Versailles was taken by a Newland Tours customer on the "Highlights of France" tour.

3) Insert two text fields, one text area, and a Submit button in the right column of the table. In the first three cells of the left column, enter the following text: *Your Email Address, Subject, Message Body.*

In this step, you are building the presentation of the table. You are not yet dealing with its data—e.g., naming the fields you've created or worrying about the form's action statement. You'll get to those shortly.

TIP *Sometimes Dreamweaver has screen redraw problems when you add or remove large contents to or from table cells. For example, during this step, the dashed border of the form may appear to cut through the table. Remember, though, that this is merely a screen refresh problem: there is nothing wrong with the underlying code. To see how the page really looks at any time, click the left-most `<table>` tag in the tag selector, which forces Dreamweaver to redraw the table.*

4) Select the `<table>` tag in the tag inspector, and use the Property inspector to change its bgcolor (background color) attribute to #eeeeee, which is a light gray.

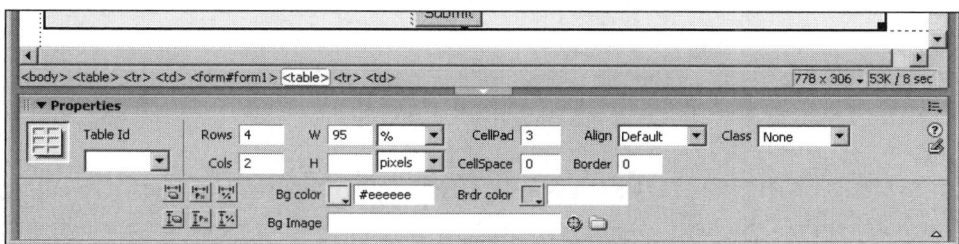

The gray background sets apart the form from the rest of the page, while also drawing attention to its text fields, which suddenly appear much whiter.

5) Insert a Heading 2 element above the table that reads, *Send Us a Message*.

The form itself is conspicuous, but until you label it, its purpose is not.

The effects of this and the preceding steps are visible in the accompanying screenshot.

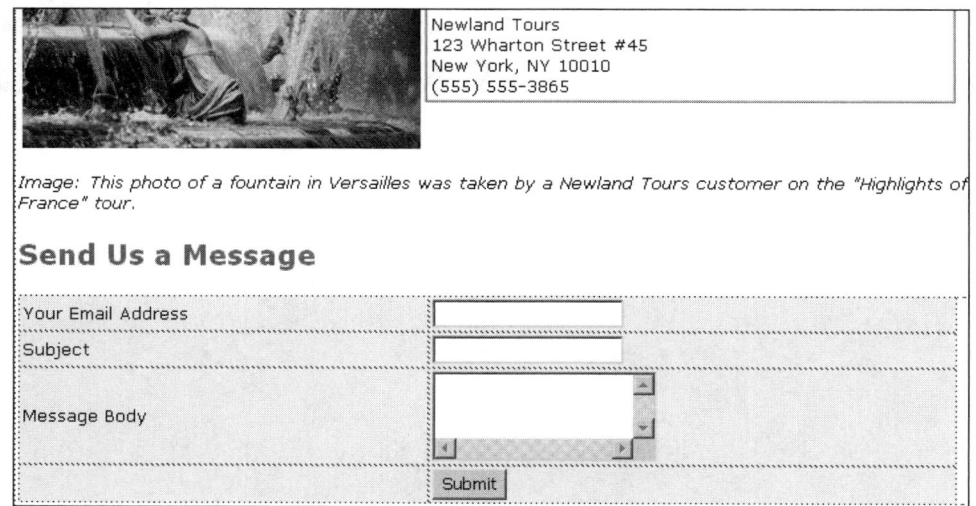

187

6) In turn, select each of the first two text fields and name them *emailAddress* and *subject*. Select the text area and name it *body*, and specify its Char Width as 55, its Num Lines as 6, and Wrap as Virtual.

In this step, you take care of much of the behind-the-scenes logic—giving each field a meaningful ID, which will make it easier to collect that data on messageSent.asp.

By customizing the text area, you make it easier for users to enter a longer message than the default text area settings made convenient.

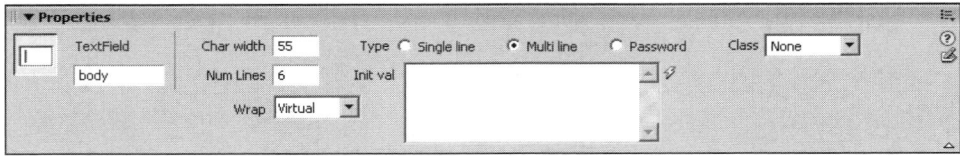

7) Select `<form#form1>` in the tag selector, and in the Property inspector, name it *frm_message*. In the Action field, type *messageSent.asp*. In the Method drop-down, select POST.

Hopefully, you had anticipated the Action and Method settings at the beginning of this task. As a review, they mean that the form will call messageSent.asp and include the data entered in the form in name-value pairs in the body of the HTTP request.

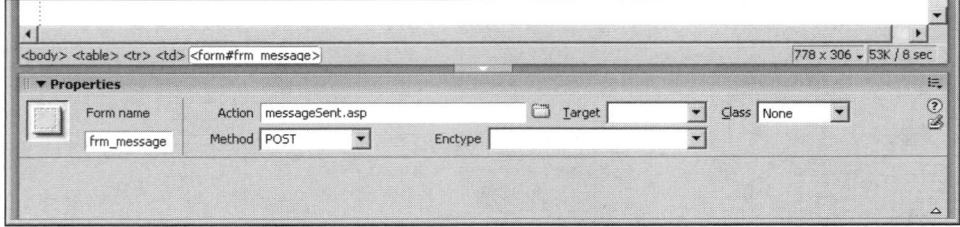

8) Save, close, and upload contact.asp.

The form is ready. To make use of it, though, you'll need to load the form values dynamically into the mail object.

EMAILING DYNAMIC FORM VALUES

Having worked through Lessons 4 and 5 and having sent form data from one page to another, you can probably complete this task without the steps printed here. Indeed, I challenge you to try it, only referring back if you get stuck or have a problem. Don't forget to come back for the final section, "Client-Side Form Validation."

But before you put the book down and give it a go on your own, I want to point out the full complexity of what you are about to do. You have learned how to send and capture data using different scopes—cookies, form, querystrings, and so on. You have learned how to display dynamic text, using ASP's `Response.Write()`, ColdFusion's `<cfoutput>`, and PHP's echo. In this lesson, you learned about objects, and in particular, how your server model has objects dedicated to sending SMTP email. Individually, passing data between pages and mail objects have nothing to do with each other.

But in this final task of the lesson, you will bring together these two disparate techniques to create a specific functionality not explicitly built into ASP or ColdFusion. You have created your own application by combining different tools and technologies (HTML, HTTP requests, and ASP/ColdFusion/PHP communication objects). In a way, this convergence stands metaphorically for all of dynamic Web site development: You combine different objects and techniques to empower the user to make use of information and communication tools in an open-ended way.

1) Open messageSent.asp in code view.
Design view won't help you here, since the code you need to change isn't even visible on the page.

2) Find the sender email address in the mail code, and replace it with the appropriate form variable, as follows:
For ASP, change the first appearance of your email address to `Request.Form("emailAddress")`.

For ColdFusion, replace `from="yourname@yourserver.com"` with `from="#form.emailAddress#"`.

As mentioned earlier, PHP doesn't have a simple, foolproof way to specify the sender, and the sender is optional for PHP anyway, so you can skip this step. Again, there are ways to specify a sender, so work with your ISP to find out how you can do it within the context of their servers.

Rather than always printing your email address in the From portion of your email address, the message will now indicate that it is from whatever value is entered in the form.

3) Continue through the code, replacing the hard-coded subject and body values with the form data for each of those values.

Because there is no field for users to enter the recipient's email address, and because for testing purposes it needs to come to you, you'll leave your own email address hard-coded as the recipient. The final code blocks should be as follows:

In ASP:

```
<%

theSchema="http://schemas.microsoft.com/cdo/configuration/"
Set cdoConfig=server.CreateObject("CDO.Configuration")
cdoConfig.Fields.Item(theSchema & "sendusing")= 2
cdoConfig.Fields.Item(theSchema & "smtpserver")="your.SMTP.server.com"
cdoConfig.Fields.Update

set cdoMessage=Server.CreateObject("CDO.Message")
cdoMessage.Configuration=cdoConfig
cdoMessage.From=Request.Form("emailAddress")
cdoMessage.To="yourname@yoursever.com"
cdoMessage.Subject=Request.Form("subject")
cdoMessage.TextBody=Request.Form("body")
cdoMessage.Send

Set cdoMessage=Nothing
Set cdoConfig=Nothing

%>
```

```
1  <!DOCTYPE html PUBLIC "-//W3C//DTD XHTML 1.0 Transitional//EN" "http://www.w3.org/TR/xhtml1/DTD/xhtml1-t
2
3  <%
4  theSchema="http://schemas.microsoft.com/cdo/configuration/"
5  Set cdoConfig=server.CreateObject("CDO.Configuration")
6  cdoConfig.Fields.Item(theSchema & "sendusing")=2
7  cdoConfig.Fields.Item(theSchema & "smtpserver")="mail.insightbb.com"
8  cdoConfig.Fields.Update
9
10 set cdoMessage=Server.CreateObject("CDO.Message")
11 cdoMessage.Configuration=cdoConfig
12
13 cdoMessage.From=Request.Form("emailAddress")
14 cdoMessage.To="jeffrey@allectomedia.com"
15 cdoMessage.Subject=Request.Form("subject")
16 cdoMessage.TextBody=Request.Form("body")
17 cdoMessage.Send
18
19 Set cdoMessage=Nothing
20 Set cdoConfig=Nothing
21 %>
22
23 <html xmlns="http://www.w3.org/1999/xhtml">
```

In ColdFusion:

```
<cfmail from="#form.emailAddress#" to="yourname@yourserver.com" fisubject=
⇒"#form.subject#">
#form.body#
</cfmail>
```

In PHP

```
<?
mail('yourname@yourserver.com', $_POST['subject'], $_POST['body']);
?>
```

4) Save and upload the page, and test the functionality by completing the form, clicking Submit, and checking your email.

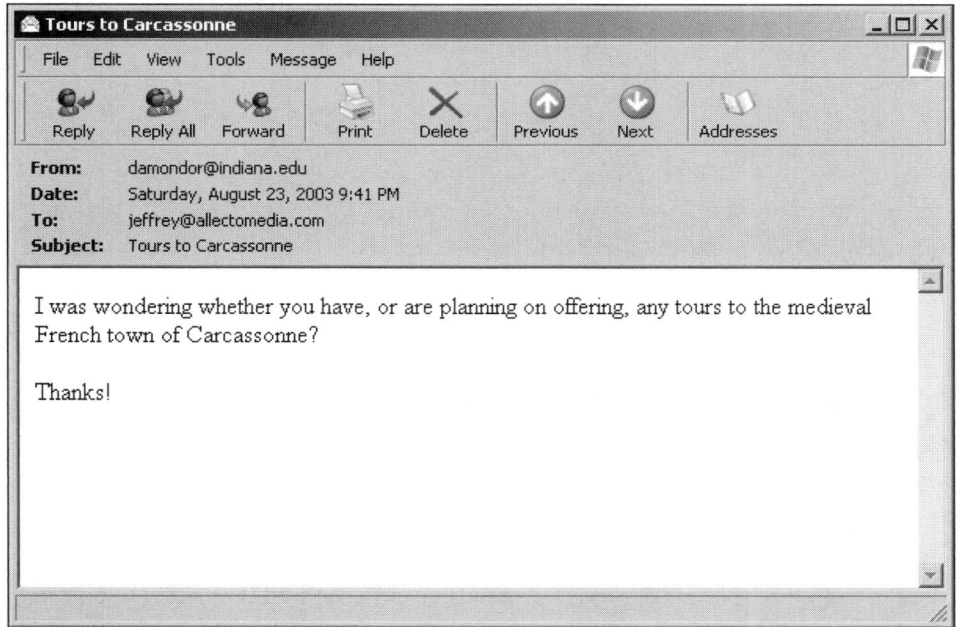

If, rather than seeing the values you entered, you see form.subject as the subject, or form.body as the body, then you probably forgot to remove the quotation marks around the dynamic variables (ASP and PHP) or you forgot to include the pound signs ## (ColdFusion).

CLIENT-SIDE FORM VALIDATION

Depending on what you entered in the form when you tested it, you may have exposed a problem. The form does not verify that users enter the correct type of data. For example, you could enter anything as the email address—nothing verifies that it meets the username@domain.com format. But Newland Tours staff won't be able to respond to messages if users forget to enter their entire email address, which could result in lost business.

In this task, you will use a simple Dreamweaver behavior that verifies the user entered the correct type of information. This verification is called form validation, and it comes in two varieties: client-side and server-side validation.

- Client-side validation verifies that data entered in the form meets the needs of the page from within the browser, the moment the user presses the Submit button and before the HTTP request is sent.

- Server-side validation occurs in a script on the server after the HTTP request is sent. Each form of validation has its own strengths and limitations.

In this task, you will deploy client-side form validation, using a Dreamweaver behavior. This behavior writes JavaScript that ensures the user entered the correct information. If the user didn't, an alert pop-up appears, preventing further progress. If the user does enter the correct information, the JavaScript lets the page proceed as programmed.

1) Open contact.asp and in design view, select the Submit button.

You want the form validation to kick in as soon as the user clicks the Submit button. Therefore, you'll attach the behavior to the Submit button. The user clicking that button becomes the event that triggers the validation script.

2) In the Behaviors panel (Window > Behaviors), click the Add Behavior (+) button, and choose Validate Form from the list.

This behavior enables you to enter a few parameters in a dialog box and then writes the requisite JavaScript for you.

192

3) In the Validate Form dialog, select the first item in the list, check the Required box, and select the Email Address radio button in the Accept group.

Here you are specifying that the user must fill in the emailAddress field of the form, and that what the user types in must be in the proper email format.

NOTE *This validation verifies only the proper email syntax. It does not ensure that the particular email address actually exists, let alone attempt to verify that it belongs to the current user.*

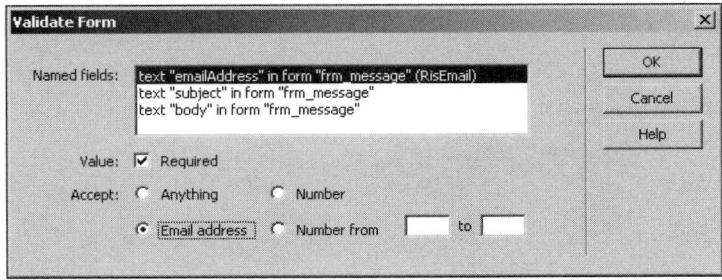

4) In turn, select each of the remaining two items in the list, and check the Required box. Leave the Accept radio setting at Anything.

Here you are forcing the user to enter a subject and body text, but you are not specifying any particular format.

The completed dialog displays (RisEmail) beside the first item, and (R) beside the remaining two.

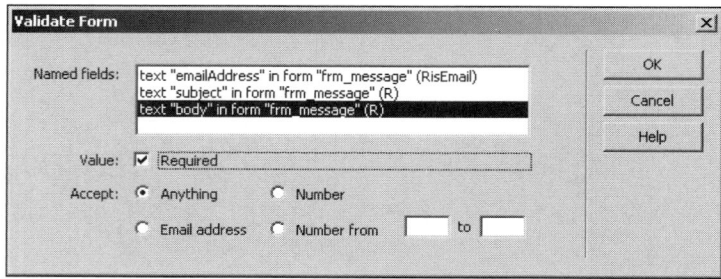

5) Click OK.

This applies the behavior to the Submit button.

6) Save, upload, and test the functionality, by leaving a field blank or by entering a non-email address in the Email address field, and press Submit.

If you break one of the validation rules, you'll see a JavaScript alert dialog. Correct the error, submit the form, and check your email.

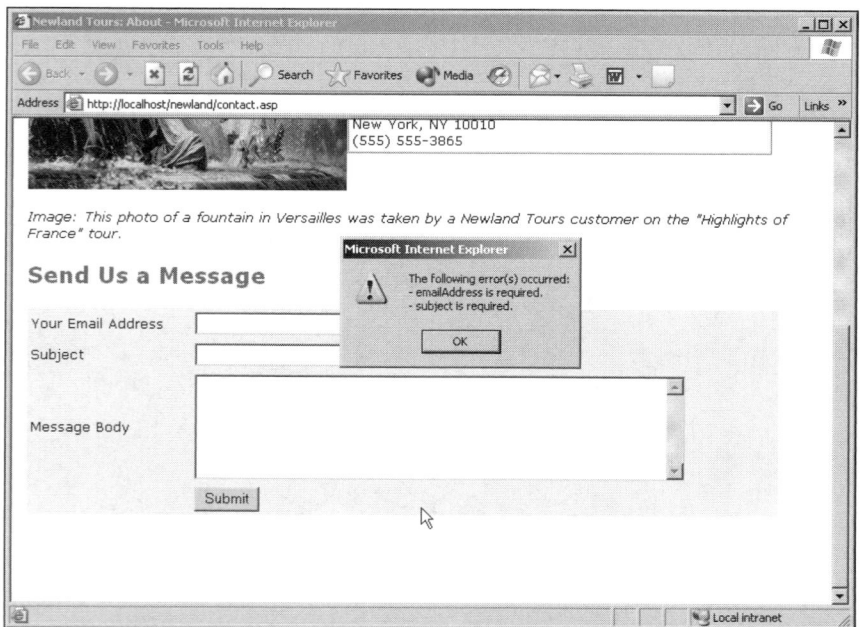

WHAT YOU HAVE LEARNED

In this lesson, you have:

- Configured your server for SMTP message service (pages 173–177)

- Learned about objects, methods, and properties (pages 178–179)

- Made use of two ASP objects (CDO.Configuration and CDO.Message), a ColdFusion tag that makes use of an object (<cfmail>), and a PHP function (mail()) (pages 180–183)

- Caused the server to generate an email message with hard-coded values (pages 180–185)

- Built a form to collect message data from the user (pages 185–188)

- Dynamically loaded user-entered data into the email message (pages 189–191)

- Applied client-side form validation to ensure the integrity of the generated message (pages 192–194)

building a tour price calculator

LESSON 7

One of the most significant benefits of dynamic Web sites is that they are capable of including self-service applications. Self-service applications are a win-win situation for businesses and customers alike. Customers don't have to go to the trouble of calling a number, pressing a sequence of numbers ("please press 3, now"), and sitting interminably on hold ("your call is important to us"), only to learn that office hours ended three hours ago. Businesses decrease incoming calls, which decreases long-distance phone charges and hours, and yet they can still serve customers 24 hours, 7 days a week.

In this lesson, you will build a tour price calculator, which enables users to obtain an estimate for the cost of a tour based on the number of adults and children going on

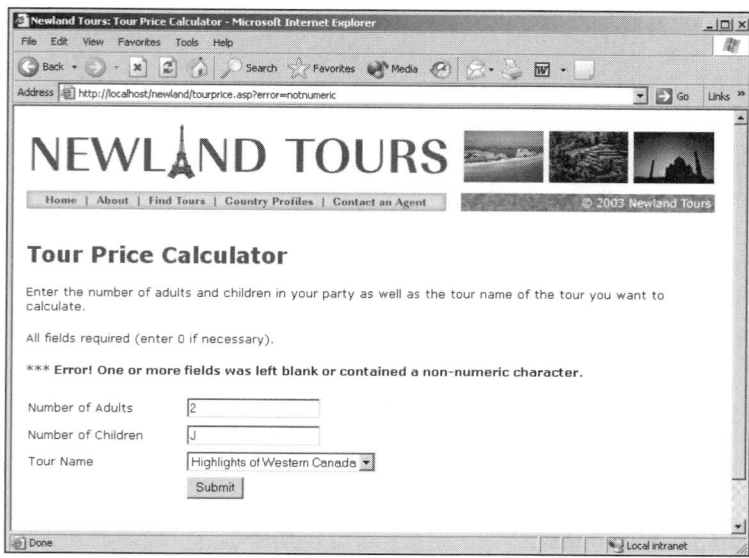

Your application both enables users to build customized estimates and ensures that they enter the correct information, displaying an error message inline if they do not.

the tour. You'll use ASP, ColdFusion, or PHP to multiply the tour price by the number of adults and children to come up with the estimate. This estimate will be output using correctly formatted currency.

The calculator won't have full functionality until the end of Lesson 9, however, because part of it uses price amounts drawn dynamically from a database. But in this lesson, you'll build the majority of the application and temporarily hard-code the price values while you nail the functionality.

But that's not all you'll do. You'll also extend your skills with form validation, this time writing custom ASP, ColdFusion, or PHP code to handle form validation on the server side, rather than the client side, as in Lesson 6. You'll create a custom cascading style sheet (CSS) class, and see how to use ASP, ColdFusion, or PHP to create a region of the page that displays conditionally: If the user does not fill in the form, an error message, written inline in HTML, appears that was hidden before.

WHAT YOU WILL LEARN

In this lesson, you will:

- Create a simple self-service application
- Collect and manipulate form data
- Display data, using a built-in function to format it as currency
- Deploy server-side form validation
- Create a custom CSS class
- Use a conditional HTML region

APPROXIMATE TIME

This lesson takes approximately two hours to complete.

LESSON FILES

Starting Files:

Lesson07/Start/newland/generic_template.asp
Lesson07/Start/newland/contact.asp
Lesson07/Start/newland/newland.css

Completed Files:

Lesson07/Complete/newland/tourprice.asp
*Lesson07/Complete/newland/tourprice_
  processor.asp*
Lesson07/Complete/newland/newland.css

CREATING THE PAGES

To begin the application, you'll create the two pages needed for it to work and rough out the static content. Once that is in place, you can add the individual pieces of functionality one at a time. Until then, though, you're doing just plain HTML authoring.

1) Open generic_template.asp, and save it as *tourprice_processor.asp*, and then save it again as *tourprice.asp*.

You have created two pages based on the template, and one of the pages, tourprice.asp, is open in Dreamweaver.

2) In the toolbar, change the page title to *Newland Tours: Tour Price Calculator*. In the main document, change the title so it reads *Tour Price Calculator*. Then type the following text as the body text:

Enter the number of adults and children in your party as well as the tour name of the tour you want to calculate.

All fields required (enter 0 if necessary).

Beneath this text you will create a form, but for now, this file is done.

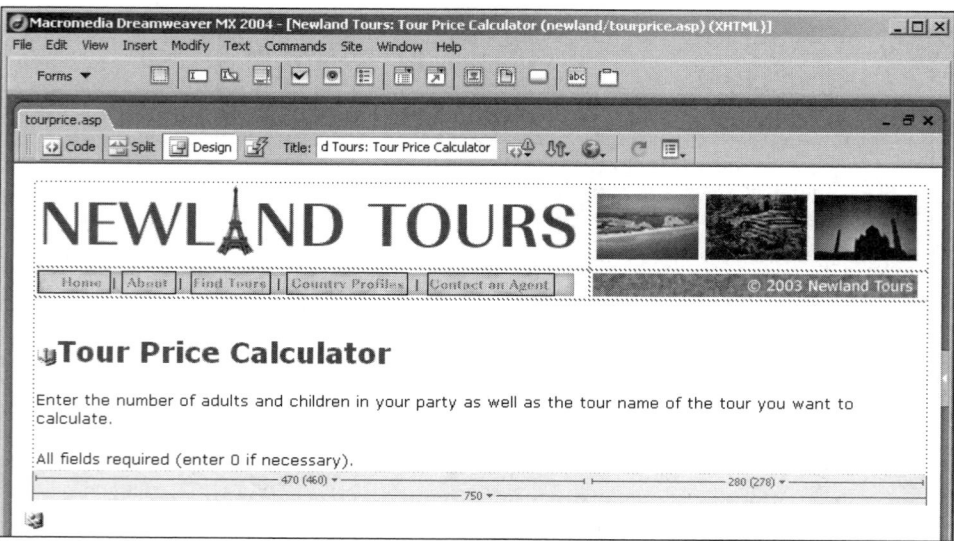

3) Save and close tourprice.asp. Open tourprice_processor.asp.

Creating the second page is much like creating the first.

4) In the toolbar, change the page title to *Newland Tours: Tour Price Calculator*. In the main document, change the title so it reads *Tour Price Calculator*. Then type the following text as the body text:

The estimated cost of your tour is XXX.

Prices include hotel, accommodation, and travel expenses during the tour. They do not include airfare to the starting destination.

Calculate another tour.

Contact one of our qualified agents.

Later in this lesson, the placeholder text string XXX will be replaced with the amount output from the ASP/ColdFusion script.

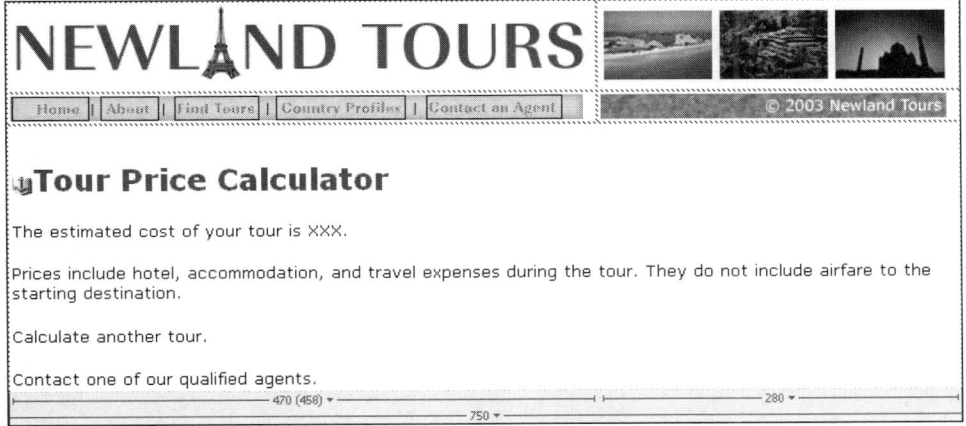

5) Select the XXX placeholder text, and click the B button in the Property inspector to apply bolding to the text.

Just because the eventual output will be generated dynamically using ASP doesn't mean that you can't format the text the way you want it to appear.

Oddly enough, rather than wrapping the text in <strong> tags, as Dreamweaver normally does, this procedure wraps the text in <span class="author"> tags. Evidently, Dreamweaver assumes that if you want bolding, you probably want to use your custom class to do it. This conversion is fairly harmless in this instance, except it is likely to confuse users with screenreaders. Since this isn't a real production site, you can let Dreamweaver do this and not worry about it. Or, if it bothers you, you can go into code view and replace <span class="author"> with <strong>.

6) Select the word Calculate, and use the Property inspector to link it to tourprice.asp. Select the word Contact and link it to contact.asp.

Visually, aside from the placeholder text, this page is ready. You'll add two significant pieces of functionality to it later in the lesson—server-side form validation and the tour price calculation itself—but these functionalities will be created with scripting and will be invisible to the user.

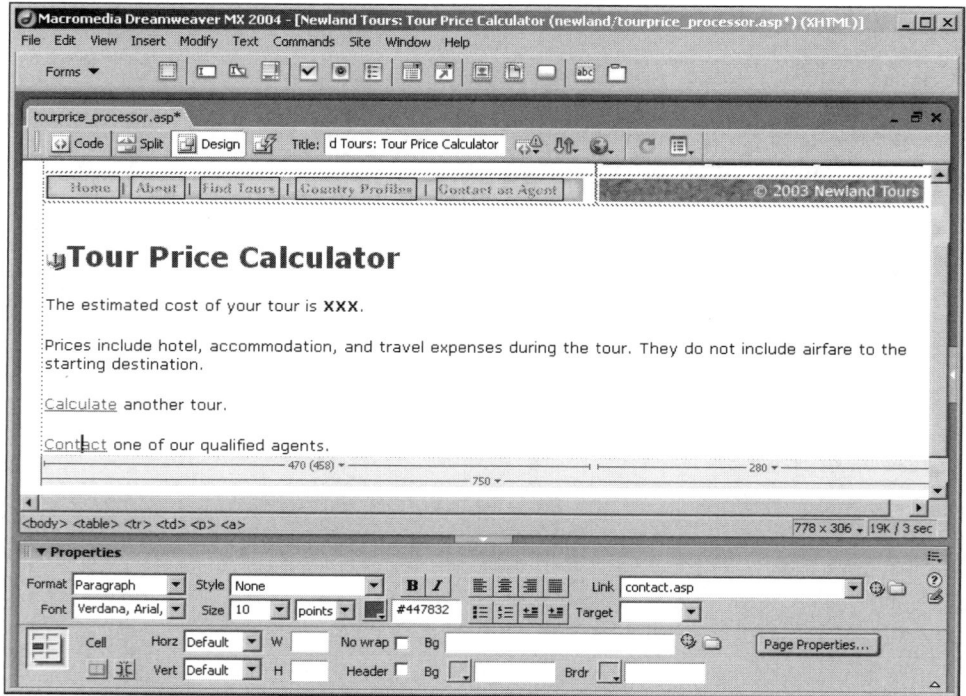

7) Save and close tourprice_processor.asp.

BUILDING THE FORM

In this task, you will build the form that users will fill out to provide the calculation script with sufficient information to create the estimate. The form that you are about to build has two items of note. It includes an embedded table, used for formatting. You saw this technique in Lesson 6, when you built the contact form. The other item of note is the use of a drop-down menu.

1) Open tourprice.asp. Position the insertion point at the end of the All fields required line, after the period. Using the Forms tab in the Insert panel, click the Form button. In the Property inspector, name the form *frm_tourprice*, specify tourprice_processor.asp as its Action, and verify that POST is selected as its Method.

Without any fields or submit button, the form cannot do anything, but it's a start.

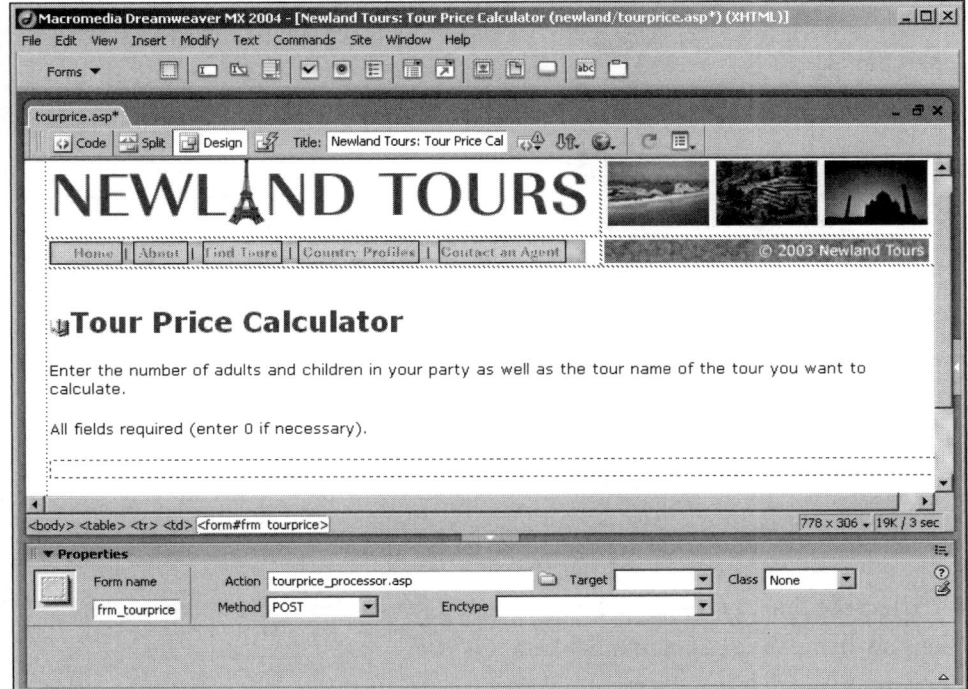

The dashed line represents form boundaries

2) With the insertion point inside the form, click the Insert Table button from the Tables tab of the Insert panel. In the ensuing dialog, specify 4 rows, 2 columns, a width of 60 percent, a border of 0, cell padding of 3, and cell spacing of 0.

When you are finished, the form stretches to accommodate the new table that appears.

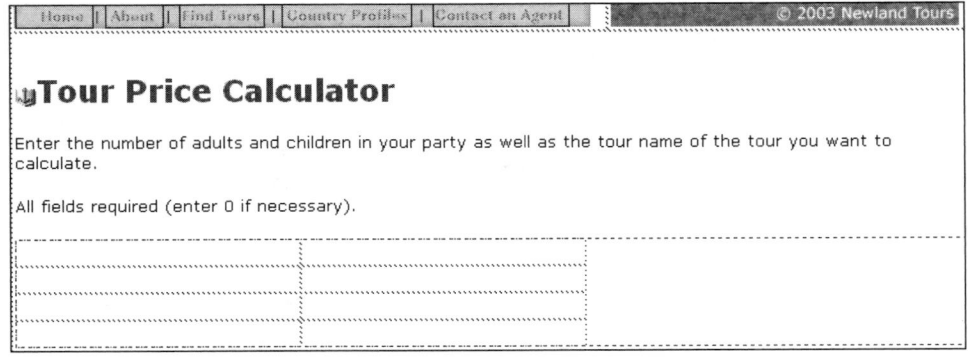

3) In the top three cells of the left column, enter *Number of Adults*, *Number of Children*, *Tour Name*. In the right column, from top to bottom, insert a text field, another text field, a list/menu, and a Submit button, using the Forms tab of the Insert panel.

The Forms tab makes building Web forms a snap. However, you still need to configure each of the form elements.

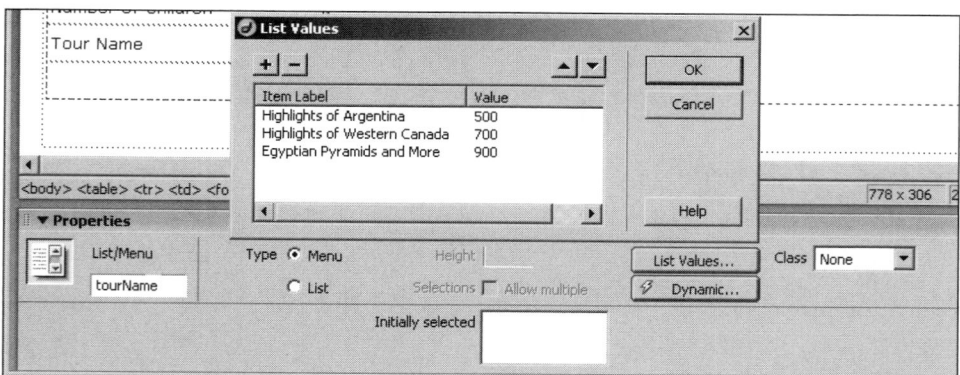

4) Select the first text field, and in the Property inspector, name it *numAdults*. Likewise, name the second text field *numChildren*.

Remember, the field names are also the variable names that ASP/ColdFusion/PHP uses to extract the data, so it is important to give them meaningful names.

5) Select the menu, and in the Property inspector, name it *tourName* and then click the List Values button. In the List values dialog, click below Item Label, and type *Highlights of Argentina*. Press Tab and type *500*. Pressing Tab to continue, enter *Highlights of Western Canada*, *700*, *Egyptian Pyramids and More*, and finally *900*.

To understand what's happening in this step, let's compare form menus with text fields. When you create a text field, you give it a name. When the user types in the

202

field, that information is the field's value. Thus, the firstName text field you created in previous lessons carried whatever value the user entered into it on the second page—the one that collects and displays the form data.

Menus work a bit differently than forms. Like text fields, they're given names, and the data associated with them is stored with that name. Thus, on the page that processes this form, `Request.Form("tourName")` (ASP), `#form.tourName#` (ColdFusion), or `$_POST['tourName']` (PHP) would retrieve this data.

But the similarity ends there. Drop-down menus are not as open-ended as text fields. With drop-down menus, users select from a finite number of options that the developer specifies. The options that the user chooses from are entered in the Item Label column of the List Values dialog. The Value column of the List Values dialog is the data value that is sent with the form. Thus, if a user chooses Egyptian Pyramids and More, then `Request.Form("tourName")` (ASP), `#form.tourName#` (ColdFusion), or `$_POST['tourName']` (PHP) would retrieve 900. You'll use that value shortly when you perform the actual calculation.

The item label does not get submitted with the form to the next page. It remains in the form itself to enable the user to make a selection. The reason that the item label and values are separate is so that you can submit a value other than the label to the script. Since you are performing mathematical calculations, you need a numeric data value, rather than a text string.

Clearly, Newland Tours offers more than three tours. Entering them one by one would be tedious, to say the least. Worse, if you wanted to add or remove a tour, you'd have to revisit the List Values dialog to fix it. There is a better way: You can dynamically load the labels and their values from a database to automatically generate this menu on the fly. You'll see how to do that in Lesson 9. But for now, you'll hard-code these values just to build the core functionality.

Another problem with the current form might have occurred to you. Right now, if a user selects Egyptian Pyramids and More, only the value 900 is sent. You can multiply that by the number of adults or children, but there is no way to send separate values for each. The whole point of the application is to provide an estimate that reflects the values of both the price for adults and for children. You'll fix this problem as well in Lesson 9, by retrieving both figures from a database.

6) Save tourprice.asp, and press F12 to test it in a browser.

The form is complete and ready to use. Before moving onto the server-side code, however, you should test it in a browser to verify that it looks as expected. You can press Submit if you like, and tourprice_processor.asp should appear, but it won't look any different than before.

When you are finished, close tourprice.asp.

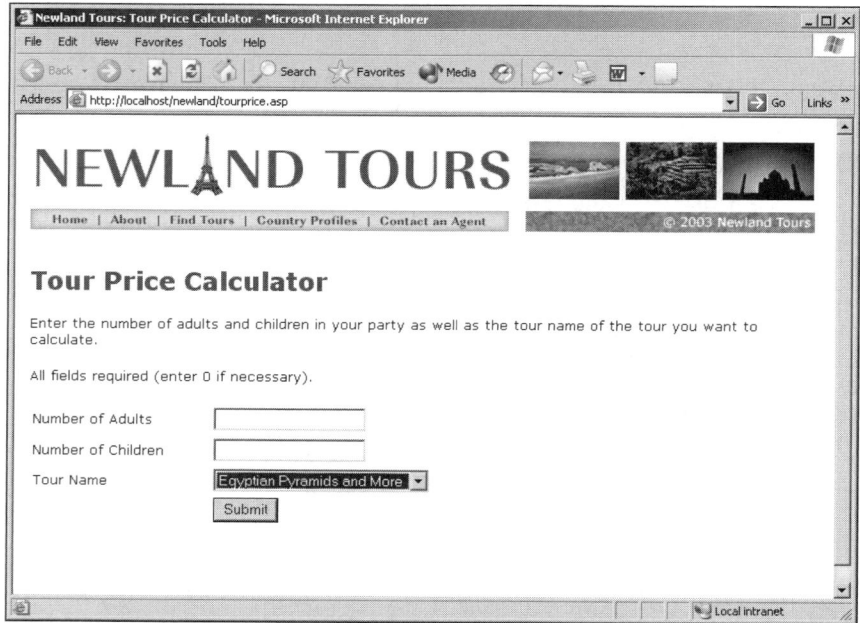

COLLECTING, PROCESSING, AND DISPLAYING THE DATA

The stage is set, and now it is time to capture the data entered on the form and perform the price calculation based on the data the user entered. You are already familiar with collecting form data and displaying it on the page, so in this task you should focus on the calculation itself.

1) Open tourprice_processor.asp. If necessary, switch to split view or code view.
To perform the calculations, you need the data, which is available on the page specified in the form's action attribute.

The switch to code view is necessary for now, because you are about to do some hand-coding, and there is no way to do so in design view.

2) ASP only: Position the insertion point at the top of the document, before the opening `<!DOCTYPE...>` tag, press Enter/Return twice, return to line 1, and type `<%@LANGUAGE="VBSCRIPT" CODEPAGE="1252" %>`.
This line is necessary for two reasons. First, it tells the server that the scripting language used is VBScript. Remember, ASP can be coded using more than one language. The most common languages for ASP are VBScript and JScript, and with ASP.NET, you have even more options. ColdFusion users don't have to worry about

this setting, because ColdFusion supports only ColdFusion Markup Language (CFML), so there is no possibility for confusion.

The second attribute, CODEPAGE, specifies the page's language. 1252 refers to English.

3) ASP only: Position the insertion point in line 2 and press Enter/Return twice to add some more space. Beginning in line 3, type the following code:

```
<%
Dim numAdult, numChild, basePrice, tourPrice
%>
```

As you know from before, <% is used to mark up ASP code that the server needs to process. The extra space just above the closing %> is to leave room for additional script, which you'll add in a moment.

The second line may look a bit odd. In ASP, whenever you want to create a new variable, you must declare it. You declare new variables using Dim. Thus, the second line announces to the server that you are creating three new variables. These variables have not yet been assigned any values—you'll give them values momentarily.

NOTE *Some languages do not require you to declare variables before you set their values. Neither ColdFusion nor PHP require you to first declare variables, so these don't have equivalents for the Dim line.*

By the end of this step, ASP users' code window should appear as in the following screenshot. ColdFusion and PHP users, just to reiterate, haven't done anything in this task yet, but that's about to change.

```
1  <%@LANGUAGE="VBSCRIPT" CODEPAGE="1252" %>
2
3  <%
4  Dim numAdult, numChild, basePrice, tourPrice
5
6  %>
7
8  <!DOCTYPE html PUBLIC "-//W3C//DTD XHTML 1.0 Transitional//EN" "http://www.w3.org/TR/xhtml1/DTD/xhtml1-t
9  <html xmlns="http://www.w3.org/1999/xhtml">
10 <head>
```

4) All users: Set three variables, numAdult, numChild, and basePrice, to the values entered in the numAdults, numChildren, and tourName form fields.

In ASP, insert the following code beginning in the empty line after the Dim line:

```
numAdult = Request.Form("numAdults")
numChild = Request.Form("numChildren")
basePrice = Request.Form("tourName")
```

In ColdFusion, enter the following code at the top of the document, before the opening <!DOCTYPE> tag:

```
<cfset numAdult = form.numAdults>
<cfset numChild = form.numChildren>
<cfset basePrice = form.tourName>
```

In PHP, enter the following code at the top of the document, before the opening <!DOCTYPE> line:

```
$numAdult = $_POST['numAdults'];
$numChild = $_POST['numChildren'];
$basePrice = $_POST['tourName'];
```

You've seen Request.Form("fieldname"), form.fieldname, and $_POST['fieldname'] in earlier lessons. This time, rather than simply printing them on the page, as you did before, you are storing those values inside new variables. The reason for this is that what needs to be printed on the page is the output of the calculation. By storing these values in descriptively named variables, the calculation is easier to code (and read).

ColdFusion users might wonder why the form variables aren't surrounded by pound signs (##) as they were in previous lessons. Pound signs are used only when ColdFusion is outputting a dynamic value to an external source, such as HTML. Without them, ColdFusion would print the variable name, rather than its value. But the pound signs are unnecessary here, because the action here is internal to ColdFusion—it is not outputting values anywhere.

5) Set a fourth variable, tourPrice, to equal the output of the calculation itself.

In ASP, insert the following code in the line below the basePrice line:

```
tourPrice = (numAdult * basePrice) + (numChild * basePrice)
```

In ColdFusion, insert the following code in the line below the basePrice line:

```
<cfset tourPrice = (numAdult * basePrice) + (numChild * basePrice)>
```

In PHP, insert the following code in the line below the basePrice line:

```
$tourPrice = ($numAdult * $basePrice) + ($numChild * $basePrice);
```

Assuming you survived seventh-grade math, you probably know what this line is doing. It is setting the value of tourPrice to equal the output of a simple calculation. The parentheses are used, as in arithmetic, to ensure that the calculations take place in the proper order.

When this line of code is resolved on the server, tourPrice has the final calculated dollar amount as its value. With that in place, all we need to do is output it into the HTML code where the XXX placeholder is, and the user will see the information that they need.

```
1  <%@LANGUAGE="VBSCRIPT" CODEPAGE="1252" %>
2
3  <%
4  Dim numAdult, numChild, basePrice, tourPrice
5  numAdult = Request.Form("numAdults")
6  numChild = Request.Form("numChildren")
7  basePrice = Request.Form("tourName")
8  tourPrice = (numAdult * basePrice) + (numChild * basePrice)
9  %>
10
11 <!DOCTYPE html PUBLIC "-//W3C//DTD XHTML 1.0 Transitional//EN" "http://www.w3.org/TR/xhtml1/DTD/xhtml1-tr
12 <html xmlns="http://www.w3.org/1999/xhtml">
```

6) Still in code view, scroll down to the XXX placeholder (around line 34 in ASP, around line 30 in ColdFusion, and around line 33 in PHP). Delete XXX and in its place enter the following code to output the value of the tourPrice variable.

In ASP:

```
<% Response.Write(tourPrice) %>
```

In ColdFusion:

```
<cfoutput>#tourPrice#</cfoutput>
```

In PHP:

```
<?php echo $tourPrice; ?>
```

Outputting a variable value is familiar to you by now. The main difference between this instance of outputting a variable and what you did in Lesson 5 is that you don't need to specify an HTTP-compatible scope—URL/querystring, form, cookie, etc. The scope of this variable is the page itself as it is processed in ASP, ColdFusion, or PHP, and the variable will be resolved and removed before the code is ever sent over HTTP to the browser.

```
25 </tr>
26 <tr>
27  <td><img src="images/navbar.gif" name="navbar" width="450" height="20" border="0" usemap="#navbarMap" a
28  <td><img name="copyright_bar" src="images/copyright_bar.gif" width="272" height="20" border="0" alt="Co
29 </tr>
30 <tr>
31  <td colspan="2">
32    <h1><br />
33      <a name="top" id="top"></a>Tour Price Calculator</h1>
34    <p>The estimated cost of your tour is <strong><% Response.Write(tourPrice) %></strong>.</p>
35    <p>Prices include hotel, accommodation, and travel expenses during the tour. They do not include airf
36    <p><a href="tourprice.asp">Calculate</a> another tour.</p>
37    <p><a href="contact.asp">Contact</a> one of our qualified agents.   </p>
38    </td>
39 </tr>
40 </table>
```

7) Save and upload both tourprice.asp and tourprice_processor.asp. Select tourprice.asp in the Site panel, and press F12 to test it.

You should always test a page's functionality as soon as you can. These two pages are ready for testing. You'll add quite a few enhancements to this application, but its core functionality works—or should.

Try several different variations. Enter numeric values in each field, choose a tour, and press Submit. You should see the output page with the calculated amount in bold. Notice that the dollar amount appears, but nothing indicates that it's a dollar amount. Both ASP, ColdFusion, and recent versions of PHP have built-in functions that enable you to output numbers in proper currency format, as you'll see in a moment.

Once you have verified that it works in the best-case scenario, when you've properly entered numbers, try to break the application by entering bad data in the form. Leave one or both fields blank, or enter a letter, such as D.

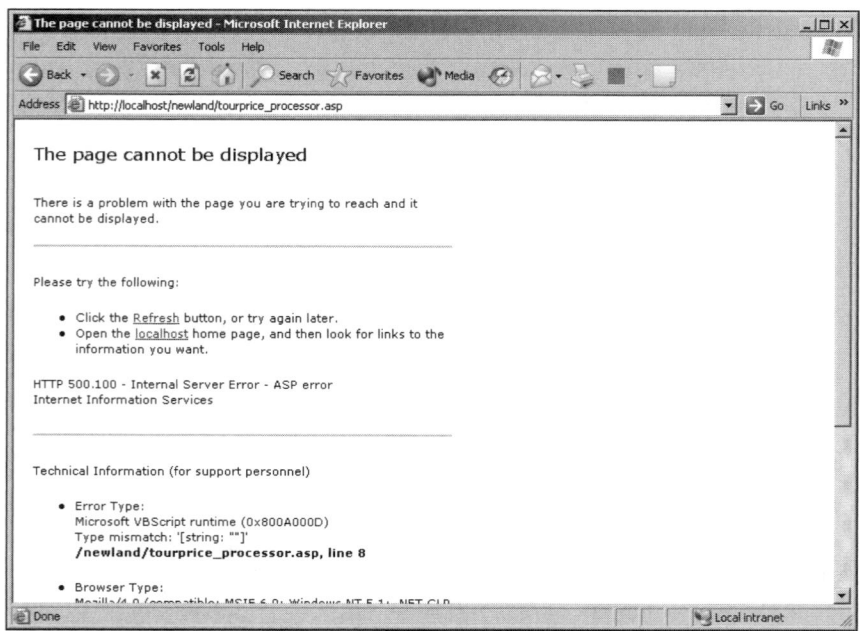

The page either returns an error message or tries to complete the calculation, anyway, returning a meaningless number. The reason is that your script multiplies and adds the contents of the form fields. If these fields have no content or contain non-numeric characters, it can't perform calculations. This application would benefit from a form validation enhancement that would ensure that users actually entered numbers in both fields, before it attempts to calculate a price.

8) Return to tourprice_processor.asp in Dreamweaver, and insert the function that converts the output number to the U.S. dollar currency format.

In ASP:

```
<% Response.Write(FormatCurrency(tourPrice)) %>
```

In ColdFusion:

```
<cfoutput>#DollarFormat(tourPrice)#</cfoutput>
```

In PHP:

```
<?php echo number_format($tourPrice,2,'.',','); ?>
```

NOTE *PHP versions 4.3 and higher have a function,* money_format() *, but this is not available in earlier versions of PHP, including the one that ships on Macintosh OS X. The only disadvantages to using* number_format() *in this context is that it won't output the dollar sign ($). You can add this manually, by entering $ between the* <strong> *(or, if you didn't change it,* <span class="author"> *tag and the opening* <?php echo... *tag.*

Functions are predefined actions that tell the interpreter how to do something. Computer languages generally have dozens of functions, if not more, built in for common tasks. Converting numeric figures to currency format is a common task, and so many languages have a function that performs this task.

Functions take the following format: FunctionName(Parameter). In some cases, there is no parameter, but the parentheses remain, as in the case of ColdFusion's Now() function, which returns the current time on the server. In the case of ASP's FormatCurrency() and ColdFusion's DollarFormat(), the lone parameter is the number that you want to format. Because the number is held in the tourPrice variable, you place that variable in the parameter.

PHP's number_format() function takes four parameters. They are, in order, the number to be formatted ($tourPrice), the number of decimal spaces to allow (2), the punctuation element used to indicate the decimal place (.), and the punctuation element used to separate thousands (,). Because the period and comma characters in the last two parameters aren't part of the function syntax, but are rather the actual text strings that PHP should print, they are enclosed in single quotes. Without the single quotes, the PHP interpreter would mistakenly attempt to read the period as the concatenation character and the comma as a separator between parameters, which would yield an error.

If you test the page now, the results are more satisfying.

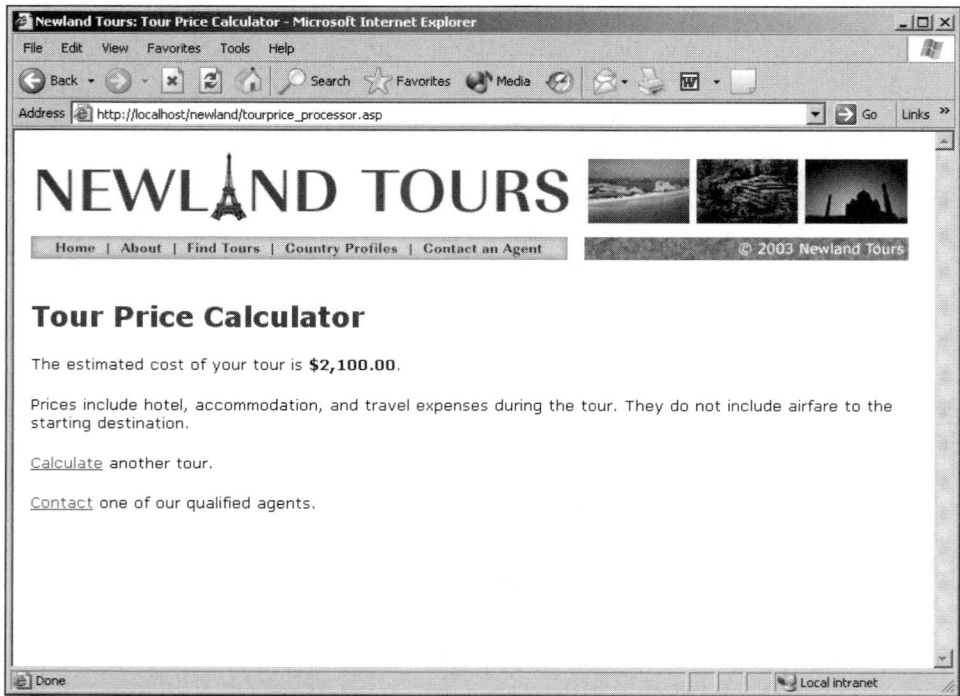

ADDING SERVER-SIDE FORM VALIDATION

As you discovered in the previous task, the application works well when the user enters numbers in both fields. But if the user leaves one blank or enters a non-numeric character, an unsightly error message appears when she or he clicks Submit. Error messages such as the one shown earlier were meant to help developers debug applications; ideally, users should never see them.

To prevent the possibility of this error occurring, you can add form validation to ensure that the requisite numbers have been entered. You used form validation with the email form in Lesson 6. That was client-side form validation—using a Dreamweaver behavior, you added a JavaScript form validation script that fired as soon as the user clicked the Submit button. That was certainly easy to deploy, but as you'll remember, the JavaScript error pop-up that appeared when the form was not filled in correctly wasn't terribly helpful.

In this task, you will add form validation on the server-side; that is, you will write some ASP, ColdFusion, or PHP code to verify that numbers were entered. If they were not, a hidden region of the HTML page will appear indicating an error. Because the error will be coded in HTML, you can make it say whatever you want, and you can also format it however you want.

The process will be as follows: The user fills out the form and clicks Submit. The page tourprice_processor.asp is requested. At the top of that page is a small form validation script, written in ASP, ColdFusion, or PHP, which verifies that numbers were entered in both fields. If numbers were entered in both fields, then the page processes as normal. If numbers were not entered in both fields, the user is redirected back to tourprice.asp, and the once-hidden HTML region with an error message is revealed.

To create this functionality, we need to write the form validation script, which you'll do in this task. Then, in the next task, you'll create the HTML error region and hide it. Finally, you'll format the text in the HTML error region using CSS.

Now that you understand the big picture, let's sketch how this form validation script is going to work. First, we are using it for flow control. That is, depending on whether the user entered the proper data, the script needs either to continue to do the calculation or to redirect the user back to tourprice.asp. Handling flow control based on conditions is easy, using if…else constructs. The following pseudocode maps out the intended functionality of the script:

```
if the user entered a non-numeric or null value in either field
  redirect the user back to tourprice.asp
else
  continue as usual
end if
```

We'll further refine this script in two ways. The first is that you don't need to spell out the else portion if you just want to continue as usual. Thus, we really only need the if half of the script.

The second refinement is that you don't merely want to redirect back to tourprice.asp; you also want to send a trigger that will change the visibility of the hidden region. In this case, a querystring/URL variable will do the job. Then, you'll add a script that looks for the presence of that URL variable, and if it is there, it will display the region. If it is not, the region will be hidden. Don't worry if this seems abstract; you'll get plenty of practice with it by the end of this lesson. The final pseudocode for the form validation script looks as follows:

```
if the user entered a non-numeric or null value in either field
  redirect the user back to tourprice.asp with a querystring
end if
```

Now that we have a plan, let's write some code.

1) Open tourprice_processor.asp. Make some room at the top of the document, before the calculation script you wrote in the previous task, for a new script.

The form validation script should be at the beginning, because you don't want ASP, ColdFusion, or PHP to attempt the calculation when you haven't even verified that the proper form values exist.

ASP users: Be sure that space for the new code is below the `<%@LANGUAGE="VBSCRIPT" CODEPAGE="1252"%>` line, which should always remain as the first line.

TIP *When building script blocks, add some extra space above and below to help set them apart visually.*

2) Create the outer shell of the script, using `if` and testing whether each of the form variables is numeric.

In ASP:

```
<%
If Not IsNumeric(Request.Form("numadults")) or Not
⇒IsNumeric(Request.Form("numchildren")) Then

End If
%>
```

In ColdFusion:

```
<cfif Not IsNumeric(form.numAdults) or Not IsNumeric(form.numChildren)>

</cfif>
```

In PHP:

```
<?php
if (is_numeric($_POST['numAdults']) == false or
is_numeric($_POST['numChildren']) == false)

?>
```

The empty line in each code block is set aside for the code you'll add in the next step.

All three languages have a function, IsNumeric() or is_numeric(), which tests whether the enclosed parameter is numeric. If it is, it returns true. If not, it returns false. Because you want to redirect if the value is not numeric, you add the word Not (ASP and ColdFusion) or specify == false (PHP) to invert the output of the IsNumeric() or is_numeric() function. Finally, because you are checking two fields, rather than one, they have to be listed separately, connecting them with or.

3) Add the inner action that is executed if the if clause evaluates to true.

In ASP, indented in the blank line beneath the if statement:

```
Response.Redirect("tourprice.asp?error=notnumeric")
```

In ColdFusion, indented in the blank line between the opening and closing <cfif> tags:

```
<cflocation url="tourprice.cfm?error=notnumeric">
```

In PHP, in the blank line beneath the opening if line:

```
{
  header("Location: tourprice.php?error=notnumeric");
  exit;
}
```

Response.Redirect() is an ASP function that sends the browser to the URL specified. Likewise, ColdFusion's <cflocation> and PHP's header("Location: …") also redirects the browser. In addition to specifying the URL, you've also added a querystring. You'll add a script back on tourprice.asp that looks for this querystring, using if…else to control the visibility of the error region.

```
1  <%@LANGUAGE="VBSCRIPT" CODEPAGE="1252" %>
2
3  <%
4  If Not IsNumeric(Request.Form("numAdults")) or Not IsNumeric(Request.Form("numChildren")) Then
5      Response.Redirect("tourprice.asp?error=notnumeric")
6  End If
7  %>
8
9  <%
10 Dim numAdult, numChild, basePrice, tourPrice
11 numAdult = Request.Form("numAdults")
12 numChild = Request.Form("numChildren")
```

4) Save and upload tourprice_processor.asp. Test tourprice.asp.

You'll see that if you don't enter numbers in both fields, not only are you stuck on tourprice.asp, but also the querystring variable appears in the Address bar. It's not being used yet, but it's there. Its presence enables both your server script and you to distinguish between when the page first loads, and when it loads because of an error.

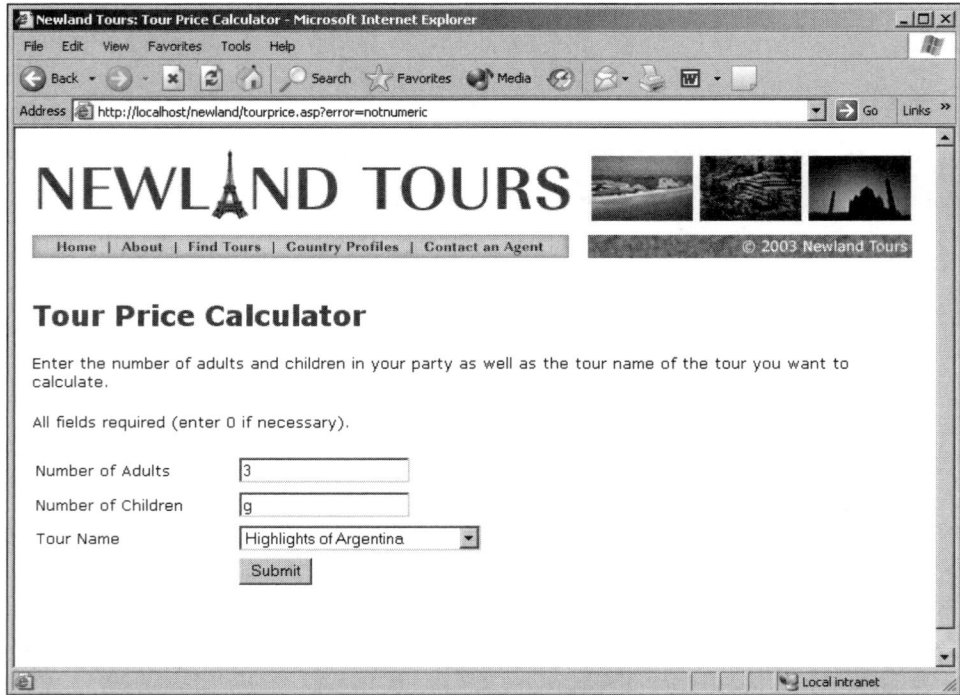

CREATING THE CONDITIONAL REGION

The idea of a region of HTML that can be shown or hidden may sound fancy, but in fact you can do it using skills you have learned in this chapter. All you do is embed standard HTML inside an if statement. If that evaluates to true, then the HTML is displayed. If it evaluates to false, then it skips the HTML and continues.

1) Open tourprice.asp. Position the cursor before the opening <form> **tag, and press Enter/Return a few times to make room for some new code.**

You should find the opening <form> tag around line 38. By inserting the conditional region here, you cause the error message to appear in a prominent location when the page reloads.

2) As before, start with the outer shell, by writing the if statement.

In ASP:

```
<%
If Request.QueryString("error") = "notnumeric" Then

End If
%>
```

In ColdFusion:

```
<cfif url.error is "notnumeric">

</cfif>
```

In PHP:

```
<?
if ($_GET['error'] == "notnumeric")

?>
```

The if statements here test to determine whether there is a querystring (or URL) variable called error, and if so, whether its value is set to "notnumeric." When the page first loads, there is no querystring or URL variable named error, so this if statement would evaluate to false. As you have seen, however, if the page has been redirected back to tourprice.asp from the form validation script on tourprice_processor.asp, the querystring exists with that value.

3) Nested between the opening and closing if lines, insert the code that tells ASP/ColdFusion to output the desired HTML.

In ASP:

```
Response.Write("<p>*** Error! One or more fields was left blank or contained
⇒a non-numeric character.</p>")
```

In ColdFusion:

```
<cfoutput><p>*** Error! One or more fields was left blank or contained a
⇒non-numeric character.</p></cfoutput>
```

In PHP:

```
{
  echo "<p>*** Error! One or more fields was left blank or contained a
⇒non-numeric character.</p>";
}
```

`Response.Write`, `<cfoutput>`, and echo can be used to output static or dynamic code. We've used them to output dynamic code thus far, but there is no reason why you can't put static code in there as well, or any combination of static and dynamic code.

```
24    <p>Enter the number of adults and children in your party as well as the tour name of the tour you want t
25    <p>All fields required (enter 0 if necessary). </p>
26
27    <%
28    If Request.QueryString("error") = "notnumeric" Then
29        Response.Write("<p>*** Error! One or more fields was left blank or contained a non-numeric character
30    End If
31    %>
32
33    <form name="frm_tourprice" id="frm_tourprice" method="post" action="tourprice_processor.asp">
34      <table width="60%"  border="0" cellspacing="0" cellpadding="3">
35        <tr>
36          <td>Number of Adults </td>
```

4) ColdFusion users only: Wrap the entire `<cfif>` script in another `<cfif>` script, so that the original `<cfif>` script only runs if the URL variable error actually exists.

```
<cfif isDefined("url.error")>
  <cfif url.error is "notnumeric">
    <cfoutput><p>*** Error! One or more fields was left blank or contained a
⇒non-numeric character.</p></cfoutput>
  </cfif>
</cfif>
```

```
24    <p>Enter the number of adults and children in your party, as well as the tour name of the tour you want
25    <p>All fields required (enter 0 if necessary).</p>
26
27    <cfif isDefined("url.error")>
28      <cfif url.error is "notnumeric">
29        <cfoutput><p>*** Error! One or more fields was left blank or contained a non-numeric character.</p><
30      </cfif>
31    </cfif>
32
33    <form name="frm_tourprice" id="frm_tourprice" method="post" action="tourprice_processor.cfm">
34      <table width="60%"  border="0" cellspacing="0" cellpadding="3">
35        <tr>
```

The function `isDefined` works much like `isNumeric`, except that rather than testing whether the parameter is a number, it tests to see whether the parameter exists.

This extra code is necessary in ColdFusion, because ColdFusion assumes that if you are testing a variable (`<cfif url.error = "notnumeric">`), then that variable exists. If it does not exist, and you attempt to test it, ColdFusion displays an error message. The error URL variable exists only when the page loads as a result of a redirection from the form validation on tourprice_processor.cfm. Thus, when the page first loads, an ugly error message dominates the page. We solve the problem by testing to ensure that url.error is defined. If it is not, then ColdFusion ignores the directions that test whether error's value is set to notnumeric. If url.error is defined, ColdFusion continues with the test, as before.

ASP and PHP differ from ColdFusion in this instance, in that if querystring.error is undefined, then the interpreter knows error can't be equal to notnumeric and it proceeds as expected.

5) Save and upload tourprice.asp. Test it in a browser.

The error message now appears when you fail to enter numbers in both fields.

There's only one problem left: The error message isn't very conspicuous, is it?

CREATING AND APPLYING A CUSTOM CSS CLASS

Making the error message more conspicuous is a matter of presentation. In XHTML, you should use CSS for presentation-related controls. XHTML has built-in styles for headings, body text, lists, and so forth, but XHTML lacks an <errormessage> tag that you can redefine with CSS. Fortunately, CSS enables developers to create custom styles, which can be applied to standard XHTML elements, such as the <p> tag.

In this task, you will create a custom CSS style, also called a class, just for error messages.

1) In the CSS Styles panel, click the New CSS Style button. In the dialog, select Class (can apply to any tag), and enter .error as the name. Use the Defined In field to verify that the new style is added to newland.css. Click OK.

The period (.) before the word error is obligatory, so don't leave it out.

You went through this process several times earlier in the book, so it should be familiar. Just remember that rather than redefining an existing tag, you are creating a custom class.

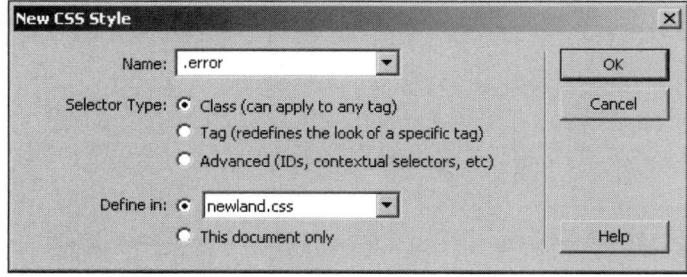

2) In the CSS Style Definition dialog, set the Weight as bold and the color as #990000, a deep red. Click OK.

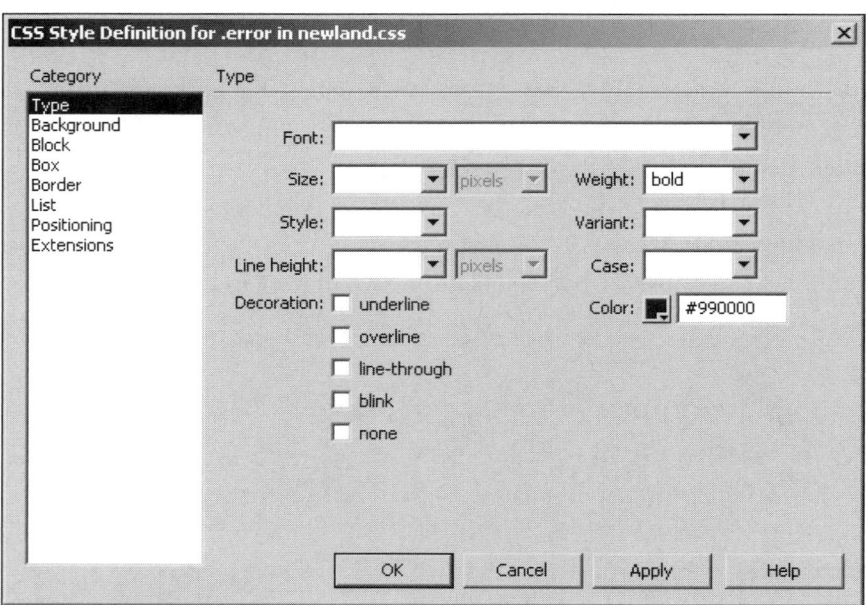

One of the advantages of CSS styles is that they inherit attributes of other styles that they don't explicitly contradict. This new class will be attached to the <p> tag that contains the error message. The <p> is already defined such that it uses a certain font, in a certain size, and so on. The .error class inherits all of that. When you create a CSS class, then, define only those attributes that are unique to that class—in this case, the fact that the text should be bold and red.

NOTE *Depending on the settings in Dreamweaver Preferences, the CSS style sheet document may have opened in Dreamweaver. If so, you can close it at this point.*

Now that the style is created, you need to apply it.

3) Using the Site panel, upload newland.css to the remote server.

Remember, the new .error style has been saved only locally, so if you don't upload the style sheet, you won't see any difference when you test the file.

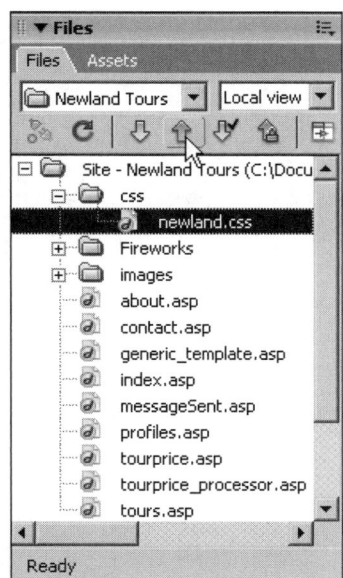

4) Back in code view, scroll to the `Response.Write`, `<cfoutput>`, **or** `<?php echo` **line that prints the error message, and modify its** `<p>` **tag so that it reads** `<p class="error">`.

To apply a CSS style to a tag, use the class attribute. Notice that the period is omitted in the class attribute.

5) ASP and PHP users only: Add a second pair of quotation marks (ASP) or a backslash (PHP) in front of each of the quotation marks in the class attribute.

In ASP, the tag should now read `<p class=""error"">`, and in PHP it should read `<p class=\"error\">`.

The second set of quotes (ASP) or backslash (PHP) is necessary, because the entire HTML string is embedded in quotes. If you use a normal set of quotation marks, ASP/PHP gets confused. By adding the extra quotes/backslash, you are communicating to ASP/PHP that it should treat these quotation marks as a part of the text string, rather than as the boundaries of the text string.

This additional step is unnecessary in ColdFusion, because the output text string in ColdFusion is enclosed in <cfoutput> tags and not quotation marks.

```
21   <td colspan="2">
22     <h1><br />
23       <a name="top" id="top"></a>Tour Price Calculator</h1>
24     <p>Enter the number of adults and children in your party as well as the tour name of the tour you war
25     <p>All fields required (enter 0 if necessary). </p>
26
27     <%
28     If Request.QueryString("error") = "notnumeric" Then
29         Response.Write("<p class=""error"">*** Error! One or more fields was left blank or contained a no
30     End If
31     %>
32
33     <form name="frm_tourprice" id="frm_tourprice" method="post" action="tourprice_processor.asp">
34       <table width="60%"  border="0" cellspacing="0" cellpadding="3">
35         <tr>
36           <td>Number of Adults </td>
```

6) Save, upload, and test the file.

For such a simple application, it took a fair amount of work. But the extra polish shows: The application is useful and usable. Now that it works, you need to remove the dummy dollar values and use real data. That requires working with databases, which is introduced in the next lesson.

WHAT YOU HAVE LEARNED

In this lesson, you have:

- Built a form using test field and drop-down menu elements (pages 198–204)

- Written a script that manipulates data the user entered (pages 204–206)

- Output the manipulated value and formatted it using a built-in function (pages 206–210)

- Written a script that performs server-side form validation (pages 210–214)

- Redirected the user to the first page, while appending a querystring (pages 212–214)

- Created and activated a conditional region, depending on the outcome of the server-side form validation (pages 214–217)

- Formatted the text in the conditional region using a custom CSS class (pages 217–220)

databases on the web

Developing dynamic Web pages is more difficult than developing static pages. Whereas static Web page development uses only a handful of technologies—XHTML, CSS, and FTP—dynamic Web page development uses these and many more, including ASP, ColdFusion, PHP, databases, servers, ODBC, and SQL, among others. In addition, dynamic Web page development, as you have already experienced, involves quite a bit more coding.

Lessons 4 through 7 introduced you to server-side scripting. You learned about passing data between pages, manipulating data, using built-in functions, displaying dynamic data, flow control using if…else statements, form validation, and more. This four-chapter introduction culminated in the code-intensive Lesson 7, where you wrote a number of scripts to build a simple application. I threw all that code at you deliberately, to help you overcome any trepidation you might have about writing server-side code, as well as to get you accustomed to the concepts and syntax of ASP, ColdFusion, and PHP.

Data in a database is stored in tables, which, at first glance, look like Excel spreadsheets.

This lesson marks a turning point in the book. I will take for granted henceforth that you are comfortable with the concepts and techniques for sending data from one page to the other, though I will continue to explain every script you produce, whether you handwrite it or use a Dreamweaver behavior. In this and the next several lessons, you will focus on working with databases. You will learn how to connect to a database, display data pulled from a database, and build forms that save data in a database.

Few people realize how deep and complex a topic databases are, until they start working with them. This lesson mainly consists of a crash course in databases, including a tour of the database I have prepared for you to use in the rest of the book, and tasks that have you connect your site to the database and display a block of text dynamically pulled from a database. While the last lesson was heavy on code, this lesson is heavy on theory, so make mental adjustments accordingly.

WHAT YOU WILL LEARN

In this lesson, you will:

- Learn core database terms and concepts
- Learn how databases are used to support Web sites
- Install and start up the MySQL database server (PHP users only)
- Tour the Newland database I have created for you
- Connect your copy of the site to the database
- Display a column of text pulled from the database on the site's homepage

APPROXIMATE TIME

This lesson takes approximately 75 minutes to complete.

LESSON FILES

Starting Files:

Lesson08/Start/newland_tours.mdb

*Lesson08/Start/newland_tours.sql
   (for PHP/MySql users only)*

Lesson08/Start/newland/index.asp

Completed Files:

Lesson08/Complete/newland/index.asp

A CRASH COURSE ON DATABASES

A tutorial-based book should keep you actively working, so I try to refrain from pausing the action for long-winded passages explaining esoterica. But you will not get very far developing dynamic Web sites if you do not have a solid familiarity (though not necessarily expertise) with databases. In this section, I'll introduce you to basic database concepts and vocabulary, using Microsoft Access as the running example. The layout of the data (and the data itself) in MySQL is the same as it is in Access. However, Access has a better user interface, so all the screenshots are from Access. I strongly encourage you to spend additional time learning to work with databases, as you continue to master dynamic Web site development. For now, this section should be enough to get you started.

Though MySQL looks radically different from Access, all of the critical concepts still apply. Some of the following discussion is Access-centric, and where MySQL has no equivalent, I'll make a note of it.

INTRODUCING DATABASE OBJECTS

In the simplest terms, a database is a system of storage for data. But in contemporary use, the term database generally means a lot more—certainly in the case of Microsoft Access or MySQL, or an enterprise-level database system, such as Microsoft SQL Server or Oracle. Each of these is a **relational database management system** (RDBMS). The RDBMS model was developed in the 1970s and 1980s to enable database managers to store data in a way that reflected relationships between different types of data. We'll return to the idea of relationships momentarily, but first you should understand the objects that make up databases.

Data in a database is stored in **tables**. At first glance, tables look like Excel spreadsheets, in that they are made of rows and columns. The columns, called **fields**, contain a single category of information. The rows, called **records**, contain a single set of information comprising one element of data for each field. For example, in a table called tbl_customers, you might expect to find fields for first name, address, city, state, postal code, phone number, and so on. Each individual customer would have her or his own record.

The accompanying figure shows a table from the Newland database as it appears in Access. This table contains basic information about countries. You can easily see each country listed in a row in the countryName field, and you'll see that each country has the same type of information listed. You can edit tables directly by clicking in a cell and typing away, but there is a better way, which is to use an interface, such as Access forms or a Web form.

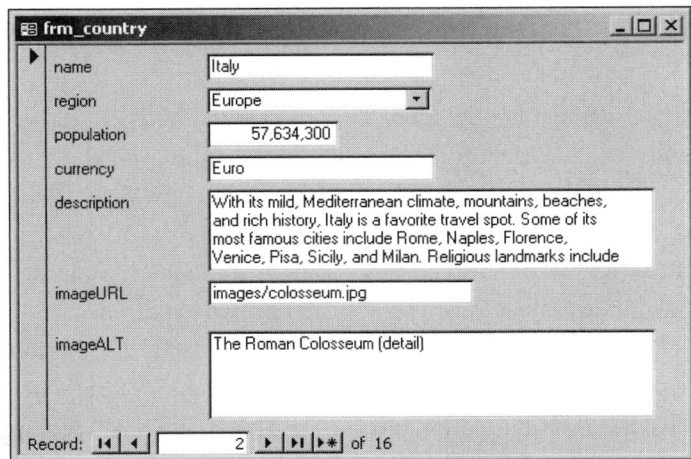

Tables aren't the only type of object you can expect to find in databases. Also of note are forms, reports, and queries. **Forms** are used to insert new data and modify existing data. The form used to build the country table shown in the preceding screenshot can be seen in the following screenshot. Forms make it easy to insert and edit information, and you can also use them to control the type of information entered, which helps ensure the integrity of the data entered. At the bottom of the form is a group of record navigation buttons, which you can use to access the record you want to edit, or to create a new record from scratch.

NOTE *By itself MySQL lacks a GUI interface. Commands are issued to MySQL through the command line. It is, however, possible to download a GUI interface for MySQL, such as phpmyadmin. However, no MySQL interface has the same level of depth and complexity as that of Access. MySQL handles the important part—data storage and access—arguably better than Microsoft Access, but MySQL's interface is minimalist, at best.*

225

Whereas forms are a means of inputting information into tables, **reports** are a means of outputting that data. You probably noticed that it was impossible to read all of the information in the table directly, because the fields weren't wide enough to accommodate all the text. You can use reports to make data presentable. Better yet, you can selectively show only some data in reports, rather than showing all of it, which makes reports much more useful.

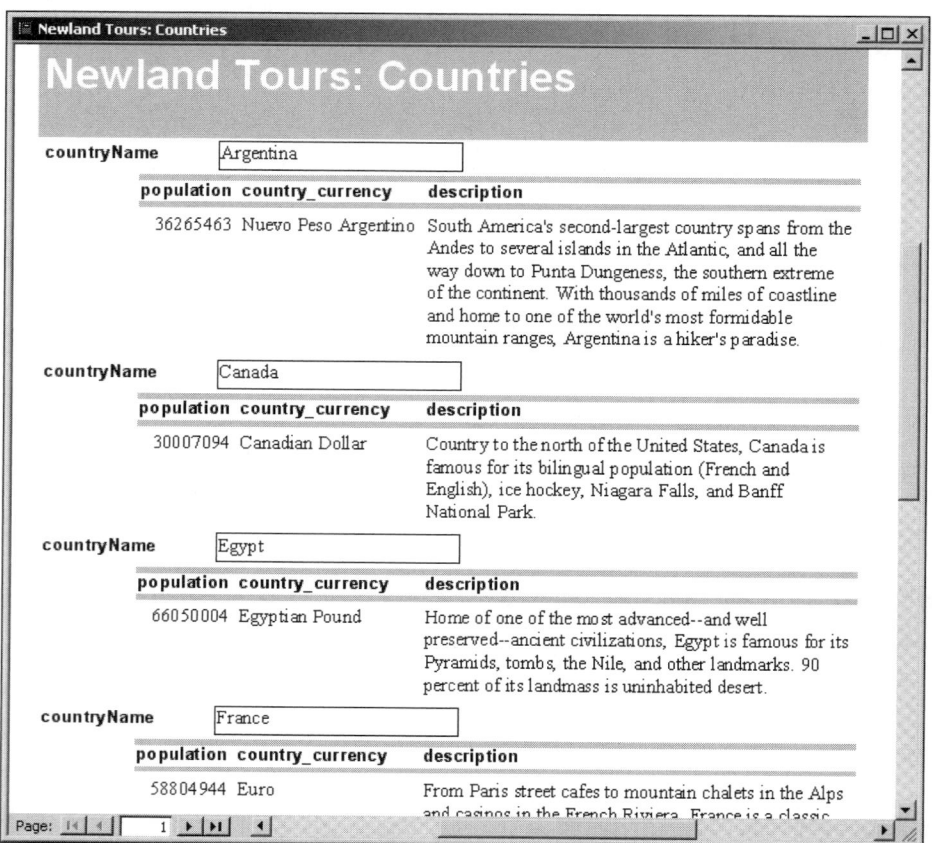

You use **queries** to show data selectively in reports. Queries are like searches: You provide certain criteria, and the database returns a report. For example, you could obtain a report of all the countries in the Newland database that begin with T, which would return Taiwan and Thailand. Queries are written in a language called **SQL**, or **Structured Query Language**. You will use SQL heavily when working with databases, beginning with this chapter, because you must use SQL to retrieve data from a database to make it available for Web pages via ASP, ColdFusion, or PHP. The reason for this is that SQL is the primary means that developers have to communicate with database systems. Access has a visual SQL editor, but you can't use it in Dreamweaver. In Dreamweaver, you can hand-code SQL or use Dreamweaver's visual SQL editor.

Familiarity with SQL is a prerequisite for dynamic Web application development. You'll learn a fair amount in this book, but for an easy-to-read and comprehensive introduction, check out *SQL: Visual QuickStart Guide* (Peachpit Press).

The SQL snippet in the accompanying screenshot retrieves all of the records in the countryName, population, country_currency, and description fields of the tbl_country table.

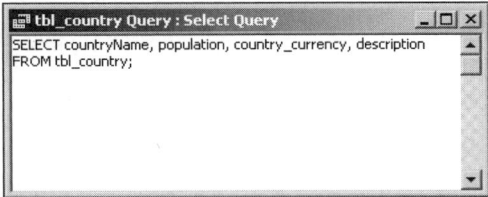

UNDERSTANDING RELATIONSHIPS

Relationships are a crucial concept when it comes to working with modern databases. They enable developers to specify how different database tables are connected with one another through shared data. By creating relationships, database designers are able to model data into tables that reflect reality and enable efficient maintenance of data over time. I have created the database file you will use for the book, and it already has many relationships in place. While you won't be creating any more relationships, you will often need to retrieve and use data from more than one table together, and you can't do this unless you understand relationships.

NOTE *The concept of relationships is not dependent on any particular database management system. That is, this discussion applies equally to Access and MySQL, as well as any database you are likely to use for Web development, including Microsoft SQL Server, Oracle, or PostgreSQL.*

It is perhaps easiest to understand relationships by following an example. Imagine you use an Excel spreadsheet to store information about financial transactions at your company. You want to store each transaction as a separate row, so you create a spreadsheet with the following columns:

f_name	l_name	str_add	city	state/prov	country	postal	cred_card	subtotal	tax	total

Over time, hundreds of records are added to this spreadsheet. Many of these records are for repeat customers. The problem is, each time a customer returns her or his address information is stored again. As time passes, some of these repeat customers move. Their new addresses are duly entered in the spreadsheet, but all of the former records have the old address. Chances are, sooner or later, someone will inadvertently use the wrong address. Updating these addresses is hard, because there are so many; and, unfortunately, in Excel there's not much you can do about this problem.

A more logical way to represent the transaction is to separate the customer from the transaction. One table would track individual sales, but the customer information would be stored in a separate table for customers. The customer table would have one and only one record for each customer. If a customer moved, you would need to update only the single record that applied to the customer, not all of the records of his or her transactions. Then, back in the transaction table, instead of listing all of the customer information, you would list a unique identifier that referenced the customer in the customer table. Databases enable you to create this type of relationship between tables.

NOTE *If you've ever wondered why catalog companies have product IDs or customer IDs that you have to refer to, this is why: Those IDs are unique numbers in their database that refer to you and only you, or to a given product and only that product.*

Thus, the customer table would look as follows:

cust_ID	F_name	l_name	str_add	city	state/prov	postal	credit_card

And the transaction table would look as follows:

transaction_ID	cust_ID	subtotal	tax	total

Notice that both tables have a field for cust_ID. The cust_ID in the customer table is a unique identifier in that table, also called the **primary key**. No two columns in this table will ever have the same cust_ID. It's possible that there will be two John Smiths, and it's possible that two people will reside at postal code 90210. But each row is guaranteed to be unique, because each row has its own unique primary key, cust_ID.

In contrast, the cust_ID in the transaction table could be repeated multiple times—this would mean that the same customer had ordered more than one time. When you use the primary key of one table as a field in a different table, it is referred to as a **foreign key**. By placing foreign keys in tables, you create **relationships** between tables. Again, the benefit of doing this is that you remove redundant information and better maintain the integrity of your data.

NOTE *To facilitate the discussion, I've simplified these tables. For example, you would normally expect to see a third table to handle products (that is, an inventory table), with product_ID used as the foreign key in the transaction table. Also, this example assumes that a customer can have only a single credit card. Obviously, you can add new tables, fields, and relationships to handle these realities.*

The following figure shows the relationships between the two tables described in this example. The line between the two tables indicates the relationship. The number 1 on the left side indicates that in the tbl_customers table, the cust_ID is unique, while the infinity character on the right indicates that cust_ID can appear many times. This is known as a one-to-many relationship.

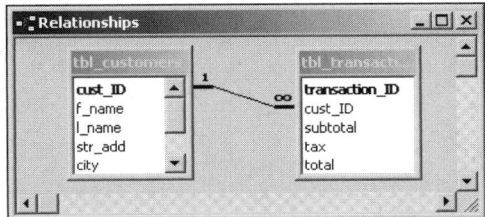

The power of relationships extends beyond preventing redundancy. For example, you can write a SQL query that pulls data out of both tables, using certain criteria. For instance, you could write a query that lists all of the first and last names of customers who spent over $100. You can also create forms that write to more than one table.

TIP *A copy of this simple database can be found on the CD-ROM in Microsoft Access format, in Lesson08/Start/transaction.mdb.*

DATABASES ON THE WEB

Now that you have a sense for what databases look like and what they can do, you should be primed to understand how they work on the Web.

Database content is used on the Web in many different ways. The simplest way—which you'll do yourself at the end of this lesson—is to display the contents of a field on the Web. But you can display more than a simple string of text. You can also display multiple fields, populate menus, and handle user authentication. In addition to reading and displaying information, you can also collect it and store it in database tables. Using this technique, you can create user registration, surveys, quizzes, and content management systems.

TIP *Content management systems let users add or modify site content without having to know any HTML, buy any special software, or worry about uploading files, using Web forms and databases. The user types the site content into a Web form. This content is then stored in a database and output to a different Web page.*

If you compare database-driven Web pages to the Access database objects discussed earlier in the lesson, you'll realize that you can effectively use Web pages and Web forms as a surrogate for database reports and forms. Pages that output and display data are like reports, while pages with Web forms can perform the same function as database forms. The advantage to such a system is that users don't need Access or MySQL (or whichever RDBMS your organization uses) to maintain its content, and users can be distributed all over the world and still have access to the data storage, thanks to the Internet. Better still, because you aren't giving users direct access to the database, you decrease the likelihood of your data being compromised (maliciously or inadvertently).

So much for the cool features; now how does it all work? Just as you have access to files sitting on your hard drive, so a user has access to files sitting on a server's hard drive. An Internet user does not have permission to start modifying files on any server—that would be a security nightmare. But you can give applications on your system access to certain files.

One way is to use Windows' ODBC, which enables you to create a **data source name** (DSN) that lets ASP or ColdFusion to read and write to your Access database. The relationship is depicted in the following figure.

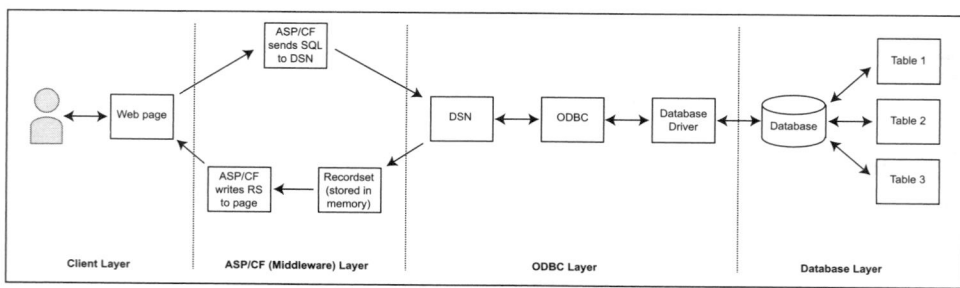

There's a lot going on in this figure. Before I deconstruct it, though, notice how far the user is from the actual data; this complex sequence enables the user to access data, but protects the data from convenient access, providing some measure of security.

Let's look at the figure in detail. You'll notice the figure is divided into four different regions: the client layer, the middleware layer, the ODBC layer, and the database layer.

The client layer includes static HTML interpreted by the browser. This static HTML may have been coded as static HTML, or as dynamic HTML, but as you know, by the time it is returned to the browser, it's all static HTML.

ODBC has all of the information needed to access the database, including the appropriate database driver and the path to the database. These two pieces of information are stored in ODBC and are referred to using the DSN.

Finally, the SQL reaches the database itself, and it looks in the proper table(s) and retrieves the appropriate information.

So much for the way in. On the way out, the data is sent back the same way it came in, until it gets to the middleware layer. At this point, the data retrieved is stored in the server's memory (RAM). It is not actually on the page yet. A set of data stored in memory as the result of a query is called a **recordset**. You use ASP or ColdFusion to output the recordset data (or any subset of it) inside the HTML, much as you did with form variables, so that the user can see it.

PHP/MySQL doesn't work exactly the same way, since it doesn't make use of ODBC. Instead, you provide the information the PHP processor needs to access the database directly in the code. I'll cover the details later in the chapter, but the gist is that PHP has a special function (`mysql_connect()`) used for connecting to a MySQL database. When you use this function, you provide a path to the database server as well as username and password credentials. Then you use another function (`mysql_select_db()`) to specify the name of the MySQL database that you want to access. MySQL can contain numerous databases; in contrast, in Access, each database is stored in its own *.mdb file. At any rate, though PHP and MySQL use a slightly different approach, the process is, in a generic way, similar.

N O T E   *ODBC drivers for MySQL are available, but Dreamweaver doesn't use ODBC to connect PHP pages to MySQL, so you don't have to worry about installing ODBC drivers for MySQL.*

DATABASE SECURITY AND THE WEB

Security is a major issue with dynamic applications that link to data sources. The integrity (and usually confidentiality) of a company's data is vital to that's company's interests. If you read the news, you know that malicious users are out there who try very hard to hack into other organizations' databases and business logic. But, ironically, an equally dangerous threat comes not from malicious users at all, but rather from well-intentioned employees making mistakes while doing their job.

Security issues are largely beyond the scope of this book, but the following bullets offer suggestions for protecting the integrity of your database from yourself and/or end users. For more information, see Macromedia's Security Development Center, a free resource containing dozens of articles, white papers, tips, tutorials, and more. It can be found at http://www.macromedia.com/devnet/security/.

To maintain the integrity of your data, consider:

- Checking all user input for correct data type and format. That is, in a field that holds phone numbers, make sure that any data a user tries to enter is composed of digits and has the correct number digits.

- Letting the database do manipulation of data (via SQL) rather than the application where possible.

- Setting proper constraints on tables and fields to prevent users from inputting bad data.

- Having users choose from a menu of permissible options rather than letting them input free-form text where appropriate.

Implementing these features doesn't guarantee that data cannot be compromised, but it is a significant step in the right direction. As you develop, be sure to keep these considerations in mind throughout the project design and development phases.

INSTALLING AND RUNNING MYSQL

This section is only for those running PHP locally on a Windows or Macintosh OS X system. If you are using ASP or ColdFusion in any configuration, or you are using PHP on a remote server (e.g., via Intranet or FTP), skip to the next section, "Touring the Newland Database."

The process of installing MySQL on Windows and Macintosh systems is quite different, so I've broken each one out into its own section.

INSTALLING AND RUNNING MYSQL IN WINDOWS

The easiest way to get MySQL running on a Windows machine is to download and use a MySQL installer. Once MySQL is installed, you can start it up and start using it.

1) Go to http://www.mysql.com, navigate to the downloads page, and download the Windows installer to your hard drive.

If necessary, unzip the file to a folder on your hard drive.

2) Double-click setup.exe to start the installation. Use the default directory, c:\mysql.

Although you can specify a different directory, doing so requires some extra work—
you'll need to create a configuration file that points to the directory you choose,
whereas if you choose the default, you don't have to worry about creating the
configuration file.

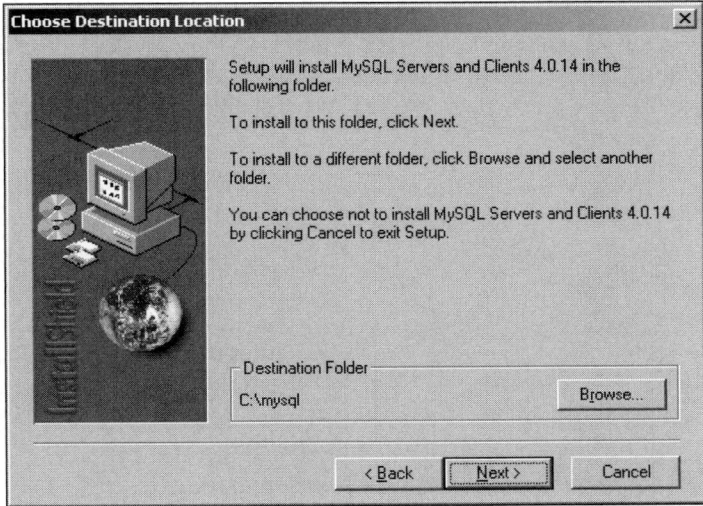

3) Continue through the installation, accepting all the defaults.

Once the installer completes, phpmyadmin is installed. However, it is not yet running.
In Windows, you run MySQL as a service. To activate the service, you use a Windows
MySQL utility called WinMySqlAdmin.

4) In Windows Explorer, look in c:\mysql\bin.

This folder contains the applications related to mysql, including WinMySqlAdmin.

5) Double-click winmysqladmin.exe.

You'll be prompted for a username and password.

Once you provide this information, WinMySqlAdmin starts up MySQL as a service.
It also places a stoplight icon in the task bar, which indicates whether MySQL is
running. The light should be green, indicating that it is running.

233

By right-clicking the traffic light, and choosing Show Me, you can see the WinMySQLadmin console, which provides information about MySQL and which can be used to specify various configuration options.

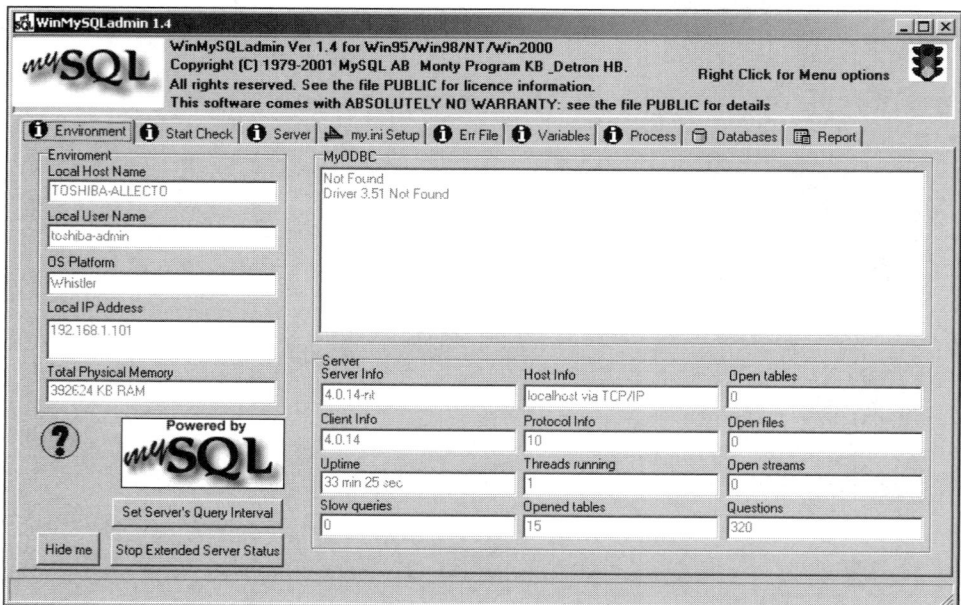

Now that you have installed MySQL and started it, you can create and populate the Newland Tours database and begin using it for site development.

6) Copy newland_tours.sql from the Lesson08/Start folder to the C:\mysql folder on your hard drive.

The exact location of the file doesn't matter too much, but in a moment you'll have to type its path, so it's best to copy it into an easily accessible directory.

7) Using Windows Explorer, navigate to C:\mysql\bin, and double-click mysql.exe to open the mysql command prompt.

The mysql> prompt appears.

8) At the mysql> **prompt, type the following to generate the newland_tours database in your copy of MySQL. Press Enter.**

```
source C:\mysql\newland_tours.sql
```

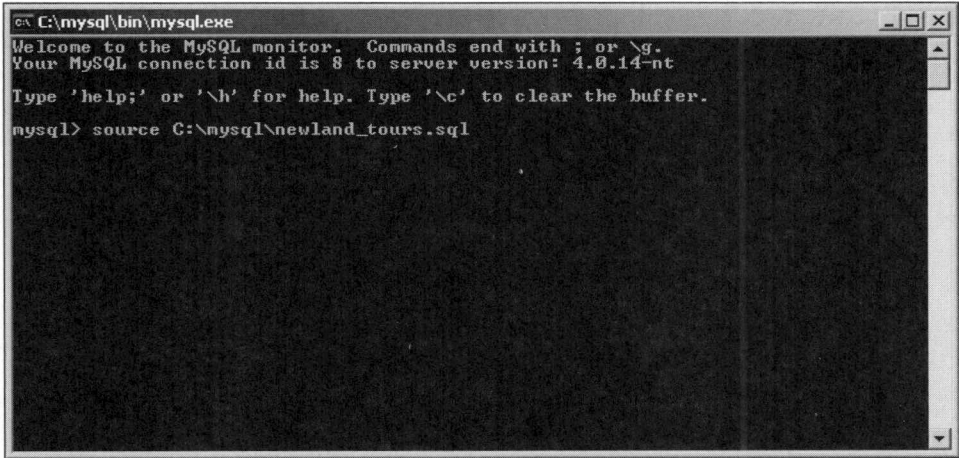

The source command is used to run one or more SQL commands stored in an external document. If you open newland_tours.sql in a text editor, you'll see all the code needed to create the newland database, tell MySQL to start using that database, provide instructions to generate each of the six tables in the database, and finally populate each of those tables with data.

Once you press Enter, MySQL goes to work, outputting dozens of success messages that fly by your screen too fast to read, until it reaches the end.

The newland_tours database is properly installed and running in MySQL. You can skip ahead to the section, "Touring the Newland Database."

Installing and Running MySQL in OS X

Installing MySQL on a Macintosh OS X is quite easy, because installers are already available. However, turning on the database requires that you go into the Terminal and type some code at the command prompt.

1) Go to http://www.mysql.com and download the installer file for Macintosh OS X.2.

The file should download directly to your desktop and auto-extract.

2) Double-click the mysql-standard-4.0.14 icon.

Note that the version number may be different.

3) In the Finder window, double-click the mysql-standard-[version].pkg file to begin installation.

The files themselves are installed in the /usr/local/mysql-[version] directory, but a symbolic link (or shortcut) is created, so that you can always access MySQL via /usr/local/mysql/. The actual program files that you'll use to run and maintain MySQL can be found in the bin subdirectory.

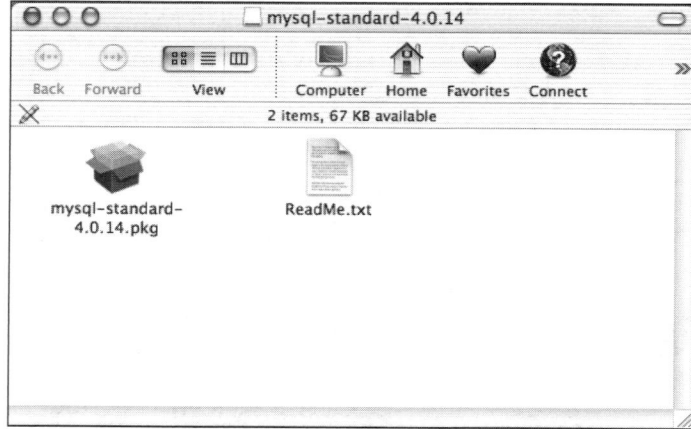

4) Continue clicking through the wizard until the software is installed.

You can accept the defaults all the way through. When it is done, MySQL is installed, but it is probably not running.

236

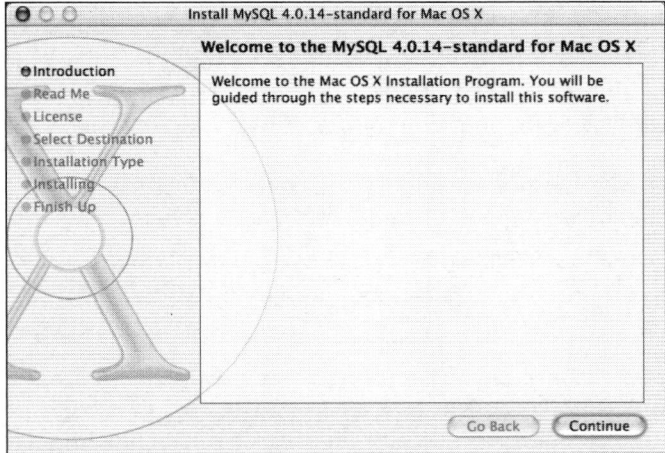

5) To start MySQL, open the Terminal (Applications/Utilities/Terminal).

Unless (and until) you install a separate interface for MySQL, you access it via the command line.

6) Log in as the root user: To do so, type su**, press Return, and when prompted, enter the root password.**

To run MySQL, you must be logged into the Terminal as the all-powerful root user. This step assumes that you have some familiarity with working in the Macintosh OS X implementation of the Unix environment.

7) Switch to the MySQL directory by typing cd /usr/local/mysql**.**

Remember, you can type ls at any time to see a listing of the files and directories within the current directory.

8) To start up MySQL, type bin/mysqld_safe &**.**

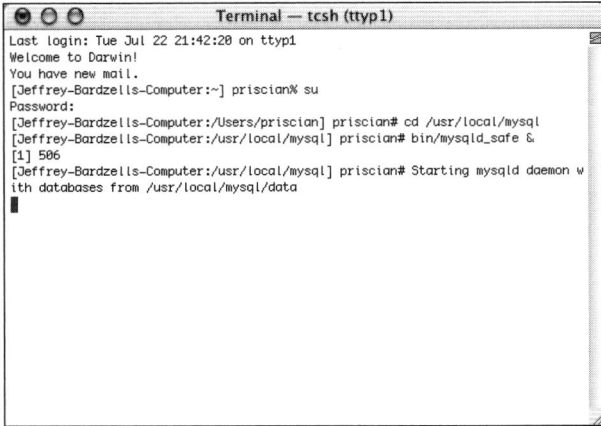

`mysqld_safe &` is the command used to start up the MySQL daemon and keep it running in the background. If this command doesn't work, try typing `./bin/mysqld_safe &` instead. If it still doesn't work, type `cd bin/` to enter the bin directory, and type `mysqld_safe &` or `./mysqld_safe &`.

As long as you are logged in, MySQL will run and will be available. As soon as you log off, shut down, or restart your Macintosh, MySQL will shutdown and will not restart unless you go back to the Terminal, log in, navigate to the usr/local/mysql directory, and re-execute the `mysqld_safe &` command from the bin directory.

TIP *You can write a simple script that executes this command for you automatically every time you log in. A quick Web search should result in a number of sample scripts.*

9) Copy the file newland_tours.sql from the Lesson08/Start folder on the CD to your desktop.

Though it doesn't matter where on your hard drive you save the file, the subsequent steps assume you save it on your desktop.

10) In the terminal window, open the mysql command line interface. To do so, assuming you are in the mysql directory (/usr/local/mysql), type the following command and press Return. Enter your password, and press Return again.

```
./bin/mysql -p
```

The mysql> prompt appears.

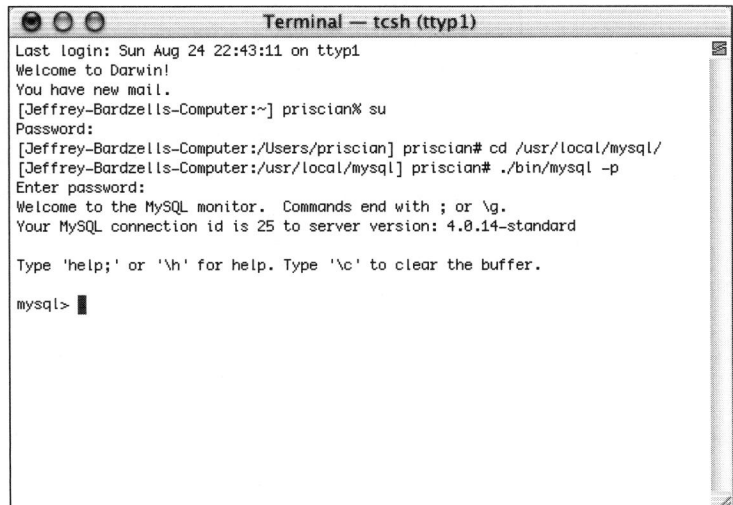

**11) At the prompt, type *source /Users/[username]/Desktop/newland_tours.sql*
and press Enter.**

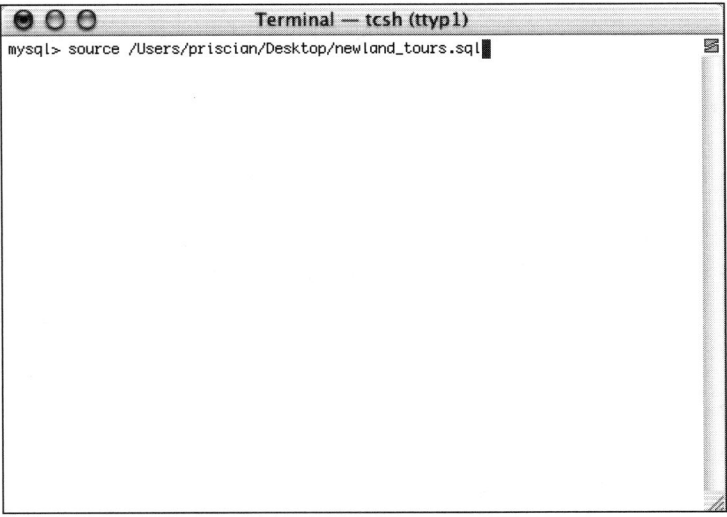

Make sure you replace [username] with your actual login name. Also, remember that
UNIX is case-sensitive.

The source command is used to run one or more SQL commands stored in an external document. If you open newland_tours.sql in a text editor, you'll see all the code needed to create the newland database, tell MySQL to start using that database, provide instructions to generate each of the six tables in the database, and finally populate each of those tables with data.

Once you press Enter, MySQL goes to work, outputting dozens of success messages that fly by your screen too fast to read, until it reaches the end.

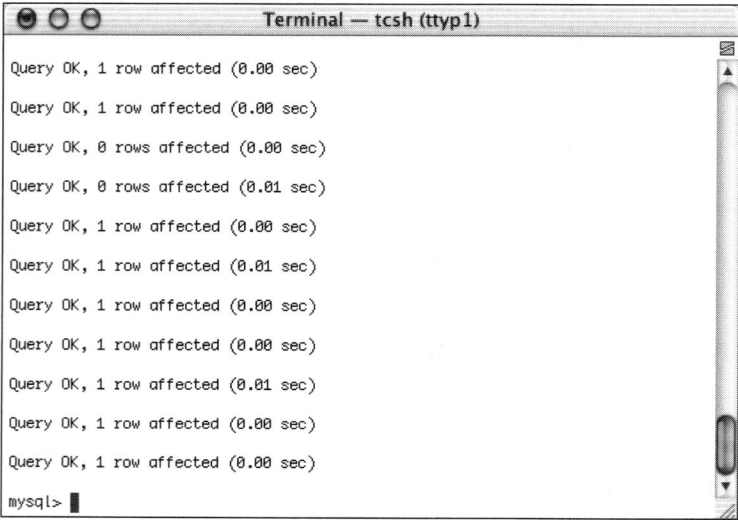

The newland_tours database is properly installed and running in MySQL. You can skip ahead to the section, "Touring the Newland Database."

INSTALLING THE NEWLAND TOURS DATABASE ON A REMOTE SERVER

Unfortunately, I can't tell you how to install the newland_tours database into a remote MySQL server. Only your ISP can tell you how to do it.

In my experience, many Linux-based ISPs offer a utility for maintaining MySQL databases remotely, called phpMyAdmin. phpMyAdmin is a Web-based interface, which lists all of the databases to which your account has access. It lets you view the data in your databases, see the SQL code used to generate each table, and it has a host of database maintenance features that make it easy to add new tables, modify existing ones, and even drop tables and even whole databases. The following screenshot provides a glimpse of phpMyAdmin.

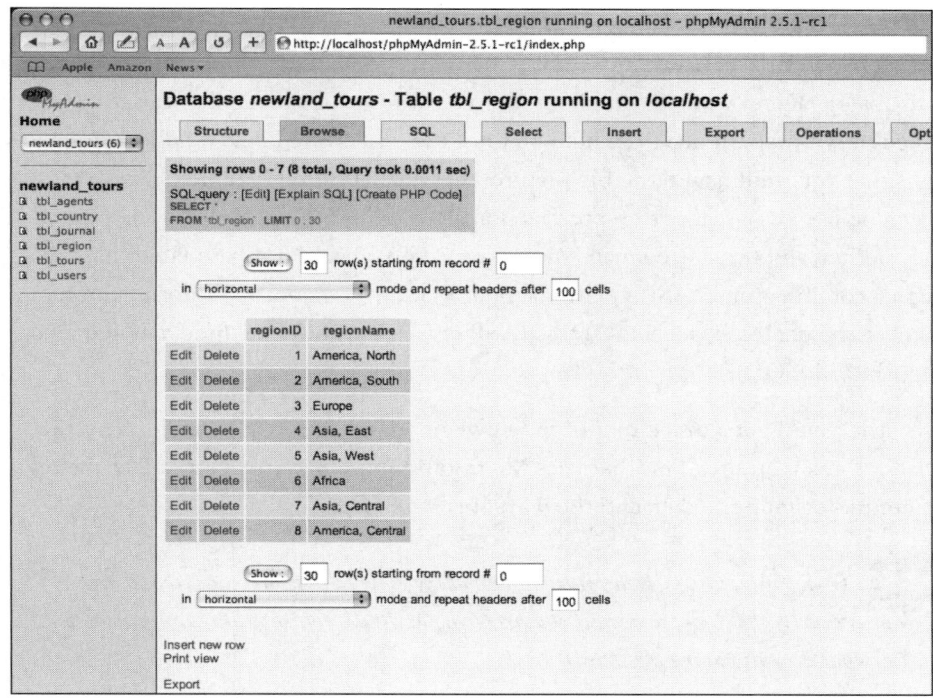

One of the benefits of phpMyAdmin is that it lets users generate tables using SQL stored in an external text file. You can use this feature to install the newland_tours database on a remote server running phpMyAdmin. Before you can do so, you'll need to copy the newland_tours.sql file from the Lesson08/Start folder on the CD to your computer. Open the file and delete the following two lines of code:

```
CREATE DATABASE newland_tours;
USE newland_tours;
```

The new first line of code should begin DROP TABLE IF EXISTS.

The reason for this change is that you create the database directly in phpMyAdmin, so these two lines of code would be redundant.

Once the file is prepared, you can install the database using phpMyAdmin. To begin, log in and create a new database called newland_tours. Follow the link to open this database in phpMyAdmin, if necessary. Click the SQL tab, and near the bottom of the page, click the Choose File button to browse to the newland_tour.sql file included in the Lesson08/Start folder on the CD. Proceed to run the file and the database will be populated.

NOTE *Those developing with local copies of MySQL may be interested to know that phpMyAdmin can be downloaded for free, at the following URL: http://www.phpmyadmin.net/*

TOURING THE NEWLAND DATABASE

DSNs, SQL, ODBC, relationships, tables, queries, forms, reports, recordsets—that's a lot to absorb! Don't worry if you don't feel as if you've mastered all of this yet. You'll get lots of experience from here on until the end of the book. The important thing is that you understand the big picture: that data is stored in tables; that the Web can be used as a read/write interface for these tables; that tables may be related to one another; and that the connection between the Web and database tables happens through a combination of ASP, ColdFusion, or PHP; SQL code; and information to connect to the database, such as ODBC (ASP or ColdFusion) or a direct connection string (PHP/MySQL).

In this task, you'll get a quick tour of the newland_tours database that will drive the Newland Tours Web site. This tour uses Microsoft Access, because its interface makes it easy to understand the data and the ways it is structured.

NOTE *Though MySQL lacks an interface anything close to that of Access, the structure of the data is exactly the same, so even if you are using MySQL, you should read through this section (without actually doing the steps.)*

1) ASP and ColdFusion users only, copy the entire Lesson08/Start/newland-asp/ folder into an appropriate location on the server (see below for details).

If you are developing ASP or ColdFusion on your local computer, and you are using Windows XP, paste the database folder into the Shared Documents folder, which you can access in My Computer. By placing the database folder and the Access database file (newland_tours.mdb) in this directory, you ensure that the proper permissions are applied so that ASP/ColdFusion and Dreamweaver can access the database.

If you are developing ASP or ColdFusion alongside IIS on your local computer, and you are using Windows 2000, paste the database folder in the C:\Inetpub\wwwroot\ newland directory. Remember, everything in wwwroot is on your local Web server and accessible through localhost.

If you are developing ColdFusion using the standalone Web server on your local computer, and you are using Windows 2000, paste the database folder in the C:\CFusionMX\wwwroot\newland directory.

If you are developing ASP or ColdFusion and are using a remote server, such as an Intranet server or at your ISP via FTP, put the newland_tours.mdb file wherever the server administrator tells you to put databases. This varies by ISP.

2) If you have Access, open newland_tours.mdb, which is inside the database folder you just copied.

If you do not have Access, then follow along reading the text and looking at the screenshots.

When you open the database file, you see a window that lists several object categories on the left side, and a group of objects on the right. The object categories are the same as the ones discussed earlier in the lesson.

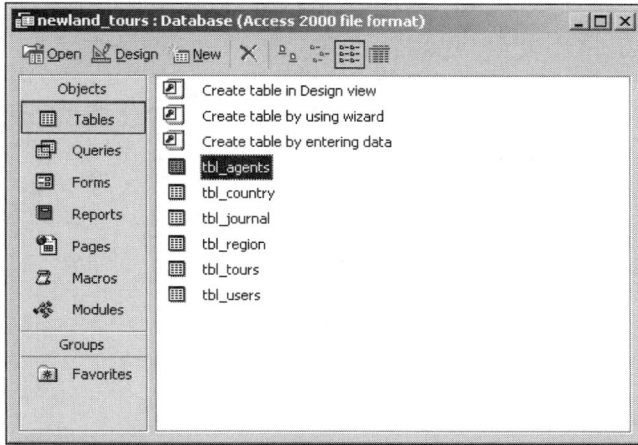

3) Click each of the objects listed on the left in turn, to see the objects that already exist in the database.

As you can see, six tables are in the Tables category, and a corresponding number of forms are in the Forms category. The remaining categories are empty.

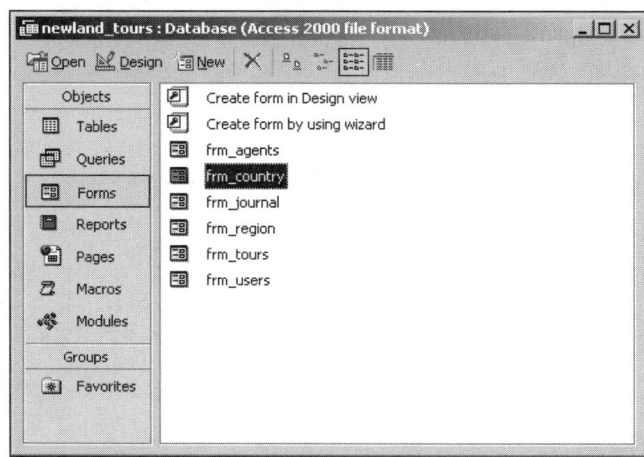

243

4) In the Tables group, double-click to open each of the tables to see what they contain.

Some of the tables have more data than others. The two tables with the most information are tbl_country and tbl_tours—these will be used to populate the Country Profile and Find a Tour segments.

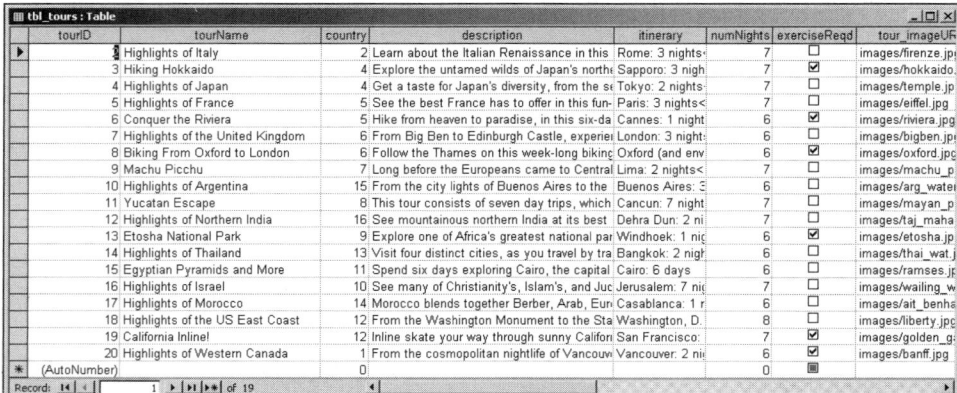

When you open tbl_journal, you'll see that it contains the text used in the Traveler's Journal section of the homepage.

The tbl_agents table is odd in that it contains only numbers, and no names as you might expect. The reason for this is that these numbers are actually foreign keys—the user is userID from tbl_users and the specialty is regionID from tbl_region.

The tbl_users table contains information used for logging in and authenticating at the site. When users register, their information is stored in this table. Notice that there are two categories in the userGroup field: admin and visitor. Users can access different areas of the site, depending on their userGroup category.

Close the tables window to return to the main screen.

5) In the Forms group, open each of the forms, navigating through records to see what they contain.

The forms, again, are convenient interfaces through which one can enter data into the tables. You won't use these in the Newland Tours site—forms aren't accessible through the Web, so you will create your own Web forms to replace them. But I used these to create the tables used in the site, and I left them in place, so you could explore them.

244

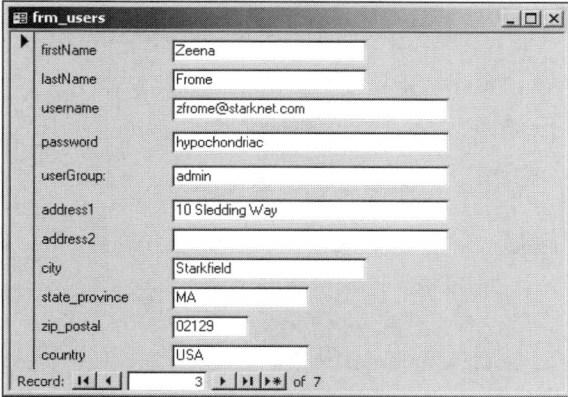

6) Click the Relationships button on the toolbar.

Access has a convenient visual interface that lets you view and modify relationships among tables.

RELATIONSHIPS
BUTTON

7) Review the relationships among the different tables.

The bold field in each table is its primary key. Foreign keys are linked to primary keys by a line. Do you remember how tbl_agents had only numbers in it? Now you can see why. The table comprises a primary key (agentID) and two foreign keys (user and specialty). Notice also that tbl_journal isn't linked to any other tables. Not every table needs to be part of a relationship.

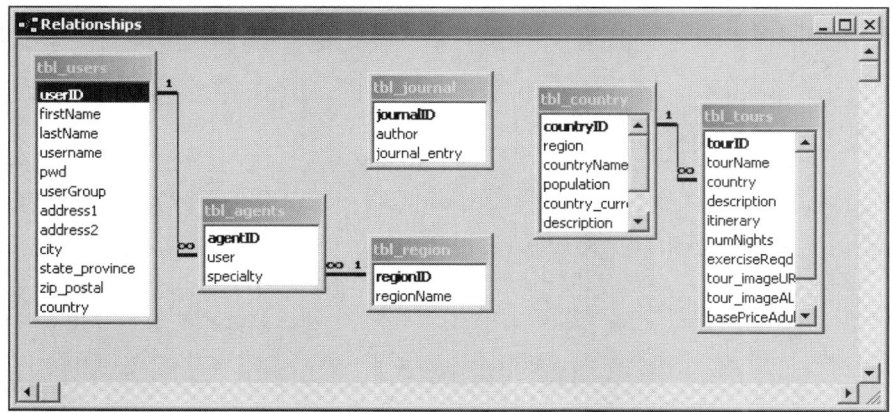

245

8) Do any further exploring without making any changes, and then close all open windows and Access.

You've now had a crash course in Access and familiarized yourself with a bona fide database.

CONNECTING TO A DATABASE

Enough theory and exploration: It's time to connect this database to your pages. As you must have gathered, a number of preliminary steps are involved to get everything set up. And the steps vary depending on how you are connecting to your server and the server technology (ASP, ColdFusion, or PHP) you are using.

For ASP and ColdFusion users, there are two steps you need to take to connect to a database. First, you have to create the DSN on the server, so you can take advantage of an ODBC connection. Remember, the DSN is simply a pointer to your database that you register on the server. Second, you have to get Dreamweaver to see this DSN, so it can ensure that scripts on individual pages can access the database through this DSN.

PHP/MySQL doesn't use ODBC or DSNs; instead, you provide the connection information—database location and name, as well as login credentials—directly in your PHP code. As you'll see, Dreamweaver lets you enter this information in a dialog, and then Dreamweaver writes a generic connection file, to which it refers every time you create a page that refers to your database.

The variations in configuring the database are so extreme that rather than attempting to create a generic set of instructions, I've separated them.

ASP USERS (RUNNING IIS LOCALLY OR CONNECTING TO A REMOTE SERVER)

This section is for all ASP users, regardless of how they connect to their server.

In this section, you will configure Dreamweaver to connect to an existing DSN. ASP users who are working locally will need to first setup the DSN, and instructions to do so are included in this section. Then they will enable Dreamweaver to connect to that DSN.

ASP users who connect to a remote server must have the administrator for that server create a system DSN for them, using the following information: The DSN should be called "newland." The database type is Microsoft Access (which uses the JET driver). The database is located in the newland/database folder in your directory. Assuming you have in fact copied the database folder to that directory, your server administrator has enough information to create the DSN for you. Unfortunately, you cannot continue until this DSN has been created. Once it has, you'll use the steps in this section to enable Dreamweaver to connect to that DSN.

246

1) Open index.asp.

It doesn't matter which page of your site is open when initially creating the connection. Dreamweaver creates the connection for the whole site. You've opened index.asp, because you will add dynamic content to that page, shortly.

2) Open the Databases panel, in the Application panel group. Click the Connection (+) button, and choose Data Source Name (DSN).

This opens the Data Source Name dialog, which is used to create a database connection for the site.

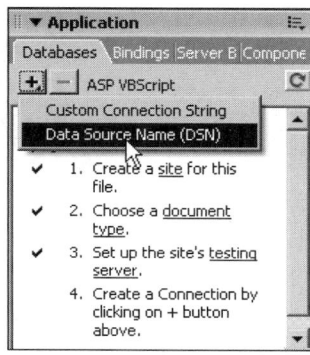

3) Users connecting to remote servers, skip to step 8 below. Users running IIS locally only: Click the Define button to begin the process of creating a System DSN.

The ODBC Data Source Administrator dialog opens. This is a Windows dialog, not a Dreamweaver dialog, which you can also access using the Control Panel.

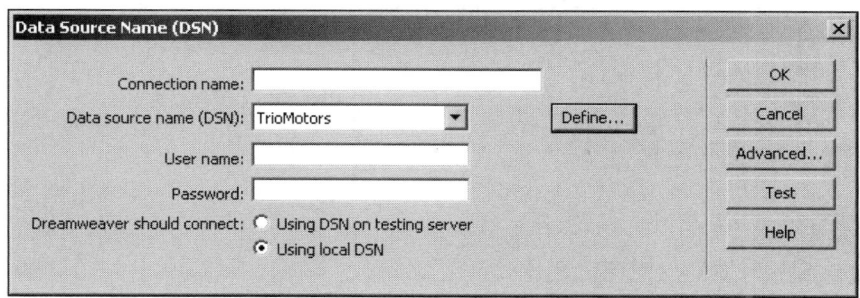

4) Click the System DSN tab.

To give Web access to your data source, you must add the DSN using the System DSN tab, and not the User DSN tab that appears by default.

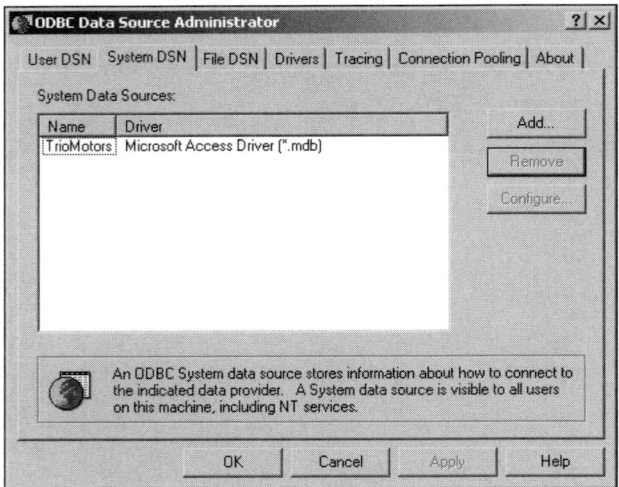

5) Click the Add button. In the Create New Data Source dialog, choose Microsoft Access Drive (*.mdb) from the dialog, and click Finish.

A DSN needs three pieces of information: The driver needed to communicate with the database, a name for the DSN, and the path to the database on the server. In this dialog, you provide the first piece of information.

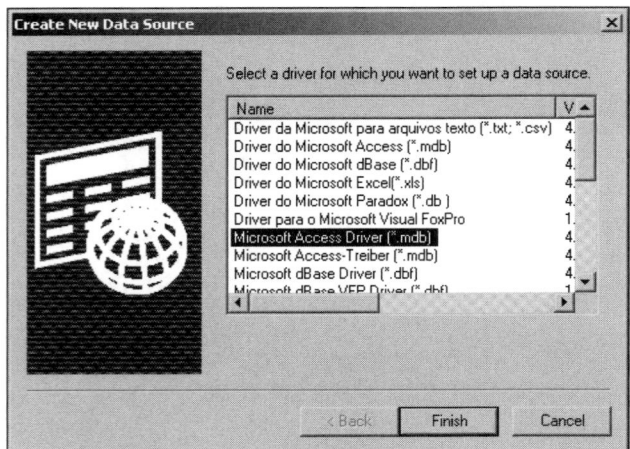

6) In the ODBC Microsoft Access Setup dialog that appears, type *newland* as the Data Source Name. Click the Select button, and in the Select Database dialog, browse to the newland_tours.mdb file, which should be in the following directory for Windows XP users: C:\Documents and Settings\All Users\Documents\database; Windows 2000 users should look in the following directory: C:\Inetpub\wwwroot\newland\database.

In this step, you are supplying a name for the DSN and the path to the database.

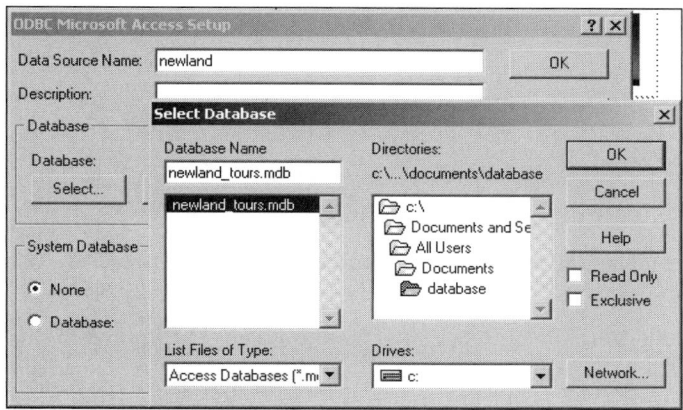

7) Click OK three times to close the windows and return to the Data Source Name dialog.

Now that the DSN is complete, you can return to Dreamweaver and use the new DSN to connect to your data source.

8) In the radio group at the bottom of the dialog, choose Using DSN on Testing Server, which erases all content in the dialog (this does not affect the DSN you created). Return to the top of the dialog, and in the Connection Name field, enter *conn_newland*. Enter newland as the Data Source Name. Click the Test button to verify the connection was made, and click OK.

By completing this dialog, you are providing Dreamweaver with sufficient information to connect to your database using ODBC.

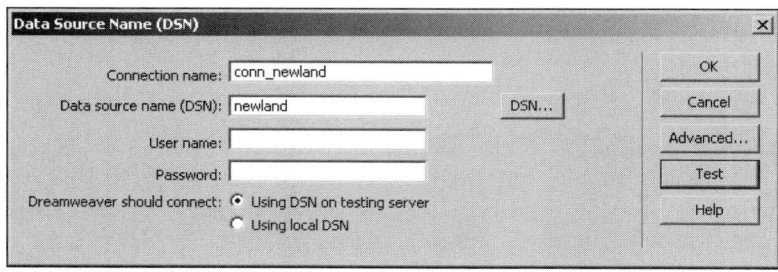

249

When you close the dialog, Dreamweaver creates a new folder in your site, called Connections, with a new file inside called conn_newland.asp. You should also notice that the Databases panel now has an expandable listing of the database and its assets.

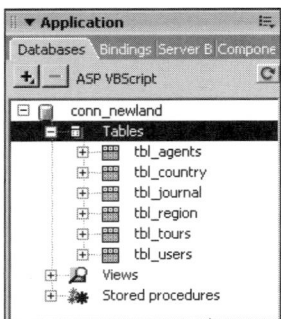

9) Select the Connections folder in the Files panel, and click the Put button to upload it to the server.

You are ready to create a recordset and start binding database data. Skip ahead to the task, "Retrieving Recordsets and Displaying Database Information."

ColdFusion Users (Running ColdFusion Locally or Connecting to a Remote Server)

This section is for all ColdFusion users, regardless of how they connect to their server.

ColdFusion users who connect to a remote server must have the administrator for that server grant them RDS login information—which consists of a password. Without RDS login, you will not be able to complete this book.

1) Open index.cfm.

It doesn't matter which page of your site is open when initially creating the connection. Dreamweaver creates the connection for the whole site. You've opened index.cfm because you will add dynamic content to that page in the next task.

2) Open the Databases panel, in the Application panel group. Click the Specify the RDS login for your ColdFusion server link, enter your password, and click OK.

RDS login grants developers permission to access the ColdFusion server, which is necessary for defining and using data sources.

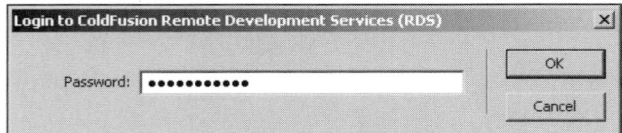

At the end of this step, if there are already many data sources existing on the ColdFusion server, they are all visible in the Databases panel.

The only problem is, the Newland database is not among them.

3) Click the Create a ColdFusion data source link (if it is available), or click the Modify Data Sources button on the right side of the Databases panel.

Regardless of whether you click the button or the link, after a moment, the ColdFusion administrator opens in a browser, to the Data Sources page. You will first need to enter the password to access the administrator.

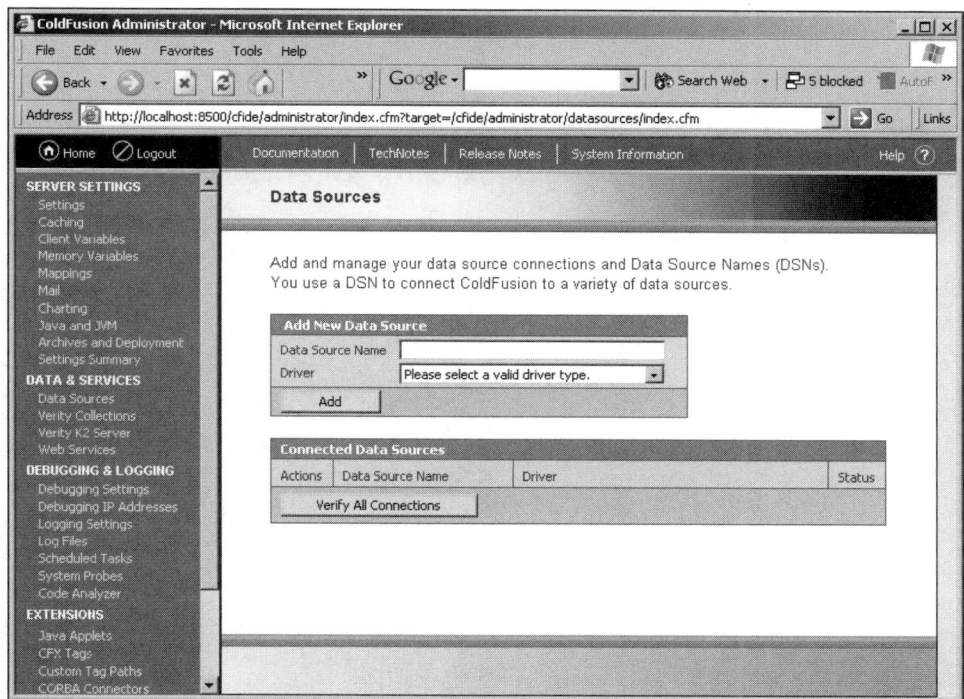

4) In the Add New Data Source box, enter *newland* as the Data Source Name. In the Driver drop-down menu, select Microsoft Access. Click Add.

A DSN consists of a name, a driver that enables the application to communicate with the database, and the path to the database. In this step, you have entered the first two of these three pieces of information.

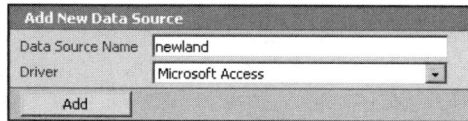

5) In the Microsoft Access Data Source box that appears, click the first Browse Server button and browse to the newland_tours.mdb file on the site. Click Submit.

For Windows XP users, browse to the following directory: C:\Documents and Settings\All Users\Documents\database\. This is the directory to which the shortcut Shared Documents points.

For Windows 2000 users running ColdFusion in standalone mode, browse to the following directory: C:\CFusionMX\wwwroot\newland\database\.

For Windows 2000 users running ColdFusion alongside IIS, browse to the following directory: C:\Inetpub\wwwroot\newland\database\.

This step provides ColdFusion with the remaining information it needs to connect to your database.

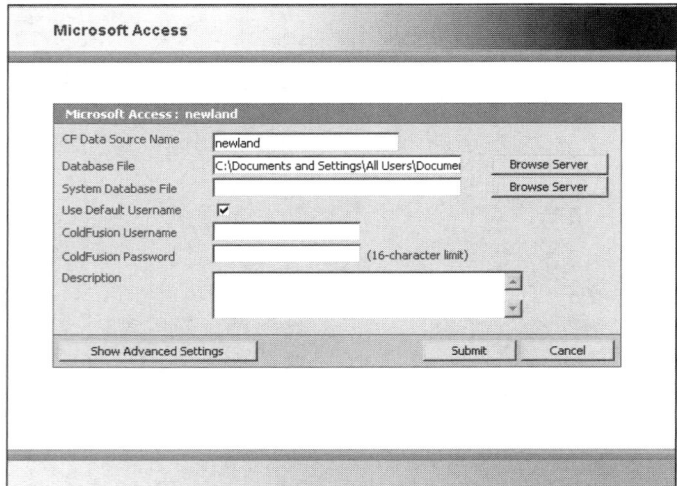

6) Close the ColdFusion Data Sources Web page to return to Dreamweaver. In the Databases panel, click the Refresh button beside the Modify Data Sources you clicked earlier. The newland DSN should show up. Click the + button beside it to expand it and explore the data source.

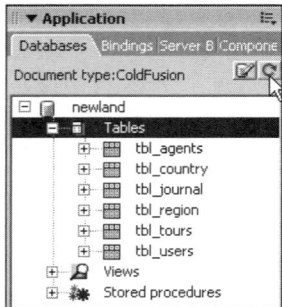

Now that you can see the contents of the newland_tours.mdb database, you know that Dreamweaver has successfully made the connection. You are ready to create a recordset and start binding database data.

Skip ahead to the section entitled "Retrieving Recordsets and Displaying Database Information."

PHP Users (Running PHP/MySQL Locally or on a Remote Server)

Because PHP doesn't make use of ODBC or DSNs, you can specify all the information you need to access your MySQL database right in Dreamweaver.

1) Open index.php.

It doesn't really matter which file is open, since Dreamweaver makes the connection available site-wide. However, at least one file must be open in the site, before you can create a connection to MySQL.

2) In the Databases tab, click the + button and choose MySQL Connection to create a new connection to MySQL.

The MySQL Connection dialog opens.

3) Specify the following information, so that Dreamweaver can make the MySQL data source available to your site.

Connection name: *conn_newland*

MySQL server: *localhost* (if developing locally) or whatever your server administrator tells you (if developing remotely)

User name and Password: the user name and password of the MySQL account that you use to access MySQL.

Database: *newland_tours*.

If you are developing on a remote server, only your server administrator will be able to tell you how you access MySQL from Dreamweaver/PHP. If you are developing locally, then just use the information you specified when you first installed MySQL. If you installed MySQL yourself and are unsure of your username and password, try root as the username and leave the password blank.

TIP *Optionally, click the Test button to make sure that Dreamweaver can actually access MySQL.*

4) Click OK.
Dreamweaver creates a Connections directory on your site, with a file in it called conn_newland.php. This file contains the information your pages will need to access MySQL. Whenever you call a database from PHP, Dreamweaver references this file.

5) Expand conn_newland in the Databases panel to explore the structure of the newland_tours database from within Dreamweaver.
Dreamweaver is actually accessing the database within MySQL and providing you with information about it. Albeit in a limited way, you can interface with MySQL via Dreamweaver.

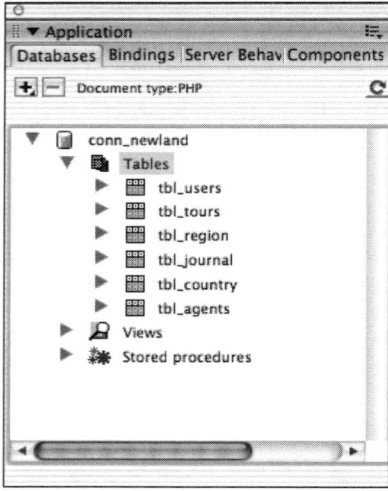

6) In the Files panel, click the Connections folder, and then click the Put button to upload it to the server.
The PHP/MySQL connection won't work unless this folder is uploaded.

RETRIEVING RECORDSETS AND DISPLAYING DATABASE INFORMATION

It seems like a long time since you made any improvements to the actual site. You've done some theory, some exploration, and some configuration. But you haven't done anything to any pages yet. In this final task of the lesson, you'll cause the Traveler's Journal to load dynamically from the database. In the browser, the homepage will look the same as it did before, but in Dreamweaver, the difference will be unmistakable.

1) With index.asp open in Design view, select the text from "Teens Discover..." down to "...putting together" at the bottom. Do not select the yellow image icon beside the T in Teens (if it appears). Press Delete.

You're going to replace this text with dynamic text, so you are just making room in this step.

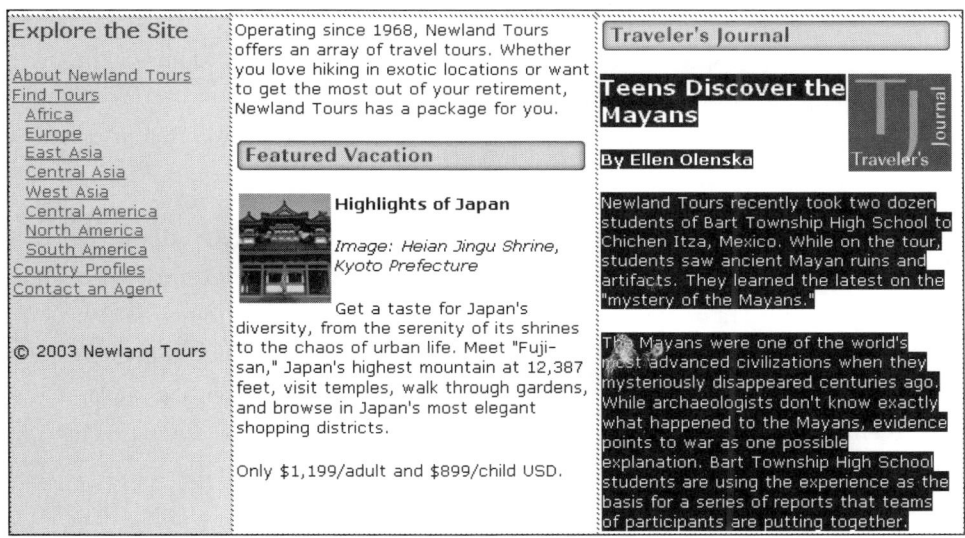

2) Click the Traveler's Journal image to select it. In the tag selector (in the bottom-left corner of the document window), right-click the `<h3>` **tag just to the left of the** `<img>` **tag, and choose Remove Tag from the menu.**

The journal entry in the database is already marked up in HTML. You need to remove the `<h3>` tag here, or the tags in the journal entry will be illegally nested inside the `<h3>` tag.

3) In the Bindings panel, click the New Binding (+) button, and choose Recordset (Query) from the menu.

At this point, you have connected your site to a data source, which means you have made it possible for Dreamweaver to write code for you that retrieves data from your database. However, you have not actually retrieved any data yet. In this and the next two steps, you'll create a recordset, which as you'll recall from the beginning of this lesson, is a collection of data that meets certain criteria and that is retrieved from a database using SQL.

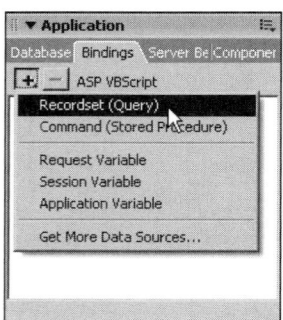

Your goal is to display the journal entry, but you don't want to display all the journal entries, only the most recent. In order to facilitate this, each journal entry has been given an unique ID (a primary key). These IDs are numbered incrementally, as the records are added. Therefore the record with the highest journalID is the most recent. You'll need to sort the data, and then retrieve the contents of the latest journal entry in order to display it. You'll take the first steps toward doing this in the next step.

4) In the Recordset dialog, enter *rs_journal* as the Name. Choose conn_newland (or newland for ColdFusion users) from the Connection drop-down. Select tbl_journal from the Table drop-down. In the Columns section, choose the Selected radio button, and Ctrl-select (Windows) or Command-select (Macintosh) journalID and journal_entry.

In this dialog, you are creating a recordset, named rs_journal. The data in this recordset is retrieved using criteria specified in SQL. You may not realize it, but you have already begun the SQL statement.

Specifically, you have specified data in the data source stored in conn_newland (that connection specifies the newland DSN). Within that data source, you are specifying that the data is in a table named tbl_journal. Going a step further, you are specifying that you only want to retrieve the journalID and journal_entry fields from that table.

256

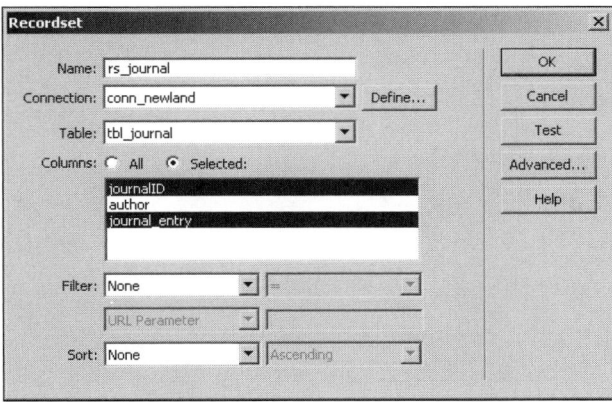

5) In the Sort drop-down menu, choose JournalID, and then choose Descending in the next drop-down menu. Click OK.

This adds the SQL necessary to sort the entries from most recent to least recent.
You have entered the information necessary to create the recordset.

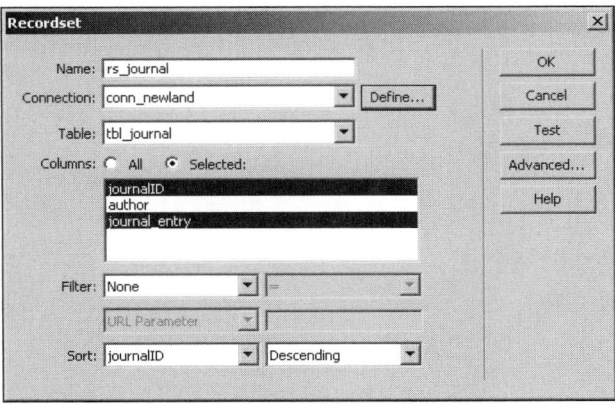

After you click OK, the recordset appears in the Bindings panel, much like form and URL variables did earlier in the book.

6) Expand Recordset(rs_journal) in the Bindings panel, and drag journal_entry so that it is just to the right of the image and release it.

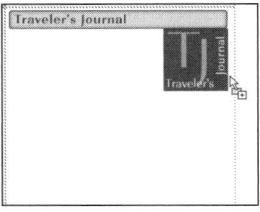

257

It may take some trial and error to order the dynamic text and the image correctly, so just keep trying till the image icon, the dynamic text, and the graphic itself look like they do in the screenshot.

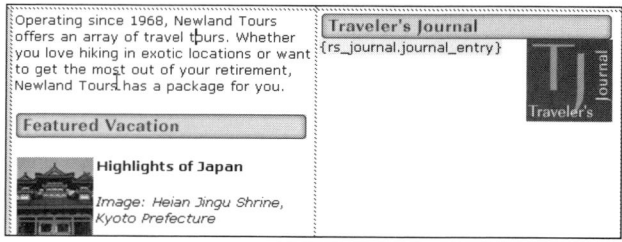

7) Choose View > Live Data from the main menu.

You already know that when you want to test a dynamic page, you can press F12 to open it in a browser, running from the server. If that is too much trouble for you, you can also view Live Data from inside Dreamweaver. This is a very convenient feature, because you can see the effects of your work right in the Dreamweaver authoring environment. It is especially handy when you are trying to format dynamic content, and Dreamweaver's pseudocode placeholders don't give you a sufficiently visual idea of how the page will look.

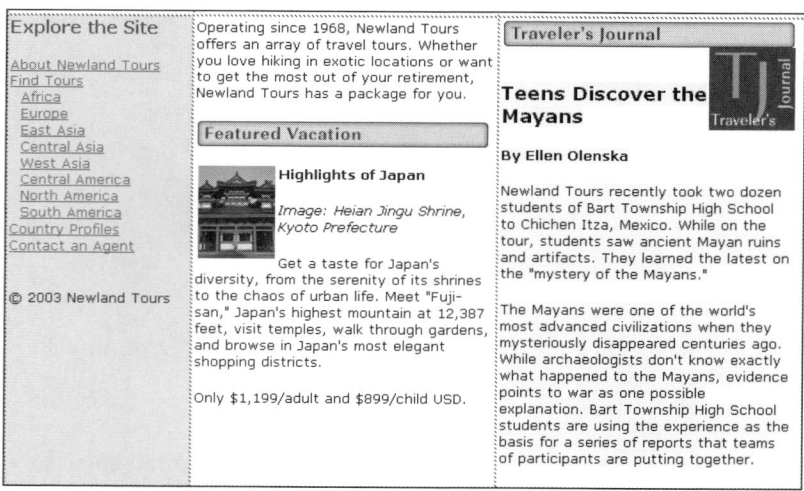

Clearly, the recordset and display of the live data worked, because you can see the database data inside of Dreamweaver. You can also see that it is correctly formatted. The formatting is possible, because I entered HTML tags in the database itself, so when the data was placed on the page, the browser (or, in this case, Dreamweaver) correctly parsed and rendered the HTML tags.

NOTE *The text is highlighted in yellow to show you that it is dynamic and cannot be edited like normal text. This yellow highlighting does not appear in the actual browser; it is merely a Dreamweaver authoring aid.*

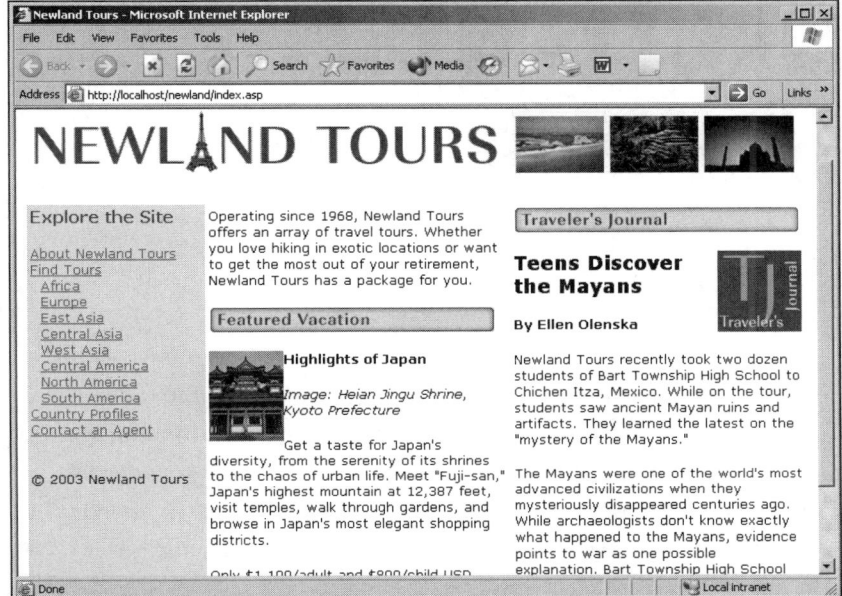

8) Choose View > Live Data again, to toggle it off. Save and upload index.asp. Press F12 to test it in a browser.

If you are seeing what's in the screenshot, then your system is fully configured, and from here forward it's all about the code.

WHAT YOU HAVE LEARNED

In this lesson, you have:

- Learned about the objects a database comprises (pages 224–227)
- Learned about database relationships (pages 227–229)
- Discovered how database content is used on the Web (pages 229–232)
- Installed MySQL on a Mac or PC (PHP users developing locally only) (pages 232–241)
- Explored the Newland Tours database in Access (pages 242–246)
- Configured your system so that Dreamweaver can connect to a database (pages 246–254)
- Displayed XHTML-formatted database content dynamically (pages 255–259)

259

completing the price calculator

LESSON 9

Back in Lesson 7, you began the tour price calculator application and created most of its functionality. As you'll recall, though, you lacked the actual data required to make it work. That data is stored in the newland_tours database (in Access or MySQL, depending on your setup). In this lesson, you will finish what you started, by working with information from the database, controlling what data is retrieved and how it is displayed.

While there will be some hand-coding in this lesson, you will also make use of some of Dreamweaver's visual features for working with database data. For example, you will learn how to populate the drop-down list in the form on tourprice.asp with dynamic data using a simple dialog.

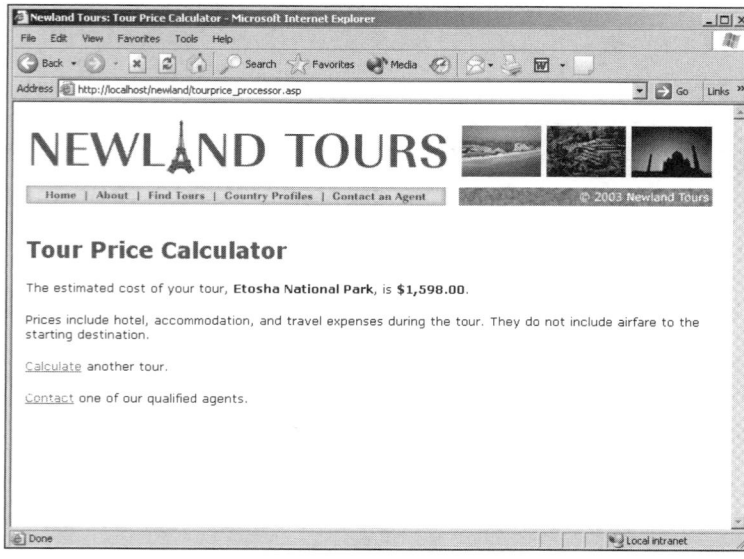

By the end of this lesson, the tour price calculator application will be fully functional with live data.

You'll also spend some more time working with SQL and creating queries. You'll see how to filter SQL queries using dynamic data, which enables you to deliver a truly customized experience to your users.

In addition, by the end of the lesson, both tourprice.asp and tourprice_processor.asp will have a number of server-side code blocks—enough to make them hard to read. You'll learn how to document these blocks using comments, making the scripts—and the documents as a whole—easier to read and maintain.

WHAT YOU WILL LEARN

In this lesson, you will:

- Dynamically populate a form menu with database data
- Filter a query using dynamic data
- Update the tour price calculation with live data
- Document your code with comments

APPROXIMATE TIME

This lesson takes approximately 45 minutes to complete.

LESSON FILES

Starting Files:

Lesson09/Start/newland/tourprice.asp

Lesson09/Start/newland/tourprice_ processor.asp

Completed Files:

Lesson09/Complete/newland/tourprice.asp

Lesson09/Complete/newland/tourprice_ processor.asp

DYNAMICALLY POPULATED DROP-DOWN MENUS

As you'll recall from Lesson 7, when the user submits the form on tourprice.asp, three pieces of data are sent: number of adults, number of children, and a dummy value for the cost of the tour. The ASP, ColdFusion, or PHP script in tourprice_processor then multiplies the number of adults by the dummy tour price and multiplies the number of children by the dummy tour price, adds the two results together, and outputs the number in HTML.

To replace the dummy values with real data takes a little work. To begin, you need to populate the drop-down menu in the form with real data. As you know, the drop-down menu can send only one piece of data, but you need to access two: the price for adults and the price for children. Therefore, rather than sending a dollar value, you'll send a unique identifier for the tour. On tourprice_processor.asp, you'll use that unique identifier to query the database for the adult price and child price for just that tour. You'll insert these values into the calculation, outputting the correct final value.

Now let's look more closely at the form menu element. As you know, each entry in a form menu has two attributes that need to be set: the label (the part users read, which is not submitted with the form), and the data (the information that is submitted as the value of the form element). It's easy enough to guess what the label should be: the tour name itself. Since there's a field in the database corresponding to the tour name, this should be easily retrieved. Now, how about the data? I said earlier that the data value that needs to be sent with the form should be the "unique identifier" for the tour. If you thought about tbl_tours' primary key when you read that, then you are thinking the right way. Remember, every database table has (or should have) a primary key, which contains a unique value for each row in that field (often this key is simply autonumbered). To summarize, each menu item's label will be the tour name, and its data value will be its primary key (tourID), both of which are stored in the tbl_tours table.

1) Open tourprice.asp. Click the New Binding (+) button in the Bindings panel, and choose Recordset (Query) from the list.

Before you can configure the menu you need to create the recordset that will make that data available so you can bind it to the form. Whenever you are working with database data, the first thing you have to do is create a recordset.

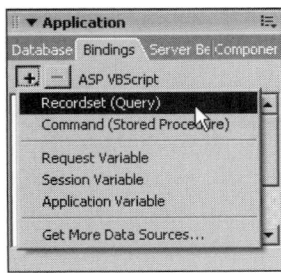

2) In the Recordset dialog, enter *rs_tourprices* as the Name. Select conn_newland as the Connection. Select tbl_tours from the Table menu. In the Columns section, select Selected, and Ctrl-select (Windows) or Command-select (Macintosh) tourID and tourName.

NOTE *ColdFusion users should select newland in the Connection field. ColdFusion does not require the separate conn_newland connections file that ASP and PHP do. In other words, whereas ASP and PHP reference conn_newland.asp/php to get directions to the newland DSN, ColdFusion accesses the newland DSN directly.*

Up to this point in the dialog, you have specified most of the information you'll need to populate the menu. You are creating a script that creates a recordset called rs_newland, which contains data obtained by going through conn_newland to find the appropriate database, and then finding the tbl_tours table, and retrieving all of the values stored in the tourID and tourName columns. You'll use the tourName data for the menu labels, and the tourID data for the menu data.

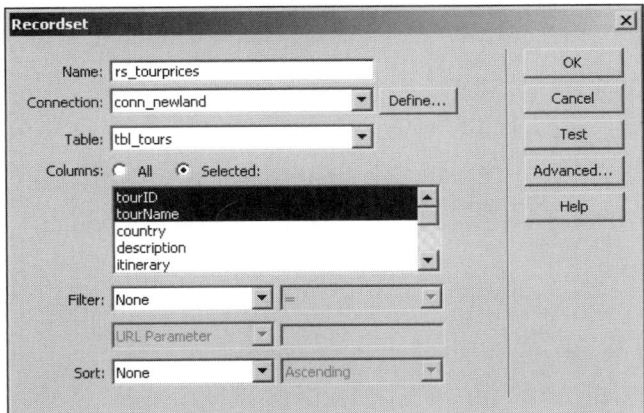

3) In the Sort drop-down menu, choose tourName, and verify that the box beside it is set to Ascending.

Unless you tell it otherwise, the database is going to display data in the order it appears in the database. However, the data was not entered in any particular order. By sorting the data by tourName ascending, you ensure that all of the tours are listed in alphabetical order, which will make it easier for your users to find the tour they want.

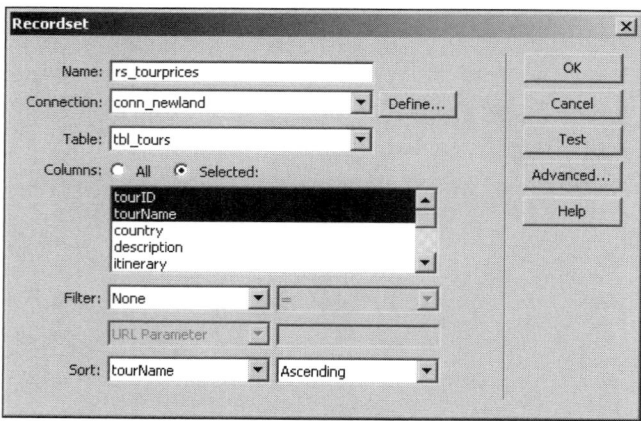

4) Click the Test button.

Clicking this button displays for you the contents (and order) of your recordset. Often, when you build queries you may need to do some trial and error. Here, you can see that all 19 tours have been retrieved, and that they are ordered alphabetically by tourName.

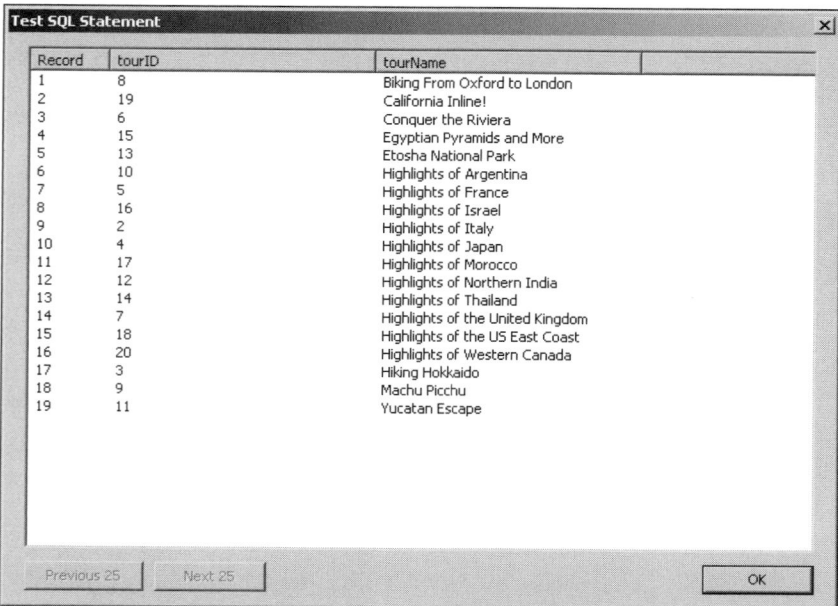

5) Click OK in the Test window to return to the dialog, and click OK.

The appearance of the document doesn't change, though if you look in the code, you'll see a new block that contains the code necessary to create the query. We'll look specifically at this code later, but you can at least see it by looking in code view—it should be just below the top of the document. The screenshot shows the code for ASP. ColdFusion users comparing their screens with the screenshot may be surprised at how much less code they have, as well as how much easier it is to read.

```
1  <%@LANGUAGE="VBSCRIPT"%>
2  <!--#include file="Connections/conn_newland.asp" -->
3
4  <%
5  Dim rs_tourprices
6  Dim rs_tourprices_numRows
7
8  Set rs_tourprices = Server.CreateObject("ADODB.Recordset")
9  rs_tourprices.ActiveConnection = MM_conn_newland_STRING
10 rs_tourprices.Source = "SELECT tourID, tourName FROM tbl_tours ORDER BY tourName ASC"
11 rs_tourprices.CursorType = 0
12 rs_tourprices.CursorLocation = 2
13 rs_tourprices.LockType = 1
14 rs_tourprices.Open()
15
16 rs_tourprices_numRows = 0
17 %>
18
19 <!DOCTYPE html PUBLIC "-//W3C//DTD XHTML 1.0 Transitional//EN" "http://www.w3.org/TR/xhtml1/DTD/xhtml1-t
20 <html xmlns="http://www.w3.org/1999/xhtml">
21 <head>
22 <title>Newland Tours: Tour Price Calculator</title>
```

6) Switch to design view, and click to select the menu in the form. In the Property inspector, click the List Values button to open the List Values dialog. In turn, select each of the label/data pairs, and click the Remove Value (minus sign) button.

At the end of this step, there should be no item labels or values in the dialog.

You added dummy data in Lesson 7 just so you could build the functionality. In this step, you are removing the dummy data, so you can add the real data you just placed in the rs_tourprices recordset.

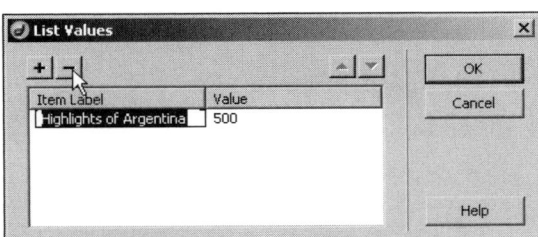

7) With the menu still selected, in the Property inspector, click the Dynamic button.

This opens the Dynamic List/Menu dialog, used to bind dynamic data to form menus.

8) Choose rs_tourprices from the Options from recordset field. Specify tourID in the Values field, and specify tourName from the Labels field. Click OK.

Dreamweaver adds the code necessary to bind the data to the menu. One important thing to note is that the resulting ASP, ColdFusion, or PHP script loops through the data pulled from the database. In other words, just as you manually entered an item label and item value one at a time in Lesson 7, so each of the 19 tour label/value pairs must be loaded into the menu one at a time. Using a programming structure called a loop, ASP, ColdFusion, or PHP goes through each tourName/tourID pairing in the recordset and adds it to the menu item.

Obviously, in addition to the initial convenience—what you just did was a lot faster than manually entering 19 label/value pairs—you have the added bonus that if the database is ever changed, this menu field is automatically and instantly updated. That means that as long as you maintain your database, Web maintenance will happen automatically.

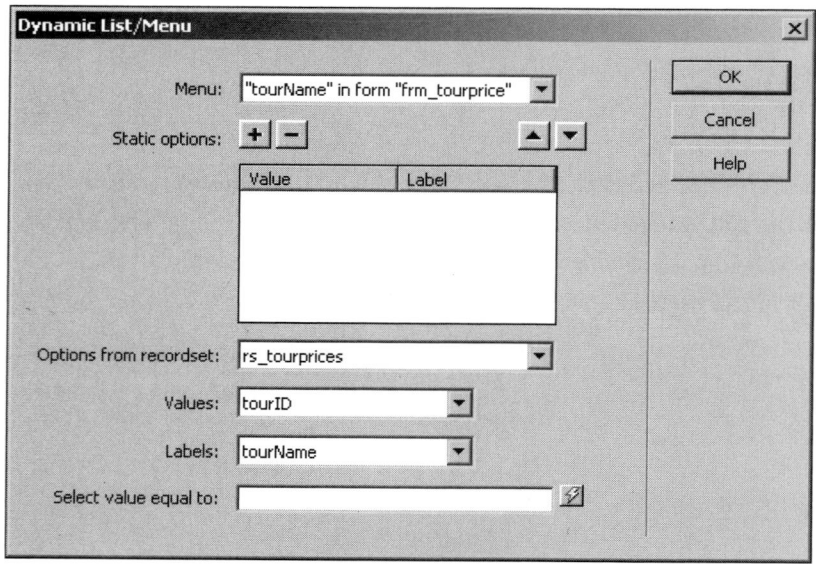

9) Save, upload, and test the page.

When you click the menu, you should see all 19 tours listed, in alphabetical order.

10) PHP users who see an "undefined index" error, as shown in the following screenshot: Amend the code in tourprice.php as follows.

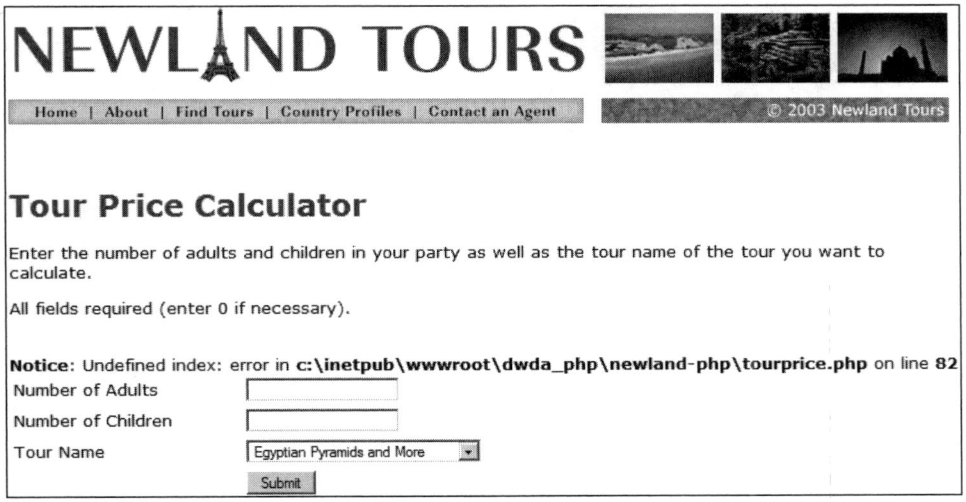

Find the following code in tours.php.

```php
<?php
if ($_GET['error'] == "notnumeric")
{
echo "<p class=\"error\">*** Error! One or more fields was left blank or contained
⇒a non-numeric character.</p>";
}
?>
```

Change that code block so that it reads as follows.

```php
<?php
if (isset($_GET['error']))
{
   if ($_GET['error'] == "notnumeric")
{
echo "<p class=\"error\">*** Error! One or more fields was left blank or contained
⇒a non-numeric character.</p>";
}
}
?>
```

The error appears on only some implementations of PHP. The cause is that you're testing whether a variable ($_GET['error']) is of a certain value (notnumeric), without actually making sure the variable exists in the first place.

The solution is to use a nested if block (that is, an if block wrapped inside another if block). The outer if block determines whether the error variable exists in the URL. If it does, then it checks to see whether its value is equal to notnumeric. But if the error variable doesn't exist in the URL, the whole operation is skipped, and so the source of the problem is avoided.

```
70    <td><img src="images/navbar.gif" name="navbar" width="450" height="20" border="0" usemap="#navbarMap" alt="Navigation Bar" />
71    <td><img name="copyright_bar" src="images/copyright_bar.gif" width="272" height="20" border="0" alt="Copyright 2004 Newland To
72    </tr>
73    <tr>
74    <td colspan="2">
75      <h1><br />
76        <a name="top" id="top"></a>Tour Price Calculator </h1>
77      <p>Enter the number of adults and children in your party as well as the tour name of the tour you want to calculate.</p>
78      <p>All fields required (enter 0 if necessary).</p>
79
80
81      <?php
82      if (isset($_GET['error']))
83      {
84          if ($_GET['error'] == "notnumeric")
85          {
86              echo "<p class=\"error\">*** Error! One or more fields was left blank or contained a non-numeric character.</p>";
87          }
88      }
89      ?>
90
91      <form name="frm_tourprice" id="frm_tourprice" method="post" action="tourprice_processor.php">
92        <table width="60%"  border="0" cellspacing="0" cellpadding="3">
93          <tr>
94            <td>Number of Adults </td>
95            <td><input name="numAdults" type="text" id="numAdults" /></td>
```

11) Complete the form and submit it.

The page, tourprice_processor.asp, should load and the calculation should still work. Of course, the tour price suddenly meets even the thriftiest of budgets. That's because the calculation is now using the tourID as the dollar amount, and all the tourIDs are under 20.

CREATING FILTERED RECORDSETS

Twice now, once each in this lesson and the preceding one, you have created recordsets and displayed their data. In both cases, you just retrieved all of the information stored in the database and bound it to the page. But you have a different problem now. To get the calculator to function properly, you need to plug in the adult and child prices for the selected tour—not all of the tours and not the first tour, but the one that the user selected.

How's that going to work? The user selected a tour from the menu on the form and submitted it. On tourprice_processor.asp, the tourID associated with that tour has been included as a form variable. Thus, when you query the database, you'll construct something along the following lines (in pseudocode):

```
Retrieve the adult price (basePriceAdult) and the child price (basePriceChild)
from tbl_tours where tourID equals the tourID submitted by the user on the form.
```

It is very helpful to formulate your intentions very clearly before attempting any sort of programming, even if the programming (in this case SQL programming) is masked behind a graphic interface: Dreamweaver's Recordset dialog.

1) Open tourprice_processor.asp. Use the Bindings panel to open the Recordset dialog.

When you create a recordset in Dreamweaver, it persists in the individual page only.

2) Enter *rs_tourprices_filtered* as the Name, conn_Newland as the Connection, tbl_tours as the Table, Selected in the Columns category, with the following fields selected: tourID, tourName, basePriceAdult, and basePriceChild.

As it stands (which you could see for yourself by clicking Test), this query returns data from all 19 records in tbl_tours in the four fields you specified. But you want the query to return only the data for the tour that the user specified in the form.

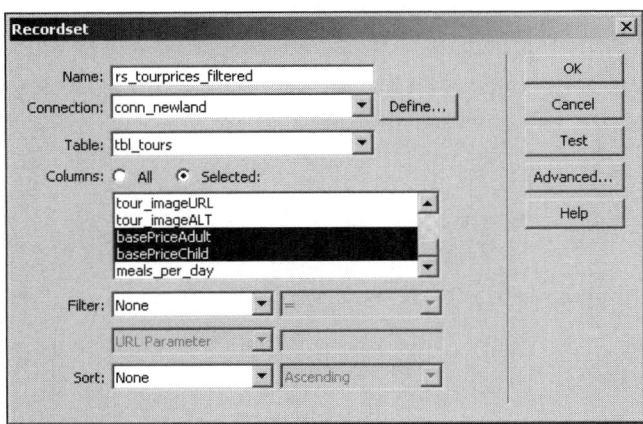

3) In the Filter category, create the following formula: tourID = Form Variable tourName by entering the appropriate choices in the four drop-down menus.

In this step, you are adding an additional criterion to the query. In pseudocode, you are saying, retrieve all the specified information from the table, but only from the record that matches the record the user selected in the form.

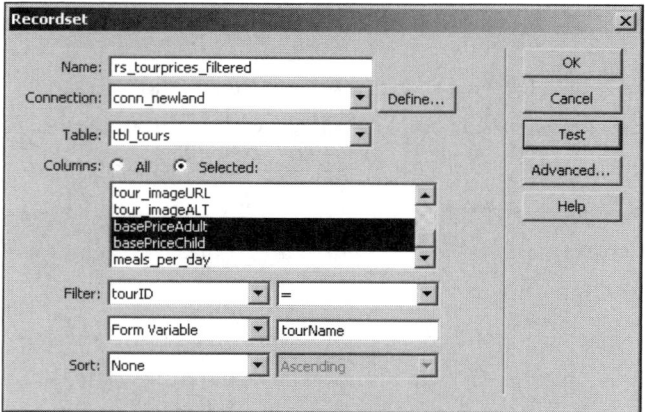

4) Click the Test button. Enter 9 in the Please Provide a Test Value dialog, and click OK.

The test this time works differently than it did in the past. This time, you must specify a test value. The reason is that the query needs a value to be sent from the form, but in the authoring environment, that data doesn't exist. So the dialog appears prompting you for a value.

This time, when the output window opens, only one tour is listed—Machu Picchu, if you entered 9. If you go back and enter different test values, you'll see different tour records that have been retrieved from the database.

5) Click OK to exit the test output, and click OK again to save the recordset.

Once again, the appearance and functionality of the page isn't changed, because creating a recordset only retrieves the data and stores it in the server's memory—you're not using it yet.

270

REVISING THE CALCULATION SCRIPT WITH LIVE DATA

Both times before, when you output data from a database, you did so directly into HTML. You output the Traveler's Journal entry into the main page in index.asp, and you output the tourName/tourID pairing into a form menu element. In this step, you don't need to output the adult and child prices anywhere that the user can see them. In fact, they need to be output into the calculation itself. As you'll see, though, you output internally to a script the same way you do to XHTML.

Before you do that, though, let's add one more simple piece of functionality: Let's display the name of the tour that users just calculated, in case they forgot or chose the wrong one.

1) In tourprice_processor.asp, switch to design view. After the word tour in the first sentence, add the following text: , *XX*,. Select XX, and apply bolding to it, using the Property inspector.

Once again, the Xs are used as placeholder text. The advantage to using this text is that you can format it the way you want your dynamic content to appear, in this case, bold.

2) Select the XX text, and switch to the Application category of the Insert bar. Click the Dynamic Data button and choose Dynamic Text from the pop-up menu.

The Application tab is used to insert common dynamic elements, such as dynamic text.

DYNAMIC TEXT

3) In the Dynamic Text dialog, expand Recordset (rs_tourprices_filtered), and click tourName. Click OK.

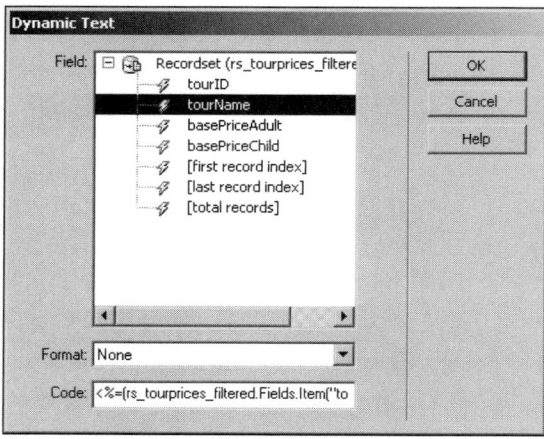

What you've just done is equivalent to dragging a binding from the Bindings panel onto the page. You should also be able to understand the code Dreamweaver outputs in the code window.

In ASP, the following is added where XX appeared before: `<%=(rs_tourprices_filtered.Fields.Item("tourName").Value)%>`. Remember, `<%=` (as opposed to `<%`) means `<% Response.Write`, so this is an output script. As you can probably guess from the rest, it is outputting the value of the `tourName` item, which is a field, in the recordset rs_tourprices_filtered.

In ColdFusion, the following code appears: `<cfoutput>#rs_tourprices_filtered.tourName#</cfoutput>`. Again, the `<cfoutput>` tag is equivalent to ASP's `Response.Write`, and what is being output is the tourName value stored in rs_tourprices.

In PHP, the following code appears: `<?php echo $row_rs_tourprices_filtered['tourName']; ?>`. The command echo is roughly equivalent to ASP's `Response.Write` and ColdFusion's `<cfoutput>`. As in the ASP and ColdFusion versions, this block is outputting the tourName value in rs_tourprices.

Reading and understanding the code is important, because in the next step, you'll have to do some hand-coding.

4) In code view, find the calculation script. Delete the line that sets the value of the basePrice variable to the form variable tourName.

The line in ASP that you are deleting is basePrice=Request.Form("tourName"), and it should be around line 34 (plus or minus) in code view.

The line in ColdFusion that you are deleting is <cfset basePrice = form.tourName>, and it should be around line 14 (plus or minus) in code view.

The line in PHP that you are deleting is $basePrice = $_POST['tourName'];, and it should be around line 12 in code view.

This line is no longer necessary, because you are not obtaining the base price from the form anymore, but rather from the database. In addition, there are two prices that you now need to use: the one for children and the one for adults.

```
25  If Not IsNumeric(Request.Form("numAdults")) or Not IsNumeric(Request.Form("numChildren")) Then
26      Response.Redirect("tourprice.asp?error=notnumeric")
27  End If
28  %>
29
30  <%
31  Dim numAdult, numChild, basePrice, tourPrice
32  numAdult = Request.Form("numAdults")
33  numChild = Request.Form("numChildren")
34  basePrice = Request.Form("tourName")
35  tourPrice = (numAdult * basePrice) + (numChild * basePrice)
36  %>
37
38  <!DOCTYPE html PUBLIC "-//W3C//DTD XHTML 1.0 Transitional//EN" "http://www.w3.org/TR/xhtml1/DTD/xhtml1-t
39  <html xmlns="http://www.w3.org/1999/xhtml">
40  <head>
```

5) Add two new lines of code that set the value of two new variables: basePriceAdult and basePriceChild.

In ASP:

```
basePriceAdult=rs_tourprices_filtered.Fields.Item("basePriceAdult").Value
basePriceChild=rs_tourprices_filtered.Fields.Item("basePriceChild").Value
```

In ColdFusion:

```
<cfset basePriceAdult = rs_tourprices_filtered.basePriceAdult>
<cfset basePriceChild = rs_tourprices_filtered.basePriceChild>
```

In PHP:

```
$basePriceAdult = $row_rs_tourprices_filtered['basePriceAdult'];
$basePriceChild = $row_rs_tourprices_filtered['basePriceChild'];
```

All of these scripts create two new variables and set the values to the appropriate adult and child prices as retrieved from the database.

```
29
30  <%
31  Dim numAdult, numChild, basePrice, tourPrice
32  numAdult = Request.Form("numAdults")
33  numChild = Request.Form("numChildren")
34  basePriceAdult = rs_tourprices_filtered.Fields.Item("basePriceAdult").Value
35  basePriceChild = rs_tourprices_filtered.Fields.Item("basePriceChild").Value
36  tourPrice = (numAdult * basePrice) + (numChild * basePrice)
37  %>
38
```

6) ASP users only: Remove *basePrice* from the *Dim* line and add *basePriceAdult* and *basePriceChild* to the list.

Since ASP requires explicit declaration of all variables, you have to remember to update that declaration whenever you change your variables.

7) Update the *basePrice* variables in the calculation line itself with the appropriate new variables.

In ASP:

```
tourPrice = (numAdult * basePriceAdult) + (numChild * basePriceChild)
```

In ColdFusion:

```
<cfset tourPrice = (numAdult * basePriceAdult) + (numChild * basePriceChild)>
```

In PHP:

```
$tourPrice = ($numAdults * $basePriceAdult) + ($numChildren * $basePriceChild);
```

Now the calculation reflects the values that you have retrieved from the database.

```
30  <%
31  Dim numAdult, numChild, basePriceAdult, basePriceChild, tourPrice
32  numAdult = Request.Form("numAdults")
33  numChild = Request.Form("numChildren")
34  basePriceAdult = rs_tourprices_filtered.Fields.Item("basePriceAdult").Value
35  basePriceChild = rs_tourprices_filtered.Fields.Item("basePriceChild").Value
36  tourPrice = (numAdult * basePriceAdult) + (numChild * basePriceChild)
37  %>
38
```

8) Save and upload tourprice_processor.asp. In the Site panel, select tourprice.asp and press F12 to test the application.

The application works as it should. The application outputs the correct calculation based on the information the user entered. Best of all, maintaining this application

274

is as easy as maintaining the database. If a price goes up and the new value is added to the database, the calculator will reflect that immediately. If you add or remove an entire tour, that will be reflected in the application as well.

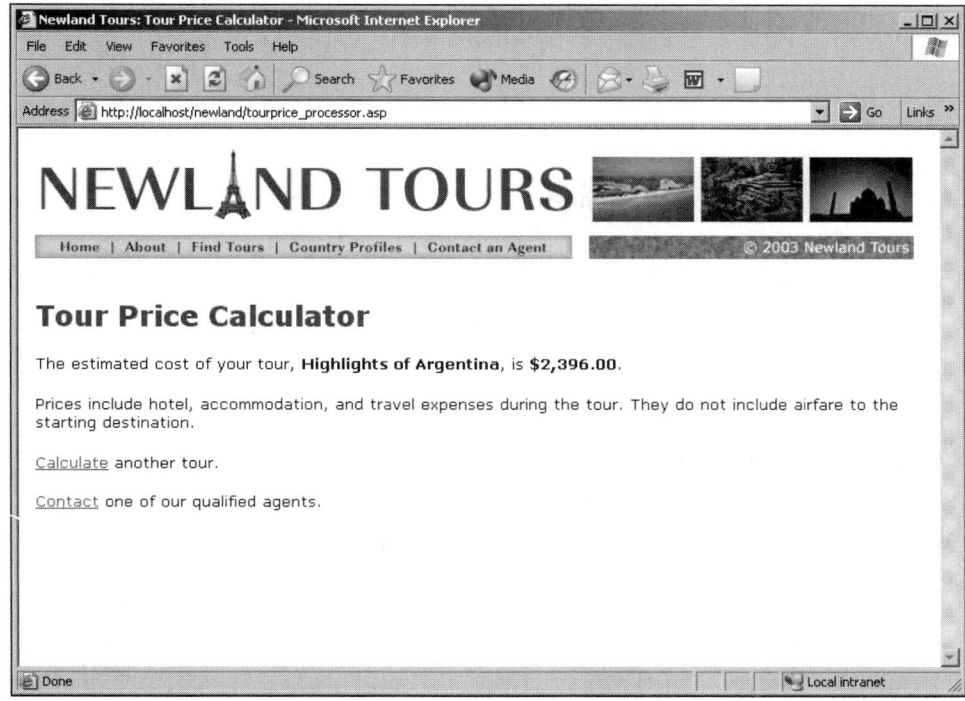

DOCUMENTING YOUR CODE WITH COMMENTS

You added quite a bit of functionality to make the tour price calculator application work. You can see the results of this work in all your Web pages. In my copy of tourprice_processor.asp, for example, the XHTML document proper doesn't start until line 39—everything above that is ASP scripts! Those using ColdFusion will discover that their XHTML documents start around line 18. For the most part, they have the same scripts that do the same things—it's just that ColdFusion requires fewer lines of code. PHP is in between—my XHTML document begins on line 28.

If you scroll through all that code at the top of tourprice.asp and tourprice_processor.asp, you should be able to interpret just about all of the scripts you'll find there (ASP and PHP users will have one exception, which I'll get to shortly). You can read these scripts not only because you are beginning to master ASP, ColdFusion, or PHP scripting, but also because they are fresh in your head. But if you came back in six months, or if someone just handed you this code today for the first time, you might not be able to look at it and know what everything is doing.

This is an important issue, because Web documents have a way of hanging around for years—often longer than the developers do. For your own sake, and the sake of your successor, you should document your code, so everyone knows what it's doing.

You document the code using comments, which are pieces of information added to code that tell readers what the code does, but which are ignored by computers interpreting the code. In this final section, you'll go through tourprice.asp and tourprice_processor.asp and comment the code blocks.

1) Open tourprice.asp. Add a comment just above the query.

In ASP, add a new line below the opening <% at the beginning of the query (just before Dim rs_tourprices), and type the following:

```
' Creates a recordset of all the tour names and IDs from the tbl_tours table in
⇒the database. This data is used later to populate the form drop-down menu.
```

In ColdFusion, type the following at the top of the document:

```
<!---Creates a recordset of all the tour names and IDs from the tbl_tours table in
⇒the database. This data is used later to populate the form drop-down menu. - -->
```

In PHP, type the following just before the line that begins mysql_select_db, which should be around line 3:

```
// Creates a recordset of all the tour names and IDs from the tbl_tours table in
⇒the database. The data is used later to populate the form drop-down menu.
```

In all three languages, comments are denoted in a special way. In ASP's VBScript, you use the single quote (') character. Everything from that character until the end of the line is commented out, or ignored by the interpreter. In ColdFusion, you wrap the comment in special comment tags. In fact, they are the same as HTML comment tags, except they use three dashes instead of two. ColdFusion comments can span multiple lines. Single-line PHP comments can be prefaced with two slashes (//) or a single hash mark (#). You can also create multiple-line comments in PHP, by wrapping the comment as follows: /* my comment */.

Because these comments are in the language of the server (VBScript, ColdFusion Markup Language, or PHP, as opposed to HTML), they are stripped out of the document before it is sent to the client. This means you can document your code as much as you like and not worry about users being able to see it.

```
1  <%@LANGUAGE="VBSCRIPT"%>
2  <!--#include file="Connections/conn_newland.asp" -->
3
4  <%
5  ' Creates a recordset of all the tour names and IDs from the tbl_tours table in the database. The data is
6  Dim rs_tourprices
7  Dim rs_tourprices_numRows
8
9  Set rs_tourprices = Server.CreateObject("ADODB.Recordset")
10 rs_tourprices.ActiveConnection = MM_conn_newland_STRING
11 rs_tourprices.Source = "SELECT tourID, tourName FROM tbl_tours ORDER BY tourName ASC"
```

2) Save and close tourprice.asp, and open tourprice_processor.asp.

Most of the scripts used in this application appear in tourprice_processor.

3) ASP and PHP users only: Add the following comment to the first block of code after the *<% LANGUAGE* declaration (ASP only) and the *<!-include* (ASP) or *require_once* (PHP) blocks, remembering to preface the comment with the ' (ASP) or // (PHP) character(s) as appropriate.

A small script generated by Dreamweaver to help with the dynamic query

Make sure you always add comments in ASP or PHP inside the <% %> or <?php ?> block.

This script is probably unfamiliar to you, because Dreamweaver added it automatically, when you created the dynamic query (that is, when you filtered the data with the criterion: where tourID = form variable tourName). This comment will remind you what it's doing there and how it got there.

ColdFusion lacks this script, because it handled its functionality in a different—and simpler—way.

```
1  <%@LANGUAGE="VBSCRIPT" CODEPAGE="1252" %>
2  <!--#include file="Connections/conn_newland.asp" -->
3  <%
4  ' A small script generated by Dreamweaver to help with the dynamic query
5  Dim rs_tourprices_filtered__MMColParam
6  rs_tourprices_filtered__MMColParam = "1"
7  If (Request.Form("tourName") <> "") Then
8    rs_tourprices_filtered__MMColParam = Request.Form("tourName")
9  End If
10 %>
11 <%
12 Dim rs_tourprices_filtered
13 Dim rs_tourprices_filtered_numRows
```

4) Find the script that creates the recordset, and add the following comment to it: *Queries the database for the tour name, adult price, and child price; data is filtered so that the only record retrieved corresponds to what the user entered in the form.*

In ASP, the query script begins with the declaration of its variables: `Dim rs_tourprices_filtered`.

In ColdFusion, the query script is easily identified, because `<cfquery>` tags surround it.

In PHP, look for the line that begins `mysql_select_db`.

Don't forget to use the proper comment syntax for your server technology.

```
1  <%@LANGUAGE="VBSCRIPT" CODEPAGE="1252" %>
2  <!--#include file="Connections/conn_newland.asp" -->
3  <%
4  ' A small script generated by Dreamweaver to help with the dynamic query
5  Dim rs_tourprices_filtered__MMColParam
6  rs_tourprices_filtered__MMColParam = "1"
7  If (Request.Form("tourName") <> "") Then
8      rs_tourprices_filtered__MMColParam = Request.Form("tourName")
9  End If
10 %>
11 <%
12 ' Queries the database for the tour name, adult price, and child price; data is filtered so that the only
13 Dim rs_tourprices_filtered
14 Dim rs_tourprices_filtered_numRows
15
16 Set rs_tourprices_filtered = Server.CreateObject("ADODB.Recordset")
```

5) Find the form validation script, and add the following comment: *Form validation script; redirects user back to tourprice.asp if form fields do not have numeric values.*

In ASP, this script begins `If Not IsNumeric`. In ColdFusion, it begins `<cfif Not IsNumeric`. In PHP, it begins `if (is_numeric`.

```
22 rs_tourprices_filtered.Open()
23
24 rs_tourprices_filtered_numRows = 0
25 %>
26
27 <%
28 ' Form validation script; redirects users back to tourprice.asp if form fields do not have numeric values
29 If Not IsNumeric(Request.Form("numAdults")) or Not IsNumeric(Request.Form("numChildren")) Then
30     Response.Redirect("tourprice.asp?error=notnumeric")
31 End If
32 %>
33
34 <%
35 Dim numAdult, numChild, basePriceAdult, basePriceChild, tourPrice
36 numAdult = Request.Form("numAdults")
37 numChild = Request.Form("numChildren")
```

6) Find the calculation script, and add the following comment: *Collects data for number of adults and children, and the prices for both adults and children; multiplies data to calculate total.*

After all you've done with this script, you should be able to find it on your own.

When you are finished, don't forget to save and upload these files.

```
31  End If
32  %>
33
34  <%
35  ' Collects data for number of adults and children, and the prices for both adults and children; multipl
36  Dim numAdult, numChild, basePriceAdult, basePriceChild, tourPrice
37  numAdult = Request.Form("numAdults")
38  numChild = Request.Form("numChildren")
39  basePriceAdult = rs_tourprices_filtered.Fields.Item("basePriceAdult").Value
40  basePriceChild = rs_tourprices_filtered.Fields.Item("basePriceChild").Value
41  tourPrice = (numAdult * basePriceAdult) + (numChild * basePriceChild)
42  %>
43
44  <!DOCTYPE html PUBLIC "-//W3C//DTD XHTML 1.0 Transitional//EN" "http://www.w3.org/TR/xhtml1/DTD/xhtml1-t
45  <html xmlns="http://www.w3.org/1999/xhtml">
46  <head>
```

WHAT YOU HAVE LEARNED

In this lesson, you have:

- Populated a menu with database data (pages 262–268)

- Created a dynamically filtered recordset (pages 269–270)

- Output the resulting data both in HTML and inside a server script (pages 271–275)

- Commented your code to make it more comprehensible (pages 275–279)

filtering and displaying data

LESSON 10

One of the many benefits of using databases is that they are scalable. At the moment, the Newland Tours database contains profiles for 16 countries. However, over time the business could grow, and contain profiles of 40 or even 60 countries. Even at 16, the complete listing of country profiles on a single Web page is too much for most users to wade through. In most cases, users are not interested in all of the countries, but rather only a subset—the ones they are considering visiting. The same applies to the tour descriptions themselves and even more broadly to most database data on the Web. Imagine going to Amazon.com if you had to download and display millions of products on a single page!

For this reason, it's important when developing dynamic Web sites to make it easy to filter data, so that users can see the data that they want to see. You can enable your

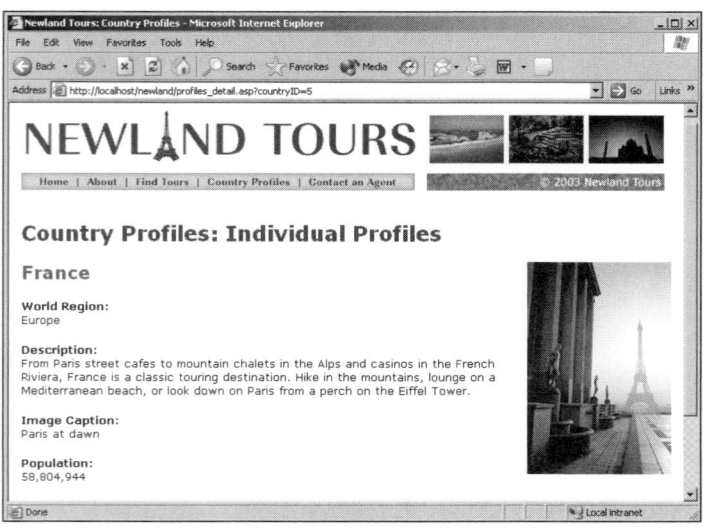

The entire country profile is pulled dynamically from the database, identified using the URL variable countryid=5, and formatted on the fly using CSS.

site's visitors to filter data in many different ways, from simple URL parameters to full-blown search engines. In this, and the next two lessons, you'll build several different interfaces that give you control over how you display data to users.

In this lesson, you will use URL parameters (also known as querystrings) to filter data. You used this technique back in Lesson 5 (Passing Data Between Pages) when you built the cat person/dog person widget. But that was a toy to demonstrate a point. In this lesson, you'll not only filter results based on a URL parameter, but you'll also dynamically generate the hyperlinks themselves, including the linked text the user sees and the unique URL parameters for each.

Like many dynamic Web applications, this one is split into two pages. On the first page, users click the URL for the country profile they want to see. On the second, the appropriate country profile is displayed. But again, the majority of the information on both pages is dynamically generated. The advantage to this approach is that once you've built the two-page application, maintaining it is as simple as updating the database itself—no one will need to revise either page if a country is added, removed, or renamed (it happens).

WHAT YOU WILL LEARN

In this lesson, you will:

- Create a two page application that filters and displays database data
- Dynamically generate URLs
- Layout multiple elements populated with dynamic data
- Display images dynamically
- Create repeating dynamic data regions
- Hand-code SQL to combine filtered data from multiple tables

APPROXIMATE TIME

This lesson takes approximately two hours to complete.

LESSON FILES

Starting Files:
Lesson10/Start/newland/profiles.asp

Completed Files:
Lesson10/Complete/newland/profiles.asp
Lesson10/Complete/newland/profiles_detail.asp

PREPARING THE INPUT PAGE

Currently, the Country Profiles page (profiles.asp) contains a listing in static HTML of many of the countries to which Newland offers tours. The countries themselves will be listed on the second page, which you have yet to add. That means that just about all of the content on this page (excluding the banner) is obsolete, so you need to delete it.

Once you have removed all of the old content, you'll need to add a list of links that will let users choose a country profile. Since this list will be dynamically generated, you'll first need to create a recordset that contains the data required to create the links, which includes the countryName and countryID fields. In this task, then, you will clear out the old content and add the recordset needed to create the list of dynamic URLs.

1) Open profiles.asp in design view.

I find it much easier to delete page content while in design view, rather than hunting around for it in code view.

2) Drag to select everything on the page starting from the horizontal rule just above Namibia all the way down to the bottom of the table.

The yellow icon (representing the image map) at the bottom outside of the table should not be selected.

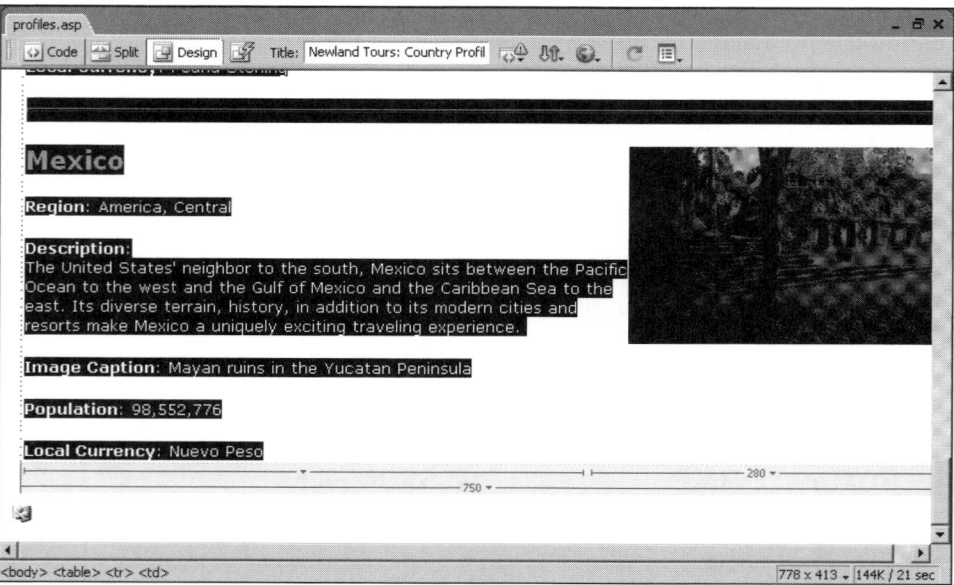

3) Press Delete.

The content is removed and the table is resized.

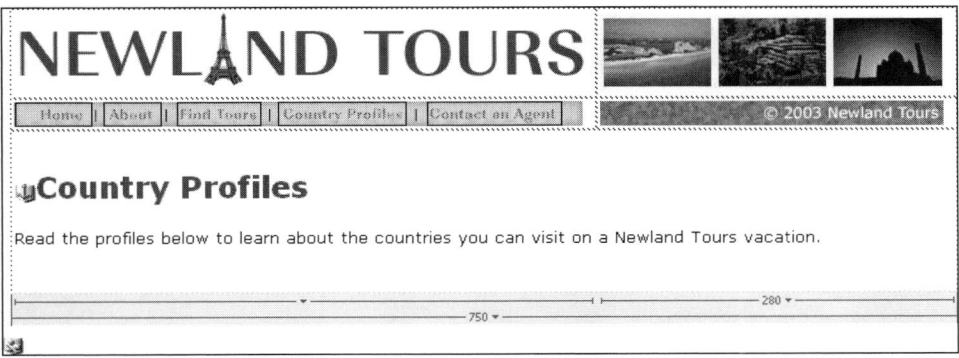

4) Replace the page heading with *Select a Country Profile*. Replace the first line of body text with *The following list shows all of the countries to which we currently offer tours. To learn more about a country, follow its link.*

Here, you are just changing the title and directions of the page to reflect the new functionality of the page.

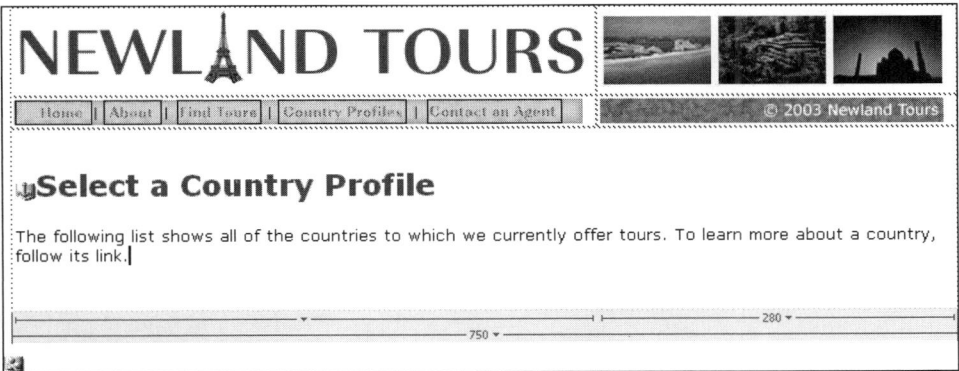

5) In the Bindings panel, click the New Binding (+) button, and choose Recordset (Query) from the list.

You should be getting familiar with the mechanics of adding new recordsets by now.

6) Name the recordset *rs_countryNames*. Choose conn_newland as the Connection. Select the tbl_country table, and select the countryName and countryID fields. Order by countryName, ascending.

You probably know what to expect at this point. Remember, if you are unsure of the data a given query will return, click the Test button to see a preview. If you click this button now, you'll see 16 countries listed in alphabetical order, ranging from Argentina to the United States.

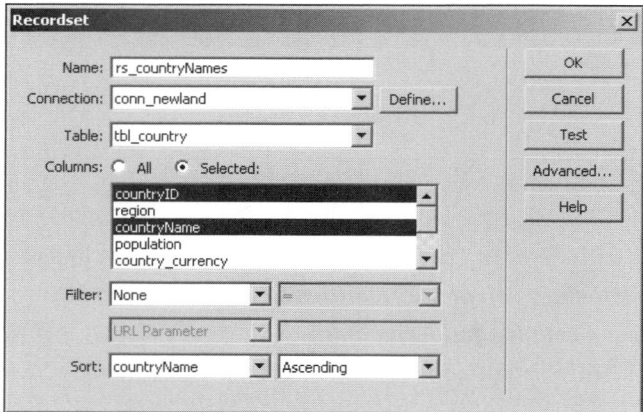

7) Save the file.

GENERATING URLS DYNAMICALLY

In this task, you'll create the list of links that users can click to view a given country profile. Because this list of links will be generated dynamically, and because all of the links will point to the same page (differentiated only by URL parameters), you need to take care of a few different things in this task. You have to output all of the country names into the page so that they are readable to the user. You have to enclose each of these in a link that points to profiles_detail.asp. And you have to append a countryID name-value pair to the URL, so that the results can be filtered on profiles_detail.asp.

1) Place the cursor in the line below the lone paragraph of body text. (Create a new paragraph if necessary.) In the Bindings panel, expand Recordset (rs_countryNames) if necessary, select countryName from the list, and click Insert.

You've done this before: You are binding the value in the countryName field of the database to this paragraph on the page.

TIP *In addition to selecting a tag and clicking the Insert button, another way to bind dynamic data to pages is to drag and drop the data element from the Bindings panel onto the page. The only disadvantage to this method is that it is easy to inadvertently bind the data to the wrong HTML element, so be sure to double-check when using this approach.*

2) Click to select the dynamic text {rs_countryNames.countryName}, and in the Link field of the Property inspector, enter *abc* (or any other text string).

In a moment, you'll add dynamic data to the URL. When you do, Dreamweaver overwrites whatever is entered in the field. However, if you don't add something to the Link field, Dreamweaver can't add the dynamic parameter to the <a> tag, because it doesn't exist. In other words, entering abc is just a temporary workaround.

285

3) With the dynamic text still selected, click the <a> tag in the tag selector, click countryID in the Bindings panel, choose a.href in the Bind To drop-down menu at the bottom of the panel, and click the Bind button.

In this step, you are binding the value of countryID to the href attribute of the <a> tag. The abc text you entered a moment ago is replaced.

TIP *I've noticed (especially when working with ColdFusion) that sometimes the Bind To menu is grayed out in this step. To work around this problem, select <a> in the tag selector before selecting regionID in the Bindings panel.*

The only problem now is that the information in the href attribute is the countryID, such as 6 or 9. You don't have any pages called 6 or 9, so the link is not yet functional.

4) In the Link field of the Property inspector, position the insertion point at the beginning (before the opening <% = in ASP, the <cfoutput> in ColdFusion, or the opening <?php in PHP), and enter the following text:

```
profiles_detail.asp?countryID=
```

Immediately following this text, the ASP, ColdFusion, or PHP code should begin. When the page is tested, the ASP, ColdFusion, or PHP code will be resolved to a single number, so in the case of Argentina, the URL will be as follows: `profiles_detail.asp?countryID=15`.

TIP *Remember, you should replace .asp with .cfm or .php, as appropriate for your server model.*

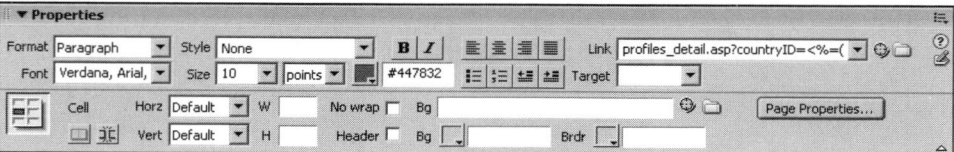

5) Save, upload, and press F12 to test the file. Roll your cursor over the link (without clicking).

There are a couple things to note about the page so far. First, only one country is listed: Argentina. That's not going to work! You'll need to add some functionality to ensure that all countries are listed, not just the first one.

On a brighter note, when you roll over the link, you should see the correct URL listed in the lower corner of your browser, so at least you know the dynamic URL binding worked.

NOTE *In Internet Explorer for Windows XP and Safari on Mac OS X, sometimes the visibility of the status bar is turned off by default, so you can't see the URL listed in the lower-left corner. In both browsers, you can toggle it back on by choosing View > Status Bar.*

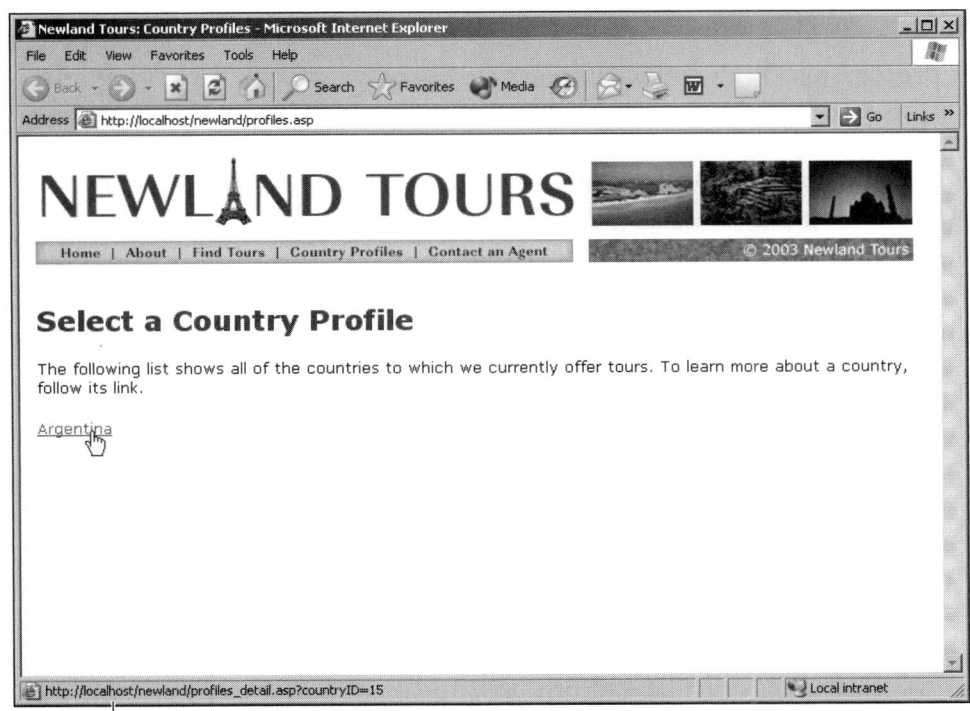

URL WITH CORRECT PARAMETER

6) Return to the page in Dreamweaver, select the dynamic text once again, then click the <a> tag in the tag selector, and in the Server Behaviors panel (Window > Server Behaviors), click the Add Server Behavior (+) button, and choose Repeat Region from the list.

287

The Repeat Region behavior will add the necessary code to ensure that multiple records, rather than just the first one, will be displayed.

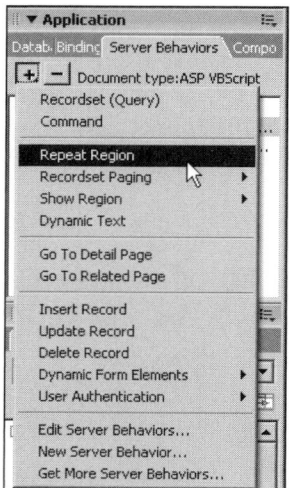

7) In the Repeat Region dialog, leave the Recordset field alone, and select All records from the Show radio group.

The Recordset option enables you to specify which recordset you want to repeat; however, there is only one on this page, so you don't have to enter any information in the field.

The Show options—Show ## Records at a time and Show All records enable you to create **recordset paging**. Some recordsets will output so many rows of data that the page becomes unmanageable, so results are broken into groups of 10 or 25 results at a time. Most search engines use this strategy. Because you only have 16 country names in your recordset, which is not too unwieldy, you can go ahead and show all of the records at once.

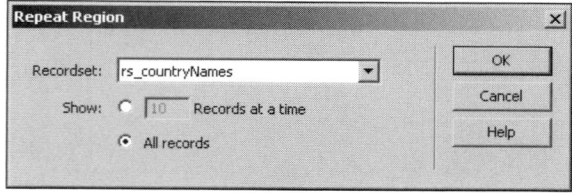

8) Save, upload, and test the file.

You should now see all 16 countries listed, and if you roll over (don't click!) each of the links, you should see a different countryID parameter for each.

The only problem is the formatting. All of the countries are listed side-by-side on a single, hard-to-read line (ASP and ColdFusion), or they are spaced too far apart (PHP).

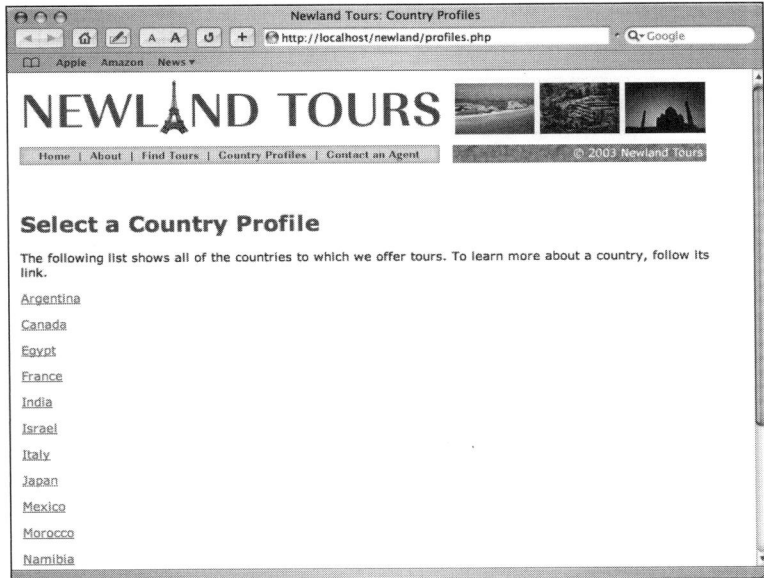

What's happening is that ASP, ColdFusion, and PHP are using a **loop** structure. In programming, loops are structures that execute over and over again until something breaks them out of the loop. Loops are flow control structures, just like if...else structures. The difference is that if...else structures execute once based on one or more conditions, while loops execute repeatedly until a given condition is met.

289

You created the loop by making the dynamic text a repeated region. A repeated region is an output block of text that is inside of a loop, causing the same region to be output multiple times. The region in this case is the country name and its link. The condition that must be met before the loop is broken and the remainder of the page is processed is that all of the records in the recordset are displayed.

9) Return to Dreamweaver, and switch to code view, finding the dynamic code just below the body text paragraph that begins "The following list shows...".

To understand why the display problem is happening, you need to look at the loop structure directly and identify why the output is not displaying correctly. As usual, I strongly encourage you to understand what's going on in all three code blocks, and not just in the server model you are using.

THE ASP BLOCK

In ASP, the code Dreamweaver wrote for us to handle this functionality is as follows:

```
<%
While ((Repeat1_numRows <> 0) AND (NOT rs_countryNames.EOF))
%>
<a href="profiles_detail.asp?countryid=<%=(rs_countrynames.fields.item
⇒("countryid").value)%>"><%=(rs_countryNames.Fields.Item("countryName").
⇒Value)%></a>
<%
Repeat1_index=Repeat1_index+1
Repeat1_numRows=Repeat1_numRows-1
rs_countryNames.MoveNext()
Wend
%>
```

This is an eyeful for nonprogrammers, but it's important to at least get the gist of what's going on. Notice that there are two ASP blocks (each with opening and closing <% %> tags). The top one contains a while statement: while is used to begin loops, and its parameter (the code in parentheses) is the condition that causes the loop to stop. In VBScript, EOF refers to end of file, so the condition says to break the loop when there are no more records to process. The bottom ASP block contains the code that actually advances through the loop one record at a time and eventually ends the loop (Wend).

Nested in between these two loop code blocks is the code that's looped; it is the link itself. Notice that after the closing </a> tag in this code, there is no <br /> tag, which would add a line break after each URL. You'll need to manually add that code at the end of that line of text to get the page to display properly. (You'll do so momentarily.)

THE COLDFUSION BLOCK

The ColdFusion block, predictably, is a lot simpler.

```
<p><a href="profiles_detail.cfm?countryID=<cfoutput>#rs_countryNames.countryID#
⇒</cfoutput>"><cfoutput query="rs_countryNames">#rs_countryNames.countryName#
⇒</cfoutput></a></p>
```

The first thing you should notice, assuming you read the deconstruction of the ASP script, is that there is no apparent loop structure. As a matter of fact, a loop is in play, but ColdFusion hides it behind the simple tag syntax. Anytime you use `<cfoutput>` and list a query as an attribute within that tag, ColdFusion automatically loops. The condition that breaks the loop—when ColdFusion reaches the end of the recordset—is implied.

The specific problem is that looping occurs only within the `<cfoutput>` tags, and there is no `<br />` or `<p>` tags inside that block to create line breaks. A secondary problem is that Dreamweaver has generated two `<cfoutput>` blocks, where only one is needed.

You'll fix both problems momentarily.

THE PHP BLOCK

The PHP block more closely resembles the ASP block:

```
<?php do { ?>
<p><a href="profiles_detail.php?countryID=<?php echo $row_rs_countryNames
⇒['countryID']; ?>"><?php echo $row_rs_countryNames['countryName']; ?></a></p>
<?php while ($row_rs_countryNames = mysql_fetch_assoc($rs_countryNames)); ?>
```

The looping structure in PHP is performed by a do...while structure. The do portion appears in the first line of the code block, and the while portion appears in the final line. In between, of course, is the line that creates the country name listing and the hyperlink with the proper countryID passed as a URL parameter.

To determine how many loops are necessary, this code block references the recordset itself, using mysql_fetch_assoc(). When you query a database using mysql_query() in conjunction with a SELECT statement, the returned data is not immediately available to PHP. To get to the data, you have to "fetch" it, using one of PHP's various functions for that purpose, including mysql_fetch_assoc(). This function returns one record (or row) of data at time, which in the preceding code block is assigned to the $row_rs_countryNames variable. Thus, to return all of the rows, you need to loop through the recordset. Every time through the loop, the value of $row_rs_countryNames changes and it outputs accordingly into HTML.

NOTE *The first time through the loop, the default value for $row_rs_countryNames is used; this value is set near the top of the document in the main query block itself, in line 6 on my page.*

Now that you understand how the code works, you probably can already see what the problem is: each time the code loops, it prints a block of text wrapped by an <p></p> tag pairing. And <p> tags are block-level HTML elements that output with extra space. In other words, you need to replace the <p> tags with a <br /> tag. You'll add it momentarily.

Thus all three server models (ASP, ColdFusion, and PHP) are not quite looping what we want, and that is why the display on the page is not right. In all cases, all we need to do is modify the code being looped over, so that there are no paragraph tags inside the loop, and so that there is a line break after each link. This obviously is an easy solution—but it is only easy if you look at the code and take a moment to understand what's going on.

The solution varies somewhat by server model.

10) All server models: Find the closing </a> tag inside the loop, and immediately after it, insert a <br /> tag.

This line break fixes the display problem from before for ASP and PHP. ColdFusion users need to complete one more step.

```
51 ') AND (NOT rs_countryNames.EOF))
52
53 .asp?countryID=<%=(rs_countryNames.Fields.Item("countryID").Value)%>"><%=(rs_countryNames.Fields.Item("countryName").Value)%></a><br />
54
55 lex+1
56 umRows-1
```

11) PHP users only: Move the opening <p> tag so that it is before the opening <?php do line; likewise, move the closing </p> tag so that it is outside the closing <?php } while line (but before the closing </td>.

This takes care of the nesting problem. Now, effectively all elements output by the loop are in a single paragraph, separated with line breaks (<br />).

The final PHP block should look as follows:

```
<p><?php do { ?>
<a href="profiles_detail.php?countryID=<?php echo $row_rs_tourNames['countryID'];
⇒?>"><?php echo $row_rs_tourNames['countryName']; ?></a><br />
<?php } while ($row_rs_tourNames = mysql_fetch_assoc($rs_tourNames));
⇒?> </p></td>
```

```
32    <p>The following list shows all of the countries to which we offer tours. To learn more about a country, follow its link. </p>
33
34    <p><?php do { ?>
35     <a href="profiles_detail.php?countryID=<?php echo $row_rs_tourNames['countryID']; ?>"><?php echo $row_rs_tourNames['countryName']; ?></a><br />
36    <?php } while ($row_rs_tourNames = mysql_fetch_assoc($rs_tourNames)); ?></p></td>
37    </tr>
```

12) ColdFusion users only: Rewrite the code so that it reads as follows (all in one line):

```
<p><cfoutput query="rs_countryNames"><a href="profiles_detail.cfm?countryID=
⇒#rs_countryNames.countryID#">#rs_countryNames.countryName#</a><br />
⇒</cfoutput></p></td>
```

You've made two different types of changes. First, you consolidated what were originally two <cfoutput> blocks into a single one. Remember, <cfoutput> can be used to output static HTML text as well as ColdFusion variables, so there is no reason to keep them separate. Now, the entire block of code that is looped is contained within the <cfoutput> tags.

With that change made, it is easier to fix the original problem—the line spacing. As with the ASP and PHP code in the preceding steps, the goal is to get all of the looping code inside one set of <p> tags, and to include a <br /> tag as a part of the loop, to create the line breaks.

13) Save, upload, and test the file once again.

The input page is both functional and attractive.

PREPARING THE OUTPUT PAGE

The input page is ready, but it points to a page that doesn't yet exist. You'll fix that in this step. You'll also create a recordset that collects data based on the URL parameter supplied when the user clicks a link on the previous page.

1) Open generic_template.asp in design view. Enter *Newland Tours: Country Profiles* as the Title in the toolbar, and save it as *profiles_detail.asp*.

Once again, our template makes the initial mock-up of a page fast and easy.

2) Enter *Country Profiles: Individual Profiles* as the first heading on the page. Then type the following text, each in its own paragraph:

Country Name:

World Region:

Description:

Image Caption:

Population:

Local Currency:

In this and the next few steps, you are building a layout to hold dynamic data.

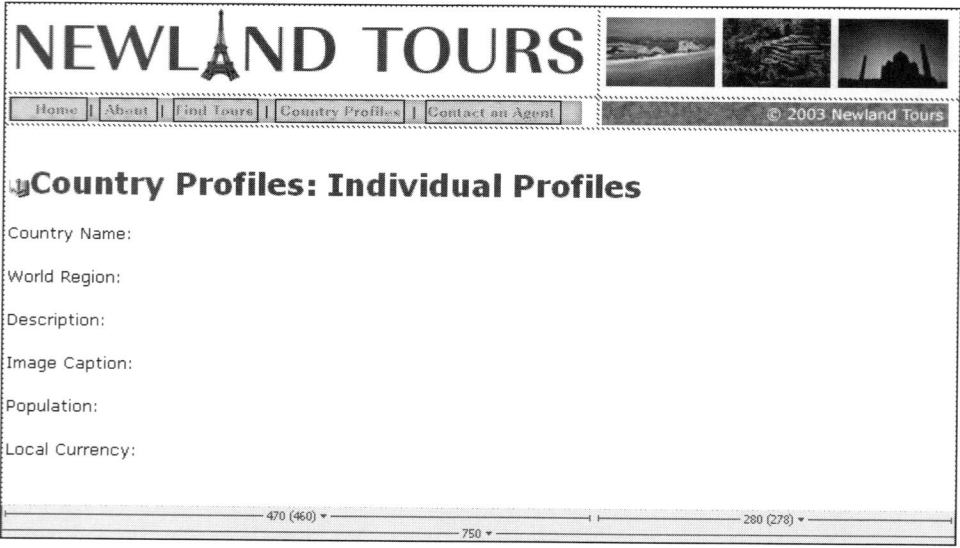

**3) Click once in Country Name, and select H2 from the Format field of the
Property inspector.**

The country name should become large and purple, as the CSS style kicks in.
You'll format the rest of the fields in the next exercise.

4) Using the Bindings panel, create a new recordset using the following information:

Name: *rs_countries*

Connection: conn_newland

Table: tbl_country

Columns: All

Filter: countryID = URL Parameter countryID

Sort: None

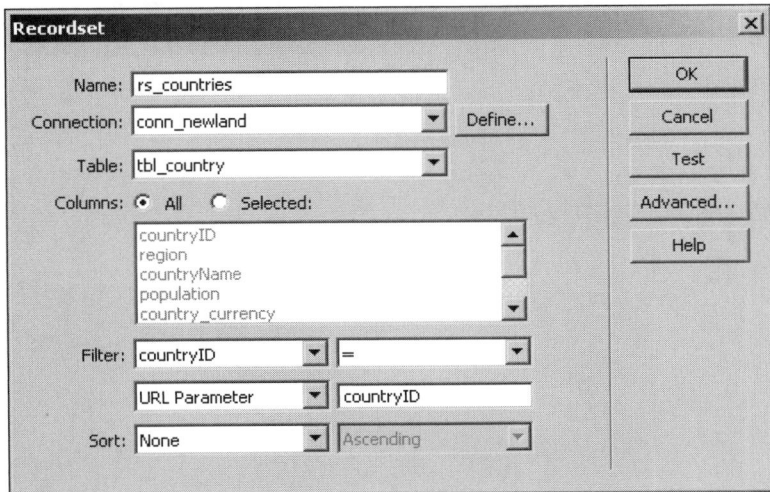

You probably know what these settings are going to accomplish, but if you are not
sure, click the Test button. Because it is filtering based on a URL parameter, you'll
need to provide a test value. Enter 3, and you'll see Taiwan.

When you are finished, the Bindings panel contains the new recordset, which you
can use to populate your page.

POPULATING PAGE LAYOUTS DYNAMICALLY

Up to this point in the book, most of the dynamic data you have displayed has been simple—usually a single item. But now you are going to output an entire country profile, comprising multiple kinds of data. To accomplish this, you'll intersperse dynamic output with the static HTML code you inserted in the previous task.

1) Position the cursor just after Country Name, and in the Bindings panel, expand Recordset(rs_countries) and click CountryName, and click Insert. In the document window, delete the placeholder words Country Name, leaving just the dynamic text. This causes the country name in the selected record to appear formatted as the redefined <h2> element.

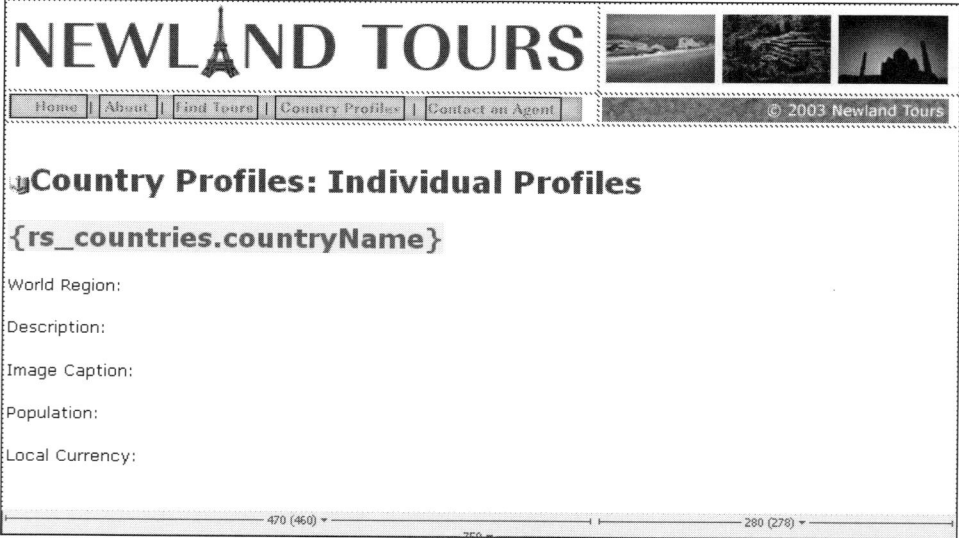

2) Position the cursor after the colon in World Region:, and press Shift+Enter (Windows) or Shift+Return (Macintosh) to insert a line break. Select World Region: and click the Bold button in the Property inspector.

NOTE *If Dreamweaver wraps the text using the* <span class="author"> *tag as it did in an earlier lesson, you can remove that tag and manually type* <strong> *tags in code view.*

You'll add the dynamic data in the line just beneath World Region, and the bolding distinguishes the category name from the data that will appear there.

The line beneath World Region should not be bold.

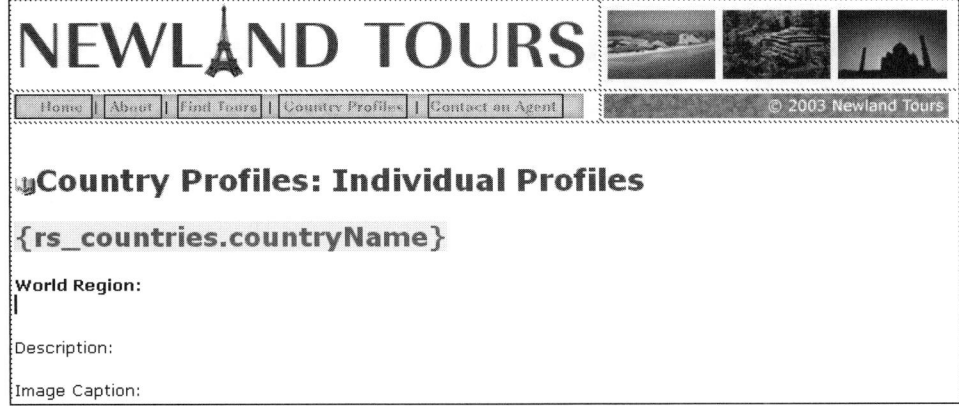

3) One at a time, format the remaining four categories in the same manner, adding a line break and bolding only the first line.

You've now made room for all of the dynamic data.

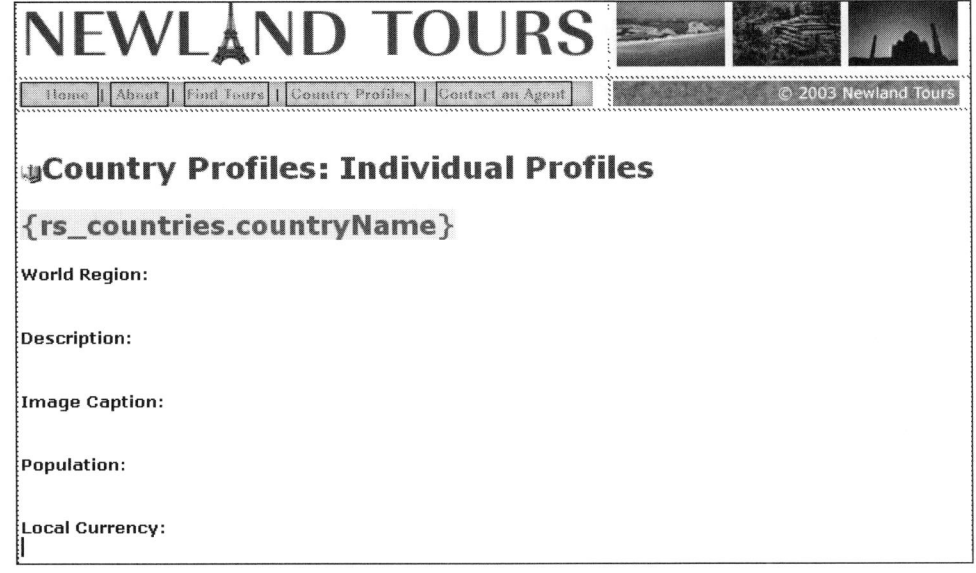

4) One at a time, bind region to the line beneath World Region; bind description beneath Description; imageALT beneath Image Caption; population beneath Population; and country_currency beneath Local Currency.

Laying out pages with dynamic data is quite easy.

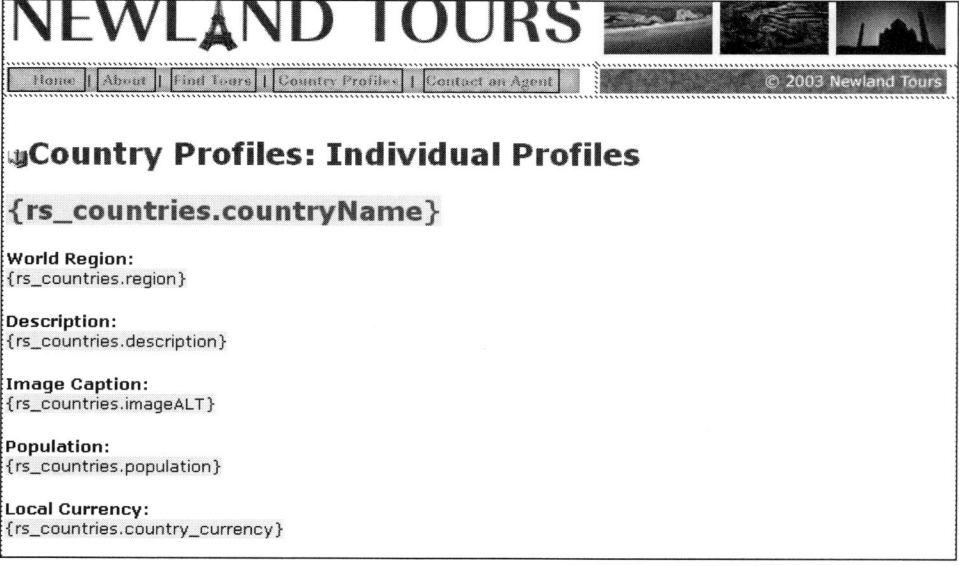

5) Save, upload, and test the file.

Not bad for a beginning, but there are several issues that you still need to work out.

You might be wondering why Canada showed up as the country. The reason is that when you created your query, Dreamweaver set the default URL parameter to 1 (in ASP, ColdFusion, and PHP), and Canada is the country in the database with that value. If Dreamweaver had not added that default value, then you would have seen an error message or a page with missing data (depending on the server model), because the query depends on a URL parameter where none existed. Had you accessed this page from profiles.asp, of course, there would have been a URL parameter.

The World Region is listed as 1, which is not terribly helpful. Why does Canada have a world region of 1, rather than something meaningful, such as North America? This has to do with the structure of the database. Remember, relational databases often have foreign keys, rather than actual data in their fields. That's what's happening in this case. Because most countries share continents with other countries, I created a separate table for continents in the database, and used the key (unique ID) in tbl_region as a foreign key in tbl_country. The result is that that key value—in this case, 1—is showing on the page, rather than the region name. To fix this, you'll need to look up the region name associated with 1 in tbl_region.

298

Finally, the population figure is listed as 30007094, but it would be easier to read as 30,007,094. You'll use a number formatting function, built into your server model to format this number correctly.

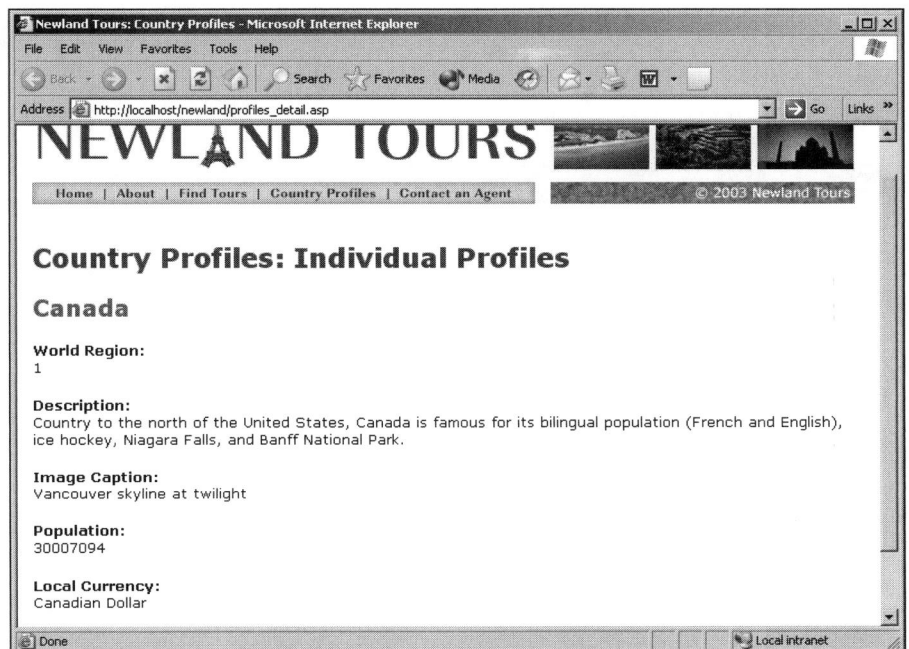

ADDING DYNAMIC IMAGES AND FORMATTING THE POPULATION NUMBER

The country profile is basically functional, so at this point, you'll add a couple of enhancements to make it look better. In this task, you'll add an image dynamically, and you'll also format the population number to make it more readable. Formatting the population number is akin to formatting a number as currency, which you did in an earlier lesson. (You'll fix the region name problem later in the lesson.)

You might wonder how it is even possible to insert an image dynamically, since you can't put a whole image inside an Access or MySQL database. You can, however, put an image's URL in a database, which is exactly what I did. Each tour and each country has an image, all of which are located in the images folder. An extra field in the database holds the image's URLs, and I entered the URLs when adding new records. To display an image, all you need to do is dynamically load its URL into an otherwise static <img> element in HTML.

1) Still in profiles_detail.asp, switch to design view, and insert the cursor just before the <h2> element {rs_countries.countryName}.

In a moment, you'll insert the image here.

2) From the main menu, choose Insert > Image. In the Select Image Source dialog, select the Data Sources radio button at the top (Windows) or the Data Sources button near the bottom (Macintosh).

Normally, when you insert images, you browse to the image and Dreamweaver inserts the path. Because this is a dynamic image you are inserting, you can't specify the path. By choosing Data Sources, you gain access to the recordset that contains the path to the dynamic image.

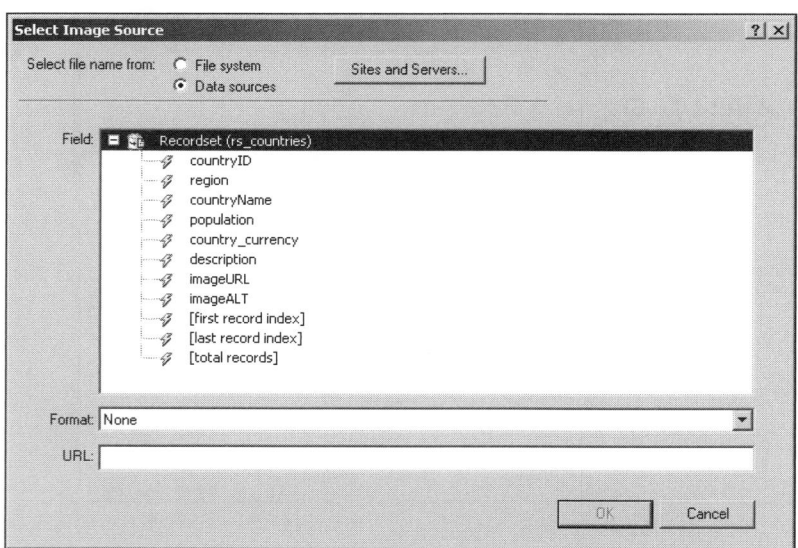

3) Select imageURL from the list, and click OK.

The dynamic image is inserted, represented by a placeholder graphic. Before moving on, though, let's take a quick look at the code.

In ASP, the following code is added:

```
<img src="<%=(rs_countries.Fields.Item("imageURL").Value)%>" />
```

In ColdFusion, the following code is added:

```
<img src="<cfoutput>#rs_countries.imageURL#</cfoutput>" />
```

In PHP, the following code is added:

```
<img src="<?php echo $row_rs_countries['imageURL']; ?> />
```

Though the technique used to insert this code is different than what you have done with the Bindings panel, the resulting code is the same. Dreamweaver creates an <img> tag with the src attribute. Rather than hard-coding a path in the src attribute, ASP, ColdFusion, or PHP retrieves that path—which is none other than a string of text in the database, as shown in the accompanying figure.

300

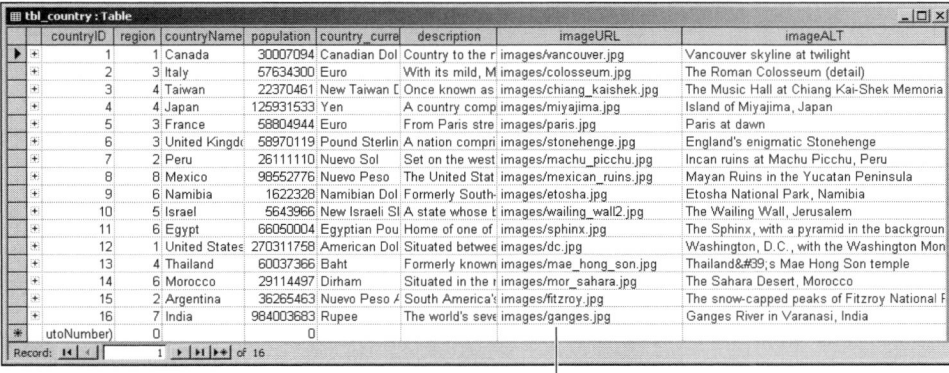

URLS STORED IN DATABASE AS TEXT STRINGS

4) Back in design view, click the dynamic image icon where you inserted the image, and use the Property inspector to change its alignment to Right.

When you are done with this step, the dynamic image icon appears on the right side, and a yellow image icon appears in its original location to indicate where the image was inserted.

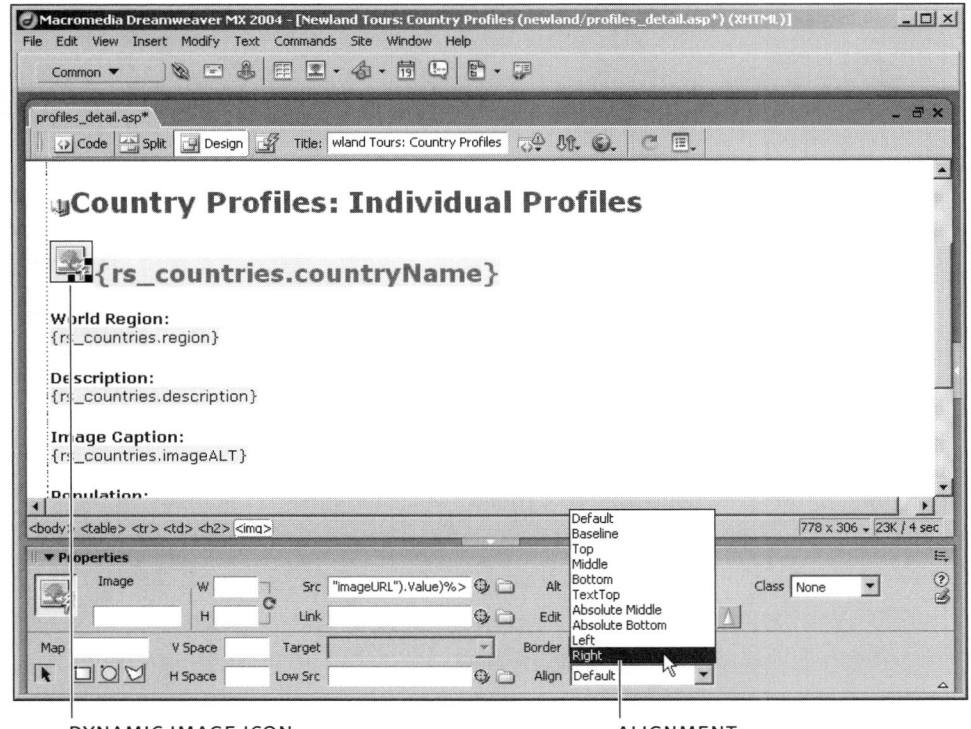

DYNAMIC IMAGE ICON   ALIGNMENT

301

Before testing this functionality, let's quickly take care of the number formatting. ASP and ColdFusion users can accomplish this task using Dreamweaver's interface, but PHP users will have to hand-code.

5) ASP and ColdFusion users: select and delete the dynamic text underneath the Population heading. Position the cursor in the now-empty line. From the Application tab of the Insert panel, choose Dynamic Text.

The dynamic text feature offers the same functionality as the Bindings panel, except that it lets you specify how to format the data.

DYNAMIC TEXT

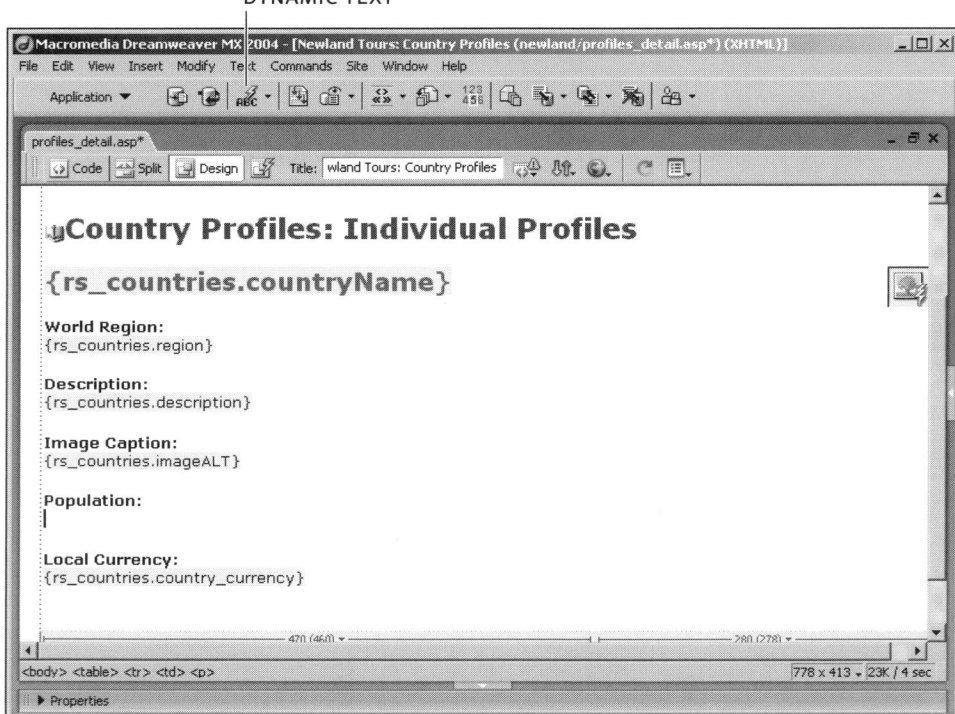

6) ASP and ColdFusion users: in the Dynamic Text dialog, select population from the list. In the Format drop-down, select Number – Rounded to Integer. Click OK.

In Lesson 7, I had you type in the function (`FormatCurrency()` or `DollarFormat()`) directly, so you could work with the code. In this step, you are doing the same thing (using a different function to format numbers, rather than currency) using Dreamweaver's visual interface.

When you are done with this step, the page in Dreamweaver looks just like it did before you deleted the original population number.

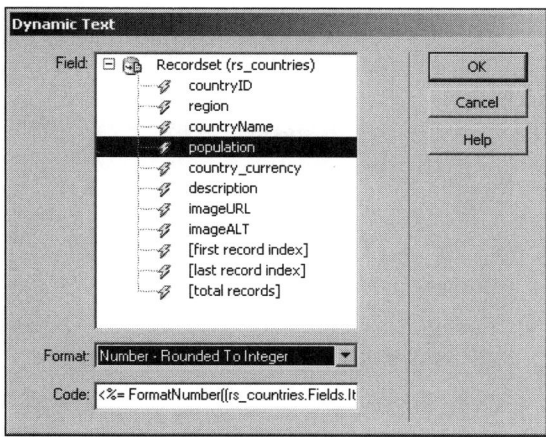

7) PHP users: switch to code view, and find the line that outputs the population:
<?php echo $row_rs_countries['population']; ?>.

This line outputs the unformatted number. In the next step, you'll wrap this in a function, which will format the number for us.

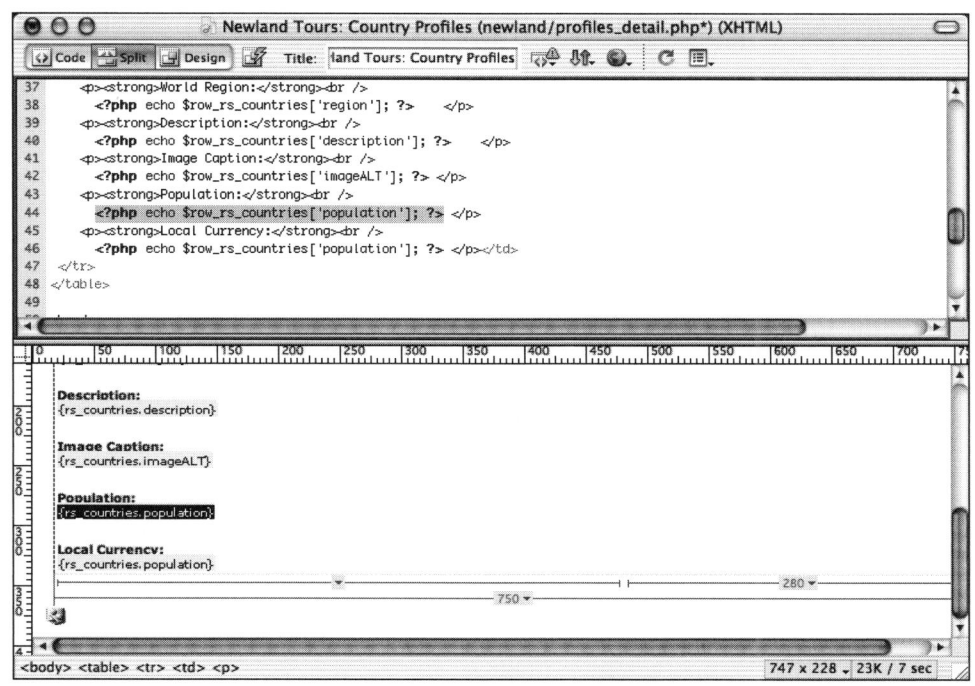

8) PHP users: revise the line you just found so that it reads as follows:

```php
<?php echo number_format($row_rs_countries['population'],0,'.',','); ?>
```

The function `number_format()` takes four parameters, each one separated by a comma. The first is the number to format; here we specify the population number as retrieved from the database. The second is the number of decimal places; we specify 0. The third is the character used for the decimal; this is academic, since we won't have any decimals, but we specified a period. Note that the period is enclosed in single quotes, so PHP knows it is a text string, and not something it should try to parse. Finally, the fourth parameter is the character used to separate thousands; here we specified a comma, again, in quotes to indicate that it is a string.

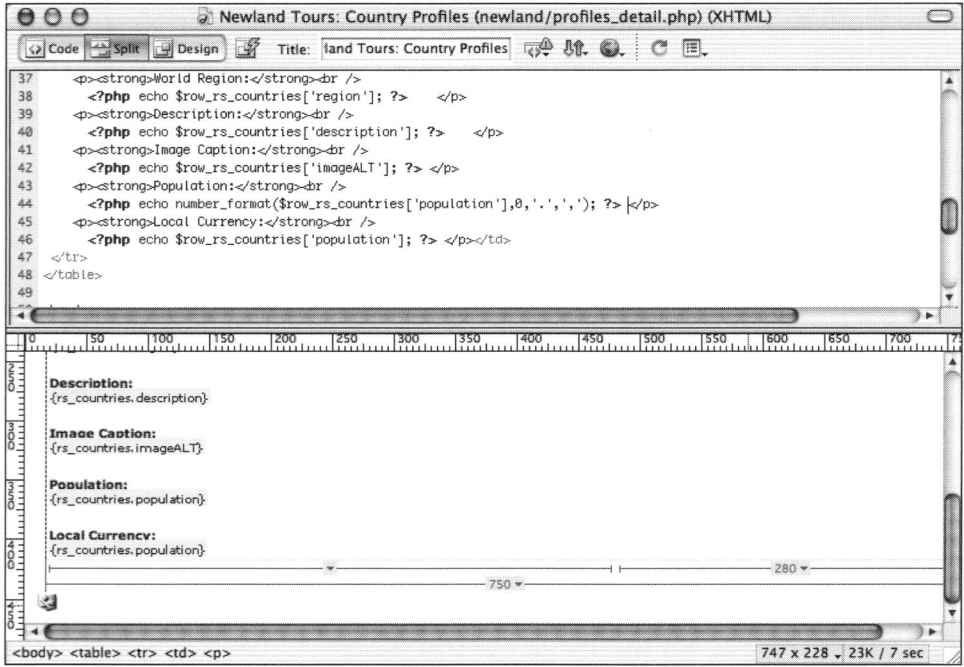

9) Save, upload, and test the file.

Both the image and the formatted number now show onscreen.

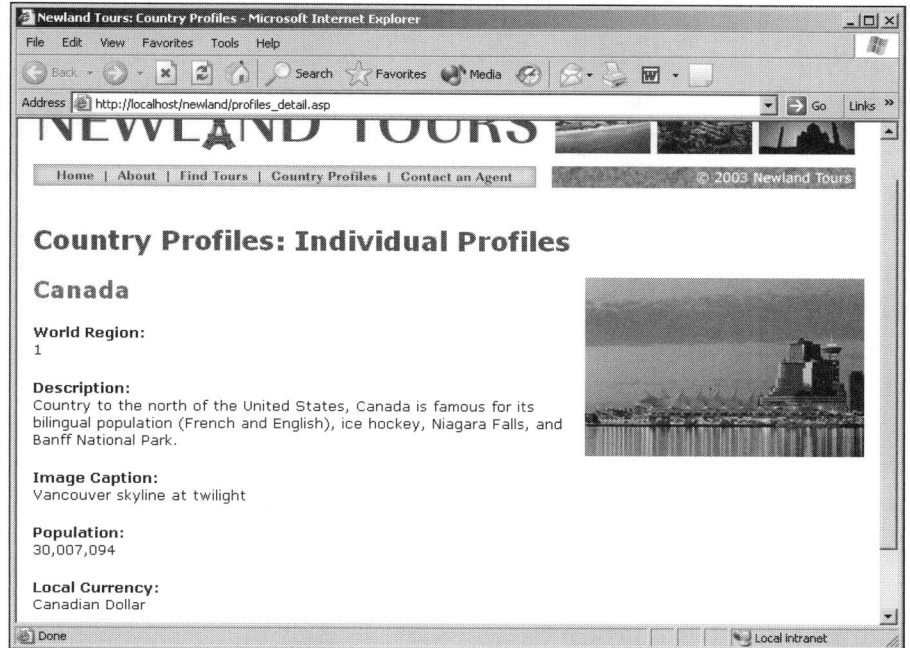

10) Still in your browser, test the functionality of these two pages by clicking Country Profiles in the navigation bar, and then clicking any country from the list.

Now at least you know Canada isn't the only country in the database!

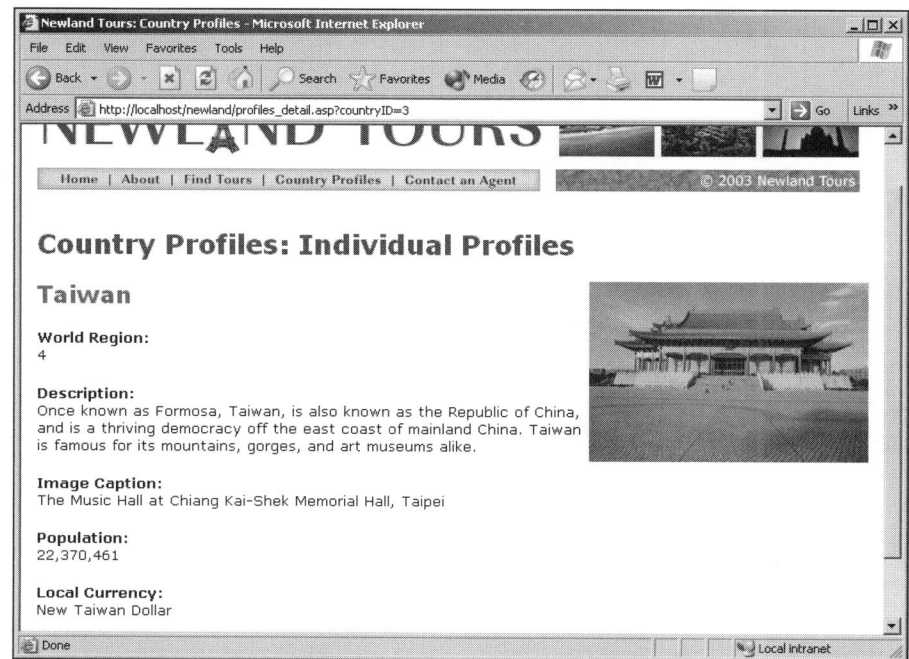

LOOKING UP FOREIGN TABLE DATA WITH SQL

This page is coming together, but you still haven't resolved the issue of the world region being displayed as a number, rather than as the name of a continent. In this task, you will solve this problem with some fancy SQL.

Let's revisit the problem, before attempting to solve it. Relationships are the corner-stone of most modern database management systems, such as Microsoft Access and MySQL. They enable people to organize their data in the most efficient format possible, by eliminating redundancy and simplifying data maintenance. Again, the way they work is that database developers put the unique key from a given table into another table as a foreign key. By doing so, developers can use a query to assemble all information from both tables, correlated to any given record. In tbl_country, there is a field for region, and its value is the unique key taken from tbl_region's unique regionID field.

Let's be more concrete. In tbl_region, the record that contains North America has a unique key of 1. The record that contains East Asia has a unique key of 4. In tbl_country, the records that contain Canada and the United States both have world regions of 1, which means both are in North America. Japan, Thailand, and Taiwan all have world regions of 4, meaning they are in East Asia. This relationship is shown in the following screenshot.

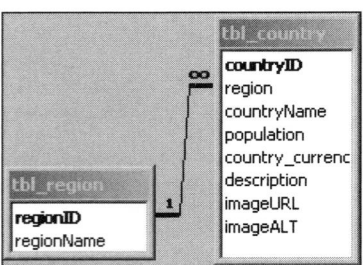

The catch, as you know, is that the only actual data from the region table is this unique key, and that is not meaningful to regular users. What you need to do is combine the data from two tables (tbl_country and tbl_region) where they intersect. Thus, if the user selects Canada, not only will the query retrieve all of the data from the Canada row in tbl_country, but it will also retrieve the data associated with the region value (1) in that table—and in the case of Canada, that data is North America.

Unfortunately, Dreamweaver's SQL builder is meant for relatively simple queries, rather than queries that combine data from two tables using a relationship. That means that you'll have to code some of the SQL by hand. Dreamweaver has an advanced SQL window that lets you hand-code SQL, but let's edit it directly in the document, so you can get some experience working with SQL.

1) In profiles_detail.asp, switch to code view. Find the SQL statement as it appears in the code, using the code listings below.

In ASP:

```
SELECT * FROM tbl_country WHERE countryID = " + Replace
⇒(rs_countries__MMColParam, "'", ",,") + ""
```

In ColdFusion:

```
SELECT * FROM tbl_country WHERE countryID = #URL.countryID#
```

In PHP:

```
SELECT * FROM tbl_country WHERE countryID = %s", $colname_rs_countries);
```

Paraphrased, all three of these statements say the same thing: Retrieve every field from tbl_country where the value in a given record's countryID field equals the countryID passed as a URL parameter.

As mentioned earlier, to prevent errors from occurring if the page is loaded and there is no URL parameter, Dreamweaver has added a default value (1). This value is stored in ASP using the MMColParam variable, in ColdFusion, it is stored in URL.countryID, and it is stored in PHP using the $colname_rs_countries variable.

This is all good so far—there's no data retrieved that we don't want. It's just that we need a little more.

```
14  Set rs_countries = Server.CreateObject("ADODB.Recordset")
15  rs_countries.ActiveConnection = MM_conn_newland_STRING
16  rs_countries.Source = "SELECT * FROM tbl_country WHERE countryID = " + Replace(rs_countries__MMColParam,
17  rs_countries.CursorType = 0
18  rs_countries.CursorLocation = 2
19  rs_countries.LockType = 1
20  rs_countries.Open()
```

TIP *Though ColdFusion and PHP users will find that their code varies from the ASP code shown in the screenshots, the steps still work as described.*

2) Inside the query, replace *tbl_country* with *tbl_country, tbl_region*, being careful to leave the remaining code intact.

Originally, the query was retrieving all of the fields from tbl_country. By making this change, you are telling it to retrieve all of the fields from both tbl_country and tbl_region.

3) Place the insertion point after *WHERE*, and insert the following code, being careful not to change the subsequent code.

```
tbl_region.regionID = tbl_country.region AND
```

```
13
14  ver.CreateObject("ADODB.Recordset")
15  nection = MM_conn_newland_STRING
16  "SELECT * FROM tbl_country, tbl_region WHERE tbl_region.regionID = tbl_country.region AND countryID = "
17  e = 0
18  ation = 2
19  = 1
20
```

This code creates a new criterion that retrieves only the record(s) from tbl_region that correspond to records that have been retrieved from tbl_country. In other words, if only Canada is retrieved from tbl_country, then only the record that has the same regionID (in the case of Canada, 1) will be retrieved from tbl_region.

The extra AND tacked onto the end means that both this criterion and the original one, which specified that only records corresponding to the URL parameter should be retrieved, must be met.

Speaking more concretely, this revised query will add two new fields to the recordset: regionID and regionName from tbl_regions. In addition, when it does, these will be correlated so that only the regionID and regionName for the active country are retrieved.

4) In the Bindings panel, click the Refresh button to verify that regionID and regionName are appended to the list.

Even though Dreamweaver's Recordset dialog doesn't let you build this code from a wizard, Dreamweaver understands it.

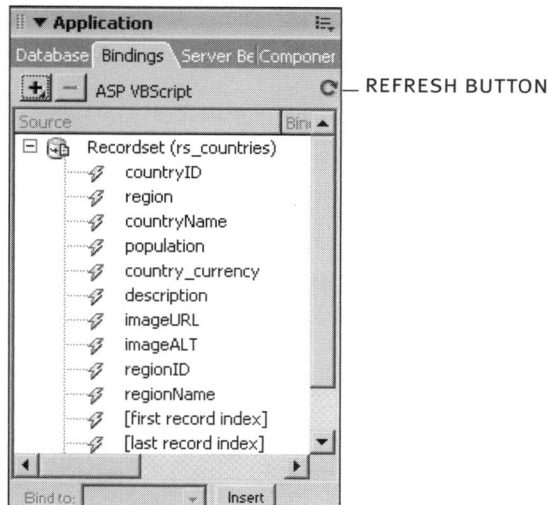

REFRESH BUTTON

5) In design view, delete the rs_countries.region dynamic text just beneath World Region, and in its place, insert the regionName field from the Bindings panel.

In this step, you are outputting the region name itself. You are confident that it will output the right region (that is, it won't say Canada is in East Asia) because of the SQL code you just wrote.

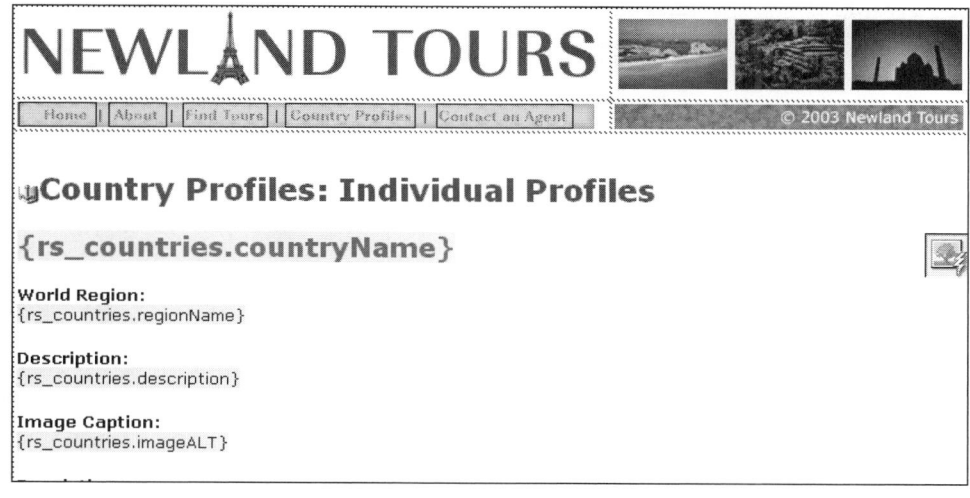

6) Save, upload, and test the file.

You now see the country's continent, rather than an arbitrary number in the World Region section.

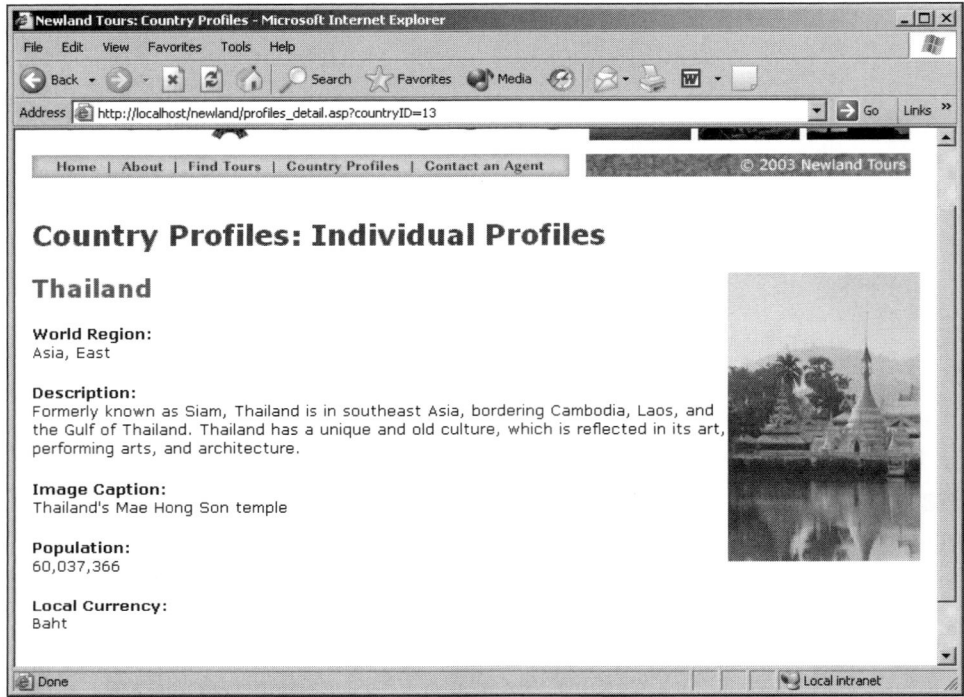

WHAT YOU HAVE LEARNED

In this lesson, you have:

- Created a recordset used to retrieve data to build a list of dynamically generated URLs (pages 282–284)

- Built the list of dynamically generated URLs (pages 284–293)

- Created a recordset used to generate the country profiles (pages 294–295)

- Created a hybrid layout using static HTML and ASP/ColdFusion/PHP scripting to display a country profile (pages 296–299)

- Deployed dynamically inserted images, and formatted a large number (pages 299–305)

- Modified SQL code by hand to combine and filter data from two different tables (pages 306–310)

building the tour descriptions

LESSON 11

When I was in college, I took a few years of Italian. On the first day of the second year, I asked the professor, "What are we learning this year?" The professor replied, "The same thing as last year, only this time I expect you to learn it." While the second year course covered much of the same grammar as the year before, it was different. We became more sensitive to nuances, more capable of expressing ourselves in the language; we began to internalize it and make it our own.

So it is with the application you'll build in Lessons 11 and 12. Much of what you'll do is already familiar, but this time around, you should both be internalizing the tasks and getting more ambitious. In the preceding three lessons, you worked with dynamic data pulled from databases, so you should be getting comfortable with the process of creating recordsets and outputting their values dynamically on pages. In addition to outputting simple text, you've output images dynamically and learned how to format numbers with commas and as currency. At the end of Lesson 10, you even looked up

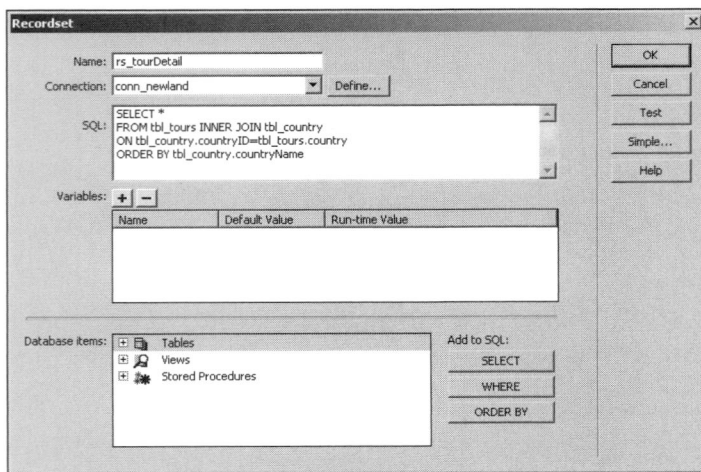

SQL can do a lot more than recall the data from a single table. In this lesson, you'll do some more advanced hand-coding in SQL, including using a structure called a join.

data from one table using criteria supplied by a different one. Such tasks are the substance of dynamic site development—things you will do again and again.

Lessons 11 and 12 build on this knowledge. As with the country profiles search-and-display application, you'll create a two-page mini-application that enables users to search and display tour descriptions. But the tours—they are, after all, the main feature of the Newland Tours Web site—need a slicker set of features. You'll implement three different means of accessing the tours (view all, view by region, or view an individual country). And you'll learn how to pass live data out of this application and into the country profile and tour price calculator applications to make this cluster of applications function a little more intelligently.

You'll push your skills in these lessons by writing your own SQL code, rather than relying on Dreamweaver's Recordset dialog. And the SQL code gets more sophisticated. You'll also start thinking more strategically about how to integrate dynamic data, server-side scripts, and SQL to accomplish certain feats. At the same time, you'll move data effortlessly among the scopes you have already learned: form, querystring/URL, local, and query. Finally, you should be comfortable intermingling HTML and ASP/ColdFusion/PHP code in creative and diverse ways.

WHAT YOU WILL LEARN

In this lesson, you will:

- Plan the search and display application for the tours
- Create a recordset with handwritten SQL code
- Design the layout for tour descriptions, and populate it with dynamic data
- Apply recordset paging, to prevent too many descriptions from showing at once
- Integrate the tour descriptions intelligently with the tour price calculator

APPROXIMATE TIME

This lesson takes approximately two hours to complete.

LESSON FILES

Starting Files:

Lesson11/Start/newland/generic_template.asp
Lesson11/Start/newland/tourprice.asp
*Lesson11/Start/newland/tourprice_
    processor.asp*

Completed Files:

Lesson11/Complete/newland/tours_detail.asp
Lesson11/Complete/newland/tourprice.asp
*Lesson11/Complete/newland/tourprice_
    processor.asp*

PLANNING THE APPLICATION

Before you develop any application, you should have a clear idea of how it's going to work. As you build, potential enhancements and usability issues no doubt will present themselves, and your idea will evolve. But before you begin, you should know what you are building. Often, I draw flowcharts, using Freehand MX, or just paper and pencil.

For this application, you can go online and see the completed version of the application. Once you know where you are headed, the steps you will take to get there make a lot more sense.

1) In a browser, open *http://www.allectomedia.com/newland_dynamic/tours.asp*, **enter** *osiris@allectomedia.com* **as the username, enter** *osiris* **as the password, and click Submit.**

The log-in is something you won't implement for several more lessons.

2) Without clicking, roll your cursor over the world region links and the View all tours link near the bottom.

Notice that the page contains three different ways to access the tour descriptions. You can display all of the tours from a world region. You can display all of the tours for a given country. Or you can display all of the tours unfiltered by clicking the View all tours link.

When you roll over the links that filter by world region, you see that the URL parameter regionID=1 (or another number) is appended to the URL. Not surprisingly, the SQL statement on the descriptions page (tours_detail.asp) filters using this parameter. But when you roll over the View all tours link, no URL parameter appears. Since no data filtering is taking place when users click this link, there is no need to send any special data to the next page.

As you have (hopefully) guessed, if you choose an individual country from the menu and click Submit, then that data is sent as a form variable and used to filter descriptions on the next page. The list of countries in this menu is, of course, dynamically generated, so that the list is always up-to-date.

3) Click a few different links and submit the form a couple of times so you get the feel for how the search and display pages work together.

Pay special attention to the URL. Notice that it contains only URL parameters when you click one of the world region links. It has no parameters when you access the page through the form, and no parameters when you access the page through the View all tours link. Notice also that you can get tours to any given country to show up in each of the three ways.

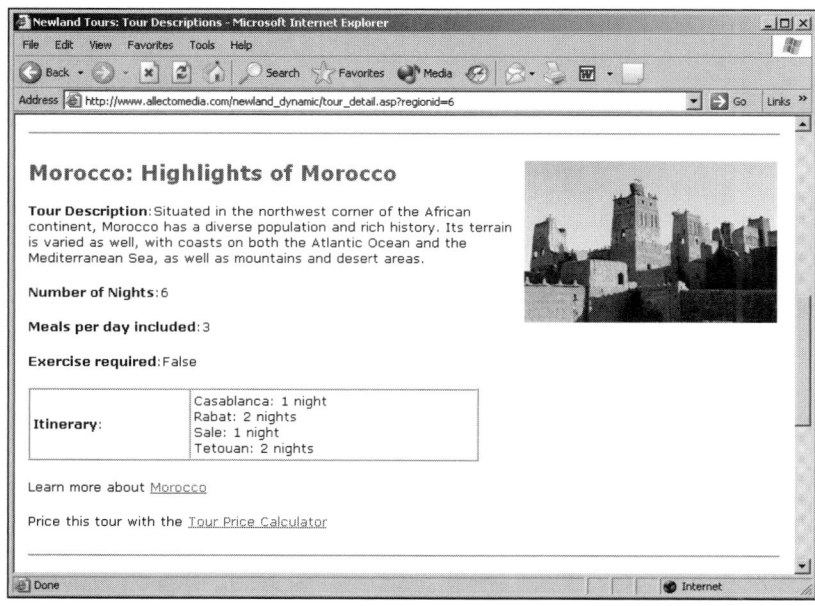

315

4) From any country's description, click the Tour Price Calculator link.

Notice that the drop-down menu that displays the tour names reflects the tour you were looking at before you clicked the link. That is, if you were reading the Highlights of Morocco tour description and click the Tour Price Calculator link, Highlights of Morocco will be preselected in the menu. This is possible in part thanks to the URL parameter (in the case of Highlights of Morocco, it's tourID=17).

In the lesson introduction, I mentioned that you would make the two applications—the search and display pairing for the tour descriptions and the tour price calculator—work together. You'll set up this collaboration later in this lesson.

Again, remember that as long as the database is maintained, the site will always display all of the tours Newland offers, and the display will meet whatever search criteria users select.

When you are finished exploring, close the browser and return to Dreamweaver.

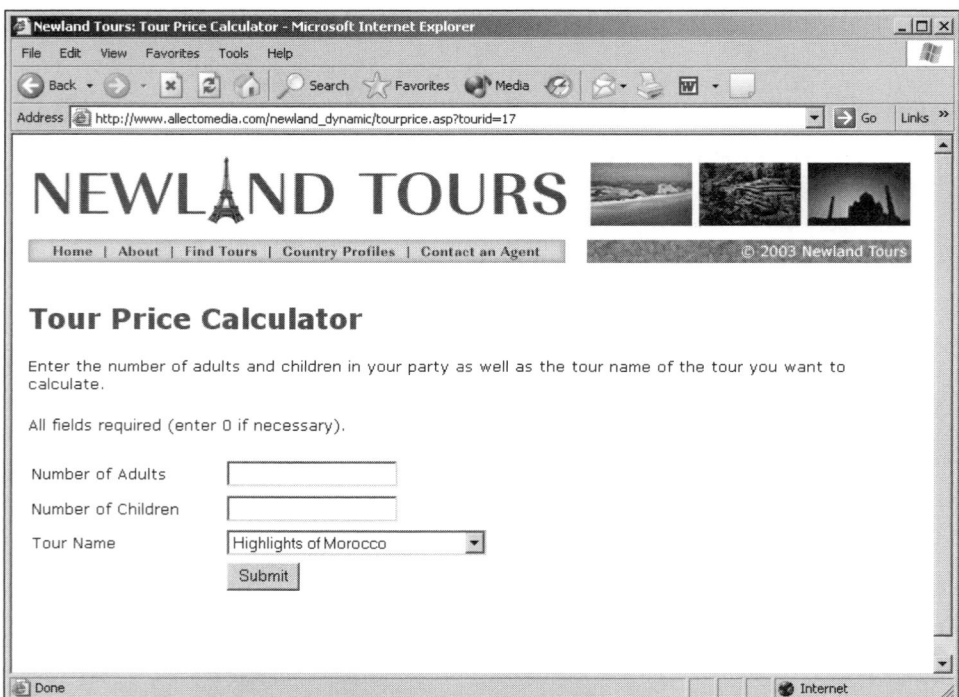

CREATING RECORDSETS WITH JOINS

In this task, you'll begin building the page that displays the tours. This is a new page in the site, so you'll start with generic_template.asp and go from there. This particular page is going to have lots of SQL—no less than three queries, in fact—and you'll build the simplest one in this lesson. This query will retrieve all of the information about all of the tours, without any filtering mechanisms.

When you create this query, you're going to use a SQL structure called a join. As you know, a relational database is split into many different tables that share different relationships. Sometimes, you will need a set of data from two or more tables that are related to one another. To collect all of this information, you use a join. If this sounds scary, don't worry: You've already done it! In Lesson 10 in the country profile page you created a join when you modified the SQL statement so that it retrieved the region name, rather than simply the region ID. (Remember the WHERE clause?)

The syntax you used in Lesson 10, which relied on WHERE, is no longer the preferred way to handle joins, though it is the easiest to understand and it will be supported in all major database management systems (like Access and MySQL) in the foreseeable future, so there is nothing wrong with using it. But there is a better way to join tables, which you will learn in this task.

1) Open generic_template.asp, use the toolbar to title the page *Newland Tours: Tour Descriptions*. Replace the placeholder title text with *Tour Descriptions*. Save the file as *tours_detail.asp*.

2) In the first line of body text, type *Find Tours: Tour Descriptions*. Highlight Find Tours and use the Property inspector to link it to tours.asp. Position the cursor at the end of the word Descriptions, and press Enter/Return twice to add two new lines. Copy the Find Tours line and paste it on the bottom line.

317

In these two steps, you are building the static part of the page. You'll place the tour descriptions in between the two Find Tours links, so users can easily return to the tour search page from the detail page.

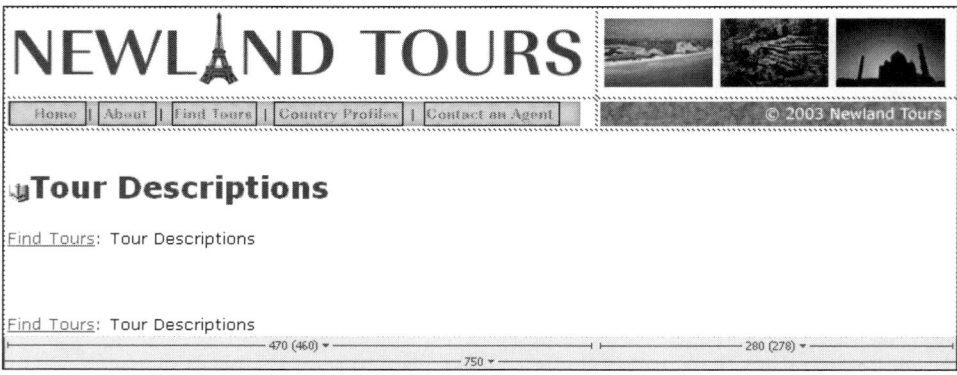

3) Add a new recordset to the page, using the following information:

Name: *rs_tourDetail*

Connection: conn_newland

Table: tbl_tours

Columns: All

You need to create a query that will pull all of the information from the tours table, so you can use it to build the descriptions. As with the country profiles, one of the fields (country) contains a foreign key, which means that it will retrieve an arbitrary number (the country's primary key), rather than the country name, which is what you really want. You'll use a join to retrieve this information, but you can't do that in this simple interface, so in this step you are building the portion of the SQL query that you can use as the basis for the more advanced query you'll write in the next step.

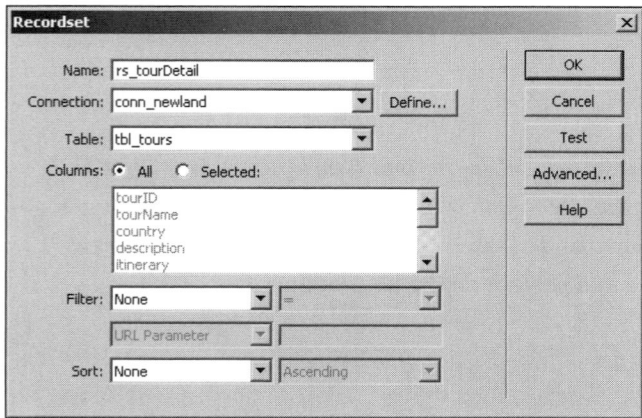

4) Click the Advanced button to open the advanced version of the Recordset dialog.

As you can see, this version of the dialog contains the SQL that you specified in the simple version of the dialog. You'll write the remaining code here in the SQL window.

TIP *You can return to the simple version of the dialog by clicking the Simple button.*

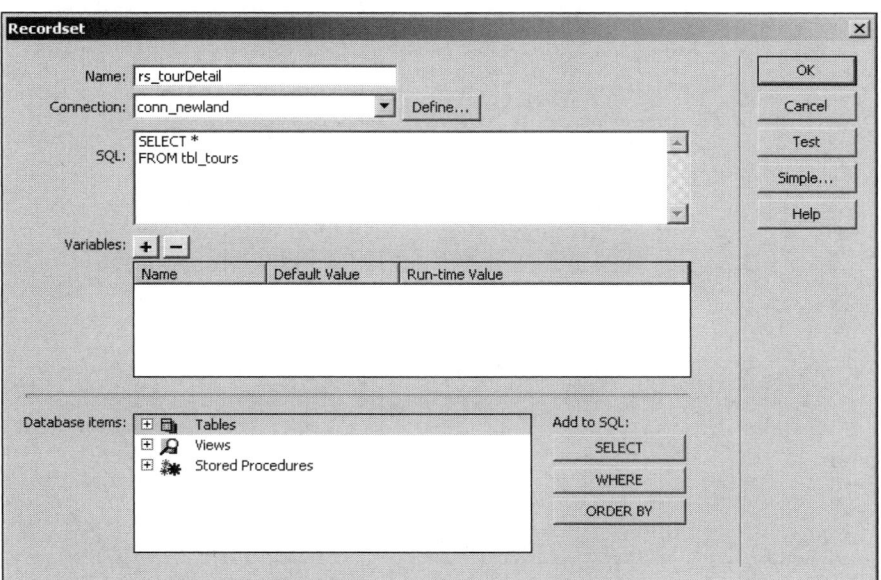

5) Change the SQL statement in the window so that it reads as follows:

```
SELECT *
FROM tbl_tours INNER JOIN tbl_country
ON tbl_country.countryID=tbl_tours.country
ORDER BY tbl_country.countryName
```

The syntax for joins is hard to read for many people. However, this query does the exact same things as the following (easier to read) query:

```
SELECT *
FROM tbl_tours, tbl_country
WHERE tbl_country.countryID=tbl_tours.country
ORDER BY tbl_country.countryName
```

That is, it selects all records and fields from both tables. When it merges the two tables, it does so by matching the value in the country field of tbl_tours with the countryID field, which is the primary key of the tbl_country table. This ensures that the correct country's data is joined to each tour. In other words, the country Argentina (and all of its data as entered in tbl_country) is associated with Highlights of Argentina.

319

Once the two tables are joined together, using the shared country/countryID value as the joining criterion, the retrieved records are listed in order by country name.

TIP *Once you've entered this SQL code, you can no longer switch back to Simple view, because that view has no way of representing the sophisticated SQL statement you just created.*

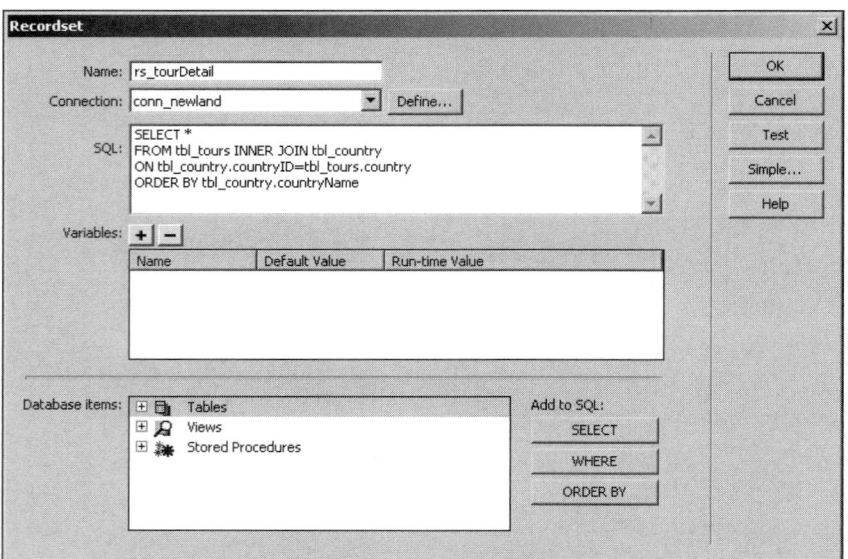

6) Click the Test button.

This brings up a large set of records. You'll need to scroll to the right to see most of the data, as it's offscreen to start.

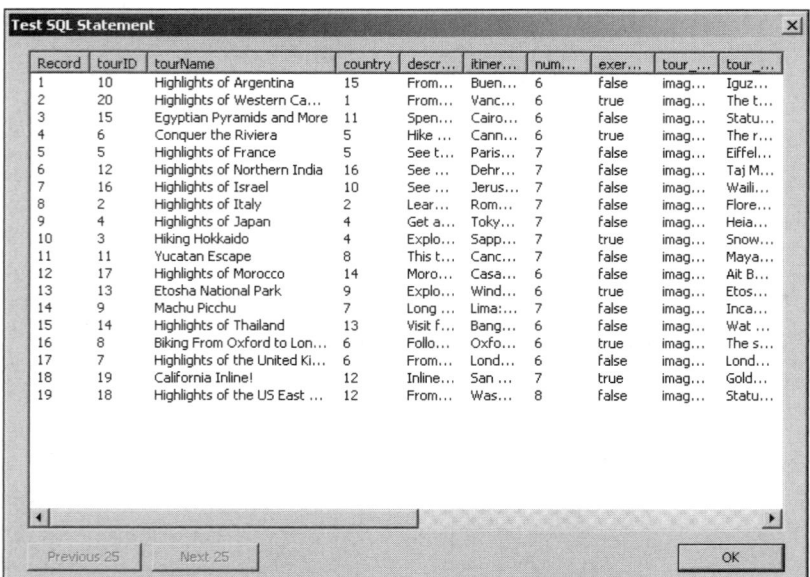

There are a couple of things to note here. First, look in the country column (it should be the fourth column from the left). Notice that it lists only numbers. If you had not done the join, and had output the country in the tour description, these would have appeared in the place of the country names. Scroll to the right, until you see the countryName column. There, you will see each of the countries listed, in alphabetical order. This column was added thanks to the join, and it means that you can output the actual country name, rather than its arbitrary primary key number.

Again, this is no different in its result than what you did in Lesson 10 with the region name. The only difference now is that you are using the best syntax (the INNER JOIN...ON...syntax) to retrieve this data.

7) Click OK twice to close the Test and then the Recordset dialogs.

In the Bindings panel, you'll see the new recordset is in place. As noted earlier, although the simple version of the Recordset dialog can't handle this SQL, Dreamweaver can. The data is correctly represented in the Bindings panel.

TIP *If you double-click the recordset in the Bindings panel to edit it, you will be taken directly to Advanced view, because Simple view cannot represent the code.*

The data is now available to the page, so you can begin laying out the tour descriptions.

BUILDING THE DESCRIPTIONS

In this task, you will prepare the tour descriptions. As with the country profiles, this activity blends together both static and dynamic elements.

1) In design view, position the insertion point between the two Find Tours lines, and choose Insert > HTML > Horizontal Rule.

The horizontal rule will be used to separate each of the tour descriptions.

2) Type the following into the document:

XX Country Name: Tour Name XX
Tour Description:
Number of Nights:
Meals Per Day Included:
Exercise Required:
Itinerary:
Learn More About XX Country Name XX
Price This Tour With the Tour Price Calculator
All Photographs © PhotoDisc

Once again, you are entering the static content first, just to provide the page with its initial structure. In the coming steps, you'll insert dynamic content in appropriate places within the page.

To add the © symbol, choose Insert > HTML > Special Characters > Copyright.

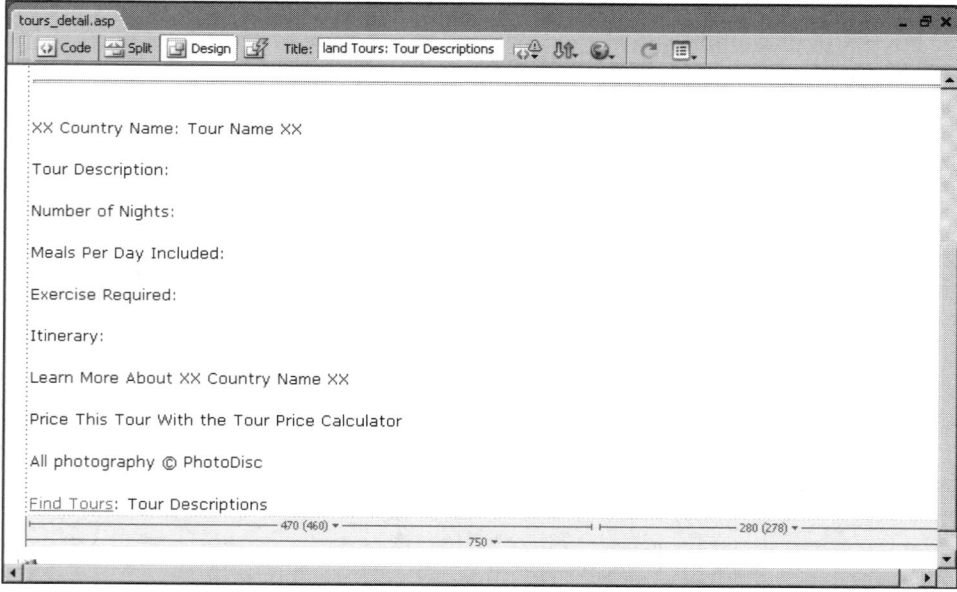

3) Click once in the XX Country Name: Tour Name XX line, and use the Property inspector's Format menu to change it to a Heading 2 element. One at a time, for each of the next five paragraphs, select the text up to (but not including) the colon, and click the Strong button in the Text category of the Insert Bar.

Here you are formatting the static HTML framework that you created in the previous step.

Because clicking the Bold button in the Property inspector results in Dreamweaver inserting `<span class="author">` tags, rather than `<strong>` tags, we're manually telling Dreamweaver to insert `<strong>` tags around these elements.

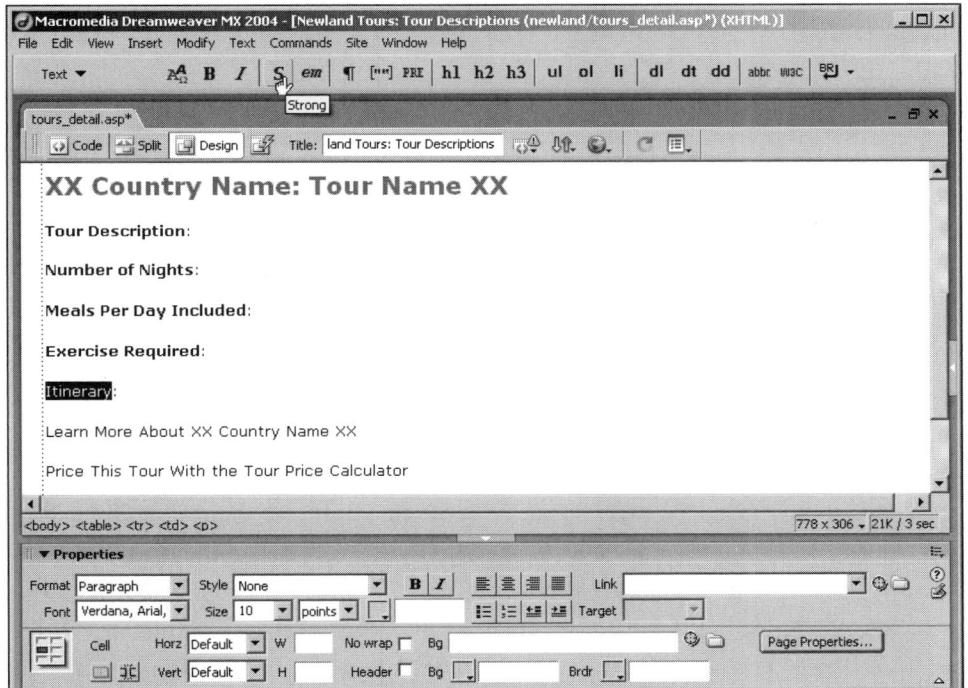

4) Select XX Country Name from the title, and replace it with countryName from the Bindings panel.

Dreamweaver replaces the placeholder text you typed with its own pseudocode to indicate the source of the dynamic text.

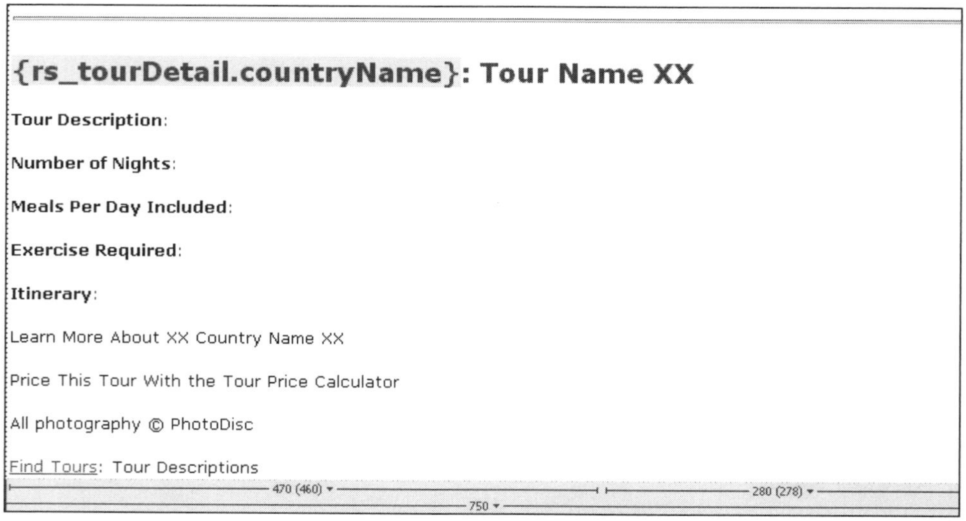

{rs_tourDetail.countryName}: Tour Name XX

Tour Description:

Number of Nights:

Meals Per Day Included:

Exercise Required:

Itinerary:

Learn More About XX Country Name XX

Price This Tour With the Tour Price Calculator

All photography © PhotoDisc

Find Tours: Tour Descriptions

470 (460) ▾   280 (278) ▾

750 ▾

---

5) Select Tour Name XX, and replace it with tourName from the Bindings panel. Choose View > Live Data to verify that one country and tour are displaying correctly. Toggle off Live Data once you have verified that it's working.

I often toggle Live Data on and off during development just to make sure there are no surprises. You should see Argentina: Highlights of Argentina in the title. The interesting thing to point out is that not only is the title derived from two different fields in a recordset, but the different fields are also derived from two different database tables. The country name comes from tbl_country, and the tour name comes from tbl_tours. The fact that the country (Argentina) is correctly correlated with the tour (Highlights of Argentina) is further confirmation that the join in your query worked.

```
Argentina: Highlights of Argentina

Tour Description:

Number of Nights:

Meals Per Day Included:

Exercise Required:

Itinerary:

Learn More About XX Country Name XX

Price This Tour With the Tour Price Calculator

All photography © PhotoDisc

Find Tours: Tour Descriptions
                  ──── 470 (460) ▾ ────      ─┤ ├─        ──── 280 (278) ▾ ────
                            ──── 750 ▾ ────
```

6) Bind dynamic data after each of the following five items (the same five you bolded in step 3, as specified below:

Tour Description: *description*

Number of Nights: *numNights*

Meals per day included: *meals_per_day*

Exercise Required: *exerciseReqd*

Itinerary: *itinerary*

This is the meat-and-potatoes step of adding most of the dynamic content to the page. It is no different than what you have done before.

```
Argentina: Highlights of Argentina

Tour Description: South America's second-largest country spans from the Andes to several islands in the
Atlantic, and all the way down to Punta Dungeness, the southern extreme of the continent. With thousands of
miles of coastline and home to one of the world's most formidable mountain ranges, Argentina is a hiker's
paradise.

Number of Nights: 6

Meals Per Day Included: 2

Exercise Required: False

Itinerary: Buenos Aires: 3 nights
Mar del Plata: 3 nights

Learn More About XX Country Name XX

Price This Tour With the Tour Price Calculator

All photography © PhotoDisc
```

7) Toggle Live Data back on.

For the most part, it seems to be coming together pretty well. The itinerary part looks sloppy, however, because the second night is on a new line, which doesn't line up with the first. A simple table will fix this.

8) Toggle off Live Data and create a table with one row and two columns to separate the static text from the dynamic text. Give it the settings shown in the screenshot. Then drag Itinerary: into the left cell, and drag the dynamic block into the right.

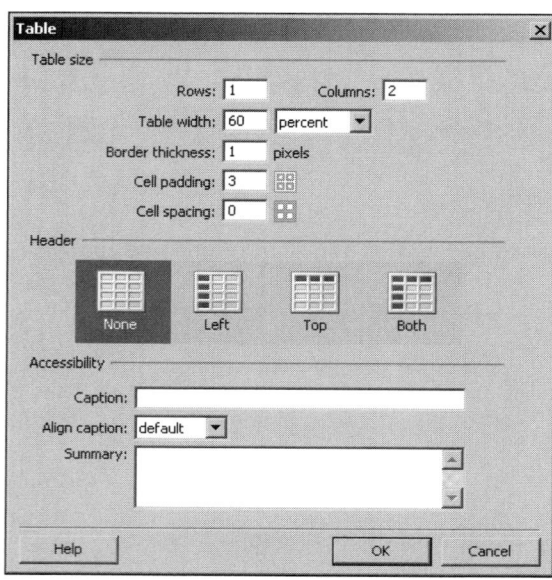

This way, when the itinerary is output on multiple lines, they'll all line up properly. You'll need to toggle Live Data back on to see the results.

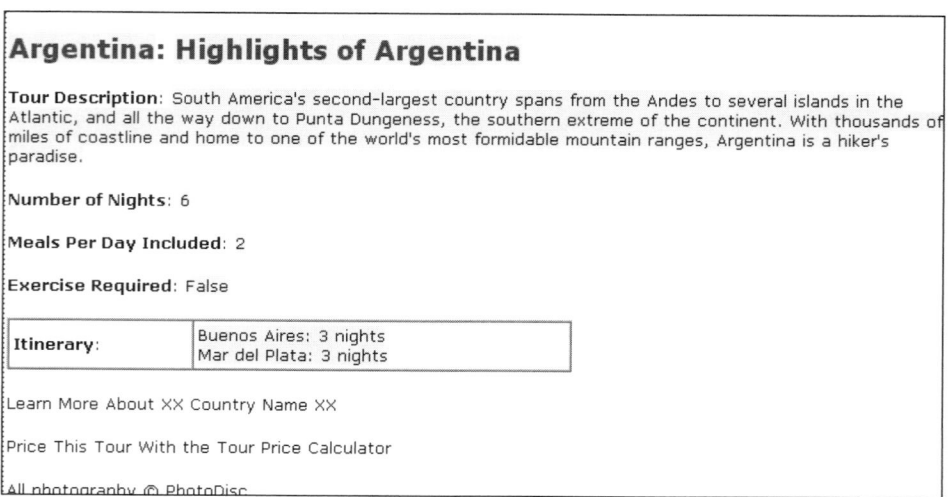

9) Select XX Country Name XX in the paragraph below the itinerary table, and replace it with countryName from the Bindings panel.

This will output the country name again. Later in this lesson, you'll add a link from this country name to its profile.

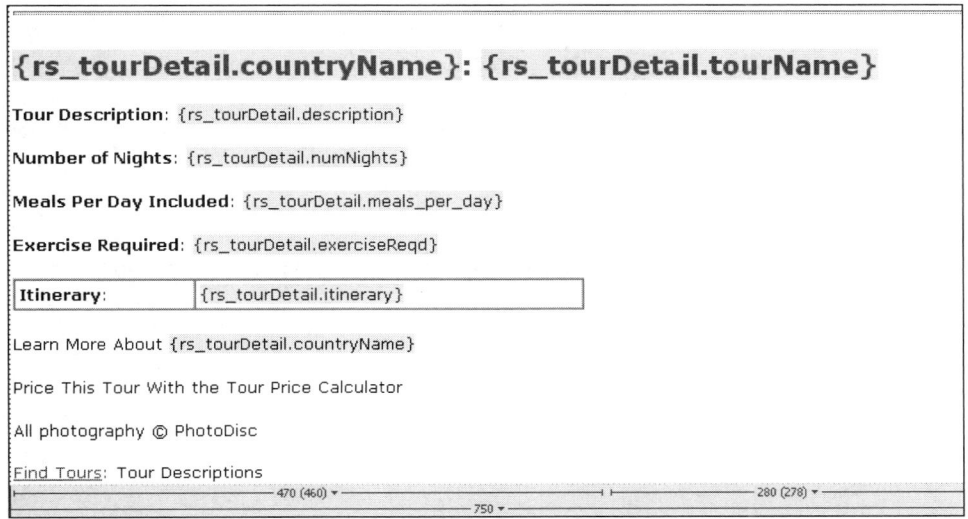

INSERTING THE IMAGES AND alt ATTRIBUTES

The tour descriptions, like the country profiles, each have an image. In this task, you'll add those images (dynamically, of course), and you'll also add alt descriptions using information stored in the database.

1) Position the insertion point just before the tour name {rs_tourDetail.countryName} in the heading near the top of the page.

The image will be positioned in the top-right corner of each tour description, much as it was with the country profiles.

327

2) Choose Insert > Image. In the Select Image Source dialog, click the Data sources radio button. Expand the recordset, and choose tour_imageURL in the list. Click OK.

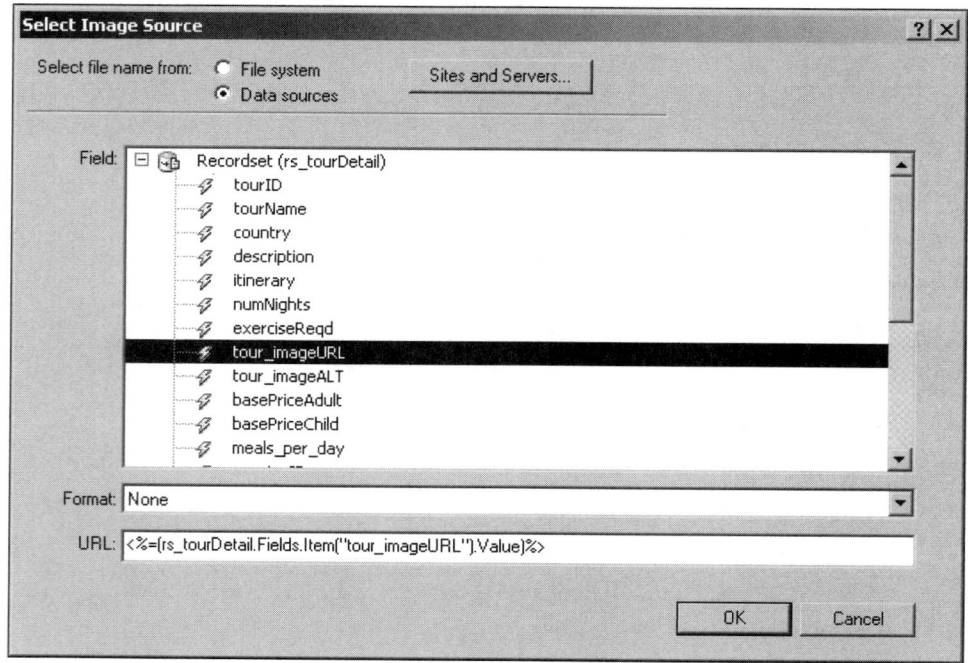

Once again, the text string that contains the URL is stored in the database. When you insert a dynamic image, what you are really inserting is a dynamic string of text, which consists of a URL pointing to an image, inside of an <img> element.

An image icon appears in the document, where the insertion point was a moment ago.

3) With the image icon still selected, set its alignment to Right in the Property inspector.

The image icon moves to the right side of the page.

To make sure that the image works as expected, you can toggle on Live Data. You should see a photo of a series of waterfalls, with a rainbow and a lake in the foreground.

NOTE *If you see some ice-capped mountains with a lake in the foreground, you selected imageURL, rather than tour_imageURL in the Select Image Source dialog. imageURL contains a link to the image for the country (that is, the image that should show up in the country profiles). A separate image is shown for the tours, and this is stored as tour_imageURL.*

Argentina: Highlights of Argentina

Tour Description: South America's second-largest country spans from the Andes to several islands in the Atlantic, and all the way down to Punta Dungeness, the southern extreme of the continent. With thousands of miles of coastline and home to one of the world's most formidable mountain ranges, Argentina is a hiker's paradise.

Number of Nights: 6

Meals Per Day Included: 2

Exercise Required: False

Itinerary:	Buenos Aires: 3 nights Mar del Plata: 3 nights

Learn More About Argentina

Price This Tour With the Tour Price Calculator

4) Select the image on the page, and in the Bindings panel, click to select tour_imageALT.

When you select tour_imageALT, the Bind To menu at the bottom of the panel becomes active, usually defaulting to img.src.

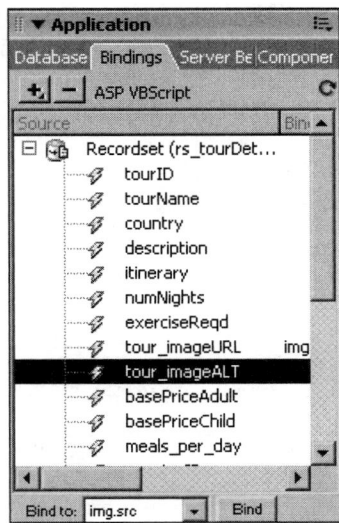

5) In the Bind To menu, change the selected option to img.alt. Click Bind.

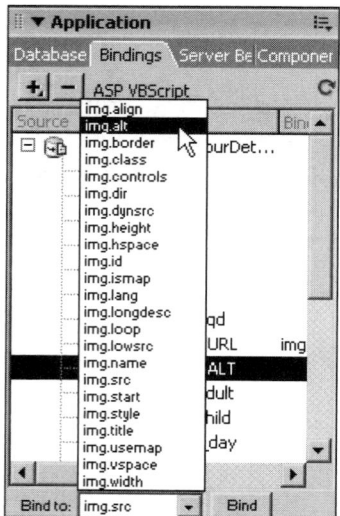

The image caption is now bound to the image as an alternate description. To confirm this, with the image selected, look in the Alt field of the Property inspector. You should see some dynamic code, and somewhere in that code, you should see `rs_tourDetail.tour_imageALT`.

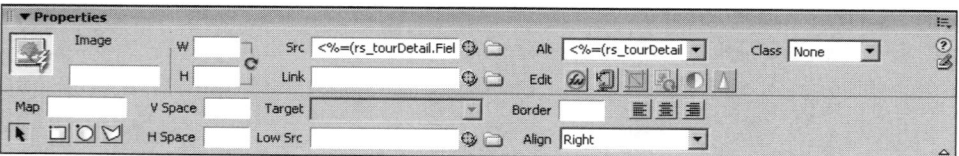

6) Save, upload, and test the file.

The page should look pretty good in a browser at this point. Depending on your browser, if you hover your cursor over the image, a tool tip may appear displaying the alt description. Also, double-check that all of the dynamic text fields look right. For example, underneath the itinerary table, you should see "Learn more about Argentina."

330

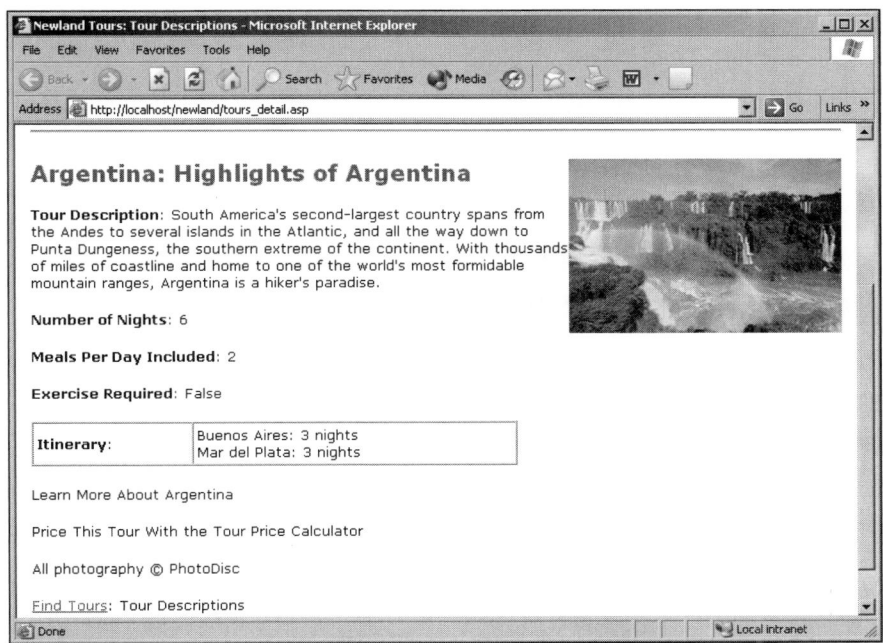

IMPLEMENTING RECORDSET PAGING

Other than the two links near the bottom of the description, which link to other applications (the country profiles and tour price calculator applications), the description is complete. One glaring problem, however, is that Newland Tours appears to only offer one tour (the one to Argentina). You need to make the output loop so that it includes each of the tour descriptions, not just the first one returned.

You used a Repeat Region server behavior in Lesson 10 to output each of the country names on profiles.asp. You'll use that behavior again with the descriptions to output more than one. The problem, though, is that unlike with the country names you output on profiles.asp, which contained a country name only, here you will be outputting an entire description, complete with an image. That could result in a long page and download time.

The functionality of the page would be better if you could limit the number of records shown, so that, for example, only five descriptions appeared at once, and users could navigate back and forth through them. This is possible—and quite easy—using a set of built-in Dreamweaver server behaviors. The Repeat Region behavior lets you limit the number of records (in this case, tour descriptions) that are displayed on a page. Another behavior, called Recordset Navigation Bar, automates the process of creating the First, Previous, Next, and Last links (or buttons) that enable users to access all of the descriptions. You'll use both behaviors in this task to create the desired functionality.

331

1) Drag to select everything from (and including) the horizontal rule through the "Price this tour with the Tour Price Calculator" paragraph.

This will be the repeated region. You don't want to include the copyright notice or the second Find Tours link in the repeated region—those should appear beneath all the tours.

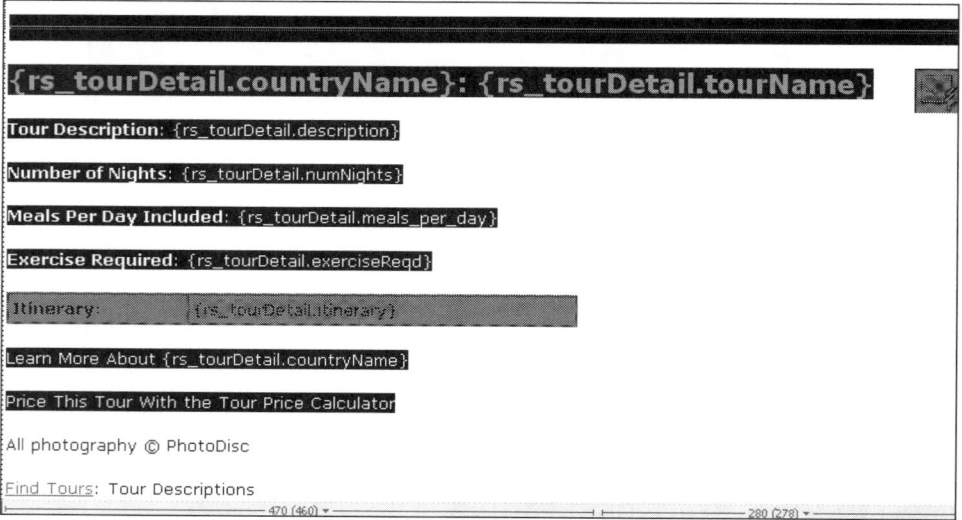

2) Use the Server Behaviors panel to add a Repeat Region behavior to the selection. In the Repeat Region dialog, enter 5 for the number of records to be shown at a time. Click OK.

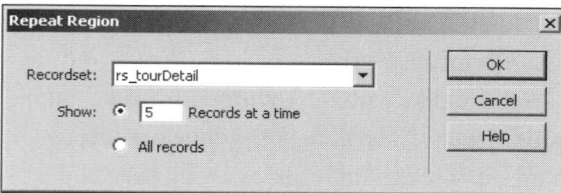

A Repeat Region square is drawn around the entire selection, indicating its boundaries.

3) Save, upload, and press F12 to test the page, to view it in a browser.

You'll see the first five records, listed alphabetically by country name. The first is still Highlights of Argentina, while the last record on the page should be Highlights of France.

332

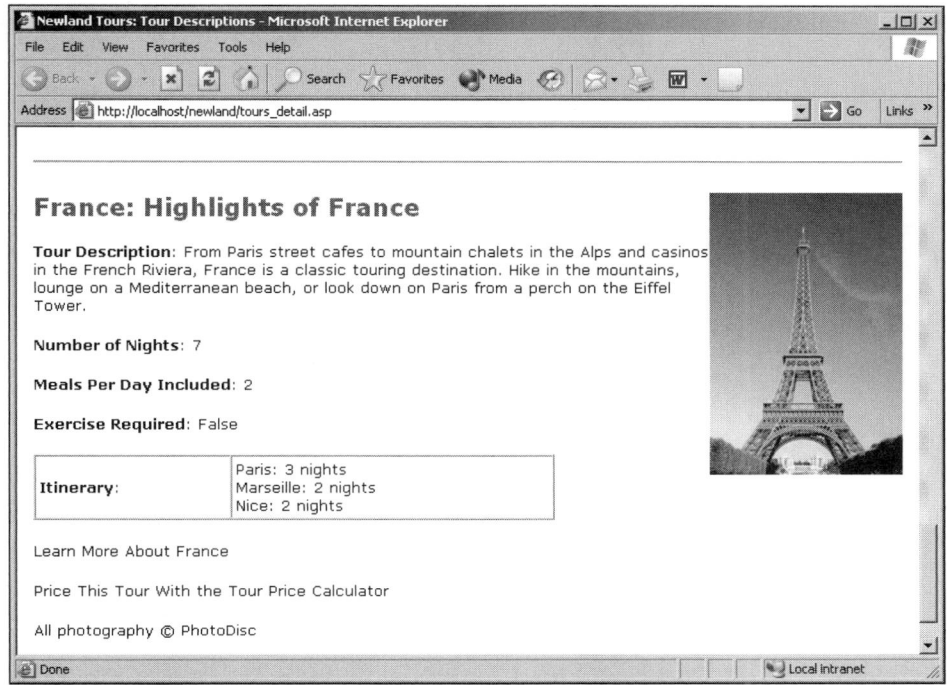

At this point, though, there is no way for you to display the next five records or skip to the end. You are stuck with only the first five tour descriptions.

4) Return to Dreamweaver, and insert an empty line beneath the Repeat Region area. With the insertion point in that empty line, choose Insert > Application Objects > Recordset Paging > Recordset Navigation Bar.

This "application object" is actually a group of server behaviors. It creates First, Previous, Next, and Last links or buttons (your choice). Each of these links tells ASP, ColdFusion, or PHP which five recordsets to show when they are clicked. In addition, if the user is viewing the first set of recordsets, the First and Previous links/buttons will be hidden, because they don't apply. Likewise, the Next and Last links/buttons won't be visible if the user is browsing the final set of records. All four links/buttons are visible in the middle.

5) In the Recordset Navigation Bar dialog, accept the defaults (rs_tourDetail as the Recordset, and Text as the Display Using option), and click OK.

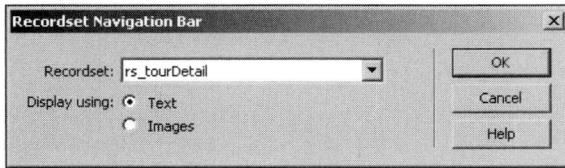

When you are finished, you'll see a new table added to the page, containing the four links. If you look in the Server Behaviors panel near the bottom, you'll also see several new behaviors, including several that begin, "Show if not…" and several "Move to XXX Record." Again, these are the individual behaviors created when you add a recordset navigation bar.

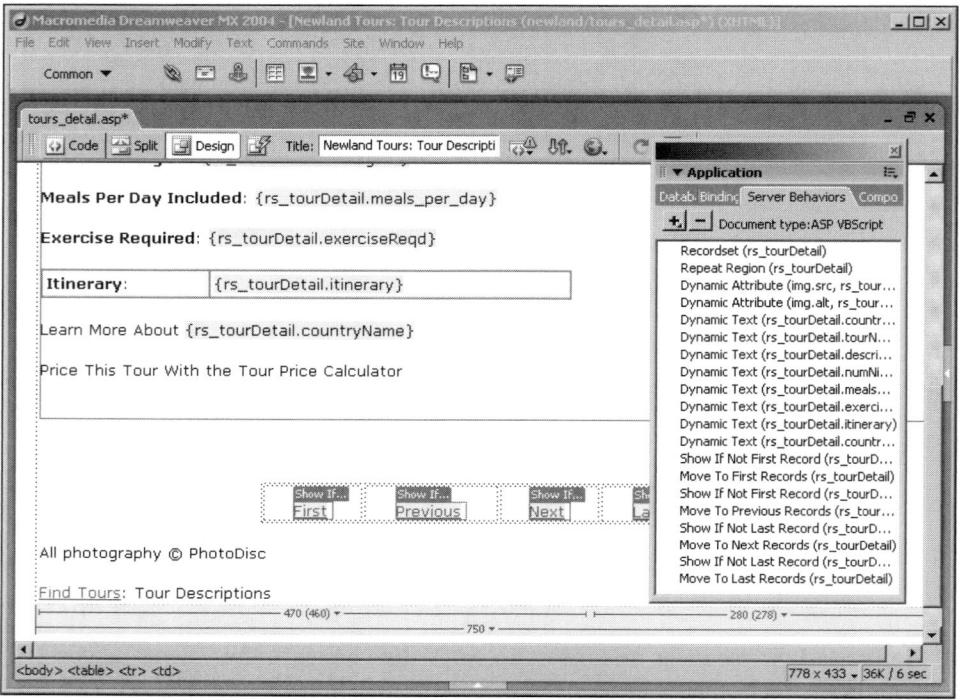

You can build this type of navigation bar manually, if you like, since all the server behaviors you need are individually available in the Server Behaviors panel, in the Recordset Paging and Show Region portions of the menu.

6) Click anywhere inside the table that contains the four links, select the right-most *<table>* tag in the tag selector, and use the Property inspector to set the cell padding to 3, the cell spacing to 0, and the border to 1.

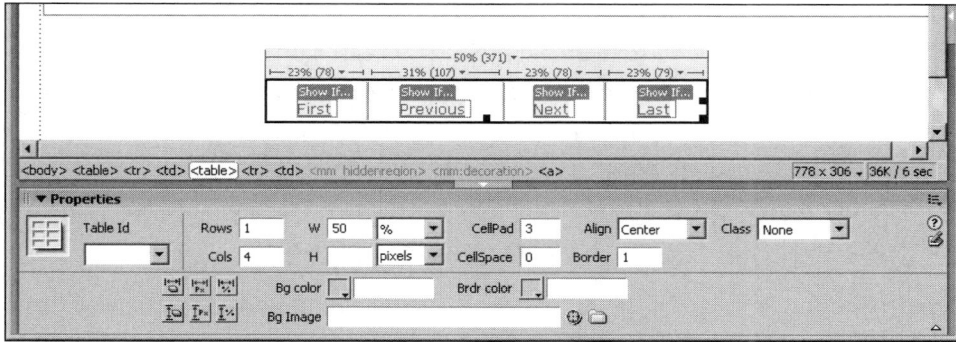

By default, the table that holds the links is invisible. Often, that's OK, but given how prominent other elements on the page are, the navigation bar is easily overlooked. By giving it a border, you make it stand out a bit more.

7) Save, upload, and press F12 to test the page. Use the navigation bar to move backward and forward through the records.

The navigation works as expected. The only problem is that the table holding the navigation bar doesn't look quite right on the first and last pages. That's because it is illegal in HTML to have table cells with no content. On the first and last pages, the conditional regions are suppressing the First/Previous or the Next/Last links, so the cells are empty. You can get around this by adding a blank space to each cell.

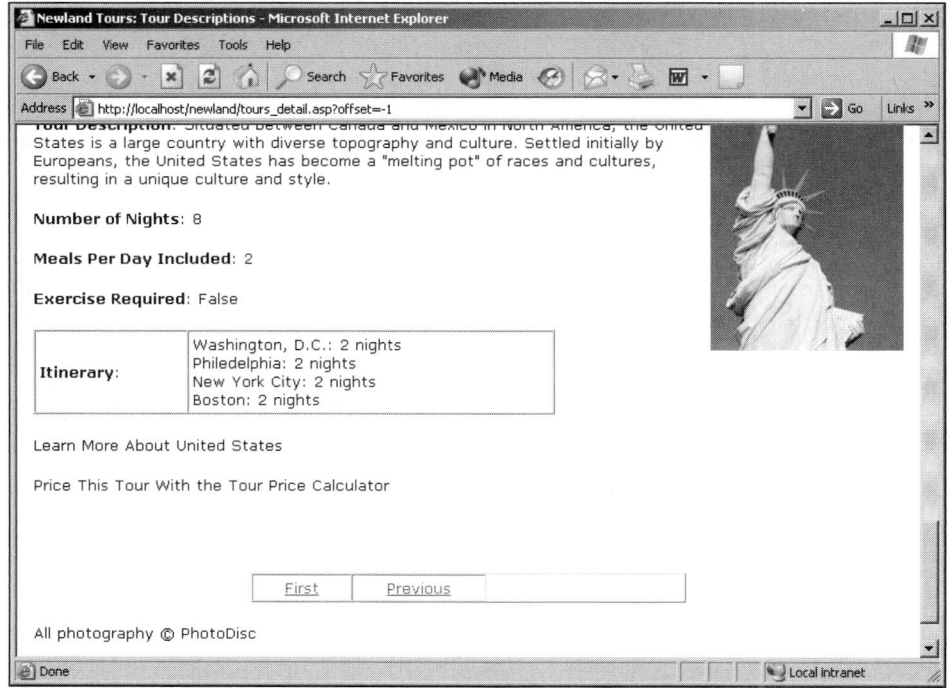

335

**8) One at a time, click after each link (ASP and PHP users) and choose Insert >
HTML> Special Characters > Non-Breaking Space. ColdFusion users will have to go
into code view and insert _ _ (the non-breaking space HTML character entity)
anywhere between each opening and closing _<td>_ and _</td>_ tag, but outside of the
<cfif> blocks contained inside.**

Though the space is obviously invisible, it fulfills the need to have some content
inside every table cell. If you test the file again, the table will look normal.

Before or after doesn't make any difference, as long as the space is entered *outside* the
conditional region. Clicking after the link in ColdFusion tends to put the link inside,
so I suggest that ColdFusion users type in the non-breaking space character manually.

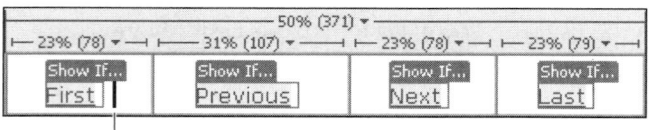

NON-BREAKING SPACE ADDED (ASP AND PHP)

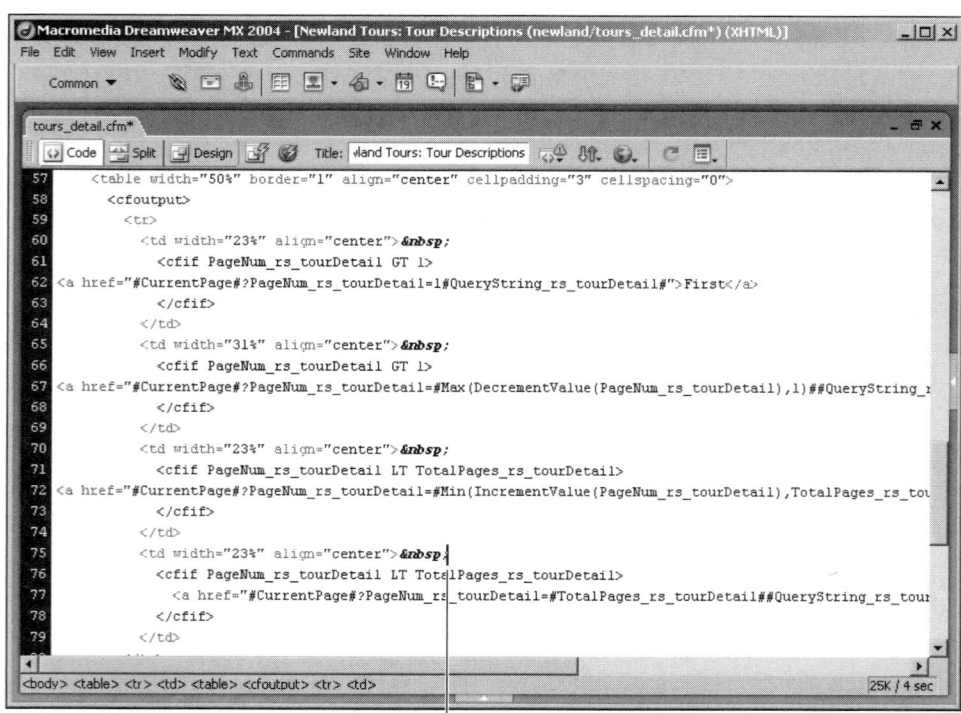

  MANUALLY ENTERED
INTO CODE (COLDFUSION)

PASSING DATA TO OTHER APPLICATIONS

Users can now browse through all of the tour descriptions, five at a time. The descriptions are laid out and attractive, and the recordset navigation bar makes it easy to go back and forth through the recordsets. Before you wrap up the lesson, you need to add two more pieces of functionality.

At the bottom of each description should be two links. The first link is a country name that takes users to the country's profile on profiles_detail.asp. The second link takes users to the tour price calculator (tourprice.asp). You can't simply create a link to these two pages, however. You need to pass data to both pages as well, so that the pages know which tour description the user was reading when she or he clicked the link.

Handling this functionality is easy in the case of the country profiles. As you'll recall, the country profiles page uses a URL parameter, countryID, to determine which country to show. This URL parameter appears when the user clicks the country name on profiles.asp. To get the same functionality, you'll need to add the same URL parameter to the link on tours_detail.asp.

The tour price calculator link will be somewhat more complicated. That page has a dynamically generated drop-down menu listing all of the tours. But if the user is reading Highlights of Italy, then clicks the Price This Tour with the Tour Price Calculator link, and arrives at the tour price calculator form, he or she wants to see the price for Highlights of Italy (not the default option of Biking from Oxford to London). Again, the solution is similar to the country profile link—you just need to send the page some extra data. But the tour price calculator is a little more complicated, because it isn't ready to receive and use that data; this is in contrast to the country profiles page, which is already expecting the countryID URL parameter. You'll take care of this (and a couple other issues) in this task.

First, let's take care of the link to the country profiles page.

1) Select the dynamic text that appears at the end of the "Learn more about" paragraph. In the Property inspector, type *abc* as a placeholder to create a link.

Just as in Lesson 10, the placeholder URL will be replaced as soon as you attach dynamic data. But you need to put something there to create the link in the first place.

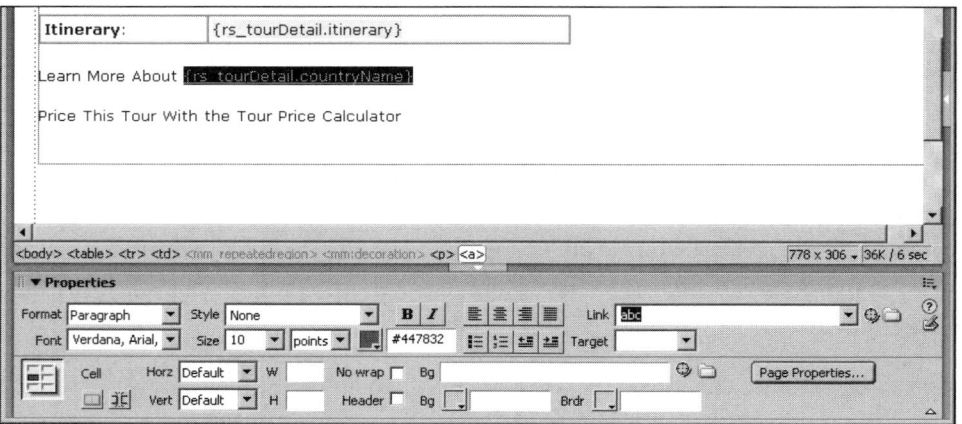

2) With the dynamic text still selected, click countryID in the Bindings panel, make sure that a.href is selected in the Bind To menu, and click Bind.

This step binds the value of countryID to the URL. Currently, the href attribute of the URL contains only a number. You need to go back and type in the main URL itself, as well as the variable name for the URL parameter.

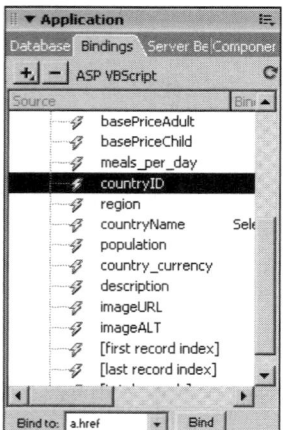

3) With the link still selected, in the Link field of the Property inspector, position the insertion point at the very beginning, before the dynamic code, and enter *profiles_detail.asp?countryID=*.

This is the link to the page itself, and after the server has resolved all the code, the countryID value will be appended just after the = sign. The profiles_detail.asp page will function correctly at this point. If you like, you can test this page and click one of the country name links, to be sure.

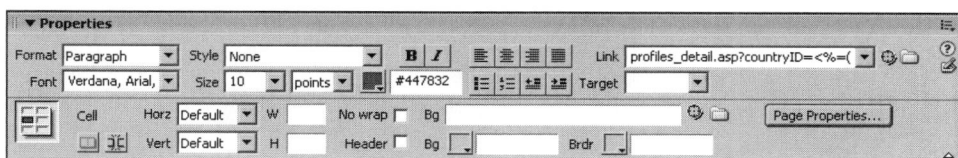

4) In the final paragraph of the description, select the words Tour Price Calculator. Enter *abc* in the Property inspector's Link field to add a link. Using the same technique as before, use the Bindings panel to bind tourID to a.href in the Bind To drop-down menu.

Once again, abc is replaced with the tourID value. You still need to go back and add the rest of the URL.

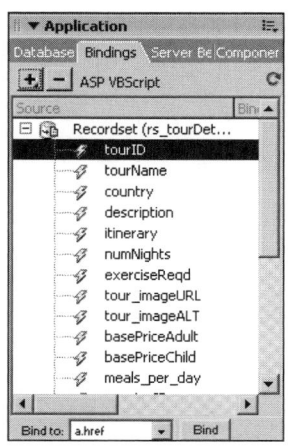

5) Position the cursor at the beginning of the Property inspector's Link field, and type the following URL before the dynamic text: *tourprice.asp?tourID=*. Save and close tours_detail.asp.

Once you have completed this step, you have added the functionality that sends the tourID value to tourprice.asp. Unfortunately, nothing on that page is expecting that value, so nothing happens.

339

6) Open tourprice.asp, and open the Bindings panel. Add a new Request.Querystring (ASP) or URL (ColdFusion and PHP) variable called tourID.

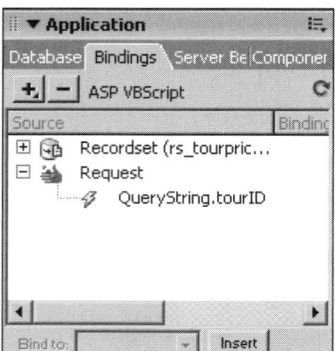

By creating this binding, you make the URL variable sent from tours_detail.asp available on this page. In the next step, you'll bind this information to the menu, so that the correct tour is highlighted automatically.

TIP *In the ColdFusion and PHP server models, previously defined URL, form, and cookie variables tend to stick around for a long time, which can be useful or annoying, depending on whether you often reuse certain variables. For example, the myPet variable from the temporary widget that you built in Lesson 5 is still listed in the Bindings panel. Old variables like these do no harm, but if the clutter starts annoying you, you might consider deleting them. To delete a binding, simply click and press the Delete key (or the Removing Binding [minus] button). If the binding you delete is the last or only binding in a category (e.g., cookie), then that whole category disappears. Deleting a binding from this panel does not affect any of the bindings you have dragged onto any page.*

7) Click to select the drop-down menu in the form, beside Tour Name. In the Property inspector, click the Dynamic button.

You've already bound dynamic data to this menu. In fact, all of the items listed in the menu are dynamically added from a database. Your goal at this point isn't to add any more items—they're all present and accounted for—but rather to set the default to match the parameter sent in the URL.

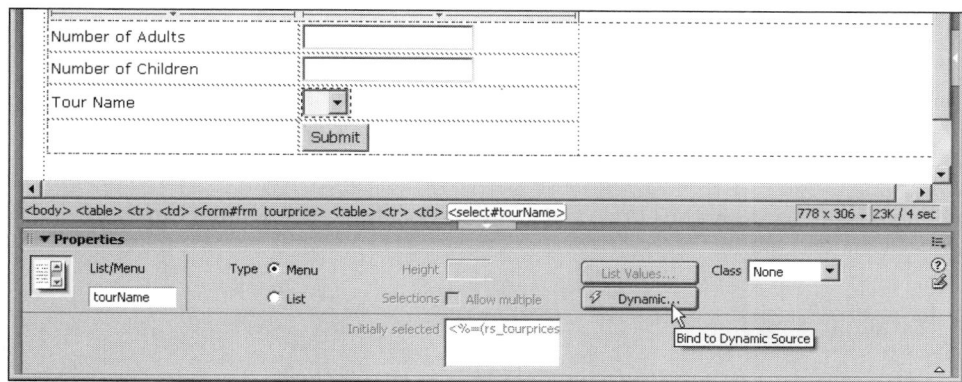

8) In the Dynamic List/Menu dialog, click the lightning bolt icon beside the Select Value Equal To field at the bottom to open the Dynamic Data dialog. In that dialog, select QueryString.tourID (ASP) or URL.tourID (ColdFusion and PHP), and click OK twice to save the settings.

As you probably recall from Lesson 9, the menu object has two main pieces of information that define it: its label (which humans can read and which are populated with tour names) and its values (which are sent with the form and which are populated with tour IDs). Here, you are setting the selected value (and hence label) to be equivalent to the value sent as a URL parameter.

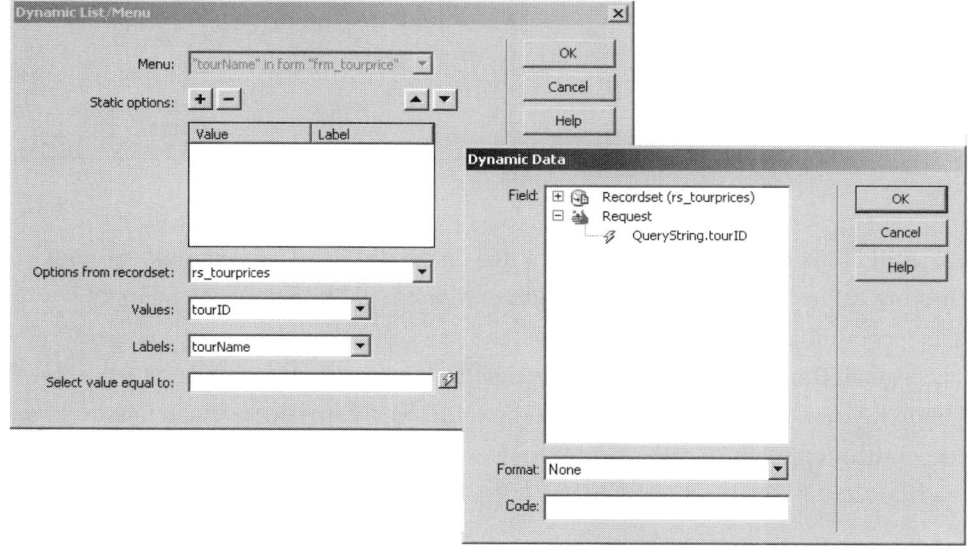

341

9) Save and upload tourprice.asp. Select tours_detail.asp in the Site panel, and press F12 to test it. Choose a random tour, and click both its country name link (which should take you to the correct profile) and its Tour Price Calculator link (which should load the proper tour name in the form menu).

Notice that the URL parameter is displayed at the bottom of the browser window, when you roll over the Tour Price Calculator link. The functionality is working pretty well, with one exception.

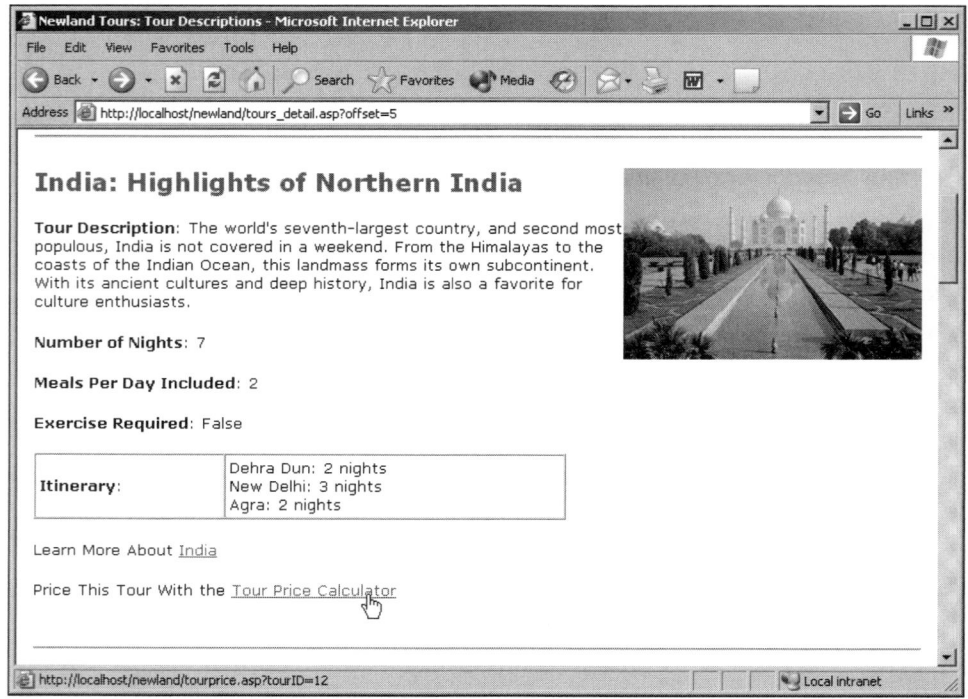

10) Still in the browser, click the Tour Price Calculator link from any tour. Without entering values for the Number of Adults or Number of Children, click Submit.

The form validation kicks in and reloads the page, displaying the error message. So far, so good. But notice that the Tour Name has reverted to Biking From Oxford to London. When the page was reloaded, the tourID URL parameter is no longer there, and so the menu fails to display the correct tour, and instead shows the first tour in the recordset.

Ideally, the form validation script on tourprice_processor.asp would send the tourID URL parameter back to tourprice.asp when it redirects the page.

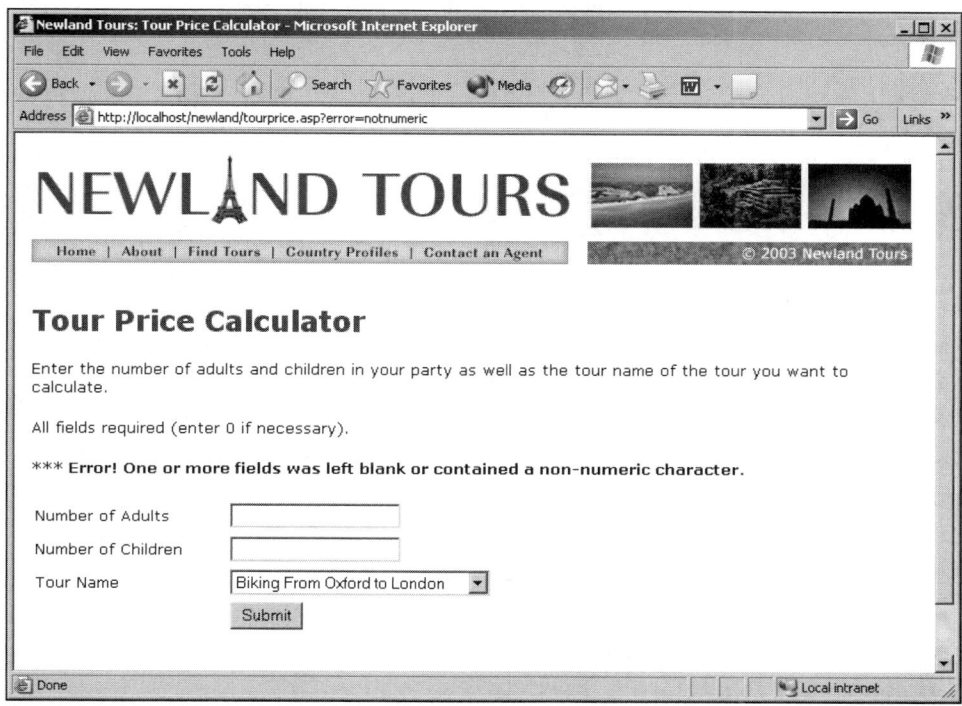

11) Close tourprice.asp, and open tourprice_processor.asp. Switch to code view. Near the top, look for the comment, *"Form validation script; redirects user back to tourprice.asp if form fields...."* In that script, locate the following code:

In ASP:

```
Response.Redirect("tourprice.asp?error=notnumeric")
```

In ColdFusion:

```
<cflocation url="tourprice.cfm?error=notnumeric">
```

In PHP:

```
header("Location: tourprice.php?error=notnumeric"
```

This piece of code is where the form validation redirects back to tourprice.asp. As you can see, it is already appending a URL parameter. You might as well add another one, to complete the functionality.

12) Change the code you just identified so that it reads as follows:

In ASP:

```
Response.Redirect("tourprice.asp?error=notnumeric&tourID=" &
⇒Request.Form("tourName"))
```

In ColdFusion:

```
<cflocation url="tourprice.cfm?error=notnumeric&tourID=#form.tourName#">
```

In PHP:

```
header("Location: tourprice.php?error=notnumeric&tourID=".$_POST['tourName']);
```

You can probably already guess what the added code does. It appends a URL variable called tourID to the page when it is redirected. The value of this tourID variable is the value of form.tourName, which is the active tour when the Submit button was pressed. As you know, since you just programmed it in steps 6 to 8 above, tourprice.asp selects the correct tour in the menu based on a URL variable called tourID.

13) Save, upload, and test the files all over again.

This time, the whole transaction should work. You seamlessly transfer from one application to another, and the page responds appropriately, thanks to some simple data transfer and preparation.

WHAT YOU HAVE LEARNED

In this lesson, you have:

- Learned the syntax for, and created SQL joins (pages 317–321)
- Laid out the tour descriptions, mixing static HTML and dynamic data (pages 322–327)
- Added images dynamically, and generated the contents of the alt attributes dynamically (pages 327–330)
- Applied the Repeat Region server behavior to enable display of multiple descriptions simultaneously (pages 331–336)
- Deployed the Recordset Navigation Bar server object (pages 333–336)
- Integrated three different applications intelligently by sending and receiving data (pages 337–344)

building search interfaces

LESSON 12

It's time to complete the tour search application you began in Lesson 11. There, you built tours_detail.asp, which displays all of the tours in an unfiltered format. In this lesson, you will build a search page that enables users to search tours in three different ways: show all, show by world region, and show by country.

The challenge is to create three independent means of searching tours, all while showing the results on the same page (tours_detail.asp). The search page (tours.asp) will contain three ways of accessing tours_detail.asp. One way is a simple URL with no URL parameters, which will show tours_detail.asp unfiltered (that is, the way it currently exists). The second way will use a URL that has additional URL variables. And the third will access the page by submitting a form, which passes form variables. Both URL and form variables will be used to filter the recordset dynamically.

To get these three different ways of getting tours_detail.asp to work, you need to set up a script in tours_detail.asp that reacts differently depending on whether it is accessed with no data (the first way), accessed with URL parameters (the second

```
9
10  If IsEmpty(Request.Form("tourCountry")) Then
11      If IsEmpty(Request.QueryString("regionID")) Then
12          rs_tourDetail.Source = "SELECT *  FROM tbl_tours INNER JOIN tbl_country  ON tbl_country.countryII
13      Else
14          rs_tourDetail.Source = "SELECT *  FROM tbl_tours INNER JOIN tbl_country  ON tbl_country.countryII
15      End If
16  Else
17      rs_tourDetail.Source = "SELECT *  FROM tbl_tours INNER JOIN tbl_country  ON tbl_country.countryID=tbl
18  End If
19
```

In this lesson you will go behind the GUI once again and work extensively with code, especially SQL code.

way), or accessed with form variables (the third way). The script will know how to filter the query that displays the tour description(s) based on the presence or absence of URL and form variables.

This may sound confusing at this early stage, but you have done most of the tasks involved in this lesson before—just never all of them together. But it's the ability to creatively combine the different techniques you learn, as well as the ability to tweak code by hand when necessary, that defines competence in ASP, ColdFusion, or PHP. In this lesson you will send and receive URL and form variables, hand-code SQL, write a nested if…else block to determine which of three SQL queries to run, use comments, and use IsEmpty() (ASP), IsDefined() (ColdFusion), or sset() (PHP) to determine the presence of variables.

WHAT YOU WILL LEARN

In this lesson, you will:

- Build a dynamic search interface that lets users search and filter data in three different ways

- Hand-code several SQL queries using joins, dynamically filtered data, and subqueries

- Show or hide the Recordset Navigation Bar, based on need

- Temporarily disable code using comments for testing and debugging

- Use built-in functions to check for the presence of URL and form variables

- Use nested if…else blocks to create a sophisticated flow control structure

APPROXIMATE TIME

This lesson takes approximately two hours and 30 minutes to complete.

LESSON FILES

Starting Files:

Lesson12/Start/newland/tours.asp
Lesson12/Start/newland/tours_detail.asp

Completed Files:

Lesson12/Complete/newland/tours.asp
Lesson12/Complete/newland/tours_detail.asp
Lesson12/Complete/newland/index.asp

PREPARING THE SEARCH PAGE AND CREATING THE SEARCH ALL LINK

In this task, you'll begin preparing the search page by removing now-obsolete content from the tours page. As it stands, tours.asp contains static listings of many of the tours. Now that you have built a dynamic listing of the tours (tours_detail.asp), this content is no longer needed on tours.asp. However, the navigation bars throughout the site point to tours.asp under the Find Tours link, so this page is perfect for containing the search interface.

The first activity, not surprisingly, is to delete all of the static tour listings. Next, you'll mock up the overall page layout. Finally, you'll create the first of three search interfaces, though in this case, "search interface" is an overstatement: It is a simple hyperlink to tours_detail.asp that causes the page to display all tours.

1) Open tours.asp, and change the Choose a Tour heading to *Find Tour*. Select everything after the heading through the bottom of the table, and press Delete. Enter the following text as body text beneath the new Find Tour page title.

Use this page to find the tour of your dreams. Once you've made a selection, check out the Tour Price Calculator.

Newland Tours offers many tours to different parts of the world. To find a tour to your desired destination, use the table below to browse by world region, by country, or view them all.

Though the page looks quite different at the end of this step, you haven't done much but replace obsolete static HTML with updated static HTML.

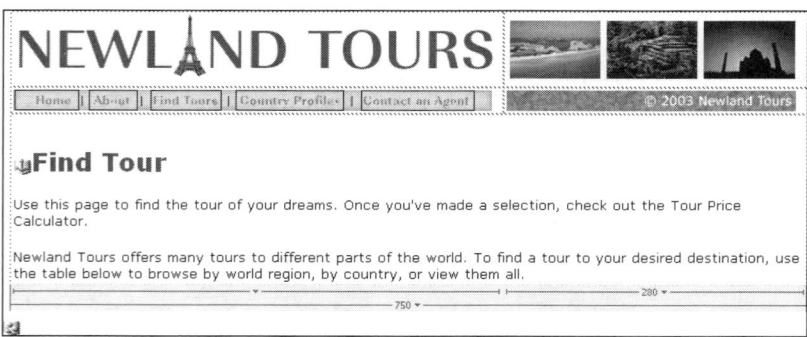

2) Link Tour Price Calculator to tourprice.asp.

Since no tour is specified, you can't send any URL parameters. But the tour price calculator application will still work; it just won't have a particular tour specified as the default in the form's drop-down menu when the page loads.

3) Create a new line beneath the second body text paragraph, and insert a table with three rows, two columns, width of 95 percent, border thickness of 1, cell padding of 3, and cell spacing of 0.

This table contains three rows, one for each kind of search. The left column will eventually contain a description of each search type, while the right column will enable the search itself.

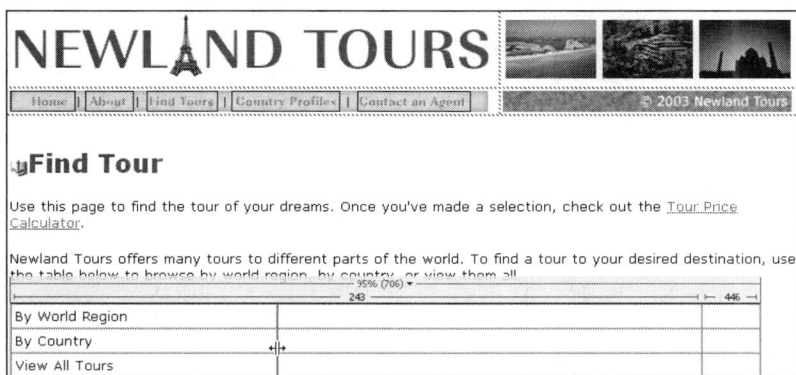

4) In order from top to bottom, type the following into the three cells in the first column: *By World Region*, *By Country*, and *View All Tours*. Drag the column divider to the left, so that the right column is wider than the left.

Once again, before you add dynamic content to a page, most often you'll build static content. Then you drop dynamic content into discrete locations within the page.

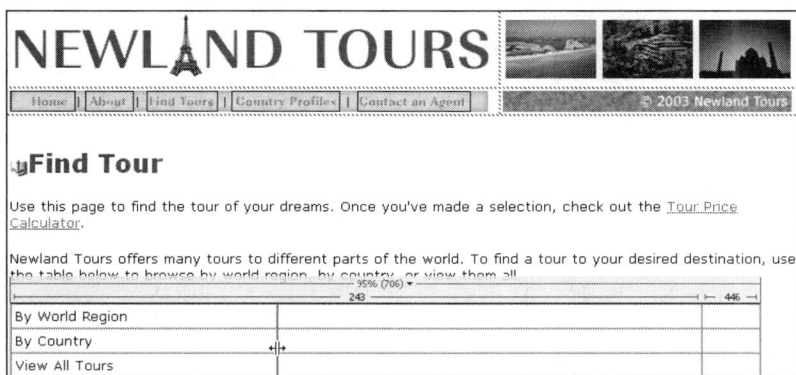

5) Drag to select View All in the View All Tours cell, and link the page to tours_detail.asp.

Clicking this link brings up the default version of tours_detail.asp—the version you completed in Lesson 11.

349

6) Save, upload, and test the file in a browser.

When you click the View All link, you'll be taken to tours_detail.asp, which should function as before. The important thing to remember for later is that when users click this link, no additional variables are sent as URL or form variables.

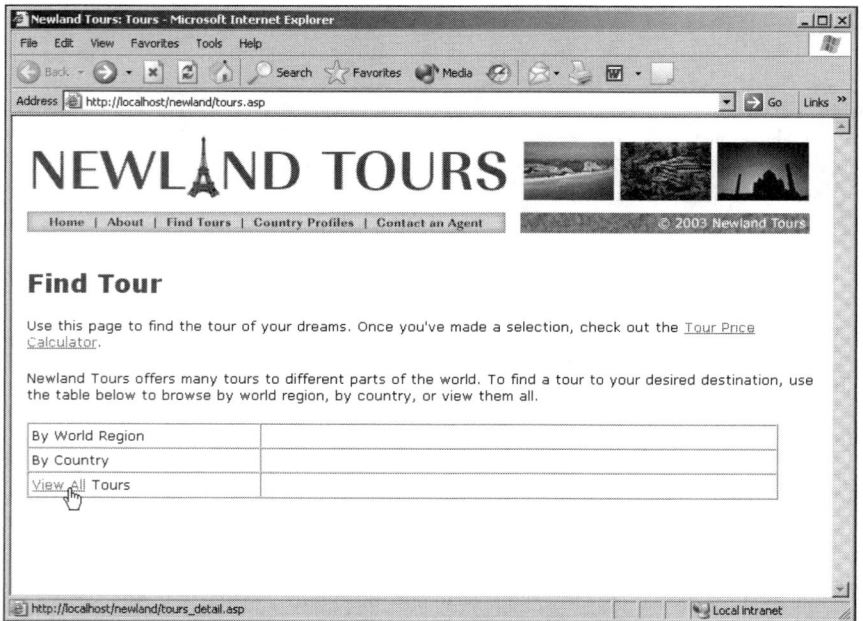

SEARCHING BY REGION: BUILDING THE INTERFACES

You are ready to create the first of the remaining two search options: searching by world region. When you are finished, you will have eight regions listed, each one linking to tours_detail.asp with a unique querystring appended containing a unique region ID. Back on tours_detail.asp, the SQL query that returns the tour descriptions will be filtered so that only the tours with that regionID will be displayed. Once you are finished, you will repeat the whole process in index.asp, to allow users to jump straight to tours in their favorite regions from the homepage. When you go to repeat the process in index.asp, I will encourage you to try to do so from memory; so as you follow the steps in tours.asp, try to internalize them.

1) Create a new recordset on tours.asp with the following settings:

Name: *rs_worldregions*
Connection: conn_newland
Table: tbl_region
Columns: All
Filter: None
Sort: regionName, Ascending

This recordset retrieves all of the region names and their unique IDs. The region names will be used to create the list of regions, while their respective IDs will be passed as URL parameters. You used a strategy similar to this with the country profiles.

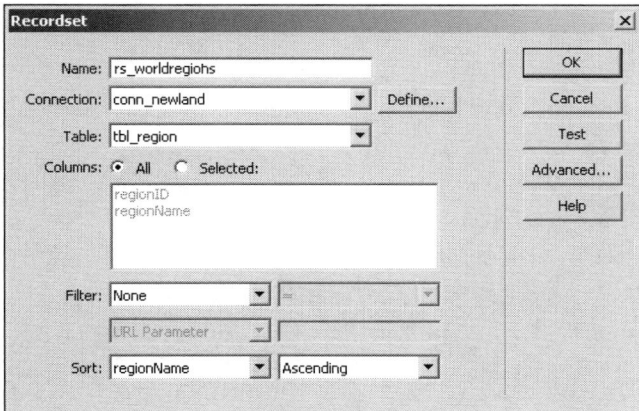

2) Position the insertion point in the empty cell to the right of By World Region. Use the Application category of the Insert panel to insert a dynamic text element. In the Dynamic Text dialog, click regionName and click OK.

If you were to test this page now, the first region name (Africa) would be output onto the page. The rest would not, because you have not designated this output as a Repeat Region. Before you do that, however, you'll need to add the hyperlink to the dynamic text.

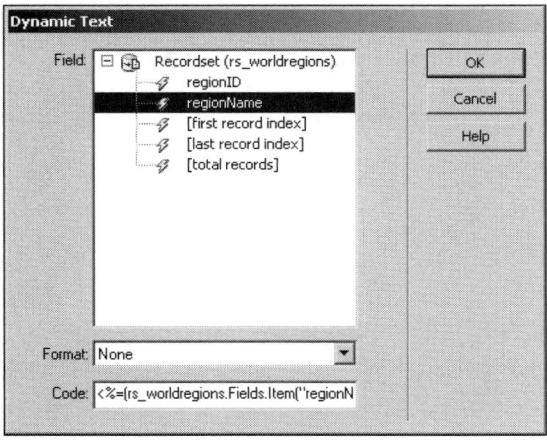

3) Click to select the dynamic text (in Dreamweaver pseudocode, you should see {rs_worldregions.regionName}). Click the Browse to File folder icon beside the Link field in the Property inspector, to open the Select File dialog. Click once to select tours_detail.asp.

In this step, you are linking to tours_detail.asp, using Dreamweaver's browse-to-link capability. Of course, it would be even easier to drag the Point to File to tours_detail.asp. But by browsing to the file, you get an added feature: Dreamweaver makes it easy to create a link that appends querystring/URL variables.

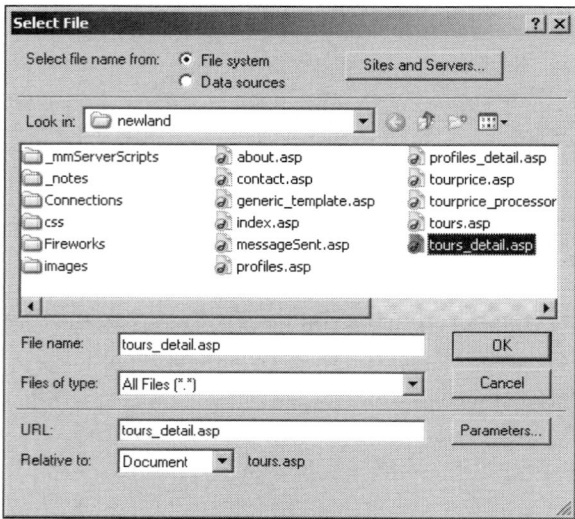

4) Still in the Select File dialog, click the Parameters button in the lower-right corner. In the Parameters dialog, type regionID as the name.

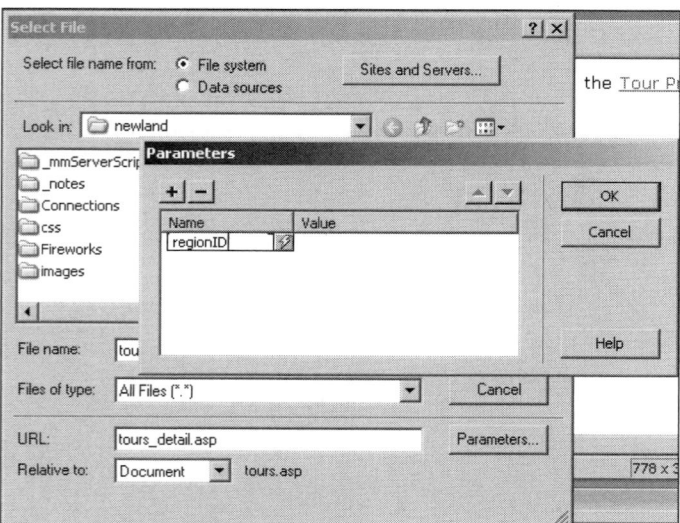

352

In this step, you are creating the regionID variable. At this point, Dreamweaver has enough information to generate the following code: `<a href="tours_detail.asp?regionID="`>. Of course, that's not enough. The regionID variable has to equal something, in this case, the current value of regionID.

5) Click the lightning icon in the Value category. Select regionID from the list and click OK to return to the Parameters dialog. Click OK two more times to return to the document.

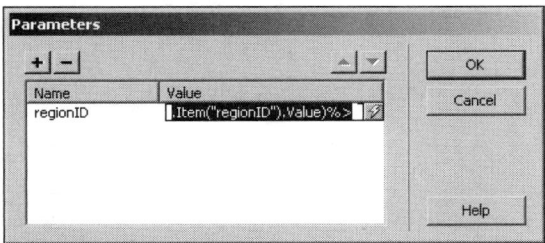

In this step, you specify the value for the regionID querystring/URL variable.

If you look in the Property inspector's Link field at this point, you'll see `tours_detail.asp?regionID=<%=(rs_worldregions.Fields.Item("regionID").Value)%>` or an equivalent line in ColdFusion or PHP.

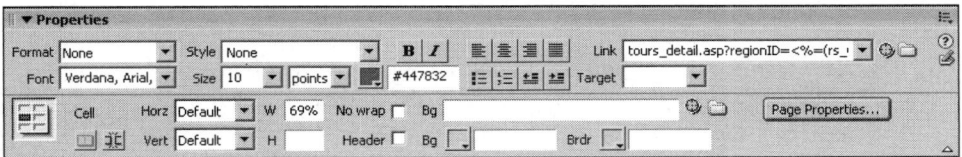

6) Click to select the dynamic code block. In the Server Behaviors panel, add a Repeat Region behavior, showing all records at once.

The Repeat Region behavior creates a loop that outputs each of the records retrieved by the query. There are eight regions in tbl_region, so each of them will be displayed now, and not just the first.

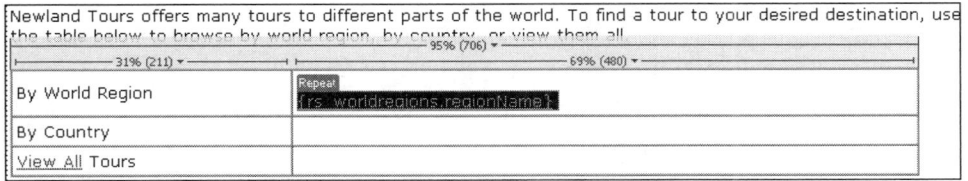

353

7) With the dynamic block selected, switch to split view if necessary. ASP and PHP users: Look just after the highlighted code for the closing </a> tag. Immediately after that, enter a line break <br /> tag. ColdFusion users, delete everything in between (but not including) the <td> ... </td> tags, and type in the following code instead:

```
<cfoutput query="rs_worldregions"><a href="tours_detail.cfm?regionID=
⇒#rs_worldregions.regionID#">#rs_worldregions.regionName#</a><br /></cfoutput>
```

This is a repeat of a problem you dealt with in an earlier lesson: without this line break, all of the regions will be output on a single line. A <br /> tag, placed inside the loop, is sufficient to format it correctly. Unfortunately for ColdFusion users, the way Dreamweaver wrote the ColdFusion to create the loop was inefficient, so instead of merely adding a <br /> tag, you had to rewrite the whole line.

```
56  0) AND (NOT rs_worldregions.EOF))
57
58  ail.asp?regionID=<%=(rs_worldregions.Fields.Item("regionID").Value)%>"><%=(rs_worldregions.Fields.Item("regionName").Value)%></a><br /
59
60  idex+1
61  _numRows-1
```

Now that the line break is in place, the records will appear in a format that looks more menu-like.

8) Save, upload, and test the file in the browser.

You should see all eight regions displayed on the page. If you click any of the links, you should be taken to tours_detail.asp, which, aside from the new URL parameter, looks and acts like it did before.

The desired filtering hasn't taken place, because you haven't changed the query on that page, which currently is written to retrieve all of the tours.

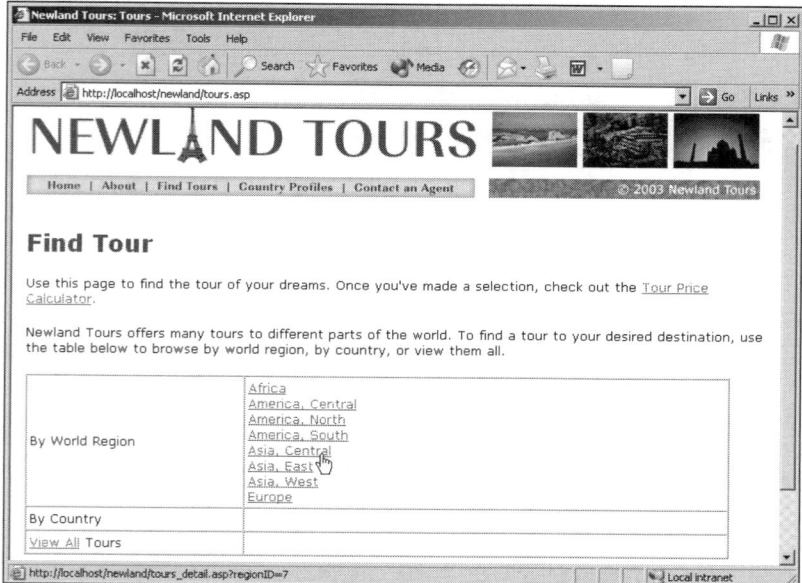

9) Repeat steps 1 through 7 to create a dynamic menu on the index page, replacing the current list of regions, taking into account the notes and variations below.

Try to do this from memory, only referring to the steps if you get stuck. This is a good test to see how well you have absorbed this knowledge. Some points to remember:

- Don't forget to create a new recordset on the page, and name it rs_worldregions. A page can have multiple recordsets, as long as they have different names.

- When you add the Repeat Region behavior, make sure you specify the correct recordset (rs_worldregions) in the Repeat Region dialog; the wrong recordset will probably show up as the default. Specifying the wrong recordset in the Repeat Region dialog will cause an error message when you test the file in a browser.

- In addition to adding a <br /> tag inside the output loop just after the closing </a> tag (and implementing the ColdFusion fix, if necessary), also insert two nonbreaking spaces (type   in code view to add each space) before the opening <a> tag, so that the list of regions is slightly indented.

- As you work on this step, the formatting of the navigation bar may look awful in Dreamweaver, because it can't fit all of its pseudocode and the Repeat Region box in the allotted design. This will go away of its own accord in a browser, so just ignore it!

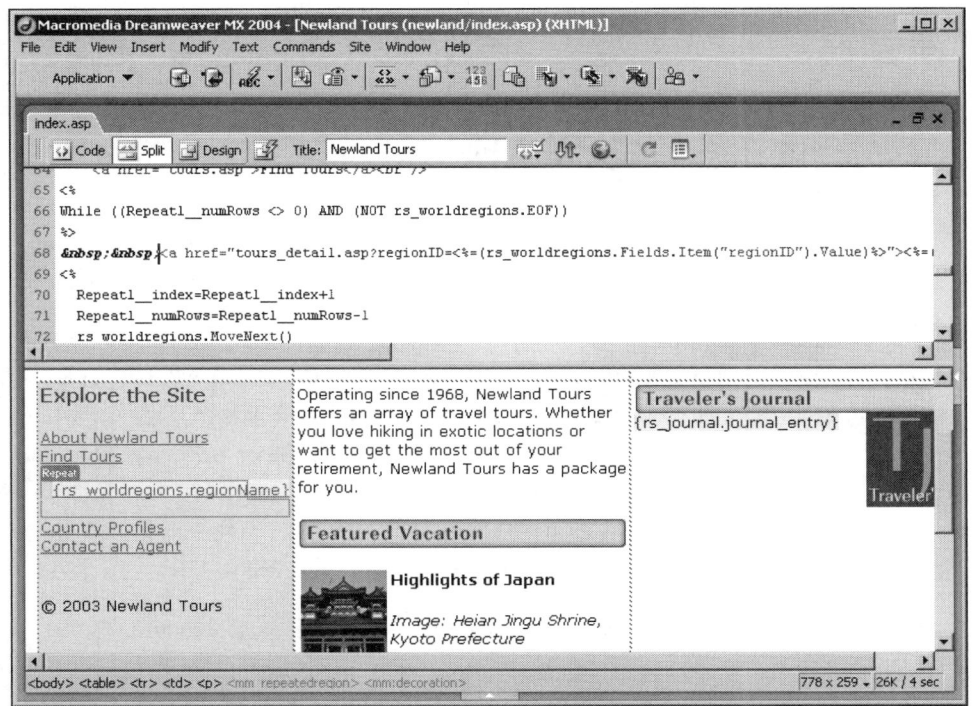

When you are finished, save, upload, and test the page in your browser, clicking a sampling of links to ensure both that you are redirected to tours_detail.asp and that a different URL parameter is appended to the URL each time.

REVISING THE QUERY AND COMMENTING CODE FOR TESTING AND DEBUGGING

The region links send URL variables to tours_detail.asp, but that page has nothing set up to do anything with those variables. In this task, you will put that functionality in place. But there is a catch.

Usually, when you bind a URL variable to the page, an error message will be displayed if a user accesses the page and that URL variable is not present. But in this case, when the user clicks the View All link, no URL parameter is sent. Later, once you've added the form that enables users to choose a country from the list, users will have another way of accessing tours_detail.asp without using URL variables. Therefore, you must set up the page in a way that it does not depend on the presence of URL variables.

When you create applications—even applications as simple as a search and results page pair—it is incumbent on you to prevent errors from occurring. Prevention often requires some strategic planning, so let's think this through before we continue building. The goal is to find a way to enable the page to return the proper results based on the type of data that is (or is not) available to it.

356

If data is available to the page (such as URL or form variables), then that data will be used only in one place: inside the SQL query as a filtering mechanism. Nowhere else on the page depends on that data. To prevent errors, you need to prevent code from running that depends on variables that don't exist. You already know that if...else structures are good at preventing or enabling certain blocks of code. Therefore, one solution to the problem is to embed multiple SQL statements in an if...else structure, with one query for each type of search. The if...else structure will ensure that only the correct query will be executed, based on the presence or absence of variables that you specify.

You'll write the if...else structure at the end of this lesson. But for now, you need to create the SQL statement that will run if a URL variable (regionID) has been sent to the page. That statement will be different from the existing SQL statement, which simply returns all records. You still need that original query, though, in case no URL parameters are sent. So you will copy the existing SQL statement and revise it to work with URL variables.

But that leads to another problem: Your code will have two incompatible queries. You'll fix that later with an if...else structure. But how do you work around the problem while you build and debug the new query? You will temporarily disable the existing query. This disabling will prevent it from running, but the code will still be there on the page when you need it for later. To create this win-win situation, you designate the original query as a comment. As you know from before, ASP, ColdFusion, and PHP ignore comments, so the code will still be there, but it won't interfere with the testing of your page. This technique, as you've learned previously, is called commenting out code, and it is a critical strategy when developing sophisticated applications.

TIP *One strategy that programmers use is to write code to solve one neatly defined problem at a time. In this case you could try to create the new query and the if...else structure simultaneously, but if something goes wrong, you may not know which section of code is the culprit. Focusing on one task at a time makes it easier to debug your code.*

In this task, you'll duplicate the original query, comment it out, and revise and test the copy.

1) Open tours_detail.asp in code view. Locate the query near the top of the page.

For me, in both ASP and ColdFusion, the query code begins around line 4. In PHP, it occurs a little later, around line 12 (look for mysql_select_db()). The goal in this step is to disturb the ASP, ColdFusion, or PHP code as little as possible, while trying to isolate the SQL code (which begins SELECT * FROM tbl_tours).

2 for ASP users) Select the entire line that begins *rs_tourDetail.Source =*. Copy this line, and paste it on the next line, so that you have two identical copies. Position the insertion point just before the first of these two lines, and enter a single quote (') character, to comment out that line.

You have copied the original query and temporarily disabled it. You are ready to start revising and testing the new query.

```
 7  Set rs_tourDetail = Server.CreateObject("ADODB.Recordset")
 8  rs_tourDetail.ActiveConnection = MM_conn_newland_STRING
 9  'rs_tourDetail.Source = "SELECT *  FROM tbl_tours INNER JOIN tbl_country  ON tbl_country.countryID=tbl_t
10  rs_tourDetail.Source = "SELECT *  FROM tbl_tours INNER JOIN tbl_country  ON tbl_country.countryID=tbl_to
11  rs_tourDetail.CursorType = 0
12  rs_tourDetail.CursorLocation = 2
13  rs_tourDetail.LockType = 1
14  rs_tourDetail.Open()
```

2 for ColdFusion users) Find the SQL statement enclosed inside the *<cfquery>* tags. If necessary, remove any line breaks, so all of the SQL is on a single line. Select the whole line of SQL, copy it, and paste it on the next line. Position the insertion point just before the first SQL statement, and type <!---. Then skip to the end of that first line and type --->.

You have copied the original query and temporarily disabled it. You are ready to start revising and testing the new query.

```
1  <cfset CurrentPage=GetFileFromPath(GetTemplatePath())>
2  <cfparam name="PageNum_rs_tourDetail" default="1">
3  <cfquery name="rs_tourDetail" datasource="newland">
4  <!---SELECT * FROM tbl_tours INNER JOIN tbl_country ON tbl_country.countryID=tbl_tours.country ORDER BY tbl_
5  SELECT * FROM tbl_tours INNER JOIN tbl_country ON tbl_country.countryID=tbl_tours.country ORDER BY tbl_count
6  </cfquery>
7  <cfset MaxRows_rs_tourDetail=5>
```

2 for PHP users) Select the entire line that begins *$query_rs_tourDetail = "SELECT*. Copy this line, and paste it on the next line, so that you have two identical copies. Position the insertion point just before the first of these two lines, and add two forward slashes (//), to comment out that line.

You have copied the original query and temporarily disabled it. You are ready to start revising and testing the new query.

```php
1  <?php require_once('Connections/conn_newland.php'); ?>
2  <?php
3  $currentPage = $_SERVER["PHP_SELF"];
4
5  $maxRows_rs_tourDetail = 5;
6  $pageNum_rs_tourDetail = 0;
7  if (isset($_GET['pageNum_rs_tourDetail'])) {
8    $pageNum_rs_tourDetail = $_GET['pageNum_rs_tourDetail'];
9  }
10 $startRow_rs_tourDetail = $pageNum_rs_tourDetail * $maxRows_rs_tourDetail;
11
12 mysql_select_db($database_conn_newland, $conn_newland);
13 //$query_rs_tourDetail = "SELECT * FROM tbl_tours INNER JOIN tbl_country ON tbl_country.countryID=tbl_tours.country ORDER BY tbl_
14 $query_rs_tourDetail = "SELECT * FROM tbl_tours INNER JOIN tbl_country ON tbl_country.countryID=tbl_tours.country ORDER BY tbl_co
15 $query_limit_rs_tourDetail = sprintf("%s LIMIT %d, %d", $query_rs_tourDetail, $startRow_rs_tourDetail, $maxRows_rs_tourDetail);
16 $rs_tourDetail = mysql_query($query_limit_rs_tourDetail, $conn_newland) or die(mysql_error());
17 $row_rs_tourDetail = mysql_fetch_assoc($rs_tourDetail);
18
19 if (isset($_GET['totalRows_rs_tourDetail'])) {
20   $totalRows_rs_tourDetail = $_GET['totalRows_rs_tourDetail'];
21 } else {
22   $all_rs_tourDetail = mysql_query($query_rs_tourDetail);
23   $totalRows_rs_tourDetail = mysql_num_rows($all_rs_tourDetail);
24 }
25 $totalPages_rs_tourDetail = ceil($totalRows_rs_tourDetail/$maxRows_rs_tourDetail)-1;
26
27 $queryString_rs_tourDetail = "";
28 if (!empty($_SERVER['QUERY_STRING'])) {
29   $params = explode("&", $_SERVER['QUERY_STRING']);
30   $newParams = array();
31   foreach ($params as $param) {
32     if (stristr($param, "pageNum_rs_tourDetail") == false &&
33       stristr($param, "totalRows_rs_tourDetail") == false) {
34       array_push($newParams, $param);
```

3) Just before the *ORDER BY* clause near the end of the statement, insert the following code:

In ASP:

```
WHERE tbl_country.region=" & Request.QueryString("regionID") & "
```

In ColdFusion:

```
WHERE tbl_country.region = #url.regionid#
```

In PHP:

```
WHERE tbl_country.region =". $_GET['regionID'] ."
```

Notice that there should be a space after the closing quotes (") in ASP and PHP, and the closing pound sign (#) in ColdFusion. That is, the word ORDER should not be directly against either the quotes or the pound sign.

Remember, in ASP, the & character is used to concatenate, or connect, text strings. The . character in PHP has the same purpose. Concatenation is necessary in both cases, because you are mixing literal strings (the majority of the SQL statements) that ASP or PHP should pass on without evaluating, and special ASP or PHP code that ASP/PHP should evaluate, such as ASP's `Request.QueryString()` *and PHP's* `$_GET()`. *Strings are in quotes, while expressions are not. Combining the two requires you to concatenate—hence the use of & and . in these code blocks. ColdFusion doesn't have this problem, because it uses hash signs (#...#) to mark up expressions that ColdFusion should evaluate.*

So what does this addition to the query do? It creates another criterion, which further limits the original search. The original search retrieves all of the information needed to build all of the tour descriptions. This query does that, too, except it limits the set to those tours whose countries share the same regionID as the one passed as a URL parameter.

Let's look at an example. Each tour has a field specifying its country. This country listing is, as you'll recall, a foreign key, which points to tbl_country. So both tours that take place in France have the countryID for France as one of their records. This shared field links the tours table to the country table, in this case, linking all tours in France to the record for the country France in tbl_country.

One of the fields that each country has is a foreign key for the region table. Thus, the record for France has a 3 in its region field, because 3 is the regionID for Europe, which contains France. Europe also contains the United Kingdom and Italy, so each of these countries' region fields also contains a 3. Japan's region value is 4, which is the regionID for East Asia. Therefore, all of the tours that list Japan as their country are related to a regionID of 4, and not of 1 or 3. Because Thailand is also in East Asia and has a regionID of 4, all of its tours are related to regionID 4.

To summarize, then, each regionID has a one-to-many relationship with countries. That is, each region may have several countries that belong to it. Likewise, each country has a one-to-many relationship with tours, which means that a single country can have multiple tours. However, no country can belong to multiple regions, and no tour can go to multiple countries. Therefore, you can write a query that retrieves tours where the tour's country belongs to a given region, and only those tours will be retrieved, and all others will be excluded.

That's what you've specified with this WHERE clause in the SQL statement. Test the file to make sure it works as expected.

4) Save, upload, and close tours_detail.asp. Select tours.asp in the Site panel, and press F12 to test that file.

You cannot test tours_detail.asp directly, because you would get an error. The SQL query that you just wrote needs the regionID URL variable to execute. If you test the page directly, that variable won't be available, which will break the SQL query and return an error.

5) Click any of the regions in the menu on the page.

After you click, you should see only tours from that region displayed on the page, so that part of the functionality works.

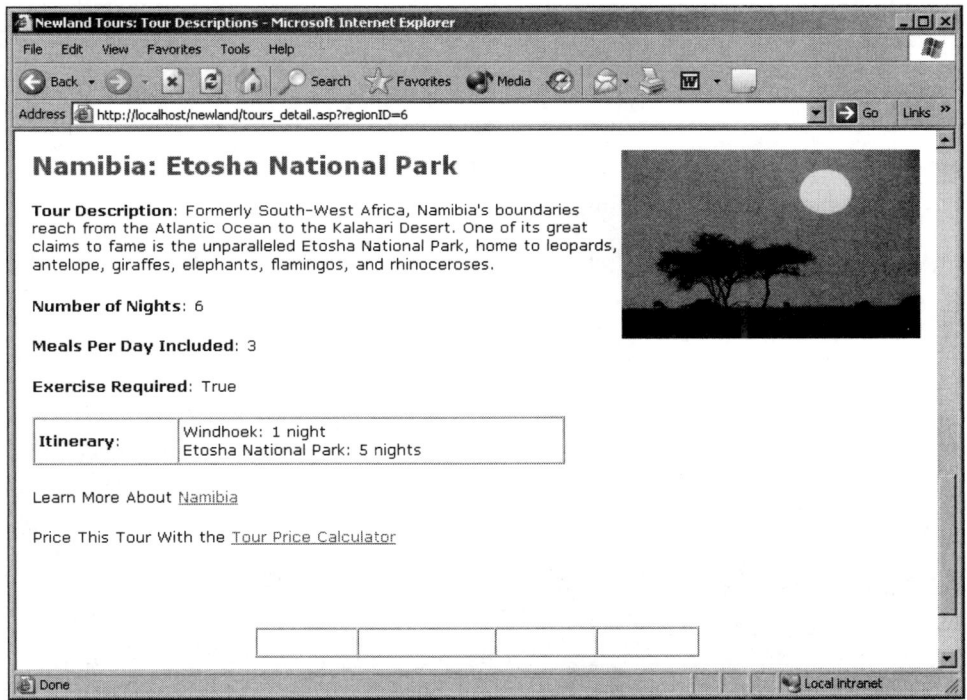

But there's some bad news as well: The Recordset Navigation Bar table is still visible. All of its cells are empty, because no region (at the moment) has more than five tours, so the page is always the first and last page. Remember, the Repeat Region server behavior on this page that displays the tours is limited to showing five records per page. It would be good to hide the Recordset Navigation Bar, when the page is the first and last page, that is, when five or fewer records are showing. But if that number ever exceeds five (say, for example, Newland adds tours to Germany, Norway, and Spain next year), the Recordset Navigation Bar needs to be made visible again.

SUPPRESSING THE NAVIGATION BAR

As always, before you start coding, you should spell out exactly what it is you are trying to accomplish. You want to show the Recordset Navigation Bar, which is stored in a table, if the number of tours displayed on the page is greater than five (that is, six or more). Remember the page is set to show only five records at a time. However, if there are five or fewer, then the Recordset Navigation Bar can't be activated, and so you don't want it to appear.

As usual, the ASP, ColdFusion, and PHP code are different, but they all use the same concept.

1) Still in tours_detail.asp, using split view and the tag selector, select the table containing the Recordset Navigation Bar.

You have selected the entire table in both design and code views. You'll need to work in code view in the next step, but you have to isolate the table, because you'll need to add code above and below it to cause it to show conditionally. Here is a case where split view simplifies finding an element buried in code.

Or as an option, you can add a few extra lines of white space above and below the table to help set it off.

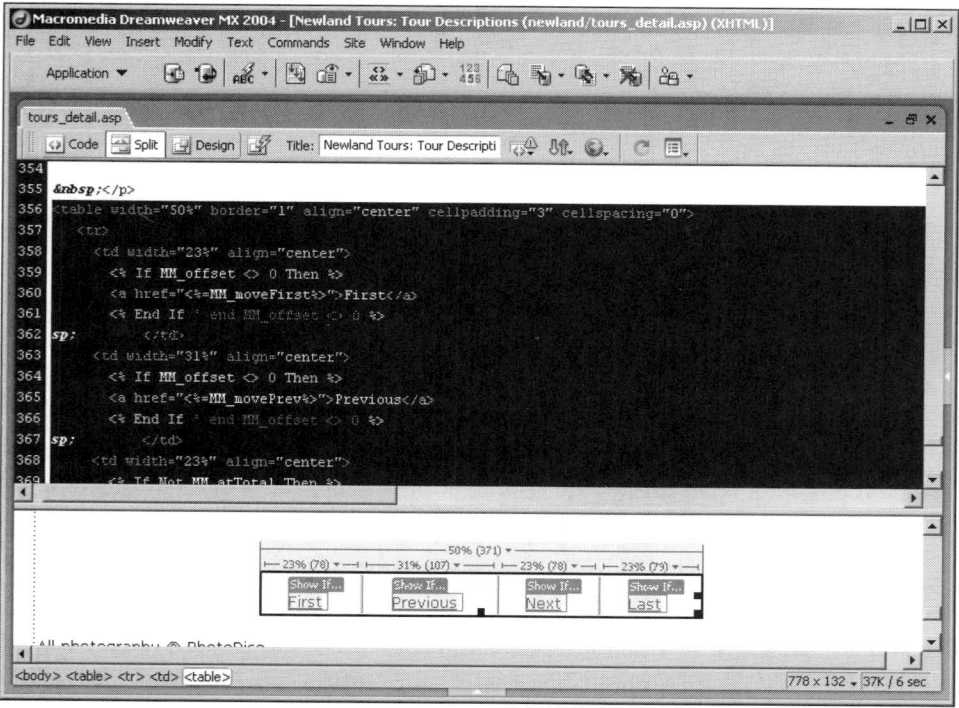

2) In code view, just before the table begins, enter the opening half of the script that controls the visibility of the table based on the number of records.

In ASP:

```
<% If (MM_atTotal = false Or Not IsEmpty(Request.QueryString("offset"))) Then %>
```

In ColdFusion:

```
<cfif rs_tourDetail.recordcount gt 5>
```

In PHP:

```
<?php if ($totalPages_rs_tourDetail != 0) { ?>
```

When you create a recordset, not only is the data in the recordset itself stored in memory on the server, so too is some basic information about that data. One piece of information available to ASP, ColdFusion and PHP is the record count, or number of records retrieved by the query. In ASP and ColdFusion, the variable that holds the total number of records is RecordCount, accessed as follows: rs_myQuery.recordcount. PHP's equivalent is mysql_num_rows(), accessed as follows: mysql_num_rows($rs_myQuery). (In both examples, rs_myQuery is the fictional name of a recordset you hypothetically created.)

Any time you are dealing with looping through records or paging through records, the RecordCount variable (ASP and ColdFusion) or mysql_num_rows() (PHP) function can be a great help. In the immediate situation, there is a catch: Scripts generated by server behaviors that you've already applied are using these variables. If you use them again, your scripts may collide in unexpected ways. Thus, you worked around these problems in the ASP and PHP scripts by working with variables created by the server behaviors.

Now let's look at the scripts themselves. In the ColdFusion version of the script, by far the most straightforward one, you are telling the server that if the record count is greater than five (the number of records you can show onscreen at any given time), then execute whatever comes after this line. What comes after it is the table that contains the Recordset Navigation Bar. If the number of recordsets is less than five (so that the if statement evaluates to false, then the script jumps ahead to the closing of the if structure (you haven't created the closing just yet) and continues. In other words, if the number of records is less than five, the table that contains the Recordet Navigation Bar does not appear. This flexible structure is convenient, because no matter what happens in the database—if new tours are added or removed— the Recordset Navigation Bar will be available if and only if it is needed.

The ASP version is written to make use of a pair of variables generated by the Recordset Navigation Bar object you inserted in the previous lesson. Understanding exactly how this line works presupposes some understanding of the VB code output by the Recordset Navigation Bar, and the nearly 300 lines of code that make up that script gets somewhat beyond the scope of what you are learning in this book. The condensed version is that the script detects when too many records were returned to fit on a page. If that's true, then the table holding the recordset navigation bar is displayed; otherwise, it is hidden.

```
361  Repeater__numRows=Repeater__numRows-1
362    num_rowTotal = num_rowTotal+1
363    rs_tourDetail.MoveNext()
364  Wend
365  %>
366
367
368  <% if (MM_atTotal = false Or Not IsEmpty(Request.QueryString("offset"))) Then  %>
369
370
371  <table width="50%" border="1" align="center" cellpadding="3" cellspacing="0">
372        <tr>
373          <td width="23%" align="center">
374            <% If MM_offset <> 0 Then %>
375            <a href="<%=MM_moveFirst%>">First</a>
376            <% End If ' end MM_offset <> 0 %>
```

The PHP version of the script is a little more complex. An existing server behavior has created the $totalPages_rs_tourDetail variable, which the script uses to keep track of the total number of pages of records, a figure that is derived from the total number of records and the number of records displayed per page. This variable is also initialized to 0, which means (odd as it may seem) that if there is one page of records, its value is 0, and if there are three pages of records, then its value is 2. Thus, you know that if this value is not 0 (the operator != means "is not equal to"), then there are two or more pages, and the recordset navigation bar is needed. Conversely, if the value is 0, then the whole if block is skipped, and the recordset navigation bar is never displayed.

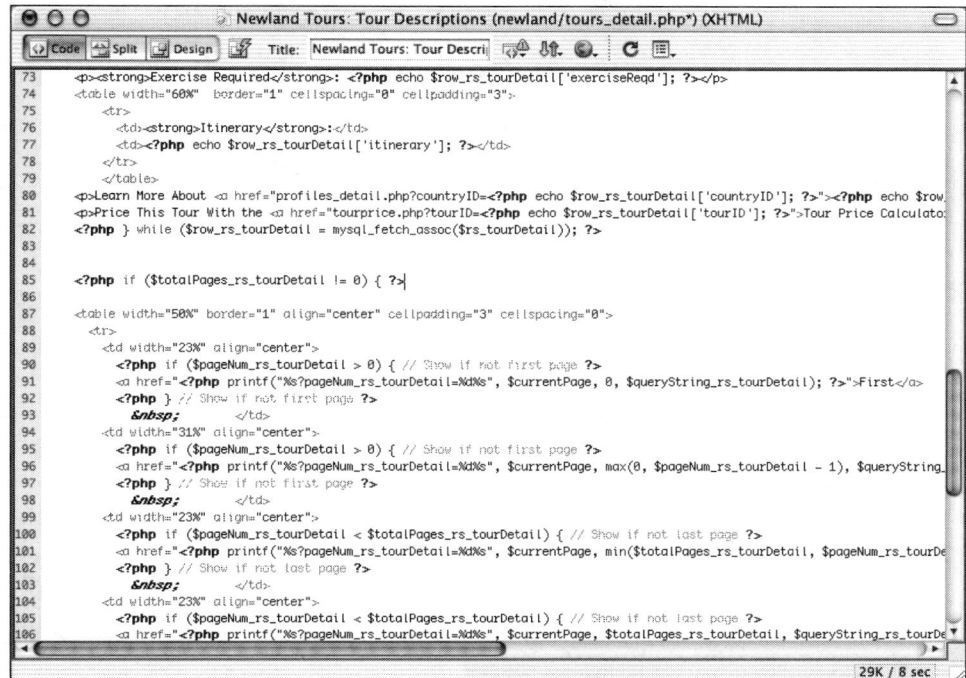

```
73    <p><strong>Exercise Required</strong>: <?php echo $row_rs_tourDetail['exerciseReqd']; ?></p>
74    <table width="60%" border="1" cellspacing="0" cellpadding="3">
75       <tr>
76          <td><strong>Itinerary</strong>:</td>
77          <td><?php echo $row_rs_tourDetail['itinerary']; ?></td>
78       </tr>
79       </table>
80    <p>Learn More About <a href="profiles_detail.php?countryID=<?php echo $row_rs_tourDetail['countryID']; ?>"><?php echo $row
81    <p>Price This Tour With the <a href="tourprice.php?tourID=<?php echo $row_rs_tourDetail['tourID']; ?>">Tour Price Calculato
82    <?php } while ($row_rs_tourDetail = mysql_fetch_assoc($rs_tourDetail)); ?>
83
84
85    <?php if ($totalPages_rs_tourDetail != 0) { ?>
86
87    <table width="50%" border="1" align="center" cellpadding="3" cellspacing="0">
88       <tr>
89          <td width="23%" align="center">
90          <?php if ($pageNum_rs_tourDetail > 0) { // Show if not first page ?>
91          <a href="<?php printf("%s?pageNum_rs_tourDetail=%d%s", $currentPage, 0, $queryString_rs_tourDetail); ?>">First</a>
92          <?php } // Show if not first page ?>
93                     </td>
94          <td width="31%" align="center">
95          <?php if ($pageNum_rs_tourDetail > 0) { // Show if not first page ?>
96          <a href="<?php printf("%s?pageNum_rs_tourDetail=%d%s", $currentPage, max(0, $pageNum_rs_tourDetail - 1), $queryString
97          <?php } // Show if not first page ?>
98                     </td>
99          <td width="23%" align="center">
100         <?php if ($pageNum_rs_tourDetail < $totalPages_rs_tourDetail) { // Show if not last page ?>
101         <a href="<?php printf("%s?pageNum_rs_tourDetail=%d%s", $currentPage, min($totalPages_rs_tourDetail, $pageNum_rs_tourDe
102         <?php } // Show if not last page ?>
103                    </td>
104         <td width="23%" align="center">
105         <?php if ($pageNum_rs_tourDetail < $totalPages_rs_tourDetail) { // Show if not last page ?>
106         <a href="<?php printf("%s?pageNum_rs_tourDetail=%d%s", $currentPage, $totalPages_rs_tourDetail, $queryString_rs_tourDe
```

3) After the closing *</table>* tag of the table you highlighted in step 6, close the if
block you opened in the preceding step.

In ASP:

```
<% End If %>
```

In ColdFusion:

```
</cfif>
```

In PHP:

```
<?php } ?>
```

This is the outer boundary of the `if` block. If the opening line evaluates to `false`, ASP, ColdFusion, or PHP looks for the closing of the block, so that it knows where to pick up again.

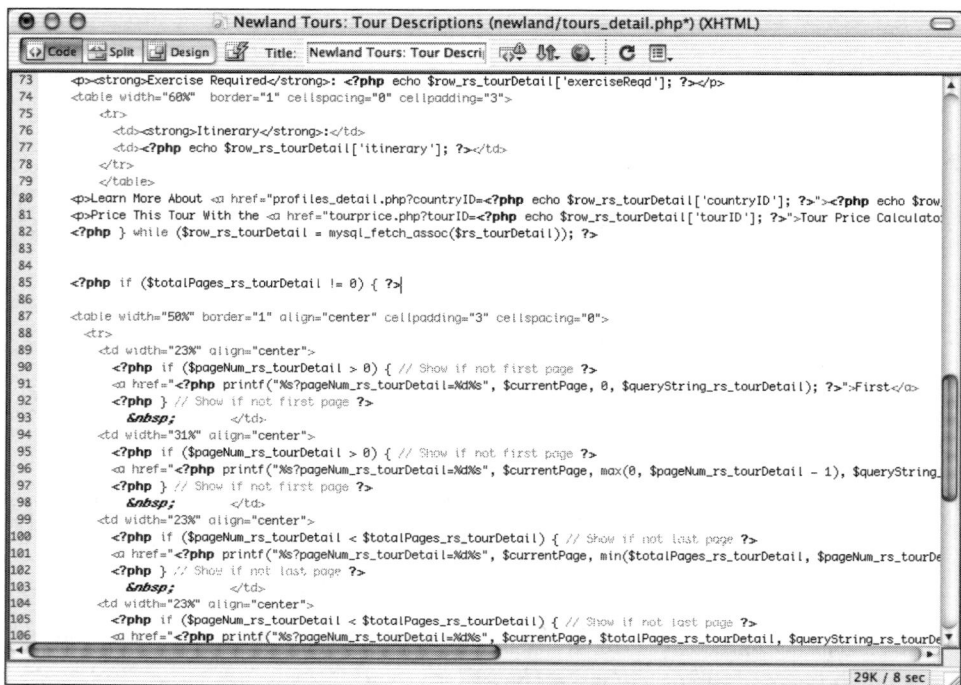

If you were to test the page at this point (remember to test through tours.asp or index.asp and click a region link), you will see that the Recordset Navigation Bar is suppressed. If you want to be extra careful, you can comment out the second SQL statement and remove the comment from the first SQL statement and test the page unfiltered. You should see all of the tours listed, and the Recordset Navigation Bar should help you move back and forth through the tours. If you do test both ways, be sure to comment the first line of SQL back out and reactivate the second line of SQL.

4) Save and close tours_detail.asp.

SEARCHING BY COUNTRY: FILTERING BY FORM VARIABLE

You have implemented the full functionality of the search by region. Implementing the search by country is similar, with a few variations. Rather than working with links and URL parameters, you will work with a form and form variables. As before, you'll create a new SQL statement to handle this filtering method.

1) Open tours.asp in design view, position the insertion point in the second row of the right-hand column, and insert a form with one list/menu element and a Submit button.

You should at this point be comfortable mocking up form elements on the page.

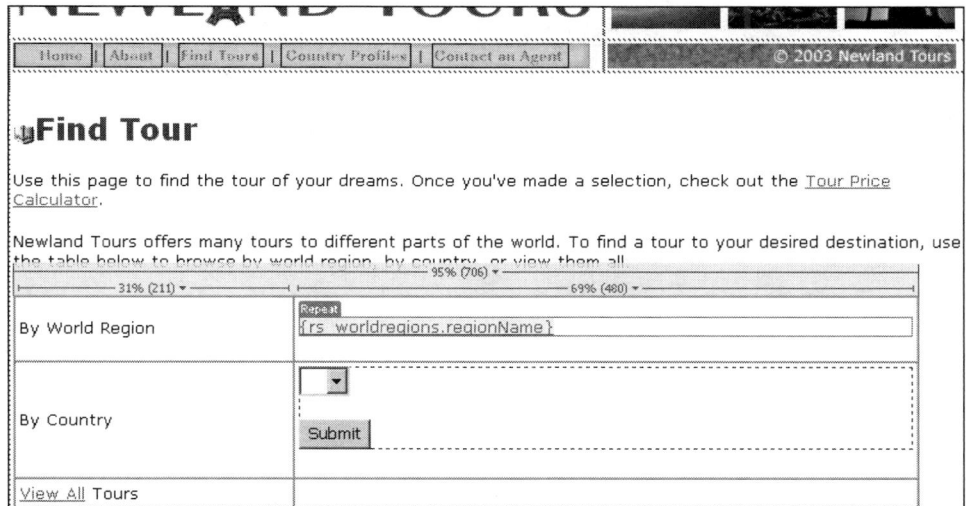

2) Select the _<form>_ tag in the tag selector, and use the Property inspector to name the form _frm_bycountry_. Specify tours_detail.asp as the action. Specify _POST_ as the method.

These settings apply to the form as a whole, and it is now ready to use. Of course, you still have to configure its elements, most notably, the menu element.

3) Use the Bindings panel to create a new recordset, using the following settings:

Name: *rs_countries*

Connection: conn_newland

Table: tbl_country

Columns: Selected, countryName

Filter: None

Sort: countryName, Ascending

If you press the Test button, you'll see that this recordset produces a list of all the countries in tbl_country in alphabetical order. You'll use this to build the drop-down menu in the form.

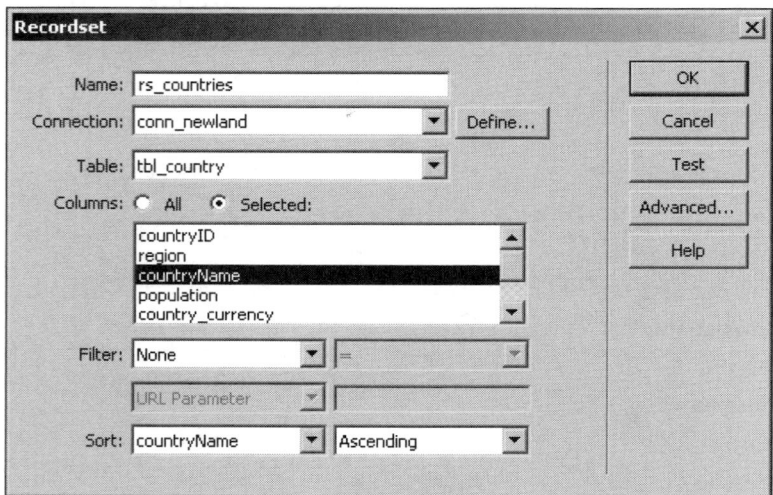

4) Click to select the menu, and in the Property inspector, name it *tourCountry*. Click the Dynamic button to open the Dynamic List/Menu dialog. Select rs_countries from the Options from recordset menu. Leave the Values and Labels at the default, countryName, and click OK.

You've done this before, so the consequence of these steps should not be a mystery. When the page is displayed in a browser, the country names will populate the menu in alphabetical order. When the user clicks Submit, tours_detail.asp will load (that was specified in the form's action attribute), and the name-value pair tourCountry=Argentina (or whichever country the user selected) will be sent as a form variable.

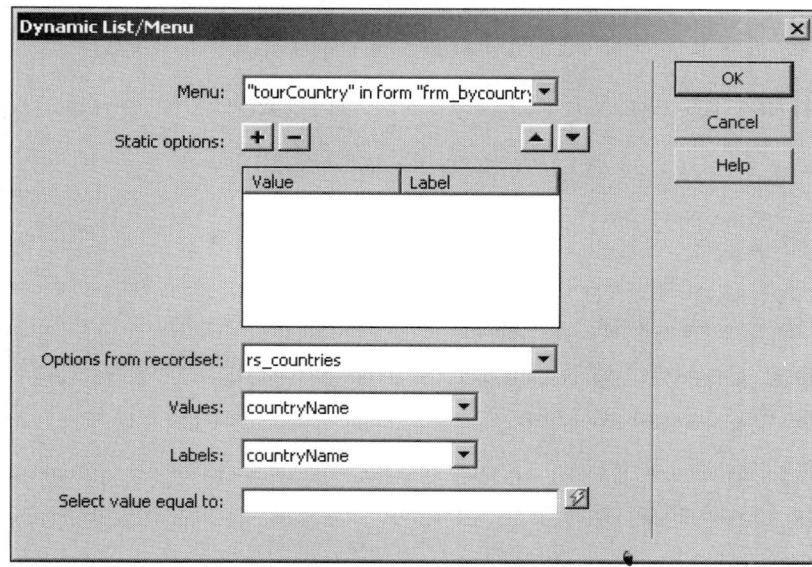

If you like, you can save and test the page in a browser, just to make sure that the menu is actually populated with country names. Don't press Submit, though, or you will get an error, because tours_detail.asp is expecting a URL variable called regionID, not a form variable called countryName.

5) Open tours_detail.asp in code view. Find the two queries (one should be commented out). Copy the second query and paste it on the next line. Comment out the second query.

Once again, you are making it possible to revise and test the new SQL statement, the one that will process the data submitted by the form.

```
1  <%@LANGUAGE="VBSCRIPT"%>
2  <!--#include file="Connections/conn_newland.asp" -->
3  <%
4  Dim rs_tourDetail
5  Dim rs_tourDetail_numRows
6
7  Set rs_tourDetail = Server.CreateObject("ADODB.Recordset")
8  rs_tourDetail.ActiveConnection = MM_conn_newland_STRING
9  'rs_tourDetail.Source = "SELECT *  FROM tbl_tours INNER JOIN tbl_country  ON tbl_country.countryID=tbl_to
10 'rs_tourDetail.Source = "SELECT *  FROM tbl_tours INNER JOIN tbl_country  ON tbl_country.countryID=tbl_to
11 rs_tourDetail.Source = "SELECT *  FROM tbl_tours INNER JOIN tbl_country  ON tbl_country.countryID=tbl_tou
12 rs_tourDetail.CursorType = 0
13 rs_tourDetail.CursorLocation = 2
14 rs_tourDetail.LockType = 1
15 rs_tourDetail.Open()
16
```

6) Change only the *WHERE* clause in the statement so that it reads as follows:

In ASP:

```
WHERE tbl_country.countryName='"& Request.Form("tourCountry") & "'
```

In ColdFusion:

```
WHERE tbl_country.countryName='#form.tourCountry#'
```

In PHP:

```
WHERE tbl_country.countryName='". $_POST['tourCountry'] ."'
```

As before, make sure there is a space between the closing single quote (') and the next clause, which begins with ORDER BY.

For the most part, this version of the query should make sense to you. You are matching the country name specified in the form with any tour that is associated with the same country name (though once again, you must go through the relationship between tbl_tours and tbl_country to access this name).

The only mysterious thing here may be the single quote (') that surrounds the dynamic content in all three server models. This is a SQL issue. Any time you are specifying a text string (as opposed to an expression or a number), it must be put in single quotes. Otherwise, the database attempts to interpret the text as if it's a function or some other special database command. By putting it in single quotes, you are telling the database not to interpret or evaluate it, but to match it with text stored in the database.

```
 8
 9 ORDER BY tbl_country.countryName"
10 HERE tbl_country.region =" & Request.QueryString("regionID") & " ORDER BY tbl_country.countryName"
11 ERE tbl_country.countryName ='" & Request.Form("countryName") & "' ORDER BY tbl_country.countryName"
12
```

7) Save and upload the file. Select tours.asp in the Site panel, and press F12 to test it. Select a country from the menu, and press Submit.

Most countries have only one tour, so you should see that tour listed when you choose a country. If you choose a country with multiple tours (France, Japan, United Kingdom, United States), you should see all of its tours.

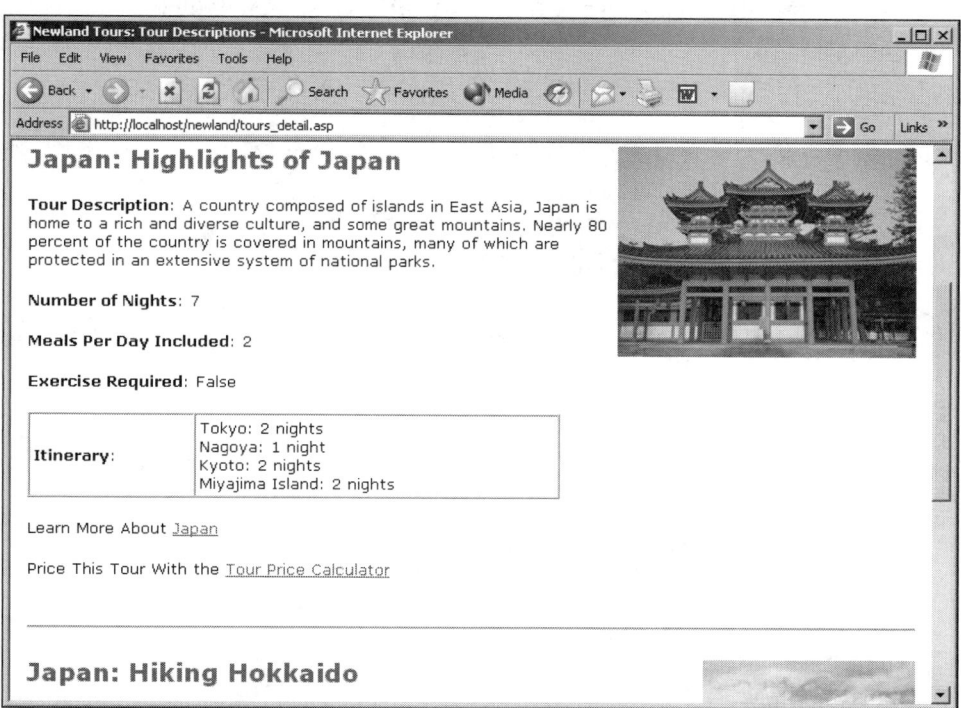

If you choose Taiwan, you'll see a blank page. The reason for this is that while Taiwan exists in tbl_country, it has no tours associated with it. In an ideal world, this discrepancy would never happen. However, it is possible that a tour to Taiwan is in the works. The person responsible for creating the country profile has already inserted this information into the database, but the tour description has not yet been finalized. In many databases, including Microsoft Access but not MySQL, you can account for this situation by retrieving only those countries that have tours associated with them in the query that populates the menu in tours.asp.

8) ASP and ColdFusion users: Open tours.asp. In the Bindings panel, double-click Recordset (rs_countries) to edit it. Click the Advanced button in the Recordset dialog. Between the *FROM tbl_country* and *ORDER BY countryName ASC*, enter the code that appears below. PHP users: skip this step but read the accompanying text.

```
WHERE EXISTS
(SELECT * FROM tbl_tours WHERE tbl_tours.country = tbl_country.countryID)
```

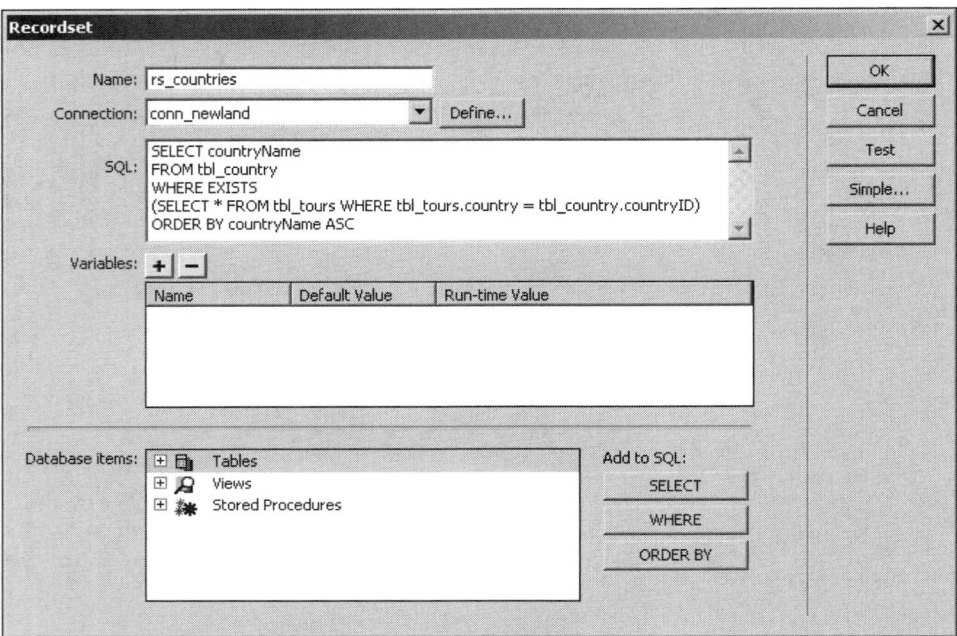

White space doesn't matter, so use line breaks as you like to make it more readable.

Let's talk about this SQL for a moment, because several things are going on. First, it uses a subquery, which is a query within a query, or more specifically here, a query used as a criterion within another query. The subquery is the part contained within the parentheses. That subquery looks for all the fields from tbl_tours where there is a match between tbl_tours and tbl_country. All of the countries in the database, except for Taiwan, fall into this category.

The EXISTS keyword is used to check for the existence of rows in a subquery result. The actual values are not retrieved, because it is simply checking for their existence. Because it finds that 15 countries exist in both locations (tbl_tours and tbl_country), it includes them in the main SELECT statement. Since Taiwan doesn't exist in both places, it is excluded.

NOTE *Although WHERE EXISTS and subqueries in general are a part of the ANSI standard for SQL, they are not supported in MySQL. If you enter this code in MySQL, you will get an error. Because of this, PHP users can't complete this step and will have to deal with this problem another way. The best solution in this case would be to have separate development and production databases and only upload data from development to production when it is ready. Of course, this project is entirely fictional anyway, so don't worry about it for the rest of this book—just don't follow the Taiwan link on tours.php.*

Click the Test button to see the results. You should now see 15, rather than 16 countries listed. Taiwan is no longer in the group. If a tour to Taiwan is added to tbl_tours, then Taiwan will be listed in the menu once again, because it would meet the EXIST criterion.

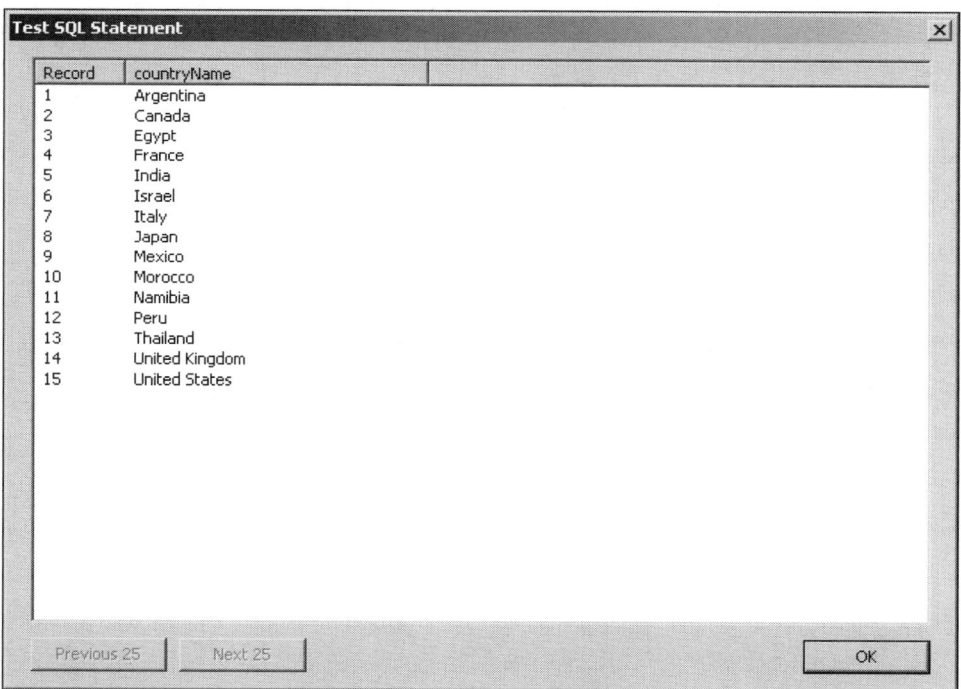

9) **Save and close tours.asp.**

SWITCHING SQL STATEMENTS ACCORDING TO ENVIRONMENTAL VARIABLES

You know from testing that each of the interfaces works—as long as two of the SQL statements are commented out. That setup is just fine for testing, when you can open the document and apply the correct commenting based on your needs, but obviously it needs help before it can go into production. You need an automated way of switching the query based on the type of search. Your first task is to identify how tours_detail.asp will know which search type the user has chosen. Then, based on that, you need to swap in the proper SQL statement. An if…else construct is perfect for swapping the correct SQL statement in, but how does it know which search type the user submitted?

Back in a previous lesson, you implemented server-side form validation. The way it worked was that it checked to see whether a form variable called numadults or numchildren existed and was numeric. If it didn't exist, or it wasn't numeric, the user was redirected back to the form on the tour price page to fix the problem. I remind you of this because it provides a strategy for determining which search type the user selected: Check for the presence or absence of certain variables, as follows:

- If no form or URL variables are present, then the user clicked the View All Tours link.
- If a URL variable is present, then the user clicked one of the Region links.
- If a form variable is present, then the user selected a country from the form menu.

With this information, you can construct the logic for the script you need to write. The following pseudocode spells out the logic. Statements in parentheses are the conclusions you can draw from certain information; however, these won't be explicitly written into the final script.

```
If no form variable exists //either the user clicked View All Tours or clicked a
⇒region link
If no URL variables exist //the user clicked the View All Tours link
Run the first query
Else a URL variable does exist //the user clicked a region link
Run the second query
Else a form variable does exist //the user selected a country from the form menu
Run the third query
```

Looking at this pseudocode, you'll notice that it will require a pair of if…else structures, one nested inside the other. That's because one of the conditions—the absence of a form variable—can be true for two different reasons: because the user clicked the View All link and there are no URL variables, or because the user clicked a region link and there is a URL variable.

1) Open tours_detail.asp in code view. Find the three lines of SQL code, and remove the comments from all of them. Add a few line breaks above and below them, to isolate them in your code.

In this step, you are preparing to wrap the if...else script around these lines of SQL. You don't want to disturb the neighboring code. Once ASP or ColdFusion determines which SQL query to execute, it will be as if the other two never existed.

```
6
7  Set rs_tourDetail = Server.CreateObject("ADODB.Recordset")
8  rs_tourDetail.ActiveConnection = MM_conn_newland_STRING
9
10
11 rs_tourDetail.Source = "SELECT *  FROM tbl_tours INNER JOIN tbl_country  ON tbl_country.countryID=tbl_tou
12 rs_tourDetail.Source = "SELECT *  FROM tbl_tours INNER JOIN tbl_country  ON tbl_country.countryID=tbl_tou
13 rs_tourDetail.Source = "SELECT *  FROM tbl_tours INNER JOIN tbl_country  ON tbl_country.countryID=tbl_tou
14
15
16 rs_tourDetail.CursorType = 0
17 rs_tourDetail.CursorLocation = 2
18 rs_tourDetail.LockType = 1
19 rs_tourDetail.Open()
```

2) Just above the top line of SQL, write the line of code that tests for the existence of the form variable.

In ASP:

```
If IsEmpty(Request.Form("tourCountry")) Then
```

In ColdFusion:

```
<cfif Not IsDefined("form.tourCountry")>
```

In PHP:

```
if (!isset($_POST['tourCountry'])) {
```

Like all if statements, this can evaluate to true or false. If it's true (that is, the form variable does not exist), then the script still has to determine whether a URL variable exists. If it's false, then we know that the user has selected a country from the form, and we can execute the third query.

375

3) Indent all three SQL statements at once, using the Tab key. Create a new line above the third SQL statement, and enter the script that will execute that line of code.

In ASP:

```
Else
```

In ColdFusion:

```
<cfelse>
```

In PHP:

```
} else {
```

When an `if` statement evaluates to `false`, the interpreter looks for any `else if` or `else` statements. If it sees them, it executes them. By adding this code here, you ensure that if the form variable is present, then the SQL statement that filters with that variable is run.

4) After the third line of SQL, close the `if...else` block.

In ASP:

```
End If
```

In ColdFusion:

```
</cfif>
```

In PHP:

```
}
```

```
 9
10  If IsEmpty(Request.Form("tourCountry")) Then
11      rs_tourDetail.Source = "SELECT *  FROM tbl_tours INNER JOIN tbl_country  ON tbl_country.countryID=tb
12      rs_tourDetail.Source = "SELECT *  FROM tbl_tours INNER JOIN tbl_country  ON tbl_country.countryID=tb
13  Else
14      rs_tourDetail.Source = "SELECT *  FROM tbl_tours INNER JOIN tbl_country  ON tbl_country.countryID=tb
15  End If
16
```

You are halfway there. In fact, if you uploaded this page now and accessed it by selecting a country and clicking Submit in the form on tours.asp, it would work as expected. But if you tried to access the page any other way, you would get an error, because it would try to execute both of the other two queries at the same time.

5) Indent the top two lines of SQL one more time. Above the first line of SQL, enter an `if` **statement that checks for the presence of the URL variable.**

In ASP:

```
If IsEmpty(Request.QueryString("regionID")) Then
```

In ColdFusion:

```
<cfif Not IsDefined("url.regionid")>
```

In PHP:

```
if (!isset($_GET['regionID'])) {
```

If this, too, evaluates to `true`, then neither the form nor URL variable is present, and the broadest SQL query—the first one—should run. That query is directly below this line, so if it is indeed true, then that query will run.

If it is `false`, then the URL variable is present, and the second SQL query should run.

6) In the line between the top two queries, enter the code necessary to activate the second query.

In ASP:

```
Else
```

In ColdFusion:

```
<cfelse>
```

In PHP:

```
} else {
```

Again, the only way this code can be executed is if the form variable is not present, but the URL variable is.

7) In the line after the second SQL statement, enter a new line to close the nested `if` **block.**

In ASP:

```
End If
```

In ColdFusion:

```
</cfif>
```

In PHP:

```
}
```

These lines complete the nested if block, the lesson, and the tour search and display application.

```
 9
10 If IsEmpty(Request.Form("tourCountry")) Then
11     If IsEmpty(Request.QueryString("regionID")) Then
12         rs_tourDetail.Source = "SELECT *  FROM tbl_tours INNER JOIN tbl_country  ON tbl_country.countryII
13     Else
14         rs_tourDetail.Source = "SELECT *  FROM tbl_tours INNER JOIN tbl_country  ON tbl_country.countryII
15     End If
16 Else
17     rs_tourDetail.Source = "SELECT *  FROM tbl_tours INNER JOIN tbl_country  ON tbl_country.countryID=tbl
18 End If
19
```

8) Save and upload this file. Test tours.asp in your browser, going back and forth trying every kind of search available.

The application should be bulletproof at this point. You should see all (and only) the tours that meet your search criteria. The Recordset Navigation Bar should show or hide, based on the number of records returned from your search. If you click a tour's country, you should see its profile. If you click a tour's Tour Price Calculator link, you should go to that application, and the tour should be preselected in the menu. In short, your users should now have a pretty slick interface through which to learn more about Newland Tours offerings.

WHAT YOU HAVE LEARNED

In this lesson, you have:

- Prepared tours.asp so that it can accommodate three different kinds of search (pages 348–350)

- Built a dynamic menu that sends data to tours_detail.asp using dynamically generated URL variables (pages 350–354)

- Replicated that dynamic menu on another page (page 355)

- Used code commenting as a strategy for testing and debugging isolated pieces of code (pages 356–359)

- Built a form with a menu populated with dynamic data (pages 358–361)

- Displayed or hid the Recordset Navigation Bar based on the number of records returned in a query (pages 362–366)

- Written an SQL query that filters data joined into two tables based on the value of a URL variable, and another that filters using a form variable (pages 367–373)

- Written an SQL query that uses the EXISTS keyword and a subquery (pages 372–373)

- Dynamically switched SQL queries based on the presence or absence of environmental variables using nested if...else structures in conjunction with IsEmpty() (ASP), IsDefined() (ColdFusion), and isset() (PHP) (pages 374–378)

authenticating users

LESSON 13

Implementing a framework that allows users to register (and log in) is one of the most common tasks for Web developers. Pages in the site are divided into those that are publicly accessible and those that require users to log in. A set of registration and log-in pages allows users to get through the barriers and access the pages requiring authentication. Creating a user authentication framework is the centerpiece of this lesson. Thanks to a series of Dreamweaver server behaviors, creating an authentication framework is much easier than you might think.

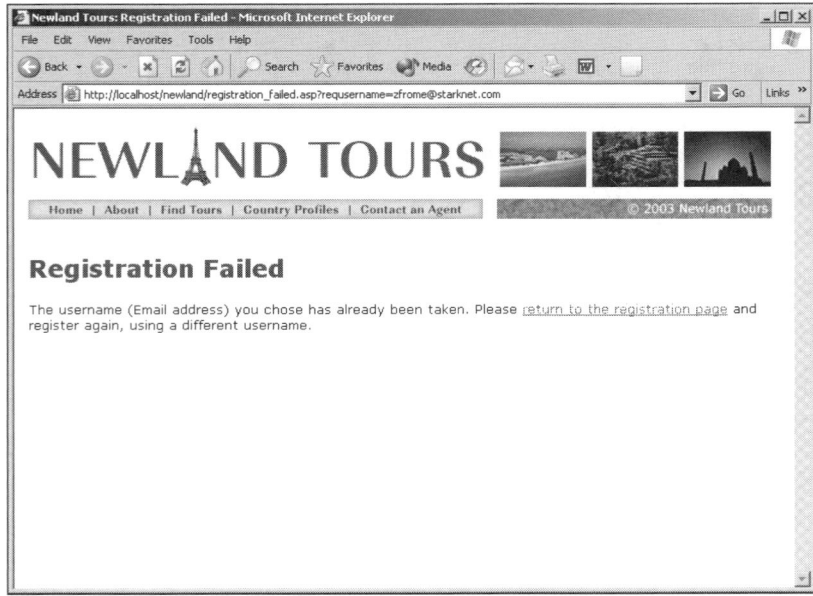

In this lesson, you'll create a complete registration and log-in system, taking into account both when things go right and when they go awry.

You might be wondering why Newland Tours would even have user authentication. Newland distinguishes three groups of users:

- Visitors who first arrive at the site and are determining whether they are interested in Newland Tours

- Visitors who are serious about travel and want to learn specific information about certain tours

- Newland Tours employees who are authorized to maintain site content

The first group can access the home, about, and contact areas of the site. To access the tour descriptions, country profiles, or tour price calculator, users first need to register to access the site. The registration is free, and Newland Tours only uses the information for marketing and promotional reasons—learning more about the users, and so on. The third group of users has access to the content-management system features of the site. This system, which you'll build later in the book, will enable Newland Tours employees to fill out Web forms to publish new content to the site, without the need to code in HTML or transfer files via FTP.

WHAT YOU WILL LEARN

In this lesson, you will:

- Learn about Web applications as entities distinguishable from the collection of pages in the site

- Create a registration page

- Create a log-in page

- Make the log-in page intercept users who have not logged in and are trying to access a restricted page

- Ensure that after users log in, they are redirected to the restricted page they tried to access

APPROXIMATE TIME

This lesson takes approximately 90 minutes to complete.

LESSON FILES

Starting Files:

Lesson13/Start/newland/generic_template.asp

Lesson13/Start/newland/index.asp

Lesson13/Start/newland/profiles.asp

Lesson13/Start/newland/profiles_detail.asp

Lesson13/Start/newland/tour_detail.asp

Lesson13/Start/newland/tourprice.asp

*Lesson13/Start/newland/tourprice_
    processor.asp*

Lesson13/Start/newland/tours.asp

Completed Files:

*Lesson13/Complete/newland/generic_
    template.asp*

Lesson13/Complete/newland/index.asp

Lesson13/Complete/newland/login.asp

Lesson13/Complete/newland/login_failed.asp

Lesson13/Complete/newland/profiles.asp

*Lesson13/Complete/newland/profiles_
    detail.asp*

Lesson13/Complete/newland/register.asp

*Lesson13/Complete/newland/registration_
    failed.asp*

Lesson13/Complete/newland/tour_detail.asp

Lesson13/Complete/newland/tourprice.asp

*Lesson13/Complete/newland/tourprice_
    processor.asp*

Lesson13/Complete/newland/tours.asp

*Lesson13/Complete/newland/application.cfm
    (ColdFusion only)*

USER AUTHENTICATION AS A WEB APPLICATION

As always, before we jump in and start using the server behaviors that create the authentication framework, it's important to understand at least conceptually how they work. Users can only access restricted pages once they've successfully logged in. To log in, a user supplies a username and password combination. ASP, ColdFusion, or PHP queries the database to see if any records contain both the username and the password together. If it does, the log-in is successful, and the user is flagged as having logged in (more on that in a moment). If there are no records with both the username and password, the log-in fails, and the user is redirected to a page indicating that log-in has failed.

Each restricted page has a script at the top that checks to verify that the user is logged in, and if so, processes and displays the page. If the user is not logged in, she or he is typically redirected to a page that enables log-in, and the restricted page never actually loads.

With one exception, you can probably understand how all this could happen in ASP, ColdFusion, or PHP. That exception is the notion of flagging a user as logged in and checking for that flag across multiple pages. Because the server forgets the user in between every page, setting and checking for the existence of the logged-in flag is problematic. You've overcome the server's forgetfulness in previous lessons by sending URL (or querystring) and form variables between pages. But these solutions are temporary, requiring you to manually send data to every page that needs it. What's needed is something more persistent.

You already worked with one type of persistent variable: the cookie. As you'll recall, a cookie is a name-value pair stored on the user's hard drive and sent to the server when the user makes an HTTP request. Using this technique, you can simulate the effect of the server remembering a user across multiple pages, simply by having pages use and respond to cookie data.

In large part to facilitate applications that need to keep track of users and data over time, ASP, ColdFusion, and PHP have special built-in features that handle much of this work for you. These features include, among others, two variable scopes: application variables and session variables.

- Application-scoped variable data: Application-scoped variable data includes any variable information that you want to set for the entire application, regardless of user. For example, if you want to specify a contact person on every page of the site, rather than hard-coding that person's name and email address onto every single page, you can define the name and address once as an application variable and bind that value to every instance of a contact address in the site. Then, if that person is replaced, you need only to change the name in one place, and the rest of the site is updated. Only ASP and ColdFusion explicitly have the application scope, though it could be simulated easily in PHP.

- Session-scoped variable data: Session variables contain information for a single user in a single session. If the user leaves the site or closes the browser for a period of time (usually about 20 minutes), then the session ends, and the information is flushed from memory.

NOTE *ColdFusion also has a built-in Client scope, which enables you to store data about a single client across multiple sessions. The Client scope is not covered in this book.*

Clearly, the session variable is perfect for handling the log-in flag. That is, once a user successfully logs in, a session variable is set indicating the successful log-in. Each page that restricts access needs merely to check for the presence of this session variable to determine whether to grant access to the page or redirect the user to a different page.

The critical concept here is persistence. Through these enhanced application features, ASP, ColdFusion, and PHP enable developers to create sites where data persists for a certain period of time, overcoming the intrinsic limitation of the stateless HTTP protocol. This persistence is crucial in many applications, not just user authentication. Imagine a Web shopping cart that forgot who you were between the pages where you entered your shipping address and credit card information! You could pay for merchandise that is then sent to someone else.

For the data to be persistent, it must be stored somewhere. Where it is stored depends on the scope of the variable. Application-scoped variables are stored on the server, typically residing in memory. For this reason, you should keep your application-scoped variables to a minimum.

Session variables, in contrast, are typically stored as cookies on the user's computer and matched to temporary session variables stored on the server. The storage of data in two locations and its subsequent matching is usually invisible to the developer; that is, while you may set and retrieve session variables, for example, you won't be both setting and retrieving server and cookie variables, because that happens behind the scenes.

To enable all of this functionality, ASP, ColdFusion, and (to a certain extent) PHP recognize the collection of pages that make up your site as a single entity, an application. Different pages are part of an application when they have access to the same session and application data. You can't see the whole application anywhere—it's not a tangible entity—but it's there. Web applications consist of sets of files that ASP, ColdFusion, or PHP manages as a group.

Both ASP and ColdFusion have a special page where you can put application-related data and scripts. ASP has global.asa, and ColdFusion has application.cfm. Although these two files are different in many particulars, their roles are comparable. Both handle application-scoped variables and events, as well as session management. Any variable, script, or functionality you add to global.asa or application.cfm is included in and available to every ASP or ColdFusion site within the same application. In most cases, global.asa or application.cfm resides in the site's root directory and therefore the application's scope is the entire site.

PHP lacks a direct equivalent to global.asa and application.cfm. However, their functionality is reasonably easy to simulate in PHP. For example, one of the most important uses of application.cfm is that it enables sessions, session-scoped variables, and session management. The ColdFusion developer enables session management in application.cfm, and ColdFusion essentially prefixes this file to every single page requested within the application. In other words, what makes ColdFusion session management work is that in the final analysis, after ColdFusion prefixes each file with the contents of application.cfm, the session-enabling code is inserted into every page at the top. In PHP (4.1 and higher), you can insert the equivalent code, a method called `session_start()`, at the top of any page to enable sessions. Or, you can create an include file with this method, and include that file at the top of every page. Thus, even though PHP isn't exactly the same as ASP or ColdFusion, the similarities are far more fundamental than their differences.

From even this brief overview, you can understand why a session management framework is so important to authentication. It enables a single entry through a log-in page to provide access to multiple pages, without requiring the developer to manually create scripts that send the data from each page to the next.

BUILDING THE REGISTRATION PAGES

Log-in presupposes a collection of valid usernames and passwords in the database. The best way to get those combinations into the database is to create a registration form that inserts them there. This is a departure from the database interaction you have been working with for the past several lessons. In those lessons, you retrieved data from the database and filtered and manipulated it for the user. Here, you are making it possible for the user to insert information into the database. Fortunately, Dreamweaver has a behavior that makes that insertion easy.

But merely inserting information is not enough. You also need to check to ensure that two people didn't use the same username. To prevent this problem, you'll use one of an entire suite of user authentication server behaviors: Check New Username. If it succeeds, the user is registered and redirected to the log-in page. If it fails, the user is redirected to a registration failed page.

1) Open generic_template.asp. Save it as *register.asp*. In the Toolbar, give it a title of *Newland Tours: Register*. Replace the placeholder heading with *Please Register to Use the Site*.

Now the page has a basic identity.

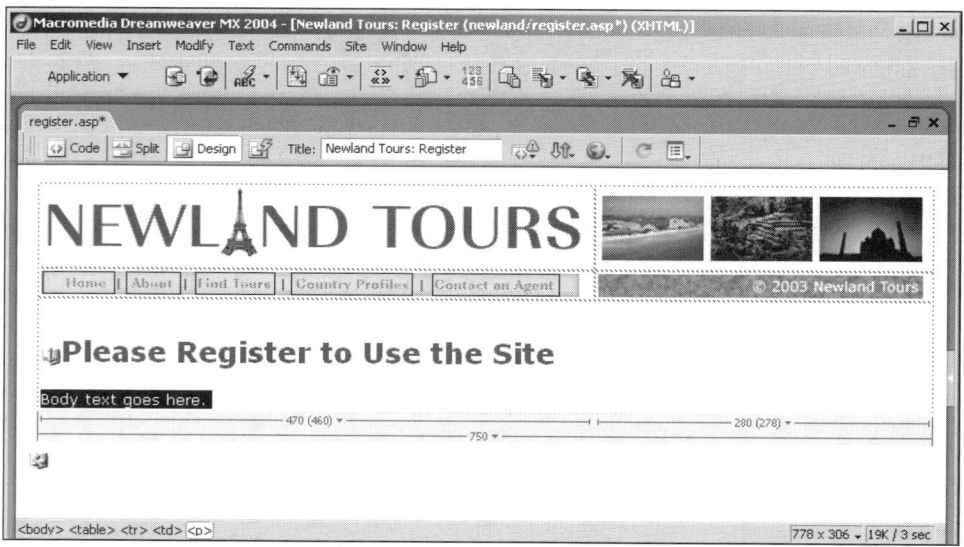

2) Delete the placeholder line of body text, and insert a form. Use the Property inspector to name the form *frm_register* (leaving the action and method attributes alone for now). With the insertion point inside the form, insert a table with 10 rows, 2 columns, a width of 95%, a border thickness of 0, a cellpadding of 3, and a cellspacing of 0.

The table will be used to structure the elements in the form.

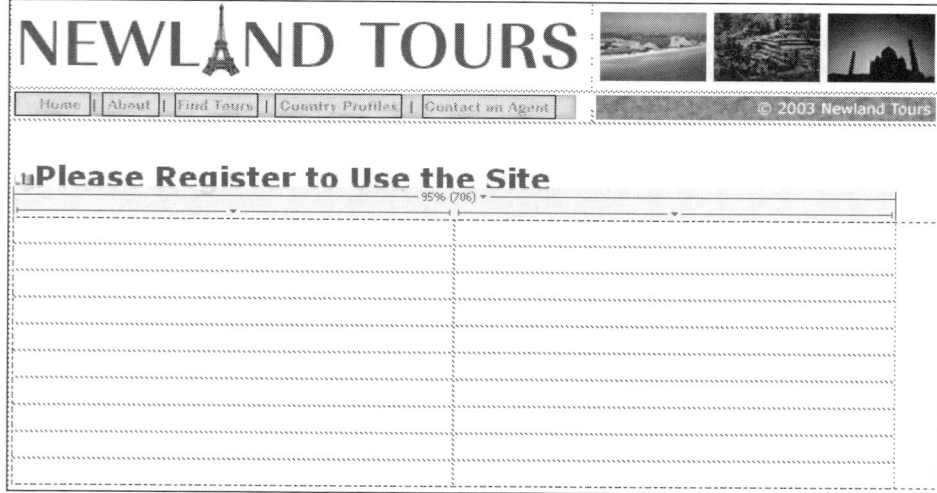

3) Insert text fields and a submit button as shown in the screenshot. Use the Property inspector to name the text fields as follows:

firstName

lastName

username

pwd

address1

city

state_province

zip_postal

country

Don't take any shortcuts in this step. You will be very sorry if you leave each of the text fields with their default name (textfield1, textfield2, etc.). You should always use descriptive names for every field, or it becomes nearly impossible to create the scripts that make use of the data from these fields. In addition, the names listed above correspond to the fields in the database where this data will go, which makes it much easier to add the server behavior that inserts the records.

Use the Char Width setting in the Property inspector to lengthen or shorten the text fields. For example, I set address1 to 55 characters wide, to make additional room in that field.

You can drag the column divider to the left, to make extra room for the right column, if needed.

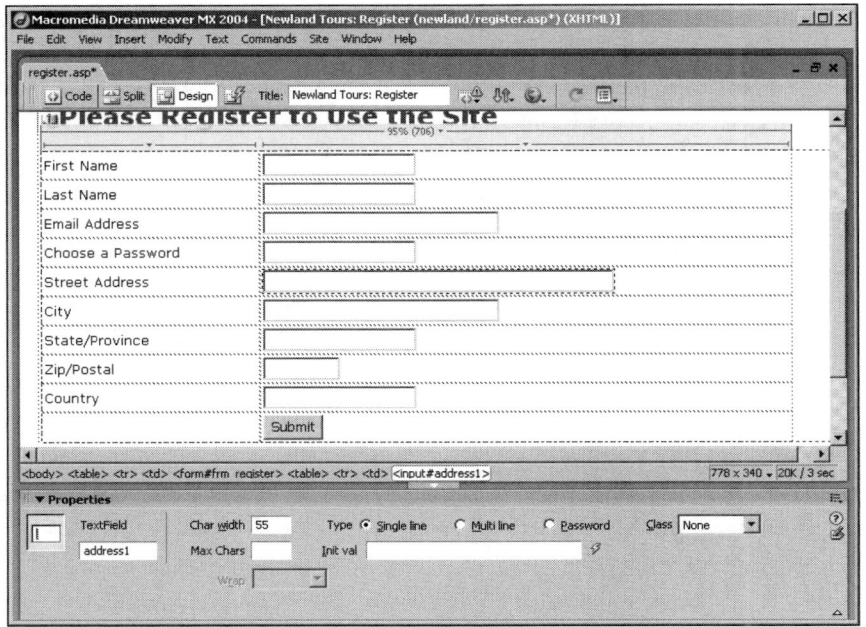

4) Position the insertion point in the empty cell to the left of the Submit button. From the Forms tab of the Insert panel, insert a hidden field element. Name it *userGroup*, and type *visitor* as its value.

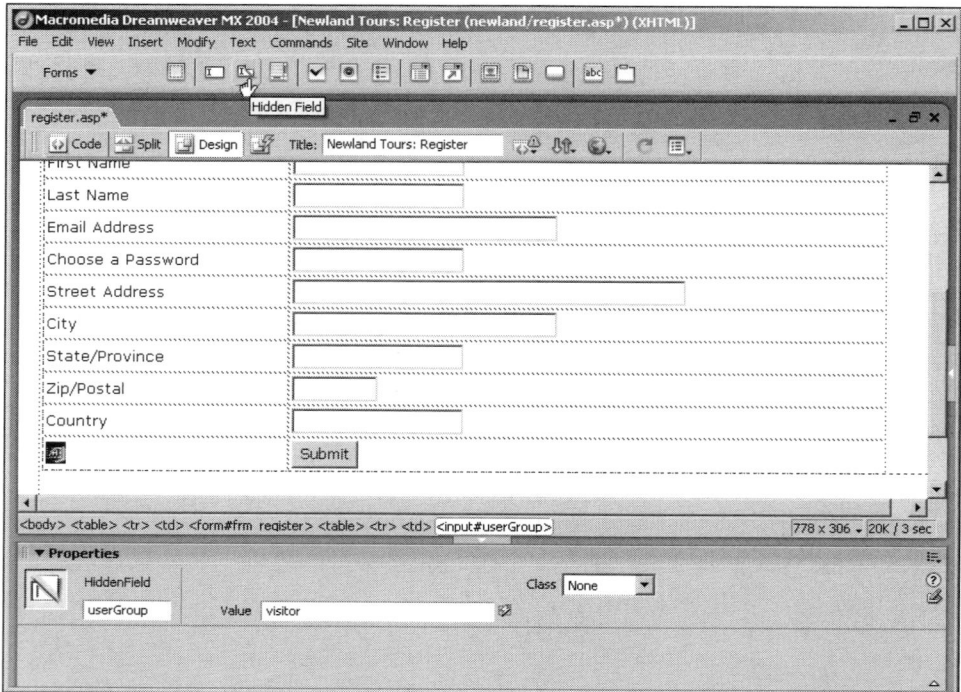

The purpose of this step is not immediately clear, unless you know what's going to follow.

Hidden fields are used in forms to pass predetermined data when the form is submitted. In this case, when the form is submitted, along with name value pairs such as firstName=Lyra and lastName=Bellacqua, the form will also pass userGroup=visitor. Unlike the firstName and lastName fields, the userGroup value is read-only, which means users won't be able to edit it.

You're probably wondering what userGroup is in the first place. Remember, the site will be set up to enable three different levels of visitors: nonregistered visitors, registered visitors, and Newland Tours employees. Two of these groups, registered guests and employees, will have different permissions. Employees will be able to access a whole set of admin pages that registered guests cannot. The catch is that both sets of users will log in using the same form. So the log-in script needs some way to distinguish between the different types of users. The way it does this is by checking which group they've been assigned to—a setting stored in their record in tbl_users of the database. But you obviously don't want users to be able to make this decision themselves—you need to ensure that everyone who registers with the public form is set up as a visitor.

To add employees to the admin group, you'll either need to build a second log-in page or existing employees will have to modify a new employee's record in the database. In the next lesson, you'll build a simple interface in the admin section of the site that enables employees to change a person's profile to be in the administrator group.

5) Click to select the Submit button, and in the Server Behaviors panel, click the Add Server Behavior (+) button to add an Insert Record behavior.

The Insert Record behavior matches data entered in the form to fields in the database, creating a new record in the database and populating it with the user-entered data.

This form will add a record to tbl_users, which you will later use in the log-in script to verify that the user is registered, as well as to determine which user group the user is a member of.

6) In the Insert Record dialog, select conn_newland as the Connection, tbl_users as the Table. In the After inserting, go to field, type *login.asp*. In the Get values from field, make sure frm_register is selected.

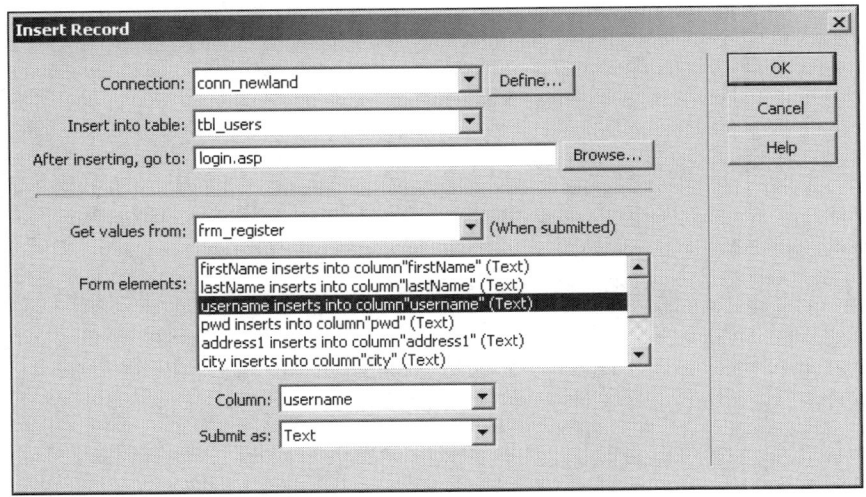

You are familiar enough with building queries that a lot of this dialog should already be familiar to you (especially the Connection and Insert Into Table settings). Like the Recordset dialog, the Insert Record dialog builds a SQL query. But unlike the Recordset dialog, the query built here does not retrieve data, but rather inserts it.

NOTE *ColdFusion and PHP users will notice that their version of the Insert Record dialog looks slightly different than the one shown here, for ASP. However, the differences are mostly cosmetic, and all variations are noted in the text, where appropriate.*

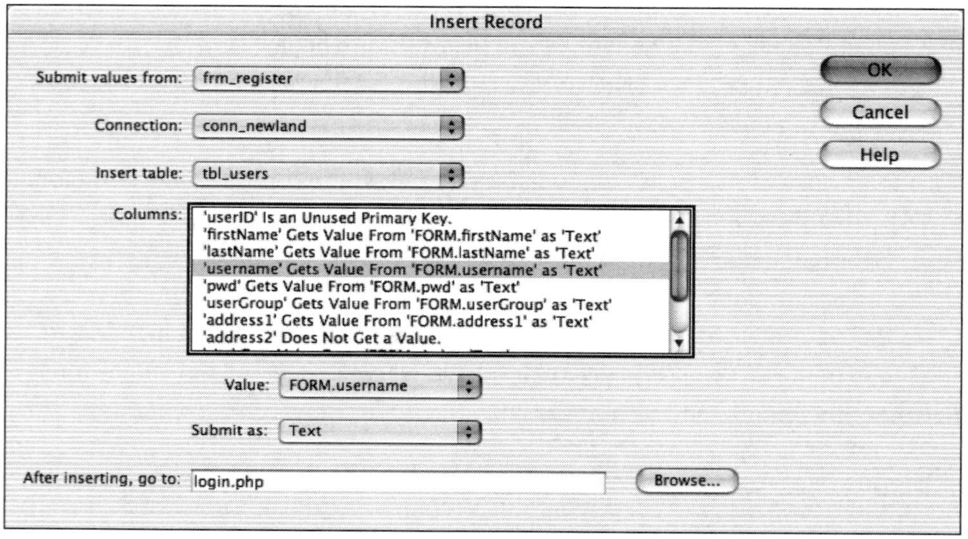

Inserting data, as mentioned earlier, is a matching activity: One item of data from a form is matched to one field in the destination table. That matching is what the lower half of the dialog is all about. Each of the items should follow this syntax: (for ASP) item_x inserts into column "item_x" (Text) or (for ColdFusion and PHP) item_x Gets Value From 'FORM.item_x' as 'Text'. One instance of item_x is the field from the form (on the left in ASP, and on the right in ColdFusion and PHP). The other is the column name in the table (on the right in ASP, and on the left in ColdFusion/PHP). The Text part refers to the variable type (e.g., text, date, integer, etc.).

In your dialog, all of the items on the left should match the items on the right, and they must be the same type. That is, if the database is expecting a number, then ASP or ColdFusion must insert a number; otherwise, ASP or ColdFusion will display an error message. In this case, the form names and the database field names match, but they don't have to: you can name your form fields differently than your database table fields. However, if they have the same name, Dreamweaver does the matching for you. If their names differ, you'll have to manually match the form fields with their corresponding table fields.

If you have any fields that don't have a corresponding column (besides userID and address2, which should not have a corresponding column or value; these should appear on for ColdFusion and PHP), select them, and choose the proper Column (ASP) or Value (ColdFusion) from the drop-down menu at the bottom of the dialog. You shouldn't have any stray fields, though, unless you entered a typo as the field name for one of the text fields in the form.

7) Click OK.
The Server behavior is applied. The form turns cyan, indicating that a Server behavior has been applied to it.

8) Click to select the Submit button again, and this time add a Check New Username server behavior, which appears in a submenu from the User Authentication section of the new Server Behavior menu.
This Server behavior ensures that the username entered in the form is unique.

9) In the Check New Username dialog, select username (or FORM.username, as ColdFusion is likely to display it) from the Username field drop-down menu, and type *registration_failed.asp* in the If already exists, go to field. Click OK.
Here, you are ensuring that the value entered in the username field doesn't already exist. Since you asked for the user's email address to use as their username, this shouldn't be a problem for legitimate users.

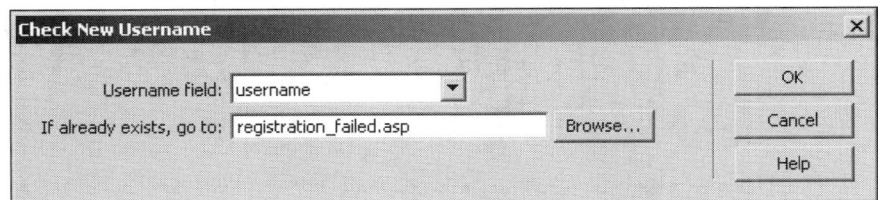

10) Back on the main page, select the Submit button once again, and from the Behaviors (not Server Behaviors) panel, add a Validate Form behavior. Make each of the fields required. In addition, make sure the username field will accept only Email Address.

Whenever you create a form, make sure you deploy some sort of form validation, whether it's a client-side JavaScript behavior such as the one used here, or a server-side script like the one you wrote earlier in the book.

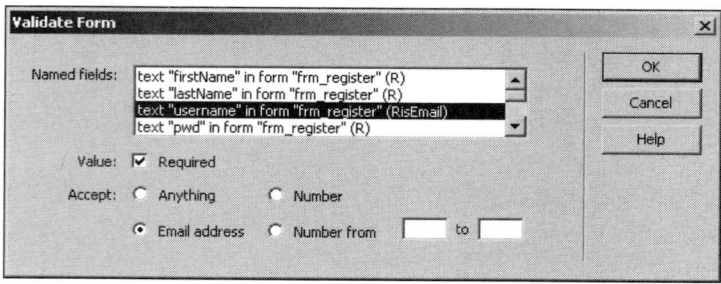

11) Save, upload, and close register.asp.

You don't need to test it now, since, whether you are successful or unsuccessful in your registration, you will be redirected to a page that doesn't yet exist.

12) Starting with generic_template.asp, create a new page called registration_failed.asp. Use the Toolbar to title it *Newland Tours: Registration Failed*. Make it look like the page shown in the screenshot. The link should point to register.asp.

Users are redirected to this page if the Check New Username Server behavior detects that the username already exists.

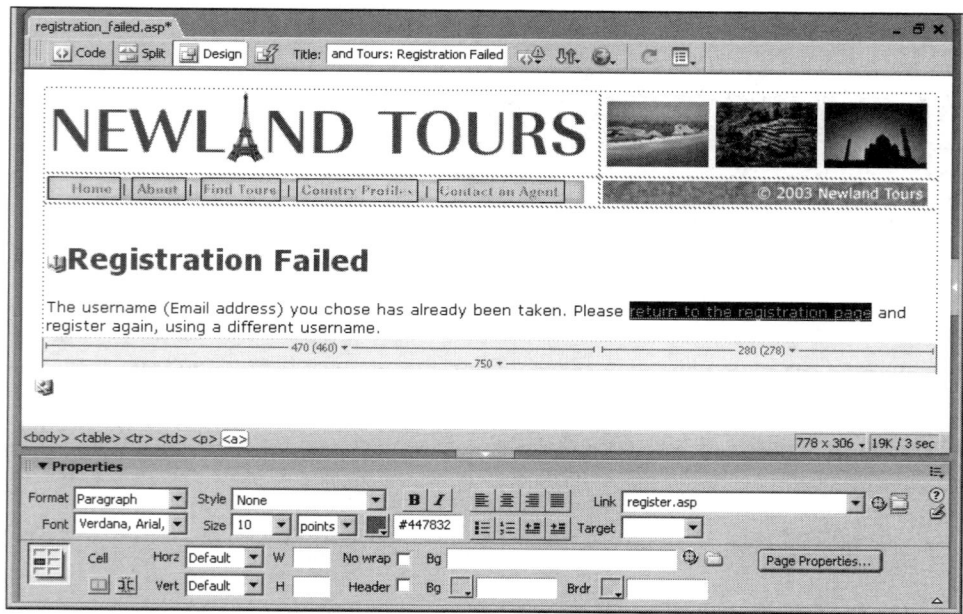

BUILDING THE LOG-IN PAGE

Now that your registration is page is functioning, you can build the log-in page. Remember, the role of the log-in page is to obtain (through a form) the user's username and password. Then, it will compare these values with the records in tbl_users. If there's a match, the log-in script sets a session variable indicating that the user is logged in. If there is no match, the user is redirected to a log-in failed page.

1) Starting with generic_template.asp, create a new file, *login.asp*. Title it *Newland Tours: Log In*. Type *Please Log In* as its heading.

Now you've created the basic page framework.

2) Replace the first line of body text with a form. Call the form *frm_login*. Inside the form, insert a table with 3 rows, 2 columns, a width of 95%, a border of 0, a cellpadding of 3, and a cellspacing of 0.

Once again, the table inside the form is used to structure the form elements. Also, as before, you don't specify the action or method attributes of the form. These are both required, but they will be completed automatically for you when you add the Server behavior, so you can leave them alone for now.

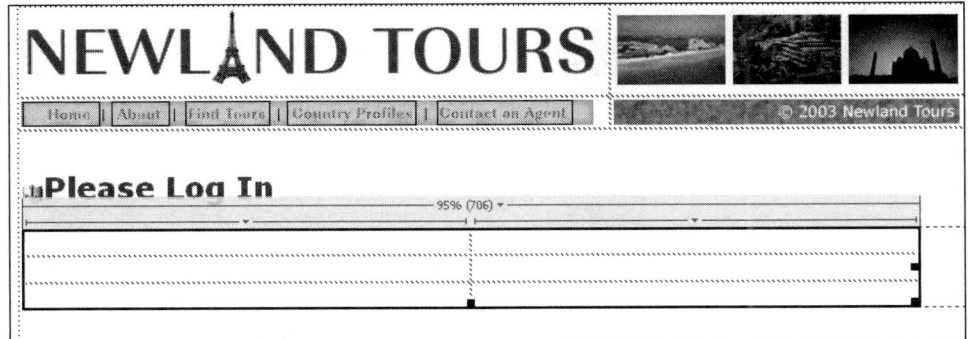

393

3) Insert the text labels, text fields, and Submit button as before. Name the text box beside Email Address *username*, and name the one beside Password, *pwd*. Make sure the pwd text field is set to the Password type in the Property inspector.

The form is built, but it doesn't do anything yet.

4) Click to select the Submit button, and use the Server Behaviors panel to add a User Authentication > Log In User behavior.

This behavior will do all the work of both verifying that the user's credentials match a pair in the database; that a session variable will be set, if the log-in was successful; and that the user will be redirected to an appropriate location, based on whether the log-in was successful.

5) In the top quarter of the Log In User dialog, verify that frm_login is the selected form, that username is set as the Username Field, and that pwd is set as the Password field. In the second quarter of the dialog, choose conn_newland as the Connection, tbl_users as the Table, username as the Username Column, and pwd as the Password Column.

With these settings, you are providing the parameters the script needs to compare the authentication entered into the log-in form with the list of registered users in the database.

6) In the third quarter of the Log In User dialog, enter *index.asp* for the successful log-in redirection, and *login_failed.asp* for the failed log-in redirection. Make sure that Go To Previous URL is checked. In the fourth quarter of the dialog, select Username, Password, and Access Level, and choose userGroup in the Get Level From menu. Click OK.

In this step, you are accomplishing two goals. First, you are specifying where the user should be redirected depending on the success or failure of the log-in.

The Go To Previous URL setting needs some explanation. There are two ways that users will access this log-in page. First, they can access it directly by following the Log In link on the homepage. But they'll also see this page if they try to access a page that requires log in, and they haven't logged in yet. That is, the log in page may intercept their progress in the site. Upon successful log in, users won't want to be redirected to the homepage—not when they clicked a link to access tours or country profiles. By checking this option, you add functionality to the script that ensures that once these users have logged in, they are redirected to the page they attempted to load before they logged in.

394

The second goal you are accomplishing is to create the separate user group functionality discussed earlier. This will enable you to distinguish between registered users who have logged in and employees who have logged in. Since these access levels are stored in the userGroup field of tbl_users, you specify that information in the Get Level From menu.

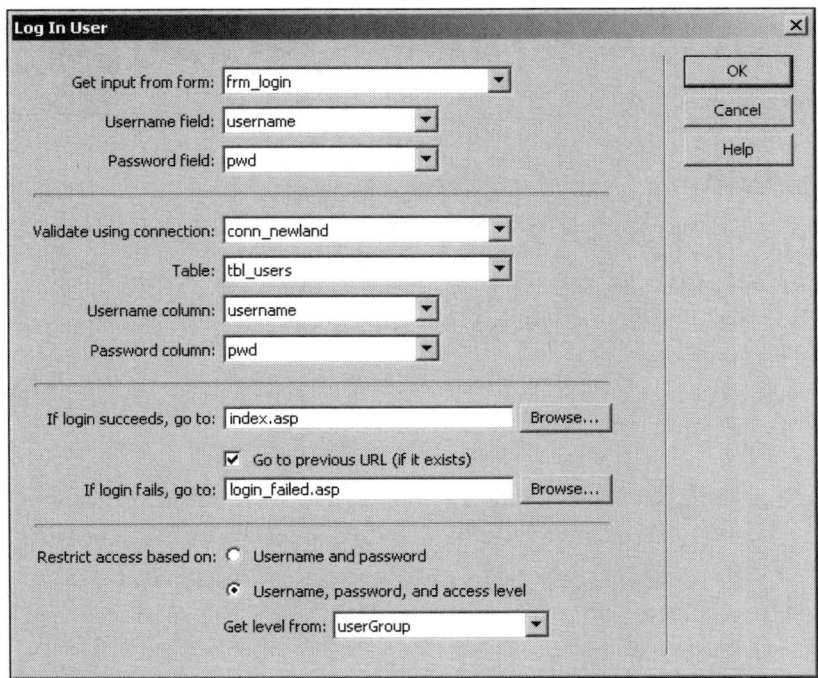

7) Click the Submit button, and add a Form Validation behavior that makes both fields required.

Every form needs some mechanism for validation.

8) Beneath the form, in regular body text, enter the following: *If you don't already have an account, please register for a free account.* **Link the word register to register.asp. Save and upload the page.**

Because the log-in page may intercept the user's path to information, and because the user may not even have realized that registration is required, adding a simple explanation with a link is a helpful usability feature.

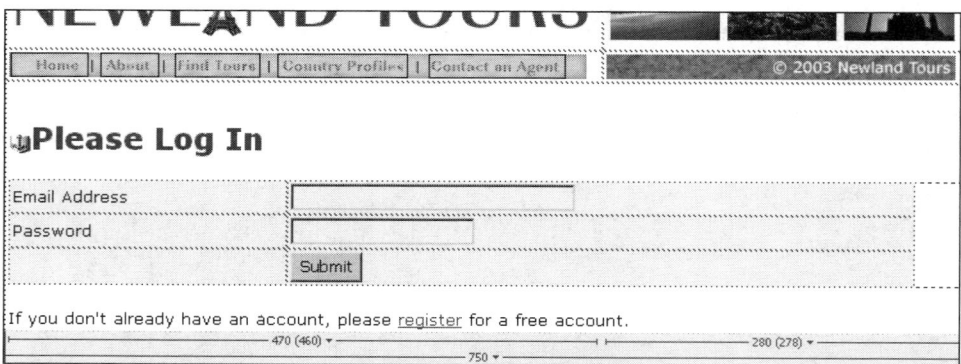

9) Starting with generic_template, create login_failed.asp. Title it *Newland Tours: Login Failed*. **Type** *Login Failed* **as the heading. Type the following as the body text:** *Your username and password combination was not recognized. Try again.* **Link the words Try again to login.asp.**

Static pages are passé, I know, but they have their uses.

ASP users can test the whole log-in application. Open register.asp, and create a profile. Then log in with your username and password. As always, try to break the application as well. Register the same name twice. Try logging in with the wrong password. Try typing your phone number instead of your email. And so on.

ColdFusion users have a quick chore to do before they can test the application: They need to create the application.cfm file that governs the Web application framework. ASP users don't have to worry about creating a global.asa file—ASP will handle session management just fine without it.

PHP users may have a quick chore of their own. Depending on your configuration, session management may not be set up properly. This problem typically crops up for Windows PHP users, but not Macintosh PHP users. See the section, "Ensuring Session Management is Enabled (Windows PHP Users Only)" later in the lesson for details.

CREATING APPLICATION.CFM (COLDFUSION ONLY)

One of the functions of the Log In User server behavior is that it creates a session variable when the user successfully logs in. The problem is, the session scope is inactive by default, which means that the log-in page won't work. You'll have to activate session management in the ColdFusion Web Application Framework. Doing so is a simple matter of creating a new file (Application.cfm), and entering a single line of code.

1) Create a new page in code view. Delete all of the code on the page, including any HTML, XML, or other tags or code.

Application.cfm is not a regular Web page, and so it should not have any code on it to begin.

2) In the first line, type the following code:

```
<cfapplication sessionmanagement="yes" setclientcookies="yes" name=
⇒"newland_tours" sessiontimeout="#CreateTimeSpan(0, 0, 20, 0)#">
```

The <cfapplication> tag effectively creates an application and enables the Web application framework. It has several attributes, many of which are optional. One required attribute is name, which is any name you want to give your application. The other attributes used here enable session management, enable the setting of cookies, and create a session timeout.

You'll note that rather than specifying a simple period of time in the `sessiontimeout` attribute, there is a function, `CreateTimeSpan()`. This function takes four parameters, standing for days, hours, minutes, and seconds. Thus, the `sessiontimeout` is set for 20 minutes. In other words, if a user is inactive or leaves the site to browse on other pages for more than 20 minutes, all session variables associated with that user are flushed. In practical terms, it means the user would have to log in again.

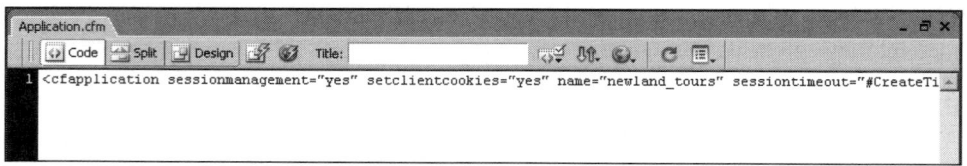

3) Save, close, and upload Application.cfm.

At this point you can test the registration and log-in features you've added in this lesson. As mentioned earlier, try to break the application, by entering every variation you can think of.

ENSURING SESSION MANAGEMENT IS ENABLED (WINDOWS PHP USERS ONLY)

When you install PHP using the default settings, session management is enabled. When PHP actually starts using sessions, it stores transaction information in a text file. This text file is already setup when you install PHP as well, or at least it is supposed to be. Unfortunately, the default setup for some versions of PHP in Windows uses the wrong path to find that text file. What results are some unseemly errors.

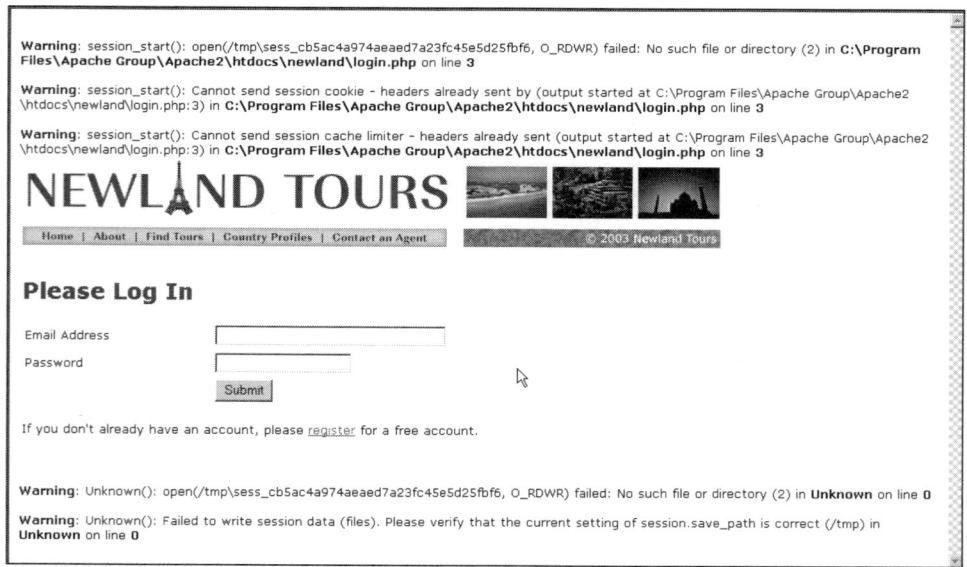

If you do not see this error when you test login.php, then you can skip ahead to the section, "Restricting Access to Pages."

If you look closely at the error, you will see that it is trying to open a file with the most unlikely path, something along the lines of /tmp\sess_ sess_6002c7a1f3cba 0838a25d6e86e596b15, O_RDWR). What makes this path so unusual is that it begins with a forward slash (/), and yet all Windows paths use backslashes (\). This is presumably a bug that comes from PHP's Unix origins; paths in Unix (including Mac OS X) are all forward slashes. Worse yet, the folder it is looking for (tmp) doesn't exist!

Fixing this problem is relatively easy, and requires two steps:

- Revise the .ini file that specifies what path PHP should use to map to the session directory
- Create the directory that the .ini file actually points to.

1) Navigate to C:\windows\php.ini. Double-click to open it in Notepad.

This file contains most of the configuration instructions for your implementation of PHP. Remember, in the Unix world, the most common interface is not the dialog box or wizard, but rather the text file.

2) Use Edit > Find to search for session.save_path. Find the path that specifies the save directory.

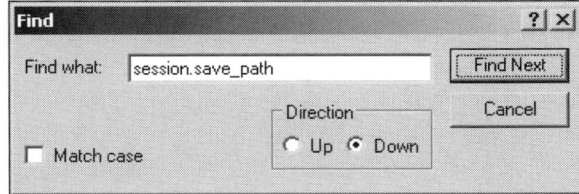

Remember, anything following a semi-colon is commented out and probably documentation. Thus, it's most likely that the first instance of session.save_path you discover will be a part of the documentation, and not the problem itself.

The instance you want is followed by a path. Your path probably varies from the one shown in the screenshot. In fact, that's the problem!

```
[Session]
; Handler used to store/retrieve data.
session.save_handler = files

; Argument passed to save_handler.  In the case of files, this is the path
; where data files are stored. Note: Windows users have to change this
; variable in order to use PHP's session functions.
; As of PHP 4.0.1, you can define the path as:
;       session.save_path = "N;/path"
; where N is an integer.  Instead of storing all the session files in
; /path, what this will do is use subdirectories N-levels deep, and
; store the session data in those directories.  This is useful if you
; or your OS have problems with lots of files in one directory, and is
; a more efficient layout for servers that handle lots of sessions.
; NOTE 1: PHP will not create this directory structure automatically.
;         You can use the script in the ext/session dir for that purpose.
; NOTE 2: See the section on garbage collection below if you choose to
;         use subdirectories for session storage
session.save_path = C:\PHP-4.3.2-Win32\temp\

; whether to use cookies.
session.use_cookies = 1

; This option enables administrators to make their users invulnerable to
; attacks which involve passing session ids in URLs; defaults to 0.
; session.use_only_cookies = 1
```

3) Revise the path so that it corresponds to the following formula:

```
C:\php-[version_number]-Win32\temp\
```

That is, type exactly what you see above, but replace [version_number] with the actual version number of your copy of PHP.

If you forgot the version number of your copy of PHP, look in the C:\ directory on your hard drive. Indeed, what you are listing there is the name of that folder, and not your version number per se, though usually the version number is a part of the directory name.

```
; NOTE 1: PHP will not create this directory structure automatically.
;         You can use the script in the ext/session dir for that purpose.
; NOTE 2: See the section on garbage collection below if you choose to
;         use subdirectories for session storage
session.save_path = C:\PHP-4.3.2-Win32\temp\

; whether to use cookies.
session.use_cookies = 1
```

4) Save and close php.ini.
You've just updated where PHP stores session information.

5) Use the Apache icon in the system tray to stop and restart Apache.
This forces php.ini to reload and actually applies the new settings.

6) In Windows Explorer, navigate to C:\php-[version_number]-Win32\ and verify that there is a folder inside called temp.

If that folder doesn't exist, create one.

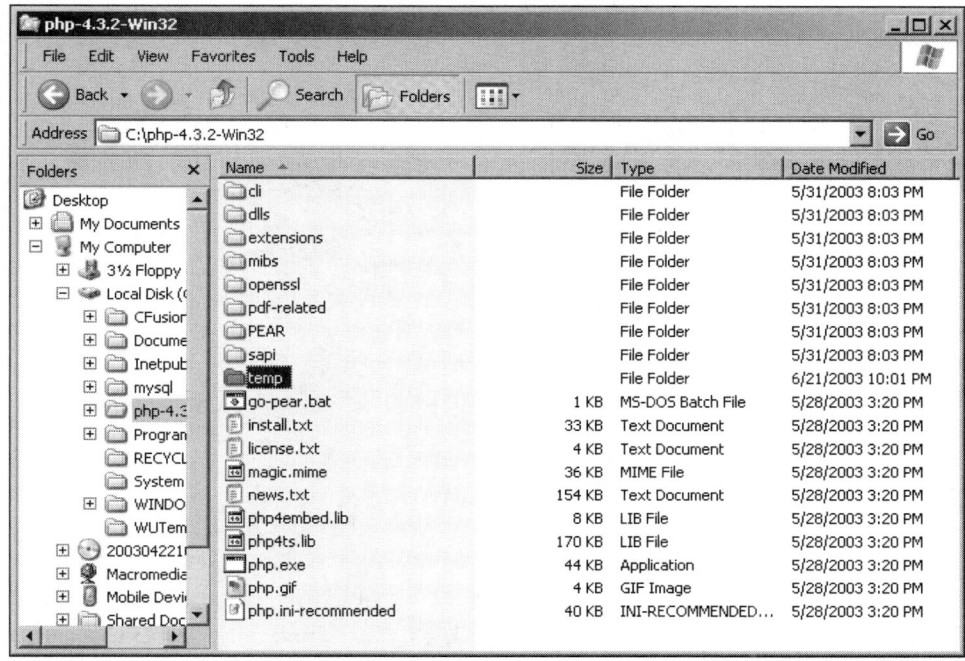

RESTRICTING ACCESS TO PAGES

By now, you should have tested your registration and log-in pages, and they should work as expected. The only thing is, until you implement page restriction features to the pages you want to block access to, your registration and log-in framework is not very useful. In this task, you will add the server behaviors that prevent users from accessing pages, unless they've first logged in.

1) Open profiles.asp.

This is one of the pages that users must log in to see.

2) Click anywhere on the page, and insert a Restrict Access to Page server behavior, found in the User Authentication submenu of the Server Behaviors menu. In the Restrict Based On group, choose Username, Password, and Access Level.

This dialog not only lets you restrict access to the page; it also lets you restrict access to a page based on a user's access level.

Of course, no such levels are defined in the Select Level(s) area, so you'll need to define some.

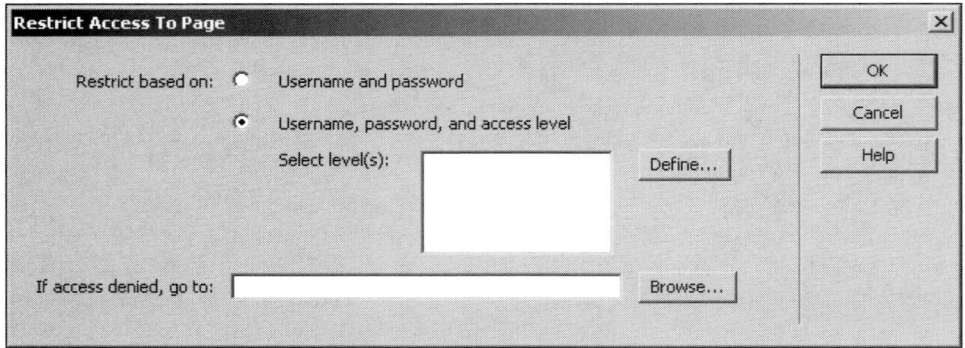

3) Click the Define button. In the Define Access Levels dialog, place the cursor in the Name field, type *visitor*, and press the + button. Repeat the process to add *admin*. Click OK.

Dreamweaver won't check to make sure these groups actually exist; it takes your word for it, so make sure you spell them correctly. These correspond to the available values in the userGroup field of tbl_users. Once it knows their names, Dreamweaver can grant access to pages to users in either or both groups, and deny access to users not in either.

4) Back in the Restrict Access to Page dialog, Ctrl-click (Windows) or Command-click (Mac) to select both visitor and admin from the Select Level(s) area. In the If Access Denied, Go To field, enter login.asp. Click OK.

You've done two things in this step. You've granted access to the page to users in either the visitor or admin group. Had you wanted to grant access to this page to only one of those groups, you would have selected only the one group. Once you've created the admin section of the site, you'll use this dialog and let in only members of the admin group.

The other thing you've done is redirect the user to login.asp if access is denied. This is how that interception described earlier happens. A user tries to access a restricted page without logging in, and she or he sees the log-in dialog. Once log-in is achieved, the restricted page she or he was trying to access appears.

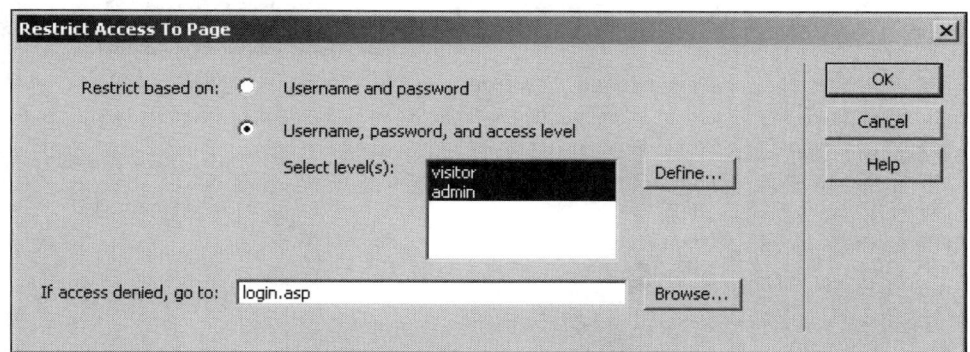

5) Repeat steps 1 through 4 for each of the following files:

profiles_detail.asp

tourprice.asp

tourprice_processor.asp

tours.asp

tours_detail.asp

Each of these pages now requires authentication as well.

6) Save and upload all of the pages you have worked on in this lesson, and, starting from the homepage (index.asp), try accessing the tours and the country profiles.

The authentication framework is fully functional. If you try to access a protected page, the login screen should appear. If you've created a registration account, use it. Or, remember you can use username: osiris@allectomedia.com and password: osiris to test. Once you've logged in, you should automatically be redirected to the page you first requested.

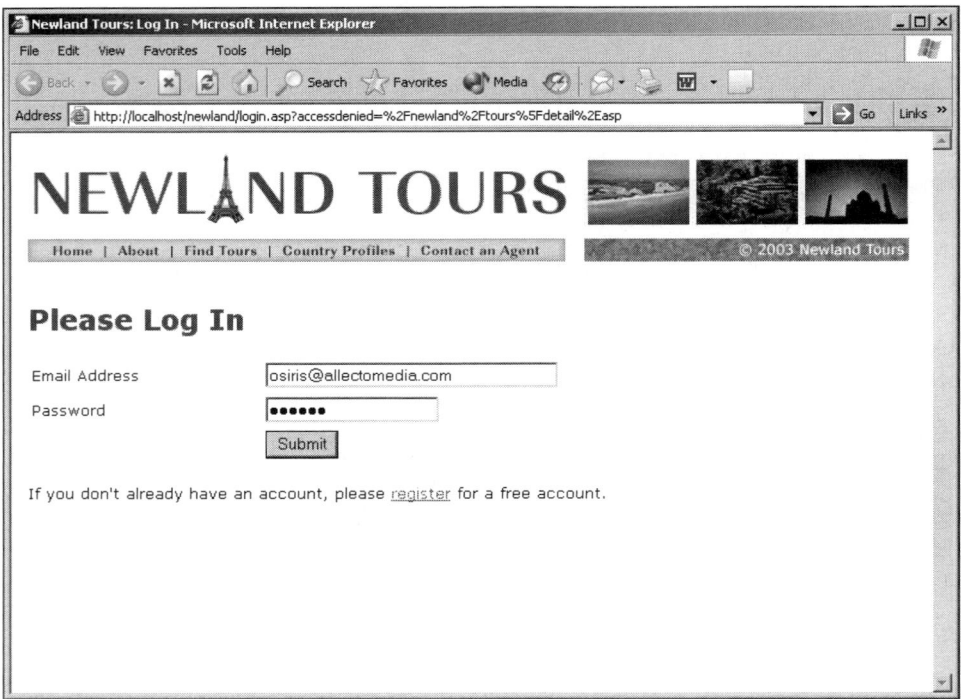

NOTE *PHP users with PHP 4.2 and higher will be disappointed to learn that instead of being redirected to the originally requested page after login, they are sent to the home page. The reason for this is that the server behavior that is supposed to cause the redirection to the originally requested page relies on a configuration setting, register_globals, to be on in order to work. Since PHP 4.2, the default setting for register_globals is off. You can go into your php.ini file and change it to on, and the site will work as expected. However, it was turned off for a reason—this setting creates a potential security hole in PHP. Thus, before you decide to go into php.ini and change the setting, I recommend that you go out on the Web and research the issue.*

7) Open index.asp, and add links at the bottom of the left navigation bar connecting to the registration and log-in pages: Register (Free!) and Log In.

Since users will be intercepted if they attempt to enter restricted pages, and since you took the time to add a link from the log-in page to the registration page, users should find everything even without these links. Still, their presence here makes it that much easier for visitors and employees alike to use the site.

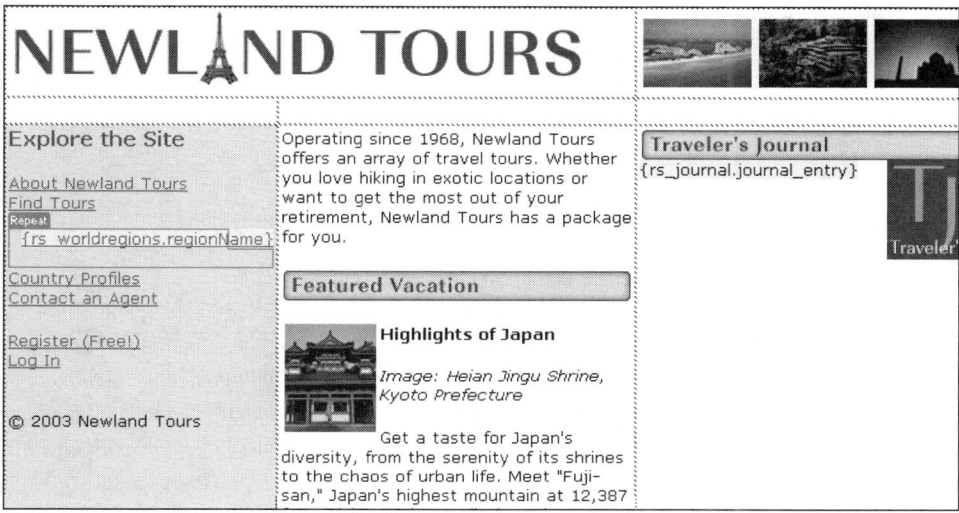

WHAT YOU HAVE LEARNED

In this lesson, you have:

- Learned about persistent data (pages 383–385)
- Created a registration page, using the Insert Record and the Check New Username server behaviors (pages 385–392)
- Built a log-in page, using the Log In User behavior (pages 393–397)
- Created pages to handle registration and log-in failures (pages 394–397)
- Applied Restrict Access to Page server behaviors to each secured page in the site (pages 401–405)

managing content with forms

LESSON 14

A content management system, as its name suggests, is an interface that facilitates the maintenance of content, including the addition of new content, the modification of existing content, and the removal of unwanted content. In this and the next two lessons, you will make steps toward building a content management system (CMS) for the Newland Tours site. You won't build a fully comprehensive CMS, which is an ambitious and often redundant task, making it of limited value in this book. But you will build enough of it to get a sense of how they work, and the know-how to start building your own.

By inserting some HTML as the default text in a text area, you can provide users a template for creating formatted text.

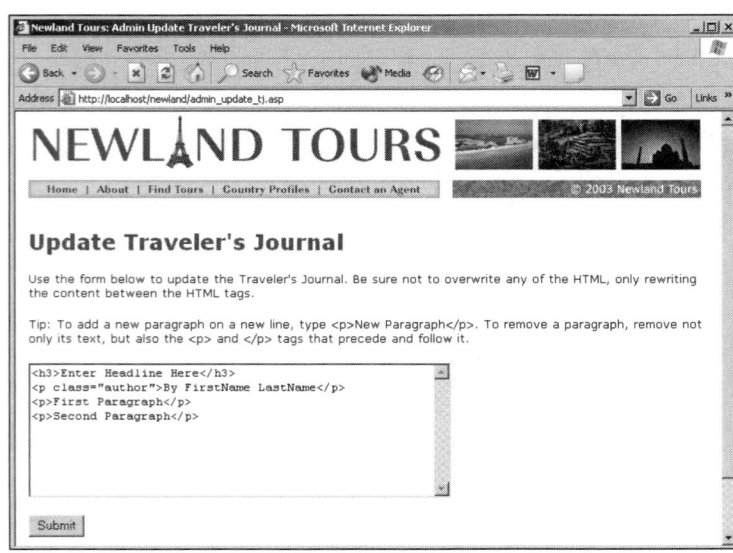

By inserting some HTML as the default text in a text area, you can provide users a template for creating formatted text.

How do CMSs work? You can look at this question as a functional question (how can Web content be maintained over the Web?) or as a technical question (how do we use available technologies to make this possible?). Whenever you face a problem like this, answer the functional question first, and then worry about the technical answer.

In practice, CMSs typically include several pages with forms on them. When users fill out the forms, whatever they entered appears on the site. You don't want these forms to be accessible to the public, which is why you created the log-in framework first. You have probably guessed how this process from form to Web works: database connectivity. You know that the contents of a Web page can be populated with database data, and you know that you can capture user-entered information from a form and put it in a database. Put two and two together, and voila! A content management system.

In 2002, Macromedia released a revolutionary new approach to content management, called Contribute. Contribute, now in its second version, enables non-technical users to maintain site content in a friendly, office productivity tool-like environment. Contribute has both advantages and disadvantages compared to a CMS using a database and ASP, ColdFusion, or PHP. As a Web editor, Contribute enables users to format content much more robustly and easily than the best database-driven CMS. And unlike database-driven sites with ASP, ColdFusion, or PHP, Contribute doesn't require significant programming up-front to achieve the most basic functionality. Because it works mainly with static sites, Contribute is generally a less expensive solution. On the down side, Contribute doesn't work with live database content. In addition, whereas updating a database-driven Web site requires a browser and Internet access, updating a site with Contribute requires Internet access and a copy of Contribute, which, though inexpensive, is not free.

As a rule, use Contribute for text- and image-heavy static sites whose contents need occasional updating, and use dynamic pages and a database for highly structured or data-oriented sites whose contents change frequently, or on sites whose contents need to be searchable. Many enterprise sites make use of both databases and server-side scripting (such as ASP, ColdFusion, or PHP) and Contribute—using each according to its strengths.

Back to the CMS we'll begin in this lesson. Content maintenance implies three abilities: inserting content, modifying content, and deleting content. If you know any SQL, you are probably aware of the INSERT, UPDATE, and DELETE statements, which make it possible to insert, modify, and delete data from a database. If you don't know SQL, don't worry: you'll get practice with each of these statements in this and the next two lessons. You will use these in your queries, rather than simple SELECT statements, to make content manageable.

The primary task remaining is to create form interfaces that serve as the front-end for the work going on in the background. Some of these, especially those for inserting data, are quite easy to create. In fact, by building the registration form, you've already created one. Updating and deleting data are a little trickier, because you have to retrieve data from the database and make it available to the user, so she or he can send the requisite queries back to the database to do the actual updating or deleting.

In this lesson, you will create the simplest portion of the CMS: the form that Newland Tours employees can use to update the Traveler's Journal on the homepage. This functionality requires only a single page, a single form, and a single server behavior (Insert Record).

WHAT YOU WILL LEARN

In this lesson, you will:

- Empower nontechnical users to add formatted content to a Web page instantly
- Create an admin section for the site, including a new template
- Use and customize a text area form element
- Track user activity with session variables and hidden fields
- Learn about SQL's INSERT statement
- Use the Insert Record server behavior

APPROXIMATE TIME

This lesson takes approximately 45 minutes to complete.

LESSON FILES

Starting Files:

Lesson14/Start/newland/generic_template.asp

Lesson14/Start/newland/index.asp

Completed Files:

Lesson14/Complete/newland/admin_ template.asp

Lesson14/Complete/newland/admin_index.asp

Lesson14/Complete/newland/admin_update_ tj.asp

Lesson14/Complete/newland/index.asp

CREATING THE ADMIN SECTION

By the time the site is complete, employees will be able to do a number of administrative tasks, which include inserting new Traveler's Journal articles, maintaining the country profiles, and maintaining the tour descriptions. All of these activities will be limited to those in the admin user group. It is a nice touch to create an administrative homepage—a single page that links to all of the different tasks that administrators can accomplish with the site.

In addition, creating the CMS features will mean creating several new pages. Each of these pages needs to have the Restrict Access to User server behavior applied to it in such a way that only members of the admin user group can get in. That could get monotonous, so to avoid that, you'll create a special admin-only template, called admin_template.asp, which is nearly identical to generic_template.asp, except that it'll have the Restrict Access to User server behavior already applied.

1) Open generic_template.asp. Use the toolbar to change the title to *Newland Tours: Admin*, and save the file as *admin_template.asp*.

You know your template is useful when you use it to create other templates!

2) Use the Server Behaviors panel to add a Restrict Access to Page behavior. In the dialog, restrict based on Username, Password, and Access Level, and make sure that only admin is selected in the Select Level(s) area. Specify *login.asp* in the If access denied field, and click OK.

All of the admin pages should require that the user log in as a member of the admin user group, so you might as well attach the Restrict Access to User behavior directly to the template.

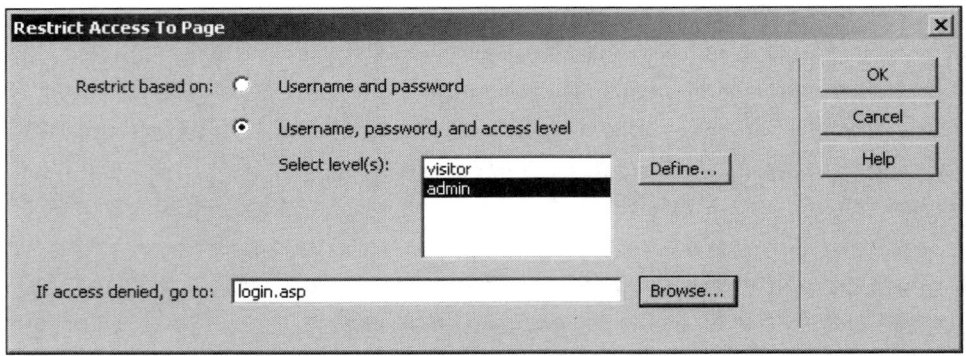

3) Choose File > Save.

You've made a change to the template, so you need to save it.

4) Choose File > Save As, and save the file as *admin_index.asp*. Change the page title to *Newland Tours: Admin Home*, and change main heading to *Admin Home*.

Employees will use this page as a starting point for administrative tasks. You'll also enable them to log in directly to this page.

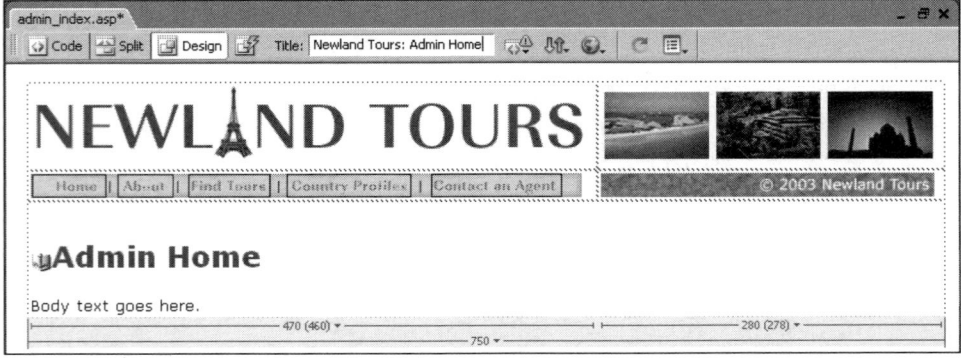

5) In the body section, enter the following lines of text:

Choose an administrative task from the list below. If you have any questions or problems, please contact the webmaster.

Update the Traveler's Journal

Add or remove a registered user to/from the Admin group

Add a new tour description

Modify or remove an existing tour description

Add a new country profile

Modify or remove an existing country profile

This is the main menu for the page. You'll add actual links as you go, but now you have the framework.

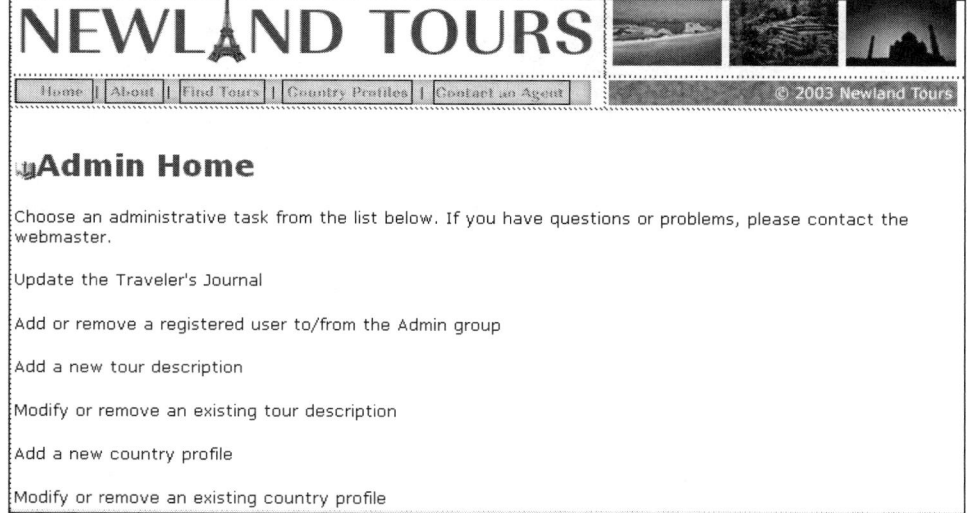

6) Link the word webmaster to your own email (don't forget the *mailto:* prefix). Save and close admin_index.asp.

Whenever you deploy a content management system, make sure you provide explicit directions and contact information, in case its users have any problems.

TIP *Developers often put admin files in a separate folder, which has different permissions. For the sake of simplicity, we'll keep everything in one place and prefix all admin pages with admin_. The topic of Web application security is beyond the scope of this book, but it is not a topic you should take lightly when you start developing dynamic applications in the real world.*

7) Open index.asp, and just below the Log In link, add a new link called Admin, which links to admin_index.asp.

Now all users—visitors and employees alike—can access what they need through the site's front door.

8) Test the new link (including log-in functionality) by pressing F12 with index.asp open and attempting to access admin_index.asp. At the log-in screen, use the following credentials to access the admin section of your site.

Username: *zfrome@starknet.com*

Password: *hypochondriac*

Though you probably created one or more of your own registration accounts in Lesson 13, remember, those are set to the visitor user group. You can't use them (yet) to access admin_index.asp. The credentials supplied above are already in the database (in tbl_users), with admin as the value in the userGroup column.

You might try logging in with your own username and password, just to verify that you *don't* get let in. If you don't have a username and password, remember that you can use osiris@allectomedia.com as the username and osiris as the password, since this user account has the visitor status.

TWO APPROACHES TO FORMATTING CONTENT STORED IN A DATABASE

Now that you have a basic framework for the admin section, you can start building its functionality. In this task, you will create a form that enables users to input new Traveler's Journal entries, which take effect immediately. The form outputs to tbl_journal, which is the same table whose contents index.asp retrieves to display the Traveler's Journal.

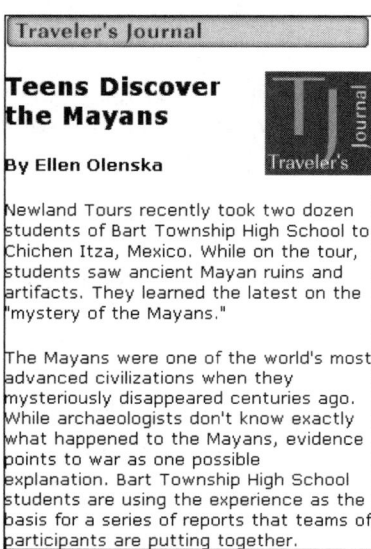

But if you look at the Traveler's Journal, you'll notice that its contents are formatted. The title is in a heading (<h3>, to be specific), the author line is in a <p> tag with the author class applied, and each subsequent paragraph is in its own set of <p> tags. How can you capture content so that it can be marked up and formatted? You can take two approaches:

- Separate each of the elements. With this approach, you create a field for the title in the form and in the database table. Then you dynamically populate an <h3> element with the contents of that record. You then add another pair of fields for the author, and so on. This is how the country profiles and tour descriptions were formatted so precisely.

- Embed HTML markup in the database table. With this approach, part of the text stored in the database is HTML markup. When the record is retrieved, so is the markup. Since the server inserts this text as a part of the page, the browser doesn't know that it is dynamically generated HTML, and it renders just like it would any other HTML.

Each approach has different advantages and disadvantages, and they are not exclusive, so you can use a hybrid approach if you like. The advantage to separating the elements is that HTML tags are hard-coded in the document, and they don't appear in the database. One disadvantage of this approach is that it's limited to paragraph-level styles. That is, it is easy to store the entire title and bind it to an <h3> element, but it would be hard to italicize one of the words in the title. Another disadvantage is that it requires more fields in both the database and the form. If someone typed the Traveler's Journal in a word processor and wanted to transfer it to a form, they would have to transfer one piece at a time.

The embedded HTML approach has its own strengths and limitations. One strength is that you can format the content to your heart's content. You can italicize words, make them bold, turn them pink, and magnify them to 100 pixels if you want. The weakness of this approach is that it requires users to hand-code HTML. One of the goals of a CMS is to make it possible for nontechnical people to maintain content, so requiring them to hand-code HTML defeats a key purpose of having a CMS.

Some commercial CMSs include basic formatting GUIs, which enable users to format using HTML without ever seeing it—they just highlight text and click a B button to make the selection bold. Such a feature set is again beyond the scope of this book, but it is possible.

NOTE *The Traveler's Journal is one element that would benefit from Macromedia Contribute: users could replace it directly and quickly, and format it as they please. We'll go ahead and build a CMS for it, because doing so will give you exposure to concepts and techniques that you'll use over and over again.*

In this task, you will take a compromise approach, in which users have to see some HTML markup, but they don't actually have to write any. They just overwrite descriptive placeholders in an already marked-up block of text that you set up as the default in a text area.

CREATING THE FORM INTERFACE

Most CMSs are form-based, so building them involves creating lots of forms. The key to developing forms is to analyze the structure of your data in the database, and make the forms match accordingly. In this case, you will be inserting a new record into a table that has only three fields, including one that's a primary key. So this form will be easy, containing only two elements and a Submit button. In this task, you'll mock up the visible part of the form.

1) Open admin_template.asp, title the page *Newland Tours: Admin Update Traveler's Journal*, change the heading to read *Update Traveler's Journal*, and save the file as *admin_update_tj.asp*.

As usual, you begin a page by mocking up its core elements.

2) Replace the placeholder body text with the following two paragraphs:

Use the form below to update the Traveler's Journal. Be sure not to overwrite any of the HTML, only rewriting the content in between the HTML tags.

To add a new paragraph on a new line, type <p>New Paragraph<p>. To remove a paragraph, remove not only the text, but also the <p> and </p> tags that precede and follow it.

Again, when you create a CMS, it is incumbent on you to document its use and train its users. Adding page directions is a simple way to meet user needs.

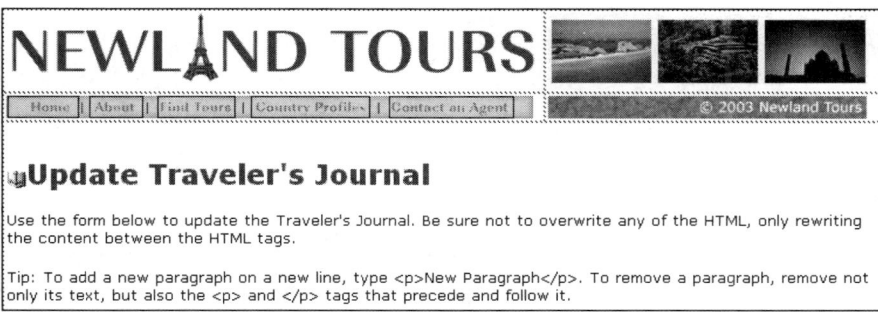

3) Below the directions, insert a new form (frm_update_tj). Inside, place a text area and a Submit button.

The text area form element is used to enable users to enter longer blocks of text than are generally allowed in a text field.

TIP *When using text areas that output to an Access database, make sure the target field's type is Memo. The normal Access Text type is limited to 255 characters and defaults to 50. The Memo type allows 65,535 characters.*

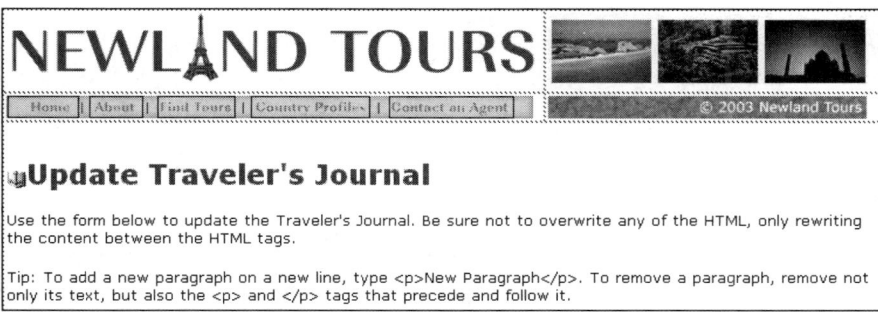

4) Select the text area, and in the Property inspector, name it *journal_entry*, set its Char Width to 55, its Num Lines to 9, and its Wrap to Virtual.

These settings give the text area a name and make it a bit larger, so users have more space to write. They also set the text to wrap automatically when it reaches the end of the line.

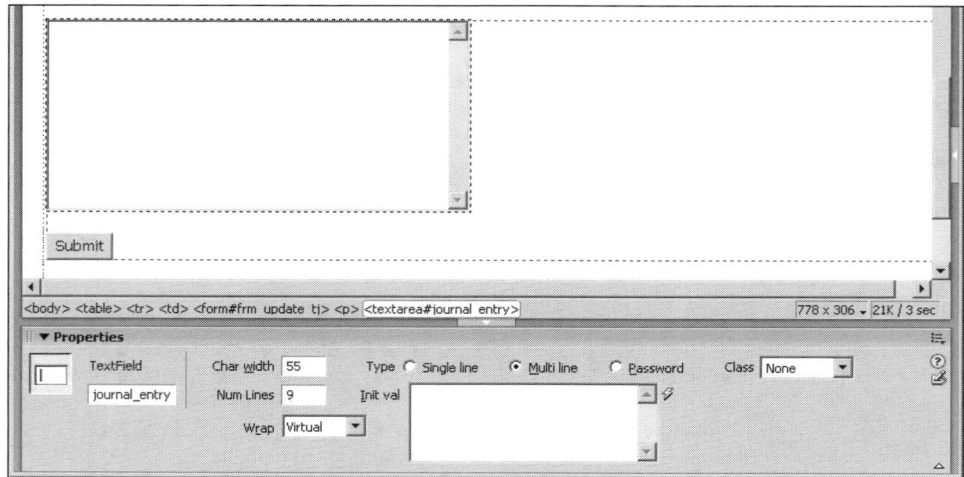

5) With the text area still selected, switch to split-design and code view (if you are not already there). Between the opening and closing *<textarea>* tags, add the following HTML. If desired, switch back to design view.

```
<h3>Enter Headline Here</h3>
<p class="author">By FirstName LastName</p>
<p>First Paragraph</p>
<p>Second Paragraph</p>
```

This HTML will be the default text that appears in the text area when the page loads. Thus, the only thing users have to do is type over "Enter Headline Here" to enter a new headline, and as long as they don't disturb the surrounding tags, the new headline will appear in the <h3> format.

NOTE *You can also enter default text in the Property inspector. To do so, select the text area, and type directly in the Init Val field. This technique is fine for two or three words, but you'd better have a strong pair of bifocals if you want to type much more. That's why I switch to code view.*

416

```
45    <p>Use the form below to update the Traveler's Journal. Be sure not to overwrite any of the HTML, onl
46    <p>Tip: To add a new paragraph on a new line, type &lt;p&gt;New Paragraph&lt;/p&gt;. To remove a par
47    <form name="frm_update_tj" id="frm_update_tj" method="post" action="">
48      <p>
49        <textarea name="journal_entry" cols="55" rows="9" wrap="VIRTUAL" id="journal_entry"><h3>Enter He
50 <p class="author">By FirstName LastName</p>
51 <p>First Paragraph</p>
52 <p>Second Paragraph</p>
53        </textarea>
54 </p>
55      <p>
56        <input type="submit" name="Submit" value="Submit" />
57      </p>
58    </form>    <p> </p></td>
59  </tr>
60 </table>
```

NOTE *Dreamweaver's design view doesn't show the <h3> and <p> tags, even though you entered them in code view. However, they will show up properly in a browser.*

6) Back in design view, notice the highlighted </p> **tag error on the page. To fix it, switch back to code view and remove the opening and closing** *<p>* **and** *</p>* **tags that surround the** *<textarea>* **tags.**

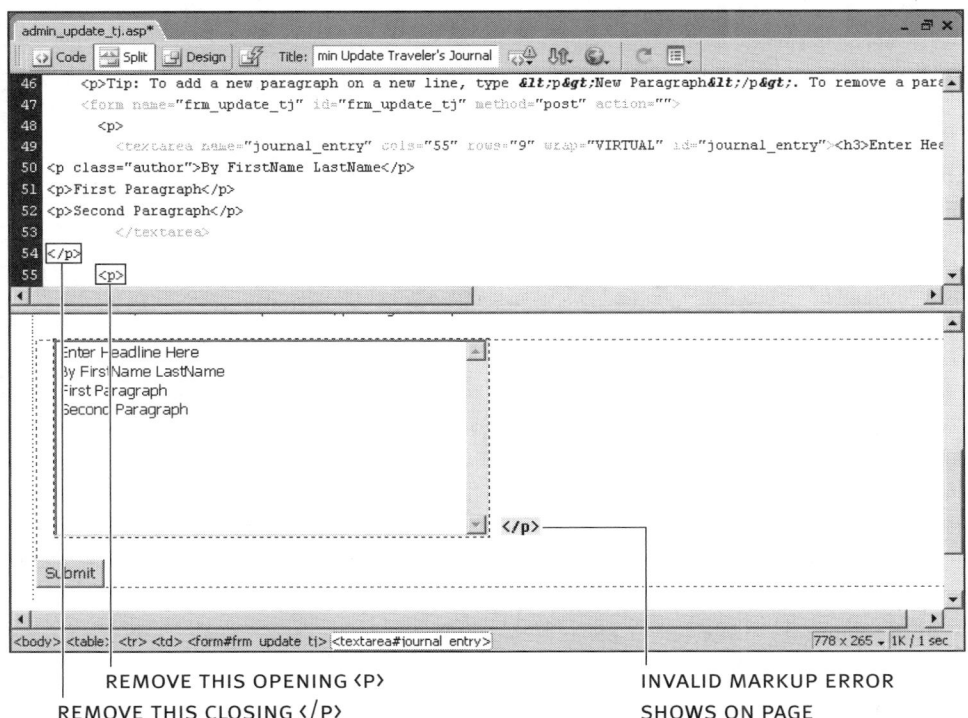

REMOVE THIS OPENING <P>
REMOVE THIS CLOSING </P>

INVALID MARKUP ERROR
SHOWS ON PAGE

The problem occurs because the text area is inserted inside <p> tags, which in itself isn't a problem, except that the default text in the text area also has <p> tags. This

417

confuses Dreamweaver, which causes the error. The fix is simply to remove the <p> tags that surround the <textarea> block element.

7) Open admin_index.asp, select Update the Traveler's Journal, and link it to admin_update_tj.asp.

Once you've created new pages, don't forget to add links to them. Save and close admin_index.asp, and save admin_update_tj.asp.

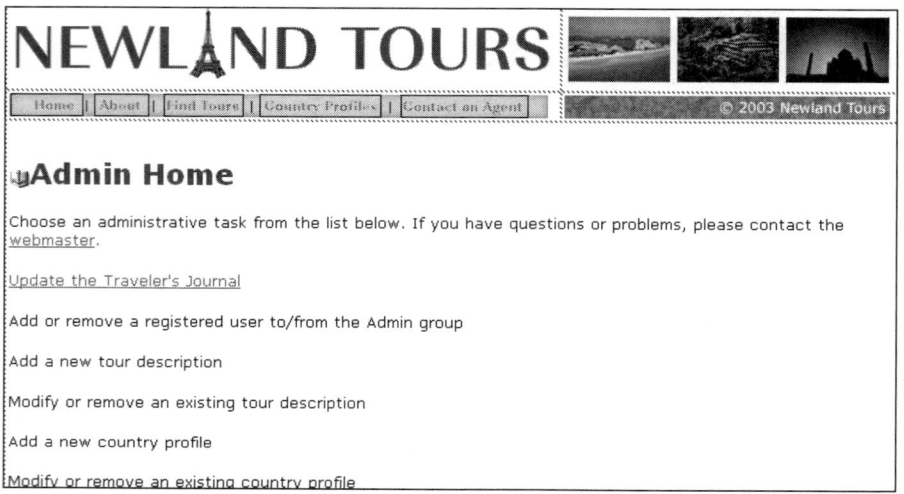

USING SESSION VARIABLES AND HIDDEN FIELDS TO TRACK USERS

One concern administrators have about a content management system is the potential for abuse. If someone manages to access the form that enables users to add a new Traveler's Journal for malicious purposes, you want to know who did it. Or, more specifically, you want to know whose account was used to do it. That way, you can identify the responsible employee (if it was an employee) or at least remove the account (if it was not). In this task, you'll capture the account used to access the admin pages, and save it with the accompanying journal_entry.

The technique you will use—and this is explained in more detail as you do it—is to capture the user's identification as it is stored in a session variable, and copy that value into the form using a hidden field. The contents of the hidden field will be submitted with the contents of the text area, and stored in the database.

1) In admin_update_tj.asp, insert a hidden field just to the left of the Submit button. Name it *author*.

This hidden field will store the name of the account used to access the page. At this stage, though, it has no value, because you haven't bound any data to it.

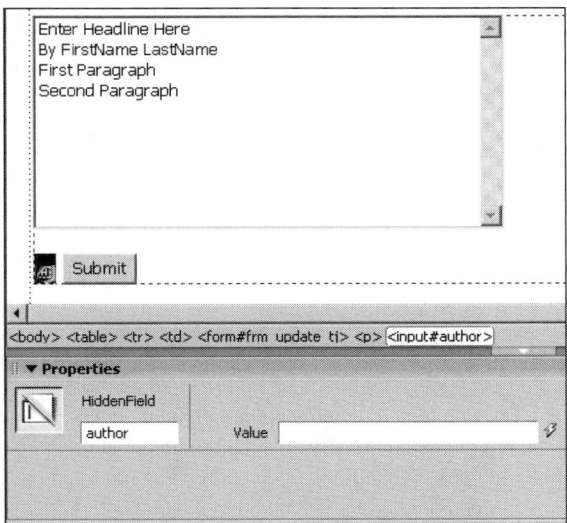

The question is, how do we find out whose account has been used? To answer that, think about what data is available to the page. This page has a Restrict Access to Page behavior attached to it. This behavior checks for the presence of a session variable set when the user successfully logged in. If that variable exists, it checks to see if its user is in the admin group. In other words, for a user to be on this page, she or he must not only be logged in with an admin account, but also the page must already know which account. Since this information is already available to the page as a session variable, all you have to do is bind that value to the hidden field, and it will be written into the database along with the form.

2) Use the Bindings panel to add a new session variable binding. In the Session Variable dialog, enter *MM_Username*, and click OK.

MM_Username is the session variable that is set when the user logs in. It is created automatically when you use the Log In User server behavior.

One thing to remember about the Bindings panel: The bindings it lists are limited to ones that you enter. In other words, even though MM_Username has been available all along as a session variable, as a part of the Restrict Access to Page server behavior, it is not listed in the Bindings panel unless you explicitly put it there.

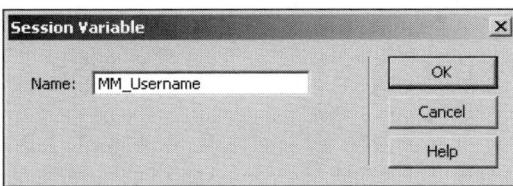

3) Select the hidden field, if necessary, then select Session > MM_Username in the Bindings panel, and click Bind.

This binds the value of MM_Username (that is, the account name used for this session's log-in) to the hidden field. You now submit the author data along with the journal entry itself.

INSERTING THE RECORD

The form is now ready, except that nothing is set to happen when the Submit button is pressed. In this task, you'll use the Insert Record server behavior to insert the data stored in the form into tbl_journal of the database, also causing the instant updating of the site.

Thanks to Dreamweaver's Insert Record server behavior, all of the SQL code will be written for you. Still, you should be familiar with the basic syntax of the INSERT statement, in case you ever need to edit it.

```
INSERT INTO tbl_table(
fieldname1 ,
fieldname2 ,
fieldname3)
VALUES(
'value1' ,
'value2' ,
'value3');
```

You might think of the Insert Record dialog (and for that matter, the Update Record dialog, though you haven't seen it yet) as a matching exercise, where you match form elements to table fields. The underlying SQL reveals why the dialog behaves this way. You specify a table in the INSERT INTO line, and then you list each of the table fields you want to insert data into one at a time, in the order you want data inserted, in parentheses.

Then you use the VALUES statement to specify the data itself that you want to insert; this data too goes inside a set of parentheses. Each piece of data that is a text string (as opposed to a number or an expression) is placed within single quotes. The individual pieces of data are separated by commas. The values at the bottom are matched in order to the fields listed at the top, so not only do the number of fields and the number of values have to match, but also you have to make sure you list them in the correct order.

TIP *One of the most common typos when building INSERT INTO SQL statements is to add a comma after the last field name or the last value. The last value should not be followed by a comma, and if it is, you will see an error message.*

1) Click to select the Submit button, and begin the process of adding an Insert Record server behavior.

This server behavior will be used to input the text area (journal_entry) and the hidden field (author) into tbl_journal's journal_entry and author fields.

2) In the Insert Record dialog, specify conn_newland as the connection, tbl_journal as the Insert Into Table, and index.asp as the After Inserting, Go To. Verify that the lower half of the dialog provides Dreamweaver with the instructions it needs to insert journal_entry into journal_entry and author into author.

This is the matching exercise part, where you specify which field of which database table is populated with which field of the form. Since you gave the form elements the same names as their destination table field names, Dreamweaver correctly matches everything for you.

You specify index.asp as the redirection page, so that users can verify that what they entered is now showing on the homepage.

Again, ColdFusion and PHP users will note that the dialog they see, though functionally the same, varies cosmetically from the one shown in the screenshot.

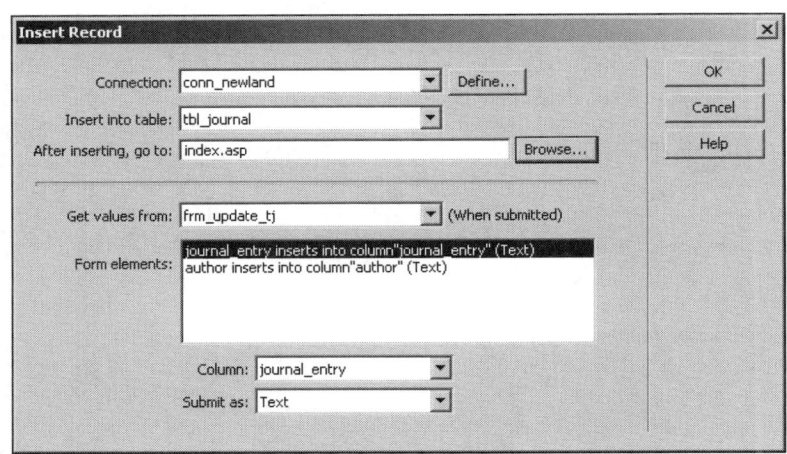

3) Test the new functionality, making sure to log in as an administrator.

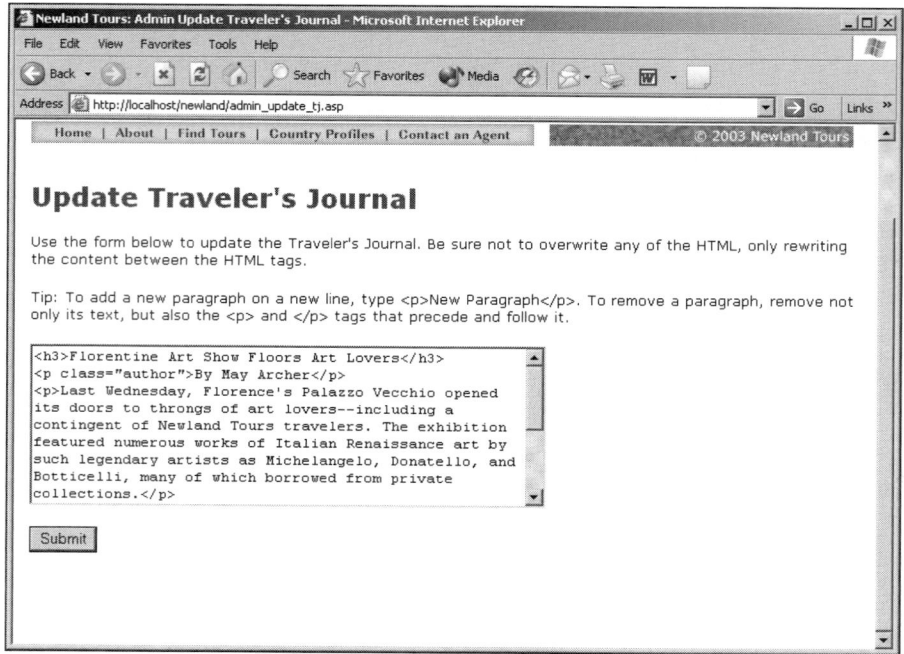

The homepage now contains whatever you entered, formatted using the specified HTML.

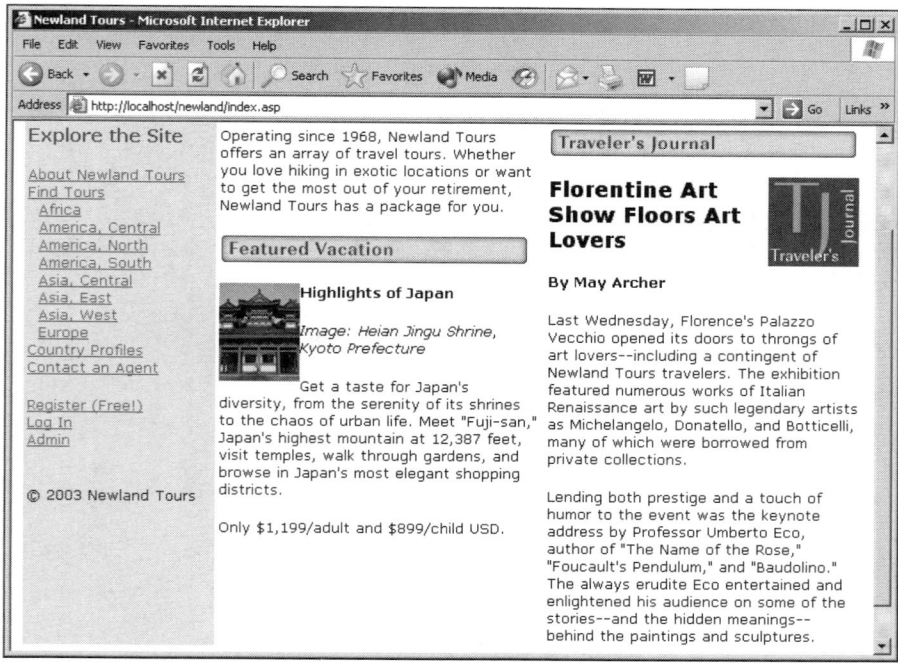

If you look in the tbl_journal table of the database, you will see both the first line of the text you entered (text entered after line breaks is not displayed in Access' table view) and the account you used to log in, which was stored as a session variable and passed through the form to the database.

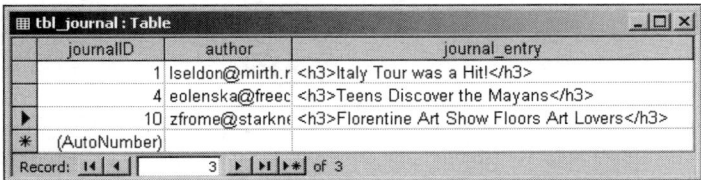

WHAT YOU HAVE LEARNED

In this lesson, you have:

- Created an admin section that makes administrative tasks conveniently accessible to users (pages 409–412)

- Repurposed generic_template.asp into a special template for the admin section (pages 409–410)

- Built a form using a text area element with HTML-formatted default text (pages 413–418)

- Designed a system to capture the identity of users updating the Traveler's Journal (pages 418–420)

- Inserted the data using the Insert Record server behavior (pages 420–423)

building update pages

LESSON 15

In this lesson, you will build an interface that lets employees change a registered user from one user group to another (from visitor to admin, or vice versa). This implies a certain workflow: To add an employee to the admin group, the employee must first register at the site, and then another employee must go in and change her or his user group. Likewise, if an employee leaves Newland Tours, another employee can easily change the former employee's user profile back to visitor. The interface will use two pages—one where the employee selects the user whose profile will be changed, and one to actually update the profile.

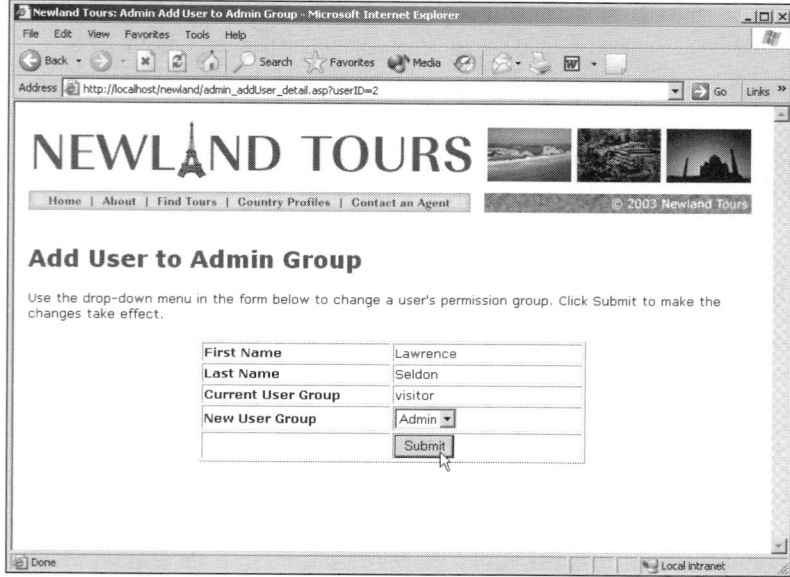

You'll enable users to update database data using a Web form, SQL's UPDATE statement, and Dreamweaver's Update Record server behavior.

Two-page applications that use this structure are referred to as master-detail page sets. A master-detail page structure is one of the most common—and useful—structures that you will master as a Web developer. The first page is the master page, because it lists many records in a summary format. Users browse this summary, and then select the record they want to learn more about or modify/delete. The second page is the detail page, because it contains detailed information about the selected record. On this page, users can learn more about a product or modify/delete a record. To summarize, the master page lists a small sampling of fields from multiple records within a database, while the detail page displays many fields from a single record.

You've already built two master-detail page sets in the course of the book: The country profile pages perfectly fit this description, and the tour description page set is a variation on the theme. But in both cases, the detail page only displayed data. In this lesson, you'll use the detail page to update data.

Updating data is slightly more complex than inserting new data, which you did in Lessons 13 and 14. When you insert new data, you identify a table and specify which data to write to which fields in that table. When updating data, you have to do the same thing to a particular, existing record; you can't just append information as a new record at the end of the table. SQL has a command—UPDATE—that you can use to accomplish this task, and Dreamweaver has an Update Record server behavior that makes it even easier.

In this lesson, you will combine the master-detail page structure with the update-record page structure. You will use several Dreamweaver behaviors to make it happen. It is vital in this lesson that you understand the big picture about what is happening: Dreamweaver behaviors sometimes make it easy for us to not worry too much about the mechanics of what's going on, but in the next lesson, you are going to replicate this structure using a more ambitious hands-on approach, so it's best now if you nail down the concepts.

WHAT YOU WILL LEARN

In this lesson, you will:

- Plan for a master-detail set, by analyzing the data needed for the application
- Create a master-detail page set, using the admin template created in the previous lesson
- Learn about SQL's UPDATE statement
- Convert the detail page to a dynamically populated form capable of updating, rather than merely displaying, contents in the database

APPROXIMATE TIME

This lesson takes approximately one hour to complete.

LESSON FILES

Starting Files:

Lesson15/Start/newland/admin_template.asp

Completed Files:

Lesson15/Complete/newland/admin_ addUser_master.asp

Lesson15/Complete/newland/admin_ addUser_detail.asp

PREPARING THE PAGES

To insert a master-detail page object, you must open the page that will become the master. In the course of completing the dialog that creates the page set, you specify the name of the detail page as well. If you haven't yet created the detail page, Dreamweaver can create one for you. But it's hard to go back and apply your template to that page. Thus, in this task, you will create the master and detail pages used in this set.

1) Open admin_template.asp, title the page *Newland Tours Admin: Add User to Admin Group*, change the heading to *Add User to Admin Group*, and save the file as *admin_addUser_master.asp*.

This page will be the master page, holding summary information about each of the registered users.

2) Replace the placeholder body text with the following. *To add a registered user to the Admin group, select her or his name from the list, and change the permission group to admin on the following page.* Save the file.

Again, providing directions now enhances the efficacy of the site and reduces tech-support calls and frustration later.

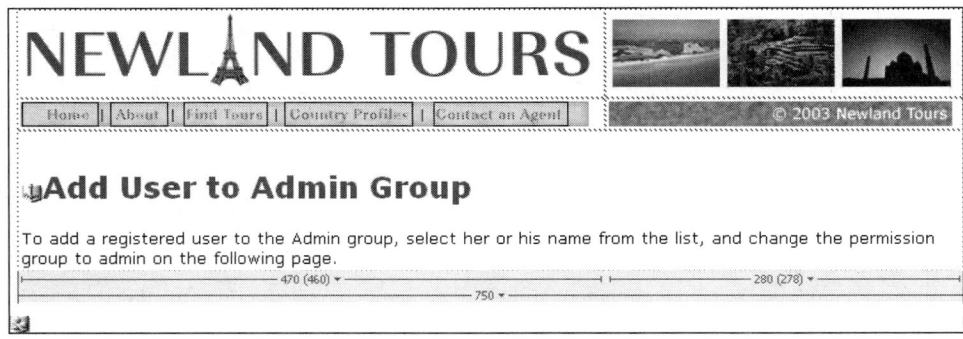

3) Open admin_template.asp, title the page *Newland Tours Admin: Add User to Admin Group*, change the heading to *Add User to Admin Group*, and save the file as *admin_addUser_detail.asp*.

This page will be the detail page, which will contain the form that employees can use to actually change a user's permission group.

4) Replace the placeholder body text with the following. *Use the drop-down menu in the form below to change a user's permission group. Click Submit to make the changes take effect.* **Save the file.**

You have now built the basic page shells to which you will add the Master-Detail Page Set object.

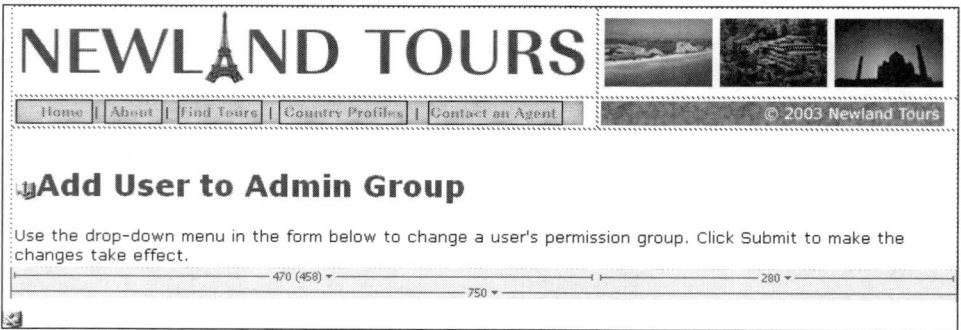

5) In admin_index.asp, link the Add or remove a registered user line to admin_addUser_master.asp.

Now users have convenient access to the new page set.

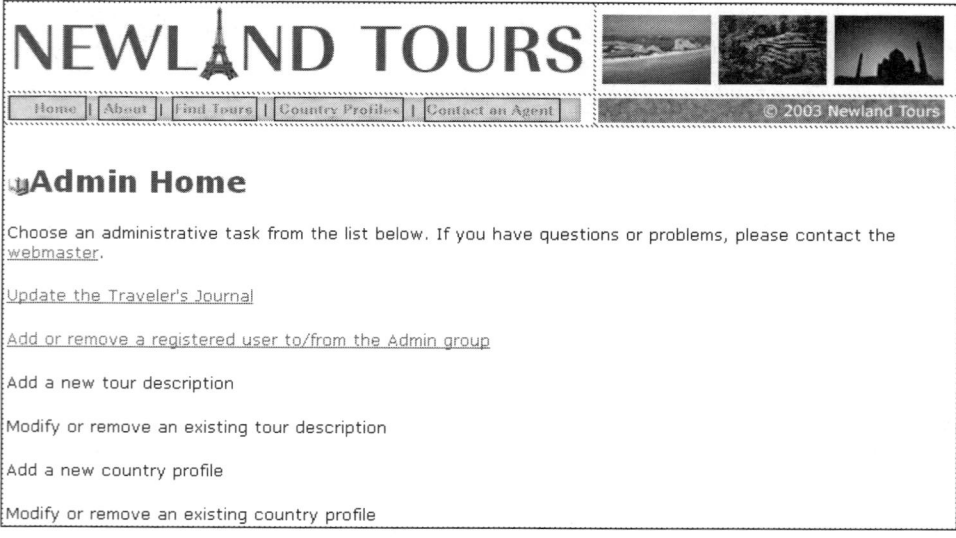

PLANNING FOR THE MASTER-DETAIL PAGES

As you saw from your earlier experiences developing the country profile and tour description master-detail page sets, creating these sets often requires quite a few server behaviors and other dynamic elements working in unison.

- You create a recordset to populate the menu on the master page.

- Because you are dealing with multiple records, you often need to create a Recordset Navigation Bar, which itself is made of several behaviors, including the behaviors from the Show Region group as well as from the Recordset Paging group.

- You output records using Dynamic Text, and apply the Repeat Region server behavior to ensure that all of the records are output.

- If the records are hyperlinked, you bind a unique querystring or URL parameter to the href attribute.

- A SQL statement that uses a dynamic value in a WHERE clause filters the recordset using criteria the user supplied on the master page.

Building master-detail pages by hand can be slow and tedious. Dreamweaver speeds up the development of this common structure with a special application object that adds all of the needed server behaviors and creates the pages for you. This server object is called a Master-Detail Page Set, and is available in the Insert > Application Object menu. This is a very convenient tool, as you'll see in this lesson.

The Master-Detail Page Set object works by collecting all of the relevant information needed to build the page set. Some of this information is derived from a query, so you'll have to create a recordset first. All told, the application object requires quite a bit of information, and a single mistake derails the entire process. For this reason, you should figure out what you want in advance. (When writing this lesson, it took me several tries in the dialog before getting it right, because I tried to cut this corner.)

The main thing you need to sort out is what information you want to appear on the master page, and likewise what information you want to appear on the detail page. This information is all retrieved from a database, so what you are doing here is determining what you should retrieve in your initial recordset.

For this master-detail page set, you want the master page to contain the following information as a menu, which should be sufficient for the employee to find and select the correct user account.

Last Name   First Name   Username   Current User Group

The detail page should include the following information.

Last Name   First Name   Current User Group

In this case, ironically, the detail page contains less information than the master page. But remember, the purpose of this detail page is not to display lots of information about the record (as you would with a product description in an online catalog), but rather to offer extended functionality to the record (in this case, the power to update the record).

At the very least, you will need to make the information shown above available to the page (via a recordset). But these four elements do not represent a complete listing of information needed from the database. Do you remember when you created the master-detail page sets for the country profile and tour descriptions that when users clicked the link a URL parameter was appended to the URL? This data for this URL parameter is needed to filter the query on the detail page, so it can display only the desired record. In this case, you need some piece of information that can cause the detail page to display one unique record. And any time you need to use something unique to identify a database record, you should immediately think of the table's primary key, in this case, userID.

To summarize, then, the recordset on which your master-detail page set will be built will require the following fields from tbl_users:

userID
firstName
lastName
username
userGroup

In addition, this data will need to be ordered alphabetically by last name to facilitate lookup, so you will need to sort on lastName, ascending. Go ahead and create this recordset now.

1) In admin_addUser_master.asp, add a new recordset, called *rs_registeredUsers*, according to the specifications just outlined.

By creating this recordset, you have made available the data needed to build the master-detail page set.

Remember, it's always a good idea to click the Test button in the Recordset dialog, just to make sure you are getting everything you need, and in the right order.

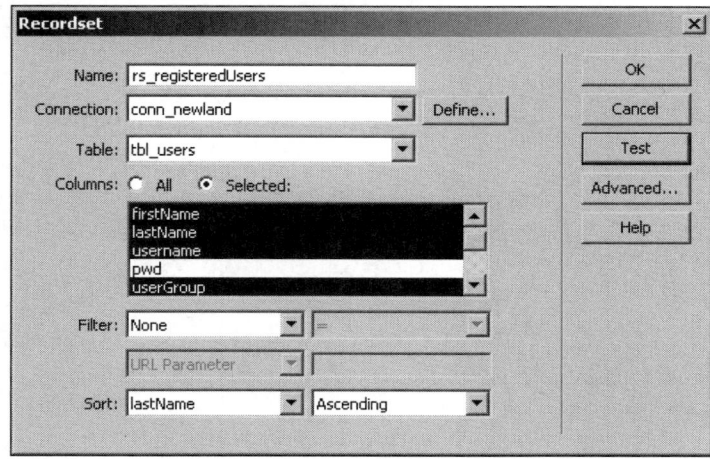

**2) Position the cursor on a new line below the directions, and choose Insert ›
Application Objects › Master-Detail Page Set.**

Selecting this option opens a large dialog.

**3) In the Insert Master-Detail Page Set dialog, make sure that rs_registeredUsers
is selected as the recordset. In the Master page fields section, select userID and
click the minus button to remove it. In the Link to detail from menu, choose
username. In the Pass unique key field, choose userID. Check Show 20 Records
at a time.**

The top half of the dialog, which you have just completed, is used to control the
appearance and functionality of the master page. The Master Page Fields section
represents all of the fields of each record that you want shown. The four selected
here correspond to the four discussed in the introduction to this task. That is, they
will appear on the page as four columns, making up a menu for the user.

The Link to detail from menu lets you specify which field's data will be hyperlinked
to the detail page. The field username is a good choice, because it is unique.

The Pass unique key menu lets you specify which piece of data will be used to filter
the data on the detail page. Again, that should be unique, so the table's primary key,
userID, is the right choice.

When you choose to show 20 records at a time, you are providing Dreamweaver with the information it needs to insert a Recordset Navigation Bar server object for you. Given that the number of registered users will likely grow to many, a recordset navigation bar is a good idea. Otherwise, employees are forced to download potentially hundreds of records all at once.

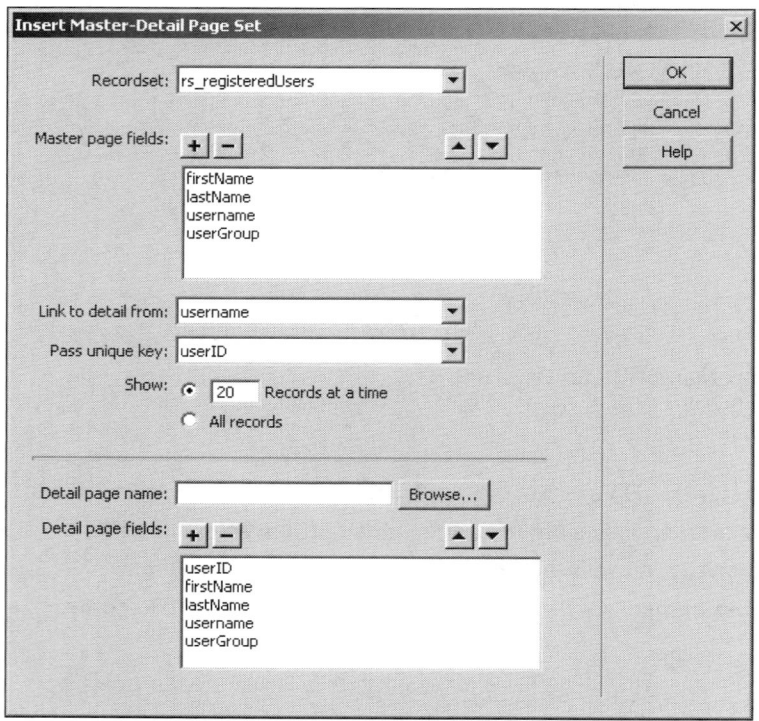

4) In the lower half of the Master-Detail Page Set dialog, type or browse to admin_addUser_detail.asp. Select userID and click the minus button to remove it. Select username and click the minus button to remove it. Click OK.

Dreamweaver may take a moment at this point, because it is adding quite a few server behaviors to two different pages. When it is done, though, the master-detail page set should be complete and functional.

The master page may be quite a bit wider now than it was before. This stretching accommodates the pseudocode strings Dreamweaver has inserted in each of the cells (for example, rs_registeredUsers.lastName). The actual data that will go in these fields is not as wide as the pseudocode, so the page will not appear stretched at all when viewed in the browser, so just disregard the stretching in Dreamweaver. Most important, do not try to fix it.

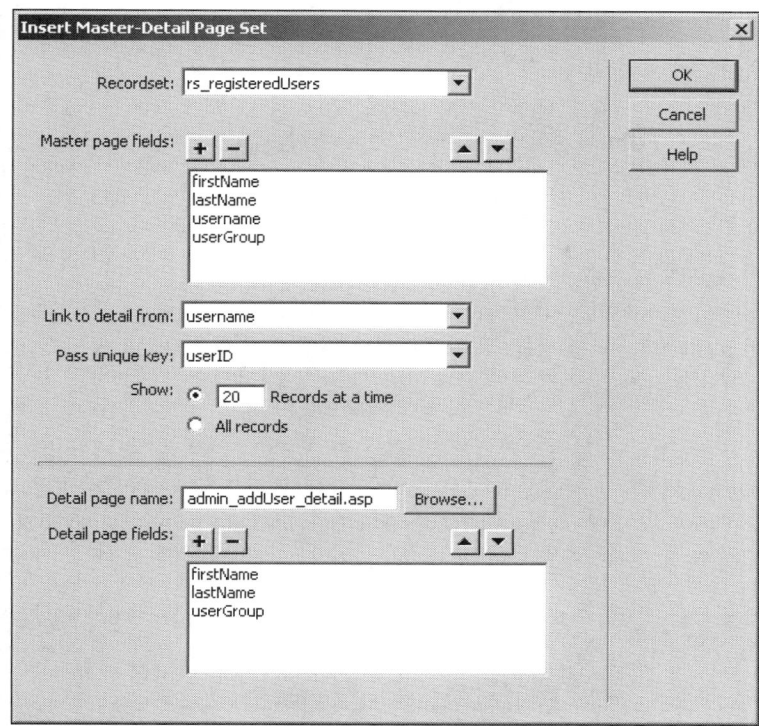

5) Switch to admin_addUser_detail.asp. Move the new table so that it is inside the main page table, just below the directions.

Dreamweaver has to guess where to put the table on the page, and it doesn't always guess correctly. Moving the table won't affect any functionality, so this change is entirely cosmetic.

433

6) Save and upload both files. Test their functionality.

You'll be intercepted by the log-in screen first. Use the following credentials to get in:

Username: *zfrome@starknet.com*

Password: *hypochondriac*

The master page contains a table with the four columns you specified. In addition, the usernames are all hyperlinked, and if you roll over the links, you'll see the URL of the detail page with the unique userID appended as a URL parameter in your browser's status bar (if it is visible).

Also, you'll see Records 1 to 5 of 5 (or however many records you have at this point in your database). This is created with the Recordset Navigation Status application object (Insert > Application Objects > Recordset Navigation Status), which is inserted automatically as a part of the Master-Detail Page Set application object.

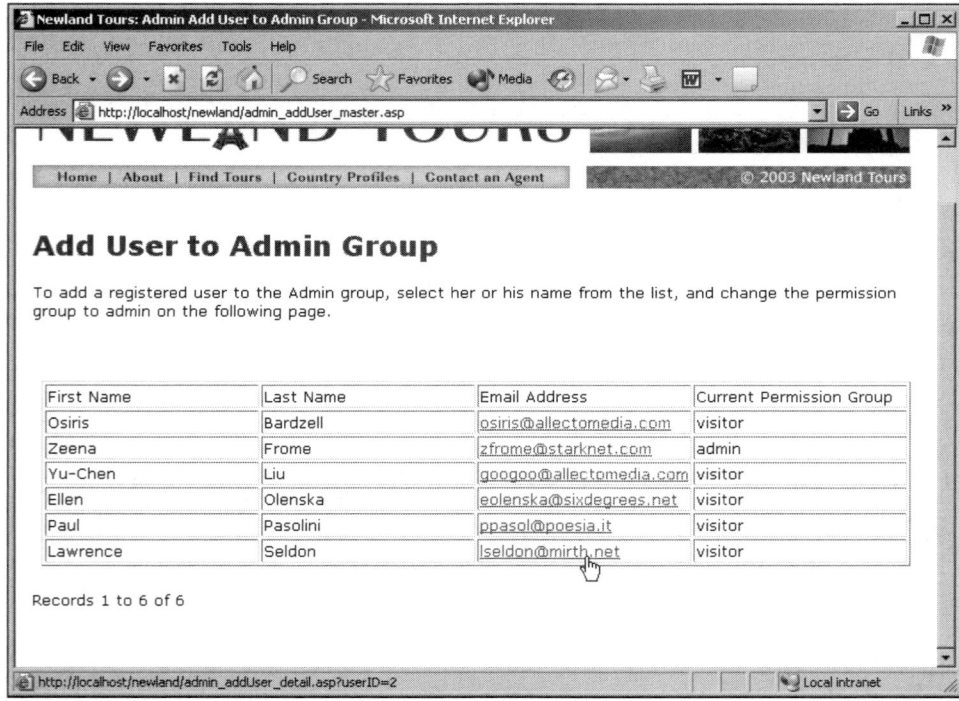

Once you've clicked one of the usernames, you'll see the detail page, with a small table containing the information that you specified in the dialog. The table is still read-only—you can't update it yet—but you can at least see that the correct record has been retrieved.

One thing you probably noticed on both pages is that the column/row headers were neither prominent nor meaningful.

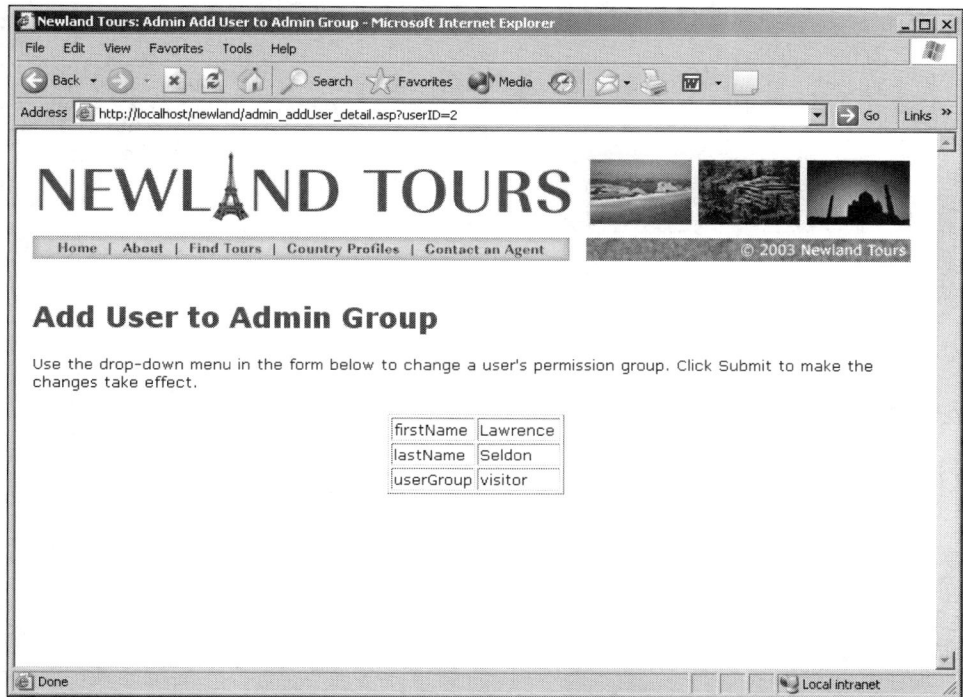

7) On admin_addUser_master.asp, one at a time, select firstName, lastName, username, and userGroup, and make them bold. Then replace each as follows:

firstName: *First Name*
lastName: *Last Name*
username: *Email Address*
userGroup: *Current Permission Group*

When it generates the table, Dreamweaver uses the database column names as the default table headers. But the database was structured to hold data, not to serve as column headings. These changes make the table easier to understand and use.

TIP *Customizing table headers also improves security. Had you not changed them, malicious users such as hackers could glean a fair amount of information about your database schema just by looking at table headings. Of course, if hackers are viewing your admin pages, you have bigger security problems than table headings! Still, the point remains that obscuring database field names from users is a good practice.*

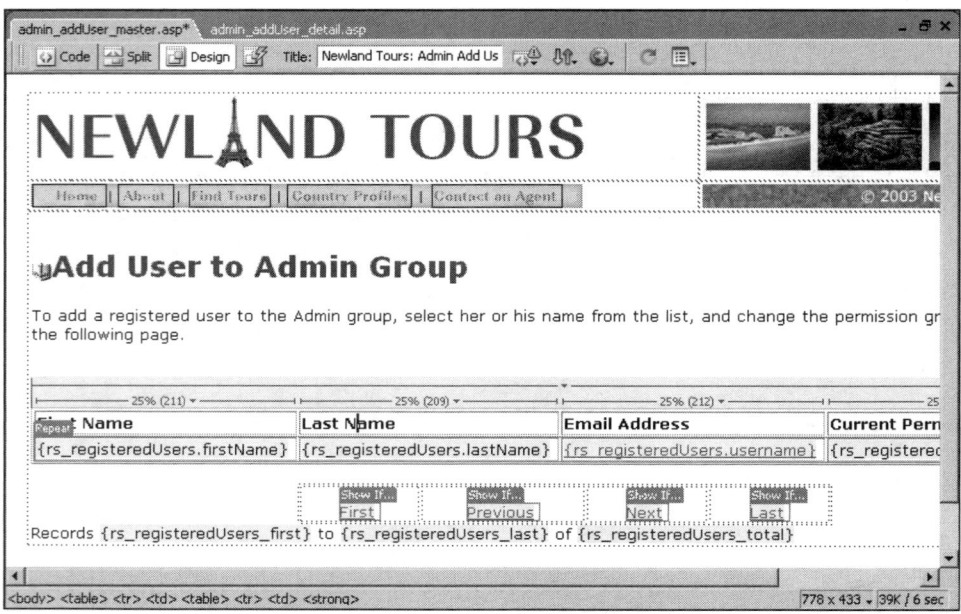

8) On admin_addUser_detail.asp, make the three row headers bold, as in the previous step, and replace the text as follows:

firstName: *First Name*

lastName: *Last Name*

userGroup: *Current User Group*

You are making these changes for the reasons described in the preceding step.

TIP *You can drag the line that separates the two columns to the right to create more space for the row headers. You might also need to increase the size of the table by dragging its right edge.*

9) Save, upload, and test the pages again, to make sure they look right.

Though the changes made were cosmetic, it never hurts to double-check the effect before moving forward.

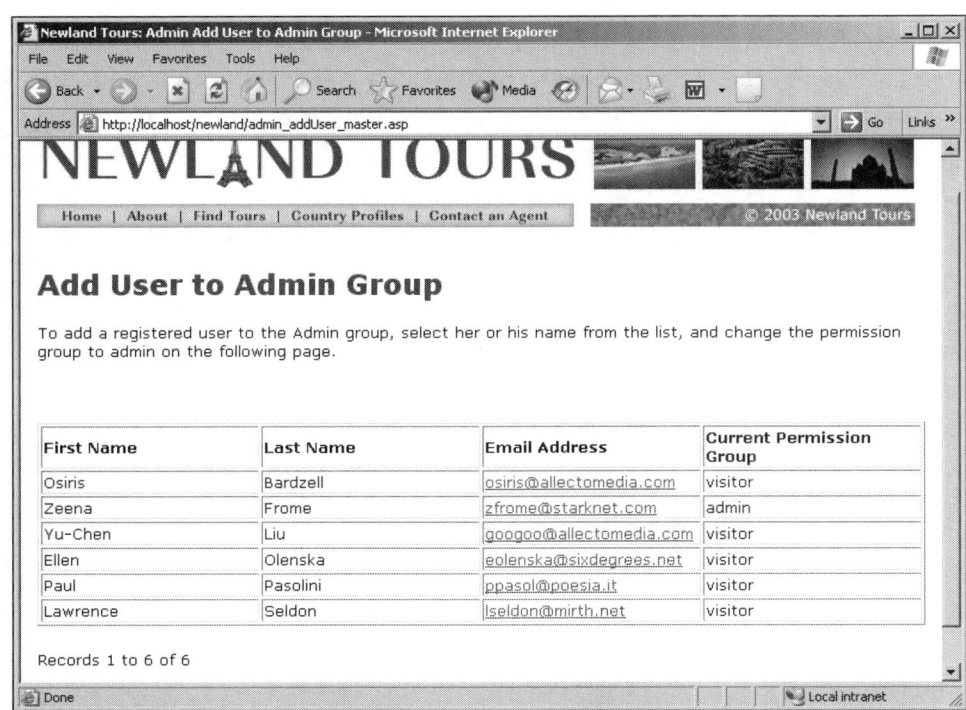

437

MAKING THE DETAIL PAGE UPDATEABLE

Other than the convenience of using a ready-made object to create master-detail pages, nothing you have done is terribly new, since you've deployed most of the functionalities aggregated on these two pages during the course of the book. But what you'll add in this task is new: You'll use the filtered display as a means of identifying the row to update.

This task should be easy, since you are merely adding a simple server behavior to a form that will have a single field. But it's not that simple. All three versions of the server behaviors wind up not working as expected, though for different reasons. The ASP version of the server behavior sends a superfluous querystring parameter that creates a conflict with another querystring. And the ColdFusion and PHP versions of the server behavior give a URL parameter an unexpected name, which might cause you to mismatch a pair of values.

I must emphasize that neither of these issues matter if you are applying the Update Record behavior to a simple page. But as you know, admin_addUser_detail.asp is not a simple page—it is a part of the great complexity of server behaviors and dynamic elements that is the Master-Detail Page Set application object.

Both sets of problems are fairly easy to fix. The important point to realize is that once again you can't rely entirely on the convenient server behaviors: You must deal with code, both to create functionality that the server behaviors can't create or to customize (and in this case fix) the code that the server behaviors generate.

1) In admin_addUser_detail.asp, create a new form (*frm_updateUser*), and place the table inside it.

You've used tables to structure form content through the book. Here, you are including dynamic content within that table, but the presence of dynamic content makes no difference to the form. The only portions affected by the form itself are form elements, and you haven't added them yet.

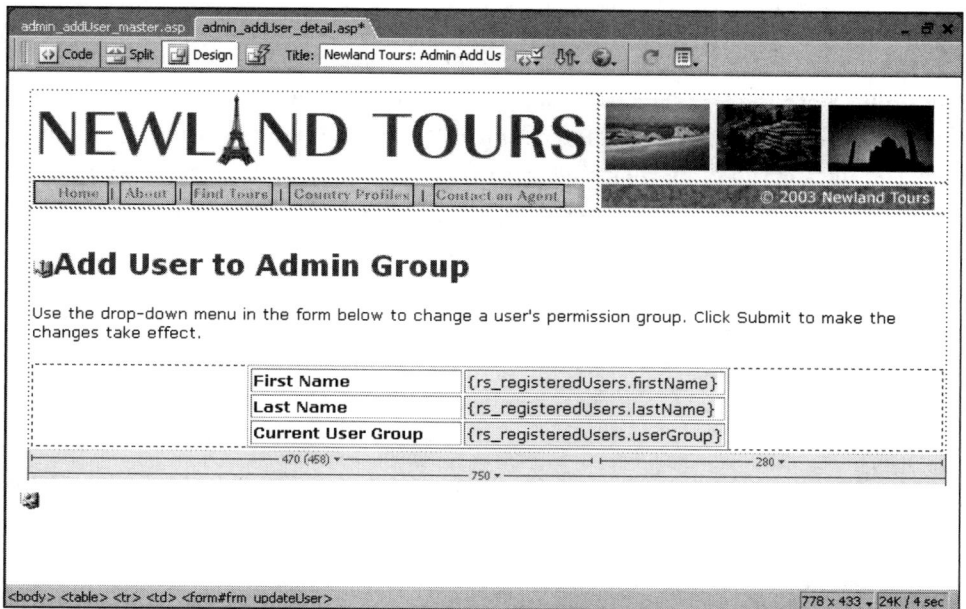

**2) Position the insertion point anywhere in the bottom row. Choose Modify >
Table > Insert Rows or Columns. In the dialog, specify 2 rows below the selection,
and click OK.**

The newly created fourth row will contain a menu enabling users to change user
groups, and the fifth row will hold the Submit button.

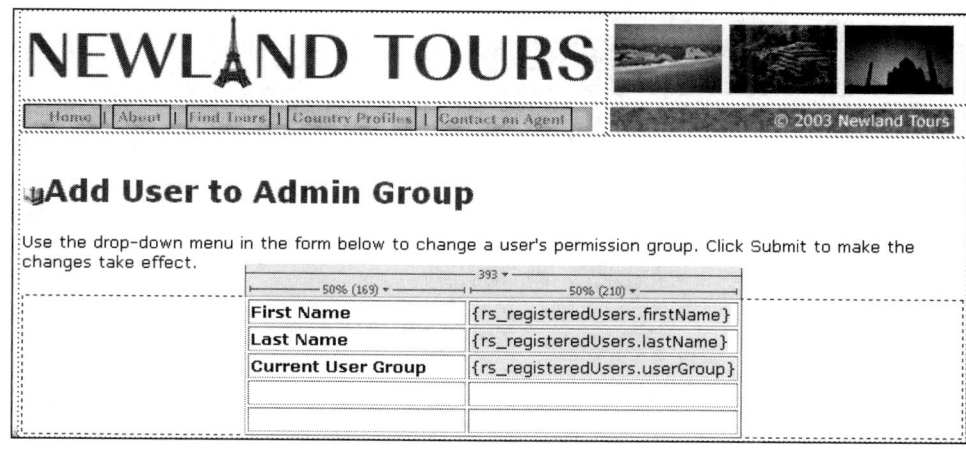

3) In the left cell of the fourth row, type *New User Group* and make it bold. In the right cell, insert a menu element. Use the Property inspector to name this element *userGroup*. Click the List Values button, and enter *Visitor* and *visitor* as the first row's item label and value, and *Admin* and *admin* as the second row's item label and value. Click OK. Back in the Property inspector click Visitor in the Initially selected area.

This menu makes it possible for the user to specify only one of two user group options. Its values are static, and if Newland Tours ever renamed or added a new user group, the HTML would have to be modified. This could be handled dynamically, of course, but that would require a new database table, joins, and all sorts of code. Sometimes, hard-coding is simply more cost-effective than doing everything dynamically.

NOTE *Make sure you do not misspell either of the values, or the affected users won't be able to log in at all!*

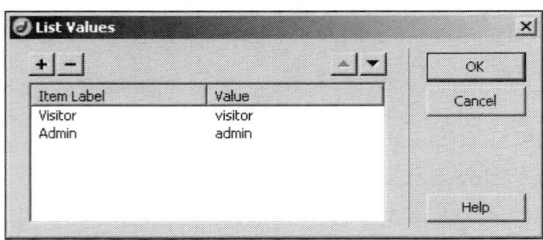

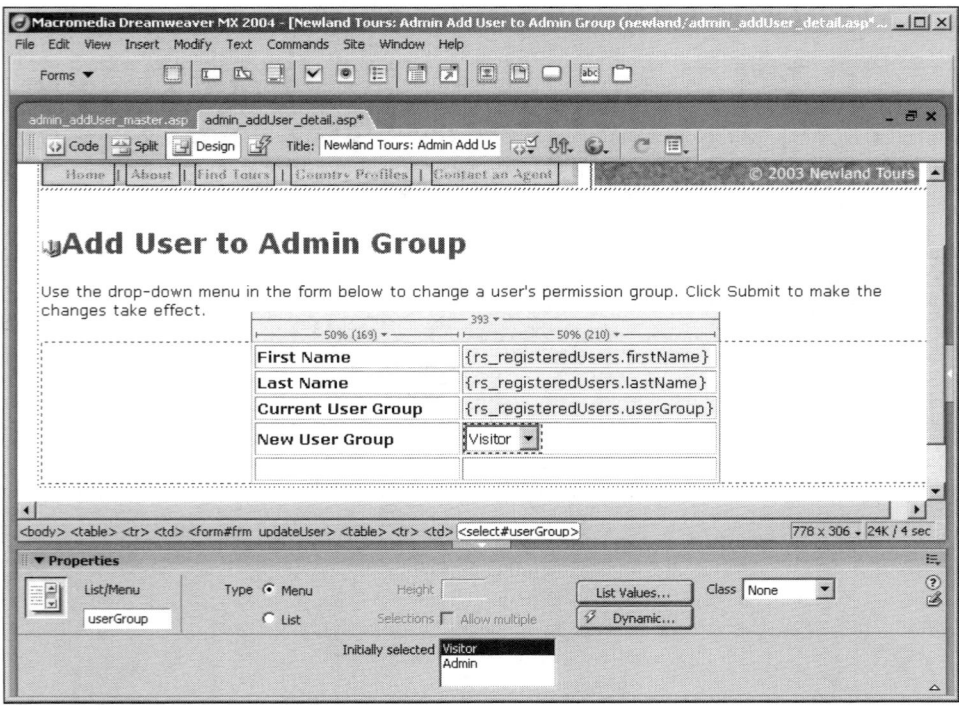

4) Place the insertion point in the right cell of the bottom row, and insert a Submit button.

Most forms don't do much without one of these.

5) ColdFusion and PHP Users Only: In the cell to the left of the Submit button, insert a hidden field element and call it *userID*. Use the Bindings panel to add a new URL variable called *recordID*. Select the hidden field in the form, and bind the new URL variable to that hidden field.

The ColdFusion and PHP versions of the Update Record server behavior require that you pass the primary key to the field you are updating. The ASP version, in contrast, requires that you do *not* pass this value.

You would think that the URL parameter passed to this page would be called userID, because that is, in fact, the value being passed, as you specified in the Insert Master-Detail Page Set dialog. In ASP, that is the name. For some reason, the ColdFusion and PHP versions of the server behavior name the URL parameter recordID, rather than userID. So when you bind the URL parameter to the userID hidden field, you have to specify the variable name Dreamweaver added to the ColdFusion/PHP code.

441

6) Click to select the Submit button, and initiate an Update Record server behavior from the Server Behaviors panel.

Updating records requires a special SQL command, called UPDATE. You have used both SELECT and INSERT in the course of this book, but you haven't looked at UPDATE yet. The server behavior will generate all of the SQL for you, but you should at least be generally familiar with the UPDATE syntax, which is as follows:

UPDATE tbl_table

SET fieldName = 'New value for this field'

WHERE keyID = '123456';

When you update a record, you specify a table. Then, you use SET to specify the new value. Finally, you use the WHERE clause to identify which row. Optionally, you can specify multiple fields to update in the SET clause; to do so, just separate each field name-new value combination with a comma.

NOTE *If you use UPDATE without a WHERE clause that specifies the row, you'll end up changing the value of every row.*

Though you won't need to in this lesson, sometimes you need to modify the SQL, and it's important to learn SQL as you learn dynamic Web site development.

The ASP, ColdFusion and PHP versions of the Update Record dialog are sufficiently different cosmetically that I'll break them down separately.

7) ASP Users Only: In the Update Record dialog, choose conn_newland as the connection, tbl_users as the Table To Update, rs_registeredUsers in the Select Record From menu, userID as the Unique Key Column (the Numeric checkbox should remain checked). In the After Updating, Go To field, enter admin_addUser_master.asp. Verify that the Form Elements area contains this text: userGroup updates column "userGroup" (Text).

With this information, you are telling Dreamweaver to write a SQL query that will update tbl_users' userGroup field with the information stored in the userGroup form element, in the row whose primary key matches the one retrieved in the rs_registeredUsers query.

Once users submit the form, they are redirected to admin_addUser_master.asp, where, as you'll recall, the summary lists each user's current user group, enabling users to make sure that the change went through.

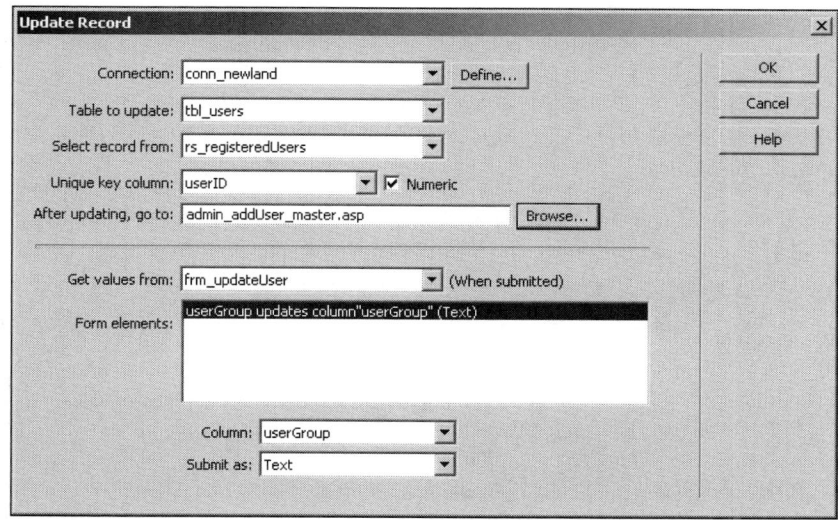

ColdFusion and PHP Users Only: In the Update Record dialog, choose newland as the Data Source and tbl_users as the Update Table. In the Columns area, make sure that the following two statements appear: 'userID' Selects Record Using 'FORM.userID' as 'Numeric'; 'userGroup' Gets Value From 'FORM.userGroup' as 'Text'; and the rest say Does Not Get a Value. Lower in the dialog, in the After Updating, Go To field, enter *admin_addUser_master.cfm*. ColdFusion users only: Make sure that Pass Original Query String is unchecked.

With this information, you are telling Dreamweaver to write a SQL query that will update tbl_users' userGroup column with the information stored in the userGroup form element, in the row whose primary key matches the one stored in the form's userID (hidden field) element.

Once users submit the form, they are redirected to admin_addUser_master.cfm, where, as you'll recall, the summary lists each user's current user group, enabling users to make sure that the change went through.

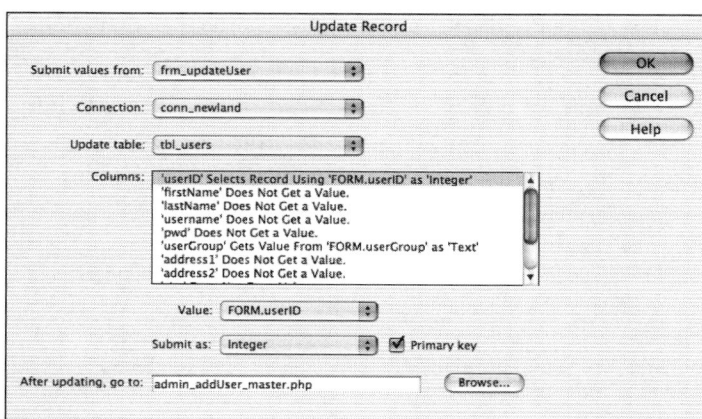

8) Save and upload the page. Then, test the page set, starting from the master page.

You should be able to select a user, change their status on the detail page, and see the change reflected when redirected to the master page. The application works to this point. There's still a problem with the ASP version, but ColdFusion and PHP users are finished with the lesson.

Once again, the login information is as follows:

Username: *zfrome@starknet.com*

Password: *hypochondriac*

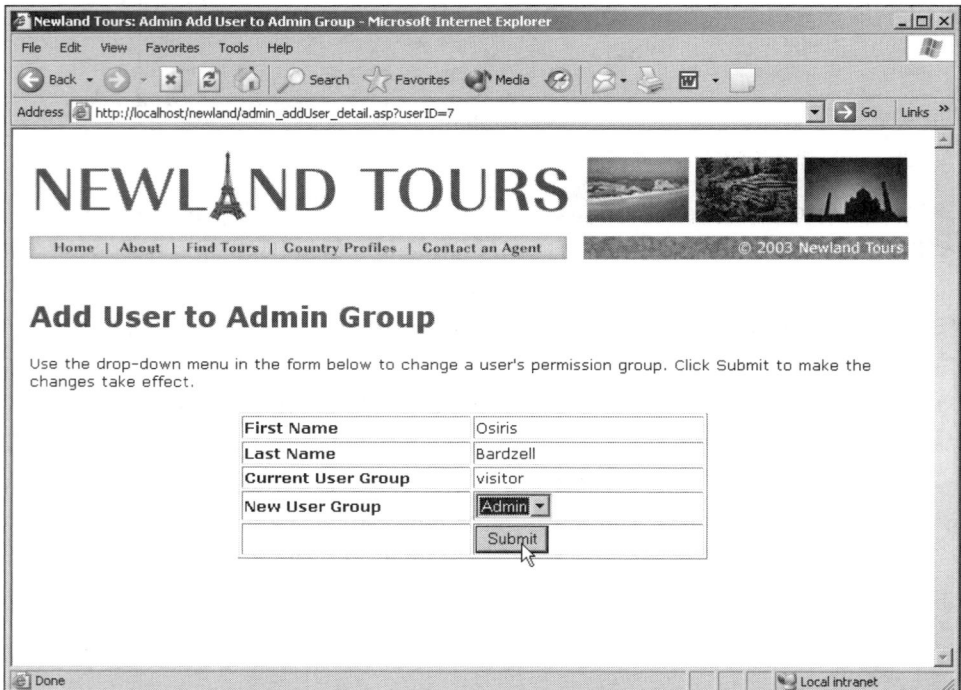

ASP users: Once you've tested the page pairing once, go ahead and try it again. The second time you try it, you get an error message. The problem is easy to spot—just look at the URL. Somehow, the querystring contains userID=# twice. This is tripping up the ASP interpreter. Click the Back button, and you'll see that one instance of userID=7 is present on the master page. But that shouldn't be there. The master page is supposed to send the URL variable, but it is not supposed to have a URL variable of its own. Why is this happening? When the form is submitted on the detail page, it passes back a URL variable to the master page. In ColdFusion, a checkbox called Pass Original Query String lets you determine whether to pass the URL variable back or not: in ASP, however, Dreamweaver assumes you want the querystring to be passed, even though you don't.

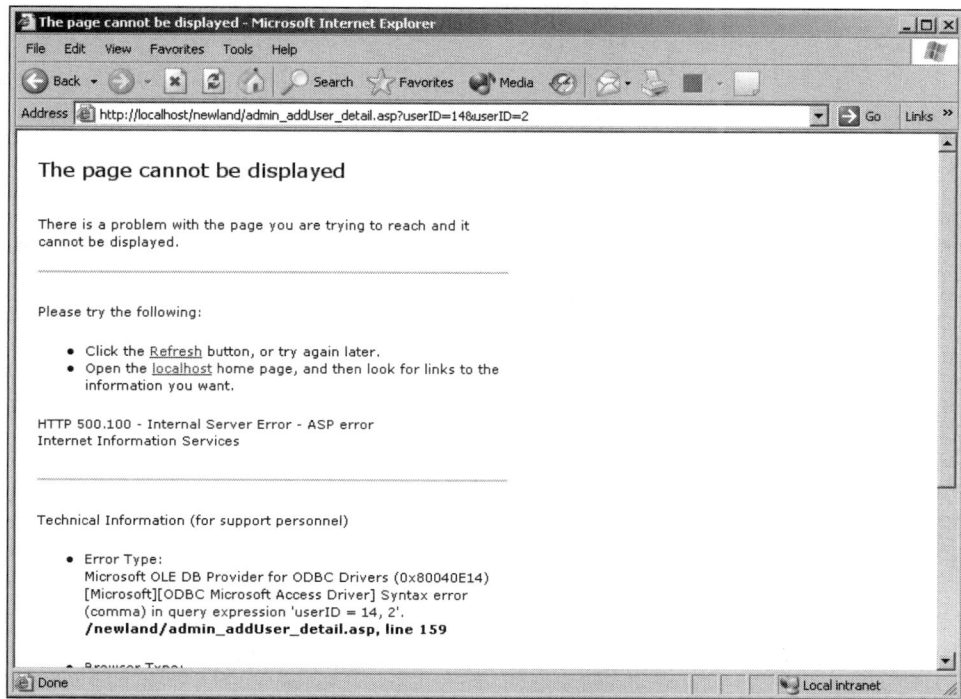

There is no way to fix this problem in a dialog or wizard. You'll have to fix it in the code itself.

9) ASP Users Only: In admin_addUser_detail.asp, switch to code view. Look for a comment, append the query string to the redirect URL. **Insert an apostrophe before the next seven lines to comment them out.**

In my version of the page, the offending code begins in line 81. If you have trouble finding it, use Edit > Find.

You'll see a nested pair of If statements. These do the work of appending the querystring, so you want to deactivate them. You could just delete them, but it's safer to comment them out, just in case you need them at some later point.

Make sure you don't inadvertently comment out the third End If, because it belongs to the parent block of code, not the portion you are commenting out.

```
73  MM_fields = Split(MM_fieldsStr, "|")
74  MM_columns = Split(MM_columnsStr, "|")
75
76  ' set the form values
77  For MM_i = LBound(MM_fields) To UBound(MM_fields) Step 2
78    MM_fields(MM_i+1) = CStr(Request.Form(MM_fields(MM_i)))
79  Next
80
81  ' append the query string to the redirect URL
82  ' If (MM_editRedirectUrl <> "" And Request.QueryString <> "") Then
83  '   If (InStr(1, MM_editRedirectUrl, "?", vbTextCompare) = 0 And Request.QueryString <> "") Then
84  '     MM_editRedirectUrl = MM_editRedirectUrl & "?" & Request.QueryString
85  '   Else
86  '     MM_editRedirectUrl = MM_editRedirectUrl & "&" & Request.QueryString
87  '   End If
88  ' End If
89
90  End If
91  %>
92  <%
93  ' *** Update Record: construct a sql update statement and execute it
94
95  If (CStr(Request("MM_update")) <> "" And CStr(Request("MM_recordId")) <> "") Then
```

Once you've commented out these lines of code, test the page set again, multiple times. It should work as expected.

WHAT YOU HAVE LEARNED

In this lesson, you have:

- Created the basic layout for each of the pages in advance (pages 427–428)

- Planned the precise data to be used in the master-detail page set (pages 429–430)

- Created a recordset sufficient to handle both pages (page 430)

- Inserted a Master-Detail Page Set application object, based on the recordset (pages 431–437)

- Converted the detail table to a form (pages 438–441)

- Applied the Update Record server behavior (pages 442–445)

- Applied fixes to ASP to make the Update Record server behavior work alongside the Master-Detail Page Set application object (pages 445–446)

hand-coding a basic cms

LESSON 16

As the final activity in the book, you'll build a content management system for the country profiles. Using it, Newland Tours employees will be able to insert new country profiles, and modify or delete existing country profiles, using simple HTML forms as their interface. You've already used UPDATE and INSERT SQL statements to manage content, so the only new SQL in this lesson is the DELETE statement.

You will hand-code a complete content management system from the ground up, enabling users to maintain site content using Web forms.

In this lesson, in contrast to the previous lessons where you built pages that inserted and updated data, you will not rely on Dreamweaver server behaviors. It is not that anything is wrong with using server behaviors, but one of the primary goals of this book is to give you the conceptual underpinnings and experience working with code that will empower you to create your own dynamic sites. And as I've stressed throughout the book, building dynamic sites usually requires some level of competence with ASP, ColdFusion or PHP code.

Although server behaviors are convenient, some of them effectively mask what's going on, enabling you to add functionalities that you don't even understand. That's great for rapid development, but not good for learning. And the code generated by the server behaviors is often incredibly complex—too complex for someone new to dynamic development to read. This complexity is often due to Dreamweaver's need for a given server behavior to work under a tremendous variety of circumstances, rather than the task itself. But it means that you often can't deconstruct the server behaviors that you add. (ColdFusion users are more likely to understand Dreamweaver's server behavior code than ASP or PHP users, due to the intrinsic nature of each language.) Avoiding server behaviors in this lesson will teach you more than you would otherwise learn.

Much of what you'll do in this lesson is not new. You'll build a group of pages that work together to handle certain functionalities. You'll create forms that collect information from the user. You'll use SQL to retrieve data from and send it to a database. You'll have a master-detail page pairing. The difference is that you'll put it all together in one lesson, and you will do all of it manually.

At the same time, the directions will be a little more high level. That is, for certain tasks you have done over and over again in this book (such as creating new pages and mocking up form interfaces), I will not provide detailed step-by-step instructions, but will assume you can manage with comparatively less guidance. That will enable the lesson to focus on the more challenging aspects of the job—connecting ASP, ColdFusion, or PHP to a database and writing the queries that will make the CMS work.

WHAT YOU WILL LEARN

In this lesson, you will:

- Build a coordinated content management system, enabling users to insert, update, and delete data

- Develop the code with minimal reliance on Dreamweaver's GUI

- Hand-write your own code to make database connections

- Make use of SQL's INSERT, UPDATE, and DELETE statements

APPROXIMATE TIME

This lesson takes approximately three hours to complete.

LESSON FILES

Starting Files:

Lesson16/Start/newland/admin_template.asp

Completed Files:

Lesson16/Complete/newland/admin_cp_ insert.asp

Lesson16/Complete/newland/admin_cp_ insert_processor.asp

Lesson16/Complete/newland/admin_cp_ master.asp

Lesson16/Complete/newland/admin_cp_ update.asp

Lesson16/Complete/newland/admin_cp_ update_processor.asp

Lesson16/Complete/newland/admin_cp_ delete_processor.asp

PREPARING THE CONTENT MANAGEMENT SYSTEM

Though it is often tempting to open Dreamweaver and start building pages right away, when you are developing a Web application, you are better served by thinking through exactly what you want to create, and at least outlining the major file assets that you need. The goal of this content management system is to create a group of pages that let users insert new country profiles, and modify or delete existing profiles.

You already should see a distinction between these two processes: When inserting a new record, you can just create a form that collects the data to be inserted, but to allow users to delete or modify existing records, the users need to be able to specify a record. In other words, the insert page doesn't require a master-detail page pairing, but both of the other two functionalities do. There's no reason, though, that the pages that enable users to modify versus delete records can't share the same master page.

Each of the three functionalities requires a script to do the actual work of inserting, updating, or removing records. The easiest way to implement these scripts is to put them on their own pages, using the _processor suffix we have used throughout the book. Once a given script is processed, we'll redirect users to the master page, so they can verify that the correct action has been taken. These pages are hidden because they are active for only the split second required to process the script before redirecting the user to another page.

NOTE *Though it is easy to store these scripts in hidden files, many developers actually put them on the same page as the form, and have the page submit the form to itself. An if...else structure near the top determines whether the form variables are present, and if so, processes the script. If not, it skips over the script and displays the page. This approach reduces the number of files on the server and keeps all the scripts that create a certain functionality in one file, but there are some advantages to keeping scripts separate. First, a good programmer can write reusable scripts, using the same script for multiple pages. Second, you can place scripts in a special folder, with special permissions on it to enhance security.*

The following figure summarizes the pages needed to create this application.

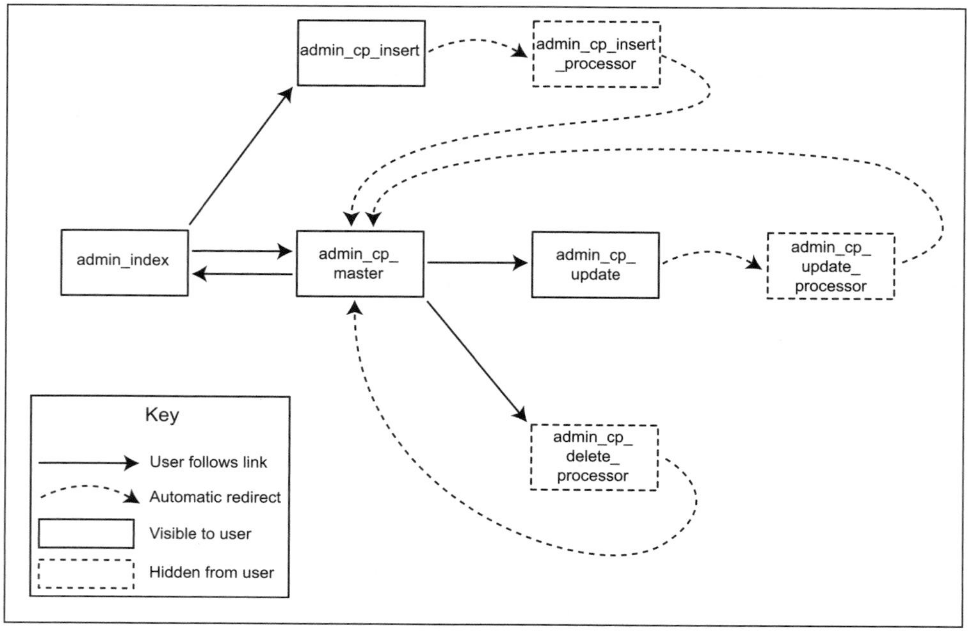

Starting from admin_index.asp, users can choose either to insert a new country profile (in which case, they are redirected to admin_cp_insert.asp) or modify/delete an existing country profile (in which case, they are redirected to admin_cp_master.asp).

The admin_cp_insert.asp page contains a blank form. Users will fill out this form when they want to create a new country profile. When they submit the form, the data is sent to admin_cp_insert_processor.asp, where it is inserted into the database and users are redirected to the master page. The new country's presence on the master page is proof that the insert action was successful.

Once on admin_cp_master.asp, users can click a link to modify an existing record, in which case they are taken to admin_cp_update.asp, which contains a form whose contents are already filled in with existing data. They can modify this data, and when they submit it, a script (on admin_cp_update_processor.asp) updates the database with the new data and redirects users back to the master page. They can view the profile again to verify that the update was successful.

Alternatively, from the master page, users can choose to delete a country profile. When they click this link, they are redirected to admin_cp_delete_processor, which contains a script that deletes the selected country and redirects users back to the master page. This process takes a fraction of a second and appears to users as if they never left the master page—it simply updates with the selected country removed.

Now that you have a firm grasp of the basic layout of the content management system, you can start building it.

1) Using admin_template.asp as the source, create each of the pages that the user will see, as follows.

admin_cp_insert.asp

admin_cp_master.asp

admin_cp_update.asp

These three pages are visible to the user, so don't delete the code and be sure to customize each accordingly. Add a page title in the toolbar, and overwrite the placeholder heading at the top of the page with something appropriate, such as "Insert a New Country Profile," "Select a Country Profile to Modify or Delete," and "Update a Country Profile."

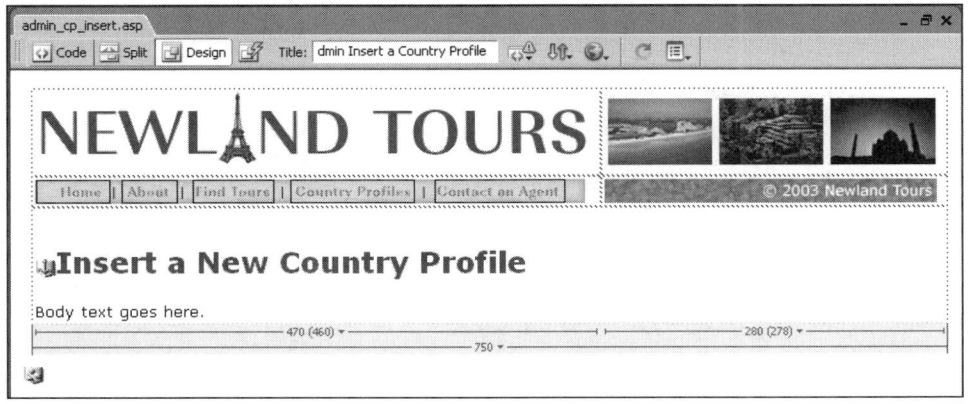

2) Create each of the hidden pages as well, saving three files (as follows). Be sure to delete all code from these pages, while in code (not design) view.

admin_cp_insert_processor.asp

admin_cp_update_processor.asp

admin_cp_delete_processor.asp

These pages should never be displayed to the user, and so they should not have any HTML code in them. They will contain only the code needed to perform the function (insert a new record, update a record, and so on).

TIP *The easiest way to complete this step is to create a new file, strip out the code, and save it three times with different filenames.*

You now have six new files. Granted, they are empty, but now that they exist, it will be easier to link to them as you build the application itself.

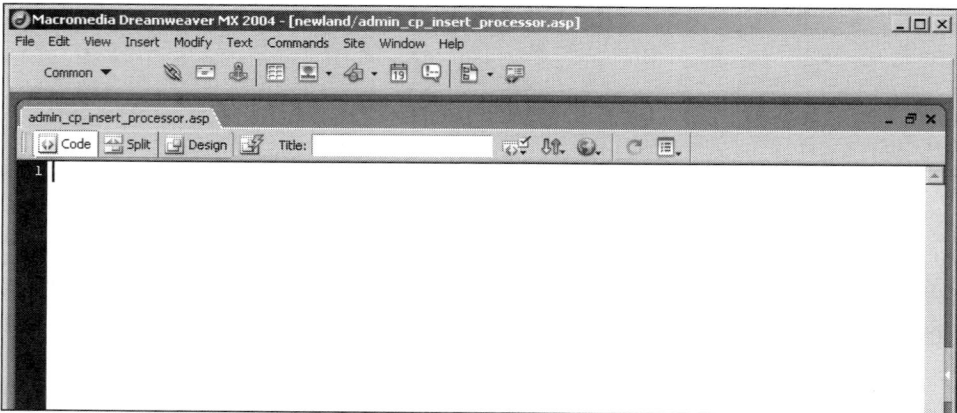

BUILDING THE FORM AND HAND-CODING A RECORDSET

In this task, you'll create the form that employees can use to insert new country profiles. You'll have the form submit its data to admin_cp_insert_processor.asp, where you'll also write the code necessary to insert the new record.

1) In admin_cp_insert.asp, create a form (Form Name: frm_insertProfile; Action: admin_cp_insert_processor.asp), and insert a table inside of it with eight rows, two columns, and a border of 1, as shown in the screenshot.

The seven items listed in the left column correspond to seven of the eight fields in tbl_country (the eighth is the autogenerated primary key).

NEWLAND TOURS

Insert a New Country Profile

Region	
Country Name	
Population (Do not use commas)	
Country Currency	
Description	
Image URL (Use this format: **images/imagename.jpg** and remember to upload the images to the images folder on the server).	
Image Alternate Description	

2) Add form elements into the right column, according to the following table:

ELEMENT TYPE	ELEMENT NAME	NOTES
List/Menu	region	Leave its type at the default, Menu, in the Property inspector
Text field	countryName	
Text field	population	
Text field	country_currency	
Text area	description	Provide enough room for users to enter a description, by setting its Char Width to 55 and its Num Lines to 9 in the Property inspector. Set its Wrap to Virtual.
Text field	imageURL	
Text area	imageALT	This doesn't need to be as large as the text area for description. Give it a Char Width of 55 as well, but leave the Num Lines blank. Set its Wrap to Virtual.

455

Once again, the element names are the same as the field names in the corresponding table, making it easier to match the two. This time, you'll be hand-coding the SQL, so you won't be using Dreamweaver's Insert Record dialog, but it's nonetheless easier if the form fields match the database table fields.

The form is almost ready, but it lacks one critical piece: The menu at the top doesn't have any data in it. It should be populated by data from tbl_region, which means you'll have to create a recordset.

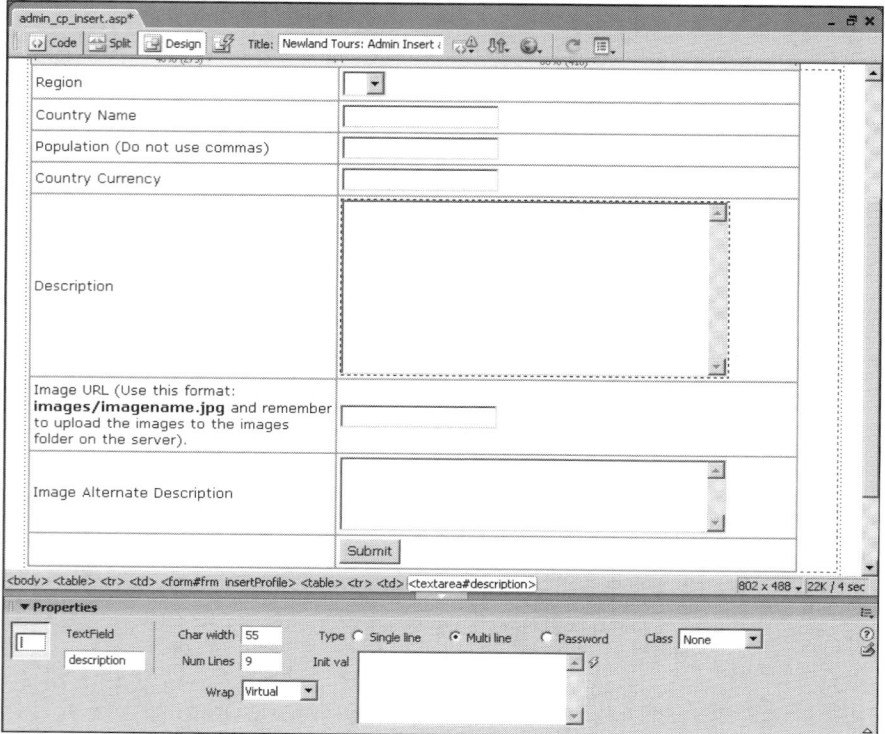

3) Switch to code view, and scroll to the portion of the document after the Restrict Access to Page server behavior but before the opening `<!DOCTYPE...>` **tag. Type the code necessary to create a connection to the database.**

In ASP:

```
<%
'Create connection object
Dim dbConn
Dim rs_regions
set dbConn = server.CreateObject("adodb.connection")
'Connect to database via DSN
dbConn.open("newland")
%>
```

In ColdFusion:

```
<cfquery name="rs_regions" datasource="newland">

</cfquery>
```

In PHP:

```
<?php
// Set up connection to MySQL
$host = "localhost";
$user = "[enter your username]";
$pwd = "[enter your password]";
$dbConn = mysql_connect($host,$user,$pwd);
// Connect to newland_tours database
$database = "newland_tours";
mysql_select_db($database);

?>
```

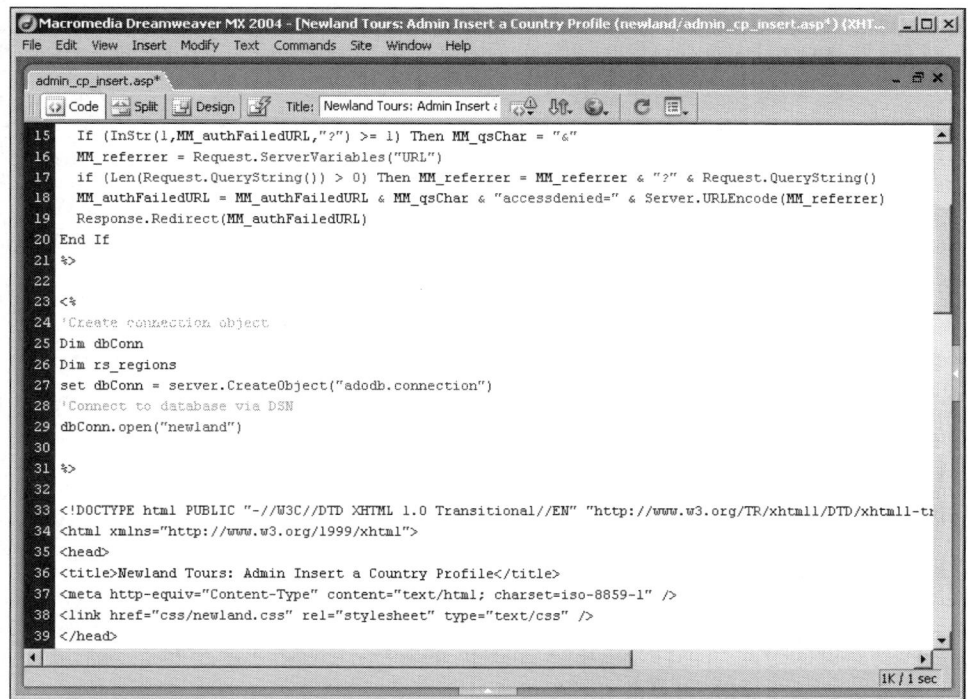

This code is sufficient to open a connection to the database. However, it doesn't actually do anything once the connection is established. You still need to add a SQL statement to make anything happen.

Let's look at the code for a moment. ColdFusion users have it fairly easy: They use the `<cfquery>` tag, give their query a name (rs_regions) and specify the data source (newland). ColdFusion figures out the rest.

ASP requires a bit more legwork. The word Dim is used to declare a new variable. Two are created here: dbConn and rs_regions. The variable dbConn will be used to create the database connection itself, and rs_regions will be used to hold the recordset. Both of these names are arbitrary, and you can call them whatever you want. The line after the Dim lines, which begins set dbConn =, tells ASP to create a new database connection object, whose name is dbConn. The next line then instructs ASP to actually open that connection to the DSN named "newland."

NOTE *ASP and PHP users might wonder why they enter (respectively) "newland" and "newland_tours" rather than "conn_newland" as they have throughout the book. In the case of ASP, the reasons is that "newland" is the DSN name that exists on the server and points to the Newland Tours database. In the case of PHP, newland_tours is the name of the database on the MySQL server. For both ASP and PHP, conn_newland, in contrast, is a connection created in Dreamweaver that uses the newland DSN (ASP) or newland_tours database (PHP) but is separate from it. Since you are coding by hand, and not going through Dreamweaver server behaviors, you specify the DSN (ASP) or the MySQL server newland_tours database directly.*

Part of the ASP framework is a group of ready-made objects designed to handle common tasks. ASP has many such objects, and you have made extensive use of them through the book (though you may not have realized it). These include the Request, Response, Session, and Application objects, among others. The Connection and Recordset objects are a part of ActiveX Data Objects, or ADO. The topic of object-oriented programming, or OOP, is beyond the scope of this book, but suffice it to say for now that you can reliably use the code developed in this lesson as a template for connecting to a database.

The PHP code, although the most verbose in the group, is fairly easy to read. The built-in mysql_connect() function is used to help PHP find the MySQL server. As the code indicates, it takes three parameters: the host, username, and password of the account you want to access. This username and password combination is the same pairing that you entered in the MySQL Connection dialog earlier in the book. Be sure to enter it in the code, where you see [enter your username] and [enter your password] in this step's code listing. Once PHP can find the MySQL server, it needs to find the database itself. To do that, you use the built-in mysql_select_db() function, whose sole parameter is the name of the database on the MySQL server.

4) Add the code necessary to retrieve the desired records in the blank line you left in the preceding step.

In ASP:

```
Set rs_regions = dbConn.Execute("SELECT * FROM tbl_region ORDER BY regionName")
```

In ColdFusion:

```
SELECT * FROM tbl_region ORDER BY regionName
```

In PHP:

```
$query_rs_regions = "SELECT * FROM tbl_region ORDER BY regionName";
$rs_regions = mysql_query($query_rs_regions);
$row_rs_regions = mysql_fetch_assoc($rs_regions);
```

This particular SQL should pose no challenge to you by this point in the book. It retrieves all of the fields in all of the records in tbl_region, and orders them alphabetically by the name of the region.

Again, the ASP and PHP might be somewhat confusing. I'll start with the ASP. Remember, dbConn is the connection object, not the recordset. This line of code creates the recordset by creating a recordset object whose contents are equal to whatever is retrieved from the query executed through the connection.

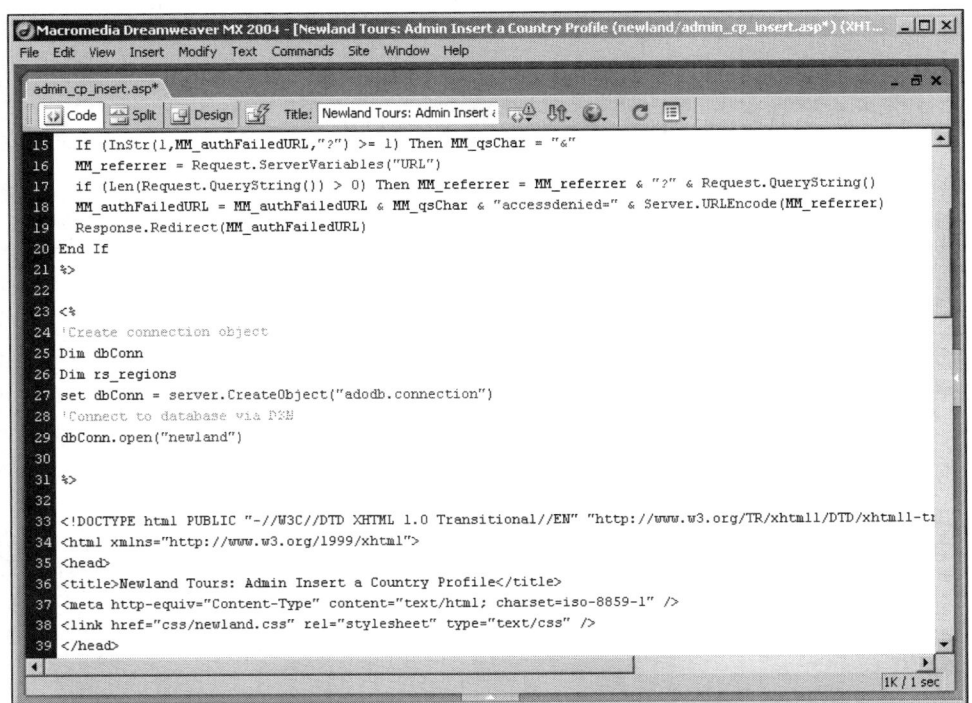

HAND-CODING A BASIC CMS

The first two lines of the PHP code query the database, as you probably guessed. And you probably also guessed that the results of the query would be a recordset stored in the $rs_regions variable. But there you would be wrong. When querying a MySQL database in PHP using mysql_query(), the result is not the recordset, but rather a number, which points to the data. The data itself is not returned. Instead, it sits in a limbo area that is neither PHP nor MySQL. Now, to get this data out of that area, you must "fetch" it, using mysql_fetch_assoc() (or one of its variants). This function retrieves the data from limbo and constructs an array to contain it. That array, in this block, is named $row_rs_regions. Once the data is in the $row_rs_regions array, it acts much like a recordset in ASP or ColdFusion—to access it, you reference $row_rs_regions.

This code is sufficient to create the recordset and make the data available to the page. If you look in the Bindings panel, you won't see this recordset listed. Dreamweaver doesn't realize it's there. Unfortunately, this also means that you won't be able to bind the recordset to the form object. You'll have to code it manually.

5) Still in code view, scroll down until you see the form. Just a few lines below it, inside the table, look for the `<select>` element, which is the menu. Press Enter or Return a few times to make some space between opening and closing tags.
The `<select>` tag creates the menu itself. To populate the menu, you use the `<option>` tag. Each option tag results in one more option in the menu. It uses the following syntax:

```
<option value="data">Label</option>
```

In this example, Label is what appears in the menu that humans can read, while data is the value that is submitted with the form. We need to bind regionName to the label and regionID to the value attribute.

```
54    <h1><br />
55      <a name="top" id="top"></a>Insert a New Country Profile </h1>
56    <form name="frm_insertProfile" id="frm_insertProfile" method="post" action="admin_cp
57      <table width="95%"  border="1" cellspacing="0" cellpadding="3">
58        <tr>
59          <td width="40%">Region</td>
60          <td width="60%">
61          <select name="region" id="region">
62
63
64          |
65
66          </select>
67          </td>
68        </tr>
69        <tr>
70          <td>Country Name </td>
71          <td><input name="countryName" type="text" id="countryName" /></td>
72        </tr>
73        <tr>
74          <td>Population (Do not use commas) </td>
```

6) In the empty space between the `<select>` **tags, type the code needed to bind database data to the** `<option>` **tag.**

In ASP:

```
<%
Response.Write("<option value=""" & rs_regions("regionID") & """>" &
⇒rs_regions("regionName") & "</option>")
%>
```

In ColdFusion:

```
<cfoutput>
<option value="#rs_regions.regionID#">#rs_regions.regionName#</option>
</cfoutput>
```

In PHP:

```
<?php
echo "<option value=\"".$row_rs_regions['regionID']."\">".$row_rs_regions
⇒['regionName']."</option>";
?>
```

```
60    <td width="60%">
61    <select name="region" id="region">
62    <%
63    Response.Write("<option value=""" & rs_regions("regionID") & """>" & rs_regions("regionName") & "<
64    %>
65    </select>
66    </td>
```

You've bound `regionID` to the value attribute, and `regionName` appears as the label in the menu.

The ASP and PHP code blocks, as usual, need additional explanation. As you know from before, `Response.Write()` and echo are the ways ASP and PHP respectively output text to the browser. In this line, you are telling the server to output a line of HTML for the `<option>` tag. When you want ASP or PHP to output a string of text, you enclose that string in quotation marks. The complication is, you don't want ASP to literally write into the browser `<option value=" rs_regions("regionID")>rs_regions ("regionName")</option>` (or the equivalent for PHP). You want ASP to evaluate `rs_regions("regionID")` and `rs_regions("regionName")`, and you want PHP to evaluate `$row_rs_regions['regionID']` and `$row_rs_regions['regionName']`. Once these have been evaluated, you want ASP and PHP to write their results ("6" and "Africa," respectively) into the browser. But if you leave that portion of the script inside quotes, ASP or PHP would simply write, rather than evaluate and output, the code.

To get around this problem, you use a technique called concatenation, which refers to the building of strings out of different pieces. Here, the pieces are string literals, such as "<option value=" and expressions, such as rs_regions("regionID") and $row_rs_regions['regionID']. You glue these pieces together with the ampersand (&) character in ASP and the period character (.) in PHP. ASP/PHP then knows to evaluate the expressions and then glue them into the string. ColdFusion uses the pound signs (#) to distinguish between string literals and expressions, eliminating the need to concatenate elements. So the final output to the browser of this code, whether you use ASP, ColdFusion, or PHP is <option value="6">Africa</option>.

ASP and PHP have another complication: Quotation marks are used in two different ways in this block of code. Like most programming languages, ASP and PHP use quotes to distinguish between strings and expressions. Everything inside of the quotes ASP and PHP ignore and output as-is. Unfortunately, the string that ASP and PHP need to output contains quotation marks: The proper syntax for the HTML attribute ASP and PHP need to output is <option value="XYZ">. In the final output of this code, the number output by rs_regions("regionID") and $row_rs_regions['regionID'] should appear in quotes, as in, <option value="6">. ASP and PHP get confused when they see the quotation marks used in the value attribute, and think that you are marking the end of the string, which in fact you are not. To solve this problem, when you want to tell ASP and PHP to write quotation marks, rather than interpret them, you insert two sets of quotation marks (ASP) or precede the quotation marks with a backslash (\) (PHP). Thus, in the ASP code you just entered, "<option value=""" &, where you see three quotation marks in a row, the first two indicate the quotation marks that ASP should write into the HTML, and the third indicates the end of the string. Likewise in the PHP code you just entered, "<option value=\""., the \" tell PHP to output one pair of quotes, while the next set of quotes (immediately preceding the period) indicated to PHP the end of the string.

Save, upload, and test the file, and look at the menu. You'll see right away that Africa has loaded, and it is alphabetically the first region in the database table. That's good. But we've got a problem. Africa is the only option in the menu! You need to cause ASP, ColdFusion, or PHP to create a new <option> tag for each record in the database. This calls for a programming structure known as a **loop**. In a loop, the same block of code is executed over and over until a condition is met. In this case, we need to create a loop that will output the <option> line over and over until it runs out of records.

7) Amend the block of code you added in step 6 so that it incorporates a looping structure.

In ASP:

```
<%
Do Until rs_regions.EOF
    Response.Write("<option value=""" & rs_regions("regionID") & """>" &
    ⇒rs_regions("regionName") & "</option>")
    rs_regions.MoveNext
  Loop
%>
```

In ColdFusion:

```
<cfoutput query="rs_regions">
<option value="#rs_regions.regionID#">#rs_regions.regionName#</option>
<cfoutput>
```

In PHP:

```php
<?php
do
{
  echo "<option value=\"".$row_rs_regions['regionID']."\">".$row_rs_regions
  ⇒['regionName']."</option>";
}
while ($row_rs_regions = mysql_fetch_assoc($rs_regions));
?>
```

```
60   <td width="60%">
61   <select name="region" id="region">
62   <%
63   Do Until rs_regions.EOF
64       Response.Write("<option value=""" & rs_regions("regionID") & """>" & rs_regions("regionName") & "<
65     rs_regions.MoveNext
66   Loop
67   %>
68   </select>
69   </td>
```

ColdFusion users need only add the query attribute to the <cfoutput> tag, and the loop is created automatically for them, behind the scenes.

ASP and PHP users, as usual, have a harder time. ASP's Do Until and PHP's do…while are looping structures. The sole parameter of each is the condition that must be met to break the loop, in both cases when the recordset runs out of records. (ASP's EOF stands for End of File.) The next line constructs the <option> element, as before. PHP uses curly braces {} to identify which code is to be looped over. ASP's MoveNext method tells ASP to advance to the next record. ASP's last line, Loop, sends ASP back to the Do Until line, while PHP's last line, with the while statement, provides the loop-breaking condition for the do half of the loop.

Test the file again in a browser, and click the menu. You'll see all of the regions listed now.

8) ASP and PHP users only: In code view, scroll all the way to the bottom of the document, and after the last line of code, </html>, insert the following script, to close and destroy the recordset.

In ASP:

```
<%
rs_regions.Close()
Set rs_regions = Nothing
%>
```

In PHP:

```
<?php
mysql_free_result($rs_regions);
?>
```

At the top of the document, you opened a connection and created a recordset. This recordset exists in the server's memory. Unless you tell it to go away, it might stay in the server's memory. Over time, you could overwhelm your server with useless recordset data that is no longer being used. The ASP code block removes all of the records from the recordset (rs_regions.Close()) and then destroys the recordset object itself (Set rs_regions = Nothing). The PHP version simply clears the $rs_regions recordset array. You add this script to the bottom of the page, of course, so that the rest of the page is processed before the recordset is destroyed. It wouldn't do your form any good if you destroyed the recordset before you had a chance to populate the menu with its data!

ColdFusion users don't have to worry about this step, because it happens automatically behind the scenes any time you deploy <cfquery>.

ADDING THE INSERT FUNCTIONALITY

The form is now fully ready. The problem is that no script yet exists to write the form data into the database. In this task, you'll write the script used to insert data. The script you'll write has the same functionality as the Insert Record behavior, but the code will be somewhat leaner, and this time around, you'll understand it.

1) Open admin_cp_insert_processor.asp in code view.

The file should be empty of all code. If not, remove any code.

Before adding code, let's review what this page should do. It should retrieve the data entered into the form and insert it as a new record into tbl_country. Once that's complete, it should redirect the user to admin_cp_master.asp.

2) Insert the code that creates the connection to the database.

In ASP:

```
<%
Dim dbConn
set dbConn = server.CreateObject("adodb.connection")
dbConn.open("newland")

%>
```

In ColdFusion:

```
<cfquery name="rs_insertCountry" datasource="newland">

</cfquery>
```

In PHP:

```
<?php
// Set up connection to MySQL
$host = "localhost";
$user = "[enter your username]";
$pwd = "[enter your password]";
$dbConn = mysql_connect($host,$user,$pwd);
// Connect to newland_tours database
$database = "newland_tours";
mysql_select_db($database);
?>
```

This is essentially the same code used in the previous task to create the recordset that populated the form menu. The difference here is that you don't even need to have a recordset returned. You are inserting data into the database, but you are not retrieving a recordset.

TIP *Because we typically use the same code over and over to connect pages to your database, many developers store the basic code for connecting to a database in a separate file, which they then include in every document. This could be a special include file, such as Application.cfm or a regular include file, accessed using something like PHP's* require_once(). *In fact, this is exactly what Dreamweaver does in the ASP and PHP models, when you "define a connection." In other words, the conn_newland source ASP and PHP users have used throughout this book is simply an include file with the basic information needed to connect to the newland_tours database.*

3) Insert the code that inserts the data into the table in the blank space you left in the previous step.

In ASP (all on one line):

```
dbConn.Execute("INSERT INTO tbl_country (region, countryName, population,
⇒country_currency, description, imageURL, imageALT) VALUES ('" &
⇒Request.Form("region") & "', '" & Request.Form("countryName") & "',
⇒'" & Request.Form("population") & "', '" & Request.Form("country_currency")
⇒& "', '" & Request.Form("description") & "', '" & Request.Form("imageURL") &
⇒"', '" & Request.Form("imageALT") & "');")
```

In ColdFusion (can be on multiple lines):

```
INSERT INTO tbl_country
(region, countryName, population, country_currency, description, imageURL,
⇒imageALT)
VALUES
('#form.region#', '#form.countryName#', '#form.population#',
⇒'#form.country_currency#', '#form.description#', '#form.imageURL#',
⇒'#form.imageALT#')
```

In PHP (on two lines):

```
$query_rs_insertCountry = "INSERT INTO tbl_country (region, countryname,
⇒population, country_currency, description, imageURL, imageALT) VALUES
⇒('".$_POST['region']."', '".$_POST['countryName']."',
⇒'".$_POST['population']."', '".$_POST['country_currency']."',
⇒'".$_POST['description']."', '".$_POST['imageURL']."',
⇒'".$_POST['imageALT']."');";
$rs_insertCountry = mysql_query($query_rs_insertCountry);
```

```
1 <%
2 Dim dbConn
3 set dbConn = server.CreateObject("adodb.connection")
4 dbConn.open("newland")
5 dbConn.Execute("INSERT INTO tbl_country (region, countryName, population, country_currency, description, im
6 Response.Redirect("admin_cp_master.asp")
7 %>
```

467

Understanding these lines is easier if you recall the basic syntax of an INSERT statement in SQL:

```
INSERT INTO tbl_table
  (field1, field2, field3)
VALUES
  ('value1', 'value2', 'value3')
```

The ASP, ColdFusion, and PHP code blocks are constructing SQL statements that use this syntax. But again, since they are replacing variables with actual values, you need to let each server know to evaluate these expressions before it inserts them into the database. As a consequence, you'll see quite a few pound signs in the ColdFusion version, and a lot of concatenation in the ASP and PHP versions.

TIP *ASP and PHP users should use code coloring to their advantage. The coloring typically changes the moment you enter an error, making it easy to spot problems before you test the page. ASP: In all cases, Request.Form should be purple, while the form field name should always be green. The ampersands (&) used to concatenate should always be blue. PHP: In all cases, string literals (including all commas and single quotes) are red, $_POST is always light blue, while periods and square brackets are always dark blue.*

NOTE *ASP and PHP use both double quotes (") and single quotes ('), which can be confusing. Content enclosed in double quotes is a part of ASP/PHP, specifically, string literals that ASP/PHP should pass without evaluating. Content enclosed in single quotes belongs to SQL and represents the values being inserted into the database.*

4) Insert the code that redirects the user to the master page once the insert is completed.

In ASP, before the closing %>:

```
Response.Redirect("admin_cp_master.asp")
```

In ColdFusion:

```
<cflocation url="admin_cp_master.cfm">
```

In PHP, before the closing ?>:

```
header("Location: admin_cp_master.php");
```

Because ASP, ColdFusion, and PHP will display an error message if they experience problems, the redirect line will only be executed if the insertion is successful.

Test the page to make sure it works (you can just make up the details about your country). Once you insert your data, you'll be sent to an as-yet incomplete admin_cp_master.asp. But there's an easy way to see whether the insertion was successful: Go to the country profiles. Updating the country profiles is the whole point of this application. You should find your newly inserted country there. Don't worry about nonsense data—you'll be building a delete application later in the lesson, and you'll need a bogus country or two to test it, so just leave your creation in the database for now.

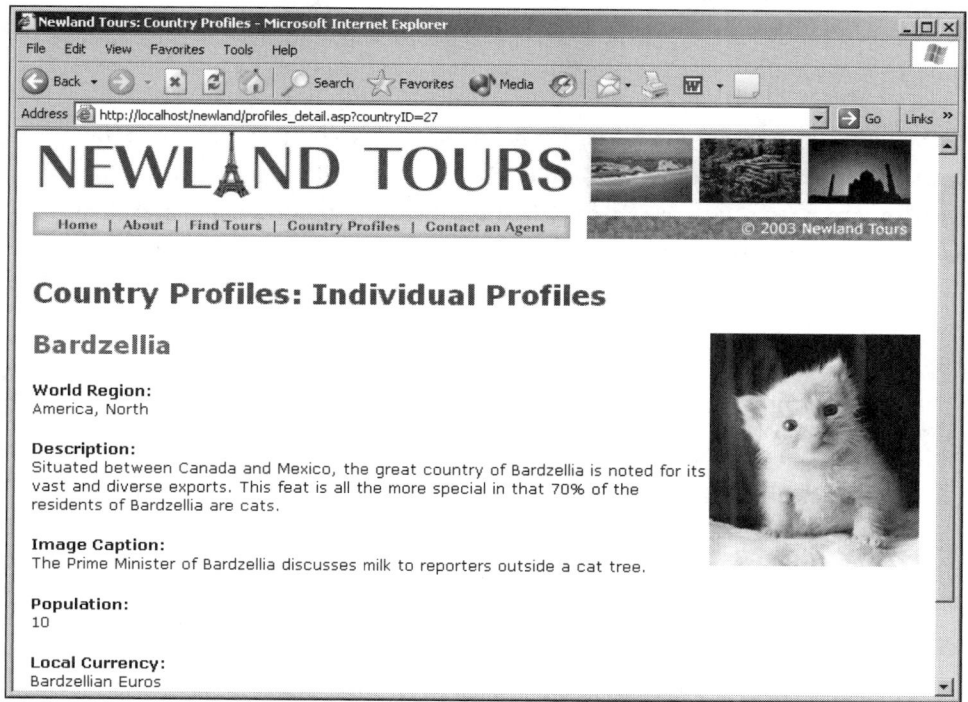

NOTE *As you test the functionality of these pages, do not enter any apostrophes in any of your descriptions. If you do, you'll see an error message. This issue is addressed later in the lesson.*

NOTE *Unless you upload an image to the images folder with the same name as the one you enter in the form, the image link will be broken.*

CREATING THE MASTER PAGE

A master-detail page pairing is necessary for the update and deletion functionality, because you have to allow the users to select which country they want to update or delete. In this task, you'll create a simple master-detail page consisting of a table with each country's name, a link to modify the country, and a link to delete the country in a row. As before, each of these links will pass a URL parameter identifying the country that the user has selected.

1) Open admin_cp_master.asp, and switch to code view.

As before, you'll create the recordset before laying out the page, and since you'll handwrite the code necessary to create the recordset, you need to be in code view.

2) Between the Restrict Access server behavior code and the beginning of the document itself (just before the `<!DOCTYPE>` tag), enter the code necessary to create a recordset (`"rs_countries"`) that retrieves the country name and ID of every record in tbl_country.

In ASP:

```
<%
Dim dbConn
Dim rs_countries
set dbConn = Server.CreateObject("adodb.connection")
dbConn.open("newland")
Set rs_countries = dbConn.Execute("SELECT countryID, countryName FROM
⇒tbl_country ORDER BY countryName ASC")
%>
```

In ColdFusion:

```
<cfquery name="rs_countries" datasource="newland">
SELECT countryID, countryName FROM tbl_country ORDER BY countryName ASC
</cfquery>
```

In PHP:

```
<?php
// Set up connection to MySQL
$host = "localhost";
$user = "[enter your username]";
$pwd = "[enter your password]";
$dbConn = mysql_connect($host,$user,$pwd);
// Connect to newland_tours database
$database = "newland_tours";
mysql_select_db($database);
$query_rs_countries = "SELECT countryID, countryName FROM tbl_country ORDER BY
⇒countryName ASC";
$rs_countries = mysql_query($query_rs_countries);
$row_rs_countries = mysql_fetch_assoc($rs_countries);
?>
```

470

```
19    Response.Redirect(MM_authFailedURL)
20 End If
21 %>
22
23 <%
24 Dim dbConn
25 Dim rs_countries
26 set dbConn = Server.CreateObject("adodb.connection")
27 dbConn.open("newland")
28 Set rs_countries = dbConn.Execute("SELECT countryID, countryName FROM tbl_country ORDER BY countryName A$
29 %>
30
31 <!DOCTYPE html PUBLIC "-//W3C//DTD XHTML 1.0 Transitional//EN" "http://www.w3.org/TR/xhtml1/DTD/xhtml1-ti
32 <html xmlns="http://www.w3.org/1999/xhtml">
33 <head>
```

Aside from the details of the SQL statement, this code is identical to that used
earlier in this lesson, so you should understand it. The query itself is also easy to
read: It retrieves the country name and unique ID, ordered by country name.

3) ASP and PHP users only: Add the code to close and destroy the recordset at the end of the document.

In ASP:

```
<%
rs_countries.Close()
Set rs_countries = Nothing
%>
```

In PHP:

```
<?php
mysql_free_result($rs_countries);
?>
```

Again, this code prevents the recordset from wasting memory on the server.

```
70 </body>
71 </html>
72
73 <%
74 rs_countries.Close()
75 Set rs_countries = Nothing
76 %>
```

4) Switch to design view, and type the following two lines of text:

Select a country to modify or delete.

Caution: Deleting is instant and permanent.

471

Again, providing directions for the user is critical to the success of your applications.

Select a Country Profile to Modify or Delete

Select a country to modify or delete.

Caution: Deleting is instant and permanent.

5) Return to code view, and below the paragraph you just created, add the code to create a new table with one row and three columns.

```
<table width="98%" border="1" cellspacing="0" cellpadding="3">
  <tr>
    <td>XX</td>
    <td>XX</td>
    <td>XX</td>
  </tr>
</table>
```

This creates the basic framework for the table. When you are done with it, its contents will be dynamically generated, with each record being mapped to a single row. Since you can't know the number of rows in advance, you'll have to loop through the recordset, creating a new row for each record.

6) Enter the appropriate code needed to create a looping structure that encloses the `<tr>` tag. The code should wrap outside the opening and closing `<tr>` tags.

In ASP:

```
<%
  Do Until rs_countries.EOF
%>
<tr>
  <td>XX</td>
  <td>XX</td>
  <td>XX</td>
</tr>
<%
  rs_countries.MoveNext()
  Loop
%>
```

In ColdFusion:

```
<cfoutput query="rs_countries">
  <tr>
    <td>XX</td>
    <td>XX</td>
    <td>XX</td>
  </tr>
</cfoutput>
```

In PHP:

```
<?php
  do {
?>
<tr>
  <td>XXX</td>
  <td>XXX</td>
  <td>XXX</td>
<tr>
<?php
  }
  while ($row_rs_countries = mysql_fetch_assoc($rs_countries));
?>
```

In this step, you are in effect creating a repeat region—you just aren't using the Dreamweaver behavior. And in spite of their cosmetic differences, all three server models use remarkably similar logic. Each has a block of code before and after the section to be looped over (the <tr> section). Each specifies a query and creates a loop that breaks only when the recordset runs out of records: ASP's EOF accomplishes this explicitly; the recordset loop is implied in ColdFusion, when you specify the query attribute in a <cfoutput> tag; and PHP tests using mysql_fetch_assoc().

Next, you need to build the contents of the table cells, which will contain a mix of HTML and ASP, ColdFusion, or PHP code.

```
54    <p>Select a country to modify or delete.</p>
55    <p><strong>Caution:</strong> Deleting is instant and permanent.</p>
56
57    <table width="98%" border="1" cellspacing="0" cellpadding="3">
58    <%
59        Do Until rs_countries.EOF
60    %>
61    <tr>
62        <td>XX</td>
63        <td>XX</td>
64        <td>XX</td>
65    </tr>
66    <%
67        rs_countries.MoveNext()
68        Loop
69    %>
70    </table>
71
72    </td>
73  </tr>
74 </table>
```

7) Create the static HTML structure using placeholders for the content inside the `<td>` tags.

```
<td>Country Name</td>
<td><a href="admin_cp_update.asp?countryID=CountryID">Modify this country's
⇒profile</a></td>
<td><a href="admin_cp_delete_processor.asp?countryID=CountryID">Delete</a></td>
```

This code is the same for both ASP and ColdFusion (except that the file extensions in the href attribute for ColdFusion/PHP should be .cfm/.php rather than .asp), because it is merely static HTML. We're using placeholders here to ensure that we get the HTML syntax right, before adding the dynamic code.

```
57    <table width="98%" border="1" cellspacing="0" cellpadding="3">
58    <%
59        Do Until rs_countries.EOF
60    %>
61    <tr>
62        <td>Country Name</td>
63        <td><a href="admin_cp_update.asp?countryID=CountryID">Modify this country's profile</a></td>
64        <td><a href="admin_cp_delete_processor.asp?countryID=CountryID">Delete</a></td>
65    </tr>
66    <%
67        rs_countries.MoveNext()
68        Loop
69    %>
70    </table>
```

8) Replace the three placeholders with dynamic output, as follows.

In ASP:

```
<td><%=rs_countries("countryName")%></td>
<td><a href="admin_cp_update.asp?countryID=<%=rs_countries
⇒("countryID")%>">Modify this country's profile</a></td>
<td><a href="admin_cp_delete_processor.asp?countryID=<%=
⇒rs_countries("countryID")%>">Delete</a></td>
```

In ColdFusion:

```
<td>#countryName#</td>
<td><a href="admin_cp_update.cfm?countryID=#countryID#">
⇒Modify this country's profile</a></td>
<td><a href="admin_cp_delete_processor.cfm?countryID=#countryID#">
⇒Delete</a></td>
```

In PHP:

```
<td><?php echo $row_rs_countries['countryName']; ?></td>
<td><a href="admin_cp_update.php?countryID=<?php echo $row_rs_countries
⇒['countryID']; ?>">Modify this country's profile</a></td>
<td><a href="admin_cp_delete_processor.php?countryID=<?php echo
⇒$row_rs_countries['countryID']; ?>">Delete</a></td>
```

You've seen plenty of ASP, ColdFusion, and PHP output code in the course of this book, so the code should be easy to read, especially if you remember that <%= in ASP is equivalent to <% Response.Write().

```
57    <table width="98%" border="1" cellspacing="0" cellpadding="3">
58    <%
59        Do Until rs_countries.EOF
60    %>
61    <tr>
62        <td><%=rs_countries("countryName")%></td>
63        <td><a href="admin_cp_update.asp?countryID=<%=rs_countries("countryID")%>">Modify this country's
64        <td><a href="admin_cp_delete_processor.asp?countryID=<%=rs_countries("countryID")%>">Delete</a></
65    </tr>
66    <%
67        rs_countries.MoveNext()
68        Loop
69    %>
70    </table>
```

9) Save, upload, and test the file in a browser.

The table has as many rows as tbl_country has records. If you hover your mouse over one of the links, you'll see not only the URL, but also the countryID parameter attached with the correct country ID.

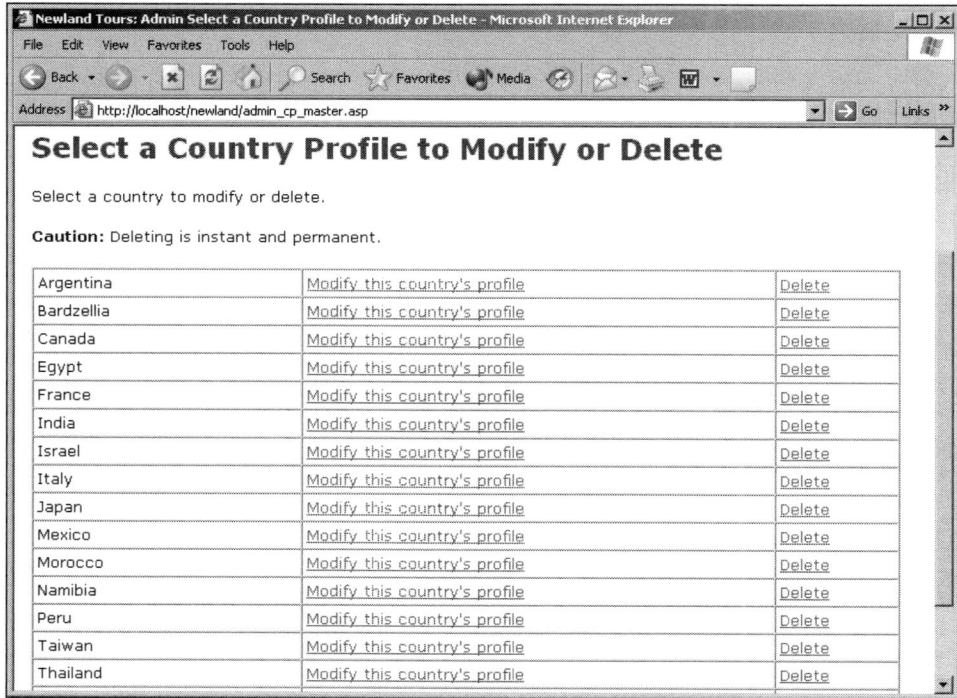

You can also close admin_cp_master.asp.

CREATING THE UPDATE RECORD DETAIL PAGE

The master page is ready, so the next step is to create the detail page. In this task, you'll build the detail page used for updating records. You won't actually need a detail page for deleting a record, because users don't need to see any details about the page—they just need a script to process the deletion.

The update page that you are about to create looks quite a bit like the page that you built enabling users to insert new country files. In fact, the page will use a modified version of the same form. The only differences are that the form fields will already be filled in on the update page, and, of course, when the user submits the form, a database record will be updated, rather than a new one created.

1) Open admin_cp_insert.asp. Choose File > Save As, and save it as admin_cp_update.asp (overwriting the original file). Change the page heading to *Update a Country Profile*, and change the page title to *Newland Tours Admin: Update a Country Profile*.

In doing so, you preserve the form you created as well as the rs_regions recordset, which retrieves all of the regions and their IDs, and populates the Region drop-down menu.

When you use this technique, you must keep in mind all of the things you will need to change. In this form, each of the fields must be automatically populated with appropriate data from the database for the chosen country; a new recordset will need to be created to facilitate this change. The action attribute of the <form> tag needs to point to admin_cp_update_processor.asp, rather than the insert processor page, and the form ought to be renamed.

2) In code view, find the opening `<form>` **tag, and set its attributes, as follows.
action (ASP):**

```
admin_cp_update_processor.asp?countryID=<%=Request.QueryString("countryID")%>
```

action (ColdFusion):

```
admin_cp_update_processor.cfm?countryID=<cfoutput>#URL.countryID#</cfoutput>
```

action (PHP):

```
admin_cp_update_processor.php?countryID=<?php echo $_GET['countryID']; ?>
```

method: post (same as before)

name: frm_updateProfile

id: frm_updateProfile

This is an easy step to overlook, so it's best to get it done right away.

```
54  <h1><br />
55    <a name="top" id="top"></a>Update a  Country Profile </h1>
56  <form name="frm_updateProfile" id="frm_updateProfile" method="post" action="admin_cp_update_processor.asp?countryID=<%=Request.QueryStri
57    <table width="95%"  border="1" cellspacing="0" cellpadding="3">
58      <tr>
```

The action attribute needs explanation. Remember, when this page first loads,
the countryID variable appears in the URL sent from the master page. A query
relies on this variable, so that it knows which country the user wants to modify.
Now, the actual updating of the database will be done on a different page:
admin_cp_update_processor.asp. However, that page, too, needs to know which
record it should update. By appending a querystring or URL parameter to the
form's action attribute, you are effectively sending this querystring variable to
the processor page.

TIP *Another common way to pass along read-only data through a form is to use a hidden
form field.*

3) Create a new recordset, rs_countryDetail, which retrieves all of the information stored about the country profile selected on the master page.

In ASP, inside the dbConn block, in a new line just below the current line that begins
Set rs_regions = :

```
Set rs_countryDetail = dbConn.Execute("SELECT * FROM tbl_country INNER
⇒JOIN tbl_region ON tbl_region.regionID=tbl_country.region WHERE
⇒tbl_country.countryID=" & Request.QueryString("countryID"))
```

In ColdFusion:

```
<cfquery name="rs_countryDetail" datasource="newland">
SELECT *
FROM tbl_country
INNER JOIN tbl_region ON tbl_region.regionID=tbl_country.region
WHERE tbl_country.countryID=#url.countryID#
</cfquery>
```

In PHP, at the end of the query block you wrote earlier, just before the closing ?>:

```
$query_rs_countryDetail = "SELECT * FROM tbl_country INNER JOIN tbl_region
⇒ON tbl_region.regionID=tbl_country.region WHERE
⇒tbl_country.countryID=".$_GET['countryID'];
$rs_countryDetail = mysql_query($query_rs_countryDetail);
$row_rs_countryDetail = mysql_fetch_assoc($rs_countryDetail);
```

```
23  <%
24  'Create connection object
25  Dim dbConn
26  Dim rs_regions
27  Dim rs_countryDetail
28  set dbConn = server.CreateObject("adodb.connection")
29  'Connect to database via DSN
30  dbConn.open("newland")
31  Set rs_regions = dbConn.Execute("SELECT * FROM tbl_region ORDER BY regionName")
32  Set rs_countryDetail = dbConn.Execute("SELECT * FROM tbl_country INNER JOIN tbl_region ON tbl_region.regionID=tbl_country.region WHERE tb
33  %>
```

477

```
45  <?php
46  // Set up connection to MySQL
47  $host = "localhost";
48  $user = "root";
49  $pwd = "priscian";
50  $dbConn = mysql_connect($host,$user,$pwd);
51  // Connect to newland_tours database
52  $database = "newland_tours";
53  mysql_select_db($database);
54  $query_rs_regions = "SELECT * FROM tbl_region ORDER BY regionName";
55  $rs_regions = mysql_query($query_rs_regions);
56  $row_rs_regions = mysql_fetch_assoc($rs_regions);
57  $query_rs_countryDetail = "SELECT * FROM tbl_country INNER JOIN tbl_region ON tbl_region.regionID=tbl_countr
58  $rs_countryDetail = mysql_query($query_rs_countryDetail);
59  $row_rs_countryDetail = mysql_fetch_assoc($rs_countryDetail);
60  ?>
```

Once again, most of this code should look familiar to you. It's worth deconstructing the SQL statement, though. Remember, tbl_country contains most of the information that Newland tracks about a country. The exception is the region name, which is stored in a different table, and linked through a relationship to tbl_country. The SQL statement therefore uses JOIN to retrieve this additional information. Also of note, this SQL statement does not retrieve all of the country profiles—only the profile that the user selected on the master page, that's ID was sent as a querystring/URL variable.

NOTE *ASP user should also Dim the new variable, rs_countryDetail, near the top of the script where the other Dim statements appear. The code should still work without it, but it's good practice to declare all variables.*

You now have all of the information about the selected country that Newland keeps. You'll use this information to populate the form on the page with live data from the database. When users submit the form, a script will replace existing database data with the information in the form. Now that this data is available, you need to bind it as the default value of each respective form element.

4) ASP and PHP Users: Scroll down to the bottom of the page, and add the code necessary to close and destroy the recordset.

In ASP:

```
<%
rs_countryDetail.Close()
Set rs_countryDetail = Nothing
%>
```

In PHP:

```
<?php
mysql_free_result($rs_countryDetail);
?>
```

Again, this frees up memory on the server, once your page no longer needs the recordset.

5) In code view, find the countryName form element. Give it a value attribute, as follows:

```
value="XX"
```

This is standard HTML, so it is the same for ASP, ColdFusion, and PHP. If you were to test the page now, the letters XX would appear in the Country Name field.

TIP *If you do test this page during the lesson, remember that it is expecting a querystring/URL parameter. If one is not supplied (and one never is when you press F12), you will see an error. To solve this problem, at the end of the URL in the Address/Location bar in your browser, type the following: ?countryID=3 and press Enter/Return. Doing so provides the necessary information for the query to run and the error is removed.*

6) Replace the XX placeholder with the dynamic value, as follows:
In ASP:

```
<%=rs_countryDetail("countryName")%>
```

In ColdFusion:

```
<cfoutput>#rs_countryDetail.countryName#</cfoutput>
```

In PHP:

```
<?php echo $row_rs_countryDetail['countryName']; ?>
```

This way, when the page loads, the proper country name appears by default in the field. If users modify it, then the country's name will be updated in the database. If the user leaves it alone, then strictly speaking, the form value will still replace the value in the database, but since they are the same, nothing will change.

```
<tr>
  <td>Country Name </td>
  <td><input name="countryName" type="text" id="countryName" value="<%=rs_countryDetail("countryName")%>" /></td>
</tr>
```

7) Using the correct ASP, ColdFusion, or PHP syntax, repeat steps 5 and 6 for each of the remaining text field elements, using the following information (provided in pseudocode):
Population: rs_countryDetail.population

Country Currency: rs_countryDetail.country_currency

Image URL: rs_countryDetail.imageURL

Now the four text fields are ready for use. You still need to take care of the two text areas.

```
74        <td>Country Name </td>
75        <td><input name="countryName" type="text" id="countryName" value="<%=rs_countryDetail("countryName")%>" /></td>
76      </tr>
77      <tr>
78        <td>Population (Do not use commas) </td>
79        <td><input name="population" type="text" id="population" value="<%=rs_countryDetail("population")%>" /></td>
80      </tr>
81      <tr>
82        <td>Country Currency </td>
83        <td><input name="country_currency" type="text" id="country_currency" value="<%=rs_countryDetail("country_currency")%>" /></td>
84      </tr>
85      <tr>
86        <td>Description</td>
87        <td><textarea name="description" cols="55" rows="9" wrap="VIRTUAL" id="description"></textarea></td>
88      </tr>
89      <tr>
90        <td>Image URL (Use this format: <strong>images/imagename.jpg</strong> and remember to upload the images to the images folder on
91        <td><input name="imageURL" type="text" id="imageURL" value="<%=rs_countryDetail("imageURL")%>" /></td>
92      </tr>
93      <tr>
94        <td>Image Alternate Description</td>
95        <td><textarea name="imageALT" cols="55" wrap="VIRTUAL" id="imageALT"></textarea></td>
96      </tr>
```

8) Between the two sets of opening and closing `<textarea></textarea>` **tags (for description and imageALT), insert the code necessary to output dynamic data as their default values.**

In ASP:

```
<%=rs_countryDetail("description")%>
<%=rs_countryDetail("imageALT")%>
```

In ColdFusion:

```
<cfoutput>#rs_countryDetail.description#</cfoutput>
<cfoutput>#rs_countryDetail.imageALT#</cfoutput>
```

In PHP:

```
<?php echo $row_rs_countryDetail['description']; ?>
<?php echo $row_rs_countryDetail['imageALT']; ?>
```

```
93  <tr>
94    <td>Image Alternate Description</td>
95    <td><textarea name="imageALT" cols="55" wrap="virtual" id="imageALT"><%=rs_countryDetail("imageALT")%></textarea></td>
96  </tr>
97  <tr>
98    <td> </td>
99    <td><input type="submit" name="Submit" value="Submit" /></td>
100 </tr>
```

The <textarea> tag uses slightly different syntax than other form element tags. Rather than having a value attribute, you place the default value between the opening and closing tags. The syntax for the ASP, ColdFusion, or PHP code is the same, though.

When you are done, save and upload the file so you can test it.

9) Select admin_cp_master.asp in the Site panel, log in, and click to select any non-African country.

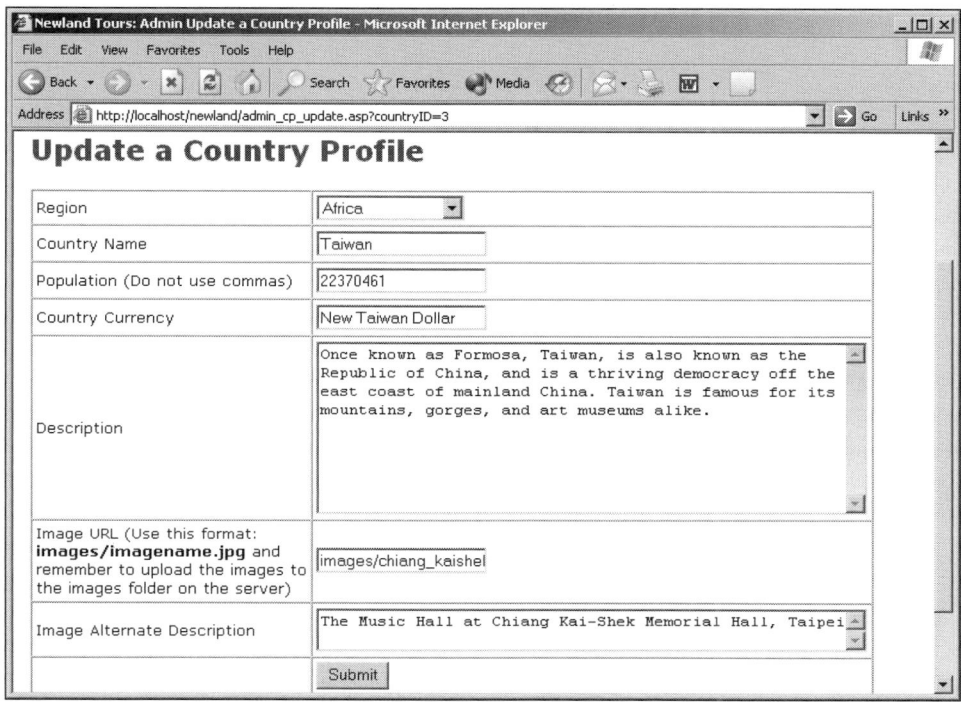

The update form appears, and all of its default values are already supplied. However, as long as you chose a non-African country, you'll see a problem: The country's region is listed as Africa. This occurs because a different recordset (rs_regions) is populating the drop-down menu, and Africa is the first region in the recordset, so it appears by default. You could change the menu, so that it displays data from rs_countryDetail, but since that has only one record, only one region would be displayed, making it impossible to change the region. And while it is unlikely that Italy will relocate to South America, you should preserve the flexibility to change regions, in case someone at Newland Tours decides to use a different regional division logic than continents, such as Northern Europe and Southern Europe, rather than simply Europe.

You might consider specifying to employees that they have to change this drop-down menu every time as appropriate, but that's poor usability. Sooner or later, an employee will forget to change it, and a country such as Mexico will be listed in Africa. The consequences of this mistake are significant: Remember that users can search by region, so they won't see Mexico if they search under Central America. And imagine the blow to credibility that a travel agent will suffer if it declares that Mexico is in Africa! This is a problem needing a solution.

But the solution is going to take some work. At the moment, the code sent to the browser (that is, after it has been processed by the ASP, ColdFusion, or PHP interpreter) for this menu element looks as follows:

```
<select name="region" id="region">
  <option value="6">Africa</option>
  <option value="8">America, Central</option>
  <option value="1">America, North</option>
  <option value="2">America, South</option>
  <option value="7">Asia, Central</option>
  <option value="4">Asia, East</option>
  <option value="5">Asia, West</option>
  <option value="3">Europe</option>
</select>
```

As you may be aware, the <select> element has an additional attribute, selected, which you can use to specify which item appears by default. So in the following list, Asia, Central would be the element that appears by default in the browser (bolding applied to make the change easier to spot).

```
<select name="region" id="region">
  <option value="6">Africa</option>
  <option value="8">America, Central</option>
  <option value="1">America, North</option>
  <option value="2">America, South</option>
  <option value="7" selected>Asia, Central</option>
  <option value="4">Asia, East</option>
  <option value="5">Asia, West</option>
  <option value="3">Europe</option>
</select>
```

What you need, then, is to insert the word selected into the code for the region corresponding to the active country. Now, the complication you face is that your menu is not hard-coded, but is rather populated by a loop, which inserts a new <option> line for each record in the rs_regions recordset.

The solution to the problem is this: Each time through the loop that populates the drop-down menu, a script will test to see whether the current record's regionID matches the region in the rs_countryDetail recordset. If it does match, then the script will output the word selected into the code. If it does not match, the script will proceed as usual. Here's how the block looks in pseudocode:

```
Loop the following code until rs_regions runs out of records
  Write the <option> line, using rs_regions.regionID as the value attribute,
  ⇒and rs_regions.regionName as the label
  If the active rs_regions.regionID equals rs_countryDetail.region
    Write the word "selected" into the code
  End If
```

Go back to beginning of loop and start next iteration

That's a lot to absorb conceptually, but once you understand the idea, the actual code is not that hard to write.

10) Update the code between the opening and closing `<select></select>` **tags for the region, as follows:**

In ASP:

```
<%
  Do Until rs_regions.EOF
%>
<option value="<%=rs_regions("regionID")%>"
<%
  If rs_regions("regionID")=rs_countryDetail("region") Then
    Response.Write(" selected")
  End If
%>
><%=rs_regions("regionName")%></option>
<%
  rs_regions.MoveNext
  Loop
%>
```

In ColdFusion:

```
<cfoutput query="rs_regions">
  <option value="#regionID#"<cfif (rs_regions.regionID EQ
rs_countryDetail.region)> selected</cfif>>#regionName#</option>
</cfoutput>
```

In PHP:

```
<?php
  do {
?>
  <option value="<?php echo $row_rs_regions['regionID']; ?>"
    <?php
    if ($row_rs_regions['regionID'] == $row_rs_countryDetail['region']) {
      echo " selected";
    }
    ?>
  ><?php echo $row_rs_regions['regionName']; ?></option>
<?php
  }
  while ($row_rs_regions = mysql_fetch_assoc($rs_regions));
?>
```

I bolded the opening and closing portions of the `<option>` tag just to make them easier to read—especially the closing angled bracket (>), which looks orphaned in ASP, ColdFusion, and PHP. (That bracket, by the way, should be orange in the code editor for all three server models.) The reason for this is that `selected` must be written before that closing bracket, so that bracket alone goes on the right of the `if` section of code, while the remainder of its tag goes on the left of the `if` section.

```
63    <select name="region" id="region">
64        <%
65        Do Until rs_regions.EOF
66        %>
67        <option value="<%=rs_regions("regionID")%>"
68            <%
69            If rs_regions("regionID")=rs_countryDetail("region") Then
70                Response.Write(" selected")
71            End If
72            %>
73        ><%=rs_regions("regionName")%></option>
74        <%
75            rs_regions.MoveNext
76            Loop
77        %>
78    </select>
```

Pay close attention to spacing when you type this code—it is important that there is a space before `selected`, so that it does not run into the `value="X"` that precedes it.

ASP and PHP users may note that this section uses different syntax for the `<option>` statement than it did in the menu you built in the insert form at the beginning of the lesson. Rather than a single ASP/PHP block that concatenates multiple elements to construct the `<option>` line, it uses multiple ASP/PHP blocks, using the ASP (<%...%>) or PHP delimiters (<?...?>). There is no functional impact to this change. The main difference is that the code is easier to understand once you add the `if` section, when broken out like this.

11) Save and upload the file. Test admin_cp_master.asp, and select a non-African country, as before.

The correct region is selected by default, and yet all of the other regions are available as well.

The update form is complete, and the worst is over.

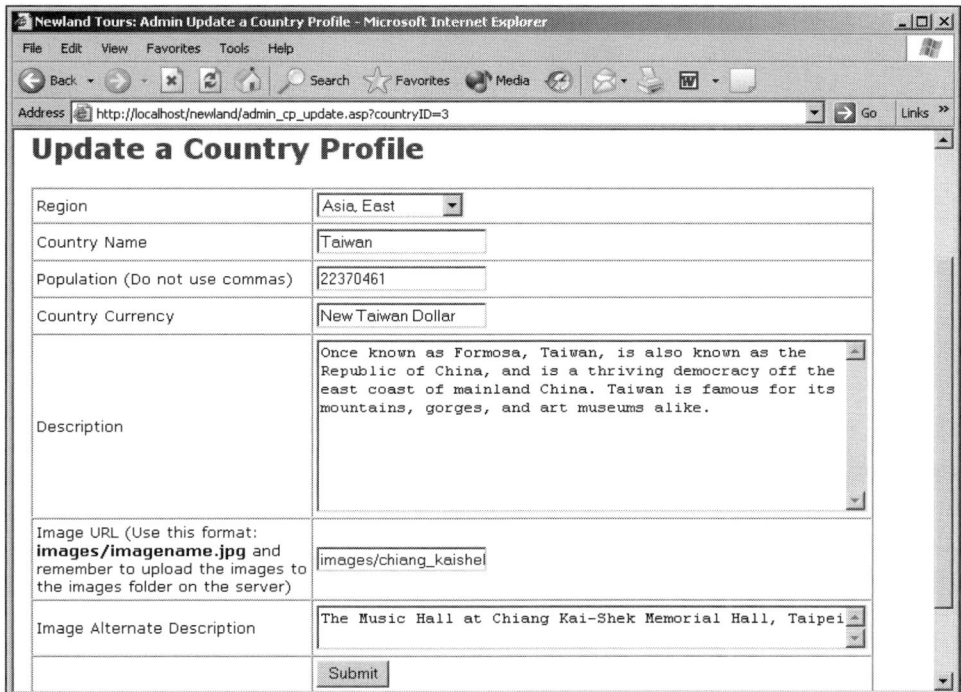

ADDING THE UPDATE FUNCTIONALITY

After the preceding task, the last two tasks will be anticlimactic. In this task, you'll create the update processor page.

1) Open admin_cp_update_processor.asp in code view. Delete any code you see.

Once again, you'll be starting from a blank slate when producing this script-only page.

2) Write the code that creates the database connection.

In ASP:

```
<%
Dim dbConn
set dbConn = server.CreateObject("adodb.connection")
dbConn.open("newland")

%>
```

In ColdFusion:

```
<cfquery name="update_cp" datasource="newland">

</cfquery>
```

In PHP:

```php
<?php
// Set up connection to MySQL
$host = "localhost";
$user = "[enter your username]";
$pwd = "[enter your password]";
$dbConn = mysql_connect($host,$user,$pwd);
// Connect to newland_tours database
$database = "newland_tours";
mysql_select_db($database);

?>
```

Now that you've got your connection, you can add the SQL.

3) Enter the code necessary to update the database in the blank line you left in the preceding step.

In ASP (all on one line):

```
dbConn.Execute("UPDATE tbl_country SET region='" & Request.Form("region")
⇒& "', countryName='" & Request.Form("countryName") & "', population='" &
⇒Request.Form("population") & "', country_currency='" & Request.Form
⇒("country_currency") & "', description='" & Request.Form("description")
⇒& "', imageURL='" & Request.Form("imageURL") & "', imageALT='" & Request.Form
⇒("imageALT") & "' WHERE countryID=" & Request.QueryString("countryID"))
```

In ColdFusion (you can use multiple lines):

```
UPDATE tbl_country
SET region='#form.region#',
  countryName='#form.countryName#',
  population='#form.population#',
  country_currency='#form.country_currency#',
  description='#form.description#',
  imageURL='#form.imageURL#',
  imageALT='#form.imageALT#'
WHERE countryID=#URL.countryID#
```

In PHP:

```php
//Update database
$query_updateCountry = "UPDATE tbl_country SET region='".$_POST['region']."',
⇒countryName='".$_POST['countryName']."', population='".$_POST['population'].
⇒"', country_currency='".$_POST['country_currency']."', description='".$_POST
⇒['description']."', imageURL='".$_POST['imageURL']."', imageALT='".$_POST
⇒['imageALT']."' WHERE countryID=".$_GET['countryID'];
$updateCountry = mysql_query($query_updateCountry);
```

Again, use code coloring to your advantage, especially ASP and PHP users. Also, make sure you don't inadvertently add a comma at the end of the element just before the WHERE clause.

```
1  <%
2  Dim dbConn
3  set dbConn = server.CreateObject("adodb.connection")
4  dbConn.open("newland")
5  dbConn.Execute("UPDATE tbl_country SET region='" & Request.Form("region") & "', countryName='" & Request.For
6  %>
```

4) Insert the line of code needed to redirect the user back to the master page.

In ASP, in the line above the closing %> tag:

```
Response.Redirect("admin_cp_master.asp")
```

In ColdFusion, in the line after the closing </cfquery> tag:

```
<cflocation url="admin_cp_master.cfm">
```

In PHP, just before the closing ?> tag:

```
header("Location: admin_cp_master.php");
```

This returns the user to the master page, so she or he can conveniently verify that the modifications took place.

```
1  <%
2  Dim dbConn
3  set dbConn = server.CreateObject("adodb.connection")
4  dbConn.open("newland")
5  dbConn.Execute("UPDATE tbl_country SET region='" & Request.Form("region") & "', countryName='" & Request.For
6  Response.Redirect("admin_cp_master.asp")
7  %>
```

5) Save and upload the file. Test the master page (F12), click a country, modify it, and click Submit. Return to that country's update page to change the value back.

The update functionality is complete and functional—at least for some of the countries. If you are using ASP, and you test using Argentina, Thailand, India, or a few others, you will see an error. The cause of the problem is that the text in the description or imageALT text areas contains an apostrophe character, which SQL misinterprets. (PHP and ColdFusion automatically escape this character, so ColdFusion and PHP users won't see this error.)

The solution to this problem is to remove all apostrophes from the text—which is not a reasonable business practice. Or is it?

In the next couple of steps, you will add some code that replaces the apostrophes with their HTML character entity equivalent (') automatically, just before the text is updated in the database. SQL will ignore the character entity (which is what we want), and when it is sent back to an HTML page, the browser correctly converts the character entity into an apostrophe. Neither the end user nor the user who maintains the Newland Tours site content will ever know that this happening behind the scenes. The only trace of this change, other than the ASP code you are about to write, is that ' will appear in the database in place of all apostrophes.

6) ASP Users Only: Return to admin_cp_update_processor.asp.

The find and replace script you'll add will appear on the processor page, just before the update is performed.

7) ASP Users Only: Add the following script after the opening `<%` and before `Dim dbConn` near the top of the page:

```
Dim description_fixed, imageALT_fixed
description_fixed = Replace(Request.Form("description"),"'","&#39;")
imageALT_fixed = Replace(Request.Form("imageALT"),"'","&#39;")
```

```
1  <%
2  Dim description_fixed, imageALT_fixed
3  description_fixed = Replace(Request.Form("description"),"'","&#39;")
4  imageALT_fixed = Replace(Request.Form("imageALT"),"'","&#39;")
5
6  Dim dbConn
7  set dbConn = server.CreateObject("adodb.connection")
8  dbConn.open("newland")
9  dbConn.Execute("UPDATE tbl_country SET region='" & Request.Form("region") & "', countryName='" & Request.For
10 Response.Redirect("admin_cp_master.asp")
11 %>
```

ASP has a built-in `Replace()` function, which takes (a) the text to be searched, (b) the string to search for, and (c) the string to replace it with as the first three parameters.

If you were to test the file now, you'd still get an error. That's because even though you've created a variable that holds the value of the two text fields, you don't insert the contents of that variable. You need to modify the SQL code.

8) ASP Users Only: Replace the two variables in the SQL statement, so that the UPDATE statement uses the fixed versions.

Replace description='" & Request.Form("description") & "', with description='" & description_fixed & "', and imageALT='" & Request.Form("imageALT") & "' with imageALT='" & imageALT_fixed & "'.

As you complete this step, notice that the description portion is followed by a comma, while the imageALT portion (the last in the series) is not.

```
8
9  rm("country_currency") & "', description='" & description_fixed & "', imageURL='" & Request.Form("imageURL"
10
```

9) ASP Users Only: Save, upload, and test the page.

This time around, even countries that have descriptions and alt descriptions with apostrophes can be updated.

Now that you know how to fix the apostrophe problem, you can fix the insert country profile pages.

10) ASP Users Only: Return to admin_cp_insert_processor.asp and apply the fix there.

The changes in code that are necessary are virtually identical to those you input into admin_cp_update_processor.asp—the only difference is that the SQL statement looks slightly different, though what you have to replace is unchanged.

ADDING THE DELETE FUNCTIONALITY

Writing the script for the delete processor page is even easier than writing the script for the update processor. Remember, users will access this page from the master page, which you have already built, so all that remains is to add the script that deletes the record from the database.

1) Open admin_cp_delete_processor.asp in code view, and remove any code.

Once again, this page will contain only a short script and a redirect elsewhere, so it needs no HTML code at all.

2) Add the code that creates the connection.

In ASP:

```
<%
Dim dbConn
set dbConn = server.CreateObject("adodb.connection")
dbConn.open("newland")

%>
```

In ColdFusion:

```
<cfquery name="delete_country" datasource="newland">

</cfquery>
```

In PHP:

```php
<?php
// Set up connection to MySQL
$host = "localhost";
$user = "[enter your username]";
$pwd = "[enter your password]";
$dbConn = mysql_connect($host,$user,$pwd);
// Connect to newland_tours database
$database = "newland_tours";
mysql_select_db($database);

?>
```

Now you can insert the code that executes a SQL statement.

3) Add the code that deletes the record specified in the URL parameter, in the space you left in the preceding step.

In ASP (all in one line):

```
dbConn.Execute("DELETE FROM tbl_country WHERE countryID=" &
⇒Request.QueryString("countryID"))
```

In ColdFusion (may be on multiple lines):

```
DELETE FROM tbl_country
WHERE countryID=#URL.countryID#
```

In PHP:

```php
$query_deleteCountry = "DELETE FROM tbl_country WHERE countryID=".$_GET
⇒['countryID'];
$deleteCountry = mysql_query($query_deleteCountry);
```

With SQL's DELETE statement, you don't have to specify each field singly, because it deletes from all fields, making it much more convenient to write. It also makes it easy to inadvertently wipe out your entire table, if you forget to specify the WHERE clause!

4) Add the redirection back to the master page, in the appropriate location.

In ASP, in the line above the closing %> tag:

```
Response.Redirect("admin_cp_master.asp")
```

In ColdFusion, in the line after the closing </cfquery> tag:

```
<cflocation url="admin_cp_master.cfm">
```

In PHP, before the closing ?> tag:

```
header("Location: admin_cp_master.php");
```

This returns the user to the master page, so she or he can conveniently verify that the deletion took place.

```
1  <%
2  Dim dbConn
3  set dbConn = server.CreateObject("adodb.connection")
4  dbConn.open("newland")
5  dbConn.Execute("DELETE FROM tbl_country WHERE countryID=" & Request.QueryString("countryID")
6  Response.Redirect("admin_cp_master.asp")
7  %>
```

5) Save and upload the file. Press F12 to open admin_cp_master.asp in a browser, and delete the country you inserted earlier in the lesson.

As promised, the country disappears instantly and permanently—don't bother trying the Back button!

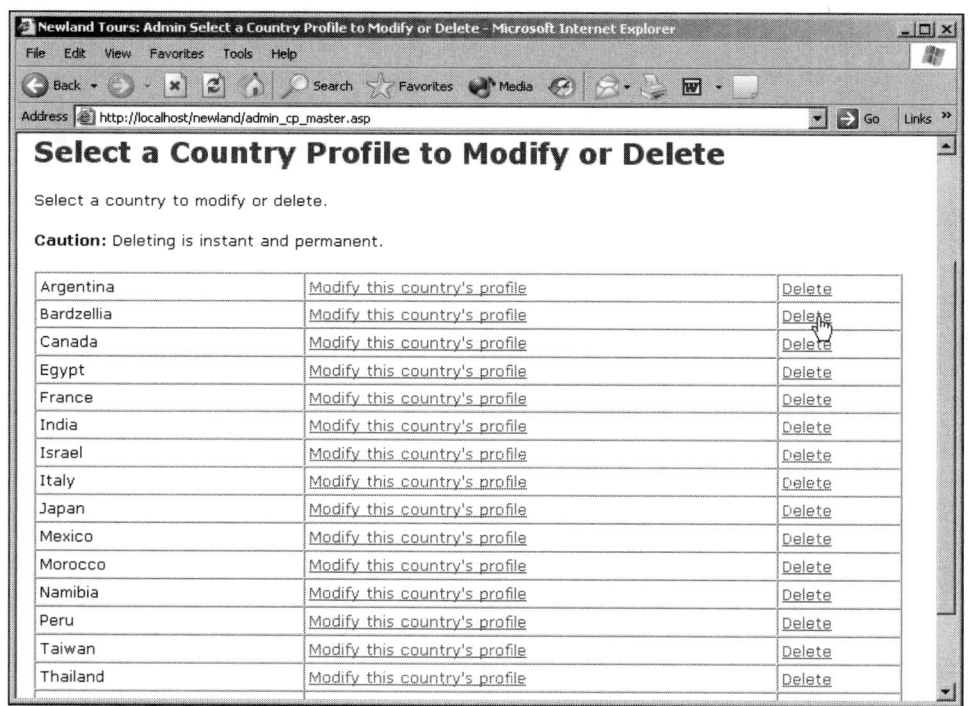

WHERE TO GO FROM HERE

With the completion of the CMS, you have also completed the instruction contained in this book. Learning dynamic Web development and programming is a significant task, one too big for a person to do over the course of a single book. However, if you got this far, you have mastered the fundamentals of dynamic application development and are ready to go out and develop database-driven sites.

If you want extra practice, use the Newland Tours site and database—they were designed specifically for learning. For example, if you want more practice building a CMS, build one for the tour descriptions.

If you are ready to return to the real world, then revisit the sites for which you are responsible, and try to identify how they might be more efficient and easier to maintain if they used dynamic scripting. You have seen and written plenty of ASP, ColdFusion, and/or PHP code in this book, and you can probably start solving problems right away. For more ambitious jobs, go to the bookstore or look online for ASP, ColdFusion, or PHP books or tutorials. You may be surprised at how much easier they are to read, now that you've built the Newland Tours site.

WHAT YOU HAVE LEARNED

In this lesson, you have:

- Designed a CMS application, including each of its pages and data flows (pages 451–454)

- Created a recordset without relying on Dreamweaver's Recordset dialog (pages 454–466)

- Written a script that inserts a new record based on a Web form (pages 466–469)

- Constructed a drop-down menu form element using a two recordsets, a loop, and an if statement (pages 469–475)

- Written a script that updates an existing record based on a Web form (pages 476–489)

- Written a script that deletes an existing record from a database table (pages 489–491)

index

real world. real training. real results.

Get more done in less time with
Macromedia Training and Certification.

Two Types of Training
Roll up your sleeves and get right to work with authorized training
from Macromedia.

1. **Classroom Training**
   Learn from instructors thoroughly trained and certified by
   Macromedia. Courses are fast-paced and task-oriented to get
   you up and running quickly.

2. **Online Training**
   Get Macromedia training when you want with affordable, interactive online
   training from Macromedia University.

Stand Out from the Pack
Show your colleagues, employer, or prospective clients that you
have what it takes to effectively develop, deploy, and maintain dynamic
applications—become a Macromedia Certified Professional.

Learn More
For more information about authorized training or to find a class near you,
visit **www.macromedia.com/go/training1**

LICENSING AGREEMENT